Tort Law

DIRECTIONS

7th Edition

CAROL BRENNAN

VERA BERMINGHAM

OXFO

UNIVERSITY

OXFORD

UNIVERSITY PRESS

Great Clarendon Street, Oxford, OX2 6DP,
United Kingdom

Oxford University Press is a department of the University of Oxford.
It furthers the University's objective of excellence in research, scholarship,
and education by publishing worldwide. Oxford is a registered trade mark of
Oxford University Press in the UK and in certain other countries

Fourth edition 2014
Fifth edition 2016
Sixth edition 2018

Impression: 1

Published in the United States of America by Oxford University Press
198 Madison Avenue, New York, NY 10016, United States of America

British Library Cataloguing in Publication Data
Data available

Library of Congress Control Number: 2020937382

ISBN 978–0–19–885392–3

Printed in Great Britain by
Bell & Bain Ltd., Glasgow

Preface

I have been teaching tort law for more years than I care to admit! I have introduced it in different institutions to a variety of students, including undergraduates studying for the LLB (as well as in disciplines such as business and social work); also to those sitting the Common Professional Examination at the graduate level, and more recently, to distance learning LLB students in the UK and abroad.

Vera Birmingham and I first conceived 'Tort Law' in the Directions series in 2006 and since that date it has been an enriching and collaborative effort. As joint authors, our aim in writing was to combine our experience and expertise in order to make the successful study of tort law accessible and achievable. Vera has now decided to step down from active involvement in the writing of this, the 7th, edition and I will be continuing with sole authorship. I will miss her support and wise counsel, however Vera's input and influence cannot be forgotten.

Tort is a subject which many students readily relate to, as some of its factual aspects may have been encountered in everyday life: for example, a claim on a motoring accident or trouble with noisy neighbours. This may be deceptive, however, because the law's solutions to these issues will not be so familiar and their mastery will require careful thought and study. The world of Internet communication increasingly raises novel questions concerning the law of defamation and privacy.

As part of the *Directions* series, this book will act as your guide to the study of tort, providing the clearest possible map through the differently named torts, while at the same time enabling you to identify the common underlying themes and uniting principles. While accessibility is a primary goal, detail is never sacrificed to that end, and you will encounter many challenging ideas and questions which can be followed up in further reading. The online resources will supply you with self-tests to build your confidence and with valuable updates, so that your knowledge is always current.

I am grateful to the anonymous referees from academic institutions around the country as well as to the many enthusiastic tort students from around the world who reliably provided me with questions and comments, thus assisting in making revisions to the 7th edition. It has been a pleasure to work with Amy Chard and Helen Swann at OUP, who offered patient flexibility, guidance, and encouragement with this new edition; and with the imaginative designers and editorial staff at OUP. Last but not least, huge thanks to colleagues, friends and family who have been stalwart in maintaining their (usually genuine) interest in the world of tort.

I have attempted to state the law as it stood on 1 October 2019.

Carol Brennan
Oxford
October 2019

New to this edition

An altered chapter order, with negligence discussed first, and trespass later in the book.

A review of current tests for duty of care in negligence and police liability in *Robinson v Chief Constable of West Yorkshire* (2018)

Poole BC v GN (2019) where the Supreme Court considers duty of care of public bodies

Supreme Court guidance on interpretation of the s 1 'serious harm' threshold in defamation in *Lachaux v Independent Print Ltd* (2019)

Commissioner of Police of the Metropolis v DSD and NBV (2018) on police liability and the ECHR

Darnley v Croydon Health Services NHS Trust (2018) on the relationship between duty of care and breach of duty

Steel v NRAM (2018) on professional negligence of a solicitor

Re A(a minor) v Calderdale & Huddersfield NHS Foundation Trust (2017) on psychiatric injury and childbirth

Spearman v Royal United Bath Hospitals NHS Foundation Trust (2017) on occupiers' liability

A controversial decision on vicarious liability in *Barclays Bank v Various Claimants* (2018)

Stocker v Stocker (2018) on defamation and social media platforms

Richard v BBC and another (2018) on privacy and police investigations

Guide to using the book

Tort Law Directions is enriched with a range of features designed to help support and reinforce your learning. This guided tour shows you how to fully utilize your textbook and get the most out of your study.

Learning objectives

Each chapter begins with a bulleted outline of the main concepts and ideas you will encounter. These serve as useful signposts to what you can expect to understand by the end of the chapter.

> **LEARNING OBJECTIVES**
>
> By the end of this chapter you should be able to:
> - analyse the functions of the defences to defamation;
> - distinguish between the different levels of protection afforded by the 'absolute' and 'qualified' defences;
> - outline the defences available for unintentional or innocent publication;

Case close up

Summaries of key and landmark cases are highlighted so you can easily pick out significant facts and details.

> **CASE CLOSE UP**
>
> **Patel v Mirza** (2016)
>
> Patel v Mirza was not a tort case but claim in contract where the parties agreed to place bets on share prices using insider information (which is an illegal activity). When the intended betting did not take place the claimant sought to recover the £620,000 he had paid the defendant and sued for breach of contract and unjust enrichment. Because the con-

Definition boxes

Key terms are highlighted in colour when they first appear and are clearly and concisely explained in definition boxes.

> ed with a savage blow out of all proportion to the incident.
>
> efendant claimed provocation as a defence after he killed the
> he defendant and his family had been subjected to a prolonged
> d woman and her family. The Court of Appeal held that con-
> nd **ex turpi causa** could be a defence to trespass to the person,
> in this case because of the disparity between the deceased's
> adly attack.
>
> **ex turpi causa (ex turpi causa non oritur actio)**
> where the law will not allow an action to proceed if it is based on an illegal cause

Thinking points

Thinking points allow you to pause and reflect on what you are reading. They give you the opportunity to form your own views and provide valuable practice in critical thinking.

> **THINKING POINT**
>
> Would the Home Office have been liable to a car owner if the boys had sailed the yacht t the mainland and walked two miles to find a car which they then vandalized?

Diagrams

A number of diagrams throughout the text provide visual representations of concepts and processes which, together with the explanatory text, help to clarify important points.

Diagram 1.1 A comparison between the tort and social security systems

	Tort system	Social security system
Speed		✓
Admin costs		✓
Periodic payment	✓	✓

Chapter summaries

The central points and concepts covered in each chapter are distilled into summaries at the end of chapters. These help to reinforce your understanding and can also be used as a revision tool.

Summary

- English law protects free speech through the defences to defamation.
- Even if defamatory and malicious, certain statements are of such social and importance that the law provides absolute protection.
- The application of the 'strict liability' rule in cases of 'unintentional' pub mitigated for an 'innocently' published statement.

The bigger picture

A selection of pointers show you how you can deepen and contextualize your legal understanding.

The bigger picture

'"Uber" is a modern business phenomenon' according to the Employment Tribu heard the first stage of a case to determine whether Uber drivers are 'workers' fo poses of entitlement to the minimum wage and holiday entitlement. In *Uber v Asl* a majority in the Court of Appeal upheld the decision of the Employment Tribuna ployment Appeal Tribunal in favour of the drivers, thus entitling them to full stat tection as 'workers' rather than independent contractors. Although not a tort ca

Knowledge-testing questions

A selection of questions is provided at the end of each chapter with answer guidance available online. These will help you to recognize any gaps in your understanding.

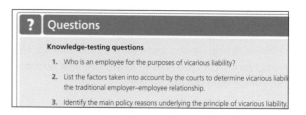

? Questions

Knowledge-testing questions

1. Who is an employee for the purposes of vicarious liability?
2. List the factors taken into account by the courts to determine vicarious liabili the traditional employer–employee relationship.
3. Identify the main policy reasons underlying the principle of vicarious liability.

Exam-style questions

End-of-chapter problem and essay-style questions will help you to develop analysis and problem-solving skills. The online resources provide answer guidance to each question.

Problem and essay questions

1. Mayuri was shopping in Arnott music centre when she noticed a number of display at greatly reduced prices. She decided to buy a CD player which co price label showing £25. As she was leaving the store the security guard a accused Mayuri of switching the labels and claimed that she had replaced th £50 price label on the CD with the label showing £25 taken from another ite display. Arnott's manager phoned the police and Mayuri was detained in his o the police arrived 30 minutes later. The manager's office was unlocked and M

Further reading

Selected further reading is included at the end of each chapter to provide a springboard for further study. This will help you to take your learning further and guide you to the key academic literature in the field.

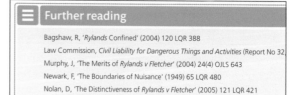

☰ Further reading

Bagshaw, R, '*Rylands* Confined' (2004) 120 LQR 388

Law Commission, *Civil Liability for Dangerous Things and Activities* (Report No 32

Murphy, J, 'The Merits of *Rylands v Fletcher*' (2004) 24(4) OJLS 643

Newark, F, 'The Boundaries of Nuisance' (1949) 65 LQR 480

Nolan, D, 'The Distinctiveness of *Rylands v Fletcher*' (2005) 121 LQR 421

Guide to the online resources

The online resources that accompany this book provide students and lecturers with ready-to-use teaching and learning resources. The resources are intended to be used alongside the book and are designed to maximize the learning experience.

 www.oup.com/uk/brennan_7e

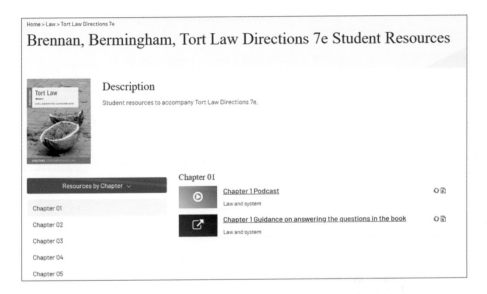

For students

Accessible to all, with no registration or password required, enabling you to get the most from your textbook.

Guidance on answering the questions in the book

Advice is provided on answering the questions at the end of each chapter, helping you to develop essential skills in analysing problems and constructing well-balanced arguments.

Podcasts

Each chapter is supplemented by a short podcast summarising the issues covered, helping to consolidate your knowledge as you work through the book.

Updates

Twice-annual updates from OUP's Law Higher Education Legal Updates service keep you up to speed on key developments in tort law, and explore their relevance from the perspective of a law student.

Self-test questions

Questions on the key topics of tort law give you the opportunity to test your learning. These automatically-marked questions test both your factual knowledge to help consolidate understanding of key topics and also offer a range of questions testing practical understanding, by putting you in the shoes of a legal practitioner facing a particular scenario.

For lecturers

Password protected to ensure only lecturers can access the resource; each registration is personally checked to ensure the security of the site.

Registering is easy: click on the 'Lecturer Resources' and complete a simple registration form which allows you to choose your own password.

Test bank

Comprising 200 multiple-choice questions with answers and feedback, this is a fully customizable resource containing ready-made assessments with which to test your students.

Acknowledgements

Grateful acknowledgement is made to all the authors and publishers of copyright material which appears in this book.

An extract from *Fairchild v Glenhaven Funeral Services* [2003] 1 AC 32 is included with permission of the Incorporated Council of Law Reporting.

Outline contents

Detailed contents

Table of cases

Table of Legislation

UK secondary legislation

European secondary legislation

International treaties and conventions

New Zealand legislation

US legislation

1 Tort: law and system

☐ LEARNING OBJECTIVES

By the end of this chapter you should be able to:

- recognize the range of activities to which tort law applies and the types of harm for which it provides compensation;

- identify the main interests protected by the law of tort;

- distinguish the law of tort from other branches of the law; and

- explain the role of policy and the human rights dimension in the law of tort;

- understand the function of tort as a form of compensation for loss;

- have an overview of the recent historical development of the tort system of compensation;

- place tort in the context of other forms of compensation; and

- analyse current debates concerning possible high levels of personal injury litigation.

1.1 What is tort?

Tort can be described as the area of civil law which provides a remedy for a party who has suffered the breach of a protected interest. The word itself is derived from the Latin *tortum*, meaning twisted or wrong. A wide scope of interests is protected by the law of tort. Currently, the tort which is the greatest source of litigation is that of negligence. Negligence concerns personal safety and interests in property, as well as some economic interests. Physical safety is also protected by the tort of trespass to the person, while ownership of property is governed by trespass to property. Other kinds of property interests are the domain of the torts of nuisance and *Rylands v Fletcher* (1868). Remedies for threats to one's reputation are provided by the tort of defamation. Recently, English law has seen significant developments concerning the protection of privacy from media intrusion.

1.2 Different torts deal with different types of harm

As you work through the chapters in this book you will discover that different torts deal with different types of harm or wrongful conduct and that the 'ingredients' for each of these diverse torts are different; each has its own particular characteristics. For example, in order to succeed in the tort of negligence a claimant must show not only that the defendant was at fault, but that he suffered damage as a result of the defendant's negligence. The tort of negligence can be contrasted with the tort of false imprisonment where, once the required ingredients of the wrong are established, a claimant will be able to succeed without proof of damage. Thus it can be said that false imprisonment is **actionable** '**per se**'.

> **actionable per se**
> without proof of damage

1.3 Tort: types of loss or harm covered

The law of tort deals with a wide range of activities and provides remedies for many different types of loss or harm. In cases of traffic accidents, injuries in the workplace, and medical negligence, the remedy sought by the claimant is likely to be damages or compensation. Tort also deals with disputes between neighbours about their use of land. If enjoyment of land is interfered with by noise or smells which are deemed to be unreasonable, this will constitute the tort of nuisance. Here, rather than seeking an award of financial compensation, the claimant may often request that the court grant an injunction, which is an order restraining the defendant from continuing to interfere with the claimant's enjoyment of his land.

Because the types of interests protected by tort are so varied and deal with many different situations in which one person causes harm to another, it is difficult to set out general principles of liability (as can be done with contract). For this reason, the study of tort can sometimes be confusing for students but, on the other hand, because tort frequently deals with everyday situations and involves the examination of interesting and exciting cases (sometimes high-profile media cases!) you will find the study of tort to be one of the most interesting and thought-provoking areas of law.

> The group litigation against Corby District Council in 2009 was brought by those who claimed that they suffered birth defects due to the inefficient disposal of toxic waste by the Council. It is a topical and valuable example of some of the principles and practice in negligence, nuisance, and breach of statutory duty. It is considered in Chapter 12 in the context of public nuisance.

1.4 Not all interests are protected by the law of tort

Where a loss is suffered as a consequence of an infringement of an interest protected by the law of tort, the defendant will be liable to pay damages to compensate for that loss. However, it is important to note that not all interests are protected by the law of tort, so that a person could suffer a loss as the result of another's conduct for which the law does not provide compensation. **Damnum sine injuria** is the Latin expression used to describe the situations where harm is suffered but the interest is not one which is protected by the law of tort and the claimant has no remedy in tort. For example, if you own a small grocery shop on the high street and a large supermarket lawfully opens a branch close by, you may suffer a loss of business and reduced profit, but the loss is not recoverable in tort because no 'legal' wrong has been committed by the supermarket.

> **damnum sine injuria**
> Latin phrase describing the situation where harm is suffered but the claimant's interest is not one which is protected by the law of tort and so the claimant has no remedy in tort.

1.5 Competing interests

You will also see that many of the interests protected by law are competing interests. The tort of nuisance provides an example: one resident may complain that the volume of his neighbour's music is so loud that it amounts to an interference with his use and enjoyment of his home or land. However, his neighbour may argue that it is he who is suffering the wrong, because he has the right to play his music in the privacy of his own home without complaint or interference from others. In these situations it is the role of the court to apply the law of tort in order to decide which of these competing interests should receive legal protection. Similarly, the clash between protection of reputation or confidence and freedom of expression is the key issue in the debate over the recent extension of the law of tort into the field of privacy.

1.6 Comparing tort to other areas of law

1.6.1 **Tort and contract**

Winfield, a leading academic expert on the law of tort, said that tort is characterized by duties 'primarily fixed by law' and owed 'towards persons generally'(*Winfield and Jolowicz on Tort*, 19th edn, Sweet & Maxwell, 2014, p 3). This definition provides grounds for distinguishing tort from another key area of civil law: the law of contract. The ideal of the contractual obligation is that, rather than being imposed by law, it is negotiated by two parties and, rather than being owed to persons generally, it is specific to the two parties to the contract.

In contrast, in the tort of negligence you will see that duties and matching rights have evolved out of the operation of the common law (supplemented in some circumstances by statute), rather than by an agreement and that they tend to belong to the population in general. We all have a duty not to drive carelessly and injure other motorists or pedestrians; and they all have the right to seek a remedy in tort if we breach this duty. However, this basis for distinguishing contract and tort is not absolute. When you come to study economic loss caused by negligent statements you will see that there are a number of cases in which the claimant has the choice of bringing his action in either contract or tort.

> ### THINKING POINT
>
> Are the contractual aspects of your day-to-day consumer transactions the result of a hard-fought bargain you have struck with the retailer or are they, perhaps, regulated by Sale of Goods Acts and other legislation?

1.6.2 Tort and criminal law

❯ THINKING POINT

In a case of battery, would it be preferable for the criminal prosecution to come before or after the tort action? See the Civil Evidence Act 1968, s 11.

The main distinction between tort and criminal law lies in the nature of their objectives. Simply put, the objective of the criminal law is to enforce the law by punishing those who break it. The objective of tort law, on the other hand, is to enforce the law by compensating those who suffer damage when the law is broken. When you begin to study tort law, you will soon become aware that its primary focus is upon the loss or damage suffered by the claimant, for the purposes of compensation, rather than upon the individual personality and motivation of the defendant. However, as with contract, the distinction described is not watertight. There are instances, such as defamation, in which the law of tort allows punishment of defendants through the use of punitive damages. On the other hand, criminal courts now have extensive powers to award compensation to victims of crime. Further, some wrongs will constitute crimes as well as torts. Examples are assault, battery, and public nuisance, and these torts can be prosecuted as criminal offences as well as being the basis for a civil tort action.

1.7 Tort and human rights

Prior to 2000, human rights law affected tort law only indirectly. Those claiming that a decision made in an English court was contrary to the European Convention on Human Rights (ECHR) could take their case to the European Court of Human Rights (ECtHR) in Strasbourg. This right still exists; however, with the coming into force of the Human Rights Act 1998 in October 2000, key articles of the Convention became binding in the United Kingdom. Statutes and case law must be interpreted and applied in a sense which is compatible with Convention rights, as far as it is possible to do so. More specifically relevant are the Articles of the ECHR which the Human Rights Act 1998 incorporates into UK law, enabling individuals to seek remedies when *public authorities* act in ways incompatible with Convention rights. The rights which are relevant to tort law and are beginning to have an impact on the development of case law are as follows:

- Article 2: right to life;
- Article 3: right to freedom from inhuman and degrading treatment;
- Article 5: right to liberty and security;
- Article 6: right to a fair trial;
- Article 8: right to respect for private and family life;
- Article 10: right to freedom of expression;
- Article 13: right to effective domestic remedy.

Because courts themselves are public authorities, the impact of the Human Rights Act can extend into all tort cases in which Convention rights may be involved. You will encounter specific examples of cases with significant human rights aspects in the relevant chapters. Privacy is currently the focus of the most heated debate among the general public, as well as in legal circles, concerning the clash between the Article 8 right to privacy and the Article 10 right to freedom of expression.

⟩ CROSS REFERENCE
See particularly Chapters 2, 11, and 15 for discussion of human rights issues. Privacy is the subject of Chapter 16.

1.8 Studying tort

The law of tort is almost entirely based on case law that has been developed by the courts over hundreds of years. Although a number of statutes have extended and changed the common law, the basic rules and principles have been laid down by judgments of the courts. In order to understand the nature and extent of tortious liability, it is essential that you are aware of the principles set down in the leading cases. Students sometimes find it difficult to extract the general principles from what seems to be a bewildering body of case law and the approach in this textbook has been to keep the number of key cases to a minimum.

However, included are all the key cases; under 'Case close-up' you will read the facts as well as explanations of the legal principles derived from them. In order to illustrate the application of the principles from the leading cases, some of the exceptions to these cases are also highlighted. Throughout the book you will find 'Thinking points' which will assist your understanding and provide topics for discussion. At the end of each chapter you will find more comprehensive 'Questions', references to the context of tort law in 'The bigger picture', and, finally, in 'Further reading', academic articles that will help to clarify your understanding of the topic of the chapters or highlight areas of ambiguity in the law.

Online Resources

www.oup.com/uk/brennan_directions7e The website associated with this textbook contains specific questions and activities, which have been designed to support the material in the chapters and to enable you to monitor your own progress in learning tort law.

1.9 The origins of tort as a system of compensation

You have seen that the overall function of tort law is to address the consequences of loss. This is accomplished in two primary ways:

(1) *Compensation*: making good the loss which would otherwise have been suffered.

If A negligently damages B's car and it will cost £1,000 to repair, tort law may provide that instead of that cost falling upon B (who is innocent of any wrongdoing) that cost should be borne by A, due to his fault or responsibility for what has befallen B. This is *loss shifting*.

Because of compulsory third-party insurance for drivers, it is very unlikely that A will be digging into his own pocket for the £1,000. Instead his motor insurers will be compensating B—using funds provided by the insurance premiums which A (and many others) have been paying for many years. The loss is not borne by any one person. This is *loss spreading*.

(2) *Deterrence*: preventing a loss in the first place by influencing behaviour.

If the *Daily Camera* fears that publishing a libellous article about a celebrity may result in extensive damages liability, lawyers will be consulted to screen articles for potentially *defamatory* material.

Another way in which deterrence may operate is through the remedy of the injunction. If neighbour A's building works are causing sleepless nights for neighbour B, an injunction obtained for the tort of *nuisance* may stipulate that no work should take place between the hours of 10pm and 6am.

Tort law has a third aim which is no less important than those above. In fact, it may be said that *justice* is a fundamental aspect of tort's aims—that is, there is a recognition that a wrong has taken place, and that this must be acknowledged and righted. We will see that some torts are actionable without proof of damage. For instance, in the case of a neighbour dispute concerning B taking an unauthorized shortcut across A's garden, a successful action in *trespass to land* by A may firmly establish the wrongfulness of this conduct, despite the absence of any tangible damage. Characterized by bilateral rights and duties, this aspect of tort is known as *corrective justice*. Tort law was summarized by Lord Bingham in *Fairchild v Glenhaven Funeral*

Services (2003) as defining 'cases in which the law may justly hold one party liable to compensate another'.

There are alternative means of accomplishing the above aims:

- Compensation for loss of earnings for those injured in accidents may come from occupational sick pay schemes or state benefits.
- Criminal penalties may be more successful in ensuring workplace safety than the law of employers' liability.
- Social responsibility or self-interest may effectively deter dangerous driving.

The focus of this chapter will be upon the compensation aim of tort law, particularly in the area of personal injury caused by accidents. We will consider whether this aim has been successfully accomplished considering the recent history of the tort system, what is known about how it operates, and any changes or developments which may address any apparent drawbacks. It is also important to consider the relative merits of other forms of compensation.

1.10 Insurance

Contrary to appearances, the opponents in most tort cases are in reality insurers who are disputing which of them will subsidize the loss in question. Under a process known as subrogation, insurers can take on the rights of the insured in order to pursue compensation. Insurance significantly supports the tort system and without it there would be little point in bringing the majority of tort claims. The prevalence of insurance as a factor in most tort claims is often cited as significantly undermining any deterrent value which tort law might have. This is certainly the view of PS Atiyah, leading authority on law and policy regarding accident compensation **subrogation**.

Insurance will generally be one of two types. Put simply, first-party (or 'loss') insurance exists to compensate the insured party for damage or injury to himself or his property howsoever caused. Third-party (or 'liability') insurance provides protection when the insured party is liable for injury done to the person or property of someone else. Liability insurance expanded in the late nineteenth and early twentieth century in parallel with the development of the tort of negligence. In 1930, legislation first required drivers to have third-party insurance (see now the Road Traffic Act 1988). The Employers' Liability (Compulsory Insurance) Act 1969 imposes similar requirements upon employers regarding work-related accident and disease. It is not surprising, therefore, that the vast majority of tort claims concern road traffic accidents and injuries sustained at work. It is presumed that the existence of insurance means that the defendants in these situations are likely to have 'deep pockets'. Insurance is now widespread, and it is likely that householders, schools, sports coaches, manufacturers, and professionals such as doctors will be similarly insured in respect of many situations in which tort claims could be made.

> **subrogation**
> a process which enables an insurer to sue a wrongdoer by taking on the rights of the insured party.

1.11 The litigation 'obstacle race'

The fact that the wrongdoer may have the means to compensate an injured party is only relevant if a successful tort claim is made. Studies done in the 1970s revealed that only 6 per cent of personal injuries in the United Kingdom resulted in the award of tort damages and, of those cases, roughly 2 per cent were the result of a court decision. All the other awards were the result of the process of negotiation and settlement, which will be discussed further later.

The process of obtaining compensation has been likened to a very challenging obstacle race, full of hurdles which may trip up the innocent competitor, ensuring that he never reaches the finishing line.

Donald Harris in the Oxford Survey (an extensive survey of accident victims in the 1970s and published in 1984) described tort litigation this way:

> a compulsory long-distance obstacle race. The victims, without their consent, are placed at the starting line, and told that if they complete the whole course, the umpire at the finishing line will compel the race-promoters to give them a prize; the amount of the prize, however, must remain uncertain until the last moment because the umpire has the discretion to fix it individually for each finisher. None of the runners is told the distance he must cover to complete the course; nor the time it is likely to take. Some of the obstacles in the race are fixed hurdles (rules of law), while others can, without warning, be thrown in the path of a runner by the race-promoters, who obviously have every incentive to restrict the number of runners who can complete the course . . .. In view of all the uncertainties, and particularly the difficulties which could be presented by the unknown, future obstacles, many runners drop out of the race at each obstacle . . . and most runners accept an offer and retire. The few hardy ones who actually finish may still be disappointed with the prize money.

A significant number of those who are injured do not even embark upon this race. Many accidents are not due to the fault of a third party, and therefore a tort claim would not be successful. The Oxford Survey revealed a number of reasons why those who could bring tort claims did not pursue them. A key one was ignorance that making a claim was even a possibility. This could be compounded by difficulties in obtaining legal advice, including the lack of the means to do so. Awareness of any or all of these obstacles would be discouraging to some victims. There may be a reluctance to bring a legal action against an employer or neighbour or a psychological need to move on following an accident. Injuries may be relatively insignificant, or the victim may feel that alternative compensation provision is preferable or adequate.

What are the obstacles and hurdles encountered by those who choose to enter the race?

- *Legal rules* The victim may be unable to establish one of the key elements of the relevant tort. We will see that a successful action in negligence is dependent on the claimant being able to establish three things: that the defendant had owed him a duty of care; that he had, in fact, been careless; and that this carelessness had caused the claimant's injury or loss. Satisfying only two out of three of these elements will not be enough. In some cases, victims will come up against statutory restrictions and limitation periods that will make a legal claim impossible.

- *Access to legal services* A sound legal case is not enough. The victim must have the financial means to pursue the case, which will usually involve obtaining legal advice. Some claimants may have legal expenses insurance and, despite falling availability, a small minority of claimants may go first to a local law centre or charity or be entitled to legal advice as a union member. Consulting a solicitor became more difficult for many with the Access to Justice Act 1999, when state-funded legal aid in personal injuries cases was abolished in all but clinical negligence cases. The Legal Aid, Sentencing and Punishment of Offenders Act 2012 (LASPO) further reduced the availability of civil legal aid. For clinical negligence, legal aid is now only available for a small number of cases in which children suffered brain injury at around the time of birth. Clinical negligence claims comprise only 1 per cent of personal injury claims and often carry the greatest potential for high damages awards but are among the hardest for claimants to win.

The ongoing reductions in legal aid have been, to some small extent, countered by conditional fee agreements (CFAs), sometimes referred to as 'no win no fee', which were gradually introduced during the 1990s, and embodied in the Access to Justice Act 1999. A solicitor who decides to take on a case may agree to require no fee or a reduced fee if the case is lost, but if the case is successful, his fee will be owed, plus an agreed 'success fee'. This is paid by the winner of the case and is calculated according to the amount of financial risk which was involved for the solicitor in taking on the case. Under LASPO the success fee can be up to 100 per cent of the basic fee, but in personal injury cases it can amount to no more than 25 per cent of the damages awarded, excluding damages for future care and loss. The loser may still have to pay the other side's costs and so will usually take out insurance to cover the possibility of loss. CFAs are now used, not only for personal injury, but in a wide range of civil litigation. The compatibility of the costs recovery scheme under the Access to Justice Act 1999 with the right to a fair trial under the ECHR Article 6 was challenged by the unsuccessful parties in the nuisance case *Coventry v Lawrence No 3* (2015)—see Chapter 12. A 5:2 majority of the Supreme Court held that despite the fact that costs payments can at times fall disproportionately on one party, the CFA scheme itself is a proportionate way of pursuing the legitimate aim of containing the costs of legal aid and improving access to justice for those with meritorious claims, and thus is compatible with the ECHR.

It is questionable whether CFAs have improved overall access to justice, particularly for those whose claims do not have at least a 70 per cent chance of winning. There are concerns that the CFA system has contributed significantly to the extensive legal costs currently being borne by the National Health Service (NHS). In 2017–18 NHS Resolution (formerly the NHS Litigation Authority) paid out £1.63 billion damages, with an additional £128 million of defence legal costs. Legal costs have been a source of concern, given the growing demands upon NHS budgets and, for the first time, these have been slightly reduced due to a strategy focused on alternative dispute resolution (ADR) and the avoidance of litigation.

In January 2010 Lord Jackson published his extensive *Review of Civil Justice Litigation Costs* in which he made a number of recommendations for reducing legal costs. The ECtHR in

▶ CROSS REFERENCE

The *Campbell* case is discussed in Chapter 16.

MGN v UK (2011) considered the CFA system in relation to the leading privacy case brought by Naomi Campbell in 2004. It concluded that the 'success fee' owed by the losing defendant newspaper in respect of Miss Campbell's legal costs was disproportionate and in breach of the Article 10 right to freedom of expression and thus unenforceable. The ECtHR strongly criticized the UK's CFA regime and recommended its revision, albeit in somewhat non-specific terms. One of Lord Jackson's recommendations which was implemented in LASPO was that lawyers' 'success fees' are no longer to be paid by the losing side.

- *Delay* The 'race' may prove to be a long one. Research published in Lord Woolf's *Access to Justice* (1996) revealed that in the early 1990s medical negligence cases took an average of five-and-a-half years from first consultation to resolution and in personal injury generally the time was four-and-a-half years. Some of this time will have been spent in gathering necessary evidence and other forms of preparation of the case. At the same time, however, it must be remembered that insurance companies as defendants have been referred to as 'repeat players'. This means that they are experienced in litigation and in some cases know that prolonging the process may cause some claimants to drop their case or to settle for considerably less than they would recover in court.

In 1998, new Civil Procedure Rules (CPR) were introduced in order to address these delays, as well as to make the civil justice system more user-friendly. Pre-action protocols now ensure greater openness between parties as well as encouraging out-of-court settlements. The courts are required to take a more proactive approach to litigation. Judges now take a leading role in managing the conduct of a case and have the power to impose sanctions on parties who unreasonably cause delay. It is not possible to say conclusively whether the problem of delay has improved under the CPR. It is apparent that litigation is now more likely to be regarded as a last resort; however, when litigation does take place, it is possible that delays and costs have just been transferred from the point targeted by the CPR to other stages in the process.

- *Uncertainty* Research shows that of the small number of those who begin a tort claim, the majority will receive at least some payment, but they may receive considerably less than they had hoped. Part of the reason for this is the process of out-of-court settlement. This involves ongoing negotiation between solicitors, with those for the defendant making an offer to resolve the claim, which may be accepted, rejected, or result in a counter-offer by the claimant. As we have seen, the experienced 'repeat player' will often be at an advantage in this procedure. It is risky because the claimant may settle for less than he would have received at trial—on the other hand, he might have lost totally. Similarly, the defendant may pay more than he would have had to, but could also have won his case in court. The settlement process is also risky because it is underpinned by costs sanctions: he who unreasonably refuses a sum offered in settlement, and is then awarded less than that sum at trial, may be penalized at the costs stage. Settlement has increased under the new pre-action protocols because the parties are better informed about each other's position and are therefore more willing to come to an agreement on the known position rather than await adjudication. The obstacle of *uncertainty* must be added to those of the *legal rules*, *access to justice*, and *delay* to provide ample deterrence to all but the most committed litigants!

1.12 No-fault liability

In 1961 it was discovered that the drug could cause severe birth defects in unborn children when it was taken by pregnant women. Eight thousand children worldwide were affected by it, some 450 of whom lived in the United Kingdom. The difficulties they had in pursuing legal remedies, in part because of the stringent requirements for proving negligence but also because of the cumbersome nature of tort litigation, gained a wide measure of public awareness. In 1973 the Royal Commission on Civil Liability and Compensation for Personal Injury, chaired by Lord Pearson, was appointed to study the system of personal injury compensation and to make recommendations for reform. The Pearson Commission conducted an impressive in-depth investigation into all aspects of the tort system, and some of the statistics produced in its 1978 Report are still of interest today. It also contained international comparisons of alternative types of compensation systems. In terms of outcomes, the Pearson Report was disappointing. It held back from recommending wholesale reform of the tort system and its cautious proposal for a no-fault scheme regarding road traffic accidents was never implemented.

1.12.1 **What is no-fault liability?**

We will see that the foundation of legal liability in the tort of negligence is the ability to establish that the claimant's injury was caused by the defendant's carelessness. Someone must be at fault in order for the claimant to obtain tort compensation. The burden is on him to prove this fault and if he fails he will be reliant on some alternative form of compensation. Fault was a basic component of the tort of negligence as it evolved during the latter half of the nineteenth century and the early part of the twentieth, prompted by a complex interplay of social and economic factors. It has been observed that 'the notion of responsibility is a powerful intuitive factor in people's attitudes to accidents and there is a deep-seated idea that those who have caused damage to others should pay' (*Winfield and Jolowicz on Tort*, 19th edn, Sweet & Maxwell, 2014, p 24).

Linked to justifications of a moral nature are the economic considerations: it may be efficient for those who benefit financially from risks that they create to pay the price when this causes loss to an innocent party. But is it truly economically efficient? The tort system brings costs of its own. The Pearson Commission estimated that it took 85p in legal and administrative costs to recover every £1 in tort compensation payments. Twenty years later costs had increased. Woolf's *Access to Justice* reported that for claims under £12,500, for every £1 claimed there was a cost of £1.35. In 2009–10, NHS patients' legal costs exceeded the damages that they received in more than one in five cases.

In 1974, the government of New Zealand adopted a radical new approach to compensation. The tort system was abolished for all personal injuries arising out of accidents. Instead a state compensation scheme was established, contributed to by employers, car owners, and the government, which enabled payments to be made on an administrative basis without proof of fault. The level of payment was partially earnings-related and originally only slightly less than that of tort. The New Zealand Accident Scheme is still a key aspect of the compensation system there; however, plans that the scheme might be extended to cover other types of personal injury have never been realized and there has been some reduction in the level of payment made. It remains, however, the most extensive no-fault scheme in the world, with extremely low administrative costs. A number of states in the United States have limited no-fault approaches to motor accidents. Germany and Sweden similarly operate partial no-fault schemes relating to drug injury compensation.

 THINKING POINT

Liam is 35 years old and has recently lost his sight due to an inherited medical condition. Tariq, also 35, was blinded in an accident at work two years ago, due to his employer's negligence. Liam's only source of financial assistance is social security benefits. Tariq, however, is in receipt of tort compensation from his employer, worth considerably more than state benefit. What differences in their needs might justify these different levels of financial support?

No-fault compensation is attractive in many ways, particularly because of its economic efficiency. There are drawbacks, however, as described by J Henderson:

> A New Zealand-type system can be criticised on several fairness grounds. First, citizens would no longer have some of the traditional methods of vindicating individual rights in our legal system . . .. Second, the anomalies are open to attack. For example, distinctions drawn between illness and accidental injury under the system cause persons similarly disadvantaged to be treated differently. Third, the measures of recovery include a number of arbitrary limits that cause persons similarly disadvantaged to receive essentially the same benefits. Finally, the procedures under the system reflect a willingness to sacrifice the interests of the individual to the greater good.

1.13 Alternative schemes

1.13.1 **Social security**

In the United Kingdom we have what is described as a 'mixed system' of compensation. The main source of compensation for accidents and work-related disease is that of state benefit (social security) because it is relatively quick, cheap, and accessible to many. The tort system, underpinned by liability insurance, is seen as supplemental to state benefit. The objectives of compensation provided by non-industrial social security benefit differ from those in tort. The tort system is committed to the principle of full compensation, as far as is possible, and has a significant earnings-related component. Basic social security, instead, makes no pretence of full compensation. That said, you should note that it is estimated that tort payouts account for little more than 25 per cent of the monetary amount of all accident compensation in this country. Diagram 1.1 compares the tort and social security systems.

Diagram 1.1 A comparison between the tort and social security systems

	Tort system	Social security system
Speed		✓
Admin costs		✓
Periodic payment	✓	✓
Flexible	✓	✓
Predictable		✓
Higher compensation for serious injuries	✓	
No industrial preference	✓	
Higher awards for bereavement	✓	
Full replacement for lost earnings	✓	

The low cost of administering the social security system was confirmed by Lord Woolf's *Access to Justice* in 1996, which calculated costs of between 8p and 12p to deliver £1 of benefit (compared, as we have seen, to as much as £1.35 for some tort claims). A distinct advantage in receiving state benefit is, of course, the lack of need to prove any fault and, unlike most tort compensation, social security is paid on a periodic basis. Social security will provide 'safety net' benefits for those in low-paid or no employment, mainly in the form of income support, housing benefit, and working tax credit, which are means-tested and may contain additional premiums for the disabled. These will often be of assistance to those who would otherwise have claimed through the tort system. You should keep in mind that there is a policy of minimizing the likelihood of double compensation and that statute provides that successful tort claimants must repay most social security benefits which they have received for up to five years after the accident.

Social security also includes the Industrial Injuries Scheme (IIS) for injuries and some diseases sustained due to employment. A fundamental development in the mixed system of compensation was the Workmen's Compensation Act 1897, which, for the first time, legislated for a scheme providing for liability of employers for workers' injuries at work, without the need for proof of fault. This was evidence of an approach to compensation characterized by 'industrial preference'—that is, creating as a special class of the injured and ill those whose loss can be linked to employment. The industrial preference has been maintained into the twenty-first century, despite both the overhaul of the benefit system following the Second World War when the welfare state was pioneered, and the doubts which were expressed about it in the Pearson Report.

The IIS provides short-term, long-term, and bereavement benefits for those injured (or who develop certain 'prescribed' diseases such as asthma or deafness) 'arising out of' employment.

This is a complex area of entitlement, but it is clear that those entitled to state benefits under the IIS will be better provided for than those without the 'industrial preference'. Financial comparisons with the tort system are equally difficult, as they depend on many different factors such as the severity and duration of the disablement, the employment status of the victim, and age. Entitlement under the tort system is not always preferable to the IIS, especially taking into account the fact that tort claimants often settle for less than they would eventually have been awarded in court.

1.13.2 **Charity**

❯ CROSS REFERENCE

Criminal injuries compensation is discussed at 1.14.1.

Although not normally thought of as compensation, it is important not to overlook the role of charity. Before the late nineteenth century, voluntary help provided by the church, community, and individuals was the main source of support for the injured and bereaved. Today, high-profile victims may be beneficiaries and we have seen the emergence of such efforts, particularly in relation to disasters such as the Paddington rail crash and London bombings. Many anonymous victims will also receive ad hoc or informal help. Charity comes from a sense of public obligation or involvement and is a form of targeted help which may provide quick payments for those facing a long wait for tort or criminal injuries scheme compensation.

The NHS itself, funded by central government out of taxation, is another benefit which UK residents may forget when comparing their situation with those under other systems. The need to subsidize the cost of their medical care is thought to be a major motivating factor in the high level of tort litigation undertaken by accident victims in the United States. The high cost to the NHS of accidents necessitated the passage of the Road Traffic (NHS Charges) Act 1999, which enables the NHS to claim back a proportion of the costs of patient care in cases when someone is liable to pay compensation. Also known as 'recoupment', this has recently been extended beyond injuries caused by motor accidents, significantly including those at work.

1.13.3 **NHS Redress Act 2006**

Medical negligence claims, while comprising only about 1 per cent of all personal injury claims, receive a lot of attention because they often result in the highest damages awards. In 2018 the largest ever damages award of £19.8 million was agreed by the NHS, to a young woman who had suffered brain damage due to oxygen deprivation as a baby. Medical, or clinical, negligence claims are difficult for claimants to pursue for several reasons. Many medical negligence claims concern birth injuries suffered by babies, and they cannot sue in their own right until they are 18 years old, although for under-18s an action can be brought on their behalf by a 'next friend'. Often the information held about the relevant event is in the possession of the NHS Trust and it may be very difficult for the claimant to obtain the necessary evidence: first, to establish that he has a cause of action in law and, second, to substantiate that action. Both liability and causation may be fiercely contested, leading to high costs. Receiving a compensation award may not be the prime motivation of the claimant in these cases. The bigger concern may be simply to find out what happened, to feel reassured that any lapses have been addressed, to receive any needed remedial care, and, most of all, to receive an apology. The debilitating process of a tort action may not be the best means of achieving this.

The NHS Redress Act 2006 provided for the establishment of a redress scheme which would allow the offer of compensation up to an upper limit of £20,000, the giving of an explanation and an apology, and the details of action taken to prevent future similar cases. It would be managed by the NHS Litigation Authority (NHSLA), the body responsible for handling negligence claims against the NHS (now renamed NHS Resolution). Many patient complaints are already dealt with within a hospital trust by ADR or mediation and there are some expectations that the new redress procedure would not be an appreciable improvement on existing provision and the Act has not yet been implemented.

1.13.4 **First-party insurance**

Many losses suffered will be covered by 'first-party' or personal insurance, taken out for his own benefit by the person who suffers the loss. Research in the mid-1990s revealed that the most common form is life insurance, which is held by over half the households in the United Kingdom, often in connection with mortgage requirements. More than 75 per cent of households held home contents insurance.

Drivers with comprehensive motor insurance will be able to claim directly from their own insurer for damage to their car, which is particularly important when no one else is responsible for the damage. Why, then, does any driver pursue a claim in tort as an alternative? One reason is that personal insurance, such as that described above, rarely covers personal injury and loss of earning capacity. At the time of the Pearson Report, only 6 per cent of accidents were covered by personal accident insurance. Another reason is that, in the absence of a 'knock-for-knock' agreement, the victim's insurer may choose to recover his losses against the liability insurer of a negligent defendant.

The Motor Insurers' Bureau, established by the insurance industry, provides compensation for those who suffer personal injury or property damage at the hands of uninsured or untraceable drivers.

The majority of those who are employed will be covered by occupational schemes, where their employer provides sick pay and they continue to receive all or part of their pay during periods of incapacity. Pensions, either occupational or personal, may provide cover if work becomes altogether impossible due to injury or if death occurs.

1.14 *Ex gratia* compensation schemes

> **ex gratia**
> payment made as a favour, rather than on the basis of a legal obligation.

1.14.1 **Criminal injuries compensation**

Many crimes, particularly violent ones, are at the same time torts. An obvious example would be a physical attack, which is likely to constitute the tort of battery. It would be very unlikely that the offender would be worth suing, and although the criminal courts have the power to

◗ THINKING POINT

It has been discovered that
the numbers who claim
under the CICS are
significantly lower than the
estimates of victims of
violent crime. Why might
victims not be taking
advantage of this
opportunity?

make a compensation order against the defendant in favour of his victim, this amount would not approach full compensation. To provide for victims of violent crime the government established the Criminal Injuries Compensation Scheme (CICS) in 1964. The main motivation for the establishment of this scheme was to demonstrate society's sympathy for the victims of crime. Itself a form of no-fault compensation, it provides a fund to which victims of violent crime can apply and, providing that the criteria for entitlement are satisfied, *ex gratia* payment will be made by a statutory body, the Criminal Injuries Compensation Authority (CICA). Compensation will be paid even if no one is convicted of the crime and although its main focus is physical injury, there is some provision for compensation for mental injury as well and dependants of deceased victims are included in the scheme. There are some significant exclusions, including most domestic violence and road traffic accidents. In some cases, the conduct and even character of the victim itself will disqualify him; for instance, if he was injured in a fight in which he had voluntarily participated. In 2017, challenges were begun on behalf of survivors of childhood sexual abuse who had been denied compensation by the CICA on the grounds that they had 'consented' to their abuse, despite being under the age at which such consent was legally possible.

Prior to 1994, criminal injury payments were calculated on a similar basis to personal injury claims under the tort system. However, since then, assessment has been according to a 'tariff' system under which the maximum award is £250,000. This is significantly less than that which might be awarded to a successful tort claimant with serious injuries; however, it must be noted that the vast majority of victims are claiming for relatively low sums. As part of a political money-saving effort, both eligibility criteria and tariffs for awards were revised, resulting in a 60 per cent fall in payouts between 2010 and 2017. It is important to note that the vast majority of applicants received £5,000 or less, with £1,000 being the minimum amount which can be claimed. Social security benefits, past and future, are deducted in full, as is compensation which the offender may have been ordered to pay by the criminal court.

1.14.2 **Specific schemes**

Occasionally situations occur involving widespread loss or injury, in which the government takes on the role of compensating its victims. A scheme is established to provide compensation at a level which, in some cases, compares favourably to what might have been obtained through the courts. Those who claim under such schemes must undertake to forego any tort action. There is no admission of fault on behalf of the government, but they indicate a level of possible responsibility which makes it both politically and economically expedient for the tort system to be bypassed. Currently, such schemes apply to vaccine damage sustained by children and for those who have contracted hepatitis C and the HIV virus from the NHS supply of contaminated blood products.

In the United States, Congress established the September 11th Victim Compensation Fund for those affected by the attacks on the World Trade Center and Pentagon. Victims of the 7 July 2005 bombings in London were compensated, some claim inadequately, by the CICS, social security, and charity.

1.15 A compensation culture?

> **'Bonkers conkers ruling',** *The Times*, **5 October 2005**
>
> So what else can we do to scare the living daylights out of our children? One serious contender for the 2004 prize for contributing to the project of boring the pants off childhood must surely be Shaun Halfpenny, the headmaster of Cummersdale Primary School in Carlisle. Mr Halfpenny decided that enough is enough, something had to be done to protect Britain's children from the scourge of that dreaded threat to our way of life—conkers.
>
> Clearly raising awareness of this public health issue has not worked. Far too many children, it seems, still suffer from the life-long trauma of grazing their knees while looking for conkers. Setting up a helpline to support victims of conkering is clearly beyond the resources available to a local primary school, so Mr Halfpenny did the next best thing.
>
> Children in his primary school have been banned from playing conkers unless they wear two pairs of safety goggles. And just to show that he is no ordinary killjoy, the headmaster went out and bought safety goggles for his pupils to wear while engaging in this highly risky adventure. To be exact, two safety goggles were purchased from the school's limited funds. It appears that children now queue up and wait for their turn to wear the goggles before they can get their hands on those risky chestnuts. No more free-for-alls as children rush off to be the first to find that extra-large shiny conker—this is safe and responsible activity at its best.

The story above is typical of many press reports about unusual policies, which have been apparently motivated by fears of legal action. Responsible for these fears are tales such as that of the mortuary technician who was reported as having been awarded £15,000 against her employer after developing a morbid fear of death; or the Scottish police dog handler who recovered £2,000 from his employers after being bitten by his own dog.

In 2004, the government's Better Regulation Task Force reported on its inquiry into the 'compensation culture'. This is a complex phenomenon to study, involving the analysis of many conflicting statistics, leading to no easy or obvious answers. The Task Force did find that the overall cost of tort claims in the United Kingdom was lower than ten other comparable economies. However, concerns continued to be raised by the insurance industry about steadily increasing numbers of claims, a rise which is mirrored by increasing insurance premiums. Certainly, we have seen that NHS Resolution has reported a significant year-on-year increase in medical negligence claims (although this is now levelling out). Assuming that this trend is real, there could be a number of different explanations. Maybe some forms of access to legal advice became more readily available due to CFAs. Some believe that the advent of the Human Rights Act has promoted the concept of 'rights', leading to a 'claims consciousness' growing

> **THINKING POINT**
>
> Is a 'compensation culture' necessarily a bad thing? What might be its benefits?

throughout society. Have judges modified legal principles in such a way as to favour claimants' cases? One possibility which must not be forgotten is that perhaps there has actually been an increase in the number of accidents and medical mishaps.

As you come to learn the details of tort law, you will see that bringing a legal action is not the same thing as winning it. The fact that people consider or attempt to recover compensation for an injury does not mean that they will be successful even if they stay the litigation course. However, perceptions (even if unfounded) of excessive or frivolous claims can have a significant impact on behaviour. For example, doctors may be reluctant to practise in certain fields, such as obstetrics, and adventure outings for schoolchildren may become a thing of the past.

In its report, *Better Routes to Regulation*, the Task Force concluded, 'the compensation culture is a myth, but the cost of this belief is very real'. Kevin Williams ('State of Fear: Britain's "Compensation Culture Reviewed"' (2005) 25(3) LS, 499–515, 513) has explained it this way:

> There is good evidence that some sorts of accident claims have risen (from a relatively low base) and that the overall cost of personal injury settlements has gone up. But there is virtually no reliable evidence about the number of bogus or exaggerated claims or whether they constitute a grave (or increasing) problem . . . .. The Task Force analysis seems to be that if we are suffering from a crisis, it is largely one of confidence arising from misplaced fears of potential defendants and their insurers, rather than from a culture which 'blames and claims' too much.

1.15.1 **Compensation Act 2006**

In 2005, the Constitutional Affairs Committee considered all the evidence which had been collected about the so-called compensation culture and resolved to address the issue in legislation. The result was the Compensation Act 2006 which, in addition to s 1, also deals with regulation of claims managers and asbestos-related damages actions.

Section 1 is a reminder to judges to consider carefully the impact that decisions about negligence liability might have in potentially deterring the organization in pursuit of certain types of activities.

 STATUTE

Compensation Act 2006, s 1: Deterrent effect of potential liability

A court considering a claim in negligence or breach of statutory duty may, in determining whether the defendant should have taken particular steps to meet a standard of care (whether by taking precautions against a risk or otherwise), have regard to whether a requirement to take those steps might:

(a) prevent a desirable activity from being undertaken at all, to a particular extent or in a particular way; or

(b) discourage persons from undertaking functions in connection with a desirable activity

CASE CLOSE-UP

Cole v Davis-Gilbert (2007)

This case provided an early illustration of the way that s 1 of the Compensation Act 2006 was to be applied by the courts. Yvonne Cole was walking across a Sussex village green on her way to a pub. She stepped into a hole hidden in the long grass and broke her ankle. Mrs Cole brought an occupier's liability action against the owners of the green and the Royal British Legion, who had organized a village fete, which had been held on the green some months ago. The hole had been made, for the purpose of supporting a maypole, by a veteran soldier using his souvenir bayonet. He had returned to the green following the fete and filled in the hole. It seems that this hole had somehow become exposed again shortly before the accident. The trial judge ruled in favour of Mrs Cole in 2005 but the Court of Appeal, subsequent to the introduction of the Compensation Act 2006, found for the defendants. According to Scott Baker LJ:

> Accidents happen and sometimes they are what can only be described as 'proper accidents', in the sense that the victim cannot recover damages because fault cannot be established . . . . If the law courts were to set a higher standard of care than what is reasonable, the consequences would quickly be felt. There would be no fetes, no maypole dancing and no activities that have come to be a part of the English village green for fear of what might go wrong.

The cases of *Bourne Leisure Ltd v Marsden* (2009) and *Tomlinson v Congleton BC* (2003) provide additional examples of the judicial reaction against the 'compensation culture'. The Compensation Act was also applied in *Hopps v Mott MacDonald Ltd* (2009) in the case of a consultant electrical engineer working in Basra who was injured in an explosion. He claimed that because of the threat levels in the aftermath of the war in Iraq his employer was negligent in not providing him with armoured transport. In determining whether the employer had done what was reasonable in the circumstances to take care of his safety the court made an analysis of the risks and considered the potential deterrent effect of a finding of liability on the employer. In the particular and unusual circumstances the employer was not negligent and s 1 of the Act applied since a finding of liability would prevent the desirable activity of the reconstruction of Iraq being undertaken and would contribute to an increasing humanitarian crisis.

> **CROSS REFERENCE**
> Both these cases are discussed in Chapter 7.

One side effect of the introduction of CFAs was the growth in claims management companies. These 'claims farmers' can be seen advertising on television for clients seeking legal advice, often in relation to personal injuries, who are then referred to solicitors. Concerns have been raised about 'ambulance-chasing' behaviour by some of these companies as well as the use of high-pressure selling tactics. There are also reports of their clients losing some or all of the compensation they have recovered in fees. The collapse of companies such as Claims Direct received much publicity, and tarnished the reputation of the legal profession. Part 2 of the Compensation Act 2006 outlined a new regulatory regime for CFAs and accordingly there is now a body concerned with claims management regulation. Currently, the Conditional Fees Order 2013 sets out the detailed framework for operation of CFAs.

1.15.2 **The Social Action, Responsibility and Heroism Act 2015**

In April 2015, the Social Action, Responsibility and Heroism Act 2015 (SARAH) came into force. It requires judges, in determining negligence and breach of statutory duty cases, to take into account whether:

- in carrying out the activity in question the defendant demonstrated a 'predominantly responsible approach' to the safety and interests of others;

- the alleged tort took place when the defendant was acting 'for the benefit of society'; and

- the alleged tort occurred when the defendant was acting 'heroically by intervening in an emergency'.

⟩ CROSS REFERENCE

See 1.11 The litigation 'obstacle race'.

Critics of the Act are quick to point out that the above are already factors which judges consider, along with all the circumstances of the case, accusing the government of pandering to a moral panic about a 'compensation crisis'. In its passage through the House of Lords, the distinguished lawyer Lord Pannick commented, 'this always was and remains the most ridiculous piece of legislation approved by Parliament in a very long time . . . a pitiful creature of a Bill'. Time will tell what impact, if any, the Act will have on the development of tort law, however at the time of writing there have been no cases reported in which SARAH has been explicitly applied.

1.15.3 **The Civil Liability Act 2018**

This legislation, which became law in December 2018, is intended to address a perceived problem with fraudulent personal injury claims and high legal fees, which may lead to generally higher insurance premiums. It institutes a framework of regular review for the 'discount rate', according to which judges take into account investment returns on lump sums when making damages awards. More controversially it orders the creation of a tariff-based system for damages awards for those suffering 'whiplash' injuries in road traffic accidents; such claims being facilitated by the establishment of a 'portal' for bringing claims. Claimants' lawyers fear that the Act's provisions limiting recoverable damages and legal costs will mean that many genuine claimants will have to act for themselves, thereby threatening their rights to justice and adequate compensation.

⟳ Summary

- The tort system is an expensive, uncertain, and time-consuming method of obtaining financial support.

- No-fault and *ex gratia* compensation is an alternative which is used selectively but there does not appear to be the political or popular will to abandon tort.

- The main alternative to the tort system is social security.

- Despite its drawbacks, there is evidence that the tort system is alive and well, and its use appears to be growing, although reports of a 'compensation culture' have been exaggerated.

- ◐ Visit the online resources to listen to a podcast summarizing the topics covered in this chapter.

The bigger picture

The perception that we live in an age of excessive legal control, particularly around issues connected to accidents and compensation, brings challenges to tort lawyers. You may wish to read Lord Young's close look at the realities of the 'compensation culture', *Common Sense, Common Safety*:

https://assets.publishing.service.gov.uk/government/uploads/system/uploads/attachment_data/file/60905/402906_CommonSense_acc.pdf

A provocatively critical stance is adopted towards the Social Action, Responsibility and Heroism Act 2015 in Mulheron, R, 'Legislating Dangerously: Bad Samaritans, Good Society, and the Heroism Act 2015' (2017) 80(1) MLR 88.

? Questions

Knowledge-testing questions

1. What are the range of needs to be fulfilled in a complaint about clinical treatment? How appropriate is financial compensation for these needs?

2. In what contexts might the Social Action, Responsibility and Heroism Act 2015 have relevant application?

Problem and essay questions

1. The tort system has been likened to a 'compulsory long-distance obstacle race'. Comment on the strengths and weaknesses of the tort system, in reference to the above statement.

2. What are the alternatives to the current tort system and how likely are they to replace that system?

 Visit the online resources for guidance on answering these questions.

 Further reading

Atiyah, P, *The Damages Lottery* (Hart 1997)

Cane, P, *Atiyah's Accidents, Compensation and the Law*, 7th edn (CUP 2006)

Conaghan, J and W Mansell, *The Wrongs of Tort (Law & Social Theory)*, 2nd edn (Pluto Press 1998)

Harlow, C, *Understanding Tort Law*, 3rd edn (Sweet & Maxwell 2005)

Harris, D, *The Oxford Survey* (Oxford Centre for Socio-Legal Studies 1984)

Jackson, R, *Review of Civil Justice Litigation Costs: Final Report* (Stationery Office 2010)

Lewis, R, 'Insurance and the Tort System' (2005) 25(1) LS 85

McIvor, C, 'The Impact of the Jackson Reforms on Access to Justice in Personal Injury Litigation' (2011) 30 CJQ 411

Matthews, J, 'Dangerous Activities' (2011) 97 PILJ 9–11

Miers, D, 'Rebuilding Lives: Operational and Policy Issues in the Compensation of Victims of Violent and Terrorist Crimes' [2006] Crim LR 695

Morgan, J, 'Abolishing Personal Injuries Law? A Response to Lord Sumption' (2018) PN 35(1) 122

Morris, A, 'Spiralling or Stabilising? The Compensation Culture and our Propensity to Claim Damages for Personal Injury' (2007) 70 MLR 349

Pearson, Lord, *Royal Commission on Civil Liability and Compensation for Personal Injury* (HMSO 1978)

Woolf, Lord, *Access to Justice: Final Report* (HMSO 1996)

2 Negligence: duty of care

Introduction

Negligence began to be recognized as a tort in its own right around the beginning of the nineteenth century. Before that time, the dominating action for personal injury was the writ of trespass. Trespass was initially concerned only with direct acts; however, during the nineteenth century the focus shifted to the distinction between intentional wrongs (trespass) and the unintentional (negligence). As we have seen, negligence was originally described in terms of a duty imposed by law and thus it will be seen that duty is one of the three key elements of negligence today.

Negligence evolved as a means of loss shifting at a time when there was little or no insurance or state welfare provision. The industrial revolution in the nineteenth century brought with it increased risks of injury to those working in factories, mines, quarries, and other dangerous situations. The development of railway transportation and mass production dramatically increased the potential for many people to be affected by the faulty conduct of strangers, at the same time that the development of incorporations meant that there would be a company to sue rather than an individual. The damage in such cases would have been personal injury or death and, to a lesser extent, property damage.

❱ **THINKING POINT**
Victorian values (laissez-faire or individualistic) are said to have implied that those who were negligent were somehow blameworthy. How might that attitude have changed as the twentieth century developed?

The Workmen's Compensation Act 1897 was the first step in the gradual introduction of compulsory compensation schemes for victims of accidents. It gave certain workers entitlement to compensation from their employers if they were injured in accidents 'arising out of and in the course of employment'. Increasingly during the twentieth century, the government took responsibility for citizens' welfare generally, particularly following the Second World War when the welfare state and the National Health Service were created. This meant that tort law was no longer the primary support for those suffering loss due to accidents.

2.1 The foundations of negligence

Winfield's definition is as follows: 'Negligence as a tort is a breach of a legal duty to take care which results in damage to the claimant.' Contained within this definition are the three key elements which must always be established for a successful action in negligence. We will study these elements separately; however, you should be aware that they are not always neatly self-contained. Often during this chapter you will be referred to Chapter 5, where the main 'problem areas' of duty of care are dealt with.

(1) *Duty of care*: Does the defendant owe the claimant a duty of care?

(2) *Breach*: Has the defendant broken that duty?

(3) *Damage*: Has that breach caused damage of a legally recognized kind to the claimant?

2.2 Duty of care

According to John Fleming 'the basic problem in the tort of negligence is that of limitation of liability' (*The Law of Torts*, 2nd edn, Clarendon Press, 1985, p 4). He points out that negligence is different from some torts such as assault or defamation in that it is not tied to a particular relationship, type of harm, or the protection of a particular interest:

> [T]o permit the imposition of liability for any loss suffered by anyone as the result of careless-ness would have imposed too severe and indiscriminate a restriction on individual freedom of action by exposing the actor to the prospect of unpredictable liability.

Prior to 1932, liability in negligence was restricted by the finding of a duty of care on a case-by-case basis—primarily in situations where there was a pre-existing relationship between the parties such as guest and innkeeper or employer and employee. In *Donoghue v Stevenson* (1932), Lord Atkin provided the first general rule for determining duty of care. The case is also significant for its groundbreaking 'narrow rule' which established that manufacturers owe a duty of care in negligence to the ultimate consumers of their products.

🔍 CASE CLOSE-UP

Donoghue v Stevenson (1932)

Mrs Donoghue and a friend went to a café in Scotland where the friend purchased a bottle of ginger beer for her. Mrs Donoghue drank some of the beer from the opaque bottle but when more beer was poured into her glass, a decomposed snail fell out. She claimed that she had suffered shock and sickness as a result and sought compensation. She could not claim in contract from the sellers because their contractual relationship was with her friend who had made the purchase. Instead she sued the manufacturers of the bottled beer in negligence.

In ruling in the plaintiff's favour on a **preliminary point of law** the House of Lords held that the existence of a contract between the defendant and the purchaser would not bar a claim in tort by Mrs Donoghue, despite the fact that she was effectively 'a third party'. This opened the way for a general duty of care of manufacturers to consumers. Lord Atkin described it thus:

> [A] manufacturer of products, which he sells in such a form as to show that he intends them to reach the ultimate consumer in the form in which they left him with no reasonable possibility of intermediate examination, and with the knowledge that the absence of reasonable care in the preparation or putting up of the product will result in an injury to the consumer's life or property, owes a duty to the consumer to take that reasonable care.

The wider importance of *Donoghue v Stevenson* lay in the test which Lord Atkin employed for the existence of a duty of care. It is known as the 'neighbour principle':

> The [biblical] rule that you are to love your neighbour becomes in law, you must not injure your neighbour; and the lawyer's question, 'Who is my neighbour?' receives a restricted reply. You must take reasonable care to avoid acts or omissions which you can reasonably foresee would be likely to injure your neighbour. Who then, in law, is my neighbour? The answer seems to be—persons who are so closely and directly affected by my act that I ought reasonably to have them in contemplation as being so affected when I am directing my mind to the acts and omissions which are called into question.

preliminary point of law
a particular issue in a case is decided without the court determining the ultimate issue in the case.

⏵ **CROSS REFERENCE**
The implications of this 'narrow rule' in *Donoghue v Stevenson* is discussed further in Chapter 10.

⏵ **THINKING POINT**
Why did Mrs Donoghue's friend not sue the café in contract for the faulty bottle of beer?

Lord Atkin was using the word 'neighbour' not to describe geographical closeness but in terms of those we might reasonably foresee as in danger of being affected by our actions if we are negligent. There are some problems with the words used in this speech. 'Omissions' are spoken of; however, you will learn that the law of negligence as a general rule does not impose a duty of care in respect of failure to act. The speech contains no specific information about what sort of damage the duty of care will relate to. You will see that the law of negligence favours loss which occurs in the form of *personal injury* or *property damage* but is less likely to impose liability for loss which is termed psychological injury or pure economic loss. The neighbour principle was not immediately or widely adopted as the definitive test for duty in the courts but over time it has become the foundation on which later approaches have been based.

Having brought her action as a 'pauper' Mrs Donoghue settled her action with the defendants for £200—a considerable amount of money at that time. A bench dedicated by lawyers now marks the site of the infamous café!

2.2.1 Policy

Before we proceed to examine the development of duty of care in the case law subsequent to *Donoghue v Stevenson*, it will be helpful to consider the way in which this concept is used by the courts. Duty of care can be broken down into *two questions*: first, one which is general and determined as a matter of law and policy, followed by one which is specific and fact-based.

(1) Is this a case of the *type* to which the law of negligence is applicable?

If so:

(2) Was it foreseeable that *this* claimant would be harmed by the defendant's act?

Comparing two significant negligence cases will illustrate what is meant by Question 1 and will introduce the important concept of *policy*.

In *Rondel v Worsley* (1969), the House of Lords confirmed that the barrister does not owe a duty of care in negligence to his clients in respect of his conduct of their case in court. This so-called immunity was gradually extended over the years to include other matters closely connected to the preparation of the court case and, as solicitors gained rights of audience, to include all advocates. Among the unanimous Law Lords' justifications for upholding the immunity were as follows: the advocate's overriding duty lies not to his client but to the court; to permit actions in negligence might result in the effective retrial of a number of cases ('collateral attacks') with a consequential impact on confidence in the administration of justice; there is a 'cab-rank rule' whereby the barrister is not at liberty to pick and choose which cases are accepted, and, lastly, the advocate must exercise his skill with complete independence, rather than in fear of a negligence claim.

🔍 CASE CLOSE-UP

Arthur JS Hall v Simons (2000)

Thirty years later the issue of advocates' immunity came before the House of Lords for re-consideration in *Arthur JS Hall v Simons* (2000). In view of the possibility that it might be decided to overrule their previous decision in *Rondel*, seven judges rather than the usual five considered the case. This time, the consensus on the matter was different. In closely argued and detailed speeches, the Law Lords reflected on the changes over the years in both professional culture and attitudes towards entitlements to remedies for wrongs and concluded that the advocates' immunity from liability for the conduct of a court case must be abolished. Lord Browne-Wilkinson reasoned as follows:

> First . . ., given the changes in society and in the law that have taken place since the decision in *Rondel v Worsley* . . ., it is appropriate to review the public policy decision that advocates enjoy immunity from liability for the negligent conduct of a case in court. Second, that the

> propriety of maintaining such immunity depends upon the balance between, on the one hand, the normal right of an individual to be compensated for a legal wrong done to him and, on the other, the advantages which accrue to the public interest from such immunity. Third, that in relation to claims for immunity for an advocate in civil proceedings, such balance no longer shows sufficient public benefit as to justify the maintenance of the immunity of the advocate.

Lord Browne-Wilkinson mentions the word *policy*. This can be defined as the *non-legal* considerations—perhaps economic, social, or ethical—which a judge may employ in deciding the outcome of a case. Policy plays a significant part in the law of negligence, particularly in relation to duty of care. When deciding whether a given situation is one in which there should be a duty of care, the judge may be estimating whether an affirmative decision would bring a flood of further similar claims which could overwhelm the courts or devalue legal credibility. This is often referred to as the *floodgates* issue. Closely related to this is the potential impact which a decision might have on the insurance industry in the future and it includes calculations about where it is most economically efficient for loss to lie. Recently judges have begun voicing concerns about the impact of negligence liability on socially beneficial activities such as school trips. Policy may also include reference to other options available to the client for obtaining redress.

⟩ CROSS REFERENCE
See also Compensation Act 2006 in Chapter 1.

McLachlin J in the Canadian Supreme Court described policy as meaning 'pragmatic' considerations (*Norsk Pacific Steamship Co Ltd v Canadian National Railway Co* (1992)). As demonstrated in *Hall v Simons* (2000), in recent years judges have become more open about expressing their views on policy matters and this transparency has let us know more about what lies behind their conclusions on the issue of duty of care. One problem with the influence of policy considerations, however, is that it involves a degree of guesswork. How much detailed evidence would need to be presented to the court before it was possible to estimate accurately a decision's likely future effect on, say, accident prevention? Thus we see that declarations of policy can be subjectively based, with judges differing on interpretations of what may be little more than informed guesswork.

⟩ THINKING POINT
Could the decision in *Hall v Simons* cause the floodgates to open? What legal approaches might be used to prevent a flood of successful negligence claims against advocates?

2.2.1.1 Expansion of the duty concept in the 1960s and 1970s

In *Donoghue v Stevenson*, Lord Macmillan observed that 'the categories of negligence are never closed' and indeed some new duty situations soon came to be recognized, for instance that due to bystanders by manufacturers of products (*Stennett v Hancock* (1939)). There was a period of general expansion of the reach of negligence during the 1960s and early 1970s.

🔍 CASE CLOSE-UP

Home Office v Dorset Yacht Co (1970)

A key case which illustrates that expansive trend is *Home Office v Dorset Yacht Co*. A group of young Borstal inmates were taken to Brownsea Island in Poole Harbour for a weekend's leave and training. During the night five of the boys escaped their guards and found their way to the claimants' yacht club, where they vandalized several yachts. When the Home Office was sued for the alleged negligence of their employees in failing to restrain the boys, the preliminary point which arose was whether the Home Office could be said to owe a duty of care in negligence in this situation.

The House of Lords held, by a majority of 4:1 in the affirmative. They recognized that in doing so they were extending the *Donoghue v Stevenson* neighbour principle into a novel set of circumstances, for two reasons. First, the wrong against the claimants had not been committed directly by the defendants (or their employees) but rather by a third party, the Borstal boys. Any liability of the defendants would then be based upon an omission—that is, their failure to control the actions of the boys. Second, there were two possible relationships of 'neighbourhood', in the *Donoghue v Stevenson* sense: that between the defendants and the boys and that between the defendants and the nearby yacht owners.

We will deal with the law relating to omissions later, but at this stage it is sufficient to point out that the court felt that this situation came within the group of cases in which there could be liability for a failure to act, that is when the wrongdoer was (or should have been!) under the care of the defendants. However, it was then necessary to focus or narrow the scope of who would be owed that duty of care, as described by Lord Diplock:

> To give rise to a duty on the part of the custodian owed to a member of the public to take reasonable care to prevent a Borstal trainee from escaping from his custody before completion of the trainee's sentence there should be some relationship between the custodian and the person to whom the duty is owed which exposes that person to a particular risk of damage in consequence of that escape which is different in its incidence from the general risk of damage from criminal acts of others which he shares with all members of the public . . ..
>
> I should therefore hold that any duty of a Borstal officer to use reasonable care to prevent a Borstal trainee from escaping from his custody was owed only to persons whom he could reasonably foresee had property situated in the vicinity of the place of detention of the detainee which the detainee was likely to steal or to appropriate and damage in the course of eluding immediate pursuit and recapture.

▶ CROSS REFERENCE

See 2.6 Omissions.

Reading between the lines, we can see that Lord Diplock's concept of duty of care is based upon reasonable *foreseeability of harm* (what would a reasonable person in the defendant's position have foreseen?) and a closeness or *proximity* of those in the yacht club who were more at risk than the general public. It must be noted that the claimants were strangers to the defendants, so in this particular case the proximity was purely geographical.

 THINKING POINT

Would the Home Office have been liable to a car owner if the boys had sailed the yacht to the mainland and walked two miles to find a car which they then vandalized?

According to Lord Reid:

> Donoghue v. Stevenson . . . may be regarded as a milestone, and the well-known passage in Lord Atkin's speech should I think be regarded as a statement of principle. It is not to be treated as if it were a statutory definition. It will require qualification in new circumstances. But I think that the time has come when we can and should say that it ought to apply unless there is some justification or valid explanation for its exclusion.

The 'justifications' and 'explanations' which Lord Reid was referring to included matters of policy. Policy in this case concerned the public interest in supporting programmes whose aim was to reform young delinquents, but which had to be balanced with private interests in personal safety and security of property.

The case of *Anns v London Borough of Merton* (1978) heralded a period, recently described as 'the heroic age of the law of negligence', in which the reach of the tort of negligence was expanded. The facts of the case concerned a local authority's liability for the negligent inspection of building plans. Here it will be seen that the ratio in *Anns* was overruled by the House of Lords in *Murphy v Brentwood DC* (1991).

▶ CROSS REFERENCE
See Chapter 5 for discussion of whether the damage was physical or purely economic.

Lord Wilberforce attempted to summarize the current principles for determining duty of care:

> [T]he position has now been reached that in order to establish that a duty of care arises in a particular situation, it is not necessary to bring the facts of that situation within those of previous situations in which a duty of care has been held to exist. Rather the question has to be approached in two stages. First one has to ask whether, as between the alleged wrongdoer and the person who has suffered damage there is a sufficient relationship of proximity or neighbourhood such that, in the reasonable contemplation of the former, carelessness on his part may be likely to cause damage to the latter—in which case a prima facie duty of care arises. Secondly, if the first question is answered affirmatively, it is necessary to consider whether there are any considerations which ought to negative, or to reduce or limit the scope of the duty or the class of person to whom it is owed or the damages to which a breach of it may give rise.

The above is sometimes referred to as 'the *Anns* two-stage test'. The first stage is satisfied by establishing whether the *Donoghue* neighbour principle can be satisfied. If so, a duty of care **prima facie** exists. The second stage involves looking at whether there are any reasons, or policy considerations, that this duty should *not* exist. Professor Cooke has likened the second stage of the *Anns* test to a 'long-stop'.

prima facie
'at first sight'; meaning that there is sufficient evidence to prove a case, unless it is disproved.

Anns was expected to lead to an increase in successful negligence actions, as there would be many more situations in which a duty of care would be found to exist. It was, indeed, followed by a number of cases which fulfilled this expectation. For example, in *Junior Books Ltd v Veitchi Co Ltd* (1983), the House of Lords held that a duty of care was owed by flooring subcontractors, who were liable to the owner of the factory whose floor they negligently laid. The court relied on the fact that the relationship between the parties was as close as it could be without being directly contractual. *Junior Books* was a controversial decision because the Law Lords were seen to have evaded the doctrine of privity of contract in order to find liability for damage which was technically pure economic loss and thus not normally allowable in negligence. The case was subsequently distinguished by later courts to the extent that it is now of historical interest only.

2.2.1.2 **The reach of negligence is restricted**

It was not long after *Anns* and *Junior Books* that judges began to make decisions which restricted this potential expansion of negligence, showing an awareness that it could open the floodgates. In *Rowling v Takaro Properties Ltd* (1988), Lord Keith said:

> a too literal application of the well-known observation of Lord Wilberforce in Anns . . . may be productive of a failure to have regard to, and to analyse and weigh, all the relevant considerations in considering whether it is appropriate that a duty of care should be imposed.

In *Yuen Kun Yeu v Att-Gen of Hong Kong* (1988), Lord Keith went further in rejecting the *Anns* test:

> [T]he two-stage test formulated by Lord Wilberforce for determining the existence of a duty of care in negligence has been elevated to a degree of importance greater than it merits, and greater perhaps than its author intended . . . .. [Their] Lordships consider that for the future it should be recognised that the two-stage test in Anns is not to be regarded as in all the circumstances a suitable guide to the existence of a duty of care.

❯ CROSS REFERENCE

For the details of *Caparo*, see Chapter 5.

The test for duty of care which is currently regarded as definitive is that described by Lord Bridge in *Caparo Industries plc v Dickman* (1990). The case itself concerned professional negligence and the question of whether auditors could be liable when their statements were relied on detrimentally by investors. However, it is important at this stage to consider the view of Lord Bridge:

> [I]n addition to the foreseeability of damage, necessary ingredients in any situation giving rise to a duty of care are that there should exist between the party owing the duty and the party to whom it is owed a relationship characterised by the law as one of 'proximity' or 'neighbourhood' and that the situation should be one in which the court considers it fair, just and reasonable that the law should impose a duty of a given scope upon the one party for the benefit of the other. But it is implicit in the passages referred to that the concepts of proximity and fairness embodied in these additional ingredients are not susceptible of any such precise definition as would be necessary to give them utility as practical tests, but amount in effect to little more than convenient labels to attach to the features of different specific situations which, on a detailed examination of all the circumstances, the law recognises pragmatically as giving rise to a duty of care of a given scope. Whilst recognising, of course, the importance of the underlying general principles common to the whole field of negligence, I think the law has now moved in the direction of attaching greater significance to the more traditional categorisation of distinct and recognisable situations as guides to the existence, the scope and the limits of the varied duties of care which the law imposes.
>
> We must now, I think, recognise the wisdom of the words of Brennan J. in the High Court of Australia in Sutherland Shire Council v. Heyman (1985), where he said:
>
> 'It is preferable, in my view, that the law should develop novel categories of negligence incrementally and by analogy with established categories, rather than by a massive extension of a prima facie duty of care restrained only by indefinable considerations which ought to negative, or to reduce or limit the scope of the duty or the class of person to whom it is owed'.

The *Caparo* 'three-stage test' comprises:

- foreseeable harm to the claimant;
- proximity or neighbourhood between the claimant and defendant; and
- that it is 'fair, just and reasonable' to impose a duty of care in this situation.

THINKING POINT

The incremental approach involves deciding new cases on the basis of similar cases already decided. Would you expect this approach to have an expanding or restricting influence on the development of the law of negligence?

It is generally accepted that Lord Bridge's third element, 'fair, just and reasonable', combines the policy factors with what is regarded as just between the parties. The three elements are given equal weight and, contrary to the position in *Anns* where there appeared to be a primary assumption of duty which could be cancelled by policy considerations, it has been argued that *Caparo* creates an assumption *against* duty, which policy considerations might overcome.

According to Lord Hoffmann in *Stovin v Wise* (1996):

> The trend of authorities has been to discourage the assumption that anyone who suffers loss is prima facie entitled to compensation from a person (preferably insured or a public authority) whose act or omission can be said to have caused it. The default position is that he is not.

At the same time as setting out his three-stage test, it is significant that Lord Bridge also endorsed an *incremental* approach to duty of care, as described by Brennan J.

CASE CLOSE-UP

Marc Rich & Co v Bishop Rock Marine Co Ltd (The Nicholas H) (1996)

In *Marc Rich & Co v Bishop Rock Marine Co Ltd (The Nicholas H)* (1996), we can see how the House of Lords put Lord Bridge's test for duty into practice. A ship, *The Nicholas H*, was carrying the claimant's cargo when she developed cracks in her hull. NKK, a marine classification society, a non-profit-making organization, was consulted in order to determine the extent of repair that would be required. An employee of NKK approved limited temporary repairs, after which the ship could resume its voyage. A few days later it sank, and all the plaintiffs' cargo was lost. Because the liability of the shipowners was limited, the plaintiffs attempted to recover the full extent of their financial loss ($5.7 million) from NKK.

The House of Lords found in favour of the defendants because no duty of care was owed by the marine classification society to the cargo owners. On a preliminary point of law, it was assumed that the defendants had acted negligently and that the cargo loss (property damage) was a foreseeable outcome of that negligence, and it was assumed that the necessary proximity between the parties also existed. But the Law Lords discussed a number of policy reasons which led them to the conclusion that it would not be fair, just, and reasonable to impose a duty in this type of case. The first was that the law of international trade, underpinned by a network of contracts and supported by insurance cover, already covered the events. To allow this to be evaded to the claimant's advantage by imposing liability on the marine classification society could undermine the whole system of international trade in the future. The insurance implications of imposing a duty of care could make international trade more effective and the settlement of disputes less efficient.

THINKING POINT

What would be the wider
implications of allowing tort
law to effectively overrule
the existing rules of
international trade?

Lord Steyn put it this way:

Is the imposition of a duty of care fair, just and reasonable?

By way of summary, I look at the matter from the point of view of the three parties concerned. I conclude that the recognition of a duty would be unfair, unjust and unreasonable
as against the shipowners who would ultimately have to bear the cost of holding classification societies liable, such consequence being at variance with the bargain between shipowners and cargo owners based on an internationally agreed contractual structure. It
would also be unfair, unjust and unreasonable towards classification societies, notably
because they act for the collective welfare and unlike shipowners they would not have the
benefit of any limitation provisions. Looking at the matter from the point of view of cargo
owners, the existing system provides them with the protection of the Hague Rules or
Hague-Visby Rules. But that protection is limited under such Rules and by tonnage limitation provisions. Under the existing system any shortfall is readily insurable. In my judgment
the lesser injustice is done by not recognising a duty of care. It follows that I would reject
the primary way in which counsel for the cargo owners put his case.

The incremental approach was impossible in *Watson v British Boxing Board of Control* (2001).
A boxer who suffered brain damage following a title fight in London alleged that the Board which
regulates boxing had been negligent in not providing a better level of ringside medical care. Lord
Phillips in the Court of Appeal described the case as a unique one because here, rather than
preventing it, the causing of physical harm was the object of the activity. The role of the defendant
was in reducing the effects of these foreseeable injuries once they occurred. Because using the
analogy of previous cases was not possible, the court considered all the circumstances of the case,
including the reliance placed upon the Board by boxers, and concluded that it was fair, just, and
reasonable to impose a duty of care. Even the fact that the Board was a non-profit-making organization (like the defendant in *Marc Rich*) was not enough to deny the justice of finding liability.

In *Darnley v Croydon Health Services NHS Trust* (2018), a patient suffering from a head injury
attended a hospital A&E department. He was told that the expected waiting time was four to
five hours, but the receptionist failed to add that he would be seen by a triage nurse within
thirty minutes. The claimant left after nineteen minutes and without treatment, his condition
worsened, and he was left with long-term disabilities which would have been avoided with
prompt treatment. In the Court of Appeal, the main issue was whether the scope of the duty
of care owed to patients by reception staff included accurate notification of waiting times. To
answer this the Court of Appeal applied the *Caparo* test. The requirements of proximity and
foreseeability were present. However, it confirmed the view of the trial judge that it would not
be fair, just, and reasonable to impose a duty of care on A&E reception staff to inform patients
accurately of waiting times.

According to the Supreme Court, the lower courts had confused or conflated the issues of duty
and breach. It was clear that the duty of care owed by a hospital to a patient included the duty
to give reasonably accurate information regarding waiting times. Because this was not a novel
situation, clearly within the scope of *Donoghue v* Stevenson, there had been no need to apply
the *Caparo* test. The 'colossal pressure' that A&E departments work under was relevant, not to

Diagram 2.1 The 'reach' of negligence

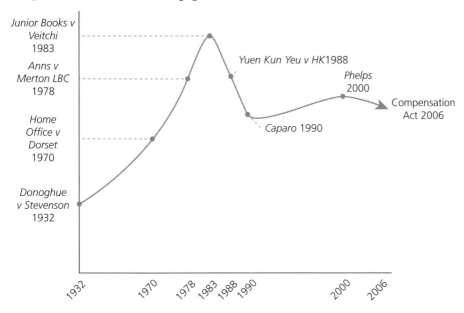

whether there was a duty of care, but rather to the question of breach. Applying the standard of 'an averagely competent and well-informed person performing the function of a receptionist at a department providing emergency medical care' the Court concluded that it had been negligent for the receptionist to fail to tell the claimant that he would be seen by a triage nurse within thirty minutes. Causation having been satisfied, liability was established.

In his leading speech in the recent key case of *Michael v Chief Constable of South Wales Police* (2015), which is discussed in detail below, Lord Toulson admitted to having doubt about the long-term impact of Lord Bridge's test in *Caparo*, while strongly endorsing the incremental approach.

Clarifying the status of *Caparo* was one of the important features of *Robinson v Chief Constable of West Yorkshire* (2018).

🔍 CASE CLOSE-UP

Robinson v Chief Constable of West Yorkshire (2018)

A 'relatively frail lady, then aged 76' was knocked over and injured during a scuffle between two police officers and a suspected drug dealer in a busy shopping centre. The simple question was whether or not a duty of care had been owed to her by the police officers; however challenging issues arose regarding the extent of police immunity from negligence actions in their crime fighting capacity. Hallett LJ in the Court of Appeal applied the *Caparo* three-part test for duty of care and concluded that, in view of previous policy decisions, that it would not be 'fair, just and reasonable' to impose a duty of care on the police in this instance.

On appeal to the Supreme Court, there was a unanimous decision finding of a duty, for the reason that this was a simple case of the breach of the duty not to cause physical injury by positive action. As discussed below, it was held that what is sometimes referred to as the 'immunity' of the police is little more than the application of the general rule against liability for the failure to protect against injury caused by a third party.

What is important here is the reiteration that the *Caparo* test is appropriate only for situations in which the established principles do not provide an answer. In the present case, however, the court is not required to consider an extension of the law of negligence. All that is required is the application to particular circumstances of established principles governing liability for personal injuries. According to Lord Hughes, 'it is neither necessary nor appropriate to treat *Caparo Industries v Dickman* . . . as requiring the application of its familiar three-stage examination afresh to every action brought. Where the law is clear that a particular relationship, or recurrent factual situation, gives rise to a duty of care, there is no occasion to resort to *Caparo*, at least unless the court is being invited to depart from previous authority.' Some of the Justices conceded that the margins of established categories can sometimes be difficult to discern; it is not always clear what will constitute a novel category.

Duty of care so far

Before moving on to look at some of the problematic aspects of duty of care, it will be helpful to recap this large and unwieldy topic.

- Duty of care is a key limiting device for the law of negligence.

- It is a matter of law and is strongly policy-based.

- The key cases on the general principles of duty of care are *Donoghue v Stevenson* and *Caparo Industries v Dickman*.

- The factors which courts take into account in determining duty of care are *foreseeability of harm*, *proximity*, and whether imposing a duty would be *fair, just, and reasonable*.

Diagram 2.1 illustrates the 'reach' of negligence.

2.3 Insurance

CROSS REFERENCE

See Chapter 1 for the tort system.

We know that the vast majority of tort actions are based upon insurance, for the simple reason that it is only the insured defendant who is likely to be able to pay compensation should he be held liable. As explained earlier, while the cases appear to be between individuals, in reality they are usually brought against the wrongdoer's insurer and are often brought by the claimant's insurer. Two areas of liability are noted for their statutory requirements of compulsory insurance.

Employers are required by the Employers' Liability (Compulsory Insurance) Act 1969 to hold liability cover for their employees and the Road Traffic Act 1988 requires motorists to be insured for damage to third parties. It is, then, no surprise to hear that the Pearson Commission discovered that 47 per cent of all tort claims concerned employers' liability and another 41 per cent were for motor accidents.

To what extent do the courts take insurance into account when making decisions about negligence liability? Judges have not always agreed on this. The traditional view is represented by Viscount Simonds in *Davie v New Merton Board Mills Ltd* (1959):

> It was at one time suggested . . . that the House should take into consideration the fact that possibly or even probably the employer would, but the workman would not, be covered by insurance, and for that reason should be the more ready to fasten upon the employer liability . . .; I will only say that this is not a consideration to which your Lordships should give any weight at all in your determination of the rights and liabilities of the parties . . . .. It is not the function of a court of law to fasten upon the fortuitous circumstance of insurance to impose a greater burden on the employer than would otherwise lie upon him.

However, in the same way that judges have become more open about discussing the policy behind their decisions, they have also begun to cite, and at times to justify, their decisions at least partly upon insurance considerations.

In *Smith v Eric S Bush* (1990), Lord Griffiths put it this way:

> What are the practical consequences of the decision on the question of reasonableness? This must involve the sums of money potentially at stake and the ability of the parties to bear the loss involved, which, in its turn, raises the question of insurance. There was once a time when it was considered improper even to mention the possible existence of insurance cover in a lawsuit. But those days are long past. Everyone knows that all prudent, professional men carry insurance, and the availability and cost of insurance must be a relevant factor when considering which of two parties should be required to bear the risk of a loss.

> **THINKING POINT**
> What effect might the prevalence of insurance have on the tort system as a means of deterrence?

He reflects an awareness that one of the functions of tort is to spread the cost of losses efficiently. It is about more than simple blameworthiness. Insurance will be relevant between the two parties in the case, but once duty is established in a certain type of situation there will be wider implications. Carol Harlow, however, has noted that in many cases judges will only be guessing about the possible future insurance considerations of certain outcomes (*Understanding Tort Law*, 3rd edn, Sweet & Maxwell, 2005, p 24). While openness about decision-making cannot be disputed, the finding of a duty of care and thus liability on the basis of perceived insurance implications could be risky when not well supported.

2.4 What kind of damage?

You will recall that the foundations of negligence law were laid in cases concerning bodily injury and property damage. Despite the amount of time given to the topic in this chapter, very little litigation actually comes before the courts concerning the issue of duty of care. That is because in cases of personal injury, death, and property damage there tends to be an assumption in favour of a duty of care. According to Lunney and Oliphant, *Tort Law: Text and Materials*, 5th edn (OUP, 2013):

> [I]n the modern law it is permissible to work on the assumption that, where a private individual commits a positive act of **misfeasance** which foreseeably causes physical harm to the person or property of the claimant, a duty of care will be owed.

> **misfeasance**
> wrongdoing

The authors go on to point out that this assumption can be rebutted in some cases and *Marc Rich* (discussed earlier) is such an example.

Negligence liability has developed to cover other types of damage as well, such as particular types of psychological injury and pure economic loss. It is now necessary to consider other situations which are also outside Lunney and Oliphant's description: when the damage is attributed not to a private individual but to a *public body* and when it is the result not of a 'positive act of misfeasance' but due to an *omission*.

2.5 Public bodies as defendants

Negligence actions against public bodies have in the past raised difficulties around the issue of duty of care. Examples of what is meant by 'public bodies' are the central government (for example, the Home Office in *Dorset Yacht*), local authorities, schools, police, or fire authorities, and 'quangos' such as Thames Water or the Milk Marketing Board. There has been a general reluctance by the courts to impose negligence liability on public bodies, based on an awareness that the actions of public bodies are subject to different considerations than those of private individuals or organizations. When allocating resources and taking decisions on risk, public bodies are likely to be both empowered and constrained by statutory authority. Judges are also aware that when liability is imposed, this will usually be indirectly underwritten by the taxpayer. As Professor Harlow has put it:

> [British judges] are more likely to take the view that the 'deep pockets' of government should not be treated as a free and bottomless insurance fund.

> **ultra vires**
> Latin phrase meaning that someone is acting beyond the powers they have been given, in this case by legislation.

Courts have at times used public law concepts such as **ultra vires** to address the problem of tort liability of public bodies. A focus on the issue of whether or not the public body was acting within its powers was suggested in *Dorset Yacht*, but case development subsequently has favoured a different approach: that of determining *justiciability*. According to this there are some aspects of public bodies' activities which can be looked into by the courts and others which are outside the scope of the courts. One approach to this distinction was described by Lord Wilberforce in *Anns v London Borough of Merton* as a choice between *policy* and *operational* decisions. The former, which are not justiciable, are ones in which the public body may be using its discretion concerning, say, the allocation of resources. In *Dorset Yacht* it would have been a policy decision that a borstal is an appropriate institution for young offenders and that a certain number of borstals were needed nationally. The operational decisions, which are justiciable, are in a more practical realm of day-to-day running of a Borstal, such as decisions made by prison officers about how to guard a particular party of youths on a given night.

The policy–operational distinction proved unworkable in practice because there was no clear consensus about which activities fell into which category. Instead, the current situation has been described by Winfield as a continuum or spectrum. At one end are matters of 'high policy' which can never be the subject of a negligence action—for instance, a Cabinet decision to go to war. At the other end are decisions which would seem to be very appropriate for a court to review in a negligence action, such as a school's educational psychologist's misdiagnosis of a child's learning difficulties. It is important to remember that just because an issue is justiciable, it does not mean that the public body will owe a duty of care to all parties concerned. The cases will show that there may be a duty to some but not to others. Neither does a finding of justiciability mean that the public body defendant will be liable in negligence: the court may impose a very high threshold on the question of breach.

THINKING POINT

Where on the spectrum of justiciability would you put the following activities and why?

(1) a decision by a local authority social worker not to take a child into care;

(2) a failure by an ambulance service to promptly dispatch an ambulance;

(3) the failure of a psychologist employed by an education authority to diagnose a pupil's dyslexia;

(4) a decision by a local authority highways department concerning dangerous obstructions in the road.

The answers given by the courts will be revealed below!

2.5.1 Liability of public bodies gathers pace

The door on tort liability of public bodies began to open with *Dorset Yacht*. However, in a number of important and high-level cases the courts continued to wrestle with the implications of negligence liability in this area.

CASE CLOSE-UP

X v Bedfordshire CC (1995)

X v Bedfordshire CC (1995) was one of a number of conjoined cases heard by the House of Lords concerning local authority liability for children's welfare. In *Bedfordshire* itself, five children in a family had been under the supervision of the local authority social services department. They were suffering a high level of neglect and mistreatment by their parents; however, the decision was made not to have them taken into care. As adults they sued the Bedfordshire County Council for damages for the personal and psychological injuries which they sustained. Lord Browne-Wilkinson indicated that although the way the initial care decision had been taken was a practical matter which was probably justiciable, it would not be fair, just, or reasonable (in *Caparo* terms) to impose a duty of care on the local authority in respect of it.

He gave a number of policy reasons which included: first, the fact that this type of decision was a delicate one which cut across a number of different disciplines; second, the local authority's power was given by the Children Act 1989 and this was not the sort of statute under which an individual should be able to sue in tort; third, there was the awareness that this was an area which might give rise to unfounded legal actions. It should be noted that when the case was appealed to the European Court of Human Rights (ECtHR) in *Z v UK* (2001), judgment was given in favour of the claimants and the UK was held neither to have protected the children from inhuman or degrading treatment (a breach of Article 3 of the European Convention on Human Rights (ECHR)) nor to have given them an effective legal remedy for this failure (a breach of Article 13).

Educational failures were the concern of *Phelps v Hillingdon LBC* (2000), where the House of Lords heard a group of conjoined cases brought against local authority education departments. One claimant had been referred to her school's educational psychologist at the age of 11 to be tested for a learning disability. Although she was later privately diagnosed as dyslexic, the problem was missed by the psychologist. As a result the claimant did not receive the sort of remedial teaching she needed, and her earning potential was diminished. The House of Lords found the defendants vicariously liable for the failure of their employee and awarded damages for the lost educational opportunities. According to Lord Slynn, 'where an educational psychologist is specifically called in to advise in relation to the assessment and future provision for a specific child and it is clear that the parents acting for the child and the teachers will follow that advice, a duty of care prima facie arises'. There were no reasons in this case to overturn that presumption.

Stovin v Wise (1996) concerned a road verge on which a bank of earth obstructed drivers' views and had been responsible for several accidents. Norfolk County Council was aware of the problem but failed to exercise its statutory power to require the landowner to remove the obstruction. The House of Lords denied a duty of care in negligence by a majority of three to two. The case was complicated by the fact that it involved an omission.

On the issue of liability of a public body, Lord Hoffmann spoke for the majority. He reflected on the inadequacy of the policy–operational distinction, because there was little predictability or consistency in allocating functions into each category. For him the significant factor in this case was that Parliament had chosen to give the council a *power* rather than a *duty* in respect of the removal of obstructions: 'the fact that Parliament has conferred a discretion must be some indication that the policy of the act conferring the power was not to create a right to compensation'. In *Gorringe v Calderdale MBC* (2004), the Law Lords reached a similar conclusion in another highways case, this time concerning a council's failure to replace a warning sign on a dangerous stretch of road.

Poole BC v GN and Another (2019) considered the issue of duty of care owed by social services departments exercising statutory functions of child protection in terms of *assumption of responsibility*. This is a concept which will be dealt with in more detail in Chapter 5 in relation to negligent misstatement. While concluding that no such duty existed in the circumstances of *Poole*, the Supreme Court was clear that assumption of responsibility can be one lens through which duty can be assessed in such cases. *X v Bedfordshire* was no longer good law, to the extent to which it appeared to give a blanket immunity to local authorities on policy grounds; each case must be examined on its own facts 'according to general principles'.

Before finishing this topic, it is interesting to observe that the same action may well be held to carry with it a duty to one of the parties involved but not to another. *JD v East Berkshire Community Health Trust* (2005) was a case in which three different sets of parents sued for the psychological injuries they had suffered due to misdiagnosis of child abuse by social services or health authorities. In *JD* itself, a boy's allergic reaction was interpreted wrongly by the social services department as indicating mistreatment by his mother and he was put on the at-risk register for some months until the mistake was discovered. His mother's claim for damages was rejected by the House of Lords for a number of policy reasons, many of which were similar to those we have seen discussed in relation to the *Bedfordshire* case. Lord Rodger, however, also felt that there could be a potential conflict of interest if a duty were owed to the mother as well as the child:

> The duty to the children is simply to exercise reasonable care and skill in diagnosing and treating any condition from which they may be suffering. In carrying out that duty the doctors have regard only to the interests of the children. Suppose, however, that they were also under a duty to the parents not to cause them psychiatric harm by concluding that they might have abused their child. Then, in deciding how to proceed, the doctors would always have to take account of the risk that they might harm the parents in this way. There would be not one but two sets of interests to be considered. Acting on, or persisting in, a suspicion of abuse might well be reasonable when only the child's interests were engaged, but unreasonable if the interests of the parents had also to be taken into account. Of its very nature, therefore, this kind of duty of care to the parents would cut across the duty of care to the children.

We are left, then, with a degree of unpredictability about when courts will impose liability on public authorities, though there appears to be a growing sympathy for claimants against education authorities. When the relationship between the claimant and defendant is that of employer and employee, the Court of Appeal was in no doubt that, despite the existence of a common law duty of care founded upon that relationship, there may be some exceptional cases where this could only be fulfilled by the exercise of a public law power (*Connor v Surrey County Council* (2010)).

> ❯ **THINKING POINT**
> What argument would you make to contradict the view of Lord Rodger in *Bedfordshire*?

🔍 CASE CLOSE-UP

Smith v Ministry of Defence (2013)

The possibility of more extensive public liability was opened up in *Smith v Ministry of Defence* (2013). The case concerned injuries and deaths suffered by five soldiers serving in the British Army in Iraq between 2003 and 2006. The claims were based upon alleged failures by the Ministry of Defence to provide adequate equipment and training as well as upon flaws in operational tactics.

❯ THINKING POINT

What would be the significance of regarding *Smith* as a case of employers' liability (see Chapter 8)?

In a striking-out action, a seven-person Supreme Court ruled on three main issues. First, the defence argument that the soldiers had been outside the jurisdiction of the UK for the purposes of the ECHR was rejected. Extraterritorial jurisdiction exists in exceptional cases, one being when individuals are under the complete control and authority of the state, as were the soldiers serving in Iraq. Second, the state's positive duties to protect the right to life under Article 2 ECHR were engaged and, while the state enjoyed a wide margin of appreciation, the question of breach remained to be judged on the detailed facts of each case. Third, combat immunity (which would mean that it would not be fair, just, and reasonable to impose a duty of care in negligence) would be narrowly construed and did not apply to preparatory activities which fell short of active conflict with the enemy, as was the situation in four of the five claims. The fifth was left to be determined at trial. Striking out was not appropriate to any of the claims.

2.6 Omissions

Although Lord Atkin in *Donoghue v Stevenson* refers to 'acts or omissions' as forming the basis of the negligence action, English law has been reluctant to impose liability for omissions, or failures to act. Another way of describing this is to say that in English law there is generally no duty to perform actions to help someone or to prevent their injury. The example is often given in terms of the possible rescue of a non-swimmer struggling in the water. The general position is that tort law would impose no liability on someone who had the means to rescue the drowning person but chose not to! This may be surprising and indeed there are many other jurisdictions, such as that of France, which provide for both civil as well as criminal liability in such situations.

Why should duty of care be restricted in the case of omissions? Read the following excerpt from the opinion of Lord Hoffmann in *Stovin v Wise* (1996) and look for the following reasons:

- invasion of freedom;
- 'why pick on me?'; and
- economic inefficiency.

There are sound reasons why omissions require different treatment from positive conduct. It is one thing for the law to say that a person who undertakes some activity shall take reasonable care not to cause damage to others. It is another thing for the law to require that a person who is doing nothing in particular shall take steps to prevent another from suffering harm from the acts of third parties (like Mrs Wise) or natural causes. One can put the matter in political, moral or economic terms. In political terms it is less of an invasion of an individual's freedom for the law to require him to consider the safety of others in his actions than to impose upon him a duty to rescue or protect. A moral version of this point may be called the 'why pick on me?' argument. A duty to prevent harm to others or to render assistance to a person in danger or distress may apply to a large and indeterminate class of people who happen to be able to do something. Why should one be held liable rather than another? In economic terms, the efficient allocation of resources usually requires an activity should bear its own costs. If it benefits from being able to impose some of its costs on other people (what economists call 'externalities') the market is distorted because the activity appears cheaper than it really is. So liability to pay compensation for loss caused by negligent conduct acts as a deterrent against increasing the cost of the activity to the community and reduces externalities. But there is no similar justification for requiring a person who is not doing anything to spend money on behalf of someone else. Except in special cases (such as marine salvage) English law does not reward someone who voluntarily confers a benefit on another. So there must be some special reason why he should have to put his hand in his pocket.

Before going on to look at case law in this area and the very important exceptions to the above rule, it is necessary to clarify what is meant by an omission in law. Obviously, many negligent courses of action involve *not* doing something. When a driver fails to stop at a red light, he has failed to put his foot on the brake pedal. This would not be treated in law as an omission, but rather just as one aspect of his negligent way of driving his car. We are often, here, looking at a defendant's failure to protect the claimant from a risk of harm caused by a third party or by himself. Another way of describing it, suggested by Lunney and Oliphant in *Tort Law: Text and Materials*, 5th edn (OUP, 2013), is the difference between 'making things worse' (which could bring liability) and 'failing to make things better' (which often does not).

 CASE CLOSE-UP

Stovin v Wise

In *Stovin v Wise*, we have seen that the cause of the danger to road users was the bank of earth projecting from land owned by British Rail (in addition to the negligent driving of one of the vehicles which crashed). Norfolk County Council was being sued for its failure, or omission, to enforce removal of the obstruction, of which it was aware. The fact that the Council's wrong was an omission was the major factor, combined with the fact that it was a public body, in concluding that there had been no duty of care. Lord Hoffmann (in the majority) and Lord Nicholls (in the minority) agreed that although there could often be uncertainty about categorizing omissions, it was correct that there should be a presumption against duty of care in these cases. Lord Nicholls said:

> [T]he recognised legal position is that the bystander does not owe the drowning child or the heedless pedestrian a duty to take steps to save him. Something more is required than being a bystander. There must be some additional reason why it is fair and reasonable that one person should be regarded as his brother's keeper and have legal obligations in that regard. When this additional reason exists, there is said to be sufficient proximity. That is the customary label.

 THINKING POINT

Discussions around duty of care often use religious terminology, such as reference to the parable of the Good Samaritan and, above, 'my brother's keeper'. Do you think that the approach of English law to the duty to rescue can be attacked as immoral or can you defend it?

What is Lord Nicholls's 'something more'? Looking at *Smith v Littlewoods* (1987) will help to provide the answers.

CASE CLOSE-UP

Smith v Littlewoods (1987)

The defendants owned a disused cinema which they were intending to demolish. Before they could do so, people began to break into the property and several times, unknown to the defendants, attempted to start fires in piles of rubbish which had accumulated. A fire was started which spread to and damaged adjoining properties. The owners of those properties sued the defendants in negligence for their failure to adequately secure the premises. The damage was done by the arsonists (who would not be worth suing), so instead the claimants sought compensation from Littlewoods, who were no doubt well insured!

According to Lord Goff:

> That there are special circumstances in which a defender may be held responsible in law for injuries suffered by the pursuer through a third party's deliberate wrongdoing is not in doubt. For example, a duty of care may arise from a relationship between the parties, which gives rise to an imposition or assumption of responsibility upon or by the defender, as in *Stansbie v. Troman* [1948] 2 K.B. 48, where such responsibility was held to arise from a contract. In that case a decorator, left alone on the premises by the householder's wife, was held liable when he went out leaving the door on the latch, and a thief entered the house and stole property. Such responsibility might well be held to exist in other cases where there is no contract, as for example where a person left alone in a house has entered as a licensee of the occupier. Again, the defender may be vicariously liable for the third party's act; or he may be held liable as an occupier to a visitor on his land. Again, as appears from the dictum of Dixon J. in *Smith v. Leurs*, 70 C.L.R. 256, 262, a duty may arise from a special relationship between the defender and the third party, by virtue of which the defender is responsible for controlling the third party: see, for example, *Dorset Yacht Co. Ltd. v. Home Office* [1970] A.C. 1004. More pertinently, in a case between adjoining occupiers of land, there may be liability in nuisance if one occupier causes or permits persons to gather on his land, and they impair his neighbour's enjoyment of his land. Indeed, even if such persons come on to his land as trespassers, the occupier may, if they constitute a nuisance, be under an affirmative duty to abate the nuisance. As I pointed out in *P. Perl (Exporters) Ltd. v. Camden London Borough Council* [1984] Q.B. 342, 359, there may well be other cases.

> These are all special cases. But there is a more general circumstance in which a defender may be held liable in negligence to the pursuer, although the immediate cause of the damage suffered by the pursuer is the deliberate wrongdoing of another. This may occur where the defender negligently causes or permits to be created a source of danger, and it is reasonably foreseeable that third parties may interfere with it and, sparking off the danger, thereby cause damage to persons in the position of the pursuer. The classic example of such a case is, perhaps, *Haynes v. Harwood* [1935] 1 K.B. 146, where the defendant's carter left a horse-drawn van unattended in a crowded street, and the horses bolted when a boy threw a stone at them. A police officer who suffered injury in stopping the horses before they injured a woman and children was held to be entitled to recover damages from the defendant. There, of course, the defendant's servant had created a source of danger by leaving his

horses unattended in a busy street. Many different things might have caused them to bolt—a sudden noise or movement, for example, or, as happened, the deliberate action of a mischievous boy. But all such events were examples of the very sort of thing which the defendant's servant ought reasonably to have foreseen and to have guarded against by taking appropriate precautions . . . . I wish to emphasise that I do not think that the problem in these cases can be solved simply through the mechanism of foreseeability . . . . [T]here is at present no general duty at common law to prevent persons from harming others by their deliberate wrongdoing, however foreseeable such harm may be if the defender does not take steps to prevent it.

The scope of the ratio in *Smith* was further defined by the Law Lords in *Mitchell v Glasgow City Council* (2009). A negligence action was brought on behalf of the deceased tenant of social housing managed by the defendants. He was murdered by a fellow tenant, following a long campaign of abuse and threats, of which the defendants had been aware. The required element of a relationship of responsibility was absent, as it would not be 'fair, just and reasonable' to impose this on a public authority coping with an onerous burden of antisocial behaviour among tenants.

2.6.1 Exceptions to no liability for omissions

The areas of exception which emerge from Lord Goff's speech are:

(1) a relationship between the parties which gives rise to an assumption of responsibility (this might be based on a contract, but not necessarily);

(2) a specific or inferred undertaking of responsibility for the claimant by the defendant;

(3) a relationship of control between the defendant and a third party; and

(4) the defendant creates or permits a source of danger to be created, which is interfered with by third parties. Additional to this is a failure of a defendant to remove a source of danger of which he is aware.

Lord Goff also refers to nuisance, vicarious liability, and occupiers' liability but they will not be dealt with at this stage.

We now consider cases which illustrate the exceptions to the basic rule about liability for omissions.

2.6.1.1 Relationship creating an assumption of responsibility

In *Mitchell v Glasgow City Council* (2009) a negligence action was brought on behalf of the deceased tenant of social housing managed by the defendants. He was murdered by a fellow tenant, following a long campaign of abuse and threats, of which the defendants had been aware. The required element of a relationship of responsibility was absent, as it would not be 'fair, just and reasonable' to impose this on a public authority coping with an onerous burden of antisocial behaviour among tenants.

In *Rabone v Pennine Care NHS Trust* (2012) a 'voluntary' patient in a hospital's mental health unit was suffering from severe depression and had known suicidal tendencies. Despite her family's doubts, doctors negligently gave her weekend leave, whereupon she killed herself. In her parents' action against the hospital, it was held that the therapeutic caring relationship had imposed upon the hospital a common law duty of care for this patient's safety.

2.6.1.2 The undertaking of responsibility for the claimant

In *Stansbie v Troman* (1948), a decorator was held liable to the homeowners for a theft of jewellery which took place when he left the house unlocked when going out for two hours to buy wallpaper. The contractual relationship between the parties was held to have created a duty on the defendant to take positive steps to protect the claimant from loss.

In *Barrett v Ministry of Defence* (1995), there had been a pattern of excessive drinking among soldiers at a remote Navy base, where drinks were very cheap. One night a soldier collapsed while drunk. The duty officer arranged for him to be taken to his room where he was left and later died due to choking on his own vomit. His widow brought a negligence action against the Ministry of Defence. The Navy was not held to be under a general duty to prevent its employees from excessive drinking; however, here a relationship of care had been undertaken.

Lord Justice Beldam in the Court of Appeal observed:

> In the present case I would reverse the judge's finding that the defendant was under a duty to take reasonable care to prevent the deceased from abusing alcohol to the extent he did. Until he collapsed, I would hold that the deceased was in law alone responsible for his condition. Thereafter when the defendant assumed responsibility for him, it accepts [*sic*] that the measures taken fell short of the standard reasonably to be expected. It did not summon assistance and its supervision of him was inadequate.

In *Kent v Griffiths* (2000), a GP made a 999 call for an ambulance to take a pregnant woman suffering from an asthma attack to hospital. The call was taken and an ambulance dispatched; however, it took thirty-eight minutes to arrive, despite two further calls by the GP, although the distance was only 6.5 miles. The patient suffered brain damage and lost her baby, and she sued the ambulance service in negligence for the damage attributable to the delay. The Court of Appeal reversed the earlier ruling against the claimant and held that the acceptance of the call created a duty of care in respect of the patient. The ambulance service was liable.

On the other hand, a failure to assume responsibility was clearly established by the lack of proximity between the defendant and the claimant's harm in *Sutradhar v NERC* (2006). A large number of people in Bangladesh had been poisoned by drinking from a well which had been contaminated by arsenic. The defendants had been commissioned by the Overseas Development Agency to test local water for minerals which might be harmful to fish. They had not been required to, nor did they ever consider, the testing of the water for arsenic. A negligence action failed in both the Court of Appeal and, unanimously, in the House of Lords. There was held to be no relationship of proximity between the claimants and the defendant that would give rise to a positive duty to test for arsenic in the water. Lord Hoffmann expressed his position strongly:

> [The] principle is not that a duty of care is owed in all cases in which it is foreseeable that in the absence of care someone may suffer physical injury. There must be proximity in the sense of a

measure of control over and responsibility for the potentially dangerous situation. Such a principle does not help the claimant . . .. The [defendant] had no control whatever, whether in law or in practice, over the supply of drinking water in Bangladesh, nor was there any statute, contract or other arrangement which imposed upon it responsibility for ensuring that it was safe to drink.

2.6.1.3 Existing relationship with wrongdoer involving control

It will be recalled that a duty of care was held to be owed to property owners in the vicinity of the Borstal camp in *Home Office v Dorset Yacht*. Again it must be emphasized that this was another example of an omission—that is, the failure of the prison authorities to prevent the boys' escape. In the House of Lords it was held that, because the custodial relationship between the prison authorities and the wrongdoers could be described as one of control, the torts committed by the boys were the responsibility of the Home Office.

The case of *Carmarthenshire County Council v Lewis* (1955) concerned a young child who ran from his nursery school premises onto the busy road which ran nearby. The plaintiff's husband swerved his car to avoid hitting the child and was himself killed when his car hit a tree. The defendant County Council and the teachers at the school were held to have been jointly in control of the child and therefore under a duty to take reasonable steps to prevent them becoming a danger to others.

2.6.1.4 Creation of or failure to remove a danger

We have seen that in *Smith v Littlewoods* the House of Lords carefully considered whether the defendants could be held liable for negligently failing to 'abate a fire risk created by third parties on their property without their fault'. Lord Goff believed that this was the sort of situation in which liability could be imposed for a failure to act. Here it was concluded that the risk of arson to the claimant's property was not reasonably foreseeable and on that basis their neighbours could not have been liable in negligence for failing to address it.

The case of *Goldman v Hargrave* (1966) was a nuisance case; however, Lord Goff used it as an example of the sort of situation in which negligence liability might be imposed for an omission. In Australia lightning struck a large tree on the defendant's land causing it to catch fire. The defendant did not sufficiently put the fire out and, when the wind changed, the fire spread to the claimant's land. This had been a hazardous state of affairs which the defendant omitted to remedy and for this Lord Goff suggested that a duty in negligence could in some circumstances be owed.

> **CROSS REFERENCE**
> See Chapter 12.

It would seem, however, that the courts are often reluctant to impose liability. In *Topp v London Country Buses Ltd* (1993), a bus driver left his bus, along with the ignition keys, in a lay-by near to a pub for a relief driver who never arrived. Some nine hours later the bus was stolen and, while being driven by the thief, hit and killed the claimant's wife. The Court of Appeal held that no duty of care arose. The theft was not foreseeable as a result of the defendants' negligence. Proximity between the bus company and the deceased was doubtful. In any case it would not be fair, just, and reasonable to impose a duty. It would appear that it was crucial to the decision that the defendants had not been aware of the nature of the clientele of the pub!

CASE CLOSE-UP

Capital & Counties plc v Hampshire County Council (1997)

The sometimes vexed position of the emergency services was at issue in this case. It concerned a number of cases against fire services who arguably had failed to prevent damage by fire. In only one of the cases was there held to have been a duty of care owed to the claimants: this was where a sprinkler system was turned off by the defendants. This positive act ultimately made the claimants' position worse, when a fire which had not been completely extinguished reignited. Students should note that merely taking the emergency call and arriving at the fire scene was not, in itself, enough to create a duty of care. There were strong policy reasons that the Court of Appeal felt that the fire service should be seen to owe a duty of care in negligence to the community as a whole, rather than individual property owners. You might wish to contrast this decision with that in *Kent v Griffiths*, discussed earlier.

 THINKING POINT

Liz is a doctor driving home from her thirty-six-hour shift at the local hospital. She sees a motorbike hit a pedestrian on a quiet road, but the rider fails to stop. Liz gets out and looks at the pedestrian and decides, wrongly, that his injuries are not serious, so she leaves him by the side of the road and drives home. Could Liz be liable in tort for the additional injury which the pedestrian suffers due to her failure to assist him?

2.7 Case study: police

Concentrating on police liability will serve as an illustration of the way the concept of duty of care has been linked to the more general evolution of negligence liability.

2.7.1 'Operational' liability

It is well established that the police can be liable in negligence when they directly injure someone due to their positive act or (in some cases) omission. For example, there is a clear duty of care upon a police driver in relation to the safety of pedestrians and other road users.

The case of *Knightley v Johns* (1982) involved a complicated chain of events. An accident occurred at the end of a one-way tunnel. When the police attended, the officer in charge ordered two motorcyclists to ride the wrong way through the tunnel, without first closing the end of the tunnel. One of the motorcyclists was hit by a car driving into the tunnel, without any fault on the part of that driver. The officer in charge was held to be solely liable in negligence for the second accident. In *Rigby v Chief Constable of Northamptonshire* (1985), the police used flammable CS gas in an operation to flush a suspect out of a building. They were liable in negligence for damage caused by the resulting fire because they had omitted to take the usual precaution of having firefighting equipment standing by.

2.7.2 **Immunity?**

The situation changes when the question is one of police liability for harm caused in the course of the 'investigation and suppression' of crime or due to resource allocation decisions. Here the courts have been slow to impose duties of care, using a range of different devices to justify their decisions.

 CASE CLOSE-UP

Hill v Chief Constable of W Yorkshire (1989)

This is a key House of Lords case which illustrates the range of principle-based and policy considerations that may come into play in duty of care decisions. Jacqueline Hill was the last victim of the serial killer Peter Sutcliffe, also known as the 'Yorkshire Ripper'. Her mother brought a tort action against the police force who had searched for the Ripper unsuccessfully over a number of years. Her case was that, had it not been for their negligence in the way they had conducted their inquiries, her daughter would not have died.

The judge at first instance struck out the case as disclosing no cause of action due to the lack of a duty of care. The claimant eventually appealed to the House of Lords. For the purpose of this **striking-out action**, the Lords assumed that there had been negligence on the part of the police. Had there been held to be a duty of care, the breach of duty point would then have been debated on the facts. They then applied the 'two-stage test' from *Anns v London Borough of Merton* in order to determine whether there could be a duty of care in this type of situation. It was agreed that the requirement of foreseeability was fulfilled in the sense that there was 'likely harm to such as Miss Hill if Sutcliffe were not identified and apprehended'. But, under *Anns*, more was needed to establish a duty of care: either a relationship of control between the police and the killer (similar to that between the prison guards and the boys in *Dorset Yacht*) or a proximity of the police to the victim. As Sutcliffe could not be said to have been under their control and there was nothing to set Miss Hill apart as being more at risk than the rest of the female population, then this element of the *Anns* equation was not fulfilled and there had not been a duty of care.

striking-out action a procedural tactic whereby one party applies to the court to strike out all or part of the other party's statement of case because it shows no reasonable grounds for bringing or defending the action.

For the avoidance of doubt, Lord Keith went on to itemize the policy reasons why there should not be a duty of care in this type of situation—in this sense tackling the second part of the *Anns* test as well as the first:

- The police's general sense of public duty would not be reinforced by negligence liability.
- Potential liability could lead to 'defensive policing'.
- Conducting murder investigations is a complex task involving decisions, often resource-dependent, on 'matters of policy and discretion'.
- Defending negligence actions would be demanding of money, time, and manpower and divert the police from their main function.
- Negligence actions would effectively reopen formerly closed cases.

Lord Templeman added:

- Internal or public inquiries are the more appropriate means of supervising the efficiency of the police.

▶ THINKING POINT

What might be the outcome if the police were to adopt an attitude of 'defensive policing'?

It is this policy reasoning which gave rise to the view that the police might hold an immunity from negligence actions concerning their role in the prevention and investigation of crime. This was applied to an extreme degree in *Osman v Ferguson* (1993). A mentally unstable teacher developed an obsession with one of his pupils. He conducted a campaign of harassment and violence against the boy's family, of which the police were aware. Eventually he seriously wounded the pupil and killed his father. A negligence action against the police was struck out at trial and this was upheld in the Court of Appeal. It was agreed that, unlike *Hill*, here there was a high degree of proximity between the claimants and the police and also that the culprit had been identified. However, the policy reasons behind *Hill* were held to apply similarly to this case and pointed away from the imposition of a duty of care. In *Osman v UK* (1999), the decision was brought before the ECtHR, which held that giving a blanket immunity to the police, according to which claims could be struck out before any investigation into the facts, was contrary to Article 6(1), the right of access to the courts. The claimants were awarded compensation to be paid by the UK government. In *Z v UK*, above, it was held that the ECtHR in *Osman* had not had the correct interpretation of the striking out of a claim when the duty criteria of *Caparo* were not satisfied. This had been a matter of the application of substantive domestic law rather than denying access to a legal remedy in a way which would engage Article 6(1).

🔍 CASE CLOSE-UP

Swinney v Chief Constable Northumbria (1997)

The Court of Appeal reconsidered the validity of the *Hill* blanket immunity in *Swinney v Chief Constable Northumbria* (1997). The claimant in this case had given the police information about someone they were seeking in connection with a murder. The claimant's name and contact details were recorded and left in a police car from where they were obtained by the alleged criminal, who then subjected the claimant and her husband to a campaign of intimidation. They suffered psychological injury and had to move house, and so sued the police in negligence on the basis that there had been a duty of care to keep her details confidential. The Court of Appeal found the required foreseeability and proximity but when they came to the policy stage, there were some aspects of the situation which had not been present in *Hill* or *Osman*. According to Ward LJ, there was at least an arguable case:

> [I]t is incontrovertible that the fight against crime is daily dependent upon information fed to the police by members of the public, often at real risk of villainous retribution from the criminals and their associates. The public interest will not accept that good citizens should be expected to entrust information to the police, without also expecting that they are entrusting their safety to the police. The public interest would be affronted were it to be the law that members of the public should be expected, in the execution of public service, to undertake the risk of harm to themselves without the police, in return, being expected to take no more than reasonable care to ensure that the confidential information imparted to them is protected. The welfare of the community at large demands the encouragement of the free flow of information without inhibition. Accordingly, it is arguable that there is a duty of care, and that no consideration of public policy precludes the prosecution of the plaintiffs' claim, which will be judged on its merits later.

In *Swinney v Chief Constable Northumbria (No 2)* (1999), the facts were examined and it was held that, apart from the duty issue, there would be no liability because the police, in leaving the information in a locked briefcase in a locked car, had not been negligent.

Another exception to the *Hill* immunity was recognized in *An Informer v A Chief Constable* (2012). The claimant was a police informer, formally authorized under the Regulation of Investigatory Powers Act 2000 to work with the police in the capacity of Covert Human Intelligence Source (CHIS). The police suspected him of involvement in money laundering activities and, while investigating this, they obtained an order under s 41 of the Proceeds of Crime Act 2002 which prohibited the claimant from accessing his bank accounts. He suffered severe financial loss as a result and consequently brought a negligence action against the police, as his employers. It was held that the close or 'special relationship' between the claimant and the police, underpinned by similar policy considerations to those in *Swinney*, brought with it a duty of care regarding the physical safety of the CHIS when he was in the course of assisting the police. This duty did not extend to protection of his financial (or, incidentally, psychological) welfare, particularly given that the losses the claimant sustained were in the course of investigation of his own possible criminality.

2.7.2.1 **The human rights dimension**

In *Van Colle v Chief Constable of Hertfordshire* (2009) (which was a conjoined appeal with *Smith v Chief Constable of Sussex Police*), the House of Lords considered the extent to which the Human Rights Act 1998 affected the possible liability of police for failure to protect. Here, a key witness in a murder trial had been threatened and then killed, and an action was brought under Article 2 (right to life). It was held that the police would be under a duty to take positive steps in such a case only when, according to *Osman v UK*, they 'knew or ought to have known of a real and immediate risk to life'. In this case, the stringent standard of foreseeability had not been satisfied and so Article 2 had not been engaged. However, in *Rabone* (discussed at 2.6.1.1 Relationship creating an assumption of responsibility) the known suicidal feelings of the mental patient constituted 'a real and immediate risk', thereby imposing on the hospital an Article 2 duty to take positive protective steps.

Q | CASE CLOSE-UP

Brooks v Commissioner of Police for the Metropolis (2005)

The basic approach of *Hill* was confirmed in *Brooks v Commissioner of Police for the Metropolis* (2005). Duwayne Brooks was violently attacked and abused by a racist gang. At the same time, he was witness to the murder of his friend Stephen Lawrence, whose case became a nationally publicized campaign against racism in the police service. Duwayne was left with post-traumatic stress following the incident. He sued the police for negligently worsening his condition in the way they treated him: allegedly as a suspect and later as a witness, but not as a victim of crime (which he was).

Before the House of Lords, three aspects to the police duty were claimed on behalf of the respondent, Duwayne Brooks:

(1)   to take reasonable steps to assess whether the respondent was a victim of crime and then to accord him reasonably appropriate protection, support, assistance, and treatment if he was so assessed;

(2)   to take reasonable steps to afford the respondent the protection, assistance, and support commonly afforded to a key eyewitness to a serious crime of violence; and

(3)   to afford reasonable weight to the account that the respondent gave and to act upon it accordingly.

This claim was struck out at first instance, reinstated by the Court of Appeal, but finally rejected by the House of Lords.

According to Lord Steyn:

> [T]he core principle of *Hill* has remained unchallenged in our domestic jurisprudence and in European jurisprudence for many years. If a case such as the Yorkshire Ripper case, which was before the House in *Hill*, arose for decision today I have no doubt that it would be decided in the same way. It is, of course, desirable that police officers should treat victims and witnesses properly and with respect: compare the Police Conduct regs 2004 (No. 645). But to convert that ethical value into general legal duties of care on the police towards victims and witnesses would be going too far. The prime function of the police is the preservation of the Queen's peace. The police must concentrate on preventing the commission of crime; protecting life and property; and apprehending criminals and preserving evidence . . .. A retreat from the principle in *Hill* would have detrimental effects for law enforcement. Whilst focusing on investigating crime, and the arrest of suspects, police officers would in practice be required to ensure that in every contact with a potential witness or a potential victim time and resources were deployed to avoid the risk of causing harm or offence. Such legal duties would tend to inhibit a robust approach in assessing a person as a possible suspect, witness or victim. By placing general duties of care on the police to victims and witnesses the police's ability to perform their public functions in the interests of the community, fearlessly and with despatch, would be impeded. It would, as was recognised in *Hill*, be bound to lead to an unduly defensive approach in combating crime.

THINKING POINT

If a duty of care is owed regarding the psychological safety of informants, according to *Swinney*, on the basis of the public interest in criminal justice, could not a similar argument be made for the psychological safety of crime victims? What difference might there be between the two groups?

In *Smith v Chief Constable of Sussex Police* (2009) the claimant suffered severe head injuries in a hammer attack. He had notified the police of the death threats he was receiving from his former partner and had repeatedly been assured by them that they had the matter in hand, although it later transpired that few steps had yet been taken to assess the problem. An application by the defendants to have the action struck out as disclosing no cause of action was upheld by a four to one majority of the Law Lords. They applied the 'core principle' first established in *Hill* and reiterated in *Brooks*, and concluded that duty was absent in this case due to concerns about 'defensive policing' and the potential drain on public resources that defending such actions could entail. It should be noted that the three judges in the Court of Appeal and Lord Bingham (who delivered a strong dissent) supported a duty of care in this situation and predicted that the so-called police immunity was likely to be tested again.

It was not long before his prediction was fulfilled, with three important cases concerning police liability in negligence.

CASE CLOSE-UP

Michael v Chief Constable of South Wales Police (2015)

This case deals with the question of police immunity in negligence but also has wider implications for the question of duty of care in general.

Joanna Michael was attacked in her home in the early hours by her former partner. He then left and she called 999 at 2.29am, saying that he had told her that he was going to return and kill her and that she expected him 'any minute literally'. Although she lived in the South Wales Police area, her call was received by the Gwent Police call centre. Her call was rated G1 (requiring an immediate response) and then forwarded to South Wales Police, a station being only five to six minutes' drive from Joanna's home. Her call was immediately referred to South Wales Police, with a summary of the situation but which did not mention the threat to kill. It was then graded G2 (response within sixty minutes). A second call was received by Gwent Police at 2.43am, with a scream, followed by the line going dead. Again the call was forwarded to South Wales and when officers responded at 2.51am, Joanna was found stabbed to death. Her ex-partner pleaded guilty to murder and was sentenced to life imprisonment.

Joanna's parents and her two children brought claims under common law negligence and breach of Article 2 ECHR, alleging that had it not been for the failures of the two police forces, her death could have been prevented. Data held by the South Wales Police recorded a history of domestic violence against Joanna committed by her killer and an investigation by the Independent Police Complaints Commission (now the Independent Office for Police Conduct) had found serious individual and organizational failures by the police in this case. The striking-out action ultimately reached the Supreme Court, where five of the seven Justices ruled in favour of the defendant police forces. Lord Toulson gave the leading speech and based his decision on two main points. First, there was not a duty of care owed because the situation did not fall under any of the exceptions to the basic rule against tort liability for omissions—specifically, the call handler had not said anything to the deceased which indicated a specific assumption of responsibility for her safety.

Second, duties owed under the Human Rights Act are owed to the public at large and do not automatically give rise to individual actions in private law. Here there was a dispute about the audibility of the part of the call referring to the threat to kill which would affect the liability under Article 2 and this remained to be determined in a trial on the facts. Lord Toulson went further, and cast doubt upon the usefulness of the *Caparo* three-part test in such situations. The element of proximity, for instance, often operates in a circular sense— with the framing of the question determining its answer. Neither did he believe that the concept of 'immunity' was helpful in such police cases; this was nothing more than an application of the general principle that a person should not be liable for failing to control the actions of another.

According to Lord Toulson: 'It does not follow from the setting up of a protective system from public resources that if it fails to achieve its purpose, through organizational defects or fault on the part of an individual, the public at large should bear the additional burden of compensating a victim for harm caused by the actions of a third party for whose behaviour the state is not responsible.'

 THINKING POINT

Lord Kerr, dissenting in *Michael*, believed that protection for an individual of precisely the sort that failed the deceased was an 'essential and critical obligation of the police force' and, as with comparable professionals, negligence liability should be possible. Do you agree? What might be the problems with this approach?

CLG v Chief Constable of Merseyside (2015) concerned the nature of any duty owed by the police to a witness in a criminal case. After volunteering to give witness statements to the police regarding a shooting, the claimants moved house following threats. Subsequently the police inadvertently revealed their new address to the CPS, who then served it on those accused of the crime. They proceeded against the police in negligence and for breach of their positive rights under the ECHR, Article 2, and their negative rights under Article 8. There was held, following *Brooks*, to be no duty of care owed to the claimants due to lack of any assumption of responsibility by the police for their safety. The Article 2 claim had been rejected by the trial judge on the grounds of lack of evidence of any imminent danger to life; and that of Article 8 was dismissed by the Court of Appeal; the release of the address had only been an isolated act of carelessness and, in any event, the Article 8 right was qualified in respect of actions 'necessary in a democratic society in the interests of preventing crime'.

The case of *Commissioner of Police of the Metropolis v DSD and another* (2018) was an action for damages and a declaration brought by two of the victims of John Worboys, the so-called 'black cab rapist'. Between 2002 and 2008 he committed over 105 rapes and sexual assaults upon women in London and the south of England, many of whom were passengers in his cab. The claims were that failure by the police properly to investigate the crimes allowed Worboys's behaviour to continue until they became victims. They based their actions on the state's alleged duty to effectively investigate. The Court of Appeal agreed with the trial judge that the police on behalf of the state did exercise a 'protective principle' under Article 3, and compensation was awarded to the claimants. In 2018 the Supreme Court rejected yet another appeal by the police, confirming that the positive duty (not limited to state actors) to reasonably investigate ill-treatment is owed not just to the public but to individuals as well.

Robinson v Chief Constable of West Yorkshire (2018) has been considered above in terms of the *Caparo* test. As an example of police liability, it should be noted that the Supreme Court regarded the decision to turn on the ordinary principles of duty of care.

In *Hill*, Lord Keith said:

> There is no question that a police officer, *like anyone else*, may be liable in tort to a person who is injured as a direct result of his acts or omissions. So he may be liable in damages for assault, unlawful arrest, wrongful imprisonment and malicious prosecution, *and also for negligence*.

According to Lord Reed in *Robinson*, cases such as *Rigby* and *Knightley*, above, which were described as 'operational' are merely 'examples of the application to the police of the ordinary common law duty of care to avoid causing reasonably foreseeable injury to persons and reasonably foreseeable damage to property'. Duty having been established, breach and causation led to a finding of liability for the defendants.

2.8 Duty to this claimant

You will recall that at the outset of this chapter, duty of care was said to be dependent on the answers to *two questions*. We have now completed discussion of the first question—that is, whether the case is one of the *types* in which a duty of care should be imposed. However, there will be some cases where we can answer 'yes' at the first stage, but the facts will raise doubts over the particular claimant involved.

This leads us to the second question: was it foreseeable that *this* claimant would be harmed by the defendant's act? It is necessary to consider this because a duty to one party does not necessarily entail a duty to all—otherwise tort liability could potentially be unlimited.

The American case of *Palsgraf v Long Island Railroad* (1928) provides an early example of the unforeseeable claimant. The defendant's employee, a porter, was assisting a passenger who was boarding a train. He jostled a package which the passenger dropped. Unfortunately, the package contained fireworks, which exploded. The explosion caused weighing scales to fall onto the plaintiff, a woman waiting for a train with her children some distance away down the platform. Her negligence action against the railroad failed because, although the defendants owed a duty of care to the nearby passengers regarding their person and property, it was unforeseeable that the plaintiff was at risk and therefore no duty was owed to her. This was because of the combination of the factors of her distance and the absence of any indication that the package contained explosives. Cardozo CJ put it this way:

> If no hazard was apparent to the eye of ordinary vigilance, an act innocent and harmless, at least to outward seeming, with reference to her, did not take to itself the quality of a tort because it happened to be wrong, though apparently not one involving the risk of bodily insecurity, with reference to someone else . . . . The orbit of the danger as disclosed to the eye of reasonable vigilance would be the orbit of the duty.

A British counterpart to *Palsgraf* is *Bourhill v Young* (1943), which dealt with the problematic topic of duty of care for psychiatric injury. A pregnant fishwife in Edinburgh was disembarking from a tram when she heard a crash between a car and a motorcyclist taking place some 50 yards away. Because it was on the other side of the tram, she did not see the crash although she later saw evidence of blood on the pavement. She suffered nervous shock as a result. She was outside the range of physical danger and psychological injury to her was not to have been foreseeable in a person of 'normal susceptibility'. The House of Lords had to consider whether or not a duty of care had been owed to her by the negligent driver.

The speech of Lord Porter is a convenient summary of the law:

> In the case of a civil action there is no such thing as negligence in the abstract. There must be neglect of the use of care towards a person towards whom the defendant owes the duty of observing care, and I am content to take the statement of Lord Atkin in *Donoghue v Stevenson*, as indicating the extent of the duty. 'You must take', he said, 'reasonable care to avoid acts or omissions which you can reasonably foresee would be likely to injure your neighbour. Who, then, in law is my neighbour? The answer seems to be—persons who are so closely and directly affected by my act that I ought reasonably to have them in contemplation as being so affected when I am directing my mind to the acts or omissions which are called in question.' Is the result of this view that all persons in or near the street down which the negligent driver is progressing are potential victims of his negligence? Though from their position it is quite impossible that any injury should happen to them and though they have no relatives or even friends who might be endangered, is a duty of care to them owed and broken because they might have been but were not in a spot exposed to the errant driving of the peccant car? I cannot think so. The duty is not to the world at large. It must be tested by asking with reference to each several complainant: Was a duty owed to him or her? If no one of them was in such a position that direct physical injury could reasonably be anticipated to them or their relations or friends normally I think no duty would be owed, and if, in addition, no shock was reasonably to be anticipated to them as a result of the defender's negligence, the defender might, indeed, be guilty of actionable negligence to others but not of negligence towards them. In the

present case the appellant was never herself in any bodily danger nor reasonably in fear of danger either for herself or others. She was merely a person who, as a result of the action, was emotionally disturbed and rendered physically ill by that emotional disturbance.

As was said in *Bourhill*, '[T]he duty is not to the world at large'. Foreseeability of risk to the claimant, or a claimant of his type, is required. In *Haley v London Electricity Board* (1965), a blind pedestrian fell on a tool which had been left guarding a trench in which the defendants were working. The barrier would have been obvious to a sighted person, but the plaintiff's white stick did not detect it and he fell over it. His injuries left him almost completely deaf. The House of Lords heard evidence about the numbers of blind people living in London and concluded that a member of that class should have been within the reasonable foresight of the defendants in considering obstacles on the pavement.

The case of *Maguire v Harland & Wolff* (2005) was a case brought on behalf of the wife of a shipyard worker who had been exposed to asbestos at work due to the negligence of his employers from 1961 to 1965. He had not suffered illness as a result. She, however, contracted asbestos-related cancer, from which she died. The only source of her exposure to asbestos was in washing his work clothes, which had been covered in asbestos dust. Although there was no dispute about the duty of care owed to her husband as an employee, the court had to decide whether there was a duty in respect of what was called 'secondary exposure'. As in *Haley*, expert evidence was offered about the extent of knowledge about the dangers of asbestos at the relevant time. On the basis of this evidence, the Court of Appeal concluded that the level of knowledge was not such as to make it reasonably foreseeable that there would be such a degree of danger to someone in the wife's position that the defendants should take precautions.

The question of whether a duty was owed to the particular claimant in question is closely related to that of remoteness. As discussed in 2.9, a question such as that considered by the court in *Bourhill* in terms of duty of care could be looked at in a different way; that is, not in terms of duty but instead as a question of *causation*, ie by asking whether damage of *this kind* was reasonably foreseeable at the time of the defendant's negligence.

> **CROSS REFERENCE**
>
> For more on remoteness, see Chapter 4.

2.9 Conclusion

In *Mutua v Foreign and Commonwealth Office* (2012), McCombe J provided a useful summary of the current approach to duty of care. Here, he refused to strike out a negligence action brought against the UK government by claimants alleging they had been subject to physical mistreatment while in detention at the time of the Mau Mau rebellion in Kenya in the 1950s. He saw *Matua* as an 'exceptional case' and therefore applied the Sutherland 'incremental approach' to the duty question. Because the allegation here was one of torture, the Supreme Court decision in *A v Secretary of State for the Home Department (No 2)* (2005) that evidence obtained by torture would be inadmissible would be relevant. The dictum in *Barrett* against striking out claims on the basis of duty on untested facts was followed. The duty formulations of both *Donoghue* and *Caparo* were considered; additionally the facts of the case which took it outside the category of omission, which would have raised a no-duty presumption.

Diagram 2.2 Negligence

Duty of care?

Yes   No → No action

Breach?

Yes   No → No action

Causation?

Yes   No → No action

Action in negligence

We have looked at a number of cases in which the courts have dealt with some complex policy debates on duty of care. You would be forgiven for thinking that such cases form a key aspect of the practitioner's workload. In fact, litigation on the topic of duty of care is relatively rare. That is because the vast majority of negligence actions pertain to either road traffic accidents or employers' liability (due to the statutory requirement for compulsory insurance in these areas). Here, duty of care is rarely contested because of the long history of established duty in these situations. We will see that, instead, breach of duty or causation would be more likely to be the source of dispute. Duty of care remains, however, highly important as perhaps the main regulator on the spread or restriction of negligence liability.

↻ Summary

- Duty of care is the first of the three main elements of negligence, as illustrated in Diagram 2.2.
- It is determined by proximity, foreseeability, and policy.
- It is most likely to be established in cases of positive acts which cause physical injury or property damage.
- Finding duty of care is not the same as finding liability.

   Visit the online resources to listen to a podcast summarizing the topics covered in this chapter.

▢ The bigger picture

Many tort cases emerge from real-life tragedies. One argument which the courts often invoke in policy discussions regarding duty of care is that an individual action for damages in the law of tort is not the appropriate remedy, but rather a public inquiry or other review would be more appropriate. You may be interested to learn more about reports and reviews which covered three key duty of care cases.

- The *Hill* case concerned the final victim of the so-called Yorkshire Ripper, Peter Sutcliffe, who was convicted of the murders of thirteen women in 1981. The conduct of the West Yorkshire Police investigation of the crimes raised serious questions, which were reviewed in two reports. The contents of the Report by Sir Lawrence Byford were released in 2006. If you're interested in the way the investigation was conducted, find out more in the following link: www.gov.uk/government/publications/sir-lawrence-byford-report-into-the-police-handling-of-the-yorkshire-ripper-case.

- The *Alcock* case (see Chapter 5) was based upon the 1989 disaster at Hillsborough football stadium. The controversy over responsibility and accountability for that event has not been resolved and following the Report of the Hillsborough Independent Panel in 2012, the original inquests into the deaths of the ninety-six victims were quashed and new inquests opened. In April 2016, twenty-seven years after the event, the second inquest reached its verdict: that the ninety-six victims had been unlawfully killed. Following this vindication of the efforts of the families and campaigners, in 2017 the Crown Prosecution Service announced six resulting criminal prosecutions. Among these was the charge against Chief Superintendent David Duckenfield (Match Commander for South Yorkshire Police on the day) of manslaughter by gross negligence; at the time of writing, no verdict has been reached. You may wish to read the account by the sociologist and Hillsborough campaigner Phil Scraton: *Hillsborough: The Truth* (Mainstream Publishing, 2016).

? | Questions

Knowledge-testing questions

1. What are the flaws, if any, in the current test for duty of care?

2. Summarize the current state of tort law regarding immunities in negligence.

3. What are the differences in objectives between human rights law and common law tort?

4. What are the situations in which there can be a duty of care in respect of omissions?

Problem and essay questions

1. Ben met his friend Olu, and they agreed they both needed a drink. They went to the pub, where Olu bought the drinks and Ben, after several pints, offered Olu a lift home. On the journey home, Ben collided with Kimberley, a 6-year-old who was trying to cross the street. The collision caused Olu to fly through the windscreen, and pushed Kimberley into the path of an oncoming car being driven by Ernie, aged 82. Kimberley sustained serious internal injuries. An ambulance was summoned to take Olu, Kimberley, and Ernie to hospital. Greta, the ambulance dispatcher, having taken the call, did not dispatch an ambulance for fifteen vital minutes, while she finished the magazine she had been reading when the call came. By the time the ambulance arrived, Olu had died. At the hospital, Kimberley's injuries were misdiagnosed by Mary, a junior doctor who was attending in A&E for the first time. Had the nature of her injuries been correctly assessed in A&E, Kimberley would have had a 40 per cent chance of full recovery. Kimberley is now paraplegic.

   Analyse the 'duty of care' aspects of this scenario.

2. According to the House of Lords in *Customs and Excise v Barclays Bank*, 'the three-fold test [in *Caparo*] . . . does not provide an easy answer to all our problems, but only a set of fairly blunt tools'.

Discuss, taking into account possible improvements which could be made to the general test.

 Visit the online resources for guidance on answering these questions.

Further reading

du Bois, F, 'Human Rights and the Tort Liability of Public Authorities' (2011) 127 LQR 589

Cornford, T, 'The Negligence Liability of Public Authorities for Omissions' (2019) 78(3) CLJ 545

Giliker, P, 'Does X Mark the Spot? University of Bristol Law School Blog' https://legalresearch. blogs.bris.ac.uk/2019/06/does-x-mark-the-spot

Goudkamp, J, 'A Revolution in Duty of Care?' (2015) 131 LQR 519

Howarth, D, 'Many Duties of Care—Or a Duty of Care? Notes from the Underground' (2006) 26(3) OJLS 449

Morgan, J, 'Nonfeasance and the End of Policy? Reflections on the Revolution in Public Authority Liability' (2019) 35(1) PN 32

Morgan, J, 'Novelty in Negligence: Policy Reasoning Survives' (2019) 78(1) CLJ 15

Mullender, R, 'Military Operations, Fairness and the British State' (2014) 130 LQR 28

Nolan, D, 'New Forms of Damage in Negligence' (2007) 70 MLR 59

Stanton, K, 'Professional Negligence: Duty of Care Methodology in the Twenty-first Century' (2006) 22(3) PN 134

Stapleton, J, 'Tort Insurance and Ideology' (1995) 58 MLR 820

Tettenborn, A, 'Wrongful Death, Human Rights and the Fatal Accidents Act' (2012) 128 LQR 327

Tofaris, S and S Steel, 'Negligence Liability for Omissions and the Police' (2016) 75(1) CLJ 128

Wilberg, H, 'Defensive Practice or Conflict of Duties? Policy Concerns in Public Authority Negligence Claims' (2010) 126 LQR 420

Witting, C, 'Duty of Care: An Analytical Approach' (2005) 25 OJLS 417

3 Breach of duty

Introduction

Establishing that the defendant owed the claimant a duty of care is the first step in formulating a negligence claim. Next, the claimant must prove that the defendant has breached that duty, that is, he has been negligent.

Negligence in this sense is determined by answering two questions:

(1) How ought the defendant to have behaved in the circumstances, ie standard of care? This has been determined by a combination of statute and common law and is described as a matter of law.

(2) Did the defendant's behaviour fall below the desired standard, ie breach? This depends on assessing what actually happened in the case and is described as a matter of fact.

3.1 Setting the standard of care

The general standard of care in negligence is objective. The conduct required is often described as that of the *reasonable man*. The reason for this lies in the primary objective of the action in negligence. It is to compensate the injured party for the harm which he has suffered. The concern is not to analyse the defendant as an individual, which in any event could be extremely difficult. This can be compared to the objective of criminal law, which might be said to be crime prevention through the punishment of offenders. This requires careful attention to the capabilities and motivations of the offender, in order to determine the level of culpability and thus punishment that is appropriate.

In *Blyth v Birmingham Waterworks Co* (1856), Alderson B described the standard of the reasonable man this way:

> Negligence is the omission to do something which a reasonable man, guided upon those considerations which ordinarily regulate the conduct of human affairs, would do, or doing something which a prudent and reasonable man would not do.

> ❱ **THINKING POINT**
>
> Why not demand a very high standard from the reasonable man? Why did Lord Macmillan not require us to imagine 'lions around every corner'?

The reasonable man is not foolhardy, but nor is he excessively cautious. He is expected to learn from experience and is not excused by being slow-witted or having a poor memory. On the other hand, the law recognizes that everyone makes mistakes.

> ❱ **THINKING POINT**
>
> The 'Man on the Clapham omnibus' (*Hall v Brooklands Auto-Racing Club* (1933)) has become 'Travellers on the London underground' (*McFarlane v Tayside Health Board* (1999)). Each term is used as a byword for an average member of the community. Presumably, some of the travellers on the underground are women!

🔍 CASE CLOSE-UP

Glasgow Corp v Muir (1943)

In *Glasgow Corp v Muir* (1943), Lord Macmillan described the reasonable man in this way:

> The standard of foresight of the reasonable man is, in one sense, an impersonal test. It eliminates the personal equation and is independent of the idiosyncrasies of the particular person whose conduct is in question. Some persons are by nature unduly timorous and imagine every path beset by lions. Others, of more robust temperament, fail to foresee or nonchalantly disregard even the most obvious dangers. The reasonable man is presumed to be free both from over-apprehension and from over-confidence.

What is reasonable to one person may not seem reasonable to another. Who decides what the reasonable person would do? What once might have been determined by a jury's application of community standards is now a matter for a judge. In making his decision he will be considering what would have been foreseeable in the circumstances of the case.

Lord Macmillan in *Glasgow Corp v Muir* put it this way:

> It is . . . left to the judge to decide what, in the circumstances of the particular case, the reasonable man would have in contemplation, and what, accordingly, the party sought to be made liable ought to have foreseen.

The circumstances in *Glasgow Corp v Muir* were that a group of picnickers were caught by the rain. They went to the manageress of a nearby tearoom, who gave them permission to bring their party into her premises. As two members of the group carried a tea urn into the hall, they lost their grip and it fell. Six children who had been buying ice cream were scalded and they sued the owners of the tearoom in negligence.

In holding that the duty of care had not been breached, the court took evidence of the weight and size of the tea urn and even heard testimony from a caterer about his experiences of carrying such items. The accident, while it could have been foreseen as a possibility, was not a reasonable probability to the extent that the manageress should have been expected to clear the hall of children in anticipation. As a reasonable person, she was entitled to go on with her own work and not supervise the picnickers.

3.1.1 Knowledge

In cases in which the state of scientific and technical knowledge may be involved, the defendant's actions will be judged on the standard prevalent in the circumstances of the time. The reasonable man would not be expected to know otherwise. In *Roe v Ministry of Health* (1954), the plaintiff suffered paralysis due to the contamination of an anaesthetic through invisible cracks in its glass ampoule. At the time of the contamination in 1947, the existence of such cracks was not known, and so not tested for. The risk became known in 1951 and by the date of the trial, preventive measures had generally been put in place. In finding the defendants not liable Denning LJ observed, 'We must not look at the 1947 accident with 1954 spectacles.' This approach was upheld by the Court of Appeal in *Japp v Virgin Holidays* (2013), where it held that the relevant safety standards of hotel glass doors were those at the time of the installation rather than that of the accident.

> **THINKING POINT**
> How might the approach in *Roe* be applied in litigation relating to present injury to health caused by smoking in the past?

However, specific knowledge possessed by the defendant cannot be discounted. In *Paris v Stepney Borough Council* (1951), the plaintiff was employed by the defendant local council in one of their garages. It was not common practice to supply safety goggles to employees doing this type of work. However, the employer was aware that the plaintiff only had the use of one eye and in those circumstances was liable when an accident at work led to the loss of sight in his good eye. According to the House of Lords there is no such thing as 'a duty of care in the air. An employer owes a special duty of care to a man known only to have one eye.' A reasonable employer with that knowledge would have supplied safety goggles to the plaintiff.

🔍 **CASE CLOSE-UP**

Nettleship v Weston (1971)

The objective standard can at times appear to work particularly harshly against a defendant. *Nettleship v Weston* (1971) is a prime example of such a case. The plaintiff, who was not a professional driving instructor, agreed to give lessons to the defendant who was a friend, having confirmed that she held fully comprehensive insurance. On her third outing, while driving in a car without dual controls and despite her teacher's attempts to avert the crash, she hit a tree. The plaintiff suffered a fractured knee.

The key issue considered by the Court of Appeal was the standard of care to be expected of the learner driver. By a 2:1 majority it was held that the standard of care expected of the learner driver was, according to Lord Denning, that of:

> an experienced, skilled and careful driver . . .. [W]e are, in this branch of the law, moving away from the concept: 'No liability without fault'. We are beginning to apply the test: 'On whom should the risk fall?' Morally the learner-driver is not at fault, but legally she is liable to be because she is insured and the risk should fall on her.

The defendant was liable to her instructor on the grounds that she had breached that standard of care. The damages awarded were reduced by 50 per cent on the grounds of the instructor's contributory negligence.

THINKING POINT

(1) What might be the policy reasons behind the decision in *Nettleship*?

(2) Should it matter in a case like this who the injured party is? Suppose it were a child passenger (Mrs Weston's son was reported to have been in the car at the time of the accident)? What about a pedestrian?

(3) Is the law in *Nettleship* actually laying down a standard which is unachievable?

3.1.2 Exceptions to the objective standard

There are some actors for whom it is not logical to expect the standard of the reasonable man to be applied. In law, children are treated as one of these exceptional groups. They are a large sector of the population who cannot realistically be expected to attain the standards of adults.

In *McHale v Watson* (1966), an Australian case which is of persuasive status in our system, the standard to be applied to a child is that of the capacity, in terms of foresight and prudence, which is 'normal for a child of the relevant age'.

Mullin v Richards (1998) involved two 15-year-old girls who were fencing with plastic rulers. This common type of horseplay resulted in a serious eye injury, when a ruler snapped and flew into the eye of one of the girls. The Court of Appeal applied the approach of *McHale* in finding that there was no breach of duty, due to the fact that the girls would not have foreseen any real likelihood of injury: 'girls of 15 playing together may play as somewhat irresponsible girls of 15'. Effectively this maintains the objective element of the test, but scales it down to the 'reasonable child' rather than the 'reasonable man'.

> **THINKING POINT**
>
> (1) What should be the upper age at which the 'reasonable child' standard should apply?
>
> (2) Are there any other problems with children as defendants?
>
> (3) What other types of defendants should be approached on a more subjective basis: the elderly, the mentally handicapped, the physically unwell?

3.1.3 Illness

To what extent are we responsible in civil law for actions which are influenced by physical illness? This will depend on the extent of our awareness of the illness and the control which we have over our actions. In *Roberts v Ramsbottom* (1980), a 73-year-old man began to drive his car, despite symptoms indicating that he had had a stroke. He caused three accidents before finally coming to rest, and his defence, based upon **automatism**, was not accepted by the court. Although the driver was not morally blameworthy, he had been negligent in continuing to drive when he had some awareness of his impaired capacities.

> **automatism**
> the psychological state whereby someone is acting mechanically, without awareness; as in sleepwalking.

It is difficult, although not impossible, to reconcile this decision with that in *Mansfield v Weetabix Ltd* (1998). There, a lorry driver did not know he was suffering from an illness in which a deficiency of glucose in his system deprived his brain of oxygen and led to him slowly becoming unconscious. This happened while he was driving a large lorry, which ploughed into the plaintiff's shop. The Court of Appeal reversed the trial judge's decision and held that the driver had not been negligent. There was no evidence that he, unlike Mr Ramsbottom, had been aware of the effects of his physical condition as he continued to drive. The standard of care expected was that of 'a reasonably competent driver unaware that he is or may be suffering from a condition that impairs his ability to drive'. Not to take his condition into account, as a key aspect of the *circumstances* surrounding the accident, would be effectively to impose strict liability.

An interesting case on medical issues arose in *Dunnage v Randall* (2015). The claimant had suffered serious burns in trying to prevent his uncle, who was suffering a schizophrenic episode, from setting fire to himself. The incident was potentially covered by the uncle's household insurance policy, but it was argued that someone suffering from extreme mental illness had so little control of his actions that he could not owe a duty of care in negligence. The Court of Appeal rejected this argument, saying that lack of rational control was not the same as lack of any physical control, as had been the situation in *Mansfield*. The law of negligence would not compromise the reasonable man standard, except in the case of children.

3.1.4 Skill

There are many situations in which the defendant may have held himself out as having a particular skill, not possessed by the usual passenger on the London omnibus or underground. These situations range from the professional (for example, medical), to the domestic. The law in these situations imposes the standard of care of the reasonable practitioner of the skill which the defendant purports to have.

A department store jewellery section provided a service for piercing ears in *Philips v William Whiteley* (1938). The plaintiff developed an infection following the procedure at the defendant's store. In the negligence claim which followed, the standard of care applied to the defendants was that of a reasonable jeweller piercing ears. The court took into account what the defendants were holding themselves out as, and also what the plaintiff should have expected. 'If a person wants to ensure that the operation of piercing her ears is going to be carried out with that proportion of skill . . . that a fellow of the Royal College of Surgeons would use, she must go to a surgeon. If she goes to a jeweller, she must expect that he will carry it out in the way that one would expect a jeweller to carry it out.' On the facts the defendants had attained the required standard of care, that of the reasonable jeweller, and were not liable.

Wells v Cooper (1958) involved an early example of what would now be termed 'do-it-yourself'. A visitor was injured when a door handle he was pulling detached from the door and caused him to fall. The handle had been fitted by the defendant occupier, who often performed simple repair jobs around the house. The standard expected of him in doing this job, which was not particularly specialized or dangerous, was that of 'the degree of care and skill to be expected of a reasonably competent carpenter'. This was said to be clearly lower than that of a professional carpenter working for pay. It was not breached by the fact that the defendant had used screws which turned out to be inadequate for the job.

The medical context is one in which a high degree of specialist skill may be required. Significantly, however, it is also one which covers a wide range of competencies and specialisms. The question of whether there is only one standard of the reasonable doctor was raised in *Wilsher v Essex HA* (1988).

🔍 CASE CLOSE-UP

Wilsher v Essex HA (1988)

The plaintiff, Martin, was born prematurely and as a result had to be cared for in a special care baby unit. One aspect of his treatment involved having his oxygen supply supplemented. He was mistakenly given too much oxygen, due to a malfunction in the machinery which was administering it. This malfunction was not noticed by either of the two doctors in charge of his care. He developed a disorder called RLF, which rendered him nearly blind.

Martin's negligence action against the health authority, representing the doctors who cared for him, carried with it two legal difficulties. One of these concerned proof of causation: had the excess oxygen caused his condition? The other legal issue which his case raised was that of standard of care. This was dealt with by the Court of Appeal, which examined the relative standards of care to be expected of a houseman (a junior level in

▶ CROSS REFERENCE

Wilsher is discussed further in Chapter 4.

▶ THINKING POINT

How can the decision in *Wilsher* be reconciled with that in *Nettleship v Weston*?

hospital medicine) and a registrar, who has a more senior and supervisory role. It was decided that it would be too subjective to apply a standard of care tailored to each individual doctor's degree of experience. The standard of care should be one appropriate to the post which the doctor holds (taking into account that the tasks undertaken by the doctor would be expected to be appropriate to his level in the hospital hierarchy). Therefore, a higher standard would be expected of a registrar than a houseman; however, a new registrar must achieve the same standard as a more experienced one.

The approach to the medical standard of care in *Wilsher* was endorsed and applied in *FB v Princess Alexandra Hospital NHS Trust* (2017). A young child was brought by his parents to an A&E department, suffering from symptoms which later transpired to be the early signs of meningitis. These were missed by a senior house officer, leading to a delay in proper diagnosis and treatment of the child's condition. She sustained brain damage and deafness as a result. The Court of Appeal rejected the finding of the lower court denying liability on the grounds that the skill required would have only been expected of a doctor at a more senior level. It held that patient history taking was a basic skill, expected to be satisfactorily exercised by a senior house officer, and that this standard had been breached. See also, *Darnley v Croydon Health Services NHS Trust* (2018) in Chapter 2.

The field of alternative medicine has raised a tricky issue on duty of care. In *Shakoor v Situ* (2001), the claimant was the widow of a man who had died after a rare complication following a course of treatment by a qualified practitioner of traditional Chinese herbal medicine. The judge had to consider what standard of care the defendant's actions should be assessed by. It held that it was not enough to require the standard of the ordinary practitioner skilled in the art of herbal medicine. The standard required should take into account the fact that the practitioner has chosen to practise alongside orthodox medicine and the defendant's conduct should reflect an awareness of research and practice in that area. The judge's interpretation of the expert evidence in this case led him to conclude that, according to this standard of care, the defendant had not been negligent.

> **CROSS REFERENCE**
>
> For more on the skills required of the medical profession, see the *Bolam* case at 3.1.7 Special standards.

3.1.5 **Risk**

How do the courts apply the standard of care to a given situation? How do we decide what a reasonable man, or woman, would have done in a particular situation? In negligence cases this judgment always has a retrospective element to it, as courts are inevitably looking at a set of circumstances which is in the past and which is extremely unlikely to recur in the same way again. *Glasgow Corp v Muir* tells us that foreseeability is the key determinant of breach. In 1947, an American judge, Learned Hand, described a new way of looking at whether a reasonable person would choose to take a risk of damage or strive to avoid that risk in a particular situation. This involves balancing two different factors which combine to determine what is reasonable behaviour, as illustrated in Diagram 3.1. Although this 'economic' approach is not

Diagram 3.1 Risk assessment A

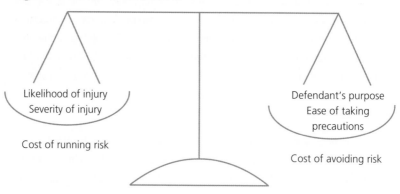

Likelihood of injury
Severity of injury

Cost of running risk

Defendant's purpose
Ease of taking precautions

Cost of avoiding risk

applied in any kind of systematic way in English courts, the consideration of different aspects is often evident in judicial reasoning.

- The magnitude of risk: this includes the likelihood of injury occurring and the severity of the injury should it occur = *cost of running the risk*.

- The importance of the defendant's purpose and the practicability of taking precautions against the risk = *cost of avoiding the risk*.

3.1.5.1 The cost of running the risk

This is made up of two elements:

(1) Likelihood of injury

What the law requires to be determined is the risk of an outcome which is reasonably foreseeable, not that of a remote outcome.

🔍 **CASE CLOSE-UP**

Bolton v Stone **(1951)**

In *Bolton v Stone* (1951), the plaintiff was injured by a cricket ball hit over the fence of a village cricket ground into the road where she was walking. Evidence indicated that balls had been hit into the road some six times in the previous thirty years. The court had to determine whether the defendant club had been negligent in continuing to play cricket on that ground. The House of Lords held that the defendants had not been negligent. Lord Oaksey said:

> The standard of care in the law of negligence is the standard of an ordinarily careful man but, in my opinion, an ordinarily careful man does not take precautions against every foreseeable risk . . . .. He takes precautions against risks which are reasonably likely to happen . . . .. There are many footpaths and highways adjacent to cricket grounds and golf courses on to which cricket balls are occasionally driven, but such risks are habitually treated by both

> the owners and committees of such cricket and golf courses and by the pedestrians who use the adjacent footpaths and highways as negligible, and it is not, in my opinion, actionable negligence not to take precautions to avoid such risks.
>
> Per Lord Reid:
>
> the test to be applied here is whether the risk of damage to a person on the road was so small that a reasonable man in the position of the appellants, considering the matter from the point of view of safety, would have thought it right to refrain from taking steps to prevent the danger.
>
> He saw this case as a difficult one lying very near the borderline of liability and requiring careful consideration of 'fact and degree' but ultimately concluded that the risk was small enough to have been disregarded by the reasonable man and thus the defendants were not liable in negligence.

(2) Severity of the injury

The second factor to be considered in assessing the cost of running a risk is the severity of the possible outcome, if the risk does materialize.

We saw in 3.1.1 Knowledge that in *Paris v Stepney Borough Council* (1951) the employee in question had already lost the sight of one eye. Therefore, an eye injury to his remaining good eye would have an extremely serious outcome for him. This should have been taken into account by his employer in evaluating the risk run by failure to provide him with protective eye goggles.

3.1.5.2 The cost of avoiding the risk

As with the cost of running the risk, this is made up of two elements:

(1) Importance of the defendant's purpose

There are many situations in which a defendant may be involved in an activity which is of importance to society and therefore there is a reluctance to place heavy restrictions by imposing negligence liability. Emergency and rescue services such as fire, ambulance, and police will often have to use speed and run risks which would not be acceptable in ordinary drivers. This does not give them a licence to be careless but means that their purpose will be taken into account in assessing breach. In *Watt v Hertfordshire CC* (1954), a fire service was summoned to the scene of an accident where a woman was trapped under a car. The only vehicle available in the station to take to the accident did not have sufficient means of securing the lifting device it was carrying. A fireman was injured when the device slid forward as the vehicle was speeding to the scene. The court held that as the defendant's purpose was the saving of a life, it was reasonable to use the available vehicle rather than delay in order to wait for the correct one. Had the defendant's purpose been a commercial one, the making of profit would not have justified the risk.

(2) Practicability of taking precautions against the risk

What would be the cost to the defendant of averting the risk? In *Latimer v AEC* (1953), the floor of the defendant's factory flooded with a combination of oil and water. Sawdust was spread over most of the floor to make it safe to walk on, but the plaintiff slipped and fell on a part of the floor which was lacking sawdust. It was held that in the circumstances the defendants had behaved reasonably. The only alternative to their action would have been to close the factory and send the workers home and, on the balance of risk, it would have been unreasonable to expect this level of precaution from the defendant. This part of the calculation can focus on financial cost to the defendant but in the case of *Watt*, above, a delay in obtaining an appropriate vehicle could have cost a life.

Available resources were considered in *Knight v Home Office* (1990). A mentally ill prisoner who was known to be at risk committed suicide, despite being observed every fifteen minutes in a prison hospital. The court recognized that the facilities to be afforded were different from what would be expected in a specialist psychiatric hospital. Lack of funds would not be a complete defence to insufficient safety precautions in a negligence case; however, the court must accept the reality that resources for prison medicine are limited. The standard of care must be tailored to the act and function to be performed. On that basis, and taking into account all the circumstances of the prisoner's death, the prison authorities had not breached the appropriate standard of care.

Knight also reminds us that a defendant might argue that he was merely following a general practice common in his field or sector of conduct. We will later (3.1.7 Special standards) see that courts can be quite deferential to the practices of professions, particularly in the medical context. However, the standard of care must ultimately be set and applied by the court, in the light of expert evidence, and there are a number of cases in which there has been no hesitation in declaring a common practice to be below standard and thus negligent. 'Neglect of duty does not cease by repetition to be neglect of duty' (*Bank of Montreal v Dominion Guarantee etc Co Ltd* (1930)).

Edward Wong Finance Co Ltd v Johnson Stokes & Master (1984) was a professional negligence case against a solicitor in which the Privy Council was called upon to consider aspects of property conveyancing in Hong Kong. It decided that despite the fact that a practice was widely accepted by most solicitors in Hong Kong, it was not reasonable and was thus negligent.

Safety regulations or internal protocols may be valuable in helping courts to assess the content of a duty of care in a given situation. *Buck and others v Nottinghamshire Healthcare NHS Trust* (2006) concerned an action brought by six psychiatric nurses who suffered injury while looking after a dangerous patient in a secure mental hospital. The Court of Appeal confirmed that evidence of NHS regulations advising on security practices in respect of dangerous patients was relevant in assessing how the hospital should have handled the patient in order to adequately protect its staff. In this case, the proper risk assessment of the patient had not been undertaken and the NHS Trust was held to be liable in negligence to its employees.

CASE CLOSE-UP

The Wagon Mound (No 2) (1967)

A situation which gave rise to two important Privy Council cases can be used to illustrate how the courts sometimes apply this so-called risk–benefit approach. A ship's chief engineer had carelessly allowed fuel oil to be spilled from his vessel during operations in Sydney Harbour. Large quantities of oil floated on the water until it reached a wharf where a number of ships were moored. At the same time, the wharf's owners were carrying on welding work. In the course of this welding, sparks and bits of hot metal were flying into the water beneath the wharf. The foreman noted a possible fire risk and ordered that the welding be stopped, until it was decided that it was safe to proceed. Two days later, a spark caused a piece of rubbish floating on the oil to catch fire and this resulted in extensive damage to the wharf and two ships.

⟩ CROSS REFERENCE
This case will be looked at in Chapter 4.

The first tort action arising from this incident was brought by the owners of the wharf (*Overseas Tankship (UK) Ltd v Morts Docks and Engineering Co Ltd*, *The Wagon Mound (No 1)* (1961)) and resulted in a highly important decision on remoteness of damage in negligence. The second tort action, reported in 1967, was brought by the owners of the damaged ships. *Overseas Tankship (UK) Ltd v Miller Steamship Co Pty*, *The Wagon Mound (No 2)* (1967) illustrates how the balancing exercise might operate when a court is deciding whether or not a defendant has breached the duty of care.

The Privy Council had to decide whether the ship's engineer had acted as a reasonable man in the circumstances. The first part of the cost–benefit equation, the *cost of running the risk*, involved consideration of the foreseeability of fire. The court speculated that the spillage of so much oil must have happened over a considerable time and a vigilant engineer would have noticed it. Expert evidence was such that 'some risk of fire would have been present to the mind of a reasonable man in the shoes of the ship's chief engineer'. Although the risk of fire was not great, the court assumed that if the oil caught fire then serious property damage was 'not only foreseeable but very likely'.

According to Lord Reid, a small risk may be neglected if there is a valid reason for doing so. Here, as regards the second part of the 'risk–benefit' equation, the *cost of avoiding the risk*, it was noted that there was no justification at all for spilling the oil; in fact, this was an expensive and illegal activity. The cost of stopping the spillage ('practicability of taking precautions') was assumed to be negligible.

The conclusion in *The Wagon Mound (No 2)* was stated by Lord Reid: 'If a real risk is one which would occur to the mind of a reasonable man in the position of the defendant's servant and which he would not brush aside as far-fetched . . . then surely he would not neglect such a risk if action to eliminate it presented no difficulty, involved no disadvantage and required no expense.' The defendants were liable in negligence. See Diagram 3.2 for an illustration of this point.

Diagram 3.2 Risk assessment B

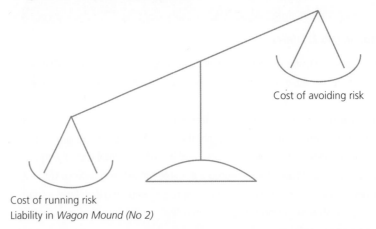

Cost of avoiding risk

Cost of running risk
Liability in *Wagon Mound (No 2)*

📖 STATUTE

Compensation Act 2006, s 1 covers the deterrent effect of potential liability

A court considering a claim in negligence or breach of statutory duty may, in determining whether the defendant should have taken particular steps to meet a standard of care (whether by taking precautions against risk or otherwise), have regard to whether a requirement to take those steps might:

(a) prevent a desirable activity from being undertaken at all, to a particular extent or in a particular way, or

(b) discourage persons from undertaking functions in connection with a desirable activity.

3.1.6 Compensation Act 2006

▶ CROSS REFERENCE

See Chapter 1 for more on the Compensation Act 2006.

We have seen that the Compensation Act 2006 addresses the problem of the so-called compensation culture.

The court is reminded that it may, but is not obligated to, take into account the wider impact of a decision it makes on standard of care. For example, finding that a local education authority has been negligent in respect of an accident on a school outing may lead to pressure from insurers and parents to curtail or abandon such outings in the future. What might be the educational implications of taking such a drastic step in order to avoid risk? The legal impact of s 1 on 'breach of duty' decisions will be awaited with interest.

Harris v Perry (2008) is a case in which the Court of Appeal reviewed a decision concerning the standard of care expected of a parent supervising children on a bouncy castle at a birthday party. The standard of care was that of the reasonably careful parent. Where the foreseeable risk was of 'less than serious' injury, the fulfilling of this duty did not require constant surveillance of the children while playing. Although the Compensation Act was not cited in the judgment, its tenor reflected an awareness that the law should not perpetuate a culture which was excessively risk-averse.

In *Lowden v Jump Zone Leisure* (2015), the defendants ran a small attraction on Brighton beach, in which the customer was flung into the air by elastic ropes attached to the customer's harness. On his second jump, the operator failed to ask the claimant if he was ready, before launching the jump. He suffered a serious neck injury. Jump Zone appealed against a finding of liability on the basis of lack of foreseeability. This was rejected by the Court of Appeal because the company's own risk assessment and guidelines recognized that to wait for confirmation of customer readiness was reasonable practice by operators.

Exercise

Walsh J in *The Wagon Mound (No 2)* (at first instance) described the taking of risks based upon foreseeability as a matter in which 'different minds would come to different conclusions'.

Rate the likelihood of injury resulting in the following circumstances on a scale of 1 (lowest) to 10 (highest) [Compare with other students]:

- going through a red light at a minor junction at 3am;
- climbing a ladder carrying a tin of paint in one hand;
- talking on a mobile phone while negotiating a roundabout;
- skiing off-piste without a guide;
- eating sausages which are two weeks past their sell-by date;
- having your ears pierced by your hairdresser;
- agreeing to take tablets which your friend (unqualified) is developing in her basement as a hangover cure;
- operating a chain saw which has a defective hand guard.

3.1.7 **Special standards**

3.1.7.1 **Sport**

Sport is an example of a situation in which participants are likely to be compelled to take extra risks in pursuit of victory, perhaps while partaking in physical contact which would not be acceptable in ordinary life. A photographer at a horse show was the claimant in *Wooldridge v Sumner* (1963). He was injured while standing at the edge of a track when a rider in the show lost control of his horse. In rejecting the claim in negligence, the court held that a competitor at a sporting event only owed a duty to a spectator not to act with reckless disregard of his safety. A momentary lapse of judgement did not constitute actionable negligence. The nature of the duty which the participant owed to the spectator was described as a duty of care, not a duty of skill and it was recognized that in sports the safety of the spectators may not be a first priority of participants. The defendant had pleaded the defence of *volenti non fit injuria*, according to which the plaintiff would have impliedly waived his action in negligence, having voluntarily agreed to attend this risky sporting event. However, it was held that the defence could only be considered once breach of duty had been established; it had not been in this case.

▶ CROSS REFERENCE

See *volenti* in Chapter 6 Defences to negligence

Standard of care in sport was further explored in *Condon v Basi* (1985), where a player in an amateur league football match was injured due to a tackle, which was a dangerous breach of the rules. The nature of the duty owed was to exercise such degree of care as was *appropriate in all the circumstances* and here 'reckless disregard' for the other's safety created liability in negligence. Sir John Donaldson MR was of the opinion that there is not a particular duty of care pertaining to sports; instead he was applying the general duty of reasonable care, 'taking into account of the circumstances in which you are placed, which, in a game of football, are quite different from those which affect you when you are going for a walk in the countryside'.

Smoldon v Whitworth (1997) was the first reported case in which a player sued a referee for injuries incurred in a rugby match. A player in an under-19s rugby match suffered severe spinal injuries when a scrum collapsed on him. The referee had not implemented the safety measures which had been adopted by the International Rugby Board to prevent such injuries in games involving young players. The Court of Appeal held that the level of care demanded was one which was appropriate in all the circumstances and 'the circumstances were of crucial importance'. In a hotly contested game of rugby the threshold of breach would be a high one, not easily crossed. Here there was evidence that the referee had ignored warnings about his conduct of the game, and was duly held to be liable in negligence. In *Vowles v Evans* (2003), comparable liability was imposed upon a referee in a professional rugby game.

▶ CROSS REFERENCE

See also Chapter 6 on defences.

You will recall that, in the case of *Watson v British Boxing Board of Control* (2001), once a duty to provide medical care to injured boxers had been imposed upon the defendants, their failure to provide ringside resuscitation equipment constituted a breach of that duty. Interestingly the court noted that, although the safety standards of the Board were claimed to be the highest in the world, it was still open to the court to determine whether even the most widely held practices were of an acceptable standard.

Sporting cases are sometimes approached not only as a question of standard of care but also in terms of the defence of *volenti*, or consent. The argument which could be made is that both participants and spectators are agreeing to run a certain amount of risk. In *Wooldridge* it was held that there can be no consent without a tort, and if the standard of care had not been breached and thus there is no tort, then there is nothing to consent to. Once the defendant's conduct is deemed negligent (whether or not within the rules of the game) then there can be no reliance on the defence of consent. This was reiterated in *Smoldon*, where the attempt to use the defence of *volenti* failed. The plaintiff had consented to the *ordinary incidents* of rugby, which did not include a game being played in contravention of the rules.

3.1.7.2 **Professional**

The legal position of the professional is similar to that pertaining more generally to *skill*. As discussed above, in setting the standard of care which must be reached, the starting point is the ability or capacity which someone is professing to have and likewise what the claimant would have been entitled to expect from him.

The professional will have a label or title which will bring with it a whole range of competencies. He is also likely to have numerous comparable peers or colleagues.

Q CASE CLOSE-UP

Bolam v Friern Hospital Management Committee (1957)

The prime example would be the medical professional. In *Bolam v Friern Hospital Management Committee*, a psychiatric patient sustained a pelvic fracture when he was given electroconvulsive treatment without first being administered a muscle relaxant. In determining whether the doctor had breached his obvious duty of care, the judge felt that the man on the Clapham omnibus would not be an appropriate comparator, because he would not be expected to have the special skills of the doctor. According to McNair J:

> Where you get a situation which involves the use of some special skill or competence . . . the test is the standard of an ordinary skilled man exercising and professing to have that special skill.

We have seen in *Wilsher* that in the medical context the standard applied will be that of other practitioners holding the same position or post as the defendant.

Supposing not all professionals agree how to behave in the relevant circumstances? According to *Bolam* it is enough for the defendant to show that the professional:

> has acted in accordance with a practice accepted as proper by a responsible body of medical men skilled in that particular art. Putting it another way round, a doctor is not negligent if he is acting in accordance with such a practice, merely because there is a body of opinion which takes a contrary view.

> ❯ THINKING POINT
>
> What might be the policy reasons behind the *Bolam* approach to professional negligence?

In *Bolam* itself, the plaintiff was unsuccessful because there were two different schools of thought on the use of muscle relaxants, and one of these supported the approach which had been adopted by the defendant.

When expert evidence is produced on both sides of the argument, how can we be sure that it is that of a 'responsible body'? The important House of Lords case of *Bolitho v City and Hackney HA* (1998) established that the court must be satisfied that 'the exponents of the body of medical opinion relied upon can demonstrate that such opinion has a logical basis'. A level of credibility must be reached before a view can be considered. It is said that *Bolitho*, and the subsequent cases which apply it, indicate a gradual shift towards greater willingness of courts to question professional practices, and there is some indication that medical negligence liability is more likely to be established, either by the courts or conceded during the process of settlement.

Bolam and *Bolitho* are cases which concern medical treatment, but their approach has also been applied to diagnosis, as in *Ryan v East London and City HA* (2001). Here the hospital trust was liable in negligence to a boy who suffered extensive surgery unnecessarily when a benign tumour was mistakenly diagnosed as malignant.

Another key aspect of medical practice pertains to communication with patients. Can the *Bolam* principle be applied to the giving of information or warning of risk to a patient?

 CASE CLOSE-UP

Sidaway v Board of Governors of Bethlem Royal Hospital (1985)

In *Sidaway v Board of Governors of Bethlem Royal Hospital*, a neurosurgeon recommended that a patient have a spinal operation to relieve neck and back pain. He neglected to tell her that the operation carried with it a one to two per cent risk of spinal damage, even if performed competently. She consented to have the operation but unfortunately sustained paralysis as a result. Her negligence action against the hospital, as vicariously liable for the surgeon, was based on her claim that if he had informed her about the risk, she would not have consented to the operation and thus not have been injured. The House of Lords, by a majority of four to one, found in favour of the defendants. Lord Bridge said:

> a decision on what degree of disclosure of risks is best calculated to assist a particular person to make a rational choice as to whether or not to undergo a particular treatment must be primarily a matter of clinical judgment. It would follow from this that the issue whether non-disclosure in a particular case should be condemned as a breach of the doctor's duty of care is an issue to be decided primarily on the basis of expert medical evidence, applying the Bolam test.

Here, expert evidence was that the risk of the severe outcome suffered by the claimant was less than 1 per cent, and non-disclosure of this level of risk would have been the practice of a responsible body of neurosurgeons. In holding that the *Bolam* test applied to this situation, the House of Lords considered and rejected a principle which is accepted by the courts in the United States, Canada, and Australia and is known as *informed consent*. According to informed consent, the standard of what should be disclosed to a patient is set by law, and is determined not only by medical practice but also by consideration of what the reasonable patient would want to know in the circumstances. In *Sidaway*, Lord Scarman dissented, preferring not the *Bolam* standard based on clinical judgement, but rather the standard of the 'prudent patient'. He felt that:

> The profession. . .. should not be judge in its own cause: . . . the courts should not allow medical opinion as to what is best for the patient to override the patient's right to decide for himself whether he will submit to the treatment offered him.

Lord Scarman's dissent was to become the basis of the following major decision by the Supreme Court thirty years later.

CASE CLOSE-UP

Montgomery v Lanarkshire Health Board (2015)

This case, where a seven-member Supreme Court departed from the decision in *Sidaway*, can be seen as the culmination of a long process in which the UK courts gradually shifted from favouring a doctor-oriented standard of care in the giving of information to that which more highly values patient autonomy. The claimant's son was born suffering from severe disabilities due to deprivation of oxygen during his birth. His mother was diabetic and thus under the care of a consultant obstetrician due to possible complications, one of which was shoulder dystocia, in which birth is impeded when the baby is too large to fit through the mother's pelvis. The chance of this occurring in her case was estimated as 9–10 per cent, but the obstetrician did not inform Ms Montgomery of this risk, nor of the alternative option of caesarean delivery.

The Justices ruled unanimously in Ms Montgomery's favour. In doing so, they were acknowledging that decision-making about treatment is no longer regarded as a matter of medical paternalism but rather depends on a partnership between patient and doctor. Law and society have evolved to the point that, according to Lord Kerr, 'patients are now widely regarded as persons holding rights, rather than as the passive recipients of the care of the medical profession; [they are] consumers exercising choices'. To ensure informed consent, the doctor must make the patient aware of *material risks*—'those which a reasonable person in the patient's position would be likely to attach significance to . . . or those of which the doctor is or should reasonably be aware that the particular patient would be likely to attach significance'.

Answering concerns about unpredictability, Lord Kerr and Lord Reed replied:

> a departure from the *Bolam* test will reduce the predictability of the outcome of litigation, given the difficulty of overcoming that test in contested proceedings. It appears to us however that a degree of unpredictability can be tolerated as the consequence of protecting patients from exposure to risks of injury which they would otherwise have chosen to avoid. The more fundamental response to such points, however, is that respect for the dignity of patients requires no less.

In *Montgomery*, the conclusion was that the risks for the patient were substantial and the exercise of reasonable care 'undoubtedly' required disclosure. The court accepted that if Ms Montgomery had been so informed, she was likely to have chosen caesarean delivery and the damage to her son would have been avoided.

> **THINKING POINT**
>
> Will the question of what constitutes a 'material risk' remain a source of dispute in clinical negligence cases?

Webster v Burton Hospitals NHS Foundation Trust (2017) illustrates an early application of *Lanarkshire* in a case involving damage sustained by a child at birth, due to a delayed delivery decision. The trial judge had denied liability, having applied to the defendants the *Bolam* standard of 'a responsible body of expert (consultant obstetrician) opinion'. The decision was overruled as having been founded on the wrong standard of care. According to Simon LJ, following *Lanarkshire*, 'in general terms the doctor's obligation (apart from in cases where this would damage the patient's welfare) is to present the material risks and uncertainties of different treatments, and to allow patients to make decisions that will affect their health and well-being on proper information'.

The issue of *disclosure of risk* can also be relevant in relation to causation, that is, the claimant's burden of establishing what he would or would not have done if properly informed.

Adams v Rhymney Valley DC (2000) reminds us that the *Bolam* test could apply to non-medical professionals as well. Parents whose three children died in a council house fire claimed that this was due to the council's negligent choice and installation of key-locking windows. The Court of Appeal applied to the defendants the standard of the reasonably skilful designer and provider of windows. This type of window had been used up and down the country and on that basis could not be considered inappropriate.

Lawyers can also reap the benefit of this generous approach. In *Moy v Petmann Smith* (2005), the *Bolam* test was applied to the question of the possible liability of a barrister in advising her client. According to Baroness Hale the duty of care had not been breached because: 'We have been shown no evidence or authority to support the view that no reasonable barrister would have given her advice in the way that Ms Perry did in this case.'

3.2 Was there a breach? Falling below standards

The basic rule is that the burden is on the claimant to establish that there has been a breach of duty. The standard of proof is the balance of probabilities. In some cases, such as road traffic accidents, the defendant may already have been convicted of a criminal offence in respect of the same set of facts. The Civil Evidence Act 1968, s 11 provides that in such circumstances the criminal conviction can be used to provide strong, although not conclusive, evidence that the defendant has been negligent.

3.2.1 *Res ipsa loquitur*

This Latin phrase means 'the thing speaks for itself'. In some cases the claimant will be significantly handicapped in his efforts to prove negligence on the balance of probabilities. In these circumstances the court may effectively give the claimant the benefit of the doubt by inferring negligence from what is known, in the absence of convincing evidence to the contrary.

Three elements must be present before the case is an appropriate one in which to apply *res ipsa loquitur*.

(1) The accident must be of the kind which does not normally happen in the absence of negligence.

Examples would be two trains colliding or a surgeon removing the wrong kidney from a patient. An early such case is *Scott v London and St Katherine's Dock Co* (1865), where the plaintiff was hit by some bags of sugar which fell out of the window of a warehouse onto his head!

(2) The cause of the accident must have been under the defendant's control.

This element is directed not at the issue of lack of care but at the fairness of imposing liability on this defendant. In *Gee v Metropolitan Railway Co* (1873), *res ipsa loquitur* was applied to an accident in which the door of a train flew open a few minutes after leaving the station, causing the plaintiff to fall out. The train doors were presumed to have been the sole responsibility of the train company at the relevant time. However, in *Easson v London & North Eastern Railway Co* (1944), a similar accident happened near the end of a journey from London to Edinburgh. In this instance the court held that there would have been too many opportunities for others to tamper with the doors, so the 'control' condition was not met.

(3) There must be no explanation of the cause of the accident.

Res ipsa loquitur is not relevant when there are sufficient facts known in order to prove negligence. This was the case in *Barkway v South Wales Transport Co Ltd* (1950). The plaintiff was injured when a bus in which he was a passenger crashed. It was established that the cause of the crash was a burst tyre and that this would not have occurred had the defendants adopted a proper system of tyre inspection. In contrast, *Thomas v Curley* (2013) was a medical negligence case in which it was held that the trial judge had correctly refused to apply *res ipsa* because there was sufficient information about how the injury had occurred.

3.2.2 **What is the effect of *res ipsa loquitur*?**

It allows the court to infer that the defendant has been negligent, but only in the absence of plausible evidence from the defendant of lack of negligence. Whether the court regards the evidence as sufficient to rebut the inference of negligence will vary from case to case.

In *Ward v Tesco Stores* (1976), yoghurt on the floor of the defendant's supermarket caused the claimant to slip and suffer injury. *Res ipsa loquitur* applied because the accident was of the type which does not happen when reasonable care is taken, the floor was the responsibility of the defendants, and there was no evidence as to how the yoghurt came to be on the floor. The evidence offered by the defendants about procedures for keeping the floors clean was not sufficient to displace the inference of negligence and they were liable. Megaw LJ in the Court of Appeal explained the outcome as follows:

> It is for the plaintiff to show that there has occurred an event which is unusual and which, in the absence of explanation, is more consistent with fault on the part of the defendants than the absence of fault; and to my mind the learned judge was wholly right in taking that view of

> **THINKING POINT**
> What would be the advantages of *res ipsa loquitur* to a claimant in a medical negligence case? On the other hand, what would be the drawbacks to relying on it?

the presence of this slippery liquid on the floor of the supermarket in the circumstances of this case; that is that the defendants knew or should have known that it was a not uncommon occurrence; and that if it should happen, and should not be promptly attended to, it created a serious risk that customers would fall and injure themselves. When the plaintiff has established that, the defendants can still escape from liability. They could escape from liability if they show that the accident must have happened, or even on balance of probability would have been likely to have happened, irrespective of the existence of a proper and adequate system, in relation to the circumstances, to provide for the safety of customers. But, if the defendants wish to put forward such a case, it is for them to show that, on balance of probability, either by evidence or by inference from the evidence which is given or is not given, this accident would have been at least equally likely to have happened despite a proper system designed to give reasonable protection to customers. That, in this case, they wholly failed to do.

Res ipsa loquitur was held to be applicable to an air crash, by the Privy Council in *George v Eagle Air Services* (2009). The three requirements were fulfilled: planes do not normally crash; the defendants had control over the aircraft, its flight, and pilot; and they had failed to give any explanation which was at least consistent with the absence of fault on their part. The defendants having failed to displace the inference of negligence, the claimants were successful.

Summary

- Breach is an objective concept, determined on a factual basis.
- Objectivity is modified in cases featuring youth and special skill.
- Risk analysis involves a balancing exercise.
- Burden of proof is on the claimant, on the balance of probabilities.

  Visit the online resources to listen to a podcast summarizing the topics covered in this chapter.

The bigger picture

The Justices in the *Montgomery* case placed emphasis on changing social and professional expectations. The Practice Guidelines published by the General Medical Council have been revised since *Montgomery*. See the following link for the new draft guidance:
www.gmc-uk.org/-/media/ethical-guidance/related-pdf-items/consent-draft-guidance/consent-draft-guidance.pdf?la=en&hash=5E54DB80171F9F78009E03FA86185000B6F87E17

Questions

Knowledge-testing questions

1. Give an example of two cases which show a departure from the 'reasonable man' test.

2. What are the four factors which courts must balance in determining whether the standard of care was breached?

3. What is the relationship between the cases of *Bolam* and *Montgomery*?

4. What is the effect of the application of *res ipsa loquitur*?

Problem and essay questions

1. Ben met his friend Olu, and they agreed they both needed a drink. They went to the pub, where Olu bought the drinks and Ben, after several pints, offered Olu a lift home. On the journey home, Ben collided with Kimberley, a 6-year-old who was trying to cross the street. The collision caused Olu to fly through the windscreen, and pushed Kimberley into the path of an oncoming car being driven by Ernie, aged 82. Kimberley sustained serious internal injuries. An ambulance was summoned to take Olu, Kimberley, and Ernie to hospital. Greta, the ambulance dispatcher, having taken the call, did not dispatch an ambulance for fifteen vital minutes, while she finished the magazine she had been reading when the call came. By the time the ambulance arrived, Olu had died. At the hospital, Kimberley's injuries were misdiagnosed by Mary, a junior doctor who was attending in Accident & Emergency for the first time. Had the nature of her injuries been correctly assessed in A&E, Kimberley would have had a 40 per cent chance of full recovery. Kimberley is now paraplegic.

   Analyse the aspects of this scenario which concern breach of duty.

2. Explain the 'balancing process' whereby the courts determine whether or not the standard of care has been met, with relevant case illustrations. To what extent do considerations of policy apply?

⊙ Visit the online resources for guidance on answering these questions.

☰ Further reading

Atiyah, P, '*Res ipsa loquitur* in England and Australia' (1972) 35 MLR 337

Fanning, J, 'Uneasy Lies the Neck that Wears a Stethoscope: Some Observations on Defensive Medicine' (2008) 24(2) PN 93

Gardner, J, 'The Negligence Standard: Political Not Metaphysical' (2017) 80 MLR 1

Heywood, R, 'R.I.P *Sidaway*: Patient-oriented Disclosure—A Standard Worth Waiting For?' (2015) 23(3) Med LR 455–66

McArdle, D and M James, 'Are You Experienced? "Playing Cultures", Sporting Rules and Personal Injury Litigation after *Caldwell v Maguire*' (2005) 13 Tort LR 193

McGrath, C, '"Trust Me, I'm a Patient . . .." Disclosure Standards and the Patient's Right to Decide' (2015) 74 CLJ 211

Turton, G, 'Informed Consent to Medical Treatment Post-*Montgomery*: Causation and Coincidence' (2019) 27(1) Med LR 108

4 Negligence: causation

LEARNING OBJECTIVES

By the end of this chapter you should be able to:

- understand the difference between the issues of causation in fact and causation in law, or remoteness;
- apply the 'but for' test and recognize the situations in which it is insufficient;
- explain the different ways in which the courts have applied the principle of *novus actus interveniens*; and
- understand the application of the 'reasonable foreseeability' test for remoteness.

Introduction

In order to bring a successful action in negligence it is not enough to establish the first two ingredients: (1) duty of care; and (2) breach of that duty. The claimant must also prove: (3) on the balance of probabilities that the breach caused his damage. If the defendant is not responsible, or partly responsible for the harm suffered, then he cannot be made liable for it—even if he has been negligent.

For example: Alfred develops a nasty rash after using Dermo-care shampoo. The manufacturers of Dermo-care have released it onto the market without proper testing, and it has been proved to cause adverse reactions in some users. However, medical evidence has established that Alfred's rash was caused by his long-standing allergy to strawberries, which he had been eating on the relevant day. Although the manufacturers of the shampoo owed him a duty of care as consumer and breached that duty, their breach did not cause his damage and therefore they are not liable to pay him compensation.

> **THINKING POINT**
> Could anyone be liable in tort for Alfred's skin complaint?

The question of causation can be divided into two issues:

(1) causation in fact; and

(2) causation in law, or remoteness.

4.1 Causation in fact

This first issue has been described by Winfield as 'primarily a matter of historical mechanics'. As its name states, it involves establishing the facts of how something came about at a given time. Causation in fact may not establish all or even the main causes, but it will permit exclusion of certain factors or persons from having contributed to a particular outcome. It will be seen that this is an aspect of negligence law which, in the past fifteen years, has seen significant adaptation and moves away from the strict orthodoxy of earlier times.

A hypothetical test is traditionally used to begin the process of establishing causation in fact. Known as the 'but for' test, it involves asking the question, 'But for the defendant's breach of duty, would the claimant's damage still have occurred?' If the answer is 'yes', then the defendant's breach generally can be eliminated as a factual cause of the damage. If the answer is 'no', then we know that the defendant's breach is at least one of the contributing causes of the damage.

Q CASE CLOSE-UP

Barnett v Kensington & Chelsea Hospital Management Committee (1969)

This case provides a clear demonstration of the application of the 'but for' test. Three nightwatchmen became ill after drinking tea. They attended the local hospital, where the casualty officer on duty did not examine them but recommended on the telephone that they return home and contact their own doctors. Some hours later, one of the men died. It turned out that he had died of arsenical poisoning and that, on the balance of probabilities, the treatment which the doctor would have given him could not have saved him. The court accepted that the casualty officer had indeed been negligent in failing to examine the patients; however 'but for' his breach, the death would still have occurred. Therefore, it was to be eliminated as a cause of the death.

The burden lies with the claimant to prove causation on the balance of probabilities. In *Pickford v ICI* (1998), a secretary was suffering from repetitive strain injury. This could have been caused by the work she had done for her former employer, ICI, but alternatively it could have had 'psychogenic' or psychological origins unconnected with her work. She was unable to establish that her injury was work-related and for that reason her negligence action failed. *Pickford* is a useful reminder of what a heavy burden the claimant bears in some cases.

> ❯ THINKING POINT
> Do you expect that duty of care would have been a disputed issue before the court in *Barnett*?

4.1.1 **Deficiencies in the 'but for' test**

▶ CROSS REFERENCE

For more on employers' liability, see Chapter 8.

Problems in the application of the 'but for' question arise in two particular circumstances: first, when the answer to the question leads to an unjust or contradictory result and, second, when it is impossible to answer the 'but for' question. A common example of the kind of situation which could lead to an unjust outcome is as follows. Two people, X and Y, simultaneously light a match in a gas-filled room and an explosion occurs. If we ask, 'But for the negligence of X would the explosion have happened?', the answer would be yes. Then if we ask, 'But for the negligence of Y would the explosion have happened?', the answer would again be yes. Applying the 'but for' test to this scenario would result in neither X nor Y being regarded as a cause and thus neither would be liable. A more appropriate outcome, to ensure a remedy in respect of the explosion, would be to regard both their actions as causes and to make X and Y *jointly and severally* liable.

Several liability occurs when two or more parties act independently to cause the same damage to a claimant. Each party is separately liable for the whole of the damage (but compensation can only be recovered once).

Joint and several liability occurs when two or more parties act together to cause the same damage to a claimant. Again, though any or all can be sued, each party is separately liable for the whole of the damage and in a case when only one is able to pay, he will be liable for the whole of the damage. A common example of joint and several liability is vicarious liability, where the employer may be held liable for the tort of his employee.

Contribution arises where there is joint and several liability and one party who pays compensation may wish to claim a portion of this from the other wrongdoers. The Civil Liability (Contribution) Act 1978, ss 1 and 2 enables the party who has paid the compensation to bring an action to recover contribution from one or more of the other parties. This action does not involve the original claimant whose loss has been satisfied; rather it is brought by the party in his own right. The usual time limit for a contribution action is two years from the original award or settlement.

▶ CROSS REFERENCE

Fairchild is discussed in 4.1.5 Current issues in causation: asbestos.

Situations in which it is not possible to accurately answer the 'but for' question vary from the simple to the complicated. In the Canadian case of *Cook v Lewis* (1952), two hunters negligently fired their guns in the direction of the claimant. One bullet hit him, but it was not established which gun had fired that bullet. In the absence of the required proof, it was held that the hunters would be jointly and severally liable. The reasoning was explained in a later House of Lords case on causation—see *Fairchild v Glenhaven Funeral Services* (2003).

Lord Nicholls said of *Cook*:

The unattractive consequence, that one of the hunters will be held liable for an injury he did not in fact inflict, is outweighed by the even less attractive alternative, that the innocent plaintiff should receive no recompense even though one of the negligent hunters injured him. It is this balance . . . which justifies a relaxation in the standard of causation required. Insistence on the normal standard of causation would work an injustice.

In the context of Lord Nicholls's reasoning, you will recall that the main preoccupation of the law of tort is to obtain a remedy for an injured party, and so creativity must be employed when the but for test fails.

The application of the 'but for' test usually involves an element of guesswork, concerning what *would have* happened in a given circumstance. Sometimes the guessing focuses on what someone might or might not have done. In *McWilliams v Sir William Arrol* (1962), the deceased's employer had been negligent in failing to provide a safety harness for a steelworker who was working at a height. He fell to his death. It was clearly established that had the defendant provided a safety harness, the worker would not have worn it. But for the defendant's breach, the damage would still have occurred and so there was no liability on the part of the employer.

CROSS REFERENCE

For more on employers' liability, see Chapter 8.

In *Allied Maples Group v Simmons* (1995), the hypothetical action under consideration was that of a third party. The plaintiff's solicitor was allegedly negligent in failing to advise his clients to request certain indemnities from the sellers of property which they were purchasing. In the event, they suffered financial loss when liabilities which would have been avoided by the indemnities fell upon them. It was unknown, at the time of trial, whether the sellers would have agreed to include the indemnities as part of the contract of sale and, the solicitor argued, because of this, it could not be proved that his negligence caused the loss.

The Court of Appeal held that because what was unknown was the hypothetical act of a third party (the sellers), all the plaintiff had to prove was that there was a substantial chance, greater than merely speculative, that if asked the sellers would have agreed to the indemnity. The quantity of compensation payable could then be adjusted to the degree of likelihood of that third party agreeing. However, the plaintiffs would have to prove on a balance of probabilities that if properly advised by their solicitors they would have requested the indemnities from the sellers. A majority of the Court of Appeal agreed with the trial judge's finding that, but for the defendant's negligence, there was a substantial chance that the plaintiffs would have been able to secure an indemnity against the losses.

4.1.2 **Loss of a chance**

In some cases, the argument will be made that the defendant's negligence increased the likelihood of a poor outcome for the claimant or deprived him of the possibility of avoiding that outcome. The courts have been reluctant to allow 'loss of a chance' to substitute for the all-or-nothing requirement that causation be proved on a balance of probabilities.

 CASE CLOSE-UP

Hotson v Berkshire Area HA (1987)

This case shows how strictly the courts have adhered to the requirement of the claimant's burden of proof. A 13-year-old boy injured his hip in a fall from a tree while at school. When taken to hospital the seriousness of his injuries was not immediately discovered.

Five days later, his condition was correctly diagnosed and treated. However, he developed a serious disability of the hip as an adult, which he claimed was caused by the delayed diagnosis. The hospital admitted negligence in terms of the original misdiagnosis but denied liability on the grounds that, according to the medical evidence, given proper treatment, the boy would only have had a 25 per cent chance of complete recovery. On the balance of probabilities, the disability would have occurred even without the defendants' negligence.

According to Lord Ackner:

> this case was a relatively simple case concerned with proof of causation, on which the plaintiff failed, because he was unable to prove, on the balance of probabilities, that his deformed hip was caused by the authority's breach of duty in delaying over a period of five days a proper diagnosis and treatment.

It has been suggested that the outcome of *Hotson* might have been different if the plaintiff's damage had been described, instead of as physical disability, as loss of a chance to avoid that disability. We will see later (4.1.5 Current issues in causation: asbestos and 4.1.5 Causation: the future) that some cases of cumulative causes have been treated as increasing risk or chance that damage might be suffered and it could be argued that in *Hotson* the defendants' negligence deprived the claimant of the small (25 per cent) chance he had of full recovery.

▶ THINKING POINT

The margin between success and failure for the plaintiff in *Hotson* was that between 25 per cent likelihood and 51 per cent likelihood. To what extent is it possible to accurately quantify the possibility of outcomes? Are you satisfied that justice is being served by this approach to causation?

🔍 CASE CLOSE-UP

Gregg v Scott (2005)

The case of *Gregg v Scott* was a clinical negligence case in which the claimant visited Dr Scott complaining of a lump under his arm. The doctor concluded that it was benign and did not order any further investigation or tests. A year later a different doctor referred the patient to a specialist for further tests and it was discovered that the lump was a symptom of cancer. The claimant was given a 25 per cent chance of ten years' survival. That chance would have been as high as 42 per cent at the time he visited Dr Scott. By a narrow three to two majority the House of Lords found in favour of the defendant. Mr Gregg's loss had been described in terms of the potential for ten years' survival. He could not prove that he had a likelihood of survival higher than 50 per cent, even at the time of his first visit to Dr Scott. The relative diminishing of his chances of survival was not a loss recognized in negligence claims.

Baroness Hale considered the implications of moving to liability for loss of a chance:

> The appellant in this case accepts that the proportionate recovery effect must cut both ways. If the claim is characterised as loss of a chance, those with a better than evens chance would still only get proportion of the full value of their claim. . . .. This would surely be a case of two steps forward, three steps back for the great majority of straightforward personal

injury claims. The complexities of attempting to introduce liability for the loss of a chance of a more favourable outcome in personal injury claims have driven me, not without regret, to conclude that it should not be done . . .

The majority of judges placed some importance upon the fact that the possible adverse outcome, death within ten years, had not actually come about. As already indicated the claimant would have been entitled to damages for any adverse outcomes which *were* caused by the doctor's negligence.

▶ THINKING POINT
Can you think of a way of describing the loss to the claimant in *Gregg* which might have resulted in a different decision by the court?

It is difficult to reconcile the decision in *Gregg* with that in *Allied Maples*, where loss of an opportunity to negotiate a better bargain was compensatable. That the latter concerned pure economic loss, while the former concerned physical injury does not seem to adequately explain the different outcomes as generally the law of tort favours physical injury over the financial.

In *Wright v Cambridge Medical Group* (2011) the defendant GP negligently delayed referral of a baby to hospital. The hospital then negligently failed to correctly diagnose her condition and she developed a disability of the hip. The claimant sued the defendant only and the trial judge found no causation, on the grounds that even had hospitalization not been delayed, the negligent diagnosis in hospital would still have occurred. The Court of Appeal disagreed on both causation and result. The court concluded that the GP's negligence was definitely *a cause* of the child's injury and, unlike *Gregg*, it was separately quantifiable from that caused by the hospital. The hospital's negligence was neither so extreme nor unforeseeable that it wiped out that of the GP. The two parties would be jointly and severally liable. This was not treated as a case of loss of chance because, in light of the decision in *Gregg*, it would only be for the Supreme Court to extend the concept into the areas of personal injury and clinical negligence.

A very different type of situation raising causation issues occurs in medical cases in which the doctor or other medical professional has been negligent in failing to explain adequately the risks of a possible course of treatment. Essential to success is the claimant's ability to establish that, had those risks been explained, the treatment would not have been consented to and the adverse outcome thereby avoided. Again, this leads to speculation about the hypothetical. In *Sidaway v Bethlem Royal Hospital* (1985), the claimant was recommended to have a spinal operation in order to relieve a painful condition. There was a chance of less than one per cent that the operation, even when performed competently, would result in moderate to severe disability. Unfortunately for the claimant this risk materialized in her case. The main legal issue in *Sidaway* was that of standard of care—that is, did the surgeon breach his duty of care to his patient in not informing her of this risk? The case was also dependent, however, on the implied assertion by the claimant that 'but for' the inadequate information, she would not have consented to the operation. Her claim ultimately failed, as a majority of the House of Lords con-

▶ CROSS REFERENCE

For more on the breach of duty, see *Sidaway* and *Bolam* in Chapter 3.

cluded that the duty had not been breached because the surgeon had 'acted in accordance with a practice accepted at the time as proper by a responsible body of medical opinion'. This aspect of *Sidaway* concerning the question of breach of duty must now be revised in view of the decision in *Montgomery v Lanarkshire* (see the *Montgomery v Lanarkshire Health Board 2015 Case Close-up* in Chapter 3).

Q CASE CLOSE-UP

▶ THINKING POINT

Would the same adverse outcome have occurred if Ms Chester had opted to have the operation at a later date? What factors would influence your answer?

Chester v Afshar (2005)

Causation was the key issue in a more recent medical consent case, *Chester v Afshar*. Here, the hypothetical question 'What would have happened if . . .?' was again the issue. A patient consulted a neurosurgeon about her back pain and was advised to undergo surgery. As in *Sidaway*, the surgery carried with it a risk, this time between one and two per cent, of serious nerve damage, even if performed without negligence. The claimant was not informed by the surgeon of this risk and following the operation she was found to have suffered the nerve damage. The trial judge concluded that the defendant had been negligent in not advising her of the risk prior to obtaining her consent and that had he done so she would not have gone ahead with the surgery at that time. However, three out of five Law Lords did not feel that the claimant could satisfy the usual tests for causation. This was because even though, had she been properly informed, she would not have agreed to the operation *at that time*, she might well have gone on to have the surgery in the future, when the risk would still have existed.

Despite this, a majority ruled in favour of the claimant. They based their conclusion on the policy grounds of upholding patient autonomy, as clearly stated by Lord Steyn:

> Standing back from the detailed arguments, I have come to the conclusion that, as a result of the surgeon's failure to warn the patient, she cannot be said to have given informed consent to the surgery in the full legal sense. Her right of autonomy and dignity can and ought to be vindicated by a narrow and modest departure from traditional causation principles.

Chester, then, is another example of the way in which the courts, on occasion of factual uncertainty, have been prepared to extend the principles of causation in order to obtain what is seen as a fair outcome. On principles of causation it is somewhat difficult to reconcile with *Gregg v Scott*. We know that these cases will be limited but the extent of their reach is as yet unpredictable. In *Environment Agency v Ellis* (2008) the defendants used an ordinary case of industrial injury to test the extent to which the courts were prepared to extend their divergence from the traditional 'but for' and all-or-nothing approach to causation. The Court of Appeal rejected any such extension into ordinary accident claims and clearly stated that it wished to limit such innovation to cases of complex industrial injury such as those caused by asbestos.

CASE CLOSE-UP

Correia v University Hospital of North Staffordshire NHS Trust (2017)

The claimant in this clinical negligence case relied on *Chester*; however, her attempt failed. She had consented to a three-stage surgical procedure; however, in her case the third stage was negligently omitted by the surgeon. Her case was that had she known of the risks of such an omission, she would not have gone ahead with the operation.

Correia is interesting because the Court of Appeal takes the opportunity to review the decision in *Chester* and to endorse its ratio as summarized in Lord Hope's speech, which begins with an acknowledgment that some medical decisions are very difficult for patients to make.

> To leave the patient who would find the decision difficult without a remedy, as the normal approach to causation would indicate, would render the duty useless in the cases where it may be needed most. This would discriminate against those who cannot honestly say that they would have declined the operation once and for all if they had been warned. I would find that result unacceptable. The function of the law is to enable rights to be vindicated and to provide remedies when duties have been breached. Unless this is done the duty is a hollow one, stripped of all practical force and devoid of all content. It will have lost its ability to protect the patient and thus to fulfil the only purpose which brought it into existence. On policy grounds therefore I would hold that the test of causation is satisfied in this case. The injury was intimately involved with the duty to warn. The duty was owed by the doctor who performed the surgery that Miss Chester consented to. It was the product of the very risk that she should have been warned about when she gave her consent. So I would hold that it can be regarded as having been caused, in the legal sense, by the breach of that duty.

In the eyes of Simon LJ in *Correia* this should be regarded as nothing more than 'a modest departure from the established principles of causation'. The Court of Appeal supported the trial judge's conclusion that the defendant's failure to specify the risks of a particular aspect of her procedure did not constitute negligence in the obtaining of overall informed consent and, importantly, that negligence in the carrying out of the procedure did not vitiate overall consent. The claimant's injury was not 'intimately linked' with a failure to warn. Further, the claimant had not convinced the court on the balance of probabilities that she would not have gone ahead with the procedure had this specific information been imparted.

Chester was again one aspect of *Diamond v Royal Devon & Exeter NHS Foundation Trust* (2019). The facts giving rise to the appeal were that the claimant had an abdominal hernia repair using the surgical mesh method. This was liable to jeopardize future pregnancies. When she consented, she had not been advised of the possible alternative of a suture repair, which the surgeon did not favour as it was likely to fail. The claimant asserted that she would have chosen the suture rather than the mesh approach, had she been properly informed.

It was held, according to the *Montgomery* approach, that the defendant had breached the duty to obtain informed consent. However causation was not established. *Montgomery* required that to establish causation the court must decide what the reasonable person in the patient's position would have done. The court believed that on the facts the claimant would have gone ahead with the mesh procedure; to do otherwise would have been irrational. The claimant had failed the 'but for' test. *Diamond* also confirmed that *Chester* created no standalone right to damages for loss of autonomy.

4.1.3 Material contribution to injury

There is a range of cases which deal with illness and injury in which it is known that one or more defendants have been negligent, but it is not possible to link them to the claimant's injury accurately.

Bonnington Castings Ltd v Wardlaw (1956) illustrates the problem. The claimant contracted pneumoconiosis due to exposure at work to silicone dust. There were two sources of the dust, one tortious (due to inadequate provision of protection by the defendant) and one non-tortious. It was impossible to attribute the disease conclusively to either source and so the but for test was of no assistance. The House of Lords ruled that this was a case in which the disease had been caused by the accumulation of dust from both sources. It was found that the dust attributable to the employer's negligence had materially contributed to this accumulation, and thus the defendant was liable—perhaps surprisingly, for the whole of the outcome. This can be explained by the fact that the resultant disease was indivisible; a totality which could not be broken down into component elements.

The issue arises of what constitutes 'material contribution'. The Court of Appeal addressed this in *Bailey v Ministry of Defence* (2008), another case of cumulative causes.

The claimant, Miss Bailey, sustained brain damage while under the care of a hospital managed by the defendants. She suffered a cardiac arrest due to aspiration of vomit and it was claimed that this would not have happened had she not been in a weakened state due to the defendants' earlier failures in her post-operative care. Breach of duty was not disputed; however, the appeal turned on the question of causation: namely had that breach been causative of her damage?

The Court of Appeal found in favour of the claimant and resolved the causation issue using the House of Lords' decision in *Bonnington Castings v Wardlaw*. *Bailey* was treated as a case of cumulative causes which operated interdependently—the claimants' weakness was caused by her inherent physical vulnerability but also by the defendants' failings in care. Although it was not possible to establish the proportion of causation which would be attributed to the defendants, it was found that 'but for' their inadequate care, Miss Bailey would have been less weak and therefore their breach had *materially contributed* to her damage. According to Lord Reid, where the contribution to the outcome was 'more than negligible', that would suffice to establish a causal link.

A more recent example comes from the Privy Council. In *Williams v Bermuda Hospitals Board* (2016) the claimant attended the defendant hospital emergency department complaining of pain. A CT scan was ordered for diagnostic purposes but there was a five-hour delay before the scan took place. His appendix ruptured, and following surgery the claimant suffered sepsis, which led to severe heart and lung damage. The negligence action alleged that had the scan occurred within a reasonable time, the damage sustained from the sepsis would have been avoided. The Privy Council concluded that the cause of the injury had been cumulative, as in *Bonnington*, and that it was more likely than not that the defendant's delay had materially contributed to the resultant damage.

Cumulative causation had not been present in, for example, *Hotson v Berkshire Area HA*. In contrast, in *Wilsher v Essex AHA*, below, the court had to consider a number of separate distinguishable potential causes.

4.1.4 **Material contribution to risk of injury**

 CASE CLOSE-UP

McGhee v National Coal Board (1973)

This was an employers' liability case brought by a worker who sustained a skin disease caused by contact with brick dust, after years of working in a brick kiln. The admitted negligence of his employers lay in the fact that they failed to provide adequate washing facilities at the end of the working day, so that the plaintiff had to cycle home covered in brick dust before he could wash it off. He alleged, but was unable to prove, that it was this extended exposure at the end of the day which had caused his disease. The case for the defendants was that, because his job involved exposure to brick dust all day long, it was more likely than not that the plaintiff's disease had been caused by 'innocent' rather than wrongful exposure. Lord Wilberforce spoke for a unanimous House of Lords in finding for the plaintiff, despite a recognition that an 'evidential gap' existed:

> [I]n the absence of proof that the culpable condition had, in the result, no effect, the employers should be liable for an injury, squarely within the risk which they created and that they, not the pursuer, should suffer the consequences of the impossibility, foreseeably inherent in the nature of his injury, of segregating the precise consequence of their default.

One single substance was known to be the cause of the plaintiff's injury in *Bonnington* and in *Bailey* different causes combined cumulatively. However, in *Wilsher v Essex Area Health Authority*, there were five separate possible factors, only one of which actually caused the damage. We have heard in Chapter 3 that the plaintiff had been given excess oxygen due to the negligence of the hospital where he had been born prematurely. He later was found to be suffering from blindness. One cause of blindness in premature babies is excess oxygen; however, there are four other potential causes, all of which were present in his case. At the trial, the plaintiff was unable to prove on a balance of probabilities that the excess oxygen had been the cause of his blindness. Both the trial judge and the Court of Appeal applied *McGhee*, enabling the plaintiff to succeed, despite his inability to close the evidential gap. However, the House of Lords distinguished *McGhee*. In that case, there had been evidence that the worker's skin disease could have been caused by an accumulation of brick dust, to which there was no doubt that the defendants had negligently contributed. In *Wilsher*, the defendants had merely added one additional possible cause to four other discrete (non-negligent) causes. In the absence of conclusive evidence that the hospital's negligence had been the operative cause, liability could not be imposed.

See, below, for another application of this approach in an asbestos case, *Sienkiewicz v Greif* (2011).

4.1.5 Current issues in causation: asbestos

Asbestos was widely used in a range of manufacturing and construction industries throughout the first half of the twentieth century. The fact that inhaling asbestos dust could cause serious and often fatal disease began to be accepted gradually in the 1930s, and by the early 1960s employers were strictly regulated in the use of asbestos. Many workers who were exposed to asbestos at a time when the risks were known and therefore foreseeable began, late in life, to develop asbestos-related diseases. The early twenty-first century has seen a growing number of legal claims against former employers which are important to victims and their families but also carry with them huge implications for the British insurance industry.

🔍 CASE CLOSE-UP

Fairchild v Glenhaven Funeral Services Ltd (2003)

The House of Lords had to deal with a complex causation issue which arose in a number of asbestos compensation claims. The claimants were suffering from mesothelioma, a cancer caused by asbestos dust. It was not known scientifically at the time whether the disease could be initiated by one fibre of asbestos or by many or exactly how the cumulative development of the disease occurred. The causation problem arose because the claimants had negligently been exposed to asbestos while working for several different employers, some of whom had gone out of business and could not now be sued. It was impossible to establish which exposure had caused their current disease. Applying the 'but for' test, the Court of Appeal had rejected all three claims.

The House of Lords, however, took a novel and controversial approach to causation, in this case of an 'evidential gap'. It unanimously allowed the appeals by the claimants, thereby permitting them to proceed against any or all of the employers who had exposed them to asbestos. This would be an example of what was described earlier as joint and several liability. It is helpful to read a long excerpt from the speech of Lord Nicholls. It illustrates the strong policy considerations which persuaded him, in what he admits is an exceptional approach, to depart from the strict causation requirements:

> I have no hesitation in agreeing with all your Lordships that these appeals should be allowed. Any other outcome would be deeply offensive to instinctive notions of what justice requires and fairness demands. The real difficulty lies in elucidating in sufficiently specific terms the principle being applied in reaching this conclusion. To be acceptable the law must be coherent. It must be principled. The basis on which one case, or one type of case, is distinguished from another should be transparent and capable of identification. When a decision departs from principles normally applied, the basis for doing so must be rational

and justifiable if the decision is to avoid the reproach that hard cases make bad law. I turn therefore to consider the departure from the normal, and the basis of that departure, in the present appeals. In the normal way, in order to recover damages for negligence, a plaintiff must prove that but for the defendant's wrongful conduct he would not have sustained the harm or loss in question. He must establish at least this degree of causal connection between his damage and the defendant's conduct before the defendant will be held responsible for the damage.

Exceptionally this is not so. In some circumstances a lesser degree of causal connection may suffice. This sometimes occurs where the damage flowed from one or other of two alternative causes. Take the well-known example where two hunters, acting independently of each other, fire their guns carelessly in a wood, and a pellet from one of the guns injures an innocent passer-by. No one knows, and the plaintiff is unable to prove, from which gun the pellet came. Should the law of negligence leave the plaintiff remediless, and allow both hunters to go away scot-free, even though one of them must have fired the injurious pellet?

[T]o impose liability on a defendant in such circumstances normally runs counter to ordinary perceptions of responsibility. Normally this is unacceptable. But there are circumstances, of which the two hunters' case is an example, where this unattractiveness is outweighed by leaving the plaintiff without a remedy.

The present appeals are another example of such circumstances, where good policy reasons exist for departing from the usual threshold 'but for' test of causal connection. Inhalation of asbestos dust carries a risk of mesothelioma. That is one of the very risks from which an employer's duty of care is intended to protect employees. Tragically, each claimant acquired this fatal disease from wrongful exposure to asbestos dust in the course of his employment. A former employee's inability to identify which particular period of wrongful exposure brought about the onset of his disease ought not, in all justice, to preclude recovery of compensation.

So long as it was not insignificant, each employer's wrongful exposure of its employee to asbestos dust and, hence, to the risk of contracting mesothelioma, should be regarded by the law as a sufficient degree of causal connection. This is sufficient to justify requiring the employer to assume responsibility for causing or materially contributing to the onset of the mesothelioma when, in the present state of medical knowledge, no more exact causal connection is ever capable of being established. Given the present state of medical science, this outcome may cast responsibility on a defendant whose exposure of a claimant to the risk of contracting the disease had in fact no causative effect. But the unattractiveness of casting the net of responsibility as widely as this is far outweighed by the unattractiveness of the alternative outcome.

I need hardly add that considerable restraint is called for in any relaxation of the threshold 'but for' test of causal connection. The principle applied on these appeals is emphatically not intended to lead to such a relaxation whenever a plaintiff has difficulty, perhaps understandable difficulty, in discharging the burden of proof resting on him.

Their Lordships were not agreed on the extent to which *McGhee* could be said to have laid down a new principle of law, but its interpretation in *Wilsher* as indicating nothing more than a 'robust and pragmatic' decision was rejected. Instead McGhee provided sound authority for accepting *material increase in risk* as adequate evidence of causation. Students should be aware that science has now rejected the 'single fibre' theory and that mesothelioma can now be regarded as a disease caused by cumulative exposure to asbestos.

Barker v Corus UK (2006) also concerned asbestos and impossibility of factual proof and repre-sented a challenge by the insurance industry to the decision in *Fairchild*. The facts differed from those in *Fairchild* in that one of the periods of the claimant's exposure to asbestos was when he was self-employed so that the negligence was that of the victim himself. The House of Lords partially reversed the ruling in *Fairchild* to the extent that it held that, although a defendant could still be liable without proof of causation, his liability could only extend to the relative proportion to which he could have contributed to the chance of the outcome. Liability was thus several rather than joint and, in this case, there was a 20 per cent discount on the overall dam-ages figure to represent the claimant's contributory negligence.

There was strong resistance to the decision in *Barker* from unions and others. It meant that claim-ants who were sick and dying might need to spend much of their remaining time trying to establish the relative extent of liability of former employers and, if it was found that some were no longer in business, they risked getting substantially less compensation than they would have done under *Fairchild*'s approach of joint liability. The Labour government quickly passed the Compensation Act 2006, s 3 of which restored the *Fairchild* position of joint and several liability in cases of meso-thelioma. This meant that any one negligent defendant could, if necessary, be ordered to bear 100 per cent liability, regardless of the extent of his involvement with the claimant. In 2009–10, legis-lation proposed the creation of an employers' liability insurance bureau to compensate those suffering from an industrial disease negligently caused by an employer who was unable to satisfy a claim, but this was not carried forward by the Conservative–Lib Dem coalition government.

In *Sienkiewicz v Grief (UK) Ltd* (2011), only one of the factors which may have caused the claimant's mesothelioma had been a single employer's negligence (the other exposure was general, non-negligent atmospheric asbestos). The Supreme Court held that, according to s 3 of the Compensation Act, the question to be asked was whether the defendant's negligence had constituted a 'material increase' in risk of the disease. This could be satisfied even when, as here, the employer's contribution to the risk was estimated to be 18 per cent.

Uncertainty as to the timing of the inception of liability in mesothelioma cases was considered in the context of insurance coverage in *BAI (Run off) and others v Durham* (2012). By a 4:1 majority the Supreme Court held that though the contracting of mesothelioma comprises the claimant's actionable injury, the defendant employer's legal responsibility begins at the time at which the claimant was first negligently exposed to the asbestos.

4.1.6 Factual causation: the future

It remains uncertain whether the *Fairchild* approach to causation will be confined to mesothelioma cases or will be extended. In *Sienkiewicz*, Lord Brown described the mesothelioma cases as 'in a category all their own' and that 'save only for mesothelioma cases, claimants should henceforth expect little flexibility from the courts in their approach to causation'. However, Peel and Goucamp remind us that future cases may bring different evidential conundrums and that *McGhee* itself, which provides authority for *Fairchild*, did not concern asbestos (*Winfield and Jolowicz on Tort*, 19th edn, Sweet & Maxwell, 2014, p 177). The Court of Appeal in *Heneghan v Manchester Dry Docks* (2018) indicated that joint and several liability could apply to other forms of asbestos-related injury (such as lung cancer) if a factual uncertainty similar to that in *Fairchild* existed.

4.1.7 **Supervening causes**

By this we mean later unconnected events causing the same or greater harm as the first tort, sometimes referred to as supervening causes.

In some cases involving two torts, the second wrongdoer may find that his breach of duty caused no additional damage to a victim and that he is therefore not liable to pay compensation. *Performance Cars v Abraham* (1962) involved an accident-prone Rolls-Royce. It was damaged in a collision due to the fault of A and, as a result, the bottom half of the car required a respray. Two weeks later, before the damage could be repaired, B collided with the same car. The damage done required a respray of the bottom half of the car. Because B created no additional damage, the liability to pay for the respray remained with A.

There may be a situation in which a second event overtakes or wipes out the effect of the damage done by a first tort. In *Baker v Willoughby* (1970), the plaintiff suffered a leg injury in a car accident attributable to the negligence of the defendant, which necessitated him taking a job in a scrap metal yard. Some three years later and before the trial regarding the accident, the plaintiff was the victim of a shooting during an attempted robbery at the yard, which resulted in the amputation of the same leg. At trial, the defendant claimed that his liability for the leg injury should cease at the time of the second injury because the injured leg no longer existed. The House of Lords held that the second event would not be treated as wiping out the original injury, which was effectively a concurrent cause of the plaintiff's eventual disability.

It is interesting to contrast *Baker* with the decision in *Jobling v Associated Dairies* (1981). There, a work injury to his back resulted in a permanent disability to the plaintiff. Three years later and, again, before the trial, he developed a spinal disease which put an end to his employment completely. On the basis of the decision in *Baker*, the plaintiff expected that the defendant's liability for the first event would be unaffected by the succeeding disease. In this case, however, a unanimous House of Lords held in favour of the defendant. The reasoning was that the disease was one of the 'vicissitudes' of life, the possible future occurrence of which is routinely taken into account by judges in calculating damages awards. When the eventuality was known to have occurred before the trial it would be irrational to ignore it.

 THINKING POINT

Is it possible to say that being the victim of a disease is a 'vicissitude' of life but that being the victim of a tort is not?

The apparent inconsistency between *Baker* and *Jobling* can only partly be explained by the fact that the first involved two torts whereas in *Jobling* a tort was followed by a naturally occurring disease. In *Baker*, it was highly unlikely that compensation would be available from those who shot the plaintiff and therefore if the first defendant's liability ceased at the time of amputation, there was a real risk of under-compensation for the plaintiff. The two cases are compared in Diagram 4.1.

Diagram 4.1 Comparing *Baker* and *Jobling*

Baker v Willoughby

D liable | D's liability continues: | Damages awarded for leg injury (shooting ignored)

① Accident C's leg injured | ② Amputation of C's leg due to shooting

Jobling v Associated Dairies

D liable | D's liability ceases: | Damages take into account supervening disease

① Accident C's back injured | ② Back disease incapacitates C

4.2 Causation in law (or remoteness)

Causation in law is often referred to as remoteness. This is concerned with the scope of a defendant's duty. Even when there is a factual link between the defendant's act and the claimant's loss, Winfield tells us:

> No defendant is responsible *ad infinitum* for all the consequences of his wrongful conduct, however remote in time and however indirect the process of causation, for otherwise human activity would be unreasonably hampered. The law must draw a line somewhere . . . not on the grounds of pure logic, but simply for practical reasons.

Often this issue arises when the defendant's negligence results in an unanticipated outcome, or one which occurs in an unusual way. In *Re Polemis* (1921) cargo was being unloaded from a ship docked in Casablanca. A plank was negligently dropped into the hold by the defendants' employee, which caused a spark, igniting gases in the hold and resulting in an explosion which destroyed the ship. The defendants were held liable for damage caused by this unexpected event on the basis that there should be liability for all the 'direct consequences' of a defendant's negligence.

Q | CASE CLOSE-UP

The Wagon Mound (No 1) (1961)

The 'direct consequences' test for remoteness prevailed until *Overseas Tankship (UK) Ltd v Morts Docks and Engineering Co Ltd; The Wagon Mound (No 1)* (1961). The facts of this case were set out in Chapter 3 when *The Wagon Mound (No 2)* (1967) was discussed in relation to breach of duty and balancing of risks. We must now look again at *The Wagon Mound* because the loss which occurred, the fire in Sydney Harbour which damaged the wharf and the ship, was not the damage which would have easily been predicted to be the result of the defendant's oil spillage. The Privy Council carefully considered the course of events and found that although some physical damage would have been foreseeable as a result of the negligence in terms of contamination of the wharf with oil, it was not foreseeable that the oil would spread until it came into contact with the welding. The fire was therefore not foreseeable and there would be no liability for it. Viscount Simonds doubted *Re Polemis*:

> It is the foresight of the reasonable man which alone can determine responsibility. The Polemis rule, by substituting 'direct' for 'reasonably foreseeable' consequence leads to a conclusion equally illogical and unjust.

It is unlikely that use of *The Wagon Mound* test will often bring about a different outcome than would that of *Re Polemis*. Both are flexible and open to judicial manipulation. Reasonable foreseeability is a concept which we have already seen to be important in establishing duty of care: it is set out in *Donoghue v Stevenson* and is one of the three parts of the *Caparo* test for duty. It is suggested by Lunney, Nolan, and Oliphant (*Tort Law: Text and Materials*, 6th edn, OUP, 2017, p 279) that in these two instances the uses of foreseeability are slightly different. When duty is the issue, we look ahead from an activity and consider a wide range of risks which might, if foreseeable, lead to the imposition of a duty of care. When remoteness is the issue, it is a case of looking back after the event, to assess whether what actually occurred was within the risk set up by the activity in question. The second use of foreseeability is thus narrower than the first.

The decision in *The Wagon Mound* has been accepted in subsequent cases as having replaced the 'direct results' test with that of 'reasonable foreseeability'. One of the most important aspects of applying that test is how to describe the damage which has occurred—in a wide or narrow sense? In *Wagon Mound* itself, we have seen that if the relevant outcome had been described as 'physical damage', it would not have been too remote because pollution and fouling of the wharf was reasonably foreseeable. Alternatively, the narrow description of damage by fire was, on balance, held to be too remote. An important early case which applied *The Wagon Mound* test was *Hughes v Lord Advocate* (1963). A group of workmen left an open manhole, guarded by paraffin lamps. Some children began playing with the lamps and dropped one of them into the manhole, where there was an explosion. This resulted in one of the children being knocked into the manhole and badly burned. The defendants' case was that this was not reasonably foreseeable and therefore not compensatable. The House of Lords did not agree. The leaving of the paraffin lamps created a risk of injury due to burns and the fact that the plaintiff's burns came about in an unlikely way was not relevant. '[T]he distinction between burning and explosion is too fine to warrant acceptance.'

Tremain v Pike (1969) is a good example of what can happen when the 'type of damage' question is set too narrowly. The claimant worked on the defendant's farm, which had, due to negligence, been allowed to become infested with rats. As a result, Tremain contracted Weil's disease (which at the time was relatively rare) from contact with the rats. His case against his employer failed on the grounds that the disease was not reasonably foreseeable, although injury due to rat bites or contamination of food might have been. It is generally accepted that a fairer result would have been obtained by describing the injury in a wider sense, leading to reasonable foreseeability and a finding of liability.

 THINKING POINT

In *Tremain v Pike*, how might the 'reasonable foreseeability' question have been posed to bring an outcome favourable to the plaintiff?

 CASE CLOSE-UP

Jolley v Sutton Borough Council (2000)

This is a more recent case in which the House of Lords reviewed *The Wagon Mound* test as applied to foreseeable injuries which come about in unlikely ways. The defendant Council was sued under the Occupiers' Liability Act 1957 for their negligence in allowing an abandoned boat to be left on their land adjacent to a block of flats. The defendants knew of the boat and put up a sign warning of danger, but failed to remove the boat for two years. Some teenage boys played on it and one used the wheel jack from his father's car to raise the boat so that it might be repaired. The jack slipped and the boat fell, leaving the claimant paralysed. The defence was raised that, although some minor injuries were reasonably foreseeable due, perhaps, to small children falling through the rotten planks on the boat, the injury that occurred was not foreseeable. It was said that the claimant was not so much playing on the boat as working on it.

The House of Lords did not accept this. The findings of fact by the trial judge were considered in the context of the precedents of *The Wagon Mound* and *Hughes v Lord Advocate*. These supported the claimant's case. For Lord Steyn these cases: 'in no way suggest[ed] that the precise *manner* in which the injury occurred nor its *extent* had to be foreseeable'.

Lord Hoffmann concluded:

> it has been repeatedly said in cases about children that their ingenuity in finding unexpected ways of doing mischief to themselves and others should never be underestimated. For these reasons, I think that the judge's broad description of the risk as being that children would 'meddle with the boat at the risk of some physical injury' was the correct one to adopt on the facts of this case. The actual injury fell within that description and we would therefore allow the appeal.

Bhamra v Dubb (2010) was an unusual case in which the caterers for a Sikh wedding supplied a meal which contained eggs. A guest died as a result of eating egg, to which he was allergic. Because the Sikh faith does not allow the eating of eggs, the Court of Appeal held that in this context it was reasonably foreseeable that guests would assume that no egg was present in the food, and so the damage which resulted was within the scope of the defendant's duty of care.

⟩ CROSS REFERENCE

For more on occupiers' liability, see Chapter 7.

In the case of financial loss, *Network Rail Infrastructure v Conarken Group* (2011) held that the question of what is reasonably foreseeable is ultimately one for the courts to decide because tortious liability to the world at large should not be determined solely by contractual terms imposed by the claimant.

4.2.1 The 'thin skull' rule

There is one situation in which the defendant will be liable for outcomes which are not reasonably foreseeable. When the loss suffered by the claimant is at least partly due to his own pre-existing deficiency, whether physical, psychological, or financial, its unforeseeability will not affect the defendant's ultimate liability. It is the defendant's bad luck if his victim turns out to have a thin or 'eggshell' skull—he must take his victim as he finds him!

 CASE CLOSE-UP

Smith v Leech Brain (1962)

This case provides a clear example. The plaintiff was splashed on his lip by molten metal, due to his employer's negligence. The burn he suffered activated a pre-cancerous condition of which he eventually died. Despite the fact that the death from cancer incited by the splash would not have been foreseeable at the time of the injury, the employer was liable for its full extent.

In *Robinson v Post Office* (1974), the plaintiff suffered a leg injury at work which necessitated a visit to the doctor for an anti-tetanus injection. Unfortunately, he suffered a severe allergic reaction to the injection and suffered brain damage as a result. The court found that although there had been some degree of carelessness on the doctor's part in administering the injection, liability remained with the plaintiff's employer. Generally speaking, if a defendant has injured someone who consequently requires medical attention, he is likely to be liable for the consequences of that treatment, even if unforeseeable.

What if the claimant, in **mitigating** his loss, has to incur extra expenditure solely because of his poor financial situation? In the past, the claimant's 'cash-flow' problems have not been given the benefit of the 'thin skull' rule. This changed with *Lagden v O'Connor* (2003). The claimant's car was damaged by the defendant and was off the road while being repaired. The claimant could not afford to pay commercial car hire rates and so entered into a delayed-credit car hire scheme. When the costs of the car hire were submitted to the defendant's insurers, they were higher than the ordinary commercial rate would have been, and the insurers declined to pay them. It was held that the insurers were liable at the higher rate. Given that the defendant had caused the loss and that paying for commercial hire was not an option for the injured party, it would not be just to expect the claimant to 'do the impossible'.

mitigation the process whereby an injured party takes steps to improve their position; for instance, seeking medical advice.

4.2.2 **Intervening events**

One way of portraying causation in tort law is to speak of a chain of events. There is a range of situations in which the defendant's act can be said to be a cause of the claimant's loss because it satisfies the 'but for' test; however, it is succeeded by another event which contributes to the eventual damage in such an important way that it can be said to break the chain of causation. It is sometimes referred to by the Latin phrase *novus actus interveniens*, or new intervening act.

We can divide these intervening acts into three different categories: (1) actions by the claimant himself; (2) natural events; and (3) actions by a third party. The criteria by which the courts decide whether or not the event has indeed broken the chain of causation differ slightly in each category.

4.2.2.1 **Actions by the claimant**

Two cases with contrasting facts well illustrate the point, summarized in Diagram 4.2. The plaintiff in *McKew v Holland* (1969) had been injured in a work-related accident for which his employer was liable. Knowing that his leg was weak, McKew descended a steep staircase with no handrail. His leg gave way and he fell down the stairs, breaking his ankle. It was held that the plaintiff's own unreasonable behaviour, in putting himself in a dangerous situation, broke the chain of causation. His employer was not liable for the effects of the second accident.

In *Weiland v Cyril Lord Carpets* (1968), the result of the defendant's negligence was that the plaintiff had to wear a neck brace, which restricted her ability to use her bifocal glasses. This caused her to miss her step on a staircase and fall down some steps, sustaining further injuries.

It was held that her conduct in walking down the steps had not been unreasonable and therefore the defendant was liable for the additional injuries caused by her fall.

An embarrassing situation confronted the plaintiff in the next case. The defendant Council was negligent in maintaining the door handles and locks of cubicles in a public lavatory and this led to a woman becoming trapped for a short time in a cubicle. In order to escape, she stood on

Diagram 4.2 **Intervening causes**

Incident 1	Incident 2
D's tort liability	D's tort liability ceases

'*Novus actus*'

Incident 1	Incident 2
D's tort liability	D's tort liability continues

No '*novus actus*'

the toilet and put her foot on the toilet roll holder, which then spun, causing her to fall and sustain an injury which, luckily, was not too serious. When she sued the Council, it was held in *Sayers v Harlow Borough Council* (1958) that due to the position she had been put in by the defendants, her action was not unreasonable enough to break the chain of causation. There was, however, a 25 per cent deduction from her damages for contributory negligence in relation to her injury.

CROSS REFERENCE
For more on contributory negligence, see Chapter 6.

The unreasonableness of the claimant's action is therefore a key criterion in determining that it breaks the chain of causation. In some cases, the claimant's action will be of the exact nature which the defendant had a duty to guard against. One case dealt with the issue of whether a suicide can be said to constitute an intervening act. In *Reeves v Commissioner of Police of the Metropolis* (2001), the plaintiff's partner had been arrested and there was evidence that he was a suicide risk, although when he was medically examined there was no evidence of mental illness. No special precautions were taken by the police and he hanged himself in his cell. The defendants conceded a duty of care to the prisoner but claimed that his own voluntary act had broken the chain of causation. This was rejected by the House of Lords. According to Lord Jauncey:

> Where . . . a duty is specifically directed at the prevention of the occurrence of a certain event I cannot see how it can be said that the occurrence of that event amounts to an independent act breaking the chain of causation from the breach of duty, even although it may be unusual for one person to come under a duty to prevent another person deliberately inflicting harm on himself. It is the very thing at which the duty was directed.

There was, however, held to have been contributory negligence by the deceased. A deduction from damages to reflect the claimant's role in his own loss is not an uncommon alternative to the finding of a break in the chain of causation.

CASE CLOSE-UP

Corr v IBC Vehicles (2008)

In *Corr v IBC Vehicles* (2008) the claimant's husband was seriously injured in a near-fatal accident at work, due to his employer's negligence. He suffered ongoing physical and psychological problems and, six years after the accident, his depression drove him to kill himself. Although, unlike *Reeves*, suicide was not a specific risk within the defendant's duty, the House of Lords upheld an earlier decision by the Court of Appeal that the defendant was liable for the suicide. Depression as a result of the accident was clearly foreseeable and the suicide was not the voluntary act of an adult of sound mind making an informed decision but was the direct result of that depression. Despite the fact that it could be described as neither reasonable nor foreseeable, the suicide did not break the chain of causation.

THINKING POINT
Suicide was a crime until 1961. Would it have made a difference to the outcome in *Reeves* and *Corr* if it were still a crime?

In *Smith v Youth Justice Board for England and Wales* (2010), a custody officer at a secure detention unit for vulnerable young people suffered post-traumatic stress disorder (PTSD) when a

15-year-old died while being restrained by her and two others. It was held that any of her employer's deficiencies in staffing and training the unit were completely eclipsed by the claimant's own negligence, in the way in which she had conducted the restraint.

4.2.2.2 **Natural events**

An unanticipated intervention might come from wind, lightning, storms, or even chemical reactions. In some cases, these are unlikely to be within the risk of the original negligence but on the other hand, should they be held to break the chain of causation they would leave the injured party without any source of redress. In *Carslogie Steamship Co Ltd v Royal Norwegian Government* (1952), the negligent defendant caused a collision which meant that the plaintiff's ship needed repairs which would take approximately ten days. It had some temporary repairs in England but then sailed to the United States where further repairs were to be undertaken. It was caught in a severe storm in the North Atlantic, which necessitated an extra thirty days' repair when it reached the United States. Despite the plaintiff's argument that it was due to the defendants that the ship was caught in the storm, the event was held to have broken the chain of causation and the defendants were only liable for the repair costs of the first collision and not for the loss of profits during the days in which it was being repaired for both the collision and storm damage concurrently.

Vacwell Engineering v BDH Chemicals Ltd (1971) concerned an extreme chemical reaction. Industrial chemicals were marketed and supplied with an inadequate warning about their explosive nature when coming in contact with water. When the plaintiffs were washing glass tubes which had contained the chemicals, a massive explosion occurred, causing loss of life and extensive property damage. Despite the fact that the type and extent of the chemical reaction were unforeseeable, it was not held to have broken the chain of causation and the defendants were liable. The nature of the chemical reaction was unforeseeable; however, it neither made the outcome too remote (as in *Hughes v Lord Advocate*) nor could it be said to constitute a new intervening act.

4.2.2.3 **Actions by third parties**

This variation may arise when a third party is responding to an opportunity provided by the defendant's act, either reacting to danger or emergency, possibly as a rescuer, or as a deliberate wrongdoer, in some cases committing a criminal act.

You will recall that rescuers are a category of claimant who are traditionally regarded favourably in the law of negligence. We have seen the way such claimants are dealt with in terms of duty of care; for example, in *Haynes v Harwood*, there was held to be a duty of care to the policeman who intervened to prevent the defendant's horses causing injury.

The status of the rescuer may instead be approached in terms of causation, with the question of whether his act broke the chain of causation. In *The Oropesa* (1943), a collision between two steamships was partially due to the fault of the defendants. The master of one set out in heavy seas in a lifeboat taking some of his crew to go to the other ship to discuss how to deal with the emergency. The lifeboat capsized, drowning nine men, including the son of the plaintiffs.

The defendants argued that the master's action of setting out in the lifeboat broke the chain of causation, but the Court of Appeal disagreed. For Lord Wright, it was not a question simply of whether the master had been negligent. This was an emergency situation created by the defendants and, for their liability to cease, a 'new cause' would be necessary, 'coming in disturbing the sequence of events, something that can be described as either unreasonable or extraneous or extrinsic'.

An example of behaviour sufficiently unreasonable to break the chain of causation arose in *Knightley v Johns*, which has been previously considered in terms of the question of police immunity and duty of care. When a road traffic accident occurred in a tunnel, due to the negligence of Johns, a police officer on the scene ordered one of his motorcyclists to ride through the tunnel against the flow of traffic. This was contrary to existing good police practice and led to a second accident which injured Knightley. In asking whether the police officer's order could be said to have intervened in the chain of causation from the first accident, the Court of Appeal placed emphasis on the fact that his was a positive act rather than a mere omission. It also asked whether the second accident could be said to have been a 'natural and probable consequence' of the negligence of Mr Johns. Here it was said to be a matter of 'common sense' that the officer's negligence was a 'new cause disturbing the sequence of events . . . which was the real cause of the plaintiff's injury and made that injury too remote from Mr Johns' wrongdoing to be a consequence of it'.

》 CROSS REFERENCE
For more on the duty of care owed by the police, see Chapter 2.

Wright v Lodge (1993) concerned an even more complicated chain of events. A Mini broke down on a foggy dual carriageway and minutes later was hit by a lorry driven at excessive speed by Lodge, injuring one of the Mini's passengers. The lorry then spun out of control into the opposite carriageway, where it was hit by several cars and a lorry. The case was referred to the Court of Appeal concerning the extent of liability of the driver of the Mini for the injuries to the passengers in the vehicles in the opposite carriageway. Despite the fact that the driver of the Mini had been partially to blame for the first collision, in not pushing her car onto the hard shoulder, her negligence did not extend to the second collision. This had been entirely due to the actions of Lodge, the lorry driver. Lord Justice Parker said:

> the presence of the lorry in the westbound carriageway was wholly attributable to Mr. Lodge's reckless driving. It was unwarranted and unreasonable. It was the violence of the swerve and the braking which sent his lorry out of control. Such violence was due to the reckless manner in which he was driving, and it was his reckless speed which resulted in the swerve, loss of control and headlong career onto, and overturn on, the westbound carriageway. It is true it would have not been there had the Mini not obstructed the nearside lane of the east-bound carriageway but . . . this is not enough.

There is an implication that, had Lodge not been driving recklessly, there would never have been the second collision and that is why his conduct was treated as breaking the chain of causation.

Rahman v Arearose Ltd (2001) indicates that an intervening act may *partially* break the chain of causation. There, the *physical* aspect of the first defendant's liability ceased at the time of the second tort but the *psychological* effects were seen as ongoing.

Rahman was working in a fast-food restaurant owned by the first defendants when he was the victim of a vicious assault which left him badly injured. In hospital, an operation was performed on his right eye and, due to the admitted negligence of the surgeon, Rahman lost the sight in that eye. In the negligence litigation which followed, the second defendants were the NHS Trust, who accepted full liability for the loss of the eye caused by their employee, the surgeon. One aspect of the case before the Court of Appeal concerned the question of which party should bear liability for Rahman's continuing serious psychological state following the event. It was impossible to determine what proportion of the psychological damage could be attributed to the assault and what to the loss of the eye. The judge at first instance described the two causes as working together in 'synergistic interaction', with each making the other worse, bringing about the claimant's state of mind. His view of the 'causative potency' of each factor led to holding the first defendant 25 per cent liable and the second defendant 75 per cent liable for the psychological head of damage. For other heads of damage, such as the physical loss of the eye, the hospital bore total liability. Another way of looking at *Rahman* is that the first and second defendants' concurrent torts made them jointly and severally liable.

It has generally been the position that when a defendant's negligence necessitates the claimant's medical treatment, the negligent administration of that treatment will only break the chain of causation if it is extreme or 'gross' (see *Robinson v Post Office*, discussed at 4.2.1 The 'thin skull' rule).

🔍 CASE CLOSE-UP

Wright v Cambridge Medical Group (2011)

This case upheld that position. The defendant GP surgery negligently delayed a child's referral to hospital; however, when she reached hospital, her condition was negligently misdiagnosed, and she sustained permanent disability. The Court of Appeal, by a majority of 2:1, concluded that the GP's negligence remained a cause of the child's ultimate injury. There was a presumption, not displaced by the defendants, that had she been referred at the correct time, she would have been competently treated by the hospital. Expert evidence indicated that even had the child been admitted two days earlier and treated the same way that she had been, the resulting damage would have been significantly less. The hospital's negligence had not been of such an extreme degree as to eclipse that of the defendant GP.

When the third party has deliberately committed a wrongful act against the claimant, there is a greater tendency to find that it has broken the chain of causation. It was put this way by Lord Sumner in *Weld-Blundell v Stephens* (1920):

> In general . . . even though A is in fault, he is not responsible for injury to C which B, a stranger to him, deliberately chooses to do. Though A may have given the occasion for B's mischievous activity, B then becomes a new and independent cause.

You will recall *Home Office v Dorset Yacht Co* in Chapter 2, which was a key case on duty of care. There, it could have been argued that the deliberate wrongful acts of the borstal trainees in vandalizing the yachts broke the chain of causation from the guards' negligent supervision, but Lord Reid was of the opinion that this was not the case. For him, this was an act which was 'very likely to happen' as a result of the negligence and this was his reasoning for holding that the damage created by the boys was not too remote.

Lord Reid's description has not been adopted by subsequent judges, who required an even higher degree of foreseeability for deliberate wrongful acts to break the chain. In *Lamb v Camden LBC* (1981), the claimant vacated his house because it was flooded due to the negligence of the defendants' workmen. While it was empty, two different groups of squatters moved in, and left considerable damage when they were evicted. Although the Court of Appeal agreed that the event was foreseeable, the outcome was still held to be too remote. Oliver LJ said, 'there may be circumstances in which the court would require a degree of likelihood amounting almost to inevitability before it fixes the defendant with responsibility for the act of a third party over whom he had and can have had no control'.

》 THINKING POINT
Judicial policy is part of the reason for the approach outlined above to deliberate wrongdoing and remoteness. What would that policy consist of?

We saw in *Stansbie v Troman* a theft that occurred when the defendant negligently failed to lock a house. Although this could not be said to have been inevitable, the promise by the decorator to lock the door reinforced liability both in terms of duty and causation. The intervention by the thief did not break the chain of causation.

4.3 Conclusion

Lord Justice Laws in *Rahman v Arearose* spoke very cogently about the basic principles behind the law of causation:

- There is a very strong link to the issue of *duty*:

[T]he real question is, what is the damage for which the defendant under consideration should be held responsible? The nature of his duty (here, the common law duty of care) is relevant; causation, certainly, will be relevant—but it will fall to be viewed, and in truth can only be understood, in light of the answer to the question, from what kind of harm was it the defendant's duty to guard the claimant.

- The law uses 'tools' in order to allocate responsibility for the claimant's damage:

Novus actus interveniens, the eggshell skull, and (in the case of multiple torts) the concept of concurrent **tortfeasors** are all no more and no less than tools or mechanisms which the law has developed to articulate in practice the extent of any liable defendant's responsibility for the loss and damage which the claimant has suffered.

tortfeasor
one who commits a tort

- The objective remains that of compensation:

The problem . . . rests in the law's attempts to contain the kaleidoscopic nature of the concept of causation within a decent and rational system for the compensation of innocent persons who suffer injury by reason of other people's wrongdoings. The common law has on the whole achieved just results, but the approach has been heavily pragmatic.

 Summary

- Causation of damage is the third essential element in the successful negligence action.
- The 'but for' test is the primary means of establishing factual causation.
- Reasonable foreseeability of damage of the relevant type (*Wagon Mound*) is required in order that the claimant's injury is not too remote.
- The chain of causation may be broken by unreasonable or unforeseeable acts or events (*novus actus interveniens*).

  Visit the online resources to listen to a podcast summarizing the topics covered in this chapter.

 The bigger picture

At the time of the *Fairchild* decision, it was uncertain whether one fibre of asbestos could lead to mesothelioma. This possibility was rejected by the High Court of Australia in *Amaca Pty Ltd v Ellis* (2010) HCA 5 in which case the *Fairchild* approach to causation was not approved and the more conventional 'but for' test was strictly applied. More extensive scientific knowledge is now available about the inception of asbestos-related disease; see J Sanders, 'Risky Business: Causation in Asbestos Cancer Cases (and Beyond?)' in R Goldberg (ed), *Perspectives on Causation* (Hart, 2011).

? **Questions**

Knowledge-testing questions

1. Explain the difference between 'causation in fact' and 'causation in law'.

2. Name two cases which illustrate the gaps in the 'but for' test?

3. What is the key rule to emerge from *The Wagon Mound (No 1)*?

4. What is the 'thin skull' rule?

Problem and essay questions

1. Ben met his friend Olu, and they agreed they both needed a drink. They went to the pub, where Olu bought the drinks and Ben, after several pints, offered Olu a lift home. On the journey home, Ben collided with Kimberley, a 6-year-old who was trying to cross the street. The collision caused Olu to fly through the windscreen, and pushed Kimberley

into the path of an oncoming car being driven by Ernie, aged 82. Kimberley sustained serious internal injuries. An ambulance was summoned to take Olu, Kimberley, and Ernie to hospital. Greta, the ambulance dispatcher, having taken the call, did not dispatch an ambulance for fifteen vital minutes, while she finished the magazine she had been reading when the call came. By the time the ambulance arrived, Olu had died. At the hospital, Kimberley's injuries were misdiagnosed by Mary, a junior doctor who was attending in Accident & Emergency for the first time. Had the nature of her injuries been correctly assessed in A&E, Kimberley would have had a 40 per cent chance of full recovery. Kimberley is now paraplegic.

Analyse the causation issues in this scenario.

2. To what extent have recent developments in causation in negligence been influenced by concerns of policy? Illustrate with case examples.

◯ Visit the online resources for guidance on answering these questions.

☰ Further reading

Green, S, *Causation in Negligence* (Hart 2015)

Morgan, J, 'Lost Causes in the House of Lords: *Fairchild v Glenhaven Funeral Services*' (2003) 66 MLR 277

Lord Neuberger of Abbotsbury, 'Loss of a Chance and Causation' (2008) 224(4) PN 206

Stapleton, J, 'Cause-in-Fact and the Scope of Liability for Consequences' (2003) 119 LQR 388

Stapleton, J, 'Occam's Razor Reveals an Orthodox Basis for *Chester v Afshar*' (2006) 122 LQR 426

Steel, S, 'On When *Fairchild* Applies' (2015) 131 LQR 363

Turton, G, 'Informed Consent to Medical Treatment Post-*Montgomery*: Causation and Coincidence' (2019) 27(1) Med LR 108

Voyiakis, E, 'The Great Illusion: Tort Law and Exposure to Danger of Physical Harm' (2009) 72 MLR 909

Negligence: duty of care problem areas

Introduction

You will recall that the origins of tort law were based upon losses in the form of physical injury and property damage. As negligence began to come to prominence in the second half of the nineteenth century, duties of care regarding physical injury and property damage continued to be recognized. However, psychological injury and economic loss went largely uncompensated, in cases where they did not occur as a consequence of physical injury or property damage. The twentieth century saw the significant development of duties of care in both of these areas and they present some of the most challenging but topical issues in the law of tort.

5.1 Psychiatric injury

5.1.1 **Definition and history**

Physical injury is often accompanied by psychological effects as well. If you are injured in an accident, you may experience pain and suffering during your recovery, or become depressed due to no longer being able to be work. If you receive tort compensation for the accident, this will also cover any psychological effects of your injury. But compensation becomes problematic when you have not suffered any *physical* injury but developed some psychological condition as a result of fearing that you would be injured or because you witnessed harm to someone else. This is the type of damage we are concerned with here.

5.1.2 Why was the law slow to allow recovery for this type of injury?

We can say that there are three main reasons.

- The first was the general lack of awareness or understanding of how the mind worked. The works of Sigmund Freud, regarded as the pioneer of modern psychiatry, were not known in England until the beginning of the twentieth century. Even then, it was widely assumed that people had more control over their mental states than we now believe. It has gradually been accepted that psychological difficulties can be as real and as disabling as physical ones. Many psychological conditions following accidents would now be given the medical diagnosis of post-traumatic stress disorder (PTSD). This term only came into general use in the 1960s, during the Vietnam War. Previously it might have been described as 'shell shock'. We will see that until very recently, psychological injury was referred to in the law reports as *'nervous shock'*.

- This leads to the second reason. Formerly, it was believed that psychological injury was very much more likely to be fraudulently claimed than the physical, which is usually visible and therefore somehow more 'real'. We now know that there is not a significant distinction to be made on this basis. Some physical conditions, for instance 'whiplash' or other types of persistent pain, can only be substantiated by the word of the sufferer, while a valid claim for psychological injury can be regarded as verified by the medical evidence of a recognized psychiatric illness.

- Third, allowing liability for psychological injury threatened to open the 'floodgates'. An example of this potential can be seen in the Hillsborough football stadium disaster. There, a shocking event was seen by thousands of people, both at the scene and on television. Permitting legal actions by even a small proportion of them might prove unmanageable for the legal system. Equally, gruesome road accidents are seen every day by people around the country. There must be some mechanism for limiting the reach of the law in such cases, or the courts might be overwhelmed.

❱ CROSS REFERENCE
Hillsborough is considered in detail at 5.1.9 The *Alcock* test.

5.1.3 The requirement for a diagnosed psychiatric condition

This is a key limiting mechanism. Mere grief, distress, or anger are not enough. Lord Oliver, in *Alcock v Chief Constable of South Yorkshire Police* (1992), put it this way:

> Grief, sorrow, deprivation and the necessity for caring for loved ones who have suffered injury or misfortune must, I think, be considered as ordinary and inevitable incidents of life which, regardless of individual susceptibilities, must be sustained without compensation.

There are cases in which the court appears not to have enforced this requirement strictly. In *Vernon v Bosley (No 1)* (1994), a father watched helplessly while attempts were made to rescue his children who were trapped in a car underwater. It was not possible to establish how much of his subsequent mental state was due to what he experienced at that time, or to 'pathological grief disorder' which developed later. Nevertheless, the court awarded him damages for his psychological injuries, without distinguishing between the two possible causes.

5.1.4 **The sudden event or its immediate aftermath**

Another qualifying factor is that the condition must be the result of the impact of a sudden event or its immediate aftermath, hence the original term, 'nervous shock'. When it is the result of any sort of prolonged exposure, say to stress, it will not qualify under this category of legal claim. In *Sion v Hampstead Health Authority* (1994), the effect on a parent of sitting by the bedside of a son who was dying, due to the defendants' negligence, was not sufficient to found a claim. As Lord Oliver said in *Alcock*:

> It would be inaccurate and hurtful to suggest that grief is made any the less real or de-privation more tolerable by a more gradual realisation but to extend the law in such cases would be to extend the law in a direction for which there is no pressing policy need and in which there is no logical stopping point.

It is possible that we are gradually seeing a relaxation in this qualifying factor. In *Walters v North Glamorgan NHS Trust* (2002), a 36-hour period between the initial medical emergency and the death of the claimant's child was held to satisfy the requirement for a sudden event (see, however, *Liverpool Women's Hospital*, at 5.1.8 Principles of liability emerge).

5.1.5 **Primary and secondary victims**

The non-recoverability of compensation for psychiatric injury was confirmed in 1888 in *Victorian Railway Commissioners v Coultas*. However, the tide was turning, as seen in the following case.

🔍 CASE CLOSE-UP

***Dulieu v White* (1901)**

Dulieu v White (1901) saw the first successful claim of this type. A barmaid was serving customers in a pub when she looked up and saw a horse and cart out of control, crashing through the wall of the pub. She was pregnant and the shock she sustained from the fright caused her to suffer a miscarriage, for which she recovered compensation. The basis of her reaction was a reasonable fear for her own physical safety. In time those in her position—namely, in fear for their own physical safety—would fall within the wider category of 'primary victims'. There is presumed to be a duty of care not to cause them physical injury and this is extended to include a duty not to cause mental harm.

A different approach is taken to the other category, that of secondary victims. We will see later (5.1.12 Primary or secondary victim?) that determining who is a primary victim is not always clear-cut; however, the term was used in later cases, such as *Bourhill v Young* and *Alcock*, both of which will be discussed later. Nearly a century after *Dulieu*, the House of Lords in *Page v Smith* (1996) discussed in detail the implications of the distinction between primary and secondary victims.

Q CASE CLOSE-UP

Page v Smith (1996)

This case involved a claim by the driver of a car which was involved in a relatively minor collision, caused by the negligence of the defendant, the other driver. Although he suffered no physical injury, he alleged that the accident caused a recurrence of ME, or chronic fatigue syndrome, which he had previously suffered from. The question before the House of Lords was whether a duty of care had been owed to the plaintiff for the type of damage suffered, and three out of five Law Lords answered in the affirmative. Lord Lloyd spoke for the majority:

> The test in every case ought to be whether the defendant can reasonably foresee that his conduct will expose the plaintiff to the risk of personal injury. If so, then he comes under a duty of care to that plaintiff. If a working definition of 'personal injury' is needed, it can be found in section 38(1) of the Limitation Act 1980: '"Personal injuries" includes any disease and any impairment of a person's physical or mental condition . . .'. There are numerous other statutory definitions to the same effect. In the case of a secondary victim, the question will usually turn on whether the foreseeable injury is psychiatric . . .. In the case of a primary victim the question will almost always turn on whether the foreseeable injury is physical. But it is the same test in both cases, with different applications. There is no justification for regarding physical injury and psychiatric injury as different 'kinds' of injury. Once it is established that the defendant is under a duty of care to avoid causing personal injury to the plaintiff, it matters not whether the injury in fact sustained is physical, psychiatric or both . . ..

> Applying that test in the present case, it was enough to ask whether the defendant should have reasonably foreseen that the plaintiff might suffer physical injury as a result of the defendant's negligence, so as to bring him within the range of the defendant's duty of care. It was unnecessary to ask, as a separate question, whether the defendant should reasonably have foreseen injury by shock; and it is irrelevant that the plaintiff did not, in fact, suffer any external physical injury.

The two main points which can be derived from *Page v Smith* are:

- psychiatric injury is not injury of a different kind than physical injury; and

- for the primary victim, reasonable foreseeability of physical injury is sufficient to bring with it a duty regarding psychiatric injury.

5.1.6 **Historical development**

But now we will take a step backwards in time, and consider how this area of law developed following the landmark decision in *Dulieu v White*. The first significant case was *Hambrook v Stokes Bros* (1925). A mother suffered (fatal) shock when she saw a driverless lorry roll down a hill and around a bend where it crashed, out of her sight but in a place where she had recently seen her children. The court felt that it would be inequitable to allow recovery when someone, like the barmaid in *Dulieu*, feared for her own safety but not, as in this case, when they unselfishly feared for the safety of a loved one.

Following the extension of liability in *Hambrook*, it became uncertain where the boundaries for 'nervous shock' recovery lay.

> ## 🔍 CASE CLOSE-UP
>
> ### *Bourhill v Young* (1943)
>
> However, some limits were set in *Bourhill v Young* (1943). A pregnant Edinburgh fishwife was getting off a tram when she heard the collision between the defendant's motorcycle and a car, some 40 yards away on the other side of the tram. The motorcyclist died at the scene and although she saw neither the event nor the body, she later saw blood on the road. Mrs Bourhill claimed that the extreme shock she experienced was responsible for the eventual stillbirth of her baby.
>
> In joining the other Law Lords who rejected her claim, Lord Porter first recognized that as a bystander the plaintiff was effectively a secondary victim, then questioned whether she had in fact suffered the required degree of shock and finally went on to explain why injury to her was not reasonably foreseeable:
>
>> In the present case the defender was never herself in any bodily danger nor reasonably in fear of danger either for herself or others. She was merely a person who as a result of the action was emotionally disturbed and rendered physically ill by that emotional disturbance. The question whether emotional disturbance or shock, which a defender ought reasonably to have anticipated as likely to follow from his reckless driving, can ever form the basis of a claim is not in issue. It is not every emotional disturbance or every shock which should have been foreseen. The driver of a car or vehicle even though careless is entitled to assume that the ordinary frequenter of the streets has sufficient fortitude to endure such incidents as may from time to time be expected to occur in them, including the noise of a collision and the sight of injury to others, and is not to be considered negligent towards one who does not possess the customary phlegm.

> ⫸ **THINKING POINT**
>
> Mrs Bourhill's failure has also been approached in terms of duty in a more general sense and also in terms of causation. Can you translate such approaches into the correct legal terminology?

5.1.7 The 'thin skull' rule

> ⫸ **CROSS REFERENCE**
>
> For more on the 'thin skull' rule, see Chapter 4.

You should be reminded at this point that the 'thin skull' rule applies to psychiatric injury in the same way as to physical injury. *Brice v Brown* (1984) confirms that if psychiatric injury would have been foreseeable in a person of ordinary fortitude, then the fact that the plaintiff suffers excessive harm due to the fact that she was prone to depression is irrelevant to her recovery of damages.

The *Bourhill* requirement for normal fortitude operated against the claimants in *Rothwell v Chemical & Insulating Co Ltd* (2007). A number of former asbestos workers claimed that their employers' negligence in exposing them to asbestos had led to anxiety and depression due to their fear that they could contract serious asbestos-related disease in the future. The House of Lords did not regard the level of exposure as sufficient to render them primary victims under *Page v Smith* and held that in the absence of a sufficient level of physical damage, anxiety itself could not constitute a 'free-standing' head of damage. Even for the claimant who suffered a more severe reaction, this would not have been foreseeable in a person of normal fortitude and therefore could not impose liability. There were obviously strong policy factors at work; the judges had an eye on the floodgates which could open if the law of negligence were extended to include fear of future disease.

5.1.8 Principles of liability emerge

From *Bourhill* onwards, foreseeability of secondary victims began to be assessed in terms of:

- time;
- space or geography;
- causation; and
- relationship to the primary victim of the negligence.

Q CASE CLOSE-UP

McLoughlin v O'Brian (1983)

This case stressed the importance of these factors.

The plaintiff's husband and three children were involved in a road traffic accident. She was told of the accident at home and travelled to the hospital, arriving about two hours after the accident, where she saw her family covered with dirt and blood and learned of the death of one of her daughters. As a consequence of what she saw, Mrs McLoughlin developed serious depression and a change of personality. Her negligence claim against the driver failed in the lower courts, but when she appealed to the House of Lords she was successful. Her psychiatric injury was foreseeable because the victims were close members of her family and her proximity in time and space to the accident was established because she witnessed the 'immediate aftermath'.

Their Lordships were not of one voice in their reasoning. For Lord Wilberforce it was a matter of policy. Despite the fact that negligence was then in an expansionist phase, he reiterated many of the reasons we have considered above for limiting negligence in this area and then proceeded to set out relatively narrow criteria which would need to be met by the claimant. Lord Bridge and Lord Scarman, on the other hand, did not want to approach the matter in terms of policy and viewed the matter more broadly. They felt that the basic requirement of reasonable foreseeability was sufficient and that this might be fulfilled in a variety of ways. An observation by Lord Bridge will be interesting to look back on after you consider the more recent law in this area:

> My Lords, I have no doubt that this is an area of the law of negligence where we should resist the temptation to try yet once more to freeze the law in a rigid posture which would deny justice to some who, in the application of the classic principles of negligence derived from *Donoghue v Stevenson* . . . ought to succeed, in the interests of certainty, where the very subject matter is uncertain and continuously developing, or in the interests of saving the defendants and their insurers from the burden of having sometimes to resist doubtful claims.

In *Galli-Atkinson v Seghal* (2003), a mother came upon the scene where her daughter had been hit by a dangerous driver and where she was told that her daughter was dead. Part of the shock she suffered was due to this experience and the other part was caused when she saw her daughter's body in the mortuary some two hours later. The Court of Appeal held that this latter part of her experience came within the definition of 'immediate aftermath'. An attempt to further stretch the concept of 'proximity', or alternatively, the timing of the 'immediate aftermath' failed in *Crystal Taylor v A Novo (UK) Ltd* (2013). The claimant's mother had been physically injured in a workplace accident. The claimant did not witness that accident, but she was present when her mother suddenly died of complications at home, three weeks later. In overruling the decision at first instance, the Court of Appeal held that it was proximity to the accident itself, rather than to the death of the primary victim, which would be required in order to support a secondary victim's claim for psychiatric injury. Any further development of liability in this area must be the responsibility of Parliament.

The reluctance of the courts to permit expansion of this head of liability was confirmed in *Liverpool Women's Hospital NHS Foundation Trust v Ronayne* (2015). The claimant alleged that he had suffered PTSD when he saw the condition of his wife, who had suffered severe complications due to the hospital's negligence in her surgery. Some ten days after the operation his wife became extremely ill, attached to a ventilator and her body became (temporarily) distressingly swollen. Although the trial judge allowed him to recover, as a secondary victim, this was reversed by the Court of Appeal, which distinguished *Walters*. Here, there had not been one sudden shocking event, or a seamless chain of events over thirty-six hours as in *Walters*, but rather a series of events. Further, there was doubt as to whether what the claimant saw could be described as horrifying; after all he was aware that his wife was seriously ill and should have prepared himself mentally.

5.1.9 The *Alcock* test

 CASE CLOSE-UP

Alcock v Chief Constable of South Yorkshire (1992)

The Hillsborough football stadium disaster was referred to earlier in the discussion of the policy concerns about floodgates. In 1989, ninety-six football supporters were killed and another 400 injured in the spectator stands when crowd control broke down and barriers collapsed at the beginning of an FA Cup match between Liverpool and Nottingham Forest. The ensuing crush was horrifying for those caught up in it but also for those watching: both thousands at the match and millions more at home on television. The main cause of the tragedy was the admitted negligence of the police, for which the Chief Constable was vicariously liable and it gave rise to a number of negligence claims which were simply settled. There were, however, other claims in which liability was disputed on the grounds that the police owed no duty to the plaintiffs in respect of the kind of damage which they suffered.

In *Alcock v Chief Constable of the South Yorkshire*, the plaintiffs were some fifteen relatives of those caught up in the crush, who all suffered psychiatric illness as a result of what they experienced that day. None had been in any physical danger themselves: all were secondary victims. The legal problem for them lay in the fact that for each plaintiff there was a lack of closeness, either to the event or to the victims themselves. For example, Mr and Mrs Copoc lost their son, but they were not at the ground and watched the event on the television, identifying his body the next day. Because they experienced the event through the medium of television, their claim lacked proximity in time and space. Another plaintiff, Robert Alcock, was at the match and was a direct eyewitness to the event's unfolding but the victim he feared for was his brother-in-law, a relationship which is considered less close than, say, parent–child.

The House of Lords held that none of the plaintiffs could recover. The judges were unanimous in this view and some of them referred with approval to the speech of Lord Wilberforce in *McLoughlin*, regarding the necessity to limit recovery by secondary victims. Lord Keith laid down his requirements for liability in this way:

> It was argued for the appellants in the present case that reasonable foreseeability of the risk of injury to them in the particular form of psychiatric illness was all that was required to bring home liability to the respondent. In the ordinary case of direct physical injury suffered in an accident at work or elsewhere, reasonable foreseeability of the risk is indeed the only test that need be applied to determine liability. But injury by psychiatric illness is more subtle, as Lord Macmillan observed in *Bourhill v Young* . . .. In the present type of case it is a secondary sort of injury brought about by the infliction of physical injury, or the risk of physical injury, upon another person.

> As regards the class of persons to whom a duty may be owed to take reasonable care to avoid inflicting psychiatric illness through nervous shock sustained by reason of physical injury or peril to another, I think it sufficient that reasonable foreseeability should be the guide. I would not seek to limit the class by reference to particular relationships such as husband and wife or parent and child. The kinds of relationship which may involve close ties of love and affection are numerous, and it is the existence of such ties which leads to mental disturbance when the loved one suffers a catastrophe. They may be present in family relationships or those of close friendship, and may be stronger in the case of engaged couples than in that of persons who have been married to each other for many years. It is common knowledge that such ties exist, and reasonably foreseeable that those bound by them may in certain circumstances be at real risk of psychiatric illness if the loved one is injured or put in peril. The closeness of the tie would, however, require to be proved by a plaintiff, though no doubt being capable of being presumed in appropriate cases. The case

of a bystander unconnected with the victims of an accident is difficult. Psychiatric injury to him would not ordinarily, in my view, be within the range of reasonable foreseeability, but could not perhaps be entirely excluded from it if the circumstances of a catastrophe occurring very close to him were particularly horrific.

In the case of those within the sphere of reasonable foreseeability the proximity factors mentioned by Lord Wilberforce in *McLoughlin v O'Brian* . . . must, however, be taken into account in judging whether a duty of care exists. The first of these is proximity of the plaintiff to the accident in time and space. For this purpose the accident is to be taken to include its immediate aftermath, which in *McLoughlin's* case was held to cover the scene at the hospital which was experienced by the plaintiff some two hours after the accident . . . .

As regards the means by which the shock is suffered, Lord Wilberforce said in *McLoughlin's* case that it must come through sight or hearing of the event or of its immediate aftermath. He also said that it was surely right that the law should not compensate shock brought about by communication by a third party.

Alcock has been said to have laid down three key requirements, all of which must be satisfied in order to establish the foreseeability necessary for the existence of a duty of care to a secondary victim:

1. *A sufficiently close relationship of love and affection with the primary victim.* This will be presumed to exist between a husband and wife and parents and children; those in other relationships will have to convince the court. Shock in a mere bystander, such as Mrs Bourhill, will not be foreseeable.

2. *Proximity to the accident, or its immediate aftermath, which was sufficiently close in time and space.* Seeing bodies in the mortuary for the purpose of identification, some nine hours after the event was held not to be sufficiently proximate in *Alcock*.

3. *Suffering nervous shock through what was seen or heard of the accident or its immediate aftermath*, or as Lord Ackner put it, 'sudden appreciation by sight or sound of a horrifying event which violently agitated the mind'. What is seen on television, or told by someone else, is not immediate enough.

4. An additional fundamental requirement must always be included: that of a sudden and shocking event, discussed above.

 THINKING POINT

In *Alcock*, Lord Ackner was not prepared to rule out a claim by a passer-by who suffers psychiatric illness as a result of witnessing a particularly horrific event. Can you think of any recent events which might qualify?

5.1.10 **Rescuers**

There is another case of major legal significance which derived from Hillsborough: *White v Chief Constable of the South Yorkshire Police* (1998).

CASE CLOSE-UP

White v Chief Constable of the South Yorkshire Police (1998)

This was a negligence action brought by a number of police officers who suffered psychiatric illness following their experiences of the tragedy. Like the plaintiffs in *Alcock*, they were never in any physical danger but were still closely involved with the events of the day. Some had been on duty in another part of the ground but were called upon to tend to the injured and dying; others dealt with relatives of the dead at the morgue. All were witnesses to gruesome and upsetting scenes and this led to their mental conditions. They all failed at first instance, because on the application of the *Alcock* test regarding secondary victims, they would fail to satisfy the requirement for close ties of love and affection.

On appeal, five of them were successful: either on the grounds that as rescuers they were foreseeable victims despite not fulfilling the *Alcock* criteria (and thus equivalent to primary victims) or because of the fact that, as employees, the defendants had breached the employer's common law duty to them. The defendants then appealed to the House of Lords, where the decision of the Court of Appeal was reversed. Lord Hoffmann spoke vividly for the majority. He was not convinced that either the employment relationship or their position as rescuers justified extending the *Alcock* criteria to accommodate these claimants. Underlying his speech was an awareness of the comparisons which might be made between the claims of the police officers in *White* and the relatives in *Alcock*:

> [The ordinary person] would think it wrong that policemen, even as part of a general class of persons who rendered assistance, should have the right to compensation for psychiatric injury out of public funds while the bereaved relatives are sent away with nothing . . . .

Prior to *White*, it had appeared that rescuers might form a special category of victims for the purposes of determining duty for psychiatric injury. In *Chadwick v British Railways Board* (1967), Mr Chadwick successfully recovered compensation when he sustained what would now be termed serious PTSD following the night he spent attempting to rescue the victims of a terrible train crash which occurred near to his house. This case can be reconciled with that of *White* on the basis that by putting himself into danger in the wrecked carriages, he could be regarded as a primary rather than secondary victim. *Dooley v Cammell Laird & Co* (1951) involved a crane operator whose shock was the result of seeing the load he was carrying drop into the hold of a ship. Although no one was injured, his fear that he had inadvertently been responsible for the injury or death of one of his workmates was the basis for his successful claim. In both *Alcock* and *White*, it was suggested that the high degree of involvement and sense of responsibility experienced in a case such as *Dooley* might take the plaintiff outside the *Alcock* restrictions. In the post-*White* legal environment, students should be wary of believing that there is a meaningful category of 'rescuers' who will predictably be treated differently for the purposes of psychiatric injury claims.

> **THINKING POINT**
>
> Many American states have what is known as a 'fireman's rule' which means that those in the rescue services are limited in their ability to bring negligence actions for injury suffered in the course of duty. What arguments can be made for and against the fireman's rule?

5.1.11 'Unique' factual situations

There are two cases which pre-dated *Alcock* in which liability for psychiatric injury was imposed and yet the 'primary victim' was an inanimate object. In *Owens v Liverpool Corp* (1939), the successful plaintiffs were mourners at a funeral who were understandably shocked when, due to a collision, the coffin fell out of the hearse and overturned, threatening to spill out its contents. *Attia v British Gas* (1988) concerned the shock suffered by a homeowner who successfully recovered from the psychological effect of witnessing the destruction of her home due to a fire negligently caused by employees of the defendant. *Winfield & Jolowicz on Tort* points out that in fact the relevant duty breached in this situation was that owed by the defendants in respect of Mrs Attia's property and therefore the case does not fit the pattern of 'pure' psychiatric injury claims. However, you might want to consider whether it would be stretching the *Alcock* criteria to imagine feeling close ties of love and affection with one's home and possessions.

What happens when the primary victim is also the wrongdoer? That situation occurred in *Greatorex v Greatorex* (2000). Here a father sued his son, mainly because the Motor Insurers' Bureau would have paid compensation on behalf of the son, who was not insured to drive. The claimant worked for the emergency services and actually attended the scene of the road traffic accident, caused by his negligent son, who also had to be rescued from the wreckage. His action in respect of psychiatric injury was unsuccessful. The judge based his decision on policy: mainly that it would be wrong to be seen to be encouraging legal actions between family members. Second, it was thought that imposing liability would in some way restrict an individual's freedom of action. It has, however, been noted that the son's purely accidental conduct in causing the accident should hardly require such protection!

5.1.12 **Primary or secondary victim?**

It has been noted earlier that the categories of primary and secondary victims are not always clear-cut. In *Page v Smith*, Lord Lloyd described the primary victim as one who was:

- directly involved in the accident and well within the range of foreseeable physical injury;

while a secondary victim was:

- in the position of a spectator or bystander.

We have seen that in *White*, the argument was accepted in the Court of Appeal that because the police officers could not be described as spectators or bystanders, they must be primary victims (although the House of Lords disagreed). We will now consider other cases in which the classification was uncertain or in which the distinction appeared to produce an unsatisfactory outcome.

W v Essex County Council (2000) was a case brought by parents who suffered psychiatric injury when they discovered that their children had been molested by a foster child, who had been placed in their care by the local authority. When entering into the fostering role, the claimants had specifically told the defendants that they did not want to be given a disturbed child. The parents were certainly never in any physical danger themselves, and so did not appear to be primary victims but, if secondary victims, they could not satisfy the second and third *Alcock* criteria. However, the court held that a duty could be owed to these claimants, most likely on the basis that, similarly to the claimant in *Dooley*, they were burdened with having unintentionally (and indirectly) been responsible for the abuse.

We have seen in *Rothwell* that the claimants' condition of apprehension of illness did not constitute physical injury and thereby allow them to be treated as primary victims. However, they did not fit into the category of secondary victim either, as their conditions were not based upon the sudden apprehension of an event affecting someone else. Unlike *W v Essex*, here their Lordships did not feel moved to stretch the principle to allow a remedy to the claimant; most likely concerns over the 'floodgates' implications were influential. Parliament, following the example of the Scottish Executive, is proposing legislation to make it easier for sufferers of asbestos-related disease to bring tort claims, if and when the potential for disease is realized sometime in the future.

Imprisonment has been the catalyst for psychiatric injury in two key cases. In *McLoughlin v Grovers* (2001), the claimant's psychiatric condition developed out of a period of imprisonment which he had to serve, due to his wrongful conviction attributable to the negligence of his defence solicitors. Negligence liability was imposed, despite the fact that many of the usual criteria for this type of case were missing: there was no shocking event as such but rather it was an extended period which contributed to the injury and, while not a spectator or bystander, neither had the claimant been in any direct physical danger. Perhaps loss of liberty can be viewed as a form of physical injury; alternatively, it is possible that the solicitor's professional status, bringing with it an *assumption of responsibility* to the claimant, was the basis for the duty of care.

5.1.13 Childbirth

The after-effects of traumatic births have recently been the subject of clinical negligence actions. In *Wild v Southend University Hospital NHS Foundation Trust* (2014) EWHC 4053 (QB) a father failed in his action in respect of damage he suffered while observing the birth of his stillborn child. It was an extended process which began with the realization that the foetus had died *in utero*, and thus was distinguished from *Walters* (above). In *Wild* it was confirmed that when negligence occurs prior to birth, the mother and the baby are to be treated as one legal entity. Thus any injury to the baby is an injury to the mother and she would be regarded as the primary victim. In contrast, a grandmother did bring a successful claim following the negligent management of the delivery of her grandchild, which she witnessed as well as the immediate aftermath. In *Re (A Child) and others v Calderdale and Huddersfield NHS Foundation Trust* (2017) EWHC 824 (QB) she was treated as a secondary victim who satisfied the *Alcock* requirements, including that of a sudden and shocking event, in order to recover for the PTSD she suffered.

THINKING POINT

What might be the impact upon medical staff and NHS resources of the decision in *Re (A Child)*?

See also *Yah v Medway NHS Foundation Trust* (2018) EWHC 2964 (QB)).

Prison authorities themselves were held liable for psychiatric injury to a prisoner in *Butchart v Home Office* (2006). The claimant was known to be in a psychologically vulnerable state when he was placed, while on remand, with a suicidal cellmate. Having been put under considerable pressure by his exposure to the cellmate, the claimant then found the body when the cellmate hanged himself. The prison authorities then placed him with a new cellmate who had just attempted suicide. The claimant suffered 'adjustment disorder' which included anxiety and distress, loss of appetite, and sleep impairment. As in *McLoughlin*, it was recognized that the case could not be fitted into the *Page* or *Alcock* model. Instead, the court treated it as more akin to the 'workplace stress' line of cases. Here, it was the custodial rather than the employment relationship which imposed a duty upon the defendants not to cause psychiatric injury to the prisoner.

5.1.14 Employment

It should be pointed out that although in most cases the risk which the primary victim faces is of accidental injury, this is not the only type of risk. In *Donachie v Chief Constable of Greater Manchester* (2004), a police officer was responsible for fitting a surveillance device to the bottom of a suspect's car. Because his employers had supplied him with a device which did not function properly, the claimant had to return repeatedly to the car, increasing the danger that he would be seen by the criminal suspect. The stress of the experience led to high blood pressure, psychiatric problems, and eventually a stroke. The police officer's status as a primary victim was confirmed by the Court of Appeal.

CROSS REFERENCE

For more on employers' liability for occupational stress, see Chapter 8.

Donachie was a case in which the psychiatric injury was caused by the breach of an employer's duty of care to his employee. Employment-related stress is an area of liability of psychiatric injury in which the negligence principles we have been considering above do not apply. In most cases, the claimant's condition will have developed over a period of time, and the primary/secondary distinction is not applicable, as the claimant himself will be the only possible victim of the negligence. The duty is owed by the employer directly to the individual worker and is dependent on the degree of foreseeability of the damage that individual suffered; therefore the objective standard of the person of ordinary fortitude would not be applied.

A case which illustrates this is *Walker v Northumberland County Council* (1995), where a social worker suffered a second nervous breakdown after struggling to cope with a heavy caseload. His employers were liable because, despite their awareness of his psychological vulnerability following his first breakdown, they had not taken necessary measures to relieve the pressures he was experiencing.

5.1.15 Imparting information

The effects of the giving of bad news has been the basis of negligence actions. Courts have been reluctant to impose liability for the way in which bad news has been delivered but less reluctant when the negligence lay in the giving of wrong information. In *AB v Tameside and Glossop Health Authority* (1997), patients were told by letter (in a rather impersonal and un-caring way) that they had been exposed to the risk of HIV infection by a health worker. Al-though a duty of care was conceded by the defendants, there was no liability, both on the grounds that there had been no breach and also because the claimants were unable to prove that their injury was caused by the means of informing them rather than by the message itself. However, in *Allin v City and Hackney HA* (1996), a hospital was liable to parents who suffered psychiatric injury, having been falsely informed that their baby had died.

5.1.16 Conclusion on psychiatric injury

In 1998, the English Law Commission reported on the state of this aspect of negligence law and recommended that for primary victims the development of the law could be left to the courts. However, as regards some secondary victims (other than rescuers or 'involuntary parti-cipants') legislation would be proposed in order that:

- the requirement for sudden shock would be removed, thereby opening up possible li-ability to claimants whose condition has developed over time;

- the second and third of the *Alcock* criteria would no longer be required, so that claimants might be successful even if they were not near to an event or its immediate aftermath and perceiving it with their own unaided senses; and

- close ties of love and affection with the direct victim (the first *Alcock* criterion) would be maintained as a condition for liability, but the category of those relationships in which these ties would be presumed would be expanded. The group would now include spouses, parents, children, siblings, and cohabitants of at least two years.

Although the importance of this aspect of the law was reinforced by the report of the Scottish Law Commission in 2004, which made its own extensive proposals, the government has indi-cated that there are no plans for legislative reform. According to Lord Steyn in *White v Chief*

Constable of South Yorkshire Police: 'the law on the recovery of compensation for pure psychiatric harm is a patchwork quilt of distinctions which are difficult to justify'. As recovery in this area becomes diversified, particularly in relation to workplace liability, Lord Steyn's observation has become increasingly accurate.

 THINKING POINT

Nicola and Archie have lived together for a year and Archie hopes that one day they might become engaged. How might the 'close tie' requirement be established should one of them be harmed and the other suffer psychiatric injury?

Table 5.1 summarizes the area of psychiatric damage and duty of care.

Table 5.1 Psychiatric damage and duty of care

| Primary/ secondary | 'Accident' n/a | 'Bystander' | | 'Employee' n/a |
		In danger primary	Not in danger secondary	
Sudden shock required?	No	Yes	Yes	No
Foreseeability of physical injury required?	Yes	Yes	Yes	No
Foreseeability of psychiatric injury required?	No	No	Yes	Yes
Indicative cases	*Rahman v Arearose* 2001	*Dulieu v White* 1901	*Alcock v South Yorkshire* 1992	*Hatton v Sunderland* 2002
		Page v Smith 1996	*Bourhill v Young* 1943	*Walker v Northumberland* 1995

5.2 Pure economic loss

5.2.1 History and background

What is pure economic loss in tort? We know that financial compensation is the main remedy sought in legal claims regarding torts. For example, if A's car is damaged by negligent driver B, a successful negligence claim will require B to pay A the financial sum which will restore A's car to its pre-accident condition. We would not describe this as 'pure economic loss' because it derives from the physical damage to the car. Pure economic loss is that which is not linked to physical injury, death, or property damage. It comes in the shape of failure to receive expected future profit or receipt of some financial benefit or it may result from the acquisition of an item of defective property, or be due to property damage sustained by a third party.

As with psychiatric injury, there has been a judicial reluctance to recognize duties of care in negligence in respect of pure economic loss. The first reason is one which we have come to recognize as a powerful aspect of policy in negligence law: fear of the floodgates. Again, like psychiatric injury, some of the situations in which pure economic loss can occur raise the prospect of what was described by a US judge, Benjamin Cardozo, in 1931 as liability: 'in an indeterminate amount for an indeterminate time to an indeterminate class'. A dramatic example of pure economic loss arose in 1998, when negligence was alleged concerning a utility company's failure to supply power to the central business district of Auckland, New Zealand for five weeks. We can imagine the extensive and unconfined financial loss which must have been sustained by the business community; and the liability which might have been incurred had the common law provided a remedy.

Another reason that duty regarding pure economic loss is restricted is that it is an area which is seen primarily as the realm of contract law. Often tort claims are made in situations in which contractual relationships exist but a claim in contract is impossible, maybe because of an exclusion clause or because of time limitation. Traditionally the courts have been reluctant to allow the law of tort to fill in gaps left by the law of contract, particularly where this could undermine the doctrine of privity of contract. We will see that this has recently become less of an obstacle than previously.

One way of understanding this aspect of duty of care is to divide it into two categories:

- loss caused by negligent acts; and
- loss caused by negligent statements.

5.2.2 Pure economic loss caused by acts

In *Cattle v Stockton Waterworks* (1875), the plaintiff was under a contractual obligation to build a tunnel for a landowner, Knight. The defendants were responsible for negligently allowing a leak in the water supply which flooded the tunnel, delaying its completion and causing the claimant loss of profit. This was held to be non-recoverable:

> There is no pretence for saying that the defendants were malicious or had any intention to injure anyone. They were at most guilty of a neglect of duty which occasioned injury to the property of Knight but which did not injure any property of the plaintiff. The plaintiff's claim is to recover the damage which he has sustained by his contract with Knight becoming less profitable, or, it may be losing a contract, in consequence of this injury to Knight's property. We think this does not give him any right of action.

Cattle v Stockton Waterworks is an early illustration of a finding of no duty owed to a plaintiff who has suffered economic loss due to physical damage to the property of a third party. Had Knight been the plaintiff, there would have been a duty of care based on damage to his tunnel.

The case of *Weller & Co v Foot and Mouth Disease Research Institute* (1966) came about following an outbreak of foot and mouth disease in the mid-twentieth century. The plaintiffs were cattle auctioneers who suffered financial loss when a local quarantine meant that they were unable to hold their weekly auctions. Their negligence action failed because they had no proprietary interest in cattle affected by the disease; their loss was solely loss of profit and for that reason not recoverable in negligence. We can also imagine how the floodgates could open in this situation as there would have been countless local businesses, such as pubs and shops, which were also affected by the quarantine.

The sometimes problematic dividing line between physical and economic damage is well illustrated in *Spartan Steel & Alloys v Martin* (1973), a case which bears close consideration.

Q CASE CLOSE-UP

Spartan Steel & Alloys v Martin (1973)

The defendant negligently drove a power shovel through the cable (significantly belonging to the utility company) which supplied electricity to the plaintiff's factory, causing a fourteen-hour power cut. The plaintiff suffered losses under three headings:

- the reduced value of metal which had to be removed from a furnace before it solidified and damaged machinery;
- profit which would have been made from that 'melt' had it been completed; and
- profit from four other future 'melts' which would have been made but for the long power cut.

▶ CROSS REFERENCE

For more on the Compensation Act 2006, see Chapter 1.

The Court of Appeal, by a majority, held that only the first two heads justified compensation. The third constituted pure economic loss because it did not flow directly from physical damage to the claimant's property. Lord Denning reviewed the policy reasons behind the reluctance to impose liability for pure economic loss. These included: the floodgates (well illustrated in the Auckland situation!), the fact that negligence law is concerned with physical and property damage ('deserving causes'), and also a feeling that people should learn to 'put up with' things rather than trying to find fault and sue. The last point is one which we have seen was later to be reflected in the Compensation Act 2006.

Additionally, Lord Denning reflected on the fact that the decision on liability cannot always be neatly assigned to the categories of duty, breach, and causation:

> The more I think about these cases, the more difficult I find it to put each into its proper pigeonhole. Sometimes I say: 'There was no duty.' In others I say: 'The damage was too remote.' So much so that I think the time has come to discard those tests which have proved so elusive. It seems to me better to consider the particular relationship in hand, and see whether or not, as a matter of policy, economic loss should be recoverable.

Unfortunately for law students, Lord Denning's simplified stance has not been widely adopted and it remains necessary to address the problem from the point of view of duty or causation.

The Canadian Supreme Court, in *Canadian National Railway v Norsk Pacific Steamship Co* (1992), felt able to take a more pragmatic approach. The facts of the case provide a good illustration of the problem of pure economic loss, despite the fact that the outcome was one which would have been unlikely in a British court.

The defendant's barge hit and damaged a railway bridge. The bridge was owned by a third party and for 80 per cent of the time it was used by the plaintiff and for the remainder by three other railway companies. The plaintiff had to re-route their trains for several weeks and sued for the costs which this brought. Had the plaintiffs owned the bridge and thus had damaged property, there would have been no issue over duty but, despite the fact that they had suffered no property damage, the court decided in favour of the plaintiff.

One judge in the majority based his decision on the strong element of foreseeability to an identifiable plaintiff (there was no danger of the floodgates opening). The other three judges were more persuaded by the proximity between the plaintiffs and the bridge owners, describing their relationship as that of a 'joint venture'. Effectively the bridge almost belonged to the railway company and for that reason, a duty was owed and compensation was appropriate. It must be noted that what appeared to be an extension of liability for pure economic loss has been retreated from in later cases in Canada and it seems that *Norsk* was an exceptional case turning on its own facts.

5.2.3 Pure economic loss suffered due to acquiring defective property

Many cases in this area arise when the claimant either fails to realize a profit or incurs expenditure arising out of a defect in either a product, land, or a building which he has acquired. This is an aspect of pure economic loss which sometimes causes confusion (even to judges) because defective property (basically the concern of contract law) can easily look like damaged property (for which there is a duty of care in negligence).

The case of *Anns v London Borough of Merton* has already been considered in the context of Lord Wilberforce's two-stage test for duty of care. The plaintiffs occupied flats in a block which, some eight years after completion, began to develop cracks and unstable floors. It was found that this was caused by having been built on foundations which were too shallow, despite prior approval by the local council. The House of Lords found that the plaintiffs had suffered 'material physical damage' and ordered the council to compensate for repair costs needed to avoid a danger to the health and safety of occupants of the building. This case came at a time of general expansion of the law of negligence and we will see that subsequent decisions rejected the position taken by the Law Lords on the issue of the type of damage which had been suffered.

Often described as the high watermark of negligence liability, *Junior Books v Veitchi* saw the House of Lords allowing a claim for repair costs and consequent loss of profits against a subcontractor who had negligently laid a floor in the plaintiff's property. This was based upon a high degree of proximity between the parties, said to be 'akin to contract'. This apparent subversion of privity of contract by tort law in *Junior Books* was controversial at the time and, while

> **CROSS REFERENCE**
> For more on the duty of care, see Chapter 2.

not specifically overruled, the case has been distinguished by later courts to the extent that it is now thought to stand alone, restricted to its own facts, and therefore to be no longer useful. In *Robinson v Jones* (2011), discussed later, both *Anns* and *Junior Books* were described as 'aberrant, indeed . . . heretical'.

5.2.4 **Reassertion of contract law**

The process of reining in legal liability in this area can be seen in several cases in which the courts both questioned the nature of the loss in question and reasserted the primacy of contract law.

 CASE CLOSE-UP

Muirhead v Industrial Tank Specialities Ltd (1985)

The plaintiff had a business plan which involved buying lobsters at a time when they were inexpensive and keeping them in tanks until a time of greater demand, when they would then be sold at a handsome profit. Unfortunately, the pumps which he purchased for his tanks, through an intermediary, were French and due to the incompatible voltage they malfunctioned and many lobsters died. The obvious contractual action was not possible due to insolvency, so instead a negligence action was brought against the French manufacturers. It was held that they were liable for not adapting the pumps to the English system, but damages were restricted to the dead lobsters (as well as certain consequential losses). They did not extend to the cost of the pumps or loss of profit on the enterprise as a whole. These were recoverable in contract or not at all.

CASE CLOSE-UP

Simaan General Contracting Co v Pilkington Glass (1988)

This case concerned the construction of a building in Abu Dhabi that featured a wall made of panels of glass which was required to be a particular shade of green representing peace in Islam. The construction of this wall was subcontracted by the plaintiff builders to a firm which ordered the glass from Pilkington. When the glass which was supplied was the wrong colour, the sheikh who had commissioned the building refused to pay the builder. The builder could not proceed in contract against the subcontractors as the firm had gone out of business, so instead he proceeded in negligence against Pilkington. It was held that there was no duty of care owed by the defendants to supply glass panels of a certain quality. The Court of Appeal was particularly persuaded that the existence of the chain of contracts between the parties was designed to exclude a direct relationship between the plaintiffs and the defendants (see Diagram 5.1). Such liability could raise difficult contractual questions, as Dillon LJ explained:

> if in principle it were to be established in this case that a main contractor or owner has a
> direct claim in tort against the nominated supplier to a sub-contractor for economic loss

occasioned by defects in the quality of the goods supplied, the formidable question would arise, in future cases if not in this case, as to how far exemption clauses in the contract between the nominated supplier and the sub-contractor were to be imported into the supposed duty in tort owed by the supplier to those higher up the chain . . ..

Diagram 5.1 *Simaan v Pilkington*

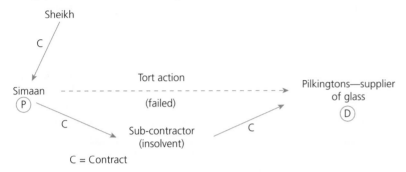

5.2.5 **The overruling of *Anns*: *Murphy v Brentwood DC***

In both *Muirhead* and *Simaan*, if we look at the essence of the claim, we can see that it originates with the supply of defective products: pumps and glass panels, respectively. Neither was 'fit for purpose' and the plaintiffs' loss of profits flowed from that defect. In *D & F Estates Ltd v Church Commissioners* (1988), the defective product consisted of poorly applied plaster. This was laid by specialist subcontractors during the building of a block of flats and, some years later, it became loose and began to flake off. The plaintiffs brought a tort action against the builder, with whom they had no contractual relationship, for the cost of repair of the plaster. The House of Lords regarded this as a case of the construction of an inherently defective building and, until such time as falling plaster caused personal injury or damage to 'other property', like carpets or furniture, there could be no liability in negligence. The mere discovery of a defect in a 'product' (pure economic loss), cannot justify using tort to circumvent the law of contract.

The Law Lords in *D & F Estates* cast doubt upon *Anns* and laid the groundwork for *Murphy v Brentwood DC* (1991). *Murphy* gave an opportunity to revisit the decision in *Anns*, in a case founded on very similar facts.

 CASE CLOSE-UP

Murphy v Brentwood DC (1991)

The plaintiff was the owner of a house which had been built on inadequate foundations leading to cracked walls. He lost profit on the sale of the house, due to the remedial work which was going to be necessary to restore the foundations, and he sued the Council who had approved the original construction plans for the house. The House of Lords held that

> *Anns* had been wrongly decided. The loss, there described as physical damage, was in fact pure economic loss, and not recoverable. The building had never existed without its defective foundations and in a sense had been condemned from the start.
>
> In likening the case to one of product liability, Lord Keith's reasoning was as follows:
>
>> The existence of a duty of that nature should not, in my opinion, be affirmed without a careful examination of the implications of such affirmation. To start with, if such a duty is incumbent upon the local authority, a similar duty must necessarily be incumbent also upon the builder of the house. If the builder of the house is to be so subject, there can be no grounds in logic or in principle for not extending liability upon like grounds to the manufacturer of a chattel. That would open up an exceedingly wide field of claims, involving the introduction of something in the nature of a transmissible warranty of quality. The purchaser of an article who discovered that it suffered from a dangerous defect before that defect had caused any damage would be entitled to recover from the manufacturer the cost of rectifying the defect, and presumably, if the article was not capable of economic repair, the amount of loss sustained through discarding it. Then it would be open to question whether there should not also be a right to recovery where the defect renders the article not dangerous but merely useless. The economic loss in either case would be the same. There would also be a problem where the defect causes the destruction of the article itself, without causing any personal injury or damage to other property.

The building in *Anns* had been held to be potentially dangerous, unlike that in *Murphy*; however, their Lordships did not feel this was a significant distinction. As the law now stands, preventative expenditure to avoid damage to persons or property is not recoverable.

5.2.5.1 Defective Premises Act 1972

The existence of the Defective Premises Act 1972 was cited in *Murphy* to support the denial of common law negligence liability. Under s 1 any 'person taking on work for or in connection with the provision of a dwelling' is under a duty to ensure that the work he takes on is 'done in a workmanlike, or, as the case may be, professional manner, with proper materials and so that as regards that work the dwelling will be fit for habitation when completed'. This duty is imposed upon builders, subcontractors, architects, surveyors, and other professionals.

⟩ CROSS REFERENCE

For more on occupiers' liability, see Chapter 7.

There have been two significant drawbacks in the utility of the Defective Premises Act 1972. First is the fact that actions under the Act are subject to a six-year limitation period which begins to run at the time of completion of the dwelling (s 1(5)), regardless of when the defect is discovered. This would have excluded claims under the Act in both *Anns* and *Murphy*. Second, s 2 excluded from the Act dwellings which were protected by an 'approved scheme', prominent among which was the one operated by the National House Building Council. At one time, s 2 applied to most new homes built in the United Kingdom; however, since the late 1980s approved schemes are considerably rarer and so the Act may have a greater range of operation.

Judicial speeches in both *D & F Estates* and *Murphy* considered what has been called the 'complex structure theory'. According to this, a building, instead of being seen as a unified structure, might instead be thought of as composed of many smaller components. If one of these malfunctioned and impacted on other parts of the building, this could be regarded as damage to 'other property' and thus potentially recoverable. An example given by Lord Bridge in *Murphy* was that of a faulty central heating boiler exploding and causing damage to the rest of the house. He went on to doubt, however, whether such a boiler could accurately be thought of as part of the structure of the building in the same sense as walls or foundations and concluded that the 'complex structure' approach offered 'no escape' from the *Murphy* principle.

 THINKING POINT

The complex structure approach can be applied to things other than buildings. Suppose a container was not suitable for hot weather conditions and melted in the hot sun, ruining its contents. Could that be regarded as damage to other property, rather than pure economic loss? See *Aswan Engineering v Lupdine* (1987).

5.3 Negligent misstatement

Cases in which the claimant has suffered pure economic loss due to a negligent statement by the defendant provide a significant *exception* to the reluctance of the law to recognize a duty of care. We will see that 'statements' include:

- advice;
- references;
- provision of information; and
- services.

Until 1964, there was a presumption, based on the House of Lords' decision in *Derry v Peek* (1889), that liability in tort was only possible for loss caused by a fraudulent rather than negligent statement. The tort of deceit required that the defendant knowingly or recklessly make a statement to the plaintiff with the intent that the plaintiff should act upon it, that the plaintiff does so act and thereby suffers loss.

5.3.1 *Hedley Byrne v Heller*

The case of *Hedley Byrne & Co v Heller & Partners* (1964) (see Diagram 5.2) gave the House of Lords the opportunity to reassess the position and the decision opened up a major new area of liability. The plaintiff, an advertising agency, wanted to know about the financial status of Easipower, on whose behalf it was considering entering into a number of advertising contracts. Through its own bankers, the agency requested references from Easipower's bank, Heller & Partners. These were supplied, confirming the creditworthiness of their client in a letter headed by this disclaimer, 'For your private use and without responsibility on the part of this bank or its officials'. On the strength of the reference, Hedley Byrne entered into contracts on behalf of Easipower and lost £17,000 when that company went into liquidation.

Diagram 5.2 *Hedley Byrne v Heller*

Their Lordships acknowledged that cases of pure economic loss were very different from those of *Donoghue* physical damage, not least in the potential for a statement to have wide dissemination and impact. But the ingredients of foreseeability and proximity could be adapted and in what he described as an application of the general principle of proximity, Lord Reid set out the 'special relationship' between parties which would give rise to a duty of care in making statements:

> where it is plain that the party seeking information or advice was trusting the other to exercise such a degree of care as the circumstances required, where it was reasonable for him to do that, and where the other gave the information or advice when he knew or ought to have known that the inquirer was relying on him.

Although the requirements for a special relationship were fulfilled in *Hedley Byrne*, the disclaimer at the top of the reference meant that there could be no liability on behalf of Heller. We will see in 5.3.12 Disclaimers that disclaimers may no longer be so effective.

 SUMMARY POINTS

Duty of care as established by the *Hedley Byrne v Heller* special relationship:

- C relied on D's skill and judgement or his ability to make careful inquiry;
- D knew, or ought reasonably to have known, that C was relying on him; and
- it was reasonable in the circumstances for C to rely on D.

5.3.2 **The ambit of *Hedley Byrne* liability**

What sort of person might find themselves subject to a duty of care when making a statement? This was considered in *Mutual Life & Citizens' Assurance Co Ltd v Evatt* (1971), where the plaintiff had requested some investment advice from his insurance company and lost money after relying on their reply. The majority of the Privy Council held that no duty arose here, because the insurance company was not in the business of giving financial advice. However, the two judges in the minority took a wider view, that specific or professional expertise in giving advice was not required and it was sufficient that the plaintiff had consulted a businessman in the course of his business and made it plain that he sought considered advice and intended to act upon that advice.

The minority view has generally been followed in subsequent cases, for example in *Esso Petroleum v Mardon* (1976). Although he was not in the business of giving advice, the fact that the defendant had special knowledge and skill regarding the operation of his garage which was not readily available to the potential purchaser was sufficient to give rise to a duty of care.

In fact, as these negotiations gave rise to a contract between the parties, *Esso Petroleum* was decided on the basis of contractual liability under s 2(1) of the Misrepresentation Act 1967. According to this, where a person enters into a contract after a misrepresentation has been made to him by another party to the contract, and he suffers a loss as a result, if the maker would have been liable in damages if the statement had been made fraudulently he shall be liable unless he can prove that he had reasonable grounds to believe and did believe that the statement was true. This is more advantageous than common law negligent misstatement because there is no need to establish a duty of care and the burden of proof is upon the maker of the statement.

> **THINKING POINT**
>
> Had the Misrepresentation Act 1967 been in force at the time of the events in *Hedley Byrne*, would the claimants have been able to bring their action under the 1967 Act?

Steel v NRAM (2018)

The defendant Ms Steel was a solicitor who was acting for a customer in a sale of commercial property and she dealt directly with an unrepresented lender, Northern Rock. She made 'grossly negligently' assurances in an email to the lender about the nature of the proposed financial transaction. Due to its reliance on her assurances the lender suffered substantial financial loss which it attempted to recover from the solicitor. In its judgment the Supreme Court reviewed a number of cases concerning *Hedley Byrne*. It concluded that it had not been reasonable for the claimant to have relied on the assurances, when it could have easily made inquiries of its own which would have revealed the true situation. Furthermore it would not have been reasonable for Ms Steel to foresee such reliance. On that basis, there was no special relationship and therefore no duty of care had existed upon the defendant in favour of the claimant. There was no liability for this negligent misstatement.

5.3.3 Causation

It is important to remember that the *Hedley Byrne* special relationship only goes to establish duty of care. The claimant must also go on to prove breach and causation. In *JEB Fasteners v Marks Bloom & Co* (1981), in the process of a takeover bid of a company, the plaintiff was supplied misleading company accounts by the defendant. He brought an action for negligent misstatement when his takeover bid proved unprofitable. The action failed because the court found that the misleading accounts had played no part in the plaintiff's actions: the takeover bid was pursued for other motives. Additionally, the plaintiffs had been unaware that the accounts were incorrect and there was no evidence that they had relied on the accounts. Effectively, the defendant's breach had not caused the plaintiff's loss.

5.3.4 **The context of the statement**

We are generally told that a *Hedley Byrne* special relationship is unlikely to arise when information is obtained 'off the cuff' or in a social situation. In these cases, the maker of the statement will not foresee that his statement might be relied upon, nor would it be reasonable for the recipient to so rely. The exercise of due care would not be expected, nor would it necessarily even be possible.

Q | CASE CLOSE-UP

Chaudhry v Prabhaker (1988)

The plaintiff was planning to buy a used car and asked advice from a friend who held himself out as being knowledgeable in this field. He agreed to help and discouraged the plaintiff from seeking advice from a qualified mechanic. When the car she purchased proved unsatisfactory, she successfully sued her friend in negligence. It must be noted, however, that a duty of care was conceded by the defendant's counsel and, had it not been so conceded, one of the judges doubted that a duty would have otherwise been found because of the potential 'hazardous' impact on relations between friends. There will be other comparable situations in which it might be unjust to impose a duty in negligence in respect of social interaction. However, a social situation in which liability was imposed on the grounds of 'assumption of responsibility' is discussed below in *Burgess v Lejonvarn* (2017).

5.3.5 **Indirect statements**

Liability under the *Hedley Byrne v Heller* exception has been extended to situations in which the statement was not made directly to the plaintiff, or was arguably made for purposes other than influencing the plaintiff. In *Smith v Eric S Bush* (1989) the defendant was a valuer who was employed by a building society to make a valuation in respect of a house which the plaintiff was proposing to purchase. The plaintiff paid the building society for the valuation, who then paid the valuer, and then the plaintiff received his report. This was then passed back to the purchaser, who proceeded on the basis of the valuation. The valuation had been negligently conducted and the house was later found to be subject to subsidence, causing pure economic loss to the purchaser.

The House of Lords found the relationship between the valuer and the purchaser to be very close, 'akin to contract'; *Hedley Byrne* would apply.

As a professional man [the valuer] realised that the purchaser was relying on him to exercise proper skill and judgment in his profession and . . . it was reasonable and fair that the purchaser should do so.

This was the foundation of the duty of care in respect of the statement which, when breached, gave rise to negligence liability. It is interesting to note that their Lordships took note of the fact that 90 per cent of domestic purchasers relied on similar valuations and specified that the decision related to that sector of the market. In the case of a more expensive house, or a commercial property, it might be expected that the purchaser would commission his own independent valuation and therefore that reliance on the building society valuation might not be reasonable.

 CASE CLOSE-UP

Caparo v Dickman (1990)

In this case the House of Lords further provided valuable detail about the situations in which the *Hedley Byrne* special relationship would arise. Caparo plc made a takeover bid for Fidelity plc and in doing so, relied upon the valuation of the company which was provided in its annual audited accounts. These were prepared by the respondent auditors, Touche Ross, and were sent to the plaintiffs in their status as existing shareholders of Fidelity. The accounts had been negligently prepared and falsely represented Fidelity as profitable. The plaintiffs sued the auditors in negligence for the loss they suffered as a result of their poor investment.

The Court of Appeal held that, as they were existing shareholders, a duty had been owed to Caparo. This was reversed by the House of Lords, which held that no duty was owed either to existing shareholders or to potential investors. The annual accounts were prepared under the Companies Act 1985, not in order to provide information for the purpose of making investment decisions, but rather to inform the shareholders whether the company was being properly managed by its directors. The accounts were freely available to the public at large and, if the compiling of these accounts was held to impose a duty of care in negligence, the scope of persons to whom that duty would be owed would be unduly wide. Despite a degree of foreseeability, the lack of proximity between the parties proved fatal to a duty of care.

Lord Oliver put it this way:

What can be deduced from the *Hedley Byrne* case, therefore, is that the necessary relationship between the maker of a statement or giver of advice (the adviser) and the recipient who acts in reliance on it (the advisee) may typically be held to exist where (1) the advice is required for a purpose, whether particularly specified or generally described, which is made known, either actually or inferentially, to the adviser at the time when the advice is given, (2) the adviser knows, either actually or inferentially, that his advice will be communicated to the advisee, either specifically or as a member of an ascertainable class, in order that it should be used by the advisee for that purpose, (3) it is known, either actually or inferentially, that the advice so communicated is likely to be acted on by the advisee for that purpose without independent inquiry and (4) it is so acted on by the advisee to his detriment. That is not, of course, to suggest that these conditions are either conclusive or exclusive, but merely that the actual decision in the case does not warrant any broader propositions.

Two cases subsequent to *Caparo* indicate how Lord Oliver's considerations are applied in practice. In *James McNaughton Paper Group Ltd v Hicks Anderson & Co* (1991) an auditor's duty of care was held not to exist when a party to a takeover bid relied on a company's draft accounts, as they had not been prepared for that purpose. However, the court was prepared to admit that a duty could exist in *Morgan Crucible Co plc v Hill Samuel Bank Ltd* (1991). This case again concerned a takeover bid and reliance by the plaintiffs upon an auditor's assessment of a company's financial status. Here, unlike *James McNaughton*, the statement was made to a single identified bidder who had emerged. There was a high degree of proximity between the parties and it was reasonably foreseeable that the statement would be relied upon.

The Court of Appeal in *James McNaughton* set out a list of criteria which may be taken into account in deciding whether, following *Caparo*, the maker of a statement may be found to be under a duty of care to the recipient of a statement:

- *The purpose for which the statement was made.* In both *Caparo* and *James McNaughton*, this was the strongest factor against the finding of a duty.
- *The purpose for which it was communicated.*
- *The state of knowledge of the maker of the statement.* Did the maker know the purpose of the statement, to whom it would be communicated, and what sort of reliance there might be upon it?
- *The size of the class to which the recipient belonged.* This is indicative of proximity and was a problem for the claimant in *Caparo*.
- *The relationship between the maker, the recipient, and any third party.* Was there an additional source of information on the matter?
- *Reliance by the recipient.* This is crucial and of course also indicates causation.

You should note that not each of these criteria will be relevant in every case, and you may have noticed that there is a degree of overlap between them.

5.3.6 **Silence and threats**

Cases can arise in which the claimant alleges that his loss has been caused by the defendant's failure to speak up or to warn him about a situation. An example is *La Banque Financière de la Cité SA v Westgate Insurance Co Ltd* (1988), where insurers failed to disclose knowledge to a bank, which they were insuring, that they had about the fraudulent activities of the agent of the bank's borrower. When the agent caused the bank to lose money due to fraud, the House of Lords decided that the insurers were not liable due to lack of causation, but in doing so assumed that in some such situations there can be a duty to speak. When there is a duty to speak, failure to do so can constitute negligent misstatement.

In *Welton v N Cornwall DC* (1997) economic loss of £34,000 was caused to the proprietor of a bed and breakfast after an environmental health inspector visited the premises and required the plaintiffs to undertake a programme of renovation to the kitchen, the majority of which turned out to have been unnecessary. The inspector had threatened to close down the business if the work was not done. The court held that the basic *Hedley Byrne* duty was owed to the plaintiff, despite the fact that the defendant's statement had the quality of a threat rather than being a reference, information, or advice.

5.3.7 **Voluntary assumption of responsibility**

Lord Reid in *Hedley Byrne* said:

> A reasonable man, knowing that he was being trusted or that his skill and judgment were being relied on, would, I think, have three courses open to him. He could keep silent or decline to give the information or advice sought: or he could give an answer with a clear qualification that he accepted no responsibility for it or that it was given without that reflection or inquiry which a careful answer would require: or he could simply answer without any such qualification. If he chooses to adopt the last course he must, I think, be held to have accepted some responsibility for his answer being given carefully, or to have accepted a relationship with the inquirer which requires him to exercise such care as the circumstances require.

The voluntary acceptance of responsibility to the recipient by the maker of the statement which Lord Reid spoke of has, since 1994, acquired an important new role in the establishment of the *Hedley Byrne* special relationship. This extension of *Hedley Byrne* has become accepted despite doubts voiced by judges, such as Lord Griffiths in *Smith v Eric S Bush* who said:

> I do not think that voluntary assumption of responsibility is a helpful or realistic test for liability.

Before looking at the problems with this test, it is necessary to consider the cases in which it gained its current status.

 CASE CLOSE-UP

Henderson v Merrett Syndicates Ltd (1994)

This case comprised a number of actions in which the defendants were managing agents who were alleged to have been negligent in handling the investments of the plaintiff 'names' in the Lloyd's insurance market. In many cases the parties were linked by contract and the plaintiffs were called 'direct names' (but some contractual actions were time-barred). However, there were also cases in which there was no privity of contract between the parties because they were separated by a third party, the members' agents, and these plaintiffs were 'indirect names'.

In the absence of possible contractual remedies, the injured parties brought negligence actions for the pure economic loss which they had suffered. The House of Lords held that there was a duty of care not to cause pure economic loss to both the direct and indirect names. There are three important aspects to the decision in *Henderson*:

(1) The existence of contractual relationships between the parties did not exclude the possibility of a duty of care in negligence. There could be concurrent duties in contract and tort. This conclusion is difficult to reconcile with the approach we saw above in *Simaan v Pilkington*, and Lord Goff recognized that there would still be many situations in which concurrent duties would not be permissible.

(2) The *Hedley Byrne* special relationship did not apply only to the giving of information and advice but also to the provision of services. Lord Goff used the example of the solicitor and client: 'Where the plaintiff entrusts the defendant with the conduct of his affairs, in general or in particular, he may be held to have relied on the defendant to exercise due skill and care in such conduct.'

(3) The foundation of the duty of care in *Hedley Byrne* was, according to Lord Goff, the assumption of responsibility to the plaintiff by the defendant. Once this was established, it was unnecessary to apply the *Caparo* test of whether it was fair, just, and reasonable to impose a duty. The managing agents were found to have expressly and impliedly assumed responsibility for the proper management of the financial affairs of the claimants and therefore were under a duty of care in negligence.

Henderson was an important case legally and also had profound implications for the parties involved; reputedly just one of the actions concerned liability by one managing agent and forty-two members' agents to 1,000 claimants and the sum at stake was £200 million.

5.3.8 **The operation of 'assumption of responsibility'**

The concept of assumption of responsibility operated to the defendant's advantage in *Williams v Natural Life Health Foods Ltd* (1998). The defendant was a director of a company which provided business plans and advice for those wanting to open franchises. After using the services of the company, the disappointed plaintiff failed to achieve the profit he had expected. He was unable to proceed in negligence against the company because it had gone into liquidation, so instead attempted to make the defendant personally liable. It was held, however, that there had been no personal dealings between the plaintiff and the defendant and no evidence that there had been any such assumption of responsibility by the defendant.

The question arises as to whether or not assumption of responsibility is subjective (consciously adopted by the maker of the statement) or objective (imposed by the law). There are, of course, many situations in which the court will find a deliberate act by the defendant indicative of the taking on of responsibility (eg *White v Jones*) Ultimately, however, Lord Bingham in *Barclays Bank* (below) provided his answer to this question when he quoted Lord Slynn of Hadley in *Phelps v Hillingdon*:

> It is, however, clear that the test is an objective one . . ., The phrase [assumption of responsibility] means simply that the law recognises that there is a duty of care. It is not so much that responsibility is assumed as that it is recognised or imposed by law.

This appears to be a well-accepted view and is illustrated by the case of *Merrett v Babb* (2001).

A surveyor, Babb, negligently valued a house. His valuation was passed by his employers to the claimant house purchaser who suffered pure economic loss as a result, due to the cost of repairing cracks in the property. When his employers went into liquidation Babb was no longer covered by their insurance, but a majority of the Court of Appeal held that by undertaking the valuation and signing the report he had assumed a professional responsibility to the claimant. Unlike the valuer in *Smith v Bush*, it was his employer's firm rather than himself who was instructed by the claimant's building society. Babb's lack of insurance was said not to be relevant to the decision (although it must have been of considerable interest to him!).

> **THINKING POINT**
>
> What would Babb have said about his legal responsibility if asked at the time of the valuation? Should 'assumption of responsibility' originate with the defendant or come from the judge?

5.3.9 Subsequent developments in liability for negligent misstatements

The following two cases illustrate the way in which the courts often apply the *Henderson* 'assumption of responsibility' test and the *Caparo* three-stage test either alternatively or so that they supplement one another.

The case of *West Bromwich Albion Football Club v El-Safty* (2006) concerned the financial consequences suffered by a football club when one of its valuable players was negligently prescribed treatment by the defendant consultant surgeon. Despite the fact that West Bromwich Albion's insurers paid for the treatment, it was held the contract for treatment was between the doctor and the player and so West Bromwich Albion could not bring an action in contract.

In the alternative tort action the Court of Appeal applied the 'expanded *Hedley Byrne* test' (derived from *Henderson*) and considered whether the doctor had assumed responsibility for the financial welfare of West Bromwich Albion. It was concluded in the negative. The doctor's only duty of care must be for the physical well-being of his patient, the player. The court then applied the *Caparo* three-stage test and, despite finding a degree of foreseeability and proximity between the doctor and West Bromwich Albion, concluded that it would not be fair, just, and reasonable to put the doctor in a situation in which he might owe the club a duty which possibly could conflict with his primary role in caring for his patient.

Q | **CASE CLOSE-UP**

Commissioners of Customs and Excise v Barclays Bank plc (2006)

In this case the House of Lords held that the assumption-of-responsibility test did not provide a clear statement of duty in a situation with no precedents. In order to protect VAT payments which were owed to the claimants by two companies, 'freezing orders' were obtained which should have alerted the bank not to allow the companies to withdraw money from their accounts. Despite receiving these orders, Barclays Bank negligently allowed the companies to withdraw money and consequently the claimants were unable to recover all the VAT which they were owed. The judge at first instance held that the defendant bank had not owed a duty of care to the claimants. This was reversed in the Court of Appeal, but the original decision was restored by the House of Lords.

The *Hedley Byrne* special relationship was not easily established on the basis of reliance, because it could not be said that the claimants would have behaved any differently had the bank obeyed the order properly; they were using the only legal means open to them to safeguard what was owed. Assumption of responsibility appeared equally inapplicable, because all the defendants did was receive the freezing order which was 'thrust upon them' by the court. Again, they had no choice in the matter. Lord Bingham said:

> I think it is correct to regard an assumption of responsibility as a sufficient but not a necessary condition of liability, a first test which, if answered positively, may obviate the need for further enquiry. If answered negatively, further consideration is called for.

Then, as was done in the *West Bromwich Albion* case, the *Caparo* three-stage test was applied. Foreseeability of possible loss by the claimants was present, but proximity between the parties was doubtful. Most importantly, it would not be fair, just, and reasonable to impose a duty of care. Such a duty would make banks liable for potentially huge sums in response to minor mistakes on their part; additionally, there are better means than the law of tort for maintaining strict standards of propriety in banking.

Lord Hoffmann recognized that there can be a flexible 'pick-and-mix' approach to determining duty of care:

> There is a tendency, which has been remarked upon by many judges, for phrases like 'proximate', 'fair, just and reasonable' and 'assumption of responsibility' to be used as slogans rather than practical guides to whether a duty should exist or not. These phrases are often illuminating but discrimination is needed to identify the factual situations in which they provide useful guidance.

A similar point had been made by Lord Steyn in *Williams v Natural Life Health Foods,* who said:

> The extended *Hedley Byrne* principle is the rationalization or technique adopted by English law for the recovery of damages in respect of economic loss caused by the negligent performance of services.

The claimants in *Patchett v Swimming Pool & Allied Trades Assn Ltd* (2009) had based their claim upon an alleged assumption of responsibility by the defendants in their trade association website which listed installers of swimming pools. The installer, C, who was chosen from the website had gone into insolvency, causing the claimants financial loss which they claimed was due to the fact that they had relied on the 'misleading and inaccurate' website.

The Court of Appeal, by a majority of 2:1, held that no duty of care had been owed for negligent misstatement. Applying the *Caparo* three-stage test, it was found that there was no relationship of proximity between the parties, akin to adviser and advisee, which would create a *Hedley Byrne* special relationship. Furthermore, it was not reasonably foreseeable that there would be reliance upon the fact that the installer's name was included on the website. The defendants would have reasonably expected an inquirer to have followed directions on the website to download an information pack, which would have indicated that C was not a full member of the organization and not covered by its warranty scheme. Therefore, it could not be said that the defendants had assumed a legal responsibility for any statement on the website, without further inquiry being made.

Similarly there was no duty of care in *Playboy Club London Ltd v Banca Nazionale del Lavoro SpA* (2016). Here, the giver of the negligent bank reference had unknowingly been dealing with the agent of a casino. They did not know the purpose of the reference or who the true recipient was; hence there was no special relationship with the claimant.

 CASE CLOSE-UP

Burgess v Lejonvarn (2017)

This case provides a recent example of an arguably generous application of the concept of 'assumption of responsibility', applied to a social relationship leading to provision of professional services.

An architect had agreed to help her friends, the respondents, with a project to landscape their garden. For no fee, she secured a contractor, who carried out the earthworks and hard landscaping. The architect intended to provide subsequent design work for which she would charge a fee. However, the project did not get that far because the respondents were unhappy with the quality and progress of the work. They brought proceedings claiming that the defendant was responsible for the defective work. On the preliminary issue to determine whether they could claim against the architect in contract or in tort, the judge determined that there was no contract, because it was not possible to identify an offer and acceptance, or consideration, and because there had been no intention to create contractual relations. He concluded that the architect owed a duty of care in negligence for pure economic loss because she possessed a special skill and had assumed a responsibility on which her friends had relied. Further, she had acted as project manager, not as a mere conduit or facilitator between the contractor and the respondents, and that just because the services had been free, did not mean that they were nothing more than informal or social.

The decision was upheld on appeal. The fact that there was no formal contract did not mean that the relationship could not be 'akin to contract'. Professional services had been provided on a professional footing, despite the absence of remuneration. Applying the ratio in *Henderson* (based on *Hedley Byrne*), there had been an assumption of responsibility by the appellant. Although Hamblen LJ did not believe it was necessary to apply the *Caparo* test for duty of care, he was of the opinion that it would be fair, just, and reasonable for a duty to arise in the circumstances.

The preliminary issue of duty having been determined in the claimants' favour, the case was then remitted for trial on the facts; see *Burgess v Lejonvarn* (2018) EWHC 3166 (TCC). In this action, the judge held that breach of duty had not been established. 'The owners' claim for negligent design and project management lacked conviction and credibility.' Despite the earlier finding of duty of care, the defendant was not liable.

> **THINKING POINT**
> Could the decision in *Burgess* have a 'chilling effect' on cooperative assistance between friends?

There remains a possibility of uncertainty over the relationship between the concept of assumption of responsibility and the more general *Caparo* test for duty of care. It is important to remember the opinion of Lord Bingham that assumption of responsibility is a 'sufficient but not necessary condition of liability'. If assumption is present, that can establish duty; if not, the court will proceed as in *Barclays Bank*, to apply the *Caparo* test as an alternative. Christian Witting in 'What are we Doing Here?' (2015) is of the opinion that the *Caparo* test should be the default test and, for the purposes of clarity, that 'the assumption of responsibility test is of real relevance in those few cases in which the evidence suggests that the defendant has voluntarily, subjectively assumed a responsibility for certain legal obligations.'

5.3.10 **Damages**

The calculation of damages in cases of pure economic loss can prove extremely problematic due to the unpredictability of property and financial markets.

South Australia Asset Management Corp v York Montague (1996) 43 All ER 365 (SAAMCO) was a so-called no-transaction situation, where the claimant lender would not have entered into the transaction in the absence of the defendant's overvaluation of a property. The lender claimed for a sum which included his total transaction losses, including those due to a fall in the property market. According to the House of Lords, in allowing the defendants' appeal, the correct measure of damages was limited to the difference between the overvaluation and correct value of the property upon which the loan was secured. This conclusion focuses on identifying the exact scope of the defendant's duty of care; here it was the provision of information about value of the property rather than the giving of advice as to whether or not to enter into the transaction at all. This was the element of the lender's loss that was attributable to the inaccurate valuation.

The SAAMCO principle was applied in *Gabriel v Little* (2017), where a firm of solicitors negligently drew up a loan facility agreement for a commercial loan transaction which their client, the claimant, had decided to enter into. This transaction was based upon the claimant's mistaken assumptions, and ultimately he lost all his money, almost £200,000, which was recovered at first instance. Allowing the defendants' appeal, the Supreme Court reduced the damages to nil on the grounds that the client's decision on whether or not to make the loan had not been within the scope of the solicitor's duty. Even had the loan facility agreement been draw up without negligence, the claimant's loss would have been the same. Although this issue is here being considered under the topic of duty of care, it could alternatively be viewed as a matter of causation. As in *Barrett v Kensington & Chelsea Hospital Management Committee* (see Chapter 4), 'but for' the defendant's negligence, the loss would still have been suffered.

In *Hughes-Holland v BPE Solicitors* (2017) SAAMCO was confirmed and here Lord Sumption clarified the position. Where a professional provides information (rather than advice), which constitutes only a portion of the basis on which a claimant has reached a decision, then there will only be liability to the extent of the financial loss suffered due to the inaccuracy of the information rather than upon the totality of the financial transaction. A way of looking at this is that the scope of the defendant's duty of care was a limited one.

5.3.11 Negligent statements relied upon by a third party

You will recall that in *Hedley Byrne*, the plaintiff (who sustained loss) was the recipient of the negligent statement (the reference). A duty of care has also been recognized when the *subject* of a statement suffers pure economic loss due to that statement being given without due care.

 CASE CLOSE-UP

Spring v Guardian Assurance plc (1994)

In *Spring v Guardian Assurance plc*, the plaintiff was a former insurance salesman whose future career was blighted when his former employers described him in a reference to another insurance company as follows: 'he is a man of little or no integrity and could not be regarded as honest'. The judge at first instance found that Spring had been incompetent but not dishonest and that the reference had been negligently compiled. The facts did not fit neatly into the *Hedley Byrne* format, because Spring, the plaintiff, was the subject rather than the recipient of the reference (see Diagram 5.3). Further, it was inaccurate to say that he had *relied* on the statement, in terms of changing his behaviour because of it. In the House of Lords, Lord Goff held that the defendants' duty was founded upon the assumption of responsibility. Despite the fact that their regulatory authority required them to write a reference, their giving of information about Spring and undertaking to convey it to the recipient imposed upon them an obligation to perform this task with due care. The other three judges in the majority based their finding on the *Caparo* three-stage test.

As Lord Woolf put it:

> The relationship between the plaintiff and the defendants could hardly be closer. Subject to what I have to say hereafter, it also appears to be uncontroversial that if an employer, or former employer, by his failure to make proper inquiries, causes loss to an employee, it is fair, just and reasonable that he should be under an obligation to compensate that employee for the consequences. This is the position if an employer injures his employee physically by failing to exercise reasonable care for his safety and I find it impossible to justify taking a different view where an employer, by giving an inaccurate reference about his employee, deprives an employee, possibly for a considerable period, of the means of earning his livelihood. The consequences of the employer's carelessness can be as great in the long term as causing the employee a serious injury.

Diagram 5.3 *Spring v Guardian Assurance*

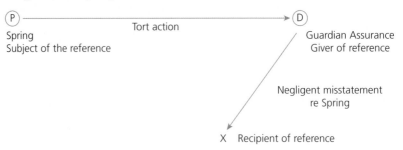

❱ THINKING POINT
Why did Spring not bring an action in defamation against his former employers?

🔍 CASE CLOSE-UP

White v Jones (1995)

This case joined *Henderson* and *Spring* as the third important House of Lords case on pure economic loss reported within a six-month period. As was the case in *Henderson*, it concerns the performance of a service and, as with *Spring*, the injured parties were not in a direct relationship with the defendant but were third parties. A family argument had provoked a father to cut his two daughters out of his will. Later, peace was made and he instructed his solicitor to draft a new will in which he would leave £9,000 to each daughter. The solicitors negligently delayed for almost two months and before they could execute the new will, the father died.

The daughters sued the solicitors for the bequests which they had lost due to the delay. Legally, their problem was that the solicitors' contractual relationship was with their client, the deceased father, and it was arguable that the duty of care relationship was the same. It should be noted that this was not a novel case: *Ross v Caunters* (1979) was a first-instance decision on a similar point of professional negligence in which a solicitor was held to owe a duty of care to the beneficiary of a will.

The House of Lords found in favour of the daughter plaintiffs, but the three majority judges' reasoning differed. Lord Goff spoke of the 'impulse to do practical justice'. If it were to be held that there was no duty of care upon the solicitor to the intended beneficiaries, there would be a gap in the law which needed to be filled. While there is authority that a solicitor does not owe a duty of care to a third party while acting for a client (see *Gran Gelato v Richcliff Ltd* (1992)), in *White* there was no conflict of interest between the client and the plaintiffs; in fact they shared an interest in having the will properly executed. There were some difficulties in speaking of reliance by the plaintiffs in *Hedley Byrne* terms; all they had was an expectation and in some cases a beneficiary might be unaware of their expectation. Lord Goff continued:

> In my opinion, therefore, your Lordships' House should in cases such as these extend to the intended beneficiary a remedy under the *Hedley Byrne* principle by holding that the

assumption of responsibility by the solicitor towards his client should be held in law to extend to the intended beneficiary who (as the solicitor can reasonably foresee) may, as a result of the solicitor's negligence, be deprived of his intended legacy in circumstances in which neither the testator nor his estate will have a remedy against the solicitor.

He recommended that the approach of the case be cautiously applied in the future and that it would be necessary for future courts to set boundaries to it, to avoid possibilities of indeterminate liability.

Lord Browne-Wilkinson used *White* as an opportunity to reflect upon the meaning of assumption of responsibility. For him, the phrase 'assumption of responsibility' refers 'to a conscious assumption of responsibility for the task rather than a conscious assumption of legal liability to the plaintiff for its careful performance'. With that responsibility for the task comes the solicitor's duty to act with 'due expedition and care in relation to the task on which he has entered'. He was confident that both foreseeability and the ingredient that it be fair, just, and reasonable to impose a duty were present. Regarding proximity, it appears that this may have been provided by the assumption of responsibility. Certainly for Lord Browne-Wilkinson, many ingredients of the *Hedley Byrne* special relationship were present.

A case which had strong similarities to *White* was *Gorham v British Telecommunications plc* (2000). A married man with two children was negligently given advice concerning his pension by a financial adviser. When he died, his wife and children found that their pension entitlements were thereby diminished. His dependants had been the intended beneficiaries of the financial advice (like the daughters in relation to the will in *White*) and on that basis the financial advisers had owed a duty of care to them in the giving of the advice. According to Pill LJ:

> The advice in this case was given in a context in which the interests of the dependants were fundamental to the transaction, to the knowledge of the insurance company representative giving the advice as well as his customer, and a duty of care was owed additionally to the intended beneficiaries.

Despite the finding that a duty of care existed, there was held to be no liability to the beneficiaries. The deceased was found to have had sufficient time to obtain correct advice and to make the appropriate pension arrangements. He had not done so, and this broke the chain of causation from the defendants' original negligence.

Financial advice connected to employment was also the core of liability in *Lennon v Metropolitan Police Commissioner* (2004). A personnel officer failed to inform a police officer of the financial implications of his transfer from one police force to another. Consequently, his service could not be regarded as continuous due to a three-week break and he lost pension rights. Despite the fact that this could be regarded as an omission, the defendant had assumed responsibility for the financial affairs of the police officer, the claimant had relied on this, and there should be legal liability for his economic loss.

A case which has similarities to both *White* and *Spring*, but which does not fit neatly into either framework, is *McKie v Swindon College* (2013). An unsolicited email was sent concerning a lecturer, Mr McKie, by his former employers, containing a number of negligently compiled, derogatory comments. When received by his present employers, it led to Mr McKie's dismissal. The email was not a reference, and so could be distinguished from *Spring*; however, the High Court instead simply applied to the situation the three-part *Caparo* test for duty of care. On this basis, there was held to be a duty of care owed to Mr McKie by his former employers and negligence liability for this misstatement was established.

> ❱ **THINKING POINT**
>
> Would the outcome in *Goodwill* have been different if the plaintiff had been the patient's partner at the time of the vasectomy?

An attempt to apply the principle of *White* to a very different context failed in *Goodwill v British Pregnancy Advisory Service* (1996). A man had had a vasectomy and was told that he was sterile. The doctor did not warn him of the possibility of 'spontaneous reversal' of the sterilization. This took place and several years later he had a sexual relationship with the plaintiff who became pregnant. She sued the defendant for the financial costs of bringing up the child, on the basis that a duty of care had been owed to her, as a third party on whose behalf the service was being performed. The Court of Appeal held that *White* could not be extended to this case. The plaintiff was unknown to the defendants at the time of the operation as she was only one of a very large class of potential future partners of the patient: the element of proximity was absent and it would not be fair, just, or reasonable to impose such far-reaching liability on the defendant.

5.3.12 **Disclaimers**

You will recall that in *Hedley Byrne v Heller*, despite the finding of a duty of care, the defendants were not held to be liable because they had headed their reference letter with a disclaimer: 'For your private use and without responsibility on the part of this bank or its officials.' This ability of an adviser to specifically exempt liability potentially represented a significant restriction on the new *Hedley Byrne* duty for pure economic loss.

However, in 1977 a statute was passed which changed the situation. According to the Unfair Contract Terms Act (UCTA), s 2(2) a person could not by means of any contract term or notice restrict his liability for loss or damage other than personal injury caused by negligence in the course of a business unless he showed that the term is reasonable. Section 11(3) specified that 'the requirement of reasonableness is that it should be fair and reasonable to allow reliance on it, having regard to all the circumstances obtaining when the liability arose or (but for the notice) would have arisen'.

In *Smith v Bush* the building society and valuer had included an exemption clause in their report: 'the surveyor's report will be supplied without any acceptance of responsibility on their part'. Lord Griffiths set out four factors to be considered in deciding reasonableness of the disclaimer under UCTA:

(1) whether the parties were of equal bargaining power;

(2) whether it would have been practicable, in terms of costs and time, for the recipient to obtain independent advice;

(3) the difficulty of the task which was the subject of the disclaimer—a difficult or dangerous task would be more likely to make a disclaimer reasonable; and

(4) the practical consequences of upholding or striking down the disclaimer, in terms of costs and also the availability of insurance.

On the facts of the case, particularly given that the valuation concerned a house of 'modest value' and parties of unequal bargaining power, the court concluded that the disclaimer was unreasonable in the circumstances, and therefore ineffective according to UCTA.

> **CROSS REFERENCE**
>
> *Smith v Bush* was discussed at 5.3.5 Indirect statements.

In *Robinson v Jones* (2011) a contractual clause which limited protection for the purchaser to the scheme provided by the National House Building Council was held to satisfy the reasonableness requirement of UCTA. Although the existence of a contract between the dissenting parties did not rule out any tortious liability, there was no evidence here of a *Hedley Byrne* assumption of responsibility.

On 1 October 2015, the Consumer Rights Act 2015 (CRA), which codified the regime of consumer rights relating mainly to contract, came into force. For students of tort, it is important to know that in relations between 'traders' and 'consumers', CRA s 62 effectively replicates UCTA s 2(2) and CRA s 65 does so for UCTA s 2(1). For a more detailed explanation, see 7.3.4 Consumer Rights Act 2015.

Lord Oliver in *Murphy v Brentwood* provided a useful account of the problem areas in negligence and his observation applies to psychiatric injury as well as pure economic loss.

> I frankly doubt whether, in searching for such limits, the categorisation of the damage as 'material', 'physical', 'pecuniary' or 'economic' provides a particularly useful contribution. Where it does, I think, serve a useful purpose is in identifying those cases in which it is necessary to search for and find something more than the mere reasonable foreseeability of damage which has occurred as providing the degree of 'proximity' necessary to support the action.

> **THINKING POINT**
>
> Had the facts of *Hedley Byrne v Heller* taken place after the Unfair Contract Terms Act 1977 came into force, would the bank have been liable for its negligent misstatement?

This chapter has illustrated many different ways in which the law has developed the 'search for something more'.

Summary

- Because the tort of negligence has its roots as a remedy for physical and property damage, it has been difficult to recover compensation for psychiatric injury and pure economic loss.

- Duty of care for psychiatric injury depends upon whether the claimant is a primary or secondary victim. If the latter, the finding of a duty is dependent on satisfying the criteria set down in *Alcock v Chief Constable of South Yorkshire*.

- Duty of care for pure economic loss is excluded when it has been suffered as a result of damage to property belonging to another or due to acquiring a defective product.

- Negligent misstatement provides a major exception to any exclusion regarding pure economic loss: a duty of care will be imposed when the *Hedley Byrne v Heller* special relationship is established or there has been found to be an assumption of responsibility by the defendant.

  🔵 Visit the online resources to listen to a podcast summarizing the topics covered in this chapter.

The bigger picture

Commissioners of Customs and Excise v Barclays Bank plc had implications for the relationship between financial institutions and those investigating criminal activities such as money laundering. You may be interested to find out more about these issues in this work by a leading legal practitioner in the field: S Platt, *Criminal Capital* (Palgrave Macmillan, 2015).

? Questions

Knowledge-testing questions

1. What is the definition of a primary, and a secondary, victim?

2. What are the *Alcock* requirements for duty of care to secondary victims?

3. What is the current state of the law regarding duty of care to rescuers?

4. What determines the *Hedley Byrne* 'special relationship'?

5. What is the important legal difference between the claimant in *Hedley Byrne* and that in *White*?

6. Name two key cases which illustrate use of the concept of 'assumption of responsibility'.

Problem and essay questions

1. Anna and Peter have agreed to take part in a charity parachute jump at Melrose Field. Stephen, the organizer, neglects to allow adequate time between each jump and as a result the parachutes of Anna and Peter become tangled. Anna lands without injury but Peter hits a power line. Among those watching the jump is Sara, Peter's sister. Lisa, Anna's partner, is late to arrive at the event, due to bad traffic and on the way she sees ambulances and fire appliances speeding towards the Field and fears the worst for Anna's safety. Mohammed, a paramedic, climbs an electricity pylon in a rescue attempt but when he reaches him, discovers that Peter is dead.

   Sara believes she is suffering from depression. Lisa is experiencing sleeplessness and is now reluctant to fly in planes. Mohammed has been diagnosed with post-traumatic stress disorder.

   Advise Sara, Lisa, and Mohammed.

2. In relation to the law of negligence, it has been observed, 'Now that courts are aware that . . . professional advice is surprisingly often careless, they [the courts] appreciate and are concerned that even small variations in the reach of liability can have significant economic impact' (Stapleton).

   How have the courts responded? Illustrate your answer with relevant case law.

🔵 Visit the online resources for guidance on answering these questions.

Further reading

Psychiatric injury

Ahuja, J, 'Liability for Psychological and Psychiatric Harm: The Road to Recovery' (2015) 23 Med LR 27

Cooke, PJ, 'Primary Victims: The End of the Road?' (2004) 25(1) Liverpool LJ 29

Descheemaeker, E, 'Rationalising Recovery for Emotional Harm' (2018) 134 LQR 602

Law Commission, *Liability for Psychiatric Illness* (Law Com No 249, 1999)

Lindsey, J, 'Psychiatric Injury Claims and Pregnancy' (2018) 26 Med LR 117

Mulheron, R. 'Rewriting the Requirement for a "Recognised Psychiatric Injury"' (2012) 32(1) OJLS 77

Nolan, D, 'The *Page v Smith* Saga: A Tale of Inauspicious Origins and Unintended Consequences' (2010) 69(3) CLJ 495

Teff, H, 'Liability for Negligently Inflicted Psychiatric Harm: Justifications and Boundaries' (1998) 57(1) CLJ 9

Pure economic loss

Barker, C, 'Wielding Occam's Razor: Pruning Strategies for Economic Loss' (2006) 26(2) OJLS 289

Gordon, E, 'Out with the Old, in with the Older? *Hedley Byrne* Reliance Takes Centre Stage' (2018) 77(2) CLJ 251

Isaacs, M, 'Understanding the Relationship between Duties in Contract and the Tort of Negligence' (2019) 35 PN 155

Morgan, J, 'The Rise and Fall of the General Duty of Care' (2006) 22 PN 206

Stanton, K, 'Professional Negligence: Duty of Care Methodology in the Twenty First Century' (2006) 22 PN 134

Stapleton, J, 'Duty of Care and Economic Loss: A Wider Agenda' (1991) 107 LQR 249

Todd, S, 'Policy Issues in Defective Property Cases' in J Neyers, E Chamberlain, and S Patel (eds), *Emerging Issues in Tort Law* (Hart 2007)

Witting, C, 'What Are We Doing Here? The Relationship between Negligence in General and Misstatements in English Law' in K Barker, R Grantham, and W Swain (eds), *The Law of Misstatements: 50 Years on from* Hedley Byrne v Heller (Hart 2015) 39

6 Defences to negligence

☐ LEARNING OBJECTIVES

By the end of this chapter you should be able to:

- recognize the conditions within which the three defences apply;
- apply the three main defences available in negligence;
- identify the other defences available for specific torts; and
- explain the overlap between the defences.

Introduction

Where a claimant establishes a successful cause of action in tort it is open to the defendant to plead one (or more) of the defences available. We have seen that the burden of establishing liability for the tort is on the claimant whereas the burden of establishing the defence is on the defendant. Where, on the balance of probabilities, a successful defence is established, the defendant's liability for the damage may be reduced or he may be totally absolved from liability. You should note that not all possible defences to an action in tort will be discussed in this chapter because some defences are specific to particular torts: for example, the defence of justification in the tort of defamation; self-defence in trespass to person; and statutory authority in the case of nuisance. These specific defences are considered in the chapters covering the torts for which they are available. Here, we are concerned with the defences having particular relevance to claims in negligence.

The defences we will look at are:

(1) contributory negligence;

(2) *volenti non fit injuria*, or consent; and

(3) *ex turpi causa non oritur actio*, or illegality.

The first of the defences, contributory negligence, operates where the claimant's own fault has contributed to the damage suffered and the damages payable are reduced in proportion to the claimant's degree of fault. The second defence to be examined is *volenti non fit injuria*, or consent, which means that no wrong is done to one who consents. A claimant who voluntarily agrees to undertake a risk of incurring harm is not permitted to sue for the consequent damage of taking that risk. It is important to note that *volenti* is a complete defence and if it succeeds the claimant gets nothing. The third defence is *ex turpi causa non oritur actio*. More commonly known as illegality, this means that no right of action arises from a disgraceful or base cause, and this applies in circumstances where the claimant was participating in an unlawful act. The effect of this defence is to completely absolve the defendant of liability for damage.

❱ **CROSS REFERENCE**
See 3.2 Was there a breach? Falling below standards.

6.1 Contributory negligence

Before the Law Reform (Contributory Negligence) Act 1945, contributory negligence was a complete defence to an action in tort and no damages were recoverable for injuries or damage caused partly by the claimant's own fault. The effect of this rule was that if a claimant could be shown to have been even slightly negligent about taking care of his own safety the defendant's fault became irrelevant and the defendant was totally absolved of liability. The harshness of the 'all-or-nothing' rule led to a gradual modification of the defence and the enactment of the Law Reform (Contributory Negligence) Act 1945, which gave the court power to apportion responsibility for damage between the claimant and the defendant, and provides that where damage is the result of the claimant's own fault then the amount awarded will be adjusted to reflect this.

 STATUTE

Law Reform (Contributory Negligence) Act 1945, s 1(1)

Where any person suffers damage as the result partly of his own fault and partly of the fault of any other person or persons, a claim in respect of that damage shall not be defeated by reason of the fault of the person suffering the damage, but the damages recoverable in respect thereof shall be reduced to such extent as the court thinks just and equitable having regard to the claimant's share in the responsibility for the damage.

6.1.1 Fault on the part of both parties

Under the Act, s 1(1) the court has power to apportion the damage where a claimant's own conduct has contributed to the accident or harm but it cannot be used to effectively defeat a claim. For the Act to come into operation there must be fault on the part of *both* parties and this means that a finding of 100 per cent contributory negligence is not permitted as the effect of this would be to defeat a claim against the defendant by holding the claimant entirely responsible. This issue was considered in *Pitts v Hunt* (1991), where the plaintiff was a pillion passenger on a motorbike driven by the defendant as they were on their way back from a disco. They had both consumed large amounts of alcohol and the plaintiff encouraged the defendant to drive his motorbike in a reckless and dangerous fashion weaving from side to side on the road and frightening pedestrians. The defendant was killed and the plaintiff was badly injured in a collision which occurred as they were driving on the wrong side of the road. The trial judge found that the plaintiff had been 100 per cent contributorily negligent. However, the finding of 100 per cent contributory negligence was not allowed because the Court of Appeal said that the Act only applies where there is fault on both sides, whereas 100 per cent reduction implies that the plaintiff was solely responsible for his injuries (had it been necessary, a deduction of 50 per cent for the plaintiff's contributory negligence would have been appropriate in the circumstances). This case will be considered again when we look at the defence of *ex turpi causa non oritur actio* which was applied to defeat the claim.

In *Jackson v Murray* (2015) the Supreme Court reviewed the approach to assessment of contributory negligence in the case of a 13-year-old girl who suffered serious injuries when she stepped out from behind her school minibus into the path of an oncoming car. The accident had occurred in the late afternoon when the light was fading and the driver failed to reduce his speed from 50 mph as he approached the bus. Although the driver ought to have kept a proper look-out and noticed the bus as being a school bus, the main cause of the accident was initially held to be the girl's recklessness in attempting to cross the road without checking that it was clear. Her contributory negligence assessed at 90 per cent was reduced to 70 per cent on appeal. It was recognized that it is not possible for a court to arrive at an apportionment which is demonstrably correct. The Supreme Court said the test to be applied by an appellate court was whether the court below had gone wrong. By a majority, it was held that the apportionment in this case had been plainly wrong and the girl's contributory negligence was reassessed at 50 per cent. According to Hale LJ, the driver was equally, if not more, blameworthy than the girl because a car could do much more damage to a person than a person could usually do to a car.

According to Lord Reed:

> It follows that the apportionment of responsibility is inevitably a somewhat rough and ready exercise (a feature reflected in the judicial preference for round figures), and that a variety of possible answers can legitimately be given. That is consistent with the requirement under section 1(1) to arrive at a result which the court considers 'just and equitable'. Since different judges may legitimately take different views of what would be just and equitable in particular circumstances, it follows that those differing views should be respected, within the limits of reasonable disagreement.

 STATUTE

Law Reform (Contributory Negligence) Act 1945 Act, s 4 provides a definition of fault

'fault' means negligence, breach of statutory duty or other act or omission which gives rise to a liability in tort or would, apart from this Act, give rise to the defence of contributory negligence.

We can see from the previous extract that 'fault' is broadly defined within the meaning of the Act; this means that it is not confined to negligent conduct but it can include a deliberate act on the part of the claimant.

> ## 🔍 CASE CLOSE-UP
>
> ### Reeves v Commissioner of Police of the Metropolis (1999)
>
> An example of the application of this provision can be seen in *Reeves v Commissioner of Police of the Metropolis*, where the harm in question was inflicted by Reeves himself, who committed suicide while in police custody. In setting out the circumstances under which a duty to take reasonable care to prevent another person deliberately harming himself is owed, Lord Hope of Craighead said:
>
> > But the duty of care may sometimes extend to preventing people injuring themselves de-liberately. The person to whom the duty is owed may be unaware of the risks to which he will expose himself by his deliberate act. Or he may be too young to appreciate them, as in *Yachuk v. Oliver Blais Co. Ltd* [1949] A.C. 386, where petrol was sold to a child aged nine who was unaware of its dangerous properties, or *Hughes v. Lord Advocate* [1963] A.C. 837, where the inquisitive children meddled with objects in the unattended shelter in the roadway without thought as to the consequences. Or he may be of unsound mind, with the result that he is at risk of doing something to himself which no rational person would do as he would appreciate that to do this would inevitably lead to injury. Or the risk that the person may commit an act of deliberate self-harm may be the result of something which the defendant has done or is doing to him.

The police, who were *liable* because they breached their duty to prevent the very act which had occurred, raised the defences of *volenti non fit injuria, novus actus interveniens*, and contribu-tory negligence. Neither the defence of *volenti* nor the *novus actus* claim was accepted but the House of Lords found that the negligence of the police and the deceased's act of intentional self-harm contributed equally to the damage. Since the purpose of the Act is to apportion the damages to reflect the claimant's own responsibility for the harm suffered, the award of dam-ages in this case was reduced by 50 per cent.

❯ CROSS REFERENCE

See 6.2 *Volenti non fit injuria*.

6.1.2 Carelessness: relates to the damage, not the cause of the accident

In determining liability for contributory negligence the question being asked is not what was the *cause of the accident*; rather, the emphasis is on what was the *cause of the damage*. Al-though the claimant's carelessness need not be a cause of the accident, it is essential to show that it contributed to the damage suffered. In *Froom v Butcher* (1976) the plaintiff was driving his car when he collided with a car driven by the defendant and as a result he suffered head and chest injuries. The defendant admitted liability for the accident but claimed that the plain-tiff's injuries were largely the result of his *own* failure to take care of his safety by not wearing a seat belt. The defendant argued that the damages awarded to the plaintiff ought to be reduced accordingly. At first instance the judge held that the plaintiff was not negligent and full damages were awarded for the injuries. However, the defendant appealed on the ground that the judge had erred in not holding that the plaintiff's failure to wear a seat belt amounted to contributory negligence. Although the negligence of the plaintiff did not contribute to the accident happening, his failure to take precautions increased the risk of harm. The Court of Appeal held that the standard of care is objective and said that in failing to wear a seat belt the plaintiff failed to take reasonable precautions for his own safety and the award of damages was reduced by 20 per cent.

According to Lord Denning:

> In most accidents on the road the bad driving, which causes the accident, also causes the ensuing damage. But in seat belt cases the cause of the accident is one thing. The cause of the damage is another. The accident is caused by the bad driving. The damage is caused in part by the bad driving of the defendant, and in part by the failure of the plaintiff to wear a seat belt. If the plaintiff was to blame in not wearing a seat belt, the damage is in part the result of his own fault. He must bear some share in the responsibility for the damage: and his damages fall to be reduced to such extent as the court thinks just and equitable.

It should be noted that in this case the plaintiff had made a conscious decision not to wear the seat belt because he feared the risk of becoming trapped in his car if an accident were to occur but, in *Condon v Condon* (1978), a plaintiff who claimed to suffer from a seat-belt phobia was not held to be contributorily negligent for failing to wear the seat belt.

 THINKING POINT

David was skating at speed along the footpath at midnight and caused Noah, a cyclist, a serious head injury when he knocked him off his bike. Noah was wearing black clothes, he was not wearing his cycling helmet, and his bike had no lights. Can David claim contributory negligence on Noah's part?

6.1.3 **Defendant must prove contributory negligence**

In *Owens v Brimmel* (1977), it was held that accepting a lift from a driver whom the plaintiff knew to have consumed large quantities of alcohol amounted to contributory negligence. The plaintiff and the defendant went on a pub crawl together and they each consumed about eight or nine pints of beer. On the journey home the defendant negligently drove into a lamp post and the defendant, who had not been wearing a seat belt, was seriously injured. However, in attempting to prove the alleged contributory negligence the defendant was unable to show, on the balance of probabilities, how the plaintiff's injury was sustained. Nevertheless, the court found the plaintiff to be 20 per cent contributorily negligent in getting into the car with a driver whom he knew to be drunk, even if at the time he himself was too drunk to know how drunk the driver was.

Another example of this principle can be seen in *Smith v Finch* (2009), where the defendant was unable to show that an approved safety helmet would have prevented the serious head injuries which the claimant suffered, or made them less severe. The claimant (Smith) sustained serious head injuries when his bicycle collided with the defendant's (Finch) motorbike at a stretch in the road where the speed limit was 30 mph. Smith claimed that Finch had ridden his motorbike along the road at an excessive speed and failed to see him. Finch contended that he had not been driving at excessive speed, and claimed that Smith had cycled out of a side road into his path and given him no reasonable opportunity to avoid a collision. He further claimed that Smith's failure to wear a cycling helmet amounted to contributory negligence on Smith's part. Unlike car seat belts and motorbike helmets, there is no legal requirement to wear a cycling helmet, but Finch relied on Lord Denning's judgment in the case of *Froom v Butcher,* where a finding of contributory negligence was made for failure to wear a seatbelt at a time before it was compulsory to do so.

▶ **CROSS REFERENCE**
See 6.1.2 Carelessness: relates to the damage, not the cause of the accident.

Griffith Williams J analysed *Froom v Butcher* and came to the conclusion that the judgment and observations of Lord Denning MR should apply to the wearing of helmets by cyclists. He quoted the following passage from the judgment of Lord Denning:

> It is compulsory for every motorcar to be fitted with seatbelts for the front seats . . . .
> Seeing that it is compulsory to fit seatbelts, Parliament must have thought it sensible to
> wear them. But it did not make it compulsory for anyone to wear a seatbelt. Everyone
> is free to wear it or not as he pleases. Free in this sense, that if he does not wear it he is
> free from any penalty by the magistrates. Free in the sense that everyone is free to run
> his head against a brick wall, if he pleases. He can do it if he likes without being pun-
> ished by the law. But it is not a sensible thing to do. If he does it, it is his own fault; and
> he has only himself to thank for the consequences.

Griffith Williams J went on to say that it does not matter that there is no legal compulsion for cyclists to wear helmets. A cyclist is free to choose whether or not to wear one because there can be no doubt that the failure to wear a helmet may expose the cyclist to the risk of greater injury; such a failure would not be 'a sensible thing to do' and so, subject to issues of causation, any injury sustained may be the cyclist's own fault and 'he has only himself to thank for the consequences'.

You should note that it is not enough to show that the claimant failed to wear a helmet; it is for the defendant to show that wearing a helmet would have prevented the injury or made it less severe. In this case no finding of contributory negligence was made because given the location of the impact on the back of Smith's head and the speed with which he had hit the ground, the wearing of a safety helmet would have made no difference to the injuries he sustained. The defendant therefore failed, on the balance of probabilities, to show that any of the injuries sustained by the claimant may have been reduced or prevented by wearing a helmet.

 THINKING POINT

Contributory negligence is based on blameworthiness. We have seen that s 1(1) of the Law Reform (Contributory Negligence) Act 1945 provides that: 'damages recoverable shall be reduced to such an extent as the court thinks just and equitable having regard to the claimant's share in the responsibility for the damage'. In the context of this statement, how would the blameworthiness of a child cyclist who failed to wear a helmet be assessed? Do you agree with the view that cycling helmets are not designed for road traffic collisions? Are cyclists more vulnerable than pedestrians?

6.1.4 **Contributory negligence and causation**

In *Jones v Livox Quarries Ltd* (1952) the plaintiff was going from his work to the canteen for lunch and, disregarding his employer's safety instructions and unknown to the driver, he was riding on the tow bar of one of the defendants' traxcavators. The vehicle stopped after turning a sharp bend and a dumper travelling close behind it ran into the traxcavator and caused the plaintiff's injuries. Although the driver of the dumper was found to be negligent in failing to keep an adequate look-out, the judge found contributory negligence on the part of the plaintiff because he had placed himself in a position of danger on the traxcavator and he was therefore one-fifth responsible for the damage he suffered. On appeal against the reduction of damages the plaintiff argued that his own negligence had not caused the damage. He claimed that his contributory negligence should not count against him because the obvious danger arising from riding on the tow bar was being thrown off, not being run into from behind and crushed by another vehicle. His appeal was dismissed on the ground that he had unreasonably exposed himself to the danger. He could not then say that that particular risk to which he had exposed himself was not the cause of his damage.

On the issue of causation Lord Denning said:

> In order to illustrate this question of causation, I may say that if the plaintiff, whilst he was riding on the towbar, had been hit in the eye by a shot from a negligent sportsman, I should have thought that the plaintiff's negligence would in no way be a cause of his injury. It would only be the circumstance in which the cause operated. It would only be part of the history. But I cannot say that in the present case. The man's negligence here was so much mixed up with his injury that it cannot be dismissed as mere history. His dangerous position on the vehicle was one of the causes of his damage.

6.1.5 **Contributory negligence involving children**

In the case of children, conduct that would be regarded as contributory negligence in the case of an adult would not necessarily be regarded as such. Age is a circumstance which must be considered in deciding if there has been contributory negligence. Although a very young child cannot be found to be contributorily negligent, depending on the circumstances of the case, an older child may be. The case of *Yachuk v Oliver Blais Co Ltd* (1949) concerned a 9-year-old boy to whom the defendants had sold a pint of petrol. The child had falsely told the defendants that his mother wanted the petrol for her car. When he used the fuel to make a burning torch for the purposes of a game he suffered severe injury for which the defendants were held liable in negligence. In supplying petrol to such a young boy, who neither knew nor could be expected to know of the dangers associated with handling it, the defendant was negligent and it was held there was no contributory negligence on the boy's part. In *Gough v Thorne* (1966), the plaintiff, a 13-year-old girl, was waiting to cross a busy road. A lorry driver stopped and beckoned her to proceed across the road and as she did so she was struck by the defendant who was driving too fast. The trial judge found that the driver was negligent but he also held that the girl had been contributorily negligent in failing to check if there was any traffic before she crossed the road. On appeal against the finding of contributory negligence the Court of Appeal held that the fact that she had relied entirely on the driver's signal to cross the road did not constitute contributory negligence. According to Lord Denning:

> A very young child cannot be guilty of contributory negligence. An older child may be; but it depends on the circumstances. A judge should only find a child guilty of contributory negligence if he or she is of such an age as reasonably to be expected to take precautions for his or her own safety: and then he or she is only to be found guilty if blame should be attached to him or her. A child has not the road sense or the experience of his or her elders. He or she is not to be found guilty unless he or she is blameworthy.

In *Jackson v Murray* (see 6.1.1 Fault on the part of both parties) the Supreme Court adopted Lord Denning's approach and held that a 13-year-old would not necessarily have the same level of judgement and self-control as an adult. The court recognized that the girl had to take account of the car approaching at speed, in very poor light conditions, with its headlights on. The assessment of speed in those circumstances was far from easy, even for an adult. It is interesting to note that in a first-instance decision on occupiers' liability the judge used the parallel of the child when considering the issue of the possible contributory negligence of a person suffering a condition of extreme mental instability. See *Spearman v Royal United Bath Hospitals NHS Foundation Trust* (2017).

▶ **THINKING POINT**

Why does the law look favourably on children? What is the aim of s 2(3)(a) of the Occupiers' Liability Act 1957 (see Chapter 7) which provides that 'an occupier must be prepared for children to be less careful than adults'?

▶ **CROSS REFERENCE**

See occupiers' liability: The Bigger Picture.

6.1.6 Contributory negligence in emergency situations

Where a defendant's negligence creates an emergency, the court is reluctant to find contributory negligence on the part of a claimant who makes a wrong decision in the agony of the moment. The conduct of a claimant in these situations is judged with the emergency in mind as in *Jones v Boyce* (1816), where the plaintiff was a passenger on the defendant's coach and, fearing that it was about to overturn, he jumped off and suffered injury. The coach did not overturn and had he stayed where he was, the plaintiff would have been safe. However, confronted with two alternatives in an emergency situation the plaintiff was not guilty of contributory negligence because he had acted reasonably in the circumstances.

6.2 *Volenti non fit injuria*

The effect of the defence of *volenti non fit injuria* ('voluntary assumption of risk') is to absolve the defendant from the legal consequences of any harm or damage on the ground that the claimant voluntarily assumed to take the risk involved. An assumption of risk may be either express or implied but in either case the defendant must show that the claimant had full knowledge of both the nature and the extent of the risk. Where the claimant accepts a lift from an obviously inebriated driver the plea of *volenti* depends on the degree of intoxication. For example,

▶ THINKING POINT
Are the risks of embarking on an aircraft journey with a drunken pilot more obvious than the risks associated with accepting a lift with a drunken driver?

the defence succeeded in *Morris v Murray* (1991) where, after a bout of heavy drinking, Murray suggested to Morris that they go for a spin in his light aircraft. Soon after take-off, the aircraft crashed, killing Murray and severely injuring Morris, who brought an action against the deceased's estate. The Court of Appeal found that the pilot's drunkenness was so extreme and obvious that the plaintiff was ***volens*** to the risk.

volens
the voluntary acceptance of a specific risk

6.2.1 Knowledge of the risk does not necessarily imply consent

In *Smith v Charles Baker & Sons* (1891) the House of Lords ruled that knowledge of the danger does not necessarily signify consent. In this case the plaintiff was employed drilling holes in a rock cutting and while he was working a crane often swung heavy stones overhead. The employee was aware that there was a risk of the stones falling and he had complained to his employer about the dangerous practice. When he was injured by a falling stone he brought an action against his employers, who pleaded *volenti non fit injuria*. Even though the plaintiff had knowledge of the danger and he continued to work, *volenti* was rejected because the court refused to accept that by continuing to work the plaintiff had voluntarily undertaken the risk of the stones falling.

6.2.2 *Volenti* in the context of employees

As we have seen in *Smith v Baker*, the courts take a cautious approach in applying the defence of *volenti* where employees are alleged to have consented in advance to accepting the risk of an employer's negligence. The realities of the employer–employee relationship are that it is one of power, where the employee is not usually free to refuse to do certain things without fearing the employer's disfavour or some other disadvantage. Although the defence will rarely be successful in an action by an employee against an employer, *volenti* was accepted by the House of Lords in *ICI Ltd v Shatwell* (1965). The plaintiff and another workman, in defiance both of their employer's orders and the statutory safety regulations, went to test some detonators without taking the required safety precautions. During the testing, an explosion occurred and the plaintiff was injured. In rejecting the plaintiff's claim in negligence against the defendant employer, the plaintiff was held to have consented to, and fully appreciated, the risk of injury. It was significant in this case that the two employees involved were in breach of statutory regulatory duties imposed on them (personally).

According to Lord Reid:

> If the claimant invited or freely aided and abetted his fellow servant's disobedience, then he was *volens* in the fullest sense.

▶ CROSS REFERENCE
See Chapter 7 for occupiers' liability

There are other examples of acceptance of the defence of *volenti* in occupiers' liability cases involving claimants who were found to have expressly or impliedly consented to take a risk that materialized and were therefore prevented from claiming damages.

For example, in *Ratcliffe v McConnell* it was held that, knowing of the risk involved, a 19-year-old student had willingly accepted the risk of injury when he took a running dive into a school swimming pool that was closed for the winter.

CROSS REFERENCE

See 7.4.6 *Volenti non fit injuria* under the 1984 Act.

6.2.3 *Volenti* in sporting activity

We have seen that in certain circumstances consent is a defence to the tort of battery. In the case of surgical procedures there is usually express consent to the interference and in the case of sporting activities there is implied consent to contact which occurs within the rules of the game.

CROSS REFERENCE

Discussed in Chapter 11.

However, the defence of consent in this context relates specifically to the tort of *trespass to person*; as far as a claim for *negligence* is concerned the defence of *volenti* is also available to those engaged in sporting activities. In negligence the claimant might not be agreeing to accept all risks associated with the sport but will only impliedly consent to accept a lower standard of care for injuries sustained in a sport played within the ordinary rules of the game. For example, in *Simms v Leigh Rugby Football Club Ltd* (1969) the plaintiff rugby league player was playing on a rugby ground that complied with the by-laws of the Rugby League. When he was thrown against a wall in the course of a tackle he was held to have accepted the risk. However, where conduct goes beyond the rules or conventions of a sporting activity consent cannot be implied. In *Condon v Basi* (1985), where the plaintiff suffered a broken leg as the result of a foul tackle in the course of a game of football, it was held that consent to reasonable contact is consent only to non-negligent behaviour. The defence of *volenti* failed and the defendant was therefore liable in negligence. In *Watson v British Boxing Board of Control* (a case we also looked at in the context of a duty of care), it was also held that although a boxer consents to injury caused by his opponent in the boxing ring, he does not consent to injury resulting from inadequate safety arrangements by the sport's governing body after being hit.

CROSS REFERENCE

For more on the special standards required in sport, see Chapter 3.

THINKING POINT

Can you think of any examples from a sporting activity where one of the players suffered an injury that was: (1) within the ordinary rules of the game; and (2) an injury which in your view was outside the rules of the game?

6.2.4 *Volenti* in the case of rescuers

Although a rescuer is technically a volunteer and has a choice whether or not to rescue, the doctrine of the assumption of risk does not apply to a rescuer when the emergency was created by the defendant's negligence. If the approach of the law to rescuers was that they assumed the risks associated with their rescue activities, rescuers would always be prevented from claiming damages. This approach would be both unfair to the rescuer and would act as a deterrent to this socially useful activity.

The approach taken by the courts can be illustrated in *Baker v Hopkins* (1959): if the defendant puts either the property or the person of a third party in a situation of danger so that the claimant is under legal or moral pressure to attempt a rescue then, if the claimant suffers harm in the process, he is not to be barred from a remedy by the defence of *volenti*. In this case the defendant employer had adopted a dangerous system of working by lowering a petrol engine down into the inside of a well. The engine discharged poisonous emissions and two of the workmen were overcome by the fumes. The plaintiff, a doctor, had volunteered to go down the well to rescue the workmen but he too was overcome by the fumes and died as a result. The Court of Appeal held that *volenti* was inapplicable because the plaintiff's actions as a rescuer were not truly voluntary. This decision can also be explained on policy grounds as it is against the public interest to deter rescue. In *Baker v Hopkins* it was suggested that in English law a person who endangered himself was, in principle, liable to be sued by his rescuer. If there is no genuine emergency the plaintiff might be *volens*, as in *Cutler v United Dairies Ltd* (1933), where the plaintiff was *volens* because there was nobody in danger when he tried to calm a horse which had bolted into a field. However, a contrasting situation occurred in another case involving bolting horses. In *Haynes v Harwood* (1935) the plaintiff was injured when he went to stop some unattended horses which had bolted in a street. The defendant was liable because, in this case, some children were at risk of injury by the horses.

6.3 *Ex turpi causa non oritur actio*

⟩ CROSS REFERENCE

See Chapter 11 for *ex turpi causa non oritur actio*.

The maxim '*ex turpi causa non oritur actio*' means 'no action may be based on an illegal cause', meaning that the courts will not assist a claimant who has been guilty of illegal conduct because it would be 'an affront to the public conscience' to do so, and might encourage others in illegal activities. On grounds of public policy the courts are unwilling to accept *volenti* in cases where the defendant alleges that the claimant agreed to undergo really serious bodily harm. For example, in *Lane v Holloway* the defence of *volenti* was not allowed in the case of an extremely violent blow returned by the defendant when an elderly drunk started a fight.

The plaintiff in *Clunis v Camden and Islington Health Authority* (1998) had been detained in hospital for treatment of a mental disorder. On 24 September 1992, the hospital discharged him into the care of the defendant health authority and on 17 December 1992 he stabbed a man to death. He pleaded guilty to manslaughter on the grounds of diminished responsibility and was sentenced to be detained in hospital for an indefinite period under the Mental Health Act 1983. The plaintiff sued the health authority, alleging that it had been negligent in discharging him and not providing adequate aftercare. He claimed damages for his loss of liberty. The health authority argued that, even assuming it had been negligent and that the plaintiff would not otherwise have committed manslaughter, damages could not be recovered for the consequences of the plaintiff's own unlawful act on the principle of *ex turpi causa non oritur actio*. This argument was accepted by the Court of Appeal, which held that a plaintiff who had been convicted of a serious offence could not, on the ground of public policy, sue a health authority for negligence in failing to treat him properly and thus prevent him committing the offence. Beldam LJ, who gave the judgment of the court said:

> In the present case the plaintiff has been convicted of a serious criminal offence. In such a case public policy would in our judgment preclude the court from entertaining the plaintiff's claim

unless it could be said that he did not know the nature and quality of his act or that what he was doing was wrong. The offence of murder was reduced to one of manslaughter by reason of the plaintiff's mental disorder but his mental state did not justify a verdict of not guilty by reason of insanity. Consequently, though his responsibility for killing Mr Zito is diminished, he must be taken to have known what he was doing and that it was wrong. A plea of diminished responsibility accepts that the accused's mental responsibility is substantially impaired but it does not remove liability for his criminal act . . . .. The court ought not to allow itself to be made an instrument to enforce obligations alleged to arise out of the plaintiff's own criminal act and we would therefore allow the appeal on this ground.

In *Vellino v Chief Constable of Greater Manchester Police* (2001) when the police arrived to enforce an arrest warrant on the claimant for failure to appear in court, he attempted to escape from their custody by jumping from a window of his second floor flat. As a result of the fall, he suffered brain damage and tetraplegia and claimed negligence on the part of the arresting officers, alleging that they had stood idly by and let him jump. The Court of Appeal held that the maxim *ex turpi causa non oritur actio* made the claim untenable because the claimant had to rely on his own criminal conduct in escaping lawful custody to found his claim.

🔍 CASE CLOSE-UP

Gray v Thames Trains Ltd (2009)

Clunis was considered by the House of Lords in *Gray v Thames Trains Ltd* in the context of the public policy expressed in the doctrine of *ex turpi causa non oritur actio*. Lord Hoffmann said the maxim *ex turpi causa* expresses not so much a principle as a policy; that policy is not based upon a single justification but on a group of reasons, which vary in different situations:

> The wider and simpler version was that you could not recover for damage which was the consequence of your own criminal act. In its narrower form, it was that you could not recover for damage which was the consequence of a sentence imposed upon you for a criminal act.

Thames Trains Ltd was responsible for a serious rail crash in which the claimant, Gray, sustained only minor physical injuries but suffered severe psychiatric injury in the form of post-traumatic stress disorder (PTSD). As a consequence of this mental disorder, Gray underwent a significant personality change which caused him to repeatedly stab a stranger to death. At the criminal trial for this offence the claimant's plea of guilty to manslaughter on the ground of diminished responsibility was accepted and he was ordered to be detained in a mental hospital under the Mental Health Act 1983. The claimant then brought an action in negligence against the train company and track operators claiming damages for: (1) loss of earnings after his detention; (2) loss of liberty and damage to reputation; and (3) feelings of guilt and remorse for the killing. Thames Trains admitted liability in negligence for damages up to the date the claimant had committed manslaughter but argued that the policy *ex turpi causa non oritur actio* barred recovery for damages after that date. The trial judge at first instance ruled that since the claim was based on the commission of a serious offence by the claimant the maxim *ex turpi causa* barred recovery for both loss of earnings and general damages in consequence of the killing. He concluded that the cause of action was inextricably bound up with the claimant's own criminal conduct and the court could not permit him to recover damages without appearing to condone that conduct.

On the claimant's appeal, the Court of Appeal agreed that he was precluded from claiming general damages but not loss of earnings. It was held that where the psychological depression suffered by a claimant as a result of the defendant's negligence led him to kill, a claim in negligence was not defeated by a manifestation of the public policy of the maxim *ex turpi causa non oritur actio* unless the claim was inextricably bound up with or linked to the claimant's criminal conduct. The question to be addressed was whether the relevant loss of earnings was inextricably linked with the claimant's crime. In concluding that the claim in question was not inextricably linked to the claimant's criminal actions, the Court of Appeal ruled that he could recover damages for loss of earnings after he committed manslaughter.

Thames Trains Ltd was successful in its appeal to the House of Lords against this finding. Their Lordships ruled that Gray's conviction for manslaughter precluded a claim for loss of earnings during his detention by reason of the public policy expressed in the doctrine of *ex turpi causa non oritur actio*.

6.3.1 Application of *ex turpi causa* in a joint criminal enterprise

The case of *Joyce v O'Brien* (2013) involved a joint criminal enterprise in which the claimant suffered serious head injuries as he and his uncle were making a getaway following the theft of two ladders. The claimant brought the action against his uncle, who had pleaded guilty to driving carelessly, and also against the uncle's insurers. The insurers defended the claim on the *ex turpi causa* principle on the ground that at the time of the accident the van was fleeing the scene of the crime. Although the injury may not have occurred but for the uncle's careless driving, the Court of Appeal held that it was foreseeable that parties engaged in criminal activities might be subject to increased risks of harm. Where such harm materialized as the result of the act of another party to the criminal enterprise, the principle of *ex turpi causa* would provide a defence. Applying the causation principle developed in *Gray v Thames Trains Ltd*, Elias LJ said that courts should recognize the wider public policy considerations for denying liability in joint enterprise cases. He stated the principle as follows:

> where the character of the joint criminal enterprise is such that it is foreseeable that a party or parties may be subject to unusual or increased risks of harm as a consequence of the activities of the parties in pursuance of their criminal objectives, and the risk materialises, the injury can

properly be said to be caused by the criminal act of the claimant even if it results from the negligent or intentional act of another party to the illegal enterprise.

He further observed that given that the doctrine is one of public policy, there should be some flexibility in its operation. The doctrine will not apply to minor traffic offences but, in most joint criminal liability cases, the nature of the principal offence will determine which acts of a co-conspirator will attract the application of the *ex turpi* doctrine. This case can be contrasted with *Delaney v Pickett* (2011), which also concerned a claimant engaged in a joint criminal activity who was seriously injured in a car crash. At the time of the accident the car was being negligently driven by the co-conspirator. An ambulance quickly arrived at the scene and as the men were being treated for their injuries they were discovered by paramedics to be in possession of cannabis. Although the accident would not have happened if the two men had not made a journey to obtain the unlawful cannabis being transported in the car, the question arose as to whether obtaining or transporting the drugs was the immediate cause of the claimant's injuries or whether they were caused by the negligent driving of his co-conspirator.

Viewed as a matter of causation, the Court of Appeal held that the accident did not happen because of the joint criminal activity; the accident was caused by negligent driving and the possession of illegal drugs was incidental to this. Although Delaney's claim was not defeated by *ex turpi causa*, this finding was of little help to him and he failed to obtain compensation for his injuries. The driver did have an insurance policy but this was avoided by the insurers for breach of its terms, so he claimed from the Motor Insurers' Bureau (MIB). This body provides compensation for injuries caused by an unidentified vehicle or a vehicle without insurance. Because the MIB agreement contains an exclusion applying to claims involving vehicles being used in the course or furtherance of a crime, the majority held that on grounds of public policy the claim against the MIB must fail.

6.3.2 'Innocent' offences and the *ex turpi causa* principle

In *Clunis* and *Gray* the *ex turpi causa* principle was applied to prevent the parties recovering damages as a consequence of their own criminal act. However, in *Griffin v UHY Hacker Young & Partners* (2010) the offence in question was committed innocently. On the basis of negligent advice from his accountants the claimant innocently contravened the Insolvency Act 1988. The offence was one of strict liability (no *mens rea* was required) so there was not necessarily any fault on the claimant's part. In his action for damages for the various losses he suffered as a result of the negligent advice, the accountants raised an illegality defence and asked the High Court to strike out the claim. The court refused to strike out the claim and held that public policy does not necessarily prevent such claims unless it is shown that there was a degree of culpability on the part of the claimant. Here it was possible that the claimant would show that he committed the offence innocently and that the offence did not give rise to a defence of *ex turpi causa*. It was also held that the level of culpability required to support an *ex turpi causa* defence based on a strict liability offence was intimately bound up with the issue of causation and since this is a developing area of law there should be a trial of the claim.

6.3.3 **Human rights and *ex turpi causa***

The case of *Hassan-Daniel v Revenue and Customs Commissioner* (2010) provides an illustration of the increasing effect of human rights on UK tort law. Mr Daniel, a drug smuggler, was stopped in the 'Nothing to declare' channel at Heathrow airport where he was found to have traces of cocaine on his person. Following his arrest and detention he was discovered to have sixteen small packets of cocaine in his digestive system. Despite being warned by staff of the risks of refusing food and almost all drink for a week, Mr Daniel died in custody. His family sued the customs authorities in negligence on the ground that with a better policy for handling such cases and with better care at the detention centre Mr Daniel's life could have been saved.

It is important to note that this claim was not based on common law negligence but on the European Convention on Human Rights (given domestic effect by the Human Rights Act 1998), which provides that everyone's right to life shall be protected by law and that no one shall be subjected to inhuman or degrading treatment. The family claimed that the cause of Mr Daniel's death was the state's failure to operate a proper system of care at the detention centre. The customs authorities raised the common law defence of illegality and sought to have the case dismissed on the ground that Mr Daniel's death was a consequence of his own illegal acts. The claimants argued that human rights are not just for the virtuous, so the question for the Court of Appeal was whether the common law defence of illegality could operate in Convention law to have the claim dismissed and prevent the case going to trial.

The Court of Appeal ruled that the common law defence of illegality does not operate in Convention law so as to bar a claim. Although the interlocutory appeal was allowed, the court reiterated that this meant no more than that the action could proceed; it did not mean that the claim would succeed. The court held that the core of the illegality defence is not criminality but causation, and referred to Lord Hoffmann's question in *Gray*, asking whether what the claimant himself did was the cause of the harm he suffered, even if there was also wrongful conduct on the defendant's part without which the harm would not have occurred.

6.4 Comment on the illegality defence in tort

Although recognizing that a discretion which makes reference to the underlying policy reasons for the illegality defence should be encouraged, the Law Commission in its Consultation Paper *The Illegality Defence in Tort* acknowledges that the manner in which the illegality defence operates in tort is difficult to predict with certainty. It notes that:

> tort cases are not strictly speaking cases of 'benefit', at least in the sense that the claimant is seeking a profit he or she hoped to make from his or her illegal activity. They are cases in which what is sought is an indemnity for losses or liabilities he or she has incurred as a result of his or her acts. Once we move away from 'benefits' to 'indemnities', it is hard to know what the limits

of the principle are. In a sense the claimant who seeks compensation for injuries incurred in the course of his or her illegal activity is seeking an indemnity from the consequences of that activity. Yet such claims are sometimes allowed, and as Evans LJ has said:

[It] is one thing to deny to a plaintiff any fruits from his illegal conduct, but different and more far-reaching to deprive him even of compensation for injury which he suffers and which otherwise he is entitled to recover at law. *Revill v Newbery* (1996)

6.4.1 Judicial approach to the illegality defence: a range of factors

The case of *Jetivia SA v Bilta (UK) Limited* (2015) involved the law of insolvency. The Supreme Court held that the illegality defence could not be raised to defend a claim where a fraud had been perpetrated by a director of the company. Even though the company was used as the vehicle for the fraud, the wrongful activity of the director could not be attributed to the company. The court recognized the need for principle, clarity, and certainty in the illegality defence to ensure that it achieved a fair and appropriate result in each case. There can be strongly held differing views across a spectrum of opinion concerning this defence but the arguments in this case were insufficiently debated, so it was not the appropriate forum to address them. According to Lord Neuberger:

In my view, while the proper approach to the defence of illegality needs to be addressed by this court (certainly with a panel of seven and conceivably with a panel of nine Justices) as soon as appropriately possible, this is not the case in which it should be decided.

Lord Neuberger's challenge was taken up in *Patel v Mirza* (2016) when a Supreme Court panel of nine justices attempted to rationalize the approach to the illegality defence.

 CASE CLOSE UP

Patel v Mirza (2016)

Patel v Mirza was not a tort case but claim in contract where the parties agreed to place bets on share prices using insider information (which is an illegal activity). When the intended betting did not take place the claimant sought to recover the £620,000 he had paid the defendant and sued for breach of contract and unjust enrichment. Because the contract was based on an unlawful act the defendant raised the defence of illegality.

The Supreme Court unanimously agreed that the claimant was not prevented from recovering his money simply because the agreement was based on an unlawful purpose. The essential rationale of the illegality doctrine, that it would be contrary to the public interest to enforce a claim if to do so would be harmful to the integrity of the legal system was reiterated. It was noted that punishment for wrongdoing was the responsibility of the criminal courts and the civil courts were generally concerned with determining private rights and obligations. Civil courts should not undermine the effectiveness of the criminal law or impose additional penalties disproportionate to the nature and seriousness of any wrongdoing.

In assessing whether a claim should fail for illegality, the majority held that the public interest is best served by a discretionary approach which allows the court to consider a range of factors such as the underlying purpose of the law that has been transgressed, any other public policy reason for denying the claim, and whether denial of the claim would be a proportionate response to the unlawful act. Although the future approach to the illegality defence will involve the consideration of 'a range of factors', the minority expressed the view that this approach required the courts to make value judgements about the respective claims of the public interest and this would lead to complexity, uncertainty, and a lack of transparency.

In *Henderson v Dorset Healthcare University NHS Foundation Trust* (2018) a woman who was released, allegedly negligently, from the defendant's psychiatric care went on to kill her mother when she was suffering a psychotic episode. Her claim was barred on the basis of illegality. The Court of Appeal doubted that *Patel*'s 'discretionary' and flexible approach to illegality would apply in a negligence case. Permission has been granted for appeal to the Supreme Court.

6.4.2 Overlap between *volenti non fit injuria* and *ex turpi causa non oritur actio*

▶ CROSS REFERENCE
See 6.1.1 Fault on the part of both parties.

The overlap that sometimes arises between the defence of *volenti non fit injuria* and *ex turpi causa non oritur actio* can be illustrated with the case of *Pitts v Hunt* (1991).

You should note at this point that in the case of motor vehicles the Road Traffic Act 1988, s 149 renders void any 'antecedent agreement or understanding' that a passenger is *volens* to the risk of negligent driving in any vehicle for which third-party insurance cover is compulsory. This provision was considered by the Court of Appeal in *Pitts v Hunt* and it was held that s 149 made the defence of *volenti* impossible in any action brought by a passenger against the driver of a vehicle on a public road. However, the defence of *ex turpi causa* applied as public policy also prevents a claimant who is engaged in illegal activity with the defendant from succeeding against the defendant for wrongs done to the claimant during the course of such activity. The key factors underlying this in *Pitts v Hunt* were that Pitts knew that Hunt did not hold a licence for the motorbike and he was not insured to use it on the road. As we have seen above, the evidence showed that both young men had consumed a large quantity of alcohol, Pitts had encouraged Hunt to ride in a way calculated to frighten other road users, and *ex turpi causa* is not determined by whether a person has been convicted of a crime. The question is whether the act in question is culpably criminal.

 THINKING POINT

What were the main reasons for denying the claimant a remedy in *Pitts*: deterrence, punishment, or some other purpose?

Exercise

According to Dillon LJ:

> It is clear for a start that the fact that a plaintiff was engaged in an illegal activity which brought about his injury does not automatically bring it about that his claim for damages for personal injury as a result of the negligence of the defendant must be dismissed.

In the context of the above statement, identify from the circumstances listed below those in which the defence of *ex turpi causa* might be dismissed:

(1) a passenger injured through the negligence of a car driver from whom he has accepted a lift knowing that the car has not passed its MOT;

(2) an armed raider escaping from a bank hold-up claiming that the driver of the getaway car drove recklessly and caused him injury; and

(3) a person seriously injured by a defective electrical product which he bought at a reduced price because he knew it had been unlawfully smuggled into the country to avoid import tax.

 ## Summary

- *Volenti* is a complete defence; therefore, contributory negligence is preferred because it is more flexible.
- *Volenti* is not easily established; the defendant must show that the claimant had full knowledge and consented to the nature and the extent of the risk.
- Assumption of risk does not apply to a rescuer when the emergency was created by the claimant's negligence.
- *Ex turpi causa* can prevent a claimant engaged in illegal activity from obtaining damages.

   Visit the online resources to listen to a podcast summarizing the topics covered in this chapter.

The bigger picture

In the following case note, N Tavares, 'Jackson v Murray: Personal Injury—Damages—Contributory Negligence' (2015) JPI Law, 3 C152–C155, the author examines apportionment for contributory negligence in accidents involving pedestrians and car drivers. He considers how, on the same set of facts, individual judges assess contributory negligence differently and observes Lord Hodge's sentiments that appellate courts are in danger of misunderstanding the findings of the trial judge.

? Questions

Knowledge-testing questions

1. In determining assessment of contributory negligence in *Jackson v Murray* (2015) how does Lord Reed describe the judicial approach to apportionment of blame?

2. To succeed in the defence of *volenti* (consent) what does the defendant need to show about the claimant's knowledge of the risk in question?

3. Does the defence of *ex turpi causa* (illegality) always bar a claim for injury sustained during an illegal activity?

4. In *Patel v Mirza* (2016) how was the essential rationale for the illegality defence explained by the Supreme Court?

Problem and essay questions

1. Explain the difference between the defences of contributory negligence and *volenti non fit injuria* and evaluate the circumstances in which voluntary assumption of risk will arise.

2. Rex and Jamie consumed large quantities of alcohol. Rex then drove his car recklessly, zooming in and out through the traffic to frighten other road users. Jamie encouraged Rex in his reckless driving and he also threw cans out of the car at passers-by. Rex and Jamie then decided to make a journey to obtain some unlawful cannabis to take to a party.

   On their way to the party, having collected the cannabis, Rex's dangerous driving caused the car to crash into an oncoming minibus carrying a group of university students. The driver of the minibus had instructed all the passengers to ensure their seat belts were securely fastened before they set off. Charles, one of the students, later unfastened his seat belt because of a seat-belt phobia. Charles was severely injured in the accident and evidence shows that if he had been wearing his seat belt his injuries would have been minor. Jamie suffered spinal injuries in the crash and he is planning to sue Rex (or his insurers) in negligence for the injuries he has suffered in the accident.

   Advise Charles and Jamie as to any defences that may be raised to their claims in negligence.

 Visit the online resources for guidance on answering these questions.

≡ Further reading

Goudkamp, J and D Nolan, 'Contributory Negligence in the Twenty-First Century: An Empirical Study of First Instance Decisions' (2016) 79 MLR 575

Kidner, R, 'The Variable Standard of Care, Contributory Negligence and *volenti*' (1991) 11 LS 1

Law Commission, *The Illegality Defence in Tort* (Law Com No 320, 2010)

Lim, E, '*Ex turpi causa*: Reformation Not Revolution' (2017) 80 (5) MLR 927

Strauss, N, 'Illegality Decisions after *Patel v Mirza*' (2018) 134 LQR 538

7 Negligence: occupiers' liability

☐ **LEARNING OBJECTIVES**

By the end of this chapter you should be able to:

● explain the scope of an occupier's liability and how it relates to other aspects of negligence;

● demonstrate a detailed knowledge of the duty of care owed by occupiers to lawful visitors under the Occupiers' Liability Act 1957;

● evaluate the duty of care owed by occupiers to trespassers under the Occupiers' Liability Act 1984 and how it relates to the previous common law duty of care; and

● outline the range of potential defendants upon whom liability may be imposed for harm caused by defective premises.

Introduction

The occupier of land or premises may be liable for injuries suffered on his premises and a buyer or tenant of a property may also be able to sue a landlord, a builder, or a local authority for harm resulting from a defect which existed in a property before its sale or lease. You will see in this chapter that although the law of tort is mainly based on case law developed by judges through the common law, the liability of occupiers for the safety of persons injured on their premises is governed by two statutes. The Occupiers' Liability Act 1957 is concerned with liability to lawful visitors and provides that all lawful entrants are owed the same 'common duty of care'. The 1957 Act did not deal with trespassers, therefore a subsequent statute, the Occupiers' Liability Act 1984, was enacted to govern the duty of an occupier to persons other than visitors (trespassers).

Table 7.1 Occupiers' liability

Duty may be owed by	Duty may be owed to
An occupier	A visitor to the premises
An occupier	A non-visitor (including a trespasser) to the premises
A seller or a lessor	A purchaser or a tenant (or his visitors) in respect of defects which existed at the time of the sale or lease
A builder, designer, or architect	A purchaser or a tenant
Building inspectors and local authorities	Purchasers or others for design faults or for negligent inspection

It is important to note that the standard of care imposed by the statutes is very similar to Lord Atkin's neighbour principle in *Donoghue v Stevenson* (1932) in common law negligence. When considering whether a duty is owed by an occupier the courts must take account of the 'right to roam' provisions of the Countryside and Rights of Way Act 2000. This Act aims to improve public access to countryside and open-air recreation, but it also provides that this right must not place any undue burden on the occupier.

Table 7.1 gives a summary of occupiers' liability.

The main focus of this chapter is on the liability of occupiers of land and buildings for harm suffered as a result of defective or dangerous premises. Liability extends to cover not just personal injury but damage to the visitor's property and damage to property of persons not themselves visitors on the premises when the damage occurred. Liability is for injury or harm caused by the state of the land itself (such as a landslide) or through the defective condition of premises. It can arise in a wide range of situations such as: a dinner guest who falls down the stairs; a service engineer injured while working on the premises; a swimmer injured through slipping on tiles at a swimming pool; or a trespasser injured while taking a shortcut across the defendant's land. However, because the average householder is unlikely to be insured against this type of risk, most claims against occupiers for accidents on their premises are brought by members of the public against businesses or local authorities.

CROSS REFERENCE

See Chapters 12 and 13 for nuisance and *Rylands v Fletcher*.

At this point you should note that a distinction is drawn between liability towards persons *on* the premises and persons *off* the premises; the duty imposed on occupiers is towards persons on the premises and not to those outside them. However, although a person who suffers harm *outside* the premises which was caused by something *on* the defendant's premises will not be able to claim in occupiers' liability, you will see in other chapters that such a claimant may have an action in nuisance or under *Rylands v Fletcher*.

7.1 The common law before 1957

Prior to the enactment of the Occupiers' Liability Act 1957, the common law distinguished between different types of visitor to the premises. The duty owed by an occupier varied according to the common law status of the entrant: the level of occupier's liability was set in a descending scale depending on the different duty owed to four different categories of entrant. The highest standard of care was owed to those, such as hotel guests, who were on the land by virtue of a *contract*. A less onerous duty was owed to *invitees*, those who had a mutual business (for example, making a contract) with the occupier, such as a customer in a shop; a still lower duty was owed to mere *licensees*, a category of entrant permitted to enter premises for some purpose of their own but not requested to be on the land by the occupier. As far as 'uninvited' persons not covered by the above categories were concerned, no duty in negligence was owed. An occupier's obligation to a trespasser was merely to refrain from deliberately or recklessly causing them harm. However, because of the harshness of the common law, if, over a period of time, the occupier permitted trespassers on his land without objecting (such as permitting people to take a short-cut), the courts began to find an 'implied permission' to be there. In this way, an entrant who could establish an implied licence became a 'licensee' rather than a trespasser and was therefore owed more than the minimal duty of care. Table 7.2 shows the different levels of duty owed.

Table 7.2 Levels of duty

Category of entrant	Level of duty owed
Contractors For example, a hotel guest	• Owed highest duty Duty to ensure that the premises were fit for the purposes of the contract
Invitees Such as a customer in a shop	• Owed less onerous duty Duty to take reasonable care to prevent damage from an unusual danger
Licensees Such as a friend invited to a party	• Owed lesser duty than invitees Duty to warn of any concealed danger or trap of which the occupier knew
Uninvited persons For example, trespassers	• No duty of care in negligence Refrain from deliberately or recklessly causing them harm

THINKING POINT

Those defined as trespassers could include: a child playing on unauthorized land; an old lady inadvertently wandering into the wrong premises; or a burglar on a housebreaking mission. Can you see the difficulties faced by the courts in dealing with accidents arising from dangerous premises, particularly in the case of children getting in through broken fences?

7.1.1 'Implied permission'

A person who claims to have entered premises under an *implied permission* must prove that an *implied licence* has been granted. For example, in *Lowery v Walker* (1911), members of the public had, for thirty-five years, used a shortcut across the defendant's field to a railway station. Although he had attempted to prevent this, he had never taken any serious action because most of the people involved were customers for his milk. When the plaintiff was savaged by a dangerous horse which had been put into the field by the defendant, the House of Lords held that he had an implied licence and was not a trespasser. However, permission may not be implied merely because the occupier knows of the entrant's presence or has failed to take the necessary steps to prevent entry. In *Edwards v Railway Executive* (1952), children had been accustomed to climbing through a fence dividing a recreation ground from a railway. The Railway Executive knew this and had taken steps to deter entry by repairing the fence whenever damage had been observed. When the plaintiff child got through the fence and was injured by a passing train, the House of Lords held that he was a trespasser and not an implied visitor. Lord Goddard observed that:

> repeated trespass of itself confers no licence. There must be evidence either of express permission or that the landowner has so conducted himself that he cannot be heard to say that he did not give it.

7.1.2 **Complications of the 'old' common law**

Defining the boundaries between the varying standards of care according to the purpose for which the entrant was on the premises became very complicated and confused. Added to this confusion, a further distinction was made between accidents caused by the *state of the premises* (to which the graded duties in Table 7.2 applied) and accidents arising from some *activity* carried out on the premises (to which the general law of negligence applied). For example, injury suffered through the collapse of an unsafe floor is caused by the state of the premises: this is said to result from 'occupancy' duty. Injury suffered on the premises which is not caused by the condition of the premises, but for instance by a negligently driven car, is said to result from the 'activity' duty. An illustration of how the general law of negligence applies to an activity on the premises is provided in *Slater v Clay Cross Co Ltd* (1956) by Lord Denning:

> If a landowner is driving his car down his private drive and meets someone lawfully walking upon it, then he is under a duty to take reasonable care so as not to injure the walker and his duty is the same, no matter whether it is his gardener coming up with his plants, a tradesman delivering his goods, a friend coming to tea, or a flag seller seeking a charitable gift.

The distinctions and confusion which had evolved in respect of an occupier's duty under the common law were highly unsatisfactory and led to much unnecessary litigation. The situation was described by David Howarth (*Textbook on Tort*, Butterworths, 1995, p 164):

> The complications became intolerable even for lawyers and the result was, first, a report from the Law Reform Committee and then the Occupiers' Liability Act 1957.

7.2 Occupiers' Liability Act 1957

The 1957 Act brings together all the previous categories of contractual entrant, invitee, and licensee into one single category of 'lawful visitors' to whom an occupier owes the 'common duty of care'. It was described by Lord Hailsham as 'a little gem of a statute'. Nevertheless, it still remains important to distinguish visitors from other entrants because, as we saw earlier, the duties of an occupier to entrants other than 'lawful visitors' (that is, trespassers) are governed not by the 1957 Act, but by the later 1984 Act. It is therefore very important to establish at the outset of a case whether the claimant is a trespasser or not, because an occupier's liability in respect of a trespasser is very different from the liability owed to a lawful entrant.

7.2.1 Who is the occupier?

 STATUTE

Occupiers' Liability Act 1957, s 1(2)

the nature of the duty imposed by law in consequence of a person's occupation or control of premises

As shown in the extract from the Occupiers' Liability Act 1957, liability is imposed on the occupier or the person in control of the premises; not necessarily on the owner. The underlying principle is that the person who could have prevented the harm is the one who should be liable, and this is most likely to be the person who is in control of the premises. Although the Act does not define 'occupier', s 1(2) provides that the persons who are to be treated as an occupier are the same as those who would at common law be treated as an occupier. Therefore, for liability to be imposed, a defendant does not need to be an owner or have a right to exclusive possession of the premises. The key question is one of *control* over the premises and, as the next case will show, there can be more than one occupier of the same premises at any one time.

7.2.2 More than one occupier in control of the same premises

In *Wheat v Lacon (E) & Co Ltd* (1966), the defendant brewing company, Lacon, were owners of a pub in which they employed Mr Richardson as their manager. They granted him and his wife a licence to use the top floor of the premises for their private accommodation and Mrs Richardson was given permission to take paying guests in this part of the building. One means of access to the private accommodation on the first floor was through a back staircase. The plaintiff and her husband were paying guests of Mrs Richardson and one evening, as it was getting dark, the husband fell down the back staircase in the private portion of the premises and was fatally injured. The handrail on the stairs was too short and did not stretch to the bottom of the staircase and although there was electric light at the top of the stairs, someone had removed the light bulb. The question then arose as to who was in occupation of that particular part of the premises. The House of Lords held that although the grant of a licence to occupy had been made to the manager, the defendants remained occupiers as they still had sufficient control over the premises to be under a duty of care. The court also held that there may be two or more occupiers of the same premises at any one time if they shared control of the premises. However, on the facts of the case the duty to the deceased had not been broken; the defendant brewery was not responsible for the unlit staircase and therefore they were not liable for the accident.

> **THINKING POINT**
>
> *Wheat* illustrates that there can be more than one occupier. Which parts of the pub would be the responsibility of (1) the manager; (2) the brewery?

7.2.3 For 'control', actual possession may not be necessary

In *Harris v Birkenhead Corporation* (1976), it was held that it is possible to become an occupier without actually taking physical possession of the premises. The case involved the compulsory purchase of a house as part of a slum-clearance programme by the local authority. Notices of entry were served on the tenant and the owner of the property by the local authority, but it was agreed to let the tenant remain in the house until a specified date. The tenant left the house and before the local authority moved in to have the property boarded up a child got in and was seriously injured when she fell from a top floor window. The local authority knew that child trespassers entered empty premises and it had taken steps to board them up to prevent children vandalizing them. In a claim for negligence the local authority argued that it could not be an occupier because it had not taken actual or symbolic possession of the house. The Court of Appeal rejected this argument and held that, even though it had not taken possession of the house, the legal right to control the state of the property had passed to the local authority when the tenant vacated the premises and it had immediately become an occupier.

7.2.4 What duty is owed?

The occupier owes a duty to all lawful visitors, but the 1957 Act provides that the duty may be limited or restricted. For example, an occupier may: set limits on the visitor's permission as to time spent on the premises; permit the visitor to be on the premises only for certain purposes; or specify that the visitor is not permitted to enter particular parts of the premises. A person who has permission only to enter a certain part of the premises has no permission to go to another part. In *The Calgarth* (1927) Scrutton LJ said that:

> When you invite a person into your house to use the staircase, you do not invite him to slide down the banisters, you invite him to use the staircase in the ordinary way in which it is used.

STATUTE

Occupiers' Liability Act 1957, s 2(1)

An occupier of premises owes the same duty, the 'common duty of care', to all his visitors, except in so far as he is free to and does extend, restrict, modify, or exclude his duty to any visitor or visitors by agreement or otherwise.

7.2.5 The 'common duty of care'

The 1957 Act requires that it is *the visitor* who must be safe in using the premises, but this does not necessarily mean that the premises themselves must be reasonably safe.

STATUTE

Occupiers' Liability Act 1957, s 2(2) provides that the common duty of care is:

A duty to take such care as in all the circumstances of the case it is reasonable to see that the visitor will be reasonably safe in using the premises for the purposes for which he is invited or permitted by the occupier to be there.

The duty covers not only risks or hazards which have been created by the occupier. Liability can even arise for mere **omissions** if the occupier fails to protect a visitor from a risk of danger on the premises. The test as to whether the duty has been fulfilled is a question of fact, and the same factors as those in an ordinary negligence action (the magnitude of the risk and the cost and practicability of taking precautions) are taken into account. The content of the duty in s 2(2) was considered by the Court of Appeal in *W Sussex CC v Pierce* (2013), where a child suffered a thumb injury on a school water fountain. The question was (bearing in mind that children do not behave like adults) whether visitors to the school were reasonably safe in using the premises, including the water fountain. The answer was yes; the school was not under a duty to safeguard children against harm under all circumstances.

In *Latimer v AEC Ltd*, the defendants' factory was flooded as the result of a heavy rainstorm and, although they spread sawdust over the affected area, there was not enough to cover the entire floor. The plaintiff employee slipped on a part of the floor that was not covered with sawdust and he claimed in negligence on the ground that a reasonable employer would have shut down the factory to avoid the risk of harm. The House of Lords rejected his claim and said that the risk of injury was too small to justify, let alone require, the drastic step of closing the factory. The likelihood of the harm occurring was a crucial factor in *Simms v Leigh Rugby Football Club Ltd* (1969), which involved a claim by a rugby league player who suffered injury to his leg when he was thrown against a wall in the course of a tackle. The defendants were not liable as the court held that an occupier does not have to guard against improbable events, even if they are foreseeable.

> **omissions**
> a failure to carry out a duty or to fulfil an act.

In *Ward v The Ritz Hotel (London)* (1992) the plaintiff was injured when he fell over a balcony in the defendants' hotel. The balustrade was about 6 inches lower than a British Standards Institution's recommendation as to the height of a balustrade. The Court of Appeal held that although the recommended standards were not legally binding, they highlighted a need for sensible safety precautions. The defendants' failure to comply provided strong evidence of negligence and they were liable under the 1957 Act. The occupier may even be liable for negligently failing to prevent deliberate injury done by one visitor to another. In *Cunningham v Reading Football Club* (1992) police officers on duty at a football match were injured by hooligans who broke off loose pieces of the concrete from the football ground and used them as weapons to hurl at the officers. Because the concrete could easily be prised up and a similar incident had happened four months previously, the risk of wrongdoing by the visitors was foreseeable and the club was held liable.

In *Sutton v Syston Rugby Club* (2011) the claimant was training with the under-16 Colts in a rugby match when, on the point of scoring, he fell and gashed his right knee on a plastic object which had become submerged in the pitch. The trial judge rejected the club's suggestion that a quick walk-over inspection of the rugby pitch before the match was sufficient to discharge its duty to take such care as was reasonable. The club's appeal was allowed. The Court of Appeal held that, before a game or training session, walking over a pitch at a reasonable pace by a coach or match organizer will satisfy a club's common law duty of care in relation to such inspection.

According to Lord Justice Longmore:

> It is important that neither the game's professional organisation nor the law should lay down standards that are too difficult for ordinary coaches and match organisers to meet. Games of rugby are, after all, no more than games and, as such are obviously desirable activities within the meaning of section 1 of the Compensation Act 2006.

The club's argument that the judge was wrong to find that the claimant had proved his case on causation (you may wish to refer to 4.1 on this point) was also considered. The evidence showed that the stub would not have been immediately visible on a casual inspection and even a reasonable 'walk-over-the-pitch' inspection would be unlikely to have revealed it. The Court therefore concluded that the claimant had been unable to prove that an inspection would, on the balance of probabilities, have revealed the stub's existence.

In *G4S Care and Justice Services (UK) Ltd v Manley* (2016) one of the questions for the Court of Appeal was whether the judge had imposed an unreasonably high standard on G4S for failing to restore a power failure within twenty minutes (which was the expected time frame for completing such repairs). The claimant, an inmate in a prison under the control of the defendant G4S, had recently been discharged from hospital following a hip replacement. He returned to prison walking with the aid of crutches and he had a weak leg.

On the evening of the accident an electricity failure or 'outage' occurred after 8.10 p.m. (Such failures were reasonably common occurrences in the prison.) Between five and ten minutes later the claimant used the intercom in his cell to report to a prison officer that he was concerned about the power going off as he had only just come out of hospital and had reduced mobility. The officer passed on the information about the power failure to a senior prison officer, but he did not stress the urgency of this particular case. During the period when the power was off the claimant needed to use the toilet and because it was dark in the cell he fell and hit his head on a cupboard.

G4S appealed against the judge's finding that the failure to restore the electricity within a reasonable time in these circumstances amounted to a breach of the duty under s 2 of the 1957 Act. The two questions for the Court of Appeal were: (1) was the judge's approach to s 2 incorrect because he had failed to consider whether the lighting conditions, as an objective fact, made the cell unsafe; and (2) had the judge imposed an unreasonably high standard of care on G4S?

In dismissing G4S's appeal the Court found that Manley had established that G4S did not take such care as was reasonable to ensure that he was reasonably safe in using the cell. The Court also found the judge had not imposed an unduly high standard of care on G4S; if they had repaired the power failure within the period of twenty minutes there would have been no breach of duty. It was during the extended period of the power failure that the accident happened and given that the claimant had reported his mobility problems to an appropriate official a timely repair was imperative.

▶ CROSS REFERENCE
For more on omissions, see Chapter 2.

7.2.6 Distinguishing 'occupancy' and 'activity' duties

The common law distinction between 'occupancy' duties and 'activity' duties was considered earlier, but it is not apparent whether this distinction still applies under the 1957 Act. From the wording of the statute it is unclear whether it covers harm arising from the state of the premises, the 'occupancy' duty, or harm suffered as a consequence of activities on the land, the 'activity' duty.

 STATUTE

Occupiers' Liability Act 1957, s 1(2)

This provides that the Act shall:

regulate the nature of the duty imposed by law in consequence of a person's occupation or control of premises.

However, s 1(1) states that the rules shall regulate the duty:

in respect of dangers due to the state of the premises or to things done or omitted to be done on them.

However, the usual view is that s 1(2) prevails. The Act applies only to the 'occupancy' duty and the 'activity' duty is covered by common law negligence. In *Ogwo v Taylor* (1988), a fireman claimed for steam injuries he suffered as he was fighting a fire in a confined space at the defendant's premises. The occupier had put the fireman at risk by carelessly creating a danger on his premises and on this basis the fireman succeeded in common law negligence, rather than occupiers' liability.

7.2.7 Does the duty vary in respect of different visitors?

As we have already seen, the nature of the duty owed by an occupier to his visitors is the same as that in common law negligence. The fundamental principle is that, depending on the magnitude and seriousness of the risk and the costs in taking precautions, a defendant who fails to take precautions that a reasonable person would take will be liable. The Act specifically provides for two categories of visitor: children and skilled visitors.

7.2.7.1 Children

 STATUTE

Occupiers' Liability Act 1957, s 2(3)(a) provides, in respect of children, that:

an occupier must be prepared for children to be less careful than adults.

The occupier's duty is to take reasonable care and, as shown in the extract from the Occupiers' Liability Act, the 1957 Act requires the occupier to take account of the fact that children are less careful than adults. A warning notice may be sufficient to alert an adult visitor to a potential danger on a premises, but this may be a totally inadequate precaution in the case of a child. In *Glasgow Corporation v Taylor* (1922), a 7-year-old child died from eating poisonous berries that he had picked from a shrub in a public park which was under the control of the corporation. The berries looked like cherries or large blackcurrants and they had a very tempting appearance to children. It was alleged that the local authority knew of the poisonous nature of the berries, but the shrub was not fenced off and no warning of the danger was given. The House of Lords held that the berries constituted an 'allurement' to the child and the fact that it had been left there constituted a breach of the defendant's duty.

Jolley v Sutton London Borough Council (1998)

In *Jolley v Sutton London Borough Council*, a derelict boat, which was left abandoned on the council's land, was found to have constituted an allurement and a trap, but these were not the causes of the accident. The immediate cause was that the plaintiff, a 14-year-old boy, and a friend decided to repair the boat and jacked it up with a car jack. The Court of Appeal had ruled that, even making full allowance for the unpredictability of children's behaviour, it was not reasonably foreseeable that the boys would work under a propped-up boat. It held that the activities of the boys and the plaintiff's serious personal injury were too remote because it occurred in an unforeseeable manner. Allowing an appeal, the House of Lords approached the question of what risk was foreseeable in the case of children in much more generous terms. The trial judge had been correct to consider the reasonable foreseeability of the wider risk that children would meddle with a dilapidated boat and be at risk of physical injury.

> **CROSS REFERENCE**
>
> See also Chapter 4 on causation.

In determining whether the common duty of care has been breached in respect of children, an occupier is entitled to assume that parents will take reasonable care for their children's safety. In *Phipps v Rochester Corporation* (1955), a boy aged 5 and his sister aged 7 went to pick blackberries in a large open space which was being developed by the defendants. It was known to the defendants that people crossed their land, but they apparently took no action. A long deep trench, which would have been obvious to an adult, had been dug in the middle of the open space. As he was crossing the open space, the 5-year-old boy fell into the trench and broke his leg. Although the trench was held to constitute a danger to a small child, the defendants were not liable. Devlin J placed the responsibility for small children primarily on their parents. In measuring the care taken by the occupiers, he said that the habits of prudent parents should also be taken into account and that both the parents and the occupier must act reasonably. Although this case is pre-1957, it is equally applicable to the common duty of care, and its reasoning was applied in *Simkiss v Rhondda Borough Council* (1983), where a 7-year-old girl fell off a steep slope which was situated opposite the block of flats where she lived. The plaintiff argued that the council should have fenced off the area to prevent children playing on the slope. The Court of Appeal took the view that the slope did not constitute a concealed danger and her father also stated in evidence that he had not considered the slope to be dangerous. It was held that the occupiers were entitled to assume that parents would have warned their children of the dangers and their Lordships concluded that if the child's father did not consider the area to be dangerous, the occupier could not be asked to achieve a higher standard of care.

THINKING POINT

Do you think the weighting given to the father's evidence in *Simkiss* was fair? Does this decision suggest that an occupier owes a lower standard of care to the child of a 'less cautious' parent? What might the court's response have been if the father had said he considered the slope to be dangerous?

CASE CLOSE-UP

Bourne Leisure Ltd v Marsden (2009)

The problem with attaching blame in cases involving young children can be summarized by the comments of Lord Justice Stanley Burnton in *Bourne Leisure Ltd v Marsden*:

> This was a tragic case, and Matthew's death has been understandably devastating for his parents. A drowning such as this is a parent's nightmare. But accidents may and do happen to young children without anyone being at fault.

Since the case concerned liability for the death of a 2-and-a-half-year-old boy, Matthew, who drowned in a pond in a holiday park operated by Bourne Leisure Limited, the focus was again on the occupier's duty to be prepared for children to be less careful than adults. The tragedy occurred while the boy's mother crossed a roadway from the family caravan to return items to a holidaymaker in a nearby caravan and did not notice that her two young children had disappeared. The boy's parents soon realized that the children were missing and began a frantic search; the mother, Mrs Marsden, went along a roadway to the camp entertainment centre and her husband searched along the roadway near their caravan. Neither of the parents was aware of the path which gave the child access to the pond where the tragedy occurred and, by the time his father found him, the child had drowned in the pond. Less than a year before this incident a 4-year-old boy had to be rescued from the pond in question and, as a result of that incident, Bourne Leisure had liaised with environmental health officers from the local authority and produced an open water policy covering all their fifty-three sites and erected a wire fence beneath the rails surrounding the pond.

The parents first claimed that Bourne Leisure should have placed an effective barrier on the site, of about 1.1 metres high, as recommended in the case of domestic ponds and schools to prevent young children who might foreseeably wander off unaccompanied by their parents, from gaining access to the pond. The trial judge rejected this aspect of the claim and accepted the reasoning contained in a written statement from an environmental health officer who had been concerned with the death of Matthew which stated:

> A pond in a school is an entirely different thing to a pond in a park. In a school, you can expect to have a number of children being supervised by very few teachers; therefore it is reasonable to take special precautions. A pond in a domestic garden is also very different, and any child in the home would be exposed to it on very many occasions. In the case of a holiday park, is it reasonable to expect the children of such young age would be under constant parental supervision? If the law required it to be fenced, how high? How do we make the fences unclimbable? What about the rivers and streams on sites, the sea itself and site roads, which are far more hazardous than ponds? . . .. this child could have strayed into the river on site, the sea, or a site road and been killed by a car or even a reversing caravan.

The second aspect of the parents' claim was that in the absence of a fence, Bourne Leisure ought to have done more to warn them of the danger of the nearby pond and drawn to their attention the risks for unsupervised children. The trial judge had found that if the parents had known about and been warned of the existence of ponds nearby, they would have been alert to the risk of danger and by failing to give warnings of that nature Bourne Leisure were in breach of their common duty of care.

Bourne Leisure appealed against this finding on the ground that its guests had received a welcome pack which included the location of the three ponds in the holiday park. They also argued that the firm had the right to expect close parental supervision of children as young as 2-and-a-half. In allowing Bourne Leisure's appeal against the finding of the trial judge, the Court of Appeal said that although an occupier ought reasonably to anticipate that small children might escape the attention of parents and wander into places of danger, it does not follow that the occupier is under a duty to take precautions against such dangers.

Lord Justice Moses said:

> three days before the death of their son they had arrived and been handed a welcome pack with a plan. The plan showed a number of sources of danger to unaccompanied children on site, in particular a number of roads, lakes, ponds, the river and the beach, just outside the site leading to the sea. Again, with commendable frankness, both parents accepted that the site was not safe for small unaccompanied children. Of course, the defendant

ought reasonably to have anticipated that small children might escape the attention of parents and wander into places of danger. But it by no means follows that the occupier is under a duty to take precautions against such dangers. If the danger is not obvious and the occupier ought to have foreseen that children may play in the area of the danger he may have to take precautions. But that situation is quite different from circumstances in which the source of danger is obvious should a small child stray from the control of even the most attentive and conscientious parent.

Sometimes these cases are bedevilled with the quest for attaching blame either to the parent or to the occupier. The occupier, it is suggested, ought to have foreseen that there will be unaccompanied small children on its site and taken precautions; faced with that accusation, the occupier blames the parent for losing control over the child. But liability is not to be attributed on the basis that one or other must be to blame. In order to escape liability the occupier is not required to prove that the parent was at fault.

As this case shows, the fact that the parents were not at fault does not mean that the defendant was in breach of duty. This line of reasoning was followed in *Edwards v London Borough of Sutton* (2016) (7.2.8) in an action brought by an adult claimant. According to Lord Justice McCombe: 'not every accident (even if it has serious consequences) has to have been the fault of another'.

7.2.7.2 Skilled visitors

In determining whether the common duty of care has been breached in respect of skilled visitors, an occupier is entitled to assume that a professional person or someone exercising a particular trade or skill will appreciate and guard against ordinary risks associated with his trade or profession.

 STATUTE

Occupiers' Liability Act 1957, s 2(3)(b) provides in respect of skilled visitors:

an occupier may expect that a person, in the exercise of his calling, will appreciate and guard against any special risks ordinarily incidental to it, so far as the occupier leaves him free to do so.

In *Roles v Nathan* (1963), two chimney sweeps were called to clean an old coke-burning boiler which was difficult to light and which smoked badly. The boiler engineer was called and advised that the flues should be cleaned and that the sweep hole and inspection chamber should be sealed before the boiler was lit. He warned the men about the dangers of working on the flues with the fires lit and of the risk of carbon monoxide poisoning if they did so. The men disregarded the warning and when the boiler was lit they carried on with their work, but they were killed by carbon monoxide fumes.

THINKING POINT

If the chimney sweeps had fallen through a rotten floorboard on their way to the boiler, would this have been covered by s 2(3)(b)?

The occupier was not liable because the defendant had discharged his duty under the Occupiers' Liability Act 1957 by warning the sweeps of the particular risks. The Court of Appeal also said that when a householder calls in a specialist to deal with a defective installation on his premises, he can reasonably expect the specialist to appreciate and guard against such dangers. Lord Denning said:

> The occupier here was under no duty of care to these sweeps, at any rate in regard to the dangers that caused their deaths. If it had been a different danger, as for instance if the stairs leading to the cellar gave way, the occupier might no doubt be responsible, but not for these dangers which were special risks ordinarily incidental to their calling.

Skills possessed by the entrant will not automatically absolve the occupier of all liability under s 2(3)(b). In *Salmon v Seafarers Restaurants* (1983), a fireman entered a fish-and-chip shop to extinguish a fire. There was an escape of gas followed by an explosion in which the fireman was injured. The defendant argued that an occupier's duty to a fireman attending a fire at his premises was limited to protecting him from special or exceptional risks over and above ordinary risks which are a necessary part of his job. The court rejected this argument. Woolf J took the view that although an occupier could expect a fireman attending a fire at his premises to be skilled in protecting himself against the risks of fire, an occupier could not be exempt from risks which would threaten a fireman who was exercising the normal skills of his profession. This approach was expressly approved by the House of Lords in *Ogwo v Taylor*, where the fireman was exercising reasonable care in using a hose when he suffered severe burns from scalding steam after he entered the roof space of the defendants' house to control a fire. The defendant argued that he was not liable because the injury was caused by the ordinary risks involved in firefighting. This was rejected by their Lordships, who said that if the fireman had taken a foolhardy and unnecessary risk in fighting the fire his own conduct might have broken the chain of causation.

7.2.8 Warning of danger

CROSS REFERENCE

See 7.3.4 Consumer Rights Act 2015.

Another factor taken into account in determining whether the common duty of care has been breached is whether there was an adequate warning of the danger. Where the warning of danger is sufficient to enable the visitor to be reasonably safe it will amount to a discharge of the occupier's duty of care.

 STATUTE

Occupiers' Liability Act 1957, s 2(4)(a)

where damage is caused to a visitor by a danger of which he had been warned by the occupier, the warning is not to be treated without more as absolving the occupier from liability, unless in all the circumstances it was enough to enable the visitor to be reasonably safe.

You will see many examples of business premises remaining open to the public during a period of reconstruction or renovation, where the occupier cordons off or fences dangerous parts of the premises to ensure that visitors are safe in using them. You will also be aware of situations where the occupier displays a warning of specific danger on the premises to alert the visitor to the potential risk so that he can take care to avoid it. However, warnings can have different purposes. They may seek to warn of the specific danger, such as a notice 'Wet Floor' or, as often seen in large supermarkets, a yellow sign showing an image of a slippery surface. Alternatively, an occupier may wish to disclaim responsibility with a notice saying 'Persons enter at their own risk. The occupier accepts no liability for injury to persons using these premises.' In some circumstances the occupier may warn of the danger and attempt to disclaim liability with the same notice; for example, a notice by a swimming pool might state: 'No running on the wet surface. No liability accepted for accidents.' You should note the important distinction between a warning notice and an exclusion of liability notice: you will see in the next section that an exclusion notice may be subject to the Unfair Contract Terms Act 1977 or the Consumer Rights Act 2015.

Although warning of the danger may discharge the duty of care (as was the case in *Roles v Nathan*), a warning notice is not enough unless in all the circumstances it enables the visitor to be reasonably safe. In *Rae v Mars (UK) Ltd* (1990), it was held that in cases of extreme danger, or where an unusual danger exists, the visitor should not only be warned, but a barrier or added notice should be placed to show the immediacy of the danger. In *Staples v West Dorset District Council* (1995), the claimant suffered injuries as a result of slipping on algae-covered rocks at the coastline. In an action against the Council he argued that he should have been warned of the danger, but here it was held that if the danger is obvious, and the visitor is able to appreciate it, there is no need for a warning sign. The duty to warn of obvious dangers was considered more recently in *Edwards v London Borough of Sutton* (2016), where the Court of Appeal referred to two well-recognized principles of law: 'First, there is the proper treatment in law of the concept of risk. Secondly, occupiers of land are not under a duty to protect, or even to warn, against obvious dangers.'

Q CASE CLOSE-UP

Edwards v London Borough of Sutton (2016)

The claimant Mr Edwards and his wife had taken up cycling as a form of exercise. On the day of the accident they cycled around a public park under control of the defendant (London Borough of Sutton) for some time before deciding to return to their van, which was parked in an adjoining car park. They wheeled their bicycles through a walkway in the park and over a small ornamental footbridge bordered by low parapets. As they crossed the bridge Mr Edwards's bicycle pulled him off balance and this caused him to fall over the side of the bridge onto large rocks in the water below. He sustained severe injuries in the fall, including a spinal injury which left him wheelchair dependent. Edwards claimed that the Borough had failed to take reasonable care to see that he, as a visitor to the park, was safe in using the bridge for a purpose for which he was permitted to use it. He claimed that the

Borough should have: installed side protection barriers to the bridge; warned of the dangers posed by the low sides of the bridge; and carried out a sufficient risk assessment of risk presented by the bridge to pedestrians. The trial judge found that in these circumstances the Borough was liable to the claimant (subject to a finding of 40 per cent contributory negligence).

On appeal the Borough argued that there was no inherent danger pertaining to the bridge which could give rise to a duty of care under the 1957 Act and there was no duty to warn of the obvious danger. The bridge had been there for many years (perhaps since the 1860s) and there was no record of any accident occurring from its use. The Borough also argued that there was no evidence that any warning would have dissuaded the claimant from crossing the bridge so any risk assessment would not have contributed to an avoidance of the accident.

In a unanimous decision the Court of Appeal allowed the Borough's appeal on the ground that it had reached the requisite standard of care, even though it did nothing in respect of the objectively dangerous state of the footbridge.

According to Lord Justice McCombe:

> One can see that an unfenced bridge or a bridge with low parapets will present more danger of a fall than would a bridge with high guard rails. There are, of course, many such unprotected bridges up and down the country in all sorts of locations. In argument, we discussed golf courses, where plank bridges, with no side rails, crossing over ditches are common and have to be negotiated by golfers with trolleys. Ornamental bridges with low walls, together with water features, are likely to be common features of decoration in public gardens. Any structure of this type presents the risk that the user may fall from it . . . .. However, while I am prepared to assume that there was objectively a 'danger' arising from the state of the premises in this respect here, does this mean that, in order to discharge the common duty of care, arising from that objective possibility of danger, no such bridges must be left open to visitors or must not be left open to visitors without guard rails or express warnings? In my judgment, the answer to this question is a clear 'no'.

However, you should note that although adult visitors do not require warnings of obvious risk, where a risk is not obvious a defendant will be in breach of the duty under s 2 for failure to provide a warning. In *English Heritage v Taylor* (2016) the 60-year-old claimant, his wife, and their grandchildren went to visit Carisbrooke Castle on the Isle of Wight. As they were walking around the historic site the claimant fell down an unmarked sheer drop of 12 feet into a moat and sustained serious head injuries. In dismissing the English Heritage's appeal against liability the Court of Appeal held that in this case the danger was not obvious and there had been no warning sign. In these circumstances a sign warning of the sheer drop would have been likely to influence the behaviour of most sensible individuals. Nevertheless, the Court was concerned that the significance of this decision should not be misunderstood and made the following comments on dangers which are obvious or not:

> In some cases, this may present an occupier of land with a difficulty. But there are many areas of life in which difficult borderline judgments have to be made. This is well understood by the courts and is taken into account in deciding whether negligence or a breach of section 2 of

the Act has been established. In this context, it is highly relevant that the common duty of care is to take such care 'as in all the circumstances is reasonable' to see that the visitor is 'reasonably' safe in using the premises for the purpose for which he is invited or permitted by the occupier to be there. The court is, therefore, required to consider all the circumstances. These will include how obvious the danger is and, in an appropriate case, aesthetic matters. If an occupier is in doubt as to whether a danger is obvious, it may be well advised to take reasonable measures to reduce or eliminate the danger. But the steps need be no more than reasonable steps. That is why the decision in this case should not be interpreted as requiring occupiers like English Heritage to place unsightly warning signs in prominent positions all over sensitive historic sites. They are required to do no more than take reasonable steps.

 THINKING POINT

Do you think a large notice written in English at the International Arrivals Terminal at Heathrow Airport stating 'Caution Wet Floor' would enable passengers to be reasonably safe? What type of notice might be more effective in warning of the danger in these circumstances?

7.2.9 Independent contractors

The general rule is that an occupier is not vicariously liable for the negligence of an independent contractor and the 1957 Act accords with this rule.

 STATUTE

Occupiers' Liability Act 1957, s 2(4)(b)

Where damage is caused to a visitor by a danger due to the faulty execution of any work of construction, maintenance or repair by an independent contractor employed by the occupier, the occupier is not to be treated without more as answerable for the danger if in all the circumstances he acted reasonably in entrusting the work to an independent contractor and had taken such steps (if any) as he reasonably ought in order to satisfy himself that the contractor was competent and that the work was properly done.

The key questions to ask in determining if the occupier has acted reasonably are:

  (1) Has he acted reasonably in entrusting the work to an independent contractor?

  (2) Has he taken reasonable care to see that the contractor was competent?

  (3) Has he taken reasonable care to check that the work was properly done?

7.2.9.1 Relevance of 'technical nature of the job' and occupier's competencies to s 2(4)(b)

The technical nature of the job to be done and the competencies of the occupier will affect the application of s 2(4)(b). The principles upon which the court will decide the issue can be illustrated by two cases decided before the 1957 Act. *Haseldine v CA Daw & Son Ltd* (1941), shows that the more technical the work, the more reasonable it will be to entrust it to an independent contractor. The plaintiff was injured when the lift in a block of flats fell to the bottom of its shaft. The accident happened as a result of the negligence of a firm of independent contractors that the defendant had employed to repair the lift. The defendant had discharged his duty by employing a competent firm of engineers to make periodical inspections of the lift. Having no technical skills meant that he could not be expected to check that the work had been satisfactorily done and he was therefore not liable. This case was distinguished in *Woodward v The Mayor of Hastings* (1945), in a claim involving a child who was injured at school having slipped on an icy step. The step had been left in a dangerous condition by a cleaner and the defendant had argued that the task of cleaning had been delegated to an independent contractor. The court held that the decision in *Haseldine v Daw* is not authority for the proposition that an occupier is always absolved from responsibility if he has entrusted work to some competent person. An occupier is bound to take that kind of care which a reasonably prudent man in his place would take; neither more nor less. The landlord of a block of flats, as occupier of the lifts, does not profess to be either an electrical or a hydraulic engineer. In *Haseldine*, the landlord was ignorant of the mechanics of his hydraulic lifts and it was his duty to choose a good expert, to trust, and then to be guided by his advice. Even assuming that the cleaner was an independent contractor, the defendants were under a duty to inspect the cleaner's work since there was no technical knowledge required to check the cleaning of a step. In these circumstances, no technical skill was required, and, according to Du Parcq, LJ:

> The craft of the charwoman may have its mysteries, but there is no esoteric quality in the nature of the work which the cleaning of a snow-covered step demands.

7.2.9.2 Independent contractors: extra-hazardous activities

The Court of Appeal has ruled that it is fair, just, and reasonable to impose liability on an occupier who allows an extra-hazardous activity to take place on his land without taking ordinary precautions to ensure that the independent contractor has public liability insurance and a proper safety plan. In *Bottomley v Tordmorden Cricket Club* (2003), as part of a fundraising event, the defendant club had allowed an independent contractor to carry out a pyrotechnic display on its land. The club was liable for the personal injuries of the claimant (a voluntary and unpaid assistant of the independent contractor), who suffered severe burns and other injuries during the display. The Court of Appeal, rejecting the club's appeal against liability, held that although the case was not about a risk caused by the state of the premises under the Occupiers' Liability Act 1957, the club was liable, along with the contractors (who had no public liability insurance), in common law negligence because of its failure to engage a competent contractor.

7.2.9.3 To what extent does the occupier need to check if the independent contractor is adequately insured?

In *Gwilliam v West Hertfordshire Hospital NHS Trust* (2002) the defendant hospital engaged an independent contractor to supply and operate a 'splat wall' for visitors bouncing from a trampoline as part of a fundraising fair on its grounds. When the claimant was injured it was discovered that the contractor's public liability insurance had expired a few days before the event.

The Court of Appeal held that the occupier owed a duty to take reasonable care to ensure that the claimant was reasonably safe and to take steps to ensure that an independent contractor, who was to supply potentially hazardous equipment, was adequately insured (on the facts of the case the defendant hospital had not breached its duty under s 2(4)(b)).

However, in *Naylor v Payling* (2004), the defendant nightclub owner was not liable for an uninsured independent contractor. The claimant suffered severe injuries while being forcibly ejected from a nightclub by a door attendant employed by the contractor responsible for security at the nightclub. The contractor had no public liability insurance, so the claimant sued the nightclub owner for failing to ensure that the contractor was adequately insured. Although the defendant had a duty of care to take reasonable steps to ensure the safety of visitors to the nightclub, this had not been breached. The nightclub owner had fulfilled his duty by checking that the independent contractor was accredited under the appropriate scheme run by the police and local government. Further, the door attendant had been employed for eighteen months before the claimant was injured and there had been no reason to doubt his competence during that period. The nightclub owner had not therefore acted negligently in selecting the independent contractor and the Court of Appeal held that, save in special circumstances, there is no free-standing duty to take reasonable steps to ensure that an independent contractor is insured.

 THINKING POINT

What are the policy reasons for not imposing a duty to ensure that the contractor is adequately insured where an occupier takes reasonable care in selecting the independent contractor?

7.3 Exclusion of liability

We have seen earlier in *Roles v Nathan* (1963) that a warning which, in all the circumstances of the case, enables a visitor to be reasonably safe in using the premises may absolve the occupier of liability. In the absence of a contract, the exclusion of liability towards a visitor may be contained in a warning sign displayed on the premises. Where a visitor enters under a contract (for example, membership of a gym) the exclusion may be contained as an express term of the contract. However, we shall below that exclusions notices are governed by the Unfair Contract Terms Act (UCTA) 1977 and (where the visitor is a 'consumer') the Consumer Rights Act 2015.

However, an occupier may also raise the defence of *volenti non fit injuria* and argue that the claimant voluntarily consented to the risk. For example, in *Simms v Leigh Rugby Football Club Ltd* (1969) the claimant, a professional rugby player, was held to have accepted the inherent risk of playing on a rugby ground that complied with the regulations of the Rugby League. Where the claimant is shown to have failed to take reasonable care for his own safety, the

⟩ CROSS REFERENCE
Defences are discussed more fully in Chapter 6.

defence of contributory negligence may be available. These defences are not specific to occupiers' liability; they are generally available in other torts.

7.3.1 *Volenti non fit injuria*

The Occupiers' Liability Act 1957 expressly preserves the defence of consent.

 STATUTE

Occupiers' Liability Act 1957, s 2(5) provides that there is no liability for:

risks willingly accepted as his by the visitor.

➤ **CROSS REFERENCE**

Tomlinson is discussed at 7.4.7 Liability for trespassers: 'self-inflicted harm'.

It can be seen from the above extract that the Act not only imposes liability on an occupier, but the visitor also has a personal responsibility to guard against his own risks in using a premises. In *Tomlinson v Congleton BC* (2003) the extent to which occupiers should be liable for injuries suffered by visitors who take obvious risks was considered and, according to Lord Hobhouse:

> It is not, and should never be, the policy of the law to require the protection of the foolhardy or reckless few to deprive, or interfere with, the enjoyment by the remainder of society of the liberties and amenities to which they are all entitled. Does the law require that all trees be cut down because some youths may climb them and fall? Does the law require the coastline and other beauty spots to be lined with warning notices? Does the law require that attractive waterside picnic spots be destroyed because of a few foolhardy individuals who choose to ignore warning notices and indulge in activities dangerous only to themselves? The answer to all these questions is, of course, no.

7.3.2 Exclusion or limitation of liability by notice

The Act provides that an occupier may exclude liability arising from the occupation of premises by imposing a condition on the visitor's entry.

7.3.3 Occupiers' Liability Act 1957

 STATUTE

Occupiers' Liability Act 1957, s 2(1) Act provides that the duty is owed except in so far as:

the occupier is free to and does extend, restrict, modify or exclude his duty . . . by agreement or otherwise.

However, it is important to note an occupier is not 'free' to restrict liability for death or personal injury resulting from negligence where the provisions of the Unfair Contract Terms Act 1977 apply. The ability of business occupiers to exclude liability under the 1957 Act has been severely restricted by the Unfair Contract Terms Act 1977 and the Consumer Rights Act 2015.

Where the premises are occupied for the business purposes of the occupier any contract term or notice purporting to exclude or restrict liability for death or personal injury resulting from breach of the 1957 Act is invalid under UCTA 1977. In the case of loss or other damage to property, an occupier cannot exclude liability unless the term satisfies the test of reasonableness.

UCTA 1977 does not apply where the visitor enters a premises pursuant to a consumer transaction, between a consumer and a trader. Exclusion clauses in consumer contracts and notices are now governed by the Consumer Rights Act 2015. According to s 2 of the 2015 Act, a 'consumer' is someone who is acting for purposes that are wholly or mainly outside that person's trade, business, craft, or profession and a 'trader' is a person or company acting for purposes relating to its trade, business, craft, or profession.

In addition to the restriction excluding liability for death or personal injury, the Consumer Rights Act 2015 (s 62) provides that the test for exclusion of liability, loss or other damage to property is one of 'fairness' (not one of 'reasonableness' as under UCTA). In determining the 'fairness test' the court takes into account factors such as the specific circumstances existing when the term was agreed, other terms in the contract, and the nature of the subject matter of the contract.

 THINKING POINT

Which of the following is an exclusion of liability: (1) 'Trespassers beware'; (2) 'The management accepts no responsibility for injuries suffered on these premises'; (3) 'Floor slippery when wet'?

7.3.4 Consumer Rights Act 2015

 STATUTE

Consumer Rights Act 2015, s 62

In the case of other damage, contract terms and notices must be fair. (1) An unfair term of a consumer contract is not binding on the consumer. (2) An unfair consumer notice is not binding on the consumer.

📖 STATUTE

Consumer Rights Act 2015, s 65

(1) A trader cannot by a term of a consumer contract or by a consumer notice exclude or restrict liability for death or personal injury resulting from negligence.

(2) Where a term of a consumer contract, or a consumer notice, purports to exclude or restrict a trader's liability for negligence, a person is not to be taken to have voluntarily accepted any risk merely because the person agreed to or knew about the term or notice.

❯ CROSS REFERENCE

See also Chapter 5.

In *White v Blackmore* (1972), the plaintiff's husband was killed while watching a motor race with his family when the wheel of a car became entangled in the safety ropes and he was catapulted 20 feet through the air. The Court of Appeal held that the Motor Racing Club and the racing organizer were not liable under the 1957 Act. A notice had been posted at the entrance and at other points about the field which stated:

> Warning to the Public, Motor Racing is dangerous . . . all persons having any connection with promotion and or organisation . . . including drivers . . . are absolved of all liabilities . . . howsoever caused to spectators or ticket holders.

A majority in the Court of Appeal concluded that the club had effectively excluded all liability arising from the accident on the ground that the deceased had entered the premises subject to the conditions contained in the notice. This case would now be decided differently because under the Unfair Contract Terms Act 1977 an occupier of premises used for the purposes of a business is no longer permitted to exclude liability for personal injuries. However, the 1977 Act does not apply where the premises are in private use and a 'private' occupier is still 'free' to restrict liability.

7.3.5 **Liability of non-occupiers**

The seller of defective premises, a landlord, a builder, or a local authority may all come within the definition of 'occupier of the premises' but where, for example, a person living in a rented flat suffers harm arising from a defect in the premises, there may be no occupier other than the claimant. In the past, it was almost impossible to sue a landlord in respect of injuries suffered on the premises. The rules of tort were also very unfavourable in respect of those wishing to bring an action against a seller for harm caused by negligence before the property was let or sold. In the 1970s the immunity which had previously been granted to landlords in respect of liability in negligence for dangers created before letting their premises began to be restricted by the courts.

7.3.6 **The Defective Premises Act 1972**

The Defective Premises Act 1972 introduced a statutory duty in negligence which gives protection against a landlord's failure to fulfil obligations to maintain and repair premises which are let or sold. This duty is owed in respect of dwellings (not commercial properties) and it is owed by, among others, builders, architects, and surveyors. The duty is owed to the party who originally commissioned the work and to those who subsequently acquire an interest in the dwelling. Liability under the 1972 Act is strict and therefore negligence on the part of the defendant does not need to be established.

CROSS REFERENCE
See also Chapter 5 for the Defective Premises Act 1972.

7.4 Occupiers' Liability Act 1984: liability for persons other than 'visitors'

7.4.1 **Trespassers: the background to the new legislation**

Until the passing of the Occupiers' Liability Act 1984, all other entrants (predominantly trespassers) were dealt with by the common law because the 1957 Act applies only to an occupier's duties in respect of visitors. Under the common law, trespassers were traditionally viewed as wrongdoers and the standard of care owed to them by occupiers was very low. In *Addie & Sons Ltd v Dumbreck* (1929) Lord Moulton said:

> Towards the trespasser, the occupier has no duty to take reasonable care for his protection or even to protect him from concealed danger. The trespasser comes on to the premises at his own risk. An occupier is, in such a case, liable only where the injury is due to some wilful act involving something more than the absence of reasonable care. There must be some act done with the deliberate intention of doing harm to the trespasser, or at least some act done with reckless disregard of the presence of the trespasser.

However, this rule produced some very harsh results, especially in the case of child trespassers or those who inadvertently strayed on to the defendant's premises. The court began to find ways of mitigating the harshness of the law, such as the concept of 'allurement' discussed earlier in *Glasgow Corporation v Taylor* (1922).

THINKING POINT
What policy considerations might have been behind the decision in *Addie v Dumbreck*?

CROSS REFERENCE
See 7.2.7 Does the duty vary in respect of different visitors?

7.4.2 **The duty of 'common humanity'**

In *British Railways Board v Herrington* (1972), the House of Lords considered the doubts expressed by the Court of Appeal about the correctness of the minimal duty set out in *Addie*. The case involved a 6-year-old child trespasser who suffered severe burns when he was trespassing on the defendant's land. The child had obtained access to an electrified railway line through a gap in the defendant's chain-link fence. The gap was used as a short-cut by members of the public and the defendants knew that in the past children had been seen on the line, but they took no action. Although a trespasser is owed a lower duty of care, their Lordships held that an occupier does owe a duty to act humanely. The plaintiff was allowed to recover in negligence because British Rail had known of the risk of injury and had failed to take the simple steps required to repair the gap in the fence. According to Lord Wilberforce:

> It must be remembered that we are concerned with trespassers and a compromise must be reached between the demands of humanity and the necessity to avoid placing undue burdens on occupiers. What is reasonable depends on the nature and degree of the danger. It also depends on the difficulty and expense of guarding against it. The law, in this context, takes account of the means and resources of the occupier—what is reasonable for a railway company may be very unreasonable for a farmer.

7.4.3 Occupiers' Liability Act 1984

Following a Law Commission Report in 1976, which recommended legislation to clarify the law in respect of persons other than visitors, the Occupiers' Liability Act 1984 was enacted. For the purposes of the 1984 Act, the term 'visitor' means 'lawful visitor' and although the term 'trespasser' is not used in the legislation, persons 'other than visitors' are in fact trespassers under the Act. The Act sets out legislative standards for the duty of care to trespassers and other 'non-visitors' (the most important category other than trespassers is that of visitors to the countryside going on to private land lawfully as a consequence of footpaths on the land being 'opened up' under certain access to the countryside legislation).

7.4.4 Existence of the duty

According to s 1(3) of the 1984 Act, the duty is owed by the occupier when:

(a) he is aware of the danger or has reasonable grounds to believe that it exists;

(b) he knows or has reasonable grounds to believe that the [non-visitor] is in the vicinity of the danger concerned or that he may come into the vicinity of the danger . . . and;

(c) the risk is one against which, in all the circumstances of the case, he may reasonably be expected to offer the [non-visitor] some protection.

In *White v St Albans District City Council* (1990), the plaintiff, a trespasser, fell into a trench and was injured while taking a shortcut across the defendant's fenced-off property. The occupier had taken precautions to stop people getting onto his dangerous premises and it was argued by the claimant that this meant he had reason to believe that someone was likely to come into the vicinity of the danger. The Court of Appeal rejected this and held that the mere fact that a defendant had taken measures to stop entry onto land containing some danger does not necessarily mean that the 'reasonable grounds to believe' element in s 1(3)(b) has been satisfied.

THINKING POINT

As we have seen, the duty owed to lawful visitors is a general duty to take steps to see that the visitor is safe in using the premises. However, in respect of trespassers, the duty under s 1(3)(a) only relates to a specific danger of which the occupier is aware. If an occupier is aware of a danger arising from the electric wiring in his premises but a trespasser is injured by falling through a loose floorboard of which the occupier was unaware and had no reason to believe presented a risk, is the trespasser likely to establish a duty in respect of that specific danger?

7.4.5 **The contents of the duty**

Once the three requirements for the existence of the duty have been satisfied, the standard which requires 'such care as is reasonable in all the circumstances' is applied. This is the same as the common duty of care.

STATUTE

Occupiers' Liability Act 1984, s 1(4)

the duty is to take such care as is reasonable in all the circumstances of the case to see that the non-visitor does not suffer injury on the premises by reason of the danger concerned.

7.4.6 *Volenti non fit injuria* **under the 1984 Act**

The courts are required to consider the defence of *volenti* at the same time as they consider the three factors outlined above to establish the existence of a duty under the Act. If the trespasser willingly accepts the risk, then no duty of care on the occupier will arise.

STATUTE

Occupiers' Liability Act 1984, s 1(6)

no duty is owed . . . to any person in respect of risks willingly accepted as his by that person.

In *Ratcliffe v McConnell* (1999), in the early hours of the morning having drunk about four pints, the plaintiff, a 19-year-old student, agreed to go swimming with two friends. They climbed over the gate of a college open-air swimming pool. Although conscious of the word 'Warning', he got undressed and took a running dive into the pool either at the point where the shallow end started or at the slope from the deep to the shallow end. He hit the top of his head on the bottom, suffering tetraplegic injuries. The Court of Appeal held that the occupiers owed no duty under s 1 of the Occupiers' Liability Act 1984. Knowing that the pool was closed for the winter, that it was dangerous to dive into water of unknown depth, and that the water level of the pool was low, the plaintiff ought to have known it was dangerous to dive into shallow water and he had therefore willingly accepted the risk as his within the meaning of s 1(6).

7.4.7 Liability for trespassers: 'self-inflicted harm'

 CASE CLOSE-UP

Tomlinson v Congleton BC (2003)

In *Tomlinson v Congleton BC*, a large lake in which swimming was dangerous was located in a park owned by the Council. Despite prominently displayed notices, oral warnings, and the safety leaflets issued by its employees, the Council was aware that its 'no swimming policy' was habitually being flaunted by members of the public. On a hot day the 18-year-old claimant went to the park with some friends and, ignoring the warning signs, he dived into the lake from a standing position. The stretch of water into which he dived was shallow and as a result he suffered appalling personal injuries. The claimant accepted that on entering the water he ceased to be a visitor and became a trespasser but he claimed damages from the Council for its breach of duty to persons other than visitors because of its failure to take reasonable care to prevent him from the known danger of swimming in the lake. The Court of Appeal found the Council liable and held that taking account of the attraction of the lake to swimmers, the frequency of exposure to danger, and the relatively inexpensive and simple deterrents available to reduce the risk of persons entering the lake, the Council had failed to discharge its duty under s 1(3)(c) of the 1984 Act. The Court of Appeal did not interfere with the judge's assessment of two-thirds contributory negligence on the part of the claimant. The House of Lords allowed the Council's appeal and held that the claimant's injury had not been caused by the state of the premises or from anything done or omitted to be done on them. According to Lord Hoffmann:

> It is relevant at a number of points in the analysis of the duties under the 1957 and 1984 Acts. Mr Tomlinson was a person of full capacity who voluntarily and without any pressure or inducement engaged in an activity which had inherent risk. The risk was that he might not execute his dive properly and so sustain injury. Likewise, a person who goes mountaineering incurs the risk that he might stumble or misjudge where to put his weight. In neither case can the risk be attributed to the state of the premises. Otherwise any premises can be said to be dangerous to someone who chooses to use them for some dangerous activity. In the present case, Mr Tomlinson knew the lake well and even if he had not, the judge's finding was that it contained no dangers which one would not have expected. So the only risk arose out of what he chose to do and not out of the state of the premises.

The risk of striking the bottom of the lake by diving into shallow water was perfectly obvious and it was his own misjudgement which had caused his injury. Lord Hoffmann further said:

> The fact that such people take no notice of warnings cannot create a duty to take other steps to protect them. I find it difficult to express with appropriate moderation my disagreement with the proposition . . . that it is 'only where the risk is so obvious that the occupier

can safely assume that nobody will take it that there will be no liability'. A duty to protect against obvious risks or self-inflicted harm exists only in cases in which there is no genuine and informed choice, as in the case of employees, or some lack of capacity, such as the inability of children to recognise danger (*British Railways Board v Herrington* [1972] A.C. 877) or the despair of prisoners which may lead them to inflict injuries on themselves (*Reeves v Commissioner of Police* [2000] 1 AC 360).

It can be seen from these cases that for the purposes of the 1984 Act, premises will not be unsafe simply because there is an obvious risk, such as drowning or, in the next case, falling from a height. In *Keown v Coventry Healthcare NHS Trust* (2006), the Court of Appeal allowed an appeal by the defendants against a first-instance decision of liability for a fire escape at the Trust hospital's premises, which could be climbed from the outside, on the ground that it constituted an inducement to children habitually playing in the grounds of the hospital. When the claimant was 11 years old he had been climbing the underside of the fire escape when he fell to the ground and was injured. Acknowledging that premises which were not dangerous from the point of view of an adult could be dangerous for a child, the court said that it would not be right to ignore a child's choice to indulge in a dangerous activity in every case merely because he was a child. The trial judge had found that the claimant had not only appreciated that there was a risk of falling but also that what he was doing was dangerous and that he should not have been climbing the fire escape. In these circumstances the Court of Appeal held that it could not be said that the claimant did not recognize the danger; the risk arose not out of the state of the premises, which were as one would expect them to be, but out of what he chose to do.

The case of *Mann v Northern Electric Distribution Ltd* (2010) is a further decision limiting the imposition of liability on occupiers where claimants have acted carelessly. Here a trespasser aged 15 suffered severe injuries when he climbed onto a transformer in an electricity substation. In considering whether the unauthorized access was reasonably foreseeable and whether the security precautions taken by the occupier were sufficient to keep the reasonable trespasser out, the Court of Appeal found that the occupier had done what was reasonably practicable to prevent unauthorized access and had therefore discharged its duty.

 THINKING POINT

To what extent do you think the decisions in *Tomlinson v Congleton BC*, *Keown v Coventry Healthcare NHS Trust*, *Bourne Leisure Ltd v Marsden*, and *Mann v Northern Electric* represent a reaction by the courts to what may be perceived as a 'compensation culture' as evidenced by the Compensation Act 2006? Do you agree with their Lordships in *Tomlinson* that a culture of blame and compensation is an interference with the liberty of citizens to enjoy the landscape and countryside?

7.4.8 **Warnings: 1984 Act**

Under the 1957 Act a warning will not absolve the occupier of liability unless, in all the circumstances of the case, the warning was enough to enable the visitor to be reasonably safe.

However, under the 1984 Act a warning will be more effective against a trespasser because the occupier is only required to take such care as is reasonable in all the circumstances to see that the trespasser does not suffer injury on the premises by reason of the danger concerned. Tables 7.3 and 7.4 compare the two Acts.

7.5 Comparing the Acts

Table 7.3 Similarities

1957 Act	1984 Act
Section 1(1) of the 1957 Act is about: 'the duty which an occupier owes to his visitors in respect of dangers due to the state of the premises or to things done or omitted to be done on them'.	Section 1(1) of the 1984 Act is about: 'whether any duty is owed by [an] occupier to [trespassers] in respect of any risk of their suffering injury on the premises by reason of any danger due to the state of the premises or to things done or omitted to be done on them; and if so, what that duty is'.
Section 2(2) of the 1957 Act, the duty is: 'to take such care as in all the circumstances . . . is reasonable to see that the visitor will be reasonably safe in using the premises'.	Section 1(4) of the 1984 Act, the duty is: 'to take such care as is reasonable in all the circumstances . . . to see that he does not suffer injury on the premises by reason of the danger concerned'.
Section 2(5) of the 1957 Act: 'the duty of care does not impose on an occupier any obligation to a visitor in respect of risks willingly accepted as his by the visitor'.	Section 1(6) of the 1984 Act: 'no duty is owed . . . to any person in respect of risks willingly accepted as his by that person'.

Table 7.4 Differences

1957 Act applies to visitors	1984 Act applies to trespassers
The 1957 Act regulates: 'the duty imposed by law in consequence of a person's occupation or control of premises'.	A duty is not automatically owed to a trespasser under s 1(3) of the 1984 Act: an occupier of premises owes a duty to [a trespasser] if— • he is aware of the danger or has reasonable grounds to believe that it exists; • he knows or has reasonable grounds to believe that [the trespasser] may come into the vicinity of the danger; and • the risk is one against which, in all the circumstances, he may reasonably be expected to offer some protection;

The 1957 Act covers personal injury and property damage (including the property of persons who are not themselves visitors) s (1)(3)(b). Liability for loss or damage cannot be excluded in the case of a visitor except 'in so far as it is fair and reasonable in the circumstances' s 2(2).

The duty under the 1984 Act is in respect of personal injury only. No duty is owed to a trespasser for property damage. Section 1(8) of the 1984 Act provides that there is no liability:

'in respect of any loss of or damage to property'.

Section 2(4)(a) of the 1957 Act provides:

'where damage is caused to a visitor by a danger of which he has been warned by the occupier, the warning is not to be treated without more as absolving the occupier from liability, unless in all the circumstances it was enough to enable the visitor to be reasonably safe'.

Section 1(5) of the 1984 Act provides:

'any duty may, in an appropriate case, be discharged by taking such steps as are reasonable in all the circumstances to give warning of the danger concerned or to discourage persons from incurring the risk'.

 ## Summary

- A wide range of potential defendants including landlords, occupiers, and those involved in the construction process may be liable for harm resulting from defective premises.

- Liability may arise under contract, in common law negligence, or under: (1) the Occupiers' Liability Act 1957, governing the duty owed to lawful entrants; (2) the Occupiers' Liability Act 1984, governing the duty owed to trespassers; and (3) the Defective Premises Act 1972, governing a landlord's failure to fulfil obligations to maintain and repair premises which are let or sold.

- The Occupiers' Liability Act 1957 is silent on the meaning of 'occupier', 'premises', and 'lawful visitors' so these terms are interpreted by reference to the common law.

- The Occupiers' Liability Act 1957 covers personal injury and damage to property, but the 1984 Act imposes liability only for personal injury.

  Visit the online resources to listen to a podcast summarizing the topics covered in this chapter.

 ## The bigger picture

Spearman v Royal United Bath Hospitals NHS Foundation Trust (2018)

This is a tragic case which illustrates the real-life dilemmas raised by occupiers' liability. The claimant was a diabetic who suffered a hypoglycaemic attack and was taken to the hospital. He was left briefly alone in a cubicle and, in a confused state of mind, he attempted to flee the hospital. He passed through various unlocked doors, into an internal fire escape where he climbed five flights to the roof and then jumped or fell to the courtyard below, sustaining serious injuries. It was held that the hospital was liable, both in statute and in common law negligence.

You may wish to read this first-instance decision in which the court was confronted by a number of occupiers' liability issues, including: was the claimant covered by the Occupiers' Liability Act 1957, what reasonable precautions should have been taken by the defendants to fulfil their duty of care, and to what extent was the claimant's mental state to be taken into account?

? Questions

Knowledge-testing questions

1. What is the common duty of care owed to lawful entrants under the Occupiers' Liability Act 1957?

2. For which particular type of visitors does the Occupiers' Liability Act 1957 vary the degree of care expected of the occupier?

3. Outline the circumstances under which an occupier may owe a duty of care to a trespasser.

4. Is damage to property recoverable under the Occupiers' Liability Act 1984?

Problem and essay questions

1. Explain the factors taken into account by the courts to determine if an occupier of premises has breached the common duty of care owed to a lawful entrant.

2. In respect of the following incidents consider the principal issues of law which will arise under the Occupiers' Liability Acts of 1957 and 1984 if the injured parties attempt to recover their losses.

   (a) Skylon Hotel commenced a major refurbishment of the hotel and put up a large notice at the entrance warning guests to take care on the premises. Ria was checking her email on the guest computer in the hotel lobby when Daniel, her 2-year-old son, strayed away. Daniel was discovered soon afterwards lying badly injured at the bottom of the hotel swimming pool, which had been emptied for maintenance.

   (b) Ronan, the electrician, forgot to check that the main power supply was switched off before he started work on replacing the electric cables. As Ronan removed the first electric cable, he suffered a severe electric shock because the cable had perforated.

   (c) James, a freelance gardener working at the hotel, began to feel unwell. He decided to have a sleep in one of the Skylon's unoccupied rooms, so he waited until the receptionist was busy checking in new guests to sneak upstairs into one of the bedrooms. The vibration of the drills on the construction work caused the ceiling in the room to collapse and cause James a broken arm.

   (d) Kathryn, a salesperson, misread her Satnav and mistakenly drove her car into the Skylon car park. She ignored the large 'No Parking' sign around the outside construction area as she stopped to make a phone call. As Kathryn was making the call a piece of negligently erected scaffolding fell onto her car and smashed the windscreen.

   🔵 Visit the online resources for guidance on answering these questions.

Further reading

Amirthalingam, K, 'Occupiers' Liability in England: Time for Some Housecleaning?' (2017) PN 46

Buckley, RA, 'The Occupiers' Liability Act 1984: Has *Herrington* Survived?' (1984) 48 Conveyancer 413

Editorial comment, 'Holiday Park Not to Blame for Toddler's Death as "Accidents May Happen"' (2009) 153(28) SJ 5

Jones, MA, 'The Occupiers' Liability Act 1984: The Wheels of Law Reform Turn Slowly' (1984) 47 MLR 713

Norris, W and Q Fraser, 'Occupiers' Liability: Issues Arising in Recent Case Law' (2015) 2 JPIL 71

Patten, K, '*"Rule of Thumb"* Guidance about the Role of Foreseeability in the Determination of Breach of Duty of Care' (2014) 164 NLJ 7590

Stevens-Hoare, M and R Higgins, 'Roam Free' (2004) 154 NLJ 1846

8 Employers' liability and non-delegable duties

LEARNING OBJECTIVES

By the end of this chapter you should be able to:

- identify circumstances where a non-delegable duty will be imposed because it is 'fair, just and reasonable' to do so;

- demonstrate an understanding of the distinction between an employer's liability for harm caused *by* his employees (vicarious liability) and liability for harm caused *to* his employees (personal liability);

- explain the non-delegable nature of the employer's duty; and

- evaluate the developments in respect of an employer's liability for occupational stress.

Introduction

When looking at employers' liability to their employees it is important to note that a duty may arise under the law of contract; employment contracts contain an implied term that an employer will take all reasonable care to ensure the health and safety of his employees. An employer may be vicariously liable for an injury caused to his employee due to the tort of another employee, without the claimant having to show that the employer was in any way at fault. In addition to vicarious liability, the employer is also under a *personal non-delegable* duty of care to take steps to ensure the safety of his employees in the workplace. As with vicarious liability, an employer is not normally liable for the torts of an independent contractor, but the non-delegable duty is to *ensure that care is taken*. Therefore, if the independent contractor is acting under the explicit instructions of the employer or if the employer is aware of the tort of the independent contractor, the duty may arise.

Alongside the common law provisions, a number of statutes such as the Health and Safety at Work etc Act 1974 and the Employers' Liability (Defective Equipment) Act

1969 were introduced to protect employees and, in certain circumstances, it used to be the case that breach of these statutory duties could give rise to a claim in tort. Where an employee can establish a breach of a statutory duty the burden of proof is shifted to the employer and the employee does not have to prove negligence: it is up to the employer to prove that he was not negligent. However, changes introduced by the Enterprise and Regulatory Reform Act 2013 mean that in future claimants will need to show the fault requirement in common law negligence.

Furthermore, various regulations arising from the EU Framework Directive on Health and Safety (89/391/EEC) set out standards of behaviour for both employers and employees which aim to improve safety and working conditions in the workplace across the European member states. These safety regulations require all employers to make suitable and sufficient assessment of risks in the workplace, provide training in the safe use of equipment, and take other safety measures. Employers must comply with the regulations and any breach gives rise to liability in what are emerging as 'Eurotorts'. We have seen that injured employees are more likely to receive compensation than victims of accidents outside the workplace because the Employers' Liability (Compulsory Insurance) Act 1969 makes it compulsory for employers to insure against workplace accidents and those injured at work may also be able to claim social security benefits.

▶ CROSS REFERENCE
See Chapter 9 on vicarious liability.

8.1 When does a common law non-delegable duty arise?

Common law non-delegable duties are an exception to the general rule that a defendant is not liable for the negligence of an independent contractor. For example, it is established that a hospital is under a direct duty of care to those admitted as patients for the negligent acts of a member of the hospital staff. As we have seen above, a non-delegable duty owed by an employer to an employee is based on the existence of a contract of employment. A non-delegable duty also arises where the defendant is engaged in an extra-hazardous activity. For example, in *Honeywill & Stein Ltd v Larkin Bros Ltd* (1934) an independent contractor engaged to take photographs in a cinema (which, at the time, involved igniting magnesium powder) negligently set the curtains on fire. The Court of Appeal held that where the task is inherently dangerous the duty on an employer is so onerous that it cannot be delegated to anyone else. A further exception to the general rule against liability for the negligence of an independent contractor is where the work carried out is on or adjoining the highway. In *Tarry v Ashton* (1876) 1 QBD 314 the occupier of a public house adjoining the highway was liable when a heavy lamp attached to the building injured a passer-by. The occupier argued that he had employed an independent contractor to keep the lamp in good repair, but it was held that the duty to maintain premises so close to the highway could not be delegated.

Q | CASE CLOSE-UP

Woodland v Essex CC (2013)

We have seen that non-delegable duties of care are inconsistent with the fault-based principles in negligence, but in this case, the Supreme Court ruled that in exceptional cases where it is fair, just, and reasonable to protect those who are inherently vulnerable such duties would be imposed. The claimant here was a pupil at a school for which Essex County Council (education authority) was responsible. During a swimming lesson, which was part of the school curriculum, she suffered a severe brain injury. The lesson did not occur on school premises, but at a pool run by another local authority. The lesson was organized and provided by a swimming teacher and a lifeguard, both of whom were employed by an independent contractor. The claimant appealed against the finding of the trial judge and the Court of Appeal that the education authority could not be said to have owed her a 'non-delegable duty of care'.

The Supreme Court took the opportunity to review the law on what have been called 'non-delegable duties of care', with Lord Sumption observing that liability for any breach on the part of the education authority was based on personal duty, not vicarious liability. He observed that the law of negligence is generally fault-based and a defendant is personally liable only for his own negligent acts or omissions. The law does not ordinarily impose personal (as opposed to vicarious) liability for what others do or fail to do. He said:

> In principle, liability in tort depends on proof of a personal breach of duty. To that principle, there is at common law only one true exception, namely vicarious liability. Where a defendant is vicariously liable for the tort of another, he commits no tort himself and may not even owe the relevant duty, but is held liable as a matter of public policy for the tort of the other . . .. The boundaries of vicarious liability have been expanded by recent decisions of the courts to embrace tortfeasors who are not employees of the defendant, but stand in a relationship which is sufficiently analogous to employment: *Various Claimants v Catholic Child Welfare Society* [2013] 2 AC 1. But it has never extended to the negligence of those who are truly independent contractors, such as Mrs Stopford appears to have been in this case.

> The issue on this appeal is, however, nothing to do with vicarious liability, except in the sense that it only arises because there is none. On the footing that the local authority was not vicariously liable for the negligence of Mrs Stopford, Ms Burlinson or Ms Maxwell, the question is what was the scope of the authority's duty to pupils in its care. Was it a duty to take reasonable care in the performance of the functions entrusted to it, so far as it performed those functions itself, through its own employees? Or was it a duty to procure that reasonable care was taken in their performance by whomever it might get to perform them? On either view, any liability of the education authority for breach of it is personal, not vicarious.

In allowing the claimant's appeal, the Supreme Court held that the education authority had assumed responsibility to her for the swimming lesson provided during the school day and it was therefore fair, just, and reasonable to hold the local authority liable. When considering whether a school owes a duty to ensure that care is taken (a non-delegable duty), Lord Sumption acknowledged that such liability would place an additional burden on providers of public services who choose to outsource certain functions.

However, he added that a non-delegable duty would be imposed only where it is 'fair, just and reasonable' to do so. If the highway and hazard cases are put to one side, a non-delegable duty of care will arise in cases where:

1. The claimant is a patient or a child, or is especially vulnerable or dependent on the protection of the defendant. Other examples are likely to be prisoners and residents in care homes.

2. There is a relationship between the claimant and the defendant: (i) which places the claimant in the actual care of the defendant; and (ii) the defendant assumes a positive duty to protect the claimant from harm. Such relationships involve an element of control over the claimant, which varies in intensity from one situation to another, but is clearly very substantial in the case of schoolchildren.

3. The claimant has no control over how the defendant chooses to perform those obligations—that is, whether personally or through employees or through third parties.

4. The defendant has delegated to a third party an integral part of the positive duty assumed towards the claimant.

5. The third party has been negligent in performing the very function assumed by the defendant and delegated to him.

> Lord Sumption also noted that the use of the term 'non-delegable' is misleading: a common law duty of care can never be delegated. It is either discharged or it is breached. However, the term is in common usage and is used to mean a duty which cannot be discharged by entrusting its performance to an apparently competent independent contractor. We have seen above that a hospital is under a direct duty of care to those admitted as patients for the negligent acts of hospital staff. In *Woodland* the court said there can be no principled distinction between the position of a hospital and a school; each of the factors which give rise to the duty in the case of a hospital applies to a school. Arguably the case is stronger in the case of a school because only children attend school, whereas adults are admitted to hospital.

In *Armes v Nottinghamshire County Council* (2017) the claimant was abused physically and sexually by foster parents with whom she was placed while in the care of the defendant local authority. The Supreme Court was asked to consider whether the criteria set out by Lord Sumption in *Woodland* placed the local authority under a non-delegable duty for the safety of children while they are in the care and control of foster parents. The Court defined non-delegable duties in the following way:

> The expression 'non-delegable duties of care' is commonly used to refer to duties not merely to take personal care in performing a given function but to ensure that care is taken. The expression thus refers to a higher standard of care than the ordinary duty of care. Duties involving this higher standard of care are described as non-delegable because they cannot be discharged merely by the exercise of reasonable care in the selection of a third party to whom the function in question is delegated.

The claimant's argument that the local authority was liable on the basis of a non-delegable duty was dismissed by the trial judge and unanimously rejected by the Court of Appeal. The Supreme Court also rejected this proposition and held that non-delegable duties in these circumstances are too broad and too demanding on local authorities. For example, local authorities need to decide whether the best interests of children in care are to allow them to stay with their families or friends. Placing them under a non-delegable duty would risk creating a conflict between the local authority's statutory duty to the children and their interests in avoiding claims in tort. The Court also pointed out that a decision to return a child in care to his or her family, would be a form of state insurance for the actions of the child's family members because a non-delegable duty would make the local authority strictly liable for the tortious acts of the child's own parents or relatives (and, indeed, their friends, relatives and babysitters, if the child were left with them).

According to Lord Reed:

> For all these reasons, I conclude that the proposition that a local authority is under a duty to ensure that reasonable care is taken for the safety of children in care, while they are in the care and control of foster parents, is too broad, and that the responsibility with which it fixes local authorities is too demanding. I therefore reach the same conclusion as the Court of Appeal on this aspect of the case, although for somewhat different reasons.

You should note that the claimant Armes also argued (successfully) that the local authority was vicariously liable for the acts of the foster parents (9.3.1.8).

8.2 Sources of an employer's liability

The common law duties and statutory provisions governing an employer's duty to protect his employees from workplace injury impose a heavy burden on employers. In the past, most of the cases taken by employees against their employers involved workplace accidents but knowledge of dangers associated with asbestos, repetitive strain injury, and, in particular, the effects of stress at work on the mental health of employees have led to an increase in litigation in these types of claim. One of the effects of this is that workplace accidents generate a very high proportion of tort claims and place injured employees in a stronger position to recover compensation than victims of other types of accident.

An injured employee seeking compensation may be able to rely on a number of causes of action: breach of the specific common law duty on employers' vicarious liability (for the negligence of a fellow employee); or breach of statutory duty (see 8.5). Although employers' liability arises from a variety of sources, the main focus of this chapter will be on the employer's liability at common law.

> **THINKING POINT**
>
> Should a person injured at work be in a more advantageous position under the tort system and receive more generous compensation than someone who suffers an identical injury outside the workplace? If so, why?

8.3 Historical background

Although employees are now considered to be in a privileged position in respect of claiming compensation for workplace injuries, this was not always the case. In fact, many of the rules on employers' liability were developed to mitigate the harshness of the common law as it developed during the time of industrialization in the early nineteenth century. At this time there was no employment protection legislation or trade unions to promote the interests of employees, and insurance for injuries in the workplace did not exist. Although the working conditions in many factories and mines were extremely hazardous and employees sometimes worked for twelve hours a day doing monotonous work at dangerous machinery, the courts were reluctant to impose liability on employers for workplace injury or to expose them to the cost of taking proper safety precautions. The legal approach was to place the responsibility on the employee to guard against the risk of injury in the workplace, as it was believed that an employer was not in any better position than his employees to ensure their safety.

8.3.1 The 'unholy trinity'

- the doctrine of 'common employment';
- the defence of contributory negligence; and
- the defence of *volenti non fit injuria*.

The three doctrines listed here, sometimes referred to as the 'unholy trinity', applied in the nineteenth century. The doctrines protected employers and prevented virtually any action by employees for workplace injury. The first of these doctrines, the doctrine of 'common employment', set down in *Priestly v Fowler* (1837), held that an employer would not be vicariously liable for harm inflicted on workers by fellow employees. This prevented an employee injured by a fellow employee from taking any action against the employer. Under this doctrine, an implied term in the contract of employment provided that an employee assumed the risk of negligence of a fellow employee in the same employment. In such circumstances, the employee was held to have known, or to ought to have known, the risks associated with his employment, including the risk of carelessness by other employees. An employer would only be held liable for negligence caused by a fellow employee if he had failed to ensure the competence of the negligent employee. The second of the 'trinity' was the defence of contributory negligence which, at the time, was a complete defence to a claim in negligence. The third doctrine, the defence of *volenti non fit injuria*, was available to an employer where the injured employee had undertaken or continued with the dangerous work in the knowledge of the potential risk of harm. Together, these doctrines provided employers with a very high level of protection.

8.3.2 Changing attitudes to employers' liability

The building of the railway system and the expansion of large factories with new machinery led to increased awareness of workplace injury and highlighted the harshness of the law towards injured employees. These factors, together with the availability of employers' insurance against workplace accidents led to a change in social attitudes. This was reflected in the courts and by the legislature, who began to take steps to enable those injured at work to receive compensation from employers.

In *Smith v Charles Baker & Sons* (1891), a case involving an employee injured by a stone which fell from an overhead crane as he was working on the construction of a railway, the House of Lords was given an opportunity to limit the scope of the *volenti* defence. The court rejected the employer's argument that voluntary acceptance of the risk could be inferred from the fact that, although he had knowledge of the danger, the employee had stayed at work. Parliament subsequently legislated for the abolition of the doctrine of common employment with the Law Reform (Personal Injuries) Act 1948, and the Law Reform (Contributory Negligence) Act 1945 provided that contributory negligence was no longer a complete defence and turned it into a partial defence by permitting the courts to apportion liability to the extent to which the plaintiff had failed to take care of his own safety.

❯ CROSS REFERENCE

See also the defence of *volenti* in Chapter 6.

Smith v Charles Baker & Sons is an illustration of how the judges began to develop techniques to mitigate the harshness of the common law by making it difficult for employers to establish the defence of *volenti*.

🔍 CASE CLOSE-UP

Wilsons and Clyde Coal v English (1938)

In this important case, the courts also developed the notion of a 'non-delegable' duty on employers. This personal (non-delegable) duty is to see that reasonable care is taken and the employer's obligation for the employee's safety is fulfilled by showing due care and skill. However, the duty is not fulfilled by delegation of that responsibility to other employees, even if they are selected with due care and skill. In *Wilsons*, the plaintiff miner was injured at the defendant's coal mine. The haulage equipment at the mine should have been stopped during travelling time but as he was travelling through the pit at the end of a day shift the plant was set in motion and the plaintiff was crushed. The defendant employers claimed that they had appointed a competent and qualified manager to control the technical management of the mine and in doing this they had discharged their duty of providing a reasonably safe system of working in the mine. The House of Lords rejected this claim and the employers were held liable, but not *vicariously* liable; the employers were liable on the ground that they could not avoid their *personal non-delegable* duty to provide a reasonably safe system of working by delegation to a competent employee. The employer's duty was stated to be 'the provision of a competent staff of men, adequate material and a proper system and effective supervision'.

The employers' non-delegable duty is commonly analysed in four elements:

(1) competent staff;

(2) adequate material;

(3) a proper system of working (including effective supervision); and

(4) a safe place of work.

The employer's duty is a general duty to take reasonable care for the physical safety of the employee; it does not extend to protecting the employee's economic welfare. In *Reid v Rush and Tompkins Group plc* (1989), it was held that an employer had no duty to arrange accident insurance for a person working abroad or to warn the employee being sent abroad of the need to take out such insurance. Nevertheless, we will see later that the scope of the employer's duty to provide a safe system of work has now been extended to safeguard an employee against psychiatric harm.

> **THINKING POINT**
> Why might the law be reluctant to extend employers' liability to the area of economic welfare of employees?

8.4 An employer's non-delegable duty

Before going on to examine each of the elements of an employer's duty, it is important to note that this duty cannot be delegated. Even when the employee is temporarily posted elsewhere to work with another employer the original employer is still under a duty to ensure the operation of a safe system of work. The non-delegable nature of the duty to provide a safe system of work can be illustrated with the case of *McDermid v Nash Dredging and Reclamation Co Ltd* (1987), which concerned an unsafe system of work on a tug. The plaintiff was an 18-year-old inexperienced deckhand employed by a company of the defendants, but the captain of the tug was employed by a third party, a different company owned by the defendants. As a result of the captain's negligence the tug's engines started unexpectedly and the plaintiff was pulled into the sea by the ropes and suffered serious leg injuries. The issue was whether McDermid's employer was liable for the captain's failure to operate a safe system when the captain was the employee of a third party. The plaintiff's employers appealed against a finding of liability and contended that the captain was not their employee. The House of Lords unanimously dismissed the appeal. According to Lord Brandon:

> My Lords, the Court of Appeal regarded the case as raising difficult questions of law on which clear authority was not easy to find. With great respect to the elaborate judgment of that court, I think that they have treated the case as more difficult than it really is. A statement of

the relevant principle of law can be divided into three parts. First, an employer owes to his employee a duty to exercise reasonable care to ensure that the system of work provided for him is a safe one. Secondly, the provision of a safe system of work has two aspects: (a) the devising of such a system and (b) the operation of it. Thirdly, the duty concerned has been described alternatively as either personal or non-delegable. The meaning of these expressions is not self-evident and needs explaining. The essential characteristic of the duty is that, if it is not performed, it is no defence for the employer to show that he delegated its performance to a person, whether his servant or not his servant, whom he reasonably believed to be competent to perform it. Despite such delegation the employer is liable for the non-performance of the duty.

8.4.1 **Defective equipment**

You may wish to note that in *Davie v New Merton Board Mills* (1959) (now overruled by statute), the House of Lords found the employer not liable when an employee suffered injury at work as he was using a defective tool provided by the employer. The plaintiff was using a metal tool provided by his employer which, because it had been manufactured at the incorrect temperature, was too hard to be safe to use. When the plaintiff struck his hammer against the tool a piece of metal flew into his left eye and caused blindness in that eye. Because the fault in the tool could not be detected with reasonable inspection and the employer had bought it from a reputable supplier, the employer was not held liable. The House of Lords ruled that the essence of the tort of negligence is a failure to take reasonable care: an employer was not taken to guarantee the safety of the equipment he provided, nor was he liable for injury caused by a defect that was undiscoverable. Viscount Simonds noted the comments of Finnemore J in an earlier case:

> Employers have to act as reasonable people, they have to take reasonable care; but if they buy their tools from well-known makers, such as the second defendants are, they are entitled to assume that the tools will be proper for the purposes for which both sides intended them to be used, and not require daily, weekly or monthly inspection to see if in fact, all is well.

The effect of this decision was to leave the injured employee without compensation where the manufacturer or supplier could not be found or was bankrupt. However, the effect of *Davie* was subsequently reversed by the Employers' Liability (Defective Equipment) Act 1969, s 1(1). The position now is that if an employee is injured in the course of his employment by a defect in equipment provided by his employer and he can prove that the defect was caused by the fault of some third party (usually the manufacturer), then the employer will be liable. The Act covers defective plant and equipment of every sort with which the employee is compelled to work and includes any plant, machinery, vehicle, aircraft, and clothing. *Coltman v Bibby Tankers* (1988) is a case which arose out of the sinking of *The Derbyshire* with the loss of all hands off the coast of Japan in 1980. It was claimed by the plaintiff that the ship was defectively constructed, and he argued that this constituted defects in equipment on the basis that the ship was 'equipment' within s 1 of the Employers' Liability (Defective Equipment) Act 1969. The court held that the meaning of the word 'equipment' was broadly defined and that for the purposes of the Act it can include ships or vessels.

8.4.2 Elements of the employer's duty

8.4.2.1 Competent staff

The employer owes a duty to employees to select competent employees, to give them proper supervision, and to ensure that they are properly trained in the use of equipment. Although the duty to select competent employees is of less importance since the abolition of the doctrine of common employment (because this means that the employer will be vicariously liable for the tort of one employee against another), this duty can be relevant. For example, it is unlikely that an employer will be vicariously liable where one employee is injured by an unforeseeable single attack or violent horseplay of another.

Nevertheless, in *Hudson v Ridge Manufacturing Co Ltd* (1957), where an employee was injured by a known practical joker who had a reputation for persistently engaging in practical jokes, the employer was liable for breach of his personal duty because he should have known about and taken steps to deal with the jester.

8.4.2.2 Adequate material

As we have seen earlier, the position of employees under the common law has been improved by the Employers' Liability (Defective Equipment) Act 1969 and, in order to give effect to the spirit of the Act, the definition of equipment is widely interpreted and was extended to include a ship upon which the employee served. In *Knowles v Liverpool City Council* (1992), where a council workman was injured by a paving stone that he was laying, the House of Lords extended the definition of equipment beyond tools used by the employee to include any materials upon which he is working.

▶ CROSS REFERENCE

For more on causation, see Chapter 4.

This duty includes not only the provision of adequate plant and equipment but also its inspection, maintenance, and proper safety protection, including instruction in the use of the equipment. However, you should note that where safety equipment has not been provided, an employer may escape liability if he can show that even if the equipment had been provided the employee would not have used it and would therefore have suffered the injury anyway. In effect, the employer would argue that the case failed on the issue of causation, as happened in the following case.

🔍 CASE CLOSE-UP

McWilliams v Sir William Arrol & Co Ltd (1962)

In this case a steel erector, who was not wearing a safety harness, fell to his death at work. Although his employers had failed (in breach of statutory duty) to provide safety harnesses, the House of Lords did not find them liable. The burden of proving that the employer's breach of duty caused the damage is on the employee and, in this case, the defendant employers were able to show that because the deceased employee had rarely, if ever, used the safety harness in the past, even if it had been provided, on this occasion it was reasonable to infer that he would not have worn it.

THINKING POINT

The evidence in the above case was strong, but did the House of Lords favour the employer by concluding that, even if the safety belt had been provided on that occasion the employee would not have worn it? Is there a possibility that, if it had been provided, the employee might have used the belt on this occasion? Do people sometimes change their minds? Should the claim have failed?

8.4.2.3 A proper system of working (including effective supervision)

An employer is under a duty to ensure a reasonably safe system of working and to give employees general safety instructions about their job. The duty will normally apply in a system of working which is regular or routine and covers: the physical layout of the job; the sequence in which the work is to be carried out; the provision, in appropriate cases, of warnings and notices; and the issue of special instructions. The question as to the nature and extent of supervision required arose in *Jebson v Ministry of Defence* (2000), where the claimant, one of a group of soldiers returning in a drunken state from a night out, fell when he tried to climb onto the roof of an army truck. Although there is no duty on the armed forces to provide a safe system of working in battle conditions, this immunity does not apply in peacetime. At first instance the defendant was found to be in breach of a duty to supervise the soldiers, but the damage was held to be too remote because it was not reasonably foreseeable that the soldier would have tried to climb onto the roof. The Court of Appeal allowed the claimant's appeal and held that under the circumstances rowdy behaviour of soldiers in high spirits was foreseeable and the employer should have taken steps, such as providing supervision, to guard against the risk.

In *Speed v Thomas Swift and Co Ltd* (1943), the employers were liable for the employee's injury because in the circumstances they had not laid out a safe system of work when he was loading a ship from a barge. The loading was normally carried out while the ship's rails were left in position, but sections of the rail had been damaged and the resulting circumstances had, on the occasion in question, made it unsafe to load the ship. Employers must warn employees of any inherent dangers in the work which they are required to do and in these circumstances it is no defence for an employer to argue that the employee himself should take precautions.

Safe systems of work were considered by the Supreme Court in *Baker v Quantum Clothing Group* (2011), where the claimant alleged her noise-induced hearing loss was a result of the employers' failure under common law negligence and/or in breach of the Factories Act 1961 to provide ear protectors. As we have seen, at common law the burden remains on the claimant to prove that the employer failed to take reasonable care to avoid the foreseeable risks of harm. However, under the 1961 Act the burden passes to the employer to prove it was not reasonably practicable to eliminate the risk of harm. Applying this test to the facts it was found that the employers had committed no breach of common law or statutory duty; it was also ruled that the Act did not impose a more stringent liability than at common law.

Employers are frequently aware that employees can be careless about taking safety precautions

The employer is not only responsible for devising a safe system of working, he is also responsible for ensuring that the system is implemented. This means that even if the system is safe the employer remains liable where it is not properly implemented. We have seen above in *McDermid v Nash Dredging* that although a safe system had been devised, the employer was liable for the captain's failure to implement the system. In deciding whether or not the duty has been breached the courts expect employers to be aware that employees can be careless about taking safety precautions and that a practice of ignoring an obvious workplace danger can evolve. The decision in *General Cleaning Contractors v Christmas* (1953) illustrates the fact that the law places the responsibility to lay down a reasonably safe system of working firmly on the employer. In this case the House of Lords took the view that if a practice of ignoring an obvious danger has been adopted by the employees, it is not reasonable to expect an individual employee to take the initiative in devising and using safety precautions. The plaintiff employee, a window cleaner, was sent to clean the windows of a club. As he was cleaning a first-floor window by standing on the windowsill and supporting himself by holding the sash with one hand, the window came down on his fingers and caused him to fall to the ground. He had been instructed by his employers in the sill method of cleaning which, if the employee was careless, carried an obvious risk of danger. Although the system had been in operation for twenty years the employers were found to have failed in their obligation to devise a reasonably safe system of work providing for an obvious danger. They did not give instructions to ensure that the windows should be tested before cleaning but left it to the initiative of individual workmen to take precautions against a common danger. According to Lord Oaksey:

> In my opinion, it is the duty of an employer to give such general safety instructions as a reasonably careful employer who has considered the problem presented by the work would give to his workmen. It is, I think, well known to employers, and there is evidence in this case that it was well known to the appellants, that their workpeople are very frequently, if not habitually, careless about the risks which their work may involve. It is, in my opinion, for that very reason that the common law demands that employers should take reasonable care to lay down a reasonably safe system of work. Employers are not exempted from this duty by the fact that their men are experienced and might, if they were in the position of an employer, be able to lay down a reasonably safe system of work themselves. Workmen are not in the position of employers. Their duties are not performed in the calm atmosphere of a board room with the advice of experts. They have to make their decisions on narrow window sills and other places of danger and in circumstances in which the dangers are obscured by repetition. The risk that sashes may unexpectedly close, as the sashes in this case appear to have done, may not happen very often, but when it does, if the workman is steadying himself by a handhold, his fall is almost certain. If the possibility is faced the risk is obvious. If both sashes are closed there is no longer the handhold by which the workman steadies himself. If either sash is kept open the handhold is available and, on the evidence in this case, is, in my opinion, reasonably safe. But the problem is one for the employer to solve and should not, in my opinion, be left to the workman. It can be solved by general orders and the provision of appropriate appliances . . . .. The appellants, knowing the risk, did nothing and have appealed to your Lordships' House with the avowed object of having this system declared to be reasonably safe. In my opinion, the system as carried on by the appellants is not reasonably safe and the appellants did not take reasonable care to ensure that it was.

8.4.2.4 **A safe place of work**

CROSS REFERENCE

See Chapter 7.

The employer must provide a safe place of work, but this duty is discharged if the employer takes reasonable steps to see that the premises are safe. In *Latimer v AEC Ltd* (1953), after a heavy rainfall the defendants' large factory was flooded and the water mixed with an oily liquid which usually collected in channels in the floor. When the mixture drained away it left the floor very slippery and, although there was insufficient sawdust to cover the entire floor, it was spread over most of the surface. A workman broke his ankle when he slipped on the untreated part of the floor. The trial judge found the defendants liable on the ground that they had not closed down the factory. However, allowing the appeal, the House of Lords held the defendants were not liable as they had acted as a reasonable employer would have acted: the danger was not such as to impose on the employer an obligation to close down the factory.

The question in *Mitchell v Co-operatives Ltd* (2012) concerned the extent of an employer's duty to provide a safe place of work for assistants working in a shop located in an area at high risk of crime and vulnerable to robberies. In an attempt to deter the robbers the employer installed various security measures, including CCTV. Nevertheless, the robberies continued and the claimants suffered post-traumatic stress and developed an anxiety state as a result of their experiences. The claimants argued that their employer should have done more to protect them by providing a full-time security guard and further surveillance equipment in the shop.

The Court of Appeal held that the employer was not required to provide a full-time guard to deter the robberies, nor was he expected to prevent the robberies taking place. When considering what was reasonable in the circumstances, Ward LJ observed:

> [There is e]vidence that the business at this particular shop was running at a loss of about £60,000 per annum and that the provision of full-time guarding would have cost £30,000 per annum. A proper approach requires a balance to be struck against the probable effectiveness of the precaution that can be taken and the expense that it involves.

 THINKING POINT

One of the main factors in the decision in *Latimer v AEC Ltd* was that the potential risk of injury was balanced against the cost to the employer of closing the entire factory for the shift in question. What does this decision highlight about the employer's duty to provide a safe place of work where there is a temporary risk of injury in the workplace?

8.4.3 **Occupational stress: a developing area of employers' liability**

CROSS REFERENCE

See also Chapter 5 on duty of care problem areas.

As we have seen, the common law in respect of employers' liability has evolved through cases involving accidents at work; however, advances in medical and scientific knowledge about the effects of asbestos, repetitive strain injury, and occupational stress have expanded to safeguard employees against these types of harm. Because of this, employers' liability is a developing area, particularly in the context of occupational stress.

As well as protecting an employee against physical injury in the workplace, an employer who knows or should know that an employee is susceptible to psychiatric injury as a result of stress at work is under a duty to take extra care to avoid such harm. In *Walker v Northumberland County Council* (1995) an area social services officer, having suffered two mental breakdowns, was dismissed on grounds of ill health. The plaintiff was off work for three months following the first nervous breakdown caused by the stress of his job. When he recovered from this breakdown and returned to work his employer promised to provide him with specific help and assistance to relieve the pressures of his job. As a consequence of the employer's failure to provide the extra help the plaintiff suffered a second nervous breakdown and was unable to return to work. He claimed damages from his employer on the ground that his ill health was caused by the extreme stress of his working conditions. It was held that the first nervous breakdown was unforeseeable but the employer was found to be in breach of its duty because, when the plaintiff returned to work after this nervous breakdown, the risk to his mental health was reasonably foreseeable; in these circumstances the standard of care required of the employer was to take extra steps to protect the plaintiff against the risk of psychiatric harm.

Q CASE CLOSE-UP

Hatton v Sutherland (2002)

Since the decision in *Walker* the increase in litigation involving cases of stress at work has led the Court of Appeal to set out guidelines to determine the nature of the duty imposed on employers in cases of excessive stress in the workplace. The leading case is *Hatton v Sutherland* (2002), which involved four conjoined appeals (three of which involved public-sector employers) against judgments holding them liable for psychiatric injury as the result of stress at work. Three of the four appeals were allowed, and the Court of Appeal laid down a number of general guidelines and stressed that the ordinary principles of employers' liability applied. Although there are no special control mechanisms (such as outlined in *Alcock* in Chapter 5) applying to claims for psychiatric injury arising from the stress of the work, an employer will only be liable if he had reason to believe that the damaging stress was foreseeable and failed to take reasonable steps to prevent it. The court in *Hatton* ruled that there are no intrinsically stressful occupations and that unless he knows of some particular problem or vulnerability, an employer is usually entitled to assume that an employee can withstand the normal pressures of a job. Taking account of any concerns that the employee himself has raised, foreseeability of the injury depends on what the employer knows (or reasonably ought to know) about the individual employee. The indications must be plain enough for any reasonable employer to realize that he should take some steps to assist the employee and in cases where an employee is known to be vulnerable, he will not be at fault for failing to inform the employer. Once the risk of harm from stresses in the workplace is foreseeable the question then arises as to what is reasonable to expect the employer to do. According to Hale LJ:

> His duty is to take reasonable care. What is reasonable depends, as we all know, upon the foreseeability of harm, the magnitude of the risk of that harm occurring, the gravity of the harm which may take place, the cost and practicability of preventing it, and the justifications for running the risk.

8.4.3.1 **When will an employer be liable for psychiatric illness caused by stress at work?**

Barber v Somerset (2004)

One of the unsuccessful claimants in *Hatton* appealed against the Court of Appeal decision and in *Barber v Somerset* this appeal was allowed by the House of Lords. The case involved a conscientious schoolteacher who, following a restructuring of staffing at the school where he was employed, was told that in order to maintain his salary level he would have to take on further responsibilities. For a six-month period Barber worked very long hours (between sixty and seventy hours a week), which included evenings and weekends. At this point he spoke about his work overload with one of the senior management team and made enquiries about taking early retirement. He was subsequently on certified sickness absence for three weeks suffering from stress and depression and on his return to work he told his managers that he was not coping with his workload. No steps were taken to assist him and as a consequence of the pressure he was under, Barber became seriously ill and had to stop working. He sued his employers, the Somerset County Council, for damages for personal injuries caused by their negligence. The trial judge found the Council liable for breach of its duty to take reasonable care to avoid injuring Barber's health and awarded him substantial damages. The Court of Appeal, however, allowed an appeal by the Council and held that the evidence before the trial judge did not sustain a finding that the school authorities ought to have foreseen that if Barber continued with his existing workload he was liable to develop a psychiatric illness. Barber then took his case to the House of Lords, where their Lordships allowed his appeal and ruled that the overall test of an employer's duty of care was that of the conduct of the reasonable and prudent employer, taking positive thought for the safety of his employees in the light of what he knew or ought to have known. The defendant Council, through the school senior management team, had known of the claimant's problems by June or July 1996, when he spoke about them to members of the team. They ought then to have taken the initiative in inquiring about the claimant's problems and attempting to ease them, and their failure to do so had been a continuing breach of the authority's duty towards the claimant. In terms of the steps the employer should take to prevent the harm, the House of Lords did not dissent from the following statement by Hale LJ in *Hatton v Sutherland*:

> It is essential, therefore, once the risk of harm to health from stresses in the workplace is foreseeable, to consider whether and in what respect the employer has broken that duty. There may be a temptation, having concluded that some harm was foreseeable and that harm of that kind has taken place, to go on to conclude that the employer was in breach of his duty of care in failing to prevent that harm (and that that breach of duty caused the harm). But in every case it is necessary to consider what the employer not only could but should have done. We are not here concerned with such comparatively simple things as gloves, goggles, earmuffs or non-slip flooring. Many steps might be suggested: giving the employee a sabbatical; transferring him to other work; redistributing the work; giving him some extra help for a while; arranging treatment or counselling; providing buddying or mentoring schemes to encourage confidence; and much more. But in all of these suggestions it will be necessary to consider how reasonable it is to expect the employer to do this, either in general or in particular: the size and scope of its operation will be relevant to this, as will its resources, whether in the public or private sector, and the other demands placed upon it. Among those other demands are the interests of other employees in the workplace. It may not be reasonable to expect the employer to rearrange the work for the sake of one employee in a way which prejudices the others. As

we have already said, an employer who tries to balance all these interests by offering confidential help to employees who fear that they may be suffering harmful levels of stress is unlikely to be found in breach of duty: except where he has been placing totally unreasonable demands upon an individual in circumstances where the risk of harm was clear.

The principles set down by the Court of Appeal in *Hatton* were reasserted in *Hartman v South Essex Mental Health and Community Care NHS Trust* (2005), where the employee's vulnerability to suffer from stress combined with information about a previous mental breakdown was provided in a confidential medical questionnaire submitted to the Occupational Health Department. Applying the *Hatton* principles, the Court of Appeal held that, under these circumstances, the employer could not be fixed with knowledge of the employee's vulnerability. It was not reasonably foreseeable to her employers that she would suffer psychiatric injury and, accordingly, they were not in breach of their duty to her.

We have seen earlier that in *Hatton* Hale LJ said that an employer who offers confidential help to employees who fear that they may be suffering harmful levels of stress is unlikely to be found in breach of duty. However, in *Daw v Intel Corporation (UK) Ltd* (2007) the Court of Appeal held that although the employer provided counselling services of which the employee decided not to avail herself, the defendant was nevertheless liable. In this case the woman was regarded as a highly efficient, conscientious, and loyal employee who had frequently complained to the defendants about her heavy workload and the conflicting pressures of her work. Notwithstanding the provision of counselling services, the employer breached its duty to her when it had become aware that the increase in her workload was having an adverse effect on her mental health, but had taken no steps to help her.

8.4.3.2 Psychiatric harm resulting from acts of fellow employees

In *Waters v Commissioner of Police of the Metropolis* (2000), the House of Lords held that where an employer knows or can foresee that an employee might suffer physical or psychiatric harm through the acts of *fellow employees* the employer owes a duty to protect its employees from such harm. In this case a female police officer made a complaint of sexual assault against a fellow police officer. Although the complaint was not pursued due to lack of evidence, after she made this complaint Waters was subjected to a campaign of victimization by other police officers and she suffered psychiatric injury as a result. Waters claimed in negligence against her employer on the ground that they carelessly failed to prevent the victimization happening. In allowing her appeal against the striking out of the claim, their Lordships ruled that she had an arguable case as it was reasonably foreseeable that following the nature of the complaint made by the officer she might suffer mistreatment. An employer owes a duty to take reasonable care to protect its employees from harm, including workplace bullying and psychiatric harm, during employment.

8.5 Breach of statutory duty

Up to this point we have been concerned with an employer's personal liability for common law negligence *to* its employees for harm suffered at work.

❱ THINKING POINT

An employer's vicarious liability for the torts committed by its employees in the course of employment is a separate topic. Vicarious liability in this context is the subject of Chapter 9.

In addition to this common law duty, employers are also subject to a large body of statutory regulation for the protection of employees. For example, it may be compulsory under statute for an employer of building workers to provide safety helmets or it may be illegal under statute to do something, such as to smoke while working with inflammable substances. However, the fact that conduct is illegal and puts an employer in breach of a statutory obligation subject to a criminal sanction (such as a fine) does not necessarily mean that the breach gives rise to civil liability in tort, even if someone is injured as a result.

Breach of statutory duty is a tort in its own right independent of any other form of tortious liability. The action for breach of statutory duty plays an important role in ensuring health and safety in the workplace so it most frequently arises in the employment context. It is not uncommon for an employee seeking compensation for a workplace injury to sue the employer both in negligence and for breach of statutory duty.

However, we saw in Chapter 7 that the Occupiers' Liability Acts 1957 and 1984 also impose statutory duties on occupiers of premises and the Consumer Protection Act 1987 imposes liability for products which cause harm to consumers, discussed in Chapter 10. These statutes create a specific form of tortious liability to provide a remedy for a breach of obligations under the Acts, but the action for breach of statutory duty is more problematic. An employer's liability for breach of statutory duty depends on whether the statute, on its proper construction, confers a right of civil action on the employee. This may be explicitly stated, but if not, the courts have to decide, as a matter of policy, whether Parliament implicitly intended to confer such a right. In determining whether a civil action for breach of statutory duty will arise, the starting point is to look to precedent or for a clearly stated parliamentary intention in the statute. In the absence of either, the following principles may assist, but in all cases the key question is to determine the fundamental purpose the legislation was intended to achieve.

8.5.1 **Did Parliament intend to create a civil action?**

The claimant must prove that Parliament intended to create a right to sue under the Act in question, but there is much uncertainty about when the courts will decide that a breach of a statutory duty gives rise to civil liability. The courts refer to the particular wording of the statute to determine the intention of Parliament. In *Lonrho Ltd v Shell Petroleum Co Ltd* (1982) the plaintiffs had complied with an oil embargo imposed by statute and subsequently sought compensation for the financial losses they suffered as the result of this compliance. The House of Lords rejected the claim on the ground that the purpose of the embargo was to use economic pressure to bring down the regime then in power and not to protect the interests of individual companies. The embargo did not give rise to civil liability.

If the statute is silent on the matter, indicators of what Parliament intended are found by looking at whether the statute was designed to protect a limited class of persons. If it was, the next question is whether it intended to confer upon members of that class a right to sue for breach. Evidence of an alternative method of enforcement is also relevant. If the Act contains another provision for enforcing the duty, this indicates that the intention of Parliament is for the duty to be enforced by those means alone, and not by a civil law action. For example, the significant factor in *Stovin v Wise* (discussed in Chapter 2) was that Parliament had chosen to give the council a power rather than a duty in respect of the removal of obstructions. According to Lord Hoffmann:

> the fact that Parliament has conferred a discretion must be some indication that the policy of the act conferring the power was not to create a right to compensation.

It is usual to describe the obligations as 'statutory duties' but in most cases the duty is not set out in the statute itself but in delegated legislation; such as the regulations below which were made under the authority of the statute.

Until recently s 47 of the Health and Safety at Work etc Act 1974 provided that breach of a duty imposed by health and safety regulations gave rise to a civil action, provided it caused damage. Section 69 of the Enterprise and Regulatory Reform Act 2013 (Civil liability for breach of health and safety duties) amends the law so that in future a breach of a duty imposed by health and safety regulations shall not be actionable unless negligence or fault on the part of the employer can be proved. This limitation on strict liability for breach of statutory duty increases the burden on claimants in cases arising after 1 October 2013, as the fault requirement in common law negligence must now be met.

8.5.2 Was the statute imposed for the benefit of a particular class of persons?

In order to establish that breach of the statutory duty gives a right of action, the claimant must first show that the obligation was imposed for the benefit of a limited class of persons. It must then be proved that, on the proper construction of the statutory provision, the claimant is a member of that class. In *Hartley v Mayoh & Co* (1954), the widow of a fireman electrocuted while fighting a fire at the defendants' factory sued for breach of statutory duty. The regulations existed for the benefit of 'persons employed' at the factory and since her husband was not a 'person employed' at the factory, it was held that she had no cause of action.

8.5.3 Was the damage caused by the breach of duty?

The claimant must prove that the defendant was in breach. The nature of the obligation needs to be determined and this can only be ascertained by having regard to the precise wording of the legislation. Some obligations are absolute, such as that formerly contained in s 14(1) of the Factories Act 1961 requiring that 'every dangerous part of any machinery shall be securely fenced', so that whether reasonable care was taken is irrelevant. Other safety obligations require measures to be taken 'so far as is reasonably practicable', which is similar to the ordinary common law negligence standard.

8.5.4 Was the damage of a kind that the statute was intended to prevent?

The claimant must show that the damage suffered is the kind of damage contemplated in the statute. This requirement is illustrated by *Gorris v Scott* (1874), where the plaintiff's sheep were swept overboard from the defendant's vessel during a storm. Statutory regulations required the sheep to be transported in pens to prevent the spread of disease. The sheep were not penned as required but the plaintiff nevertheless failed in his action; the object of the regulations was to prevent the spread of contagious disease, not to afford protection from the perils of the sea.

8.5.5 **The Eurotort**

Statutory control of health and safety has been strongly influenced by the implementation of EU directives. The so-called Eurotort action was established by *Francovich v Italy* (1993). Here it was held that a claimant is able to bring an action in a national court where it is alleged that damage has been suffered due to the state's failure to implement an EU directive. In England and Wales this action will take the form of breach of statutory duty and a successful example of such an action is *Delaney v Secretary of State for Transport* (1951).

At the time of writing, the future relationship between the United Kingdom and the EU is highly uncertain but it is hoped that any alterations in domestic employment safety protection will not be impending immediately.

 ## Summary

- The various aspects of an employer's duty described in this chapter are not separate and distinct duties but part of a *single* duty on employers to take reasonable precautions to ensure the safety of their employees.
- The employer's responsibility for the safety of his employees at work is personal and non-delegable.
- An employer's liability arises not only for failure to adopt a safe system of working, but also when a safe system is operated negligently.
- An employer who becomes aware that stress at work is having an adverse effect on the mental health of an employee is under a duty to take positive steps to prevent the harm. This is a developing area of liability.

  ○ Visit the online resources to listen to a podcast summarizing the topics covered in this chapter.

 ## The bigger picture

Goldscheider v Royal Opera House (2019)

A viola player brought an action against his employers, the Royal Opera House, for breach of safety regulations. In a rehearsal of the opera *Die Walküre*, he was seated in front of the brass section of the orchestra when the sound level reached 132 decibels, roughly equivalent to a jet engine. He suffered hearing loss which ended his musical career. The Court of Appeal upheld the trial judge's finding that Goldscheider was entitled to compensation for 'acoustic shock'. There were a number of precautions which should have reasonably been taken, such as the placement of transparent acoustic screens.

The defence case had partially relied on the Compensation Act 2006 s 1, suggesting that in such cases the court should take into account the possible deterrent effect a judgment might have on a desirable activity. This was rejected by the Court, due to the preventive measures that the defendants could have taken. *Goldscheider* illustrates the development of employee health and safety law, by bringing the orchestra pit and other live music venues into the equivalent category of protection of the factory floor and other more industrial working environments.

? Questions

Knowledge-testing questions

1. Outline the distinction between an employer's liability for harm caused *to* his employees (personal liability) and liability for harm caused *by* his employees (vicarious liability).

2. Explain your understanding of the term 'non-delegable duty' on employers.

3. How do changes introduced by the Enterprise and Regulatory Reform Act 2013 disadvantage an employee injured in a workplace accident?

4. List the factors outlined by Lord Sumption in *Woodland v Essex County Council* that are relevant to determining whether it would 'fair, just and reasonable' to impose a non-delegable duty.

Problem and essay questions

1. The general rule is that a defendant is not liable for the negligence of an independent contractor. Explain the exceptional circumstances in which such liability would be imposed.

2. Amjid was Head of Human Resources at Tara Finance plc. The increasingly competitive nature of the business and a reduced workforce meant that Amjid had to work excessively long hours. Amjid's colleagues noticed that he frequently remained in the office late into the evening to cope with his workload and that he sometimes came in at the weekend. It was apparent to his colleagues that Amjid was suffering from extreme work-related stress but because Amjid feared losing his job he did not inform his manager about his stress.

   Advise Amjid who has now suffered a complete mental breakdown and is unable to work.

 Visit the online resources for guidance on answering these questions.

☰ Further reading

Dobson, N, 'Non-Delegable Duty of Care' (2014) 111(3) LSG 17

Giliker, P, 'Vicarious Liability, Non-Delegable Duties and Teachers: Can You Outsource Liability for Lessons?' (2015) PN 31 259

Marshall, D, 'Wound Up' (2009) 153(15) SJ 9

Mullany, NJ, 'Containing Claims for Workplace Mental Illness' (2002) 118 LQR 373

Tofaris, S, 'Vicarious Liability and Non-delegable Duty for Child Abuse in Foster Care: A Step Too Far?' (2017) 79(5) MLR 884 [this article is also relevant for the topic in Chapter 9]

9 Vicarious liability

☐ LEARNING OBJECTIVES

By the end of this chapter you should be able to:

- distinguish vicarious liability from the personal liability of an employer;
- explain the tests used to distinguish between an employer and an independent contractor and identify relationships 'akin to employment';
- demonstrate an understanding of the rules on an employer's vicarious liability for the tort of its employee; and
- evaluate the justifications for the departure from the 'fault-based' principle in tort.

Introduction

You will see that throughout this book the torts discussed concern particular types of conduct regarded by the common law as blameworthy. In respect of these wrongs the general rule is that liability is based on the personal fault of the wrongdoer himself. A person is liable only for his own acts, and liability will not usually be imposed unless the defendant has negligently or intentionally caused the harm or damage to the claimant. There are, however, circumstances where one party, who cannot be said to be at fault or have personal blame, will be held liable for the damage caused by the tort of another. This is known as vicarious liability and it most commonly arises in the case of employers. Under this principle a blameless employer is liable for a wrong committed by his employee 'while acting in the course of his employment'.

Vicarious liability may also arise in the law of agency and in partnership law and we will look briefly at these aspects of liability later in the chapter. Meanwhile, you will notice in a number of the cases discussed in this chapter that in the nineteenth century the term 'servant' was used to denote an employee and the employer was denoted as 'master'. One of the reasons for the use of this terminology is that at that time the work of a servant was mainly manual and carried out under the master's instruction. This terminology has become outdated and the terms employer and employee are now used as they reflect the modern workforce containing many skilled workers and professional employees.

It is important to note the following two points before proceeding further:

- vicarious liability does not mean that the employer is liable instead of the employee; the primary liability is that of the employee who committed the wrong and vicarious liability is thus a form of secondary liability. For reasons of policy discussed below, the courts have considered it desirable to give claimants injured as the result of an employee's tort an action against the employer as well; and

- alongside vicarious liability for the torts committed by his employees, an employer owes his employees a non-delegable personal duty that arises from the employer's responsibility for the management of his organization. The employer's personal liability (which is the subject of Chapter 8) normally requires fault on the part of the employer, whereas vicarious liability will be imposed without the claimant having to show that the employer is in any way at fault.

Before going on to consider the conditions for vicarious liability to arise, the justifications for departing from the usual fault-based liability will be considered.

There is no single universally accepted and applicable argument for justifying vicarious liability, but the most accepted justifications are:

- The 'benefit and burden' principle: the employer's business obtains the benefit arising from the employee's work so it should also bear the costs of damages resulting from the enterprise.

- The employer is in the best position to know, or to find out, the nature and cost of accidents associated with the business and to take insurance against these risks.

- The employer has responsibility for ensuring that its employees are effectively trained to carry out their work safely.

- The principle of vicarious liability means that the employer is more likely to be careful in selecting employees and to provide incentives to encourage them to take care.

- The effect of the employer bearing the cost of liability insurance is to spread the loss, as the extra cost can be passed on to the public in the form of higher prices.

- The employer is better able to pay compensation and is also more likely to have liability insurance: the 'deep-pocket' argument.

Vicarious liability will not be imposed on an employer unless the following criteria are met:

- there must be an employer–employee relationship (which must be distinguished from an employer's relationship with an independent contractor);

- the employee must have committed a tort; and
- the tort must be committed while acting in the course of employment.

9.1 An employee or an independent contractor?

Historically, employers were not liable for torts committed by their independent contractors. At this point you should note that the question of whether the worker is an employee or an independent contractor also arises in contexts totally unrelated to vicarious liability. The rules on taxation are very different depending on whether the worker is an employee or an independent contractor and for the purposes of social security contributions and benefits, the status of a worker also needs to be determined: employees have certain rights, such as the right not to be unfairly dismissed, that do not extend to independent contractors. Indeed, some commentators have rightly argued that determining who should count as an employee really ought to vary depending on the purpose for which the question is asked.

▶ THINKING POINT
The definition of 'employee' is important for national insurance, tax, and welfare benefit systems. Should the definition of 'employee' be different for the purposes of the law of tort?

The legal definition of an employee was someone working under a 'contract of service' (a contract of employment). This employer–employee relationship was distinguished from an employer's relationship with a self-employed independent contractor, where the agreement was described as a 'contract for services'. However, today's working relationships often fall outside the traditional pattern and the status of an employment relationship can be difficult to define. In the case of casual or contract workers, home workers, those employed through an employment agency, and those working in the so-called gig economy (such as an Uber driver, or delivery person) the formerly essential distinction between the two types of contract can be unclear.

We will now go on to consider the approaches which have been taken by the courts in determining the employment relationship for the purposes of vicarious liability. Note that in *Various Claimants v Barclays Bank* (2018), below, the existence of a so-called 'independent contractor exemption' is doubted.

9.1.1 Tests used to determine who is an employee for the purposes of vicarious liability

9.1.1.1 The 'control' test

The traditional test used to distinguish employees from independent contractors was the 'control' test. Under this test, if the employer controlled the actual performance of the work and 'how' it was to be done the worker was regarded as an employee.

As long ago as the case of *Cassidy v Ministry of Health* (1951), it was held that a health authority is vicariously liable for the professional negligence of its staff; although it was unclear whether the plaintiff's injury was caused by the negligence of the assistant medical officer, the house surgeon, or one of the nurses, the Court of Appeal held that despite the lack of control over professionals, the hospital was vicariously liable for the professional negligence of its staff. Somervell LJ pointed out that, although the master of a ship may be employed by the owners, they had no power to tell him how to navigate his ship. So the absence of control in the case of an expert was not a barrier to the existence of a contract of service.

This is no longer considered a suitable or reliable test. The current approach to the control test was summarized in *Various Claimants v Catholic Child Welfare Society* (2013), by Lord Phillips:

> Today it is not realistic to look for a right to direct how an employee should perform his duties as a necessary element in the relationship between employer and employee. Many employees apply a skill or expertise that is not susceptible to direction by anyone else in the company that employs them. Thus the significance of control today is that the employer can direct what the employee does, not how he does it.

In assessing whether or not persons are employees, this test takes into account the extent to which they are integrated into the business of the employer. In *Stevenson, Jordan & Harrison v Macdonald & Evans* (1952), Lord Denning said that:

> under a contract of service, a man is employed as part of the business, and work is done as an integral part of the business; whereas, under a contract for services, his work, although done for the business, is not integrated into it but is only accessory to it.

Lord Denning used the examples of a ship's captain, a chauffeur, and a staff reporter to illustrate an employee, contrasted with a ship's pilot, a taxi driver, and a contributor to a newspaper who are independent contractors. This test proved vague to apply, as it relied on integration as a single concept, but the reality is that integration is established by considering various factors. Therefore a further test was developed: the 'economic reality' test. Regardless of how the parties themselves classified the relationship, the court examined the reality of the working relationship and asked: is this person in business on his own account?

9.1.1.2 **The 'economic reality' test**

In *Ready Mixed Concrete (SE) Ltd v Minister of Pensions* (1968), a concrete-manufacturing company introduced a scheme whereby its concrete would be transported by a team of lorry owners described as 'owner-drivers'. The agreement between the lorry owners and the company provided that they would be paid a fixed mileage rate for the service and it also specified their employment status to be self-employed independent contractors. Although lorry owners were required to paint the lorries in the company's colours and wear the company's uniform, the drivers owned the lorries and bore the financial risk of the enterprise. In a dispute about whether the lorry owners were employees or independent contractors, the economic reality test was applied and on the facts of the case it was found that the lorry owners were unlikely to be acting as agents or employees of the company but were, in reality, independent contractors working under a contract for services. The key factors influencing the court in reaching its conclusion were that the drivers (1) owned and maintained the lorries; (2) were free to hire other drivers in the event of holiday or sickness; and (3) took the chance of profit and bore the risk of loss.

In *Market Investigations Ltd v Minister of Social Security* (1969), the basic question was said to be whether the worker was performing the service as a person in business on his own account, or as an employee working for an agreed wage, whose employer took the risk of loss and the chance of profit. The working relationship was determined by examining the underlying 'economic reality' of the relationship between the parties and the relevant factors to be considered in determining this are:

- whether the person uses his own premises and equipment;
- whether he hires his own helpers;
- the degree of financial risk he takes;
- the degree of responsibility, if any, which he has for investment and management;
- whether and how far he has an opportunity of profiting from sound management in the performance of his task.

The court pointed out, however, that no exhaustive list of the relevant considerations to determine the question has been compiled, and no single test has been devised which is capable of application in all cases. Even written terms of the contract categorizing the working relationship are not conclusive and, although an important consideration, the wording of the contract is only one factor to be taken into account. If, on balance, the other factors in an agreement point to a different type of relationship, the courts will accept it, even if the parties themselves have given a different label to their relationship.

In *Ferguson v John Dawson & Partners (Contractors) Ltd* (1976), the plaintiff was described as a labour-only subcontractor working as part of the 'lump' labour force working on the defendant's building site. When he suffered injury at work the plaintiff argued that he was an employee for the purposes of statutory safety regulations owed by employers to their employees. The employer contended that in the employment contract the parties had characterized their relationship as that of employer–independent contractor and that, as an independent contractor, the plaintiff was responsible for his own safety. This was rejected by the Court of Appeal as, apart from the label the parties had given their working relationship, all the other surrounding circumstances were indistinguishable from an employer–employee relationship and the defendant was liable.

In conclusion, the approach of the court now is, instead of relying on a single test, to consider a wide range of factors in each particular case. How much weight will be given to the different factors will depend on the facts of each case. In *Market Investigations Ltd v Minister of Social Security*, warning against the risk of a rigid application of the factors for consideration, Cooke J said:

> No exhaustive list has been compiled and perhaps no exhaustive list can be compiled of the considerations which are relevant in determining that question, nor can strict rules be laid down as to the relative weight which the various considerations should carry in particular cases.

9.1.2 Who is liable when an employee is hired to another employer?

It is quite common for an employer to lend (or hire) its employee to another employer on a temporary basis and the question then arises as to which of the two employers will be vicariously liable for the torts of the borrowed employee. In *Mersey Docks and Harbour Board v Coggins and Griffiths (Liverpool) Ltd* (1947), a mobile crane and a driver had been hired out to a firm of stevedores under a contract which stipulated that the driver was to be the employee of the stevedores. In spite of this term, the employee's original employer, the Harbour Board, paid his wages and retained the right to dismiss him. The hirer, Coggins and Griffiths, directed the tasks which were to be performed by the driver but not how he was to operate the crane. In the course of his work the driver negligently injured the plaintiff and the question to be determined was whether the firm of stevedores or the Harbour Board were vicariously liable. In addressing the question, the court held that the control test was still important (although this might not be the case today), but said that other factors to be considered include:

- the type of machinery that had been loaned: the more complicated it is, the more likely the main employer will remain liable;
- who is the paymaster and who pays the employees' national insurance contributions;
- the duration of the alternative service with the temporary employer;
- which employer retains the power of dismissal;
- whether the employers themselves have attempted to regulate the matter.

Applying these factors, the original employer, the Harbour Board, was held liable as it still had the immediate direction and control of how the crane was worked. It is important to note that the burden of proof rests upon the permanent employer to shift prima facie responsibility to the hirer, and this burden can sometimes be a heavy one.

In *Hawley v Luminar Leisure* (2006), a security services provider successfully shifted the burden to the temporary employer (a nightclub). Luminar had contracted with ASE Security Services Ltd for the supply of doormen for their nightclub. Despite the claimant's attempt to show he wanted no trouble, the doorman punched him so hard in the face that he fell to the ground and suffered injuries which resulted in brain damage. Hawley sued both Luminar and ASE on the basis that they were each responsible for failing to carry out a proper investigation into whether the doorman was a suitable person to be employed in that capacity and for failing to train or supervise him. The Court of Appeal considered a number of factors, including who exercised control over the doormen, who paid them, and to whom they were responsible while working at Luminar's clubs. The prima facie responsibility for the hired employee was held to have shifted from ASE, the general employer, to Luminar, the temporary employer, because Luminar had exercised considerable control over how the doorman carried out his duties.

9.1.2.1 There can be dual vicarious liability

It had traditionally been assumed that where an employee was lent by one employer to work for another, vicarious liability for the employee's negligence had to rest with one employer or the other, but not both. However, in *Viasystems Ltd v Thermal Transfer Ltd* (2005), the Court of Appeal held that there can be dual vicarious liability and it is possible for two separate employers to be vicariously liable for the tort of a single employee. In this case, the claimants engaged the first defendants to install air conditioning at their factory. The first defendants subcontracted ducting work to the second defendants, who then contracted with the third defendants to provide fitters and fitters' mates on a labour-only basis. At the time of the accident, a fitter's mate negligently caused damage to the fire-protection sprinkler system that resulted in a flood which caused extensive damage. There was no question that the fitter's mate was negligent and the issue to be decided was which of the employers was vicariously liable.

The Court of Appeal found that there was no authority binding it to hold that dual vicarious liability was legally impossible and ruled that entire and absolute control of the employee was not a precondition of vicarious liability. The inquiry should concentrate on the relevant negligent act and then ask whose responsibility it was to prevent it; the question in this case was to ask who was entitled to exercise control over the relevant act or operation of the fitter's mate. On the facts, both the second and third defendants had been entitled, and if they had the opportunity obliged, to prevent the mate's negligence and accordingly both employers were vicariously liable.

Viasystems was considered in *Hawley*, above, where the Court of Appeal said the decision as to whether an employee remains an employee of the general employer for the purposes of vicarious liability or whether he is deemed to be a temporary employee of the hirer turns on the facts of the individual case. In *Hawley* it was concluded that the temporary employer should be liable, although in *CCWS*, below, the Supreme Court noted that the facts of *Hawley* could have supported a finding of dual vicarious liability.

9.1.3 **Vicarious liability outside the traditional employer–employee relationship: relationships akin to employment**

The question of whether the Catholic Church is vicariously liable for the actions of its clergy was considered in *JGE v Trustees of the Portsmouth Roman Catholic Diocesan Trust* (2012). The Church denied vicarious liability for acts of child sexual abuse carried out by one of its priests and challenged the allegation that it was the employer of its clergy. The Church claimed that priests are not employees of the Church; they are office holders rather than employees. The priest accused of the sexual abuse had no employment contract with the trustees: there was no wage agreement, no mechanism for the trustees to dismiss or discipline him, and no mechanism by which they could control him. The Court of Appeal upheld the first instance, finding that the relationship between a parish priest and his diocese was akin to an employment relationship, even though the priest received no wage and was rarely supervised. When considering vicarious liability in respect of persons not formally employed, the court held that it was not appropriate to apply tests of employment laid down in cases dealing with unfair dismissal, or taxation, or discrimination. Lord Justice Davis said:

> I would conclude that, although this was most certainly not an employment relationship or even a contractual relationship, the relationship between the bishop and Father Baldwin was

sufficiently akin to that of employment: and at all events was one such whereby, given the degree of control and connection and given the objectives of the bishop in the appointment of Father Baldwin which it was intended he should further and promote, vicarious liability in respect of his activities in the parish is capable of arising.

🔍 CASE CLOSE-UP

***Various Claimants v Catholic Child Welfare Society (CCWS)* (2013)**

In this case, the Supreme Court confirmed that it is possible for two or more different employers each to be vicariously liable for a single wrongful act of an employee.

CCWS involved 170 men who alleged they were victims of physical and sexual abuse between 1958 and 1992 by brothers of a religious order, at a residential institution for boys. The claims were brought against two groups of defendants: the first were the Middlesbrough Defendants, the body responsible for the school (which had taken over the management of the school in 1973 and inherited the liabilities of the school before that date). The second defendants, the Brothers of the Christian Schools (the Institute) had deployed teachers at the school, including the headmaster and a number of the staff. The judge's finding, upheld by the Court of Appeal, was that since the brothers of the Institute were employed by the Middlesbrough Defendants at the time the abuse took place, only they could be vicariously liable. However, the Supreme Court disagreed and ruled that the Institute was also vicariously liable for the alleged abuse committed by the brothers. The manner in which the Institute carried on its affairs led the Justices to approach this case as if the Institute were a corporate body existing to perform the function of providing a Christian education to boys. According to Lord Phillips:

> This is not a borderline case. It is one where it is fair, just and reasonable . . . for the Institute to share with the Middlesbrough Defendants vicarious liability for the abuse committed by the brothers.

This case also raised the issue of the relationship between the Institute and the brother teachers and the extension of the scope of vicarious liability to relationships 'akin to employment' (discussed below).

Even though the brothers were bound to the Institute by their vows rather than contract, and transferred all their earnings to the Institute, the Institute was found vicariously liable for their acts of sexual and physical abuse of children. The Supreme Court introduced a two-stage test for vicarious liability in which both questions must be answered in the affirmative.

1. Is the relationship between the two parties one which is capable of giving rise to vicarious liability? and

2. If so, is there a close connection that links the relationship and the act or omission of the wrongdoer?

The first question relates to the establishment of the employment or 'akin to employment' relationship. Lord Phillips went on to set out five considerations, in fact justifications for vicarious liability, the consideration of which will help to answer the first questions:

1. the employer is more likely to have the means to compensate the victim and can be expected to have insured against that liability;

2. the tort will have been committed as a result of activity being taken by the employee on behalf of the employer,

3. the employee's activity is likely to be part of the business activity of the employer,

4. the employer, by employing the employee to carry on the activity will have created the risk of the tort committed by the employee, and

5. the employee will, to a greater or lesser degree, have been under the control of the employer.

The second question will be dealt with in more detail under 'course of employment', below.

In *Cox v Ministry of Justice* (2016) and the companion appeal of *Mohamud v WM Morrison Supermarkets* (discussed at 9.3.1.4 Criminal conduct) the Supreme Court considered in detail the sort of relationship which has to exist between an employer and an employee before the employer can be made vicariously liable. In *Cox* the claimant, a catering manager at a prison, suffered injury through the negligence of a prisoner working in the kitchen. The defendant denied liability and argued that, unlike employees, prisoners have no interest in furthering the objectives of the prison service. The Supreme Court rejected this argument and in applying the tests from *CCWS* concluded that finding vicarious liability here did not even represent a significant extension of the common law. The defendant need not be carrying out a commercial or profit-making enterprise in order to be vicariously liable. Although setting prisoners to work serves the purpose of rehabilitation, penal policy also aims to ensure that convicted prisoners contribute to the cost of their upkeep. A prisoner undertaking such work for nominal wages is not only integral to the prison's mission but may even be bound into a closer relationship with the prison service than would be the case for an employee, thus making a stronger case for imposing vicarious liability.

❱ CROSS REFERENCE

See 8.1.

 CASE CLOSE-UP

***Armes v Nottinghamshire County Council* (2017)**

As a child the claimant had been physically and sexually abused by foster parents, into whose care she had been placed by the defendant County Council. In allowing the appeal against a finding against vicarious liability, much reliance was placed on the reasoning behind *Cox v Ministry of Justice*, above. Control was one consideration. In the nature of the complex relationship, close control could not be exercised over the foster parents. However the local authority controlled who the foster parents were, supervised their fostering, and controlled some aspects of day-to-day family life, such as holidays and medical treatment. But the Supreme Court noted, 'More fundamentally, it is important not to exaggerate the extent to which control is necessary in order for the imposition of vicarious liability to be justified'.

The integration test was also considered by the Supreme Court in *Armes*. The childcare provided by the foster parents was an integral part of the local authority's organization of its childcare services. The foster parents were not carrying on an independent business of their own because the local authority carried out the recruitment, selection, and training of foster parents. Therefore, the abuse carried out on the claimant was committed in the course of an activity undertaken for the benefit of the local authority.

As well as satisfying the control test and the integration test, the commission of the wrongful acts was within a risk created by the local authority by assigning those activities to the individuals in question and placing a vulnerable child in their care.

The policy reasons set out by Lord Phillips in *Various Claimants* for justifying the imposition of vicarious liability took into account the enterprise liability and risk factors created in this case. The foster parents provided care to the child as an integral part of the local authority's childcare services, and where close control cannot be exercised children are particularly vulnerable to abuse. The need for social justice identified by Lord Phillips to ensure compensation for harm suffered by innocent claimants was an important factor since most foster parents have insufficient means to be able to meet a substantial award of damages.

According to Lord Reed:

> Considering next the issue of risk creation, the local authority's placement of children in their care with foster parents creates a relationship of authority and trust between the foster parents and the children, in circumstances where close control cannot be exercised by the local authority, and so renders the children particularly vulnerable to abuse. Although it is generally considered to be in the best interests of children in care that they should be placed in foster care, since most children benefit greatly from the experience of family life, it is relevant to the imposition of vicarious liability that a particular risk of abuse is inherent in that choice. That is because, if the public bodies responsible for decision-making in relation to children in care consider it advantageous to place them in foster care, notwithstanding the inherent risk that some children may be abused, it may be considered fair that they should compensate the unfortunate children for whom that risk materialises, particularly bearing in mind that the children are under the protection of the local authority and have no control over the decision regarding their placement. In that way, the burden of a risk borne in the general interest is shared, rather than being borne solely by the victims.

THINKING POINT

Do you agree with Lord Hughes's dissenting judgment that: (1) finding the local authority vicariously liability would extend vicarious liability for family and friend foster parents; (2) this would result in undesirable family litigation in the courts?

In 2018 the Court of Appeal again had to consider whether there existed a relationship between a wrongdoer and the defendant sufficient to create vicarious liability. The significance of the following case lies in the doubt which the court cast up on the long-standing employee/

CROSS REFERENCE

See 8.1 Case of **Woodland v Essex CC** (2013).

independent contractor distinction. These concepts may no longer be meaningful in the context of today's style of working.

 CASE CLOSE-UP

Various Claimants v Barclays Bank (2018)

Over a hundred women brought an action against Barclays Bank, claiming that they had been sexually assaulted in the course of pre-employment medical checks. These were performed on the Bank's behalf by a former GP, who was employed by the Bank as an independent contractor over a period from 1969 to 1984. The question for the courts was whether there existed a relationship between the Bank and the doctor to found vicarious liability, no longer a 'defence' of being an independent contractor. At first instance, the two-part test was applied, as in *Mohamud* and *Cox*, and vicarious liability was confirmed on both counts. Barclays Bank then appealed, alleging that part one of the test: is the relationship one of employment or 'akin to employment?' had been wrongly interpreted.

In the Court of Appeal, Irwin LJ applied Lord Phillips's five criteria to determine the first question on the relationship between the defendant and the wrongdoer:

1. Barclays 'had more means to satisfy the claims than the . . . estate of Dr Bates', but that the judge had been correct to give this little weight in her initial judgment. It was stated that 'no liability could be founded on this consideration alone'.

2. Medical examination, while of some benefit to the employees, was 'clear beyond doubt that its principal benefit was to the prospective employers'.

3. In selecting employees 'there could hardly be a clearer example' of an activity being part of a defendant's business activity. In providing Barclays with a medical assessment on physical suitability, this was integral to Barclays' business.

4. The process of pre-employment medical examinations put the employees in a position of risk.

5. The question of control was 'perhaps the most critical factor'. Had the doctor 'to a greater or lesser degree been under the control' of Barclays? He had conducted a general health examination of the employees, and did so against a standard formula set by the defendants

According to Irwin, LJ:

> I accept the submission . . . that the law now requires answers to the specified questions laid down in *Cox* and *Mohamud*, and affirmed in *Armes*, rather than an answer to the question: was the alleged tortfeasor an independent contractor? No doubt where the answers to the *Cox*/*Mohamud* questions are such that vicarious liability cannot be established, the relationship may often be that of independent contractor. But that question of definition appears to me no longer to be the test. If the Supreme Court had intended it to survive

as such, it seems unlikely, given that formerly this was a decisive test, that the Court would have failed to say so.

Moreover, it seems clear to me that, adopting the approach of the Supreme Court, there will indeed be cases of independent contractors where vicarious liability will be established. Changes in the structures of employment, and of contracts for the provisions of services, are widespread. Operations intrinsic to a business enterprise are routinely performed by independent contractors, over long periods, accompanied by precise obligations and high levels of control. Such patterns are evident in widely different fields of enterprise, from construction, to manufacture, to the services sector.

9.1.4 **Vicarious liability outside the employer–employee relationship: principal–agent**

Outside the employment relationship, there is a further context in which vicarious liability will arise. Where the owner of a vehicle allows another person to drive it in his presence or where a person has authority to drive the vehicle on behalf of, or for the purposes of, the owner, the vehicle owner will be vicariously liable. The term used by the courts to define the vehicle owner in these circumstances is 'principal' and the driver is termed his 'agent' and the principal is vicariously liable for his agent's negligent driving. In *Ormrod v Crossville Motors* (1953), the driver had authority to drive the defendant's car on the defendant's behalf and for the defendant's purposes from Birkenhead to Monte Carlo so that he and the driver could eventually use the car on holiday. The driver caused an accident for which the defendant, although not the driver's employer, was held vicariously liable on the ground that the driver was pursuing not only his own interests but the defendant's as well. Important factors in reaching this decision were that the driver was furthering the defendant's interests; as owner of the car, the defendant had asked the driver to take it from Birkenhead to Monte Carlo and he planned to use it jointly with the driver on the holiday.

The principal–agent relationship from which vicarious liability arises in these cases is based on the delegation of 'a task or a duty'. In *Morgans v Launchbury* (1973), the defendant wife owned a car which was used as the family car. The husband promised her that he would never drive the car if he was drunk, but he would get a friend to drive instead. On one occasion when the husband got drunk, he asked a friend to drive him and the plaintiffs home. As a result of the friend's negligent driving an accident occurred in which the husband was killed, and the plaintiffs were injured. In determining whether the wife was vicariously liable for the negligence of the friend, the Court of Appeal held that since the friend had permission to use her car, the wife was vicariously liable. The House of Lords reversed the decision and held that she was not vicariously liable on the ground that the wife had no interest or concern in the purpose of the journey. Mere permission to drive without the owner having some concern or interest in the use of the car is insufficient to impose vicarious liability; there must be an express or implied request to drive in performance of a task or duty for the benefit of the owner.

9.2 There must be a tort

The employer can only be liable if the employee commits a tort and the tort must be committed in the course of the employee's employment. Although negligence is the tort most commonly giving rise to vicarious liability, an employer could also be vicariously liable for an employee's intentional tort such as theft. For example, in *Morris v CW Martin* (1966), the employer was liable when one of its employees stole the plaintiff's mink coat which she had left to be cleaned. In *Poland v Parr & Sons* (1927), the employer was liable in trespass to the person when one of his employees, who reasonably believed that some children were stealing the company's property, struck and injured one of the children.

In *Majrowski v Guy's and St Thomas's NHS Trust* (2006), the House of Lords ruled that the common law principle of strict liability for another's wrongs was just as applicable to breaches of statutory obligation. Under the Protection from Harassment Act 1997, conduct amounting to harassment of another is an offence giving rise to a civil action. Mr Majrowski claimed that he had been bullied, intimidated, and harassed by his departmental manager, acting in the course of her employment. He claimed for damages against the Trust for breach of statutory duty under the Protection from Harassment Act 1997. The judge at first instance struck out his claim on the grounds that the Act did not create a statutory tort for which an employer could be vicariously liable.

Mr Majrowski's appeal against the decision was permitted by the Court of Appeal and upheld by the House of Lords, which ruled that where a claim met the 'close connection' test, an employer might be vicariously liable for breach of a statutory duty placed solely and personally on the employee for harassment committed in the course of employment.

 THINKING POINT

In *Majrowski*, the NHS Trust argued that the burden on employers, insurers, and the administration of justice would be wholly unjustified if vicarious liability was imposed for an employee's harassment committed in breach of the Protection from Harassment Act 1997. Can you identify what any of these burdens might be?

WM Morrison Supermarkets plc v Various Claimants (2018) will be discussed below regarding the issue of 'course of employment'. However also resolved here by the Court of Appeal was that vicarious liability could be incurred simultaneously for breach of statutory duty under the Data Protection Act 1998, the common law tort of misuse of private information, and the equitable wrong of breach of confidence.

9.3 The tort must be committed in the 'course of employment'

The definition of 'course of employment' is crucial because the general rule is that if an employee committed the tort within the course of his employment the employer is liable; if the employee acted outside the scope of employment the employer is not liable. The question of whether an act is within or outside the course of employment is one of fact and there is no exhaustive definition of what falls within the scope of employment; each case depends on its particular facts. We shall now go on to examine the factors considered by the courts in determining the issue but you should be aware that following the decision in *Lister v Hesley Hall Ltd* (2001) the modern approach (on public policy grounds) is to expand the concept of course of employment as a means of enabling victims of the employee's tort to obtain compensation.

▶ CROSS REFERENCE

For more on *Lister* and subsequent application of its principles, see 9.3.1.5 Policy and the 'close connection' test.

9.3.1 Distinguishing between authorized and unauthorized acts

In distinguishing between authorized and unauthorized acts, one of the guidelines traditionally used by the courts is that formulated by an eminent tort lawyer, Professor Salmond, where they ask whether the wrongful act is either:

> (i) a wrongful act authorized by the master, or (ii) a wrongful and unauthorized mode of doing some act authorized by the master.

This test was applied in *Century Insurance Co Ltd v Northern Ireland Road Transport Board* (1942), in the case of carelessness of the driver of a petrol tanker, who lit a cigarette and carelessly discarded a lighted match, which caused an explosion and a fire. His act of lighting the cigarette and throwing away the lighted match at that moment was said to be negligent in performing his task of delivering petrol, and he was therefore acting in the course of employment. Although discarding the lighted match could not in itself be said to be connected with the performance of his job, the negligent act could not be looked at in isolation from the surrounding circumstances and it was held to be an unauthorized way of doing what he was employed to do. It is outside the course of employment for an employee to perform an act that is not connected with what he has been employed to do such as in *Beard v London General Omnibus Co* (1900), where a bus conductor, in the driver's absence, decided to turn the bus around for the return journey. It was not an improper manner of performing his duties because conductors were not employed to drive buses and he was therefore acting outside the course of his employment.

9.3.1.1 A journey which takes an employee on 'a frolic of his own' is outside the scope of employment

Many of those claiming in vicarious liability against employers have suffered injuries caused by employees driving company vehicles at the time of the accident. In these cases, problems arise when the employee is not driving in the course of the employer's business when the accident occurs, but is pursuing his own interests. Vicarious liability will not be imposed where the employee has taken an unauthorized deviation from the authorized journey while driving a vehicle provided by his employer. The employer's liability depends on the extent to which a deviation from the authorized route would be considered a separate and independent journey; the degree of a deviation could be so minor as to be treated as within the course of employment or it might be entirely new and separate, which takes the employee outside the course of employment. In *Joel v Morrison* (1834), the test was said to be whether the employee was engaged on the employer's business or 'on a frolic of his own'.

In *Harvey v RG O'Dell Ltd* (1958), a 5-mile journey from a workplace (which did not have a canteen) to get a midday meal during working hours was held to be incidental to the employee's work and was therefore within the course of employment. However, it is a question of degree as to the extent to which the journey takes the employee outside the scope of employment. In *Hilton v Thomas Burton* (1961), it was outside the scope of employment for an employee to use the company car to drive fellow employees to a café in order to have refreshments. In this case the plaintiff's husband, a fellow employee, was killed in an accident as they were returning from the café. However, because the driver was doing something that he was not employed to do, the employer was not vicariously liable.

> **THINKING POINT**
>
> Why might it have been decided that the employees in *Harvey* were in the course of employment but those in *Hilton* were outside the course of employment?

The defendant employer was not liable in *Storey v Ashton* (1869), when a 6-year-old child was run over by a horse and cart driven by one of his employees. Two of the defendant's employees had been instructed to deliver some wine and to bring back some empty bottles to the employer's offices. On the return journey one of the employees persuaded the other that, since it was by then after hours, they should set off in a different direction to visit relatives. The employer was not liable because at the time of the accident, the driver was not acting in the course of employment, but was on a new and independent journey which was entirely for his own business.

9.3.1.2 Travelling: from home to work and between workplaces distinguished

A distinction is made between an employee travelling between home and work, which will not generally be in the course of employment, and an employee travelling in the employer's time from home to a workplace other than the regular workplace or between workplaces, which will be within the course of employment. In *Smith v Stages* (1989), a **peripatetic** lagger was working at a power station in the Midlands when his employer sent him and another employee to perform an urgent job in Wales. Having worked without sleep, they finished the job two days early and decided to drive straight home. As they were travelling back together in the car, they were both injured when the employee driving the car crashed into a wall. The driver was uninsured and the plaintiff sued the employer on the basis of vicarious liability. The trial judge

peripatetic

someone who travels from place to place in the course of their employment (or some other type of activity), such as a music teacher working in more than one school.

held that the accident had not occurred in the course of employment, but the Court of Appeal reversed this decision and held that the employers were liable. The employers' appeal to the House of Lords was dismissed on the ground that Mr Stages was required by his employers to make the journey so that he could work at the power station in Wales. Lord Goff said the fact that the men were travelling back early was immaterial, since they were still being paid wages to travel there and back. Lord Lowry thought the crucial point was that the employees were 'on duty' at the time of the accident.

9.3.1.3 Acts expressly prohibited by the employer

Vicarious liability may be imposed even though the employee performs an act which is expressly prohibited by the employer. Although this may seem unfair, if an act expressly prohibited by an employer had the effect of taking an employee outside the course of employment, it would be easy for employers to avoid liability; an employer could simply issue specific instructions that employees 'must not be negligent' in order to avoid vicarious liability. If the prohibition applies to the way in which the employee performs his duties, rather than limits the scope of what the employee is employed to do, then the prohibition will not be effective.

 THINKING POINT

If an employer is vicariously liable for negligence when an employee is driving from one workplace to another, why is an employer not liable for an employee's negligence when driving to work?

In *Twine v Bean's Express Ltd* (1946), van drivers were expressly prohibited by their employer from giving lifts to unauthorized passengers. The plaintiff's husband, an unauthorized passenger in a company van driven by the defendant's employee, was killed as a result of the driver's negligence. The Court of Appeal held that it was not possible to say that in giving Mr Twine a lift the driver was acting within the scope of his employment or doing improperly that which he was employed to do. In these circumstances the employer was not vicariously liable as the employee was doing something totally outside the scope of his employment and from which the employer derived no benefit. The express prohibition on giving lifts was not only a prohibition but it was also a limiting factor on the scope of the driver's employment.

When the court is considering whether the prohibited act is in the course of employment the purpose for which the act is done is a factor to be taken into account. We have seen in *Twine* that the employer derived no benefit from the passenger's presence. This decision was distinguished in the next case we will look at, *Rose v Plenty* (1976), where the employer had exhibited signs at the depot prohibiting the milkmen from employing children to assist in delivering the milk and from giving lifts on the milk van. Despite his employer's express instruction not to do so, a milkman employed the plaintiff, a 13-year-old-boy, to help deliver milk from a van. When the boy was injured as the result of the milkman's negligence, the employer was held liable as the prohibition affected the manner in which the milk was delivered and it did not limit the scope of those duties; the milkman was still delivering milk with the assistance of the boy. It was held that where the prohibited conduct is performed in furthering the employer's business or to benefit the employer in some way, it is usually within the course of employment.

THINKING POINT

Ita, a computer programmer employed by Tecpro, spent the day working at the premises of one of Tecpro's clients, Global. Having finished her work at Global, Ita agreed to drive Global's manager, Ben, to the train station in Tecpro's van. Would Tecpro be vicariously liable for injuries suffered by Ben if Ita negligently crashed the van as she drove him to catch his train?

9.3.1.4 Criminal conduct

As we have seen in Professor Salmond's test for vicarious liability, his second question is whether the employee commits a wrongful and unauthorized mode of doing some act authorized by the employer. *Morris v CW Martin & Sons Ltd* (1966), concerning a mink stole which was sent for dry cleaning and was stolen by one of the employees in a firm of cleaners, is an example of a case where the employee's act constituted an unlawful mode of doing his job and the Court of Appeal held that the employer was vicariously liable for the employee's theft.

Where the employee's wrongdoing involved a deliberate assault the courts are reluctant to find that the employee was acting in the course of employment. In *Warren v Henlys* (1948), a pump attendant at a petrol station mistakenly thought that the plaintiff was attempting to drive away without paying for some petrol. He made this accusation to the plaintiff and, following an argument, the plaintiff was assaulted and injured by the pump attendant. In an action brought by the plaintiff, the employers were not held liable as the assault by the pump attendant was, on the facts, found to be a mere act of personal vengeance and outside the course of employment. Similarly, in *Keppel Bus Co Ltd v Sa'ad bin Ahmad* (1974), the employer was not vicariously liable when, following a quarrel on a bus, the bus conductor struck and injured a passenger.

9.3.1.5 Policy and the 'close connection' test

However, the above cases should now be considered in the light of the House of Lords' approach to vicarious liability in *Lister*, the Court of Appeal analysis of these principles in *Mattis v Pollock*, and the propositions set out in *Various Claimants v Catholic Child Welfare Society* (2012), where Lord Phillips noted that: 'The law of vicarious liability is on the move.' The Supreme Court has expanded the law of vicarious liability even further through the decisions in *Cox v Ministry of Justice*, *Mohamud v WM Morrison Supermarkets*, and *Armes v Nottinghamshire County Council*.

The cases that follow illustrate that the test does not simply focus on whether the employee commits a wrongful act or adopts an unauthorized mode of doing some act authorized by the employer. The courts will take an evaluative approach and consider whether the acts complained of are so closely connected with what the employee was employed to do within 'field of activities' assigned to him or her that it would be fair and just to hold the employer vicariously liable.

Lister v Hesley Hall Ltd (2001)

In this case, the House of Lords reviewed the application of the Salmond test, which focused on whether the employee's wrongful act was either authorized by the employer or an improper way of doing what was authorized. Their Lordships held that the proper approach in cases of serious criminal conduct is not to ask the simplistic question of whether the acts were modes of doing authorized acts but to adopt a broad approach to the question of the scope of an employee's employment. In determining 'course of employment' for vicarious liability, the question to be asked is whether the employee's act was *so closely connected* with what he was employed to do that it would be fair and just to hold the employer liable.

The claimants in *Lister* attended a school for boys with emotional and behavioural difficulties which was managed by the defendants. The boys boarded in the annex to the school, where they were subjected to systematic sexual abuse by the warden responsible for their care. The House of Lords allowed the appeal and held that the defendants had entrusted the care of the children to the warden and the abuse had been inextricably interwoven with the carrying out of his duties: his torts had been so closely connected with his employment that it would be fair and just to hold the defendants vicariously liable. The fact that the employment provided the perpetrator with the opportunity to be at the annex where the abuse took place was not enough in itself to make the employer liable. Nevertheless, experience shows that the risk of the acts carried out on the boys is inherent in the nature of the work that the warden was employed to do, and it therefore constituted a sufficient connection between the wrongful acts and his employment.

Lister overruled the decision in *Trotman v North Yorkshire County Council* (1999), which had applied the Salmond test in the case of a teacher who used school trips to commit sexual assaults on a dependent child. The Court of Appeal in that case refused to hold the employer vicariously liable on the ground that the perpetrator was not acting in the course of employment; his conduct was said to be a negation of the task of caring for the plaintiff and not an unauthorized mode of carrying out an authorized task. In *Lister*, the House of Lords held that the Court of Appeal had asked the wrong question and all future cases involving claims of vicarious liability will need to be considered in the light of the 'close connection' test in *Lister*.

The test is directed to the connection between the employee's duties and his wrongdoing. The question is whether the wrongdoing was so closely connected with what the employee was employed to do that it would be fair and just to hold the defendant liable. One of the criticisms of the 'close connection' test is that it will lead to uncertainty in the law because it is vague and offers no guidance on the type or degree of connection required. However, in *Lister* it appears that the House of Lords wanted to compensate the claimants and do 'practical justice' in finding the employer vicariously liable. The finding of vicarious liability in *Lister* on the ground that the wrongful acts of abuse were inextricably interwoven with the warden's duties of protecting pupils in his care has widened the scope of vicarious liability for sexual abuse of children.

9.3.1.6 **Application of the 'close connection' test**

The interpretation of the 'close connection' test set down in *Lister* was applied by the House of Lords in *Dubai Aluminium v Salaam and others* (2003), where the issue of vicarious liability arose in a case concerning the liability of a partnership for a fraudulent partner acting for his own benefit. Their Lordships held that the personal innocence of the other co-partners could not be taken into account when determining their vicarious liability for the dishonest partner. Their Lordships widened the principle in *Lister* to include not just intentional torts, but also breaches of equitable duty which were so closely connected with the acts that the employee was authorized to do in the course of the firm's business. It is important to recognize that this case reflects the policy factors which influenced the decision in *Lister* in considering whether, in all the circumstances, it was just and reasonable to hold the employer liable. Future application of the 'close connection' test will be in the context of the facts in each case.

Lister was applied by the Court of Appeal in *Mattis v Pollock* (2003). The owner of a nightclub was held vicariously liable when Mattis, the claimant, suffered paraplegia following a stabbing by a 'bouncer' employed by the club. The doorman, Cranston, who was involved in a fight with other customers in the nightclub, was forced to flee when the claimant intervened. The doorman went home to arm himself with a knife and, intent on revenge, he returned to the vicinity of the club, where he stabbed the claimant. The evidence showed that Cranston had a history of behaving aggressively and the assault on the claimant was held to be 'so closely connected' with what Pollock (the owner of the nightclub) authorized or expected of his employee in the performance of his employment as doorman that it would be fair and just to conclude that he was vicariously liable for the claimant's damage. In reaching its decision the Court of Appeal focused on the House of Lords' decisions in the above cases, and in setting out the principles relating to vicarious liability, Judge LJ said:

> The essential principle we derive from the reasoning in the *Lister* and *Dubai Aluminium* cases is that Pollock's vicarious liability to the claimant for Cranston's attack requires a deceptively simple question to be answered. Approaching the matter broadly, was the assault 'so closely connected' with what Pollock authorized or expected of Cranston in the performance of his employment as doorman at his nightclub, that it would be fair and just to conclude that Pollock is vicariously liable for the damage the claimant sustained when the doorman stabbed him?

It is interesting to consider two Privy Council cases from the Caribbean with opposite outcomes on the issue of course of employment. In *Att Gen of the British Virgin Islands v Hartwell* (2004) an off-duty police officer used his service revolver to shoot at two people in a bar due to personal jealousy. Vicarious liability was not established as his actions had no connection to his professional duties. In *Bernard v Att Gen of Jamaica* (2004), however, the police officer had announced himself as police before the wrongful shooting, later purporting to make an arrest. According to the Privy Council, 'taking into account the dominant feature of this case, viz that the constable at all material times purported to act as a policeman, the risks created by the police authorities reinforce the conclusion that vicarious liability is established'. It can be seen that a meticulous analysis of the facts is necessary to make the distinctions in such cases.

You will recall that in *CCWS*, introduced above in terms of the establishment of the employment relationship, where the two fundamental questions for vicarious liability were set out, question two is: 'is there a close connection that links the relationship and the act or omission of the wrongdoer?' In finding that the necessary close connection between the defendant and the wrongdoers existed in *CCWS*, Lord Phillips identified a common theme emerging from the authorities in the United Kingdom, Canada, and Australia:

> Starting with the Canadian authorities, a common theme can be traced through most of the cases to which I have referred. Vicarious liability is imposed where a defendant, whose relationship with the abuser put it in a position to use the abuser to carry on its business or to further its own interests, has done so in a manner which has created or significantly enhanced the risk that the victim or victims would suffer the relevant.

The application of the 'close connection' test and the way in which it focuses on the relationship between defendant and the wrongdoer and the acts of abuse can also be seen in *Maga v Trustees of the Birmingham Archdiocese of the Roman Catholic Church* (2010). The question here was whether a Catholic priest's sexual abuse of the claimant had been so closely connected with his employment as a priest that it would be fair and just to hold the Archdiocese which had employed him vicariously liable. The trial judge had found that the Catholic Church was not vicariously liable for the actions of the priest on the ground that he did not meet the claimant as part of his priestly duties and had not involved him in the activities of the Church itself. The priest had instead cultivated the claimant solely for the purpose of sexual abuse. The Court of Appeal reversed the first-instance decision, with Lord Neuberger observing that the issue, although very much fact-dependent, is ultimately one of law rather than of inference from facts. Here there was a sufficiently 'close connection' between the priest's employment at the Church and the abuse which he inflicted on the claimant, and it was fair and just to impose vicarious liability for the abuse on his employer, the Archdiocese. You will also see in the cases discussed below that the Supreme Court is not prepared to leave an innocent victim without a remedy (the wrongdoer is unlikely to have sufficient means to pay compensation) when a vicariously liable defendant is likely to be solvent or covered by insurance.

🔍 CASE CLOSE-UP

Mohamud v WM Morrison Supermarkets (2016)

The case involved an employee's attack on a customer at a petrol station where the Supreme Court considered whether the nature of the employee's job and his wrongful conduct made it right for the employer to be held liable. When Mohamud entered the kiosk at a supermarket petrol station, he was subjected to an unprovoked violent attack by the sales assistant. This began as racist verbal abuse in the kiosk; then the assistant followed the customer to his car and physically assaulted him.

The circumstances led the Court of Appeal to conclude that the employee's attack was personally motivated and had nothing to do with his employment. His duties did not involve the clear possibility of confrontation with customers or the use of force (unlike the doorman in *Hawley*, who was employed to keep order at the nightclub). The Supreme Court unanimously disagreed and allowed the claimant's appeal. According to Lord Toulson, the court has to consider two matters. The first question is what functions or 'field of activities' have been entrusted to the employee, or, in everyday language, what was the nature of his job. The second question is whether there was sufficient connection between the position in which he was employed and his wrongful conduct to make it right for the employer to be held liable. In the present case, it was the employee's job to attend to customers and his conduct in answering the claimant's request in a foul-mouthed way and ordering him to leave was inexcusable, but within the 'field of activities' assigned to him.

What happened in the attack thereafter was an unbroken sequence of events. In this type of case Lord Toulson said that the employee's motives were 'neither here nor there'. In reviewing how the law in this area has developed, what stage it has reached, and whether it is in need of significant change, the Court approved a broad approach being taken to the 'close connection' requirement as highlighted by the court in *Lister*.

An interesting recent development came in *Morrison Supermarkets v Various Claimants* (2018). This was an action brought against their employer by more than 5,500 employees of the well-known supermarket chain. In pursuit of a grudge against his employer, an IT auditor at Morrisons had copied co-workers' personal data and later, uploaded it to a file-sharing site and disclosed it to three newspapers. He was convicted of fraud and breach of the Data Protection Act 1998 (DPA) and sentenced to eight years' imprisonment. A group of employees brought tort actions against Morrison, as vicariously liable for breach of confidence and misuse of private information.

The Court of Appeal confirmed that the DPA had not expressly or by implication excluded vicarious liability, and that there could be concurrent liability under the Act and the common law. On the question of whether the wrong had been within the course of employment, the Court discounted defendant arguments that either the place of the wrong (some of the employee's activities took place at home) or motive were conclusive in this determination. The course of employment could be maintained, whether the wrong was in pursuit of greed as in *Lloyd*, personal gratification as in *Lister* or harming the employer as in the current case. The floodgates implications of 'Doomsday or Armageddon scenarios of data breaches on a massive scale caused by either corporate system failures or negligence by individuals acting in the course of their employment' were acknowledged by the Court but it concluded that this was best addressed by appropriate insurance rather than any limitation on common law remedies.

Also decided in October 2018 by the Court of Appeal was *Bellman v Northampton Recruitment* (2018). Here, the current generous judicial trend in vicarious liability persisted in the case of an after-party following the office Christmas get-together. After consuming considerable amounts of liquid 'seasonal cheer', the managing director got into an argument over a workplace issue, began to lecture the group about his position, ended up punching an employee who suffered serious brain damage, and then brought an action based on vicarious liability.

Overturning a first-instance decision in favour of the defendants, Lady Justice Arden examined the overall context. The questions Lord Toulson asked in *Mohamud* were to be applied. 'The first question is what functions or "field of activities" have been entrusted by the employer to the employee, or, in everyday language, what was the nature of his job.' It is to be approached 'broadly', looking beyond specific tasks given to the employee. Here the wrongdoer's remit and authority had been 'very wide'. The second of Lord Toulson's questions was whether there was a sufficient connection between the field of activities and the wrongful conduct in order that the employer be vicariously liable. The Court of Appeal disagreed with the first-instance interpretation of the facts. On the night in question, the managing director was attempting to exercise his managerial authority, albeit with the use of blows. Although the attack took place at a different venue from the official office party, there was a 'sufficient connection' between the wrongdoer's position as the most senior employee in the company (abusing his seniority) and the nature of the dispute, to render the assault as being within the course of employment. It can be suggested that *Bellman* is perhaps at the outer boundary of liability.

9.3.1.7 Fact-sensitive nature of the test for vicarious liability

We have seen above that the 'close connection' was criticized because it created uncertainty in the law. In *Dubai Aluminium Co Ltd v Salaam*, Lord Nicholls recognized that the application of the *Lister* test as to whether an employer is vicariously liable inevitably involves an element of value judgement, but he said a rigid test would not be effective in determining the issue. In her article 'Vicarious Liability in the Supreme Court' (2016) Professor Paula Giliker notes:

> In accepting imprecision, the Supreme Court leaves the law subject to uncertainty. We may regard this as the acceptable price of ensuring that the victims sexually abused by priests can obtain compensation when the original culprits have either disappeared or have passed away. The question remains, however, to what extent it is equally acceptable in the context of vicarious liability claims generally. One prediction may be made. The scope of the doctrine of vicarious liability will continue to be tested as claimants gain greater confidence that claims, which previously would have had no likelihood of success, may under the new regime be deemed just and fair. This is good news for tort victims, but likely to be less welcome to employers, who now find themselves strictly liable for the acts and omissions of a growing number of individuals for actions varying from the negligent carrying of kitchen supplies to racist attacks. One is left to wonder where, after three Supreme Court decisions in four years, this leaves the legal development of the doctrine of vicarious liability.

According to Giliker, the generous approach to the imposition of vicarious liability in recent Supreme Court decisions is justified because it enables innocent victims to obtain compensation. However, it seems to leave key value judgements with the trial judge, possibly creating uncertainty in the law.

This was echoed by Lady Justice Asplin in *Bellman*: 'The question of whether there is a sufficient connection between the position in which the wrongdoer is employed and his wrongful conduct so as to make the employer liable under the principle of social justice requires the court to conduct an evaluative judgment.'

9.3.1.8 The mere fact that his employment provided the employee with the opportunity to commit a tort is not sufficient to make an employer vicariously liable

A distinction needs to be made between the vicarious liability of an employer for fraud and other types of wrongdoing and an employer's liability where the employee merely uses the opportunity of his employment to commit a tort (usually involving fraud and dishonesty). In *Credit Lyonnais Bank Nederland NV v Export Credits Guarantee Department* (2000), the question was whether the employer was vicariously liable for one of its employees who had assisted in a fraudster's deceit by underwriting guarantees (in itself non-tortious conduct). The employee's act was only one aspect of the fraudulent conduct; the other features of the deceit were carried out by a third party who never had authority to act on behalf of the employer. The House of Lords refused to combine the separate acts of the two fraudsters and held that an employer could not be vicariously liable for the tort of an employee unless the acts were within the employee's actual or **ostensible authority**. The mere fact that his employment provided the employee with the opportunity to facilitate fraud was not sufficient to make an employer vicariously liable as in *Lister*.

> **ostensible authority**
> apparent authority

THINKING POINT

Would Horizon Tennis Club be liable to the owner of a valuable watch stolen from the club's changing room by the head gardener, who was expressly prohibited from entering the club house in the course of his gardening activities?

9.4 Indemnity

While we have seen that an employer can be sued for the tort of its employee, it is also possible for the employer who pays damages to a claimant to recover these from the employee. In *Lister v Romford Ice* (1957), an employee took his father with him as mate on his employer's lorry. The father was injured as a result of the son's negligence, for which his employer was vicariously liable. However, as we have seen earlier, vicarious liability does not mean that the employer is liable instead of the employee; vicarious liability is treated as joint and several liability, which means that the employee remains liable. The House of Lords held that employees are obliged by their contract of employment to indemnify their employer against any liability which results from the employee's responsibility for damage caused. However, in England, in the interests of good labour relations, no such claim for indemnity would be made against an employee in the absence of deliberate wrongdoing.

 Summary

- Vicarious liability imposes liability without the need to prove fault on the part of the defendant.
- The rationale for the rule is based on the fact that economic activity carries a risk of harm to others and employers can best afford to compensate parties injured as a result of their employees' negligence.
- Recent Supreme Court decisions illustrate that this is an area of law which is expanding and is strongly influenced by policy considerations.

- *Lister* held that the question of whether an employee is acting in the course of employment is to be addressed by application of the 'close connection' test, and *Various Claimants v Catholic Child Welfare Society* held that the criteria to establish vicarious liability involved a synthesis of two stages.

- *Majrowski* held that where an employee's act of harassment in breach of a statutory duty imposed on the employee meets the 'close connection' test, the employer could be vicariously liable.

Visit the online resources to listen to a podcast summarizing the topics covered in this chapter.

The bigger picture

'"Uber" is a modern business phenomenon' according to the Employment Tribunal which heard the first stage of a case to determine whether Uber drivers are 'workers' for the purposes of entitlement to the minimum wage and holiday entitlement. In *Uber v Aslam* (2018) a majority in the Court of Appeal upheld the decision of the Employment Tribunal and Employment Appeal Tribunal in favour of the drivers, thus entitling them to full statutory protection as 'workers' rather than independent contractors. Although not a tort case, when you read it you will see that many of the elements considered by the judges in the assessment were identical to those used in determining employee status for the purposes of vicarious liability: control, payment, ownership of vehicles, risk, and more. *Uber* reinforces two points relevant to vicarious liability: first, defining 'employment' is an issue which extends across a wide range of legal and practical situations and second, working styles and methods are ever-evolving and that the law must be adaptable.

? Questions

Knowledge-testing questions

1. Who is an employee for the purposes of vicarious liability?

2. List the factors taken into account by the courts to determine vicarious liability outside the traditional employer–employee relationship.

3. Identify the main policy reasons underlying the principle of vicarious liability.

4. Explain the tests used to determine if the employee was acting within the scope of employment for the purposes of vicarious liability.

Problem and essay questions

1. Explain the circumstances in which an employer will be vicariously liable for the tort of an employee.

2. Springfield Florists has a clear and well-publicized policy prohibiting staff from carrying passengers in company vehicles. Ben, Springfield's delivery man, is provided with a company van. Ben regularly delivers flowers in the evening on his way home from work

and sometimes he gives his friend Ali a lift in the company van. One evening as Ben was leaving to deliver flower arrangements to a hotel, he agreed that if Ali helped carry the flowers into the hotel Ben would give him a lift home in the van. Through Ben's negligence the van crashed on the return journey and Ali suffered serious injuries. Ali is claiming in negligence against Springfield florists.

Contrary to the policy prohibiting staff from carrying passengers in Springfield vehicles, Ed, one of the florists, invited the two boys from the local school to accompany him to the flower market, where he offered to buy them lunch. Ed drove to a very secluded part of the flower market, where he committed acts of sexual assault against the boys.

Advise Springfield Florists as to its liability (if any) to Ali and the boys.

 Visit the online resources for guidance on answering these questions.

Further reading

Bell, J, 'The Basis of Vicarious Liability' (2013) 72 CLJ 17

Giliker, P, '*Lister* Revisited: Vicarious Liability, Distributive Justice and the Course of Employment' (2010) 126 LQR 521

Giliker, P, 'Vicarious Liability in the UK Supreme Court' (2016) 7 *UK Supreme Court Yearbook* 152

Lord Hope, 'Tailoring the Law on Vicarious Liability' (2013) 129 LQR 514

Tofaris, S, 'Vicarious Liability and Non-delegable Duty for Child Abuse in Foster Care: A Step Too Far?'

Williams, K, 'Vicarious Liability of the Roman Catholic Church for Sexual Abuse by a Priest' (2010) 26 PN 113

10 Product liability

□ **LEARNING OBJECTIVES**

By the end of this chapter you should be able to:

● explain how the traditional common law developed to provide consumers with a remedy in tort for harm caused by defective products;

● identify the limitations of the tort system in providing compensation to a victim of harm caused by a defective product;

● explain the justifications for the imposition of strict liability on manufacturers and producers for defective products; and

● evaluate the scope and limitations of the Consumer Protection Act 1987.

Introduction

CROSS REFERENCE
Economic loss is discussed in Chapter 5.

This chapter is concerned with the liability of manufacturers and producers for personal injury or damage to property caused by a defective product. We will examine how the law concerning 'product liability' has developed and how it is applied in seeking to define, limit, and apportion responsibility for defective products which cause harm. Before the emergence of the common law and the statutory framework on 'product liability', a consumer injured by a product that he had bought could bring an action against the retailer for breach of contract. The benefit of seeking a remedy in contract is that liability is strict, in the sense that where a term in the contract is breached, or where there is breach of the implied term that goods sold under the Consumer Rights Act 2015 be of satisfactory quality, fit for purpose, and as described, the claimant is not required to show negligence on the part of the retailer. Not only will the claimant be able to recover in contract for personal injury and property damage caused by the defective product; under contract law the claimant will also be compensated for the cost of replacing the product itself. In the law of tort there is no recovery for harm caused to the product itself, which is regarded as pure economic loss.

Consumer protection in tort is concerned with protecting consumers against harm caused by 'unsafe' products, not about compensation for defects in the product itself. Product liability (ginger beer) was the basis of the claim in *Donoghue v Stevenson*, where the court recognized that a legal relationship outside contract law could arise if a relationship of proximity exists between a consumer and the manufacturer of the product. However, liability in the tort of negligence is restricted to consequential harm, which means that there is no recovery for harm caused to the product itself. The principle that recovery for quality defects is through the law of contract only was reiterated in *Murphy v Brentwood District Council* (1991), where the House of Lords said that the cost of replacing a defective product will be classified as pure economic loss and it is therefore not recoverable in tort. However, the main disadvantage of bringing an action in contract is that normally only the parties to the contract can sue. So, for example, a person injured by a product bought for him as a gift, would not have an action against the retailer (as seen in *Donoghue v Stevenson*). Similarly, a bystander injured by a defective product would be unable to bring an action in contract against the retailer because he is not a party to the contract.

10.1 The common law position

▶ CROSS REFERENCE

The 'neighbour principle' is discussed in Chapter 2.

Before *Donoghue v Stevenson* (1932), in the absence of a contractual relationship, it was not clear whether a duty of care was owed in respect of a product which caused harm, unless there was something inherently dangerous in the product itself. In *Donoghue v Stevenson*, because the drink had been bought for the plaintiff by a friend, there was no contractual duty between her and the manufacturer of the ginger beer. In this landmark decision, however, the House of Lords held that, even in the absence of a contract, a manufacturer can be liable to the ultimate consumer where a product has caused physical damage. It is from *Donoghue v Stevenson* that common law negligence developed. The 'wide *ratio*' of the decision is the neighbour principle, which judges in later generations interpreted as creating a general principle of liability in negligence. However, the 'narrow *ratio*' of the case is that a manufacturer owes a duty of care to the ultimate consumer of a product, even when the party who suffers the harm caused by the product is prevented from bringing an action against the manufacturer under the contract.

Nevertheless, because liability in negligence requires proof of fault on the part of the manufacturer, there are a number of difficulties which must be overcome by a consumer. A claimant seeking to prove that a manufacturer was negligent may find it very difficult to find out exactly what happened and obtain evidence of fault on the part of the manufacturer. The defect may have been caused by negligence during the manufacturing process but it could also be as a result of a defect in the design of the product. In many situations, such as in the manufacture of pharmaceutical or technological products, obtaining evidence of fault on the part of the manufacturer will be extremely difficult. We will now go on to consider the details of liability for defective products under the common law and then examine liability under the Consumer

Protection Act 1987 (CPA 1987), but it is important at this point to note that the statutory protection does not replace the common law tort of negligence; it supplements it by providing the consumer with a further possible cause of action over and above the common law. The focus of the Act is to protect against products which cause harm to the consumer and you will see later that the main restrictions on the scope of the Act relate to property damage. Because of these restrictions, where a defective product causes damage to property the consumer will need to rely on the common law.

Generally speaking, there is no tort action where a product is merely defective and has not caused any physical damage. The law of contract provides the basis of protection for products which are defective in quality, though not dangerous.

10.1.1 The 'narrow *ratio*' in *Donoghue v Stevenson*

As we have seen earlier, the element of this decision which provided the foundations for a general duty of care in negligence is known as the 'wide *ratio*' but the specific facts of the case concerned a duty of care in respect of liability for harm caused by a defective product. This element of the decision is known as the 'narrow *ratio*' and the duty is expressed as follows by Lord Atkin:

> a manufacturer of products, which he sells in such a form as to show that he intends them to reach the ultimate consumer in the form in which they left him with no reasonable possibility of intermediate examination and with the knowledge that the absence of reasonable care in the preparation or putting up of the products will result in an injury to the consumer's life or property, owes a duty to the consumer to take reasonable care.

We shall now examine more closely each of the elements of the narrow *ratio*.

10.1.1.1 'a manufacturer'

Although the original case related narrowly to a manufacturer's liability, subsequent cases have interpreted the meaning of 'manufacturer' very broadly and extended it beyond the maker of a product to include distributors, suppliers, and repairers of goods. In *Stennett v Hancock and Peters* (1939), where part of a wheel from a passing lorry flew off and injured the plaintiff's leg, the definition of a manufacturer was held to include the *repairer*. The court found that the owner of the lorry was not at fault but the repairers were found liable for their careless re-assembly of the wheel. Liability has also been found to arise in the case of *suppliers* in circumstances where a supplier would normally be expected to check for safety before selling the goods. For example, in *Andrews v Hopkinson* (1957), a second-hand car dealer was held liable because the defective steering on an 18-year-old car could easily have been discovered by a competent mechanic. This principle has even been extended to *distributors*, such as in the case of *Watson v Buckley, Osborne, Garrett & Co* (1940). Here the distributors who failed to test a hair dye themselves before they advertised it as harmless were held to be negligent.

10.1.1.2 'of products'

The definition of a product has been extended beyond food and drinks to include all manufactured products capable of causing damage. It seems to encompass every article, including underwear, gas, food and drink, hair dye, and even lifts (*Haseldine v Daw* (1941)). In *Grant v Australian Knitting Mills Ltd* (1936), the plaintiff contracted dermatitis through wearing woollen underpants which had been manufactured by the defendants. The disease was caused by invisible excess sulphites which had been negligently left in the underwear during the manufacturing process. The defendant argued that *Donoghue v Stevenson* could be distinguished on the ground that the ginger beer was to be consumed internally, whereas the underpants were to be worn externally. However, the Privy Council held the defendants liable on the ground that no distinction can be logically drawn between a noxious thing taken internally and a noxious thing applied externally.

The only exceptions as to what items come within the definition of 'products' appears to be buildings, which are in a category of their own. However, things attached to buildings, or the raw materials to be used in constructing buildings, may well be regarded as products.

10.1.1.3 'which he sells'

You will see from the previous paragraph that almost any type of transfer or exchange may come within the definition of 'sells' for the purposes of manufacturers' liability for dangerous or defective products.

10.1.1.4 'the ultimate consumer'

The ultimate consumer is construed very widely to include any user of the product and even persons less obviously at risk may be within the scope of the manufacturer's duty. For example, in *Barnett v H and J Packer & Co* (1940), the plaintiff, the proprietor of a sweet shop, was injured by a piece of metal protruding from a sweet. When he sued the manufacturer of the sweets he was held to be a 'consumer' and the defendant was liable. The extent to which the class of plaintiffs to which the definition of consumer has been extended can be illustrated by *Stennett v Hancock and Peters* (at 10.1.1.1 'a manufacturer'), where a pedestrian was held to be within the rule in *Donoghue v Stevenson*.

10.1.1.5 'with no reasonable possibility of intermediate examination'

> **THINKING POINT**
> Consider products you have purchased which might be reasonably expected to have been given 'intermediate examination'.

'With no reasonable possibility of intermediate examination' has been widely interpreted by the courts. A mere opportunity for intermediate examination will not exonerate the defendant; there must be a reasonable probability of intermediate inspection. The question, therefore, is whether the defendant can reasonably expect that the consumer will undertake an inspection before using the product. In *Griffiths v Arch Engineering Co* (1968), the plaintiff workman was injured by a portable grinding tool which he borrowed from the first defendants, but the tool was actually owned by the second defendants. The court held that the first defendants were liable because they had an opportunity to examine the tool and failed to do so, but the second defendants were equally liable, because they had no reason to suppose that such an examination would, in fact, be carried out.

Therefore, a manufacturer, who has no reason to believe that an intermediate inspection will take place, whether by a third party or the consumer, will be liable. The product need not reach the ultimate consumer in a sealed package for the duty to arise; in *Grant v Australian Knitting*

Mills (discussed at 10.1.1.2 'of products') it was held that for the rule to apply: 'the customer must use the article exactly as it left the maker, that is in all material features, and use it as it was intended to be used'.

10.1.2 Adequate warning and causation

A warning of danger, provided it is adequate in the circumstances, may be evidence of reasonable care on the part of the manufacturer. In *Kubach v Hollands* (1937), a manufacturer sold a chemical to the second defendants (retailers), which was accompanied with an invoice containing an express statement that the chemical must be 'examined and tested by user before use'. Before selling the chemical to a science teacher, the retailer failed to observe the manufacturer's instructions to test the product before it was labelled. When the chemical was used in a school experiment and exploded, injuring a schoolgirl and her father, the retailer was liable. The manufacturers were not liable because they had given an adequate warning and the retailer had ignored it. Although the ordinary rules of causation and remoteness of damage in negligence apply in all of these cases, at this point you should note that in order to establish liability for a defective product, there must be sufficient evidence that the defect existed when the product left the manufacturer; if the fault might have occurred after it had been manufactured rather than during the manufacturing process itself, the manufacturer will not be liable. In *Evans v Triplex Safety Glass Co Ltd* (1936), the plaintiff bought a Vauxhall car fitted with a windscreen made of 'Triplex Toughened Safety Glass'. A year later when he was driving the car, with his wife and son as passengers, the windscreen suddenly and for no apparent reason cracked and disintegrated. The occupants of the car were injured and brought an action against the manufacturers of the windscreen. In this case the defendants were not liable because the windscreen might have been interfered with and the defect introduced by any one of a range of alternative causes other than a defect in manufacture. The factors taken into account in reaching this decision were the lapse of time between the purchase of the windscreen and the accident and the possibility that the glass may have been strained as it was being screwed into its frame. In circumstances such as these, where the product has been in circulation a long time so that there has been both a probability of intermediate examination and a possibility that something caused the defect in the product after it left the manufacturer, it will be difficult for the claimant to prove that the harm was caused by the manufacturer's negligence.

> **THINKING POINT**
>
> To what extent do the above cases suggest that the common law has interpreted the law in favour of the consumer?

10.1.3 Design defects

The focus of the cases examined so far has been directed towards defects which occur in the process of manufacture of the product. However, defects can also occur at the product design stage; for example, the development of a new drug which causes unintended harmful side effects. Because of the difficulties in obtaining evidence or documents showing negligence at the design stage of a product, design defects pose particular problems for a claimant trying to establish negligence on the part of the manufacturer. Not only is there difficulty in showing fault in the design of the product but, in the case of drugs or other medical products, the claimant also needs to prove causation. Showing that the drug in question caused the particular harm

> **THINKING POINT**
>
> What are the main justifications for imposing strict liability on manufacturers and producers to consumers injured by defective products?

▶ CROSS REFERENCE
See Chapter 1 for more on the thalidomide case.

or side effect from which the claimant is suffering can present a considerable stumbling block. There may be other factors which potentially caused the harm or the claimant may be taking other drugs or receiving medical treatment that produced the side effects. It was the result of a very prominent and poignant drug injuries case, the thalidomide tragedy, that prompted widespread calls for a change in the law. The thalidomide drug was prescribed for pregnant women to relieve the symptoms of morning sickness, but it produced appalling side effects and it is estimated that about 10,000 children worldwide were born deformed as a result of their mothers taking the drug. When British parents brought claims in negligence against the drug company they experienced considerable difficulty in showing that the company failed to take reasonable care in manufacturing the drug and this led to widespread public debate about the failure in the tort system to provide compensation, which ultimately led to the introduction of a strict liability regime for defective products. We have seen that pressure for reform came about by Law Commission proposals and the Pearson Commission Report on Civil Liability and Compensation for Personal Injury in the 1970s. This growing pressure for strict liability for harm caused by defective products was followed by the Council of European Communities Directive 85/374/EEC requiring harmonization of product liability laws in member states and, in response, the UK government enacted the CPA 1987.

Following the referendum of June 2016, the UK formally left the EU on 31 January 2020. It is likely, however, that the existing consumer protections legislation will remain in place for the foreseeable future.

We will now go on to examine civil liability arising under Part I of the Consumer Protection Act 1987.

10.2 Consumer Protection Act 1987

Under the Act, Part I of which came into effect on 1 March 1988, anyone supplying defective products within the European Union (even if they are imported from outside) is strictly liable in tort if the defect causes injury to person or property. As we have seen, the fault-based system under common law focuses on the behaviour of the defendant and it is generally more difficult for a claimant to prove his case. Strict liability, however, focuses on the product itself, rather than on the person behind the product, and this means that a considerable degree of the burden of proof is shifted from the claimant to the defendant. Although the most notable feature of the Act is that the claimant does not have to show fault on the part of the defendant, it does provide the producer with a number of defences. As we will see, the most important and controversial of these defences is the 'development risks' defence. The Act does not rule out any other liability arising in contract or tort generally but it does add a further possible basis of claim to the law concerning defective products. The new strict liability statutory tort is, in effect, a supplement to the traditional fault-based liability. However, perhaps the biggest question at this point is whether or not this Act, hailed as introducing 'strict liability' on producers, really has achieved that. Only by looking closely at the requirements of the cause of action may we draw any conclusions.

10.2.1 Who can be liable under the Act?

Liability for damage caused wholly or partly by a defective product is imposed on three principal categories of defendant:

- the producer—under ss 1(2) and 2(2)(a);
- the 'own brander'—under s 2(2)(b); and
- the importer of a product into Europe—under s 2(2)(c).

10.2.1.1 Producers

Producers are usually manufacturers of the product, but a manufacturer of a 'component part' of the final product is also classified as a producer. Where products have not been manufactured but have been 'won or extracted' from other sources, the persons who mine or otherwise obtain raw materials (such as coal) come within the meaning of producers. Persons who undertake an industrial or some other process which alters the essential characteristics of the product (such as canned vegetables or processed foods and drinks) are also included in the definition of producer, but the extent to which this applies is not clear. It is questionable whether freezing fresh vegetables, for example, alters the essential characteristics of the product.

10.2.1.2 Own branders

'Own branders' is the term used to describe suppliers who put their own name or distinguishing trade mark on a product to hold themselves out as producers of the product. For example, large supermarkets frequently market goods or clothing made to their specifications by other manufacturers and when they sell these under their own brand labels (such as M&S food or clothing) they are holding themselves out as the producer. However, the retailer would not be holding itself out as the producer if the label stated: 'made from pure silk for M&S'.

10.2.1.3 Importers of goods to a member state

'Importers'—any persons who import goods into the European Union in the course of business, in order to supply to others—are treated as producers. The supplier (retailer or distributor) of goods is not generally liable under the Act, but where a consumer has bought a defective product which does not provide information on the identity of the producer, the supplier then becomes liable under s 2(3).

Other suppliers include: wholesalers, retailers, and repairers, but these are only liable in circumstances where they do not identify the producer, importer, or own brander within a reasonable time after being requested to do so by the injured party. Liability is joint and several, which means that both, or more, defendants may be sued; the consumer can therefore trace the producer through the entire chain of supply and any person in the line of manufacture or distribution of the product is potentially liable without proof of fault.

THINKING POINT

As we have seen, under the Act any person in the chain of manufacture or supply of the product which caused the harm is potentially liable without proof of fault. In what particular circumstances might this benefit the consumer?

STATUTE

CPA 1987, s 7

liability shall not be limited or excluded by any contract term, by any notice or by any other provision.

10.2.2 **What is a product?**

As you will see later, the definition of the term 'product' is not restricted to consumer goods, but includes all movables. Primary agricultural produce (such as unprocessed meat or vegetables) was originally excluded but the Act has now been modified and all primary agricultural produce and game are now covered by the legislation.

As in the common law, buildings are not covered by the Act but their component parts are included so that, for example, a manufacturer of a defective wooden beam would be liable for injury if the defect led to the collapse of a floor.

STATUTE

CPA 1987

The basic definition of 'product' is found in s 1(2):

includes any goods or electricity and . . . includes a product which is comprised in another product.

'Goods' are defined in s 45(1) as:

Substances, growing crops, and things comprised in land by virtue of being attached to it and any ship, aircraft or vehicle.

Pure information is not covered by the Act because it is thought that a 'product' must be in some tangible form, but the producer may be liable in respect of information contained in deficient printed instructions or warnings which accompany a product and thereby make it unsafe.

THINKING POINT

We have seen that pure information is not a product. Would the driver of a car using a satnav map that provided incorrect information and caused him to crash into another car, be able to claim under the Act?

10.2.3 **What is a 'defective' product?**

The key element in bringing a claim under the Act is defining what is meant by a 'defect' because the claimant must: (1) show that there was a defect in the product which made it unsafe; (2) show that the damage or harm suffered was caused wholly or partly by that defect. You will see later that under s 3(1) a product is defective when its safety is not as 'persons generally are entitled to expect'. However, what persons generally are entitled to expect may be a very different standard to that which 'consumers' are entitled to expect. Because the standard that persons generally are entitled to expect is set by the court, not only will consumers' expectations about a product's safety be taken into account, but the view of the manufacturers will also be considered. A consumer may expect a product to be perfectly safe, but a manufacturer may argue that this expectation is unreasonably high; for example, where a medicine used to treat a life-threatening condition carries some small risk of unintended side effects, a manufacturer may argue that the benefits to the consumer far outweigh the small risk of an adverse effect. The question, therefore, in determining the standard of safety the public is legitimately entitled to expect, is to ask: do the benefits in the product outweigh the risk of harm to the consumer? So, depending on all the circumstances, this means that in some cases, the standard of safety which persons are entitled to expect in a product will be lower.

STATUTE

CPA 1987

Section 3(1) provides that a product is defective where its safety:

is not such as persons generally are entitled to expect . . . .

Section 3(2) provides:

In determining . . . what persons generally are entitled to expect in relation to a product all the circumstances shall be taken into account . . . .

The factors which the court is required to take into account under s 3(2) include the following:

- the manner in which and purposes for which the product has been marketed and its get-up (packaging or presentation);
- the use of any mark in relation to the product and any instructions or warnings given with it;

- what might reasonably be expected to be done with or in relation to the product; and
- the time the product was supplied by the producer.

▶ CROSS REFERENCE
See 10.2.4 Standards of safety that 'persons generally' are entitled to expect.

Although liability under the Act is strict, many of the above factors—for example, misuse of the product by the consumer, the effect of a warning which may make a potentially 'unsafe' product safe, and the fact that the safety of the product is judged at the time it left the producer rather than when it reached the consumer—are all taken into account in common law negligence. However, in *Abouzaid v Mothercare (UK) Ltd* (2000) and *A and others v National Blood Authority and others* (2001) fault-based arguments were rejected. The court emphasized that the legislation was intended to eliminate the need to prove fault or negligence on the part of the manufacturer and to make it easier for claimants to prove their case.

STATUTE

CPA 1987, s 3(2)

and nothing in this section shall require a defect to be inferred from the fact alone that the safety of a product which is supplied after that time is greater than the safety of the product in question.

You should note that the provisions of s 3(2)(c) mean that just because a product which was supplied at a later date is safer, does not necessarily mean that a product is assumed to be defective.

10.2.4 Standards of safety that 'persons generally' are entitled to expect

In *Abouzaid v Mothercare (UK) Ltd*, the standard that persons generally are entitled to expect was considered by the Court of Appeal. The case concerned an elasticated strap on a sleeping bag intended to be fitted to a pushchair. When attempting to fit the strap, it sprang back and the buckle struck the plaintiff in the eye and caused him severe injury. The court found that the defendants would not have been liable in common law negligence because although the danger was present, it was not a risk which a reasonable manufacturer should have appreciated (see remoteness of damage). The case therefore turned on whether the product was defective as defined in s 3 of the Consumer Protection Act. Applying the test of what persons generally are entitled to expect, the product was held to be defective within the meaning of the Act because there were no warnings and the strap could not be secured safely. Although liability was borderline, the vulnerability of the eye and the serious consequences that could follow from such an injury were important factors in considering the standard of safety persons generally are entitled to expect; the court held that members of the public were entitled to expect better.

The public expectation test was again considered in *A and others v National Blood Authority and others* (2001).

🔍 CASE CLOSE-UP

A and others v National Blood Authority and others (2001)

The case involved a number of claimants who in the 1970s and 1980s had received blood from infected donors because they suffered from haemophilia or other blood disorders or while undergoing surgery. As many as 30,000 people may have been affected nationally, of whom 3,000 have died. It was accepted that the blood, which was infected with hepatitis C, was a product within the meaning of the Act. At the time of the transfusions, the risk of infection was known but the defendants claimed that since it was impossible at that particular time to detect the virus, even though it was known, the risk was unavoidable. The court held that the avoidability or otherwise of the risk was not, in this case, a relevant circumstance. A factor that was considered to be relevant was that while the risk of infection was known to medical professionals, it was barely known at all by the public at large. Burton J observed:

> I do not consider it to be arguable that the consumer had an actual expectation that blood being supplied to him was not 100% clean, nor do I conclude that he had knowledge that it was, or was likely to be, infected with Hepatitis C. It is not seriously argued by the Defendants, notwithstanding some few newspaper cuttings which were referred to, that there was any public understanding or acceptance of the infection of transfused blood by Hepatitis C. Doctors and surgeons knew, but did not tell their patients unless asked, and were very rarely asked. It was certainly, in my judgment, not known and accepted by society that there was such a risk . . . .

Thus, the public at large were entitled to expect that the blood transfusions would be free from infection and because the blood and blood products contaminated with the hepatitis C virus were defective within the meaning of s 3 of the CPA 1987, the defendants were liable.

As a result of the catastrophic consequences of this contamination of UK blood supplies with lethal viruses in July 2017 the government announced a UK-wide inquiry into the contaminated blood scandal to establish the causes of the 'appalling injustice' that took place in the 1970s and 1980s.

The issue of what constitutes a 'defective product' was considered in *Wilkes v DePuy International Ltd* (2016).

A patient received a hip replacement, with a prosthesis manufactured by DePuy. It fractured after three years and had to be replaced. The claimant brought an action under the CPA 1987 on the basis that the prosthesis constituted a defective product. Hickinbottom J in the High Court revisited *A v National Blood Authority* in which safety 'not such as persons generally are entitled to expect' was interpreted as a 'legitimate expectation' of safety. He regarded this as an 'unnecessary and unhelpful gloss on the Act':

> In considering whether a product suffered from a defect, the court must assess the appropriate level of safety, exercising its judgment, and taking into account the information and the circumstances before it, whether or not an actual or notional patient or patients, or indeed other members of the public, would in fact have considered each of those factors and all of that information.

The judge stressed that safety is 'inherently and necessarily a relative concept' and there cannot be a 'sensible expectation that any medicine or medicinal product is entirely risk-free'. The court considered a 'constellation of factors' which combined to lead to the fracture and concluded that this was not down to a defect in the prosthesis at the time it was put on the market. The claimant had failed to convince the court that its safety was not such as persons generally were entitled to expect.

The decision in *Wilkes*, albeit at first instance only, has been seen as a timely reminder that the CPA 1987, while regarded as a strict liability statute, does not guarantee that products attain a standard of absolute safety.

10.2.5 Who can recover under the Act?

Liability is to a 'consumer' and there is no distinction between those using the product and mere bystanders. This means that anyone who has suffered damage caused wholly or partly by a defect in a product, or a dependant or relative of such a person, can bring an action. The Act provides that death and personal injury are covered by the Act and you should note that personal injury damages, however small, are recoverable. This is not the case with property damage, which is not recoverable unless it is valued over £275.

 STATUTE

CPA 1987, s 5(1)

This section provides that for the purposes of liability under the Act damage means:

> death or personal injury or any loss of or damage to any property . . .

The main restrictions on the right to recover relate to property damage.

 STATUTE

CPA 1987, s 5(2)–(4)

Section 5(2) provides that damage to, or loss of, the defective product itself, including damage to a product caused by a defective component, is not recoverable.

Section 5(3) provides that 'property' must be of a type ordinarily intended for private use and the claimant must have intended to use it mainly for his own private purposes.

Section 5(4) provides that property damage below £275 is excluded.

The provisions of s 5(3) were considered in *Renfrew Golf Club v Motocaddy Ltd* (2015), where the question was whether a golf clubhouse came within the definition of property ordinarily intended for private use or occupation.

This case concerned a golf trolley manufactured in China, imported into the EU by Motocaddy and sold under their brand name. The golf trolley was purchased and used by a member of the golf club for approximately two years. On one occasion when the trolley was left overnight in the clubhouse at Renfrew Golf Club it caught fire because of what seemed to be an electrical fault in the trolley's motor. This caused a fire which extensively damaged the clubhouse and Renfrew Golf Club claimed against Motocaddy in common law negligence and under the CPA 1987.

Under the CPA, Motocaddy was the 'own brander' (s 2(2)(b)) and also the importer of the golf trolley into Europe (s 2(2)(c)). The golf trolley was claimed to be defective under s 3(1) because of failure to test and failure to fit proper electronic safety mechanisms in its motor.

However, the claim failed because under s 5(3) the damage to the clubhouse was not property ordinarily intended for private use or occupation. Lord Philip said:

> the clubhouse, in common with many golf clubhouses, was used for a material amount of economic or commercial activity. Moreover, I am unable to accept that Parliament intended that a building, the use of which was available to seven hundred members as well as others, could be described as being subject only to private use. In these circumstances I do not consider that the clubhouse was of a description of property ordinarily intended for private use or occupation.

THINKING POINT

(1) Would a home computer used by a lecturer to write all her lectures and teaching materials be considered 'property ordinarily intended for private use'?

(2) If the computer did come within the meaning of s 5(3) and had an electrical fault causing burns to the lecturer's hands and damage to his watch valued at £100, what damage would be compensated under the Consumer Protection Act?

10.2.6 Defences

STATUTE

CPA 1987, s 4(1)(a)–(f)

Section 4(1)(a): the defect was the inevitable effect of the producer acting in compliance with the law—although likely to be extremely rare, this defence would cover a situation where, for example, legal requirements stipulate that an additive or an ingredient should be contained in a product.

Section 4(1)(b): the person proceeded against did not supply the product to anyone—this would apply if the defendant could show that goods were stolen or that a 'fake' product has been supplied.

Section 4(1)(c): the defendant did not supply the product in the course of a business or for profit—the focus of protection in this section is on those not acting 'with a view to profit' and to ensure that liability is imposed on businesses and not on private individuals, for example, those who sell home-made products at charity events.

Section 4(1)(d): the defect did not exist in the product at the time it was supplied—this defence will apply where the defendant can show that the defect did not exist at the time the product was put into circulation for example, in the case of perishable foods or medicines which must not be used beyond a specified date.

Section 4(1)(e): 'development risks' defence—this is similar to the *Roe v Ministry of Health* 'state of the art defence' in negligence.

Section 4(1)(f): the producer of a component can escape liability by showing that the defect was in the subsequent product and not the component part.

Apart from general arguments concerning proof of causation, of the six defences provided in s 4 the most controversial is the s 4(1)(e) 'development risks' defence.

10.2.6.1 Section 4(1)(e) 'development risks' defence

▶ CROSS REFERENCE

See more on *Roe v Ministry of Health* in Chapter 3.

This defence is similar to the 'state of the art' defence (see *Roe v Ministry of Health*) in common law negligence and it is one of the most widely criticized aspects of the Act. The inclusion of this defence was optional under the Directive and it has not been uniformly adopted by the other member states. Section 4(1)(e) provides it is a defence for the producer to show that:

> the state of scientific and technical knowledge at the relevant time was not such that a producer of products of the same description as the product in question might be expected to have discovered the defect if it had existed in his products while they were under his control.

The Directive seems to indicate that the defence will only apply where there is no known method of discovering the risk and where the producer can establish that at the time of circulation of the product the *general* knowledge available was not such as to enable the existence of the risk to be discovered. The main criticism of s 4(1)(e) is that the defence under the Act appears to be more generous to the manufacturer and easier to establish than intended by the Directive. The Consumer Protection Act only requires the defendant to show that *the producer of products of the same description* might be expected to have discovered the existence of the defect at the time of circulation. This means that instead of showing that on the basis of the scientific and technical knowledge available at the time, *no one* could have discovered the defect, under s 4(1)(e) the defendant only has to show that *no producer of similar products* could have discovered the defect. The defendant is permitted to refer to what might have been expected in comparable producers and if the defendant can show that he has exercised the standard of care of a reasonable producer he will not be liable.

The potential conflict between the words in the Directive and s 4(1)(e) of the Consumer Protection Act was examined by the European Court of Justice in *Commission v UK* (1997), and the defence as enacted and applied was not found to be inconsistent with the Directive. Subsequently, the Directive was interpreted in favour of the consumer in *A and others v National Blood Authority and others*, where the defendant sought to rely on the defence on the ground that, although the risk was known, the scientific knowledge which existed at the time could not enable the defect to be discovered. In a no-fault regime, Burton J refused to take into account the costs or impracticality of avoiding the risk and held that once the existence of the defect was known, there was a risk the defect would cause harm. The fact that the risk was unavoidable was therefore irrelevant, he stated:

> It would, in my judgment, be inconsistent with the purpose of the Directive if a producer, in the case of a known risk, continues to supply products simply because, and despite the fact that, he is unable to identify in which if any of his products it will occur or recur, or more relevantly, in a case such as this where the producer is obliged to supply, continues to supply without accepting the responsibility for any injuries resulting, by insurance or otherwise.

In *Abouzaid v Mothercare (UK) Ltd* the defendant tried to argue that at the time the product was put into circulation the scientific or technical knowledge did not exist to enable them to discover the defect in the elastic strap. They sought to rely on the absence of any recorded accidents of this type on the Department of Trade database but the Court of Appeal held the defect was present, whether or not previous accidents had occurred. Records of comparable accidents at the relevant time probably did not constitute technical knowledge.

Diagram 10.1 summarizes the effect and scope of the CPA 1987.

CROSS REFERENCE
See 10.2.4 Standards of safety that 'persons generally' are entitled to expect.

Diagram 10.1 Overview of the Consumer Protection Act 1987

Who can be liable?
Producers
Own branders
Importers into Europe

What is a product?
Not restricted to consumer goods but includes electricity, building materials, etc. However, buildings are not within the scope of the Act

What is a defective product?
Products do not have to be absolutely safe, but only as safe as 'persons generally are entitled to expect' taking into account all the circumstances

Factors to be considered in determining liability under the Consumer Protection Act for products which cause harm

Who can recover under the Act?
Anyone who suffers death or personal injury and loss or damage to property caused by unsafe products. Note restrictions in respect of property damage: only 'property' ordinarily intended for private use is covered and property damage below £275 is not covered

Are defences provided under the Act?
The Act provides various defences. The most controversial of these is the 'development risks defence' s 4(1)(e)

10.3 Limitation of actions

A claim under the Act cannot be made outside the limitation period, which is more than ten years after the defective product was released on to the market. Within those ten years, the claimant must bring his action within three years of being injured or becoming aware (or should reasonably have become aware) of the injury or damage (and the defect and the producer's identity) which has been caused by the defective product. In the case of personal injuries, the court has discretion to extend the three-year period but in all circumstances, however strong the claimant's case, the ten-year period is an absolute cut-off point and the court has no discretion to extend this deadline. This provision is to prevent the risk of mass claims arising from design defects which only come to light after many years.

> **THINKING POINT**
>
> (1) Why might the Act be underutilized? (2) How far can we say that the Consumer Protection Act is truly strict liability?

In *O'Byrne v Aventis-Pasteur* (2010) a 5-year-old boy suffered brain damage caused by a childhood vaccine which was alleged to be defective. Proceedings against the defendant were commenced within the ten-year limitation period under the EU Product Liability Directive in the mistaken belief that it was the producer of the vaccine. Where a defendant is named in error in the original proceedings, domestic law allows for a new defendant to be substituted and the question here was whether these provisions are compatible with the strict ten-year limitation period under the EU directive. The Supreme Court held that a national rule allowing substitution of defendants could not permit a producer to be sued after expiry of the ten-year limitation period. Consequently, the expiry of the ten-year limitation period meant this claim was out of time.

Summary

- English law on product liability has been developed both through the common law and the wider EU context.
- The CPA 1987 involves a strict liability regime for defective products on a wide range of potential defendants.
- There are limits on the scope of the Act such as cases where the loss concerns damage to property not intended for private use and where the ten-year 'cut-off' limitation period applies; these restrictions do not apply in common law negligence.
- After appearing to be underutilized, the Consumer Protection Act has given rise to several cases in recent years.

  Visit the online resources to listen to a podcast summarizing the topics covered in this chapter.

The bigger picture

The contaminated blood inquiry

The use of contaminated blood products from the late 1970s until early 1990s has affected as many as 30,000 patients in the United Kingdom bringing death and serious illness to thousands. It led to the product liability case above, *A and others v National Blood Authority and others* (2001) and is now the subject of a public inquiry.

First announced in July 2017, it began hearings under the chairmanship of Sir Brian Langstaff in September 2018 and is projected to last for at least two years. The inquiry will be considering evidence from approximately 2,500 people, most of whom were infected with, or affected by, contaminated blood products such as Factor VIII or IX. Victims and relatives want to know why warnings about the safety of the medicine may have been ignored, why plans to make the United Kingdom self-sufficient in blood products were scrapped, and why many documents and patient records appear to have been lost or destroyed. Ahead of the inquiry, the government announced increased financial support for people in England affected by the tragedy, to a total of £75m from an earlier £46m.

You may wish to read more on the background to the scandal or to follow the proceedings of the Inquiry at: www.infectedbloodinquiry.org.uk

? Questions

Knowledge-testing questions

1. Which particular weakness in common law negligence for harm caused by a defective product led to the introduction of the CPA 1987?

2. What is the meaning of a defective product under s 3(1)(a) of the Act?

3. What are the limitations on recovery of property damage under the Act?

4. Outline the 'development risks' defence.

Problem and essay questions

1. Does the CPA 1987 improve on recovery in common law negligence in respect of defective products which cause harm?

2. The day after Emad had a new floor fitted by EuroTiles in his home-based recording studio he telephoned the company to complain about a strong chemical odour emanating from the tiles. The odour aggravated his asthma and made Emad feel ill. He was advised to leave his kitchen window open and assured by the salesperson that the odour would disappear when the adhesive on the tiles dried out. However, the adhesive did not dry out and after two weeks it seeped through the floorboards and damaged Emad's underfloor sound system. It has now transpired that the adhesive had not dried properly because the incorrect solvent had been used by the manufacturer who supplied the product to EuroTiles. Emad has suffered a severe asthma attack and the cost of rectifying the damage to his underfloor sound system is expected to be in excess of £10,000.

   Advise Emad.

Visit the online resources for guidance on answering these questions.

Further reading

Fairgrieve, D, G Howells, and M Pilgerstorfer, 'The Product Liability Directive: Time to Get Soft?' (2013) 4 JETL 1

Howells, G and M Mildred, 'Infected Blood: Defect and Discoverability' (2002) 65 MLR 95

Newdick, C, 'Liability for Defective Drugs' (1985) 101 LQR 405

Newdick, C, 'The Development Risk Defence of Consumer Protection Act 1987' (1988) 47 CLJ 455

11 Trespass to the person and to land

Introduction

Trespass is one of the oldest torts. The tort developed in ancient times before the existence of a police force to give protection against physical interference with person or property. Traditionally, one of the main functions of trespass was to vindicate rights and to act as a deterrent to protect against invasion of a citizen's interests in land, person, or property. Persons wronged by someone committing an unjustifiable interference with person or property were not left without a remedy, nor did they have to resort to taking the law into their own hands to protect their interests; the tort of trespass provided a cause of action for such wrongs.

Trespass takes three forms: trespass to the person, trespass to land, and trespass to goods, all of which are actionable per se, which means that a claimant does not need to prove damage to bring an action in trespass. In effect, the tort of trespass protects civil rights and in many cases an infringement of these rights will not cause physical damage but may, nevertheless, lead to a loss of dignity. For example, a person wrongfully detained as he is leaving a shop and questioned about whether the goods in his bag have been paid for, may not be able to show damage as a result of the detention. However, because personal integrity is so highly regarded, an action in the tort of trespass to the person may be available for unlawful restriction on freedom of movement.

You will see that many modern cases of trespass to the person are taken against the police or other public officials; in some of these cases the main reason for taking the action is to vindicate the claimant's rights rather than to obtain an award of damages in compensation.

At this stage it is important to note that all forms of trespass require a direct and intentional interference, such as hitting a person or entering the land of another. The torts of negligence and nuisance cover unintentional or negligent conduct and indirect interferences, such as noise or fumes emanating from land which interfere with the use or enjoyment of land of another. The focus of this chapter is on trespass to the person, a tort concerning the intentional infliction of harm without a direct interference which is known as the tort in *Wilkinson v Downton*, and trespass to land. We will start by examining trespass to the person.

11.1 Trespass to the person

The ancient tort of trespass distinguished between direct and indirect interferences; direct interferences were protected by trespass but where the interference was indirect the action had to be taken just in 'case', from which the tort of negligence developed. The extent to which the old distinction between trespass and case is relevant to the new law on trespass and negligence can be seen from the facts of *Scott v Shepherd* (1773), where the defendant threw a lighted firework into a market stall. Eventually, after several stallholders had instinctively thrown it from stall to stall, it injured the plaintiff. Although this injury was not a direct result of the defendant's throwing of the firework and the action should have been brought in case, the courts were prepared to extend the definition of direct injury to give the plaintiff a remedy because the inappropriate form of action had been chosen for the claim. It was held that the link between the defendant's act of throwing the firework had not been broken by the instinctive reaction of others throwing it on.

In addition to the distinction between the directness and indirectness of the interference, another important distinction between trespass and case was that trespass was a tort of strict liability while negligence required proof of fault. The courts then began to take into account the element of fault underlying a defendant's behaviour. For example, in *Stanley v Powell* (1891) the defendant fired a shot in circumstances where he had acted neither intentionally nor negligently. In a freak accident, the shot he fired had ricocheted off a tree and hit the plaintiff. In holding that trespass was not actionable in the absence of intention or negligence the court confirmed that trespass to the person is a fault-based tort. It was further held that the burden of proof in negligence was on the plaintiff but in trespass the burden of disproving fault was on the defendant. *Fowler v Lanning* (1959) is another case where neither intention nor negligence was alleged by the plaintiff, who was injured by a shot from the defendant's gun during a shooting party. His statement of claim simply recorded that 'the defendant shot the plaintiff' because, he argued, in trespass the burden of disproving negligence lay on the defendant. The claim was struck out as disclosing no cause of action on the ground that it lacked an allegation of intention or negligence. In this decision Diplock J removed the supposed advantage of a trespass action—that the defendant had the burden of proving that he was not at fault—whereas in negligence the burden was on the plaintiff to prove fault on the part of the defendant.

11.1.1 Direct and intentional acts

The following case illustrates that, today, the general principle is that direct intentional acts of interference are dealt with by the tort of trespass but where acts are *un*intentional and *in*direct the action lies in negligence. In *Letang v Cooper* (1965), the plaintiff suffered injury when the defendant negligently drove his car over her legs as she was sunbathing in a hotel car park. It was more than three years later that the plaintiff sued the defendant for her injury but because (under the Limitation Act 1980) personal injury actions for 'negligence, nuisance or breach of duty' must be brought within three years and other tort actions are barred only after six years, in an effort to prevent her action from being statute barred, the plaintiff sued in trespass. In the Court of Appeal, Lord Denning, with whom Danckwerts LJ agreed, held that actions for personal injuries should no longer be divided into trespass (where the harm is direct) and case (where indirect harm is suffered) but according to the nature of the defendant's conduct. If the conduct was intentional, it was trespass; where the conduct was negligent, the cause of action is in negligence and not trespass. The views expressed by Lord Denning and Danckwerts LJ, that in circumstances where the contact between the plaintiff and defendant was unintentional the action must be brought in negligence, were approved by the Court of Appeal in *Wilson v Pringle* (1987). According to Croom-Johnson LJ:

> It is the act and not the injury which must be intentional. An intention to injure is not essential to an action for trespass to the person. It is the mere trespass by itself which is the offence.

 THINKING POINT

Jay threw a stone at Kay which hit her in the eye. He also carelessly left his skateboard on the pavement outside his house, causing Ella to fall over it. Which forms of action in tort are open to Kay and Ella? Might there also be criminal liability for either of these acts?

11.2 Assault, battery, and false imprisonment

11.2.1 Assault

The tort of trespass to the person has three elements: assault, battery, and false imprisonment, as illustrated in Diagram 11.1. It is important to note that an assault requires no physical contact; it is essentially conduct which causes the claimant a reasonable *apprehension* of an *immediate* application of force which constitutes a battery. This can be illustrated

Diagram 11.1 Trespass to the person

by *Stephens v Myers* (1830), where the plaintiff was the chairman of a parish meeting at which it was resolved, by a large majority, to expel the defendant. The defendant became increasingly vociferous and moved towards the plaintiff saying that he would rather pull him out of the chair than be expelled. As the defendant moved to unseat the plaintiff he was prevented by the churchwarden from doing so and the question to be decided was whether the defendant's threat was sufficient to put the plaintiff in reasonable apprehension of an immediate battery. In finding the defendant was liable in assault Lord Tindal CJ stated that:

> though he was not near enough at the time to have struck him, yet if he was advancing with intent, I think it amounts to an assault in law.

However, where the plaintiff has no reasonable belief that the defendant has the intention or the ability to carry out the threat immediately, no assault is committed. In *Tuberville v Savage* (1669), where the defendant placed his hand on his sword and said: 'If it were not Assize time, I would not take such language from you', it was held that by his own words the defendant had negated the possibility of a battery. More recently, this principle was applied in *Thomas v National Union of Mineworkers* (1986), where picketing miners made violent threats and gestures at working miners who were being taken into the colliery in buses. There was no liability in assault because there was no danger of an immediate battery since the working miners were safely in vehicles protected by police barricades.

⟩ **THINKING POINT**

Orla quietly crept up behind Sanjeev and hit him on the back of the head with a stone. Has she committed an assault? Has she committed a battery?

11.2.2 Battery

A battery is the actual infliction of unlawful force on another person. As well as bodily integrity, the tort of battery protects the claimant's dignity. An action can be brought where there is indignity without suffering physical injury but where the claimant's rights have been infringed. An example of such an indignity could be unlawfully taking a person's fingerprints or wrongfully seizing a person's arm to detain him in a shop on suspicion of shoplifting. In these cases, the claimant may only want to establish a principle, rather than seek compensation and because of this they sue in trespass rather than negligence. Trespass, as we have seen, is actionable per se (it is not necessary to prove damage) but in order to succeed in negligence the claimant must show that damage or harm has been suffered.

11.2.2.1 What type of contact amounts to 'force'?

The application of any physical contact, no matter how trivial, is sufficient 'force'. This can be seen from the case of *Collins v Wilcock* (1984), where a woman police officer tried to question a woman whom she suspected of **soliciting** contrary to the Street Offences Act 1959. When she took hold of the woman's arm in order to detain her and administer a caution the woman scratched the police officer's arm. On appeal against her conviction for assaulting a police officer in the execution of her duty, the question to be decided was whether the police officer had gone beyond the scope of her duty in detaining the woman in circumstances short of arresting her. It was held that the officer had gone beyond the scope of her duty and, without exercising powers of arrest, the officer's action in touching the woman amounted to a battery. You should note that a distinction is made between a restraint in these circumstances and a touching to attract a person's attention or in the ordinary conduct incidental in everyday life. Goff LJ said the fundamental principle is that every person's body is **inviolate**, but he pointed out that bodily contact was not actionable if it was regarded as: 'falling within a general exception embracing all physical contact which is generally acceptable in the ordinary conduct of daily life'.

> **soliciting**
> to seek to obtain something by persuasion or entreaty, or it can mean to approach a person with an offer of sexual services.

> **inviolate**
> free or protected from violation, injury, or desecration.

11.2.2.2 An 'act' and an 'intention' to commit the act is required

The intention required in battery is that the defendant must have intended to commit the act that constitutes the trespass. An intention to hurt the plaintiff is not necessary so, for example, in *Nash v Sheen* (1953), the defendant hairdresser was liable in battery when a tone rinse which caused a rash was given to a plaintiff who had requested a permanent wave. In *Livingstone v Ministry of Defence* (1984), the defendant soldier in Northern Ireland intended to hit someone other than the victim when he fired a baton round. However, because his action in firing the baton was intentional, even though he was aiming at a rioter when he fired, the soldier was found liable in battery when he missed his target and struck the plaintiff.

> **THINKING POINT**
> A large crowd was jostling at the bus stop and as Kofi went to board the bus he bumped into Nico, causing him to fall to the ground. Can Nico sue Kofi in battery?

In *Wilson v Pringle* (1987), it was held that unless it is self-evident from the act itself, the plaintiff must show the contact to be hostile. In this case the defendant, a 13-year-old schoolboy, admitted that as an act of ordinary horseplay in a school corridor he pulled the plaintiff's schoolbag from his shoulder. This caused the plaintiff to fall and suffer a hip injury and he applied for a summary judgment on the ground that the defendant's admission of horseplay amounted to a clear case of battery to which there was no defence. The trial judge accepted this view and granted summary judgment. The defendant appealed against this decision to the Court of Appeal, which held the trial judge had been wrong to grant summary judgment as the admitted facts did not automatically amount to a battery. Croom-Johnson LJ stated:

> That touching must be proved to be a hostile touching. That still leaves unanswered the question 'when is a touching to be called hostile?' Hostility cannot be equated with ill-will or malevolence. It cannot be governed by the obvious intention shown in acts like punching, stabbing or shooting. It cannot be solely governed by an expressed intention, although that may be strong evidence. But the element of hostility, in the sense in which it is now to be considered, must be a question of fact for the tribunal of fact. It may be imported from the circumstances.

THINKING POINT

Neighbours Homer and Barney were having a dispute over a boundary wall when Barney lost his temper and threw a stick at Homer. The stick missed Homer and hit Marge, a passer-by. Has Barney committed a battery?

This decision has been criticized for failing to define what is meant by 'hostile'. As you will see from the extract noted above, the court gave a number of examples of what is not hostile, but it appears that the definition of hostile in this context seems to mean little more than that the defendant wilfully interferes with the claimant in a way in which the claimant is known to object. The test has not been well received in the House of Lords. In *Re F* (1990), Lord Goff defined battery as any intentional physical contact which was not 'generally acceptable in the ordinary conduct of daily life' and he doubted whether it is correct to say that the touching must be hostile for the purpose of battery. He stated that:

> In the old days it used to be said that, for a touching of another's person to amount to a battery, it had to be a touching 'in anger' (see Cole v Turner (1794) 6 Mod. 149, *per* Holt CJ); and it has recently been said that the touching must be 'hostile' to have that effect (see Wilson v Pringle [1987] QB 237, 253). I respectfully doubt whether that is correct. A prank that gets out of hand; an over-friendly slap on the back; surgical treatment by a surgeon who mistakenly thinks that the patient has consented to it—all these things may transcend the bounds of lawfulness, without being characterized as hostile. Indeed the suggested qualification is difficult to reconcile with the principle that any touching of another's body is, in the absence of lawful excuse, capable of amounting to a battery and a trespass.

On the basis of the current state of the case law it is preferable to treat incidental contact as justified by implied consent, and to treat the label 'hostile' as now historical.

11.2.2.3 Emotional distress: conduct 'calculated to cause harm'

In *Wilkinson v Downton* (1897), the conduct which could amount to a battery was extended to include situations where *no* contact or physical force is used. Liability can arise where words calculated to cause physical injury (including psychiatric harm) are spoken, such as in this case where the defendant, as a practical joke, told the plaintiff that her husband had been seriously injured in an accident. As a result of hearing this information, the plaintiff suffered a severe nervous disorder and for a time her life was thought to be in danger. At the time this case was decided, however, there was: (1) no recovery in negligence for psychiatric harm; and (2) the specific requirements for assault and battery—the application, or threat, of force—were not present, so the claimant could not claim in trespass to the person. On the particular facts of the case, the court distinguished *Wilkinson v Downton* from trespass to the person and found the defendant liable for wrongful interference. The conduct was not merely negligent but was intended to cause harm. Liability will arise under the principle established in *Wilkinson v Downton* where an act wilfully calculated to cause physical damage does actually cause such harm.

Q | CASE CLOSE-UP

Rhodes v OPO (2015)

In this case the Supreme Court considered whether *Wilkinson v Downton* could be used to stop the publication of a father's semi-autobiographical book on the ground that it would cause psychological harm to his son. The son, an 11-year-old, suffered from symptoms of Asperger's syndrome and a number of learning disabilities; his mother, divorced from his father and living in another jurisdiction, claimed that if their son were to read his father's account of the sexual abuse he suffered in childhood and his subsequent mental health difficulties, it was likely to have an adverse effect on the boy, possibly resulting in 'enduring psychological harm'.

Acting on behalf of the son, the mother claimed an injunction to prevent the book's full publication on the ground that it would cause intentional harm to him according to the principle in *Wilkinson v Downton*. She also claimed that because both parents had agreed 'to use their best endeavours to protect the boy from any information concerning the previous history of either parent which would have a detrimental effect on the child's well-being' the father was under a duty of care to the boy, which publication of the book would breach. In rejecting all claims, the negligence action was dismissed on the grounds of lack of duty of care. Bean J held that parental duties of care towards their children only arose when they were acting in specific capacities such as occupier, driver, or supervisor of small children. The Court of Appeal (discussed below) approached the question of duty of care by applying the 'three-part test' in *Caparo Industries plc v Dickman*: though the requirements of foreseeability and proximity were satisfied, it would not be 'fair just and reasonable' to impose a blanket duty of care upon the parental role.

The Court of Appeal allowed the mother's appeal by justifying an injunction under the 'obscure' tort of intentional harm in *Wilkinson v Downton*. Arden LJ was of the opinion that actionable wrongs extend beyond the 'false words and threats' situation. As for the question of intention in *Wilkinson*, unlike the other intentional torts, here the requirement of intention pertains not to the physical intention in committing the act itself (for example, hitting someone or locking a door) but rather to the act's outcome. Arden LJ considered a line of authority from *Wilkinson* which indicates that the defendant need not desire the outcome of psychiatric injury or even be reckless as to its causation, but the defendant 'wilfully does an act calculated to cause psychiatric harm, and causes that harm, intent is imputed'.

The Supreme Court unanimously rejected the mother's claim. In examining the proper scope of *Wilkinson v Downton* for intentionally caused psychological harm the three elements of liability were recognized: a conduct element, a mental element, and a consequence element. The issues in this case related to the first and second elements (it is common ground that the consequence required for liability is physical harm or recognized psychiatric illness).

The conduct element of *Wilkinson* requires words or conduct directed towards the claimant. The Court of Appeal had been wrong to treat publication of the father's book as conduct directed towards the boy. Publication of the book was not directed towards his son; it was directed at a wider audience. Although vulnerable children need to be protected, there was every justification for the publication of the book. According to Lady Hale:

> A person who has suffered in the way that the father has suffered, and has struggled to cope with the consequences of his suffering in the way that he has struggled, has the right to tell the world about it. And there is a corresponding public interest in others being able to listen to his life story in all its searing detail. Of course vulnerable children need to be protected as far as reasonably practicable from exposure to material which would harm them, but the right way of doing so is not to expand *Wilkinson v Downton*.

The necessary mental element for *Wilkinson* is intention to cause physical harm or severe mental or emotional distress. This approach strikes a just balance. The mental element requires actual intention inferred from the facts: intent should not be imputed and recklessness should not be included in the definition. The father in this case did not have the necessary intention to cause psychiatric harm or severe mental or emotional distress to his son.

▶ CROSS REFERENCE

The mother's claim under the relatively new action of misuse of private information was not applicable because the information was about, and belonged to, the father. This is considered in Chapter 16.

Q   CASE CLOSE-UP

Khorasandjian v Bush (1993); *Hunter v Canary Wharf Ltd* (1997)

To amount to an act 'calculated to cause harm' under *Wilkinson v Downton* there must be both actual harm and an intent to cause damage. The principle was extended in *Khorasandjian v Bush* (1993) by the Court of Appeal in a case involving intentional harassment by telephone calls by a former boyfriend of the plaintiff. There was a risk that the cumulative effect of the unrestrained telephone calls would cause the plaintiff physical or psychiatric damage and she therefore succeeded in her action. In *Hunter v Canary Wharf Ltd* (1997), the House of Lords was prepared to preserve the rule in *Wilkinson v Downton* as a general **cause of action** but it anticipated that claimants in these cases ought to rely on new **statutory provisions** contained in the Protection from Harassment Act 1997 rather than the common law. In *Rhodes v OPO*, Lord Neuberger said of the rule in *Wilkinson*: 'the narrow restrictions on the tort should ensure that it is rarely invoked anyway'.

cause of action

a factual situation or the existence of a set of circumstances that gives rise to a legal claim and entitles one party to obtain a remedy against another.

statutory provisions

a legal provision set out in an Act of Parliament or statutory instrument.

11.2.2.4 Situations involving a 'course of conduct'

The question of whether damages could be recovered for intentionally causing distress falling short of psychiatric injury was again considered in *Wong v Parkside Health NHS Trust* (2003). In this case, a campaign of rudeness and unfriendliness by colleagues was not regarded as the intentional infliction of harm, and in refusing to develop a general tort of harassment from the rule in *Wilkinson v Downton* the Court of Appeal held that there was no tort of intentional harassment which gave a remedy for anything less than physical damage or a recognizable psychiatric injury. Although this decision restricts the principle in *Wilkinson v Downton*, the Protection from Harassment Act 1997 might provide a remedy for intentional harassment where a claimant has been the victim of a 'course of conduct'. For example, there may be a remedy under the Act where the intentional harassment is perpetrated by a fellow employee. In *Majrowski v Guy's and St Thomas's NHS Trust* (2006), it was held that an employer could be **vicariously liable** under the Act for harassment committed by one of its employees in the course of employment. You should note also that in *Wainwright v Home Office* (2003) Lord Hoffmann said of *Wilkinson v Downton*: 'This is a case which has been far more discussed than applied.' However, this special little tort may still be relied on to seek a remedy where there is a single act of harassment (which is not covered by the Act) rather than a 'course of conduct'.

> **vicarious liability** arises out of one person's relationship to another. This can mean that a party can be liable without being at fault. For example, an employer is generally liable to a third party for the torts of his employee committed in the course of his employment.

11.2.2.5 Emotional distress alone not enough to establish liability

As we have seen in *Wilkinson v Downton*, there may be liability if severe emotional distress causes bodily harm and the defendant either intended this or was reckless as to the consequences of his act, but this does *not* mean that damages for distress *falling short of psychiatric injury* are recoverable. In cases where no contact or physical force is used, emotional distress is not enough to establish liability for intentionally inflicted bodily harm. In *Wainwright v Home Office* (2004) a mother went to visit her son who was in prison on remand. She was accompanied on the visit by another son but because the prison governor suspected that the prisoner in question was dealing in drugs in prison he gave instructions that anyone who wanted to visit him had to consent to be strip-searched. Although the mother and son agreed to be strip-searched, the mother was emotionally distressed and the son, who had physical and learning difficulties, suffered post-traumatic stress disorder as a result of the search.

▶ **CROSS REFERENCE**
Wainwright v Home Office is also discussed in Chapter 16.

The manner in which the prison officers carried out the strip-searches breached the Prison Service Rules and both the mother and son claimed damages for an invasion of their privacy and the intentional infliction of harm which amounted to trespass to the person. The trial judge found in favour of the claimants and awarded damages in each case but the Court of Appeal allowed the defendant's appeal. The claimants then appealed to the House of Lords, which ruled that the infliction of humiliation and distress by conduct calculated to humiliate and distress was not, without more, **tortious** at common law. Even if there was an intention to cause harm, *Wilkinson v Downton* was not authority for the proposition that damages for distress falling short of psychiatric injury were recoverable. In this case, the prison officers' deviation from the procedure laid down for strip-searches was not calculated to cause harm. The officers' conduct showed no evidence of intention to cause distress or to increase the humiliation necessarily involved but was merely the result of 'sloppiness' in the manner in which they carried out the strip-searches. Their Lordships also rejected a general right of privacy in English common law and stated that the coming into force of the Human Rights Act 1998 weakens the argument for saying that a general tort of invasion of privacy is needed. According to Lord Scott of Foscote:

> **tortious**
> having the nature of a tort

The important issue of principle is not, in my opinion, whether English common law recognises a tort of invasion of privacy. As Lord Hoffmann has demonstrated, whatever remedies may have been developed for misuse of confidential information, for certain types of trespass, for certain types of nuisance and for various other situations in which claimants may find themselves aggrieved by an invasion of what they conceive to be their privacy, the common law has not developed an overall remedy for the invasion of privacy. The issue of importance in the present case is whether the infliction of humiliation and distress by conduct calculated to humiliate and cause distress, is without more, tortious at common law. I am in full agreement with the reasons that have been given by Lord Hoffmann for concluding that it is not. Nor, in my opinion, should it be. Some institutions, schools, university colleges, regiments and the like (often bad ones) have initiation ceremonies and rites which newcomers are expected to undergo. Ritual humiliation is often a part of this. The authorities in charge of these institutions usually object to these practices and seek to put an end to any excesses. But why, absent any of the traditional nominate torts such as assault, battery, negligent causing of harm etc, should the law of tort intrude? If a shop assistant or a bouncer or barman at a club is publicly offensive to a customer, the customer may well be humiliated and distressed. But that is no sufficient reason why the law of tort should be fashioned and developed with a view to providing compensation in money to the victim.

However, cases of intentionally inflicted emotional distress will now have to be considered in light of the House of Lords decision in *Majrowski v Guy's and St Thomas's NHS Trust* (2006).

11.2.3 **False imprisonment**

11.2.3.1 **A complete restraint on freedom of movement**

False imprisonment is the unlawful constraint on the freedom of movement of another, but it does not require incarceration or the use of force. However, the unlawful constraint on freedom of movement must be total and if there is any reasonable means of escape then there is no false imprisonment. For example, in *Bird v Jones* (1845), the defendants, in order to provide seating for spectators at a regatta, wrongfully cordoned off a footpath on Hammersmith Bridge. The plaintiff insisted on his right to use a part of the footpath that had been cordoned off, but he was prevented from doing so by the defendant and was told that he could go back the way he had come. He refused to do this and claimed in false imprisonment. It was held that since the plaintiff had a way out and decided not to take it there was no total restraint on his liberty and there was therefore no false imprisonment. *R v Bournewood Community and Mental Health NHS Trust* (1998) concerned an autistic man (known as HL) who was unable to speak and had limited understanding. HL had been discharged from a psychiatric hospital into the home of paid carers with whom he had lived for three years. On one occasion at the day-care centre he attended on a weekly basis, HL's condition deteriorated and he became particularly agitated. Staff were unable to contact HL's carers on that day, so he was given sedatives and taken to hospital where the psychiatrist diagnosed him as requiring in-patient treatment. For three months HL was denied contact with his carers.

The responsible medical officer considered HL was 'compliant' in his admission. He had not resisted admission or tried to run away so the hospital claimed that he not been 'detained' but lawfully admitted as an informal patient. By a majority of the House of Lords held that a patient in an open, unlocked ward was not, in fact, detained. Although the reality was that HL was sedated and if he had attempted to leave the medical staff would have prevented him from doing so by detaining him compulsorily under the Mental Health Act 1983, he was still not 'detained'. The House of Lords had considered the issue of unlawful detention under English common law so HL's carers decided to take a human rights claim to the European Court of Human Rights (the Human Rights Act 1998 was not yet in force). The question was whether HL's detention was a deprivation of liberty under Article 5. Under the European Convention on Human Rights (ECHR) it was held that HL's inability to challenge the detention and the absence of procedural safeguards amounted to a breach of Article 5.

11.2.3.2 Reasonable restriction is not false imprisonment

Where a plaintiff's liberty is subject to a reasonable condition it is not false imprisonment to restrain the claimant until that condition is fulfilled. In *Robinson v Balmain Ferry Co Ltd* (1910), the plaintiff was a lawyer who missed a ferry and decided that he could not wait twenty minutes for the next boat. He was directed to the turnstile which was at the exit and when he refused to pay the one penny exit charge at the turnstile the defendant's employee refused to let him through. It was held that there was no false imprisonment because the condition of paying a penny to leave was a reasonable one in the circumstances and the condition had been brought to the plaintiff's attention. There is no false imprisonment where the plaintiff consents to the confinement. This principle can be illustrated with the case of *Herd v Weardale Steel, Coal and Coke Co* (1915), where the plaintiff, a miner, objected to carrying out what he believed to be dangerous work and, five hours before the end of the shift, he demanded to be brought up to the mine surface. The employer refused to authorize the lift to be operated until the scheduled time at the end of the shift. The House of Lords held that this was not false imprisonment because the plaintiff had voluntarily descended into the mine. An alternative explanation for this decision is that there was no positive act to restrain the plaintiff and trespass does not lie for a 'mere omission', but if the employers had refused to operate the lift at the end of the shift it would then have amounted to false imprisonment.

The omission principle was considered in *Iqbal v Prison Officers Association* (2010), where prisoners claimed false imprisonment because they had to spend an extra six hours of their day locked in their cell as the result of an unannounced strike by prison officers. In affirming *Herd*, the Court of Appeal said that as a general principle a defendant was not to be held liable in tort for the result of his inaction; here the mere failure of the prison officers to carry out their responsibilities involved no positive action on their part.

 THINKING POINT

In *Iqbal* Lord Justice Sullivan accepted that some positive act is implicit in the concept of restraint, and that a distinction can and should be drawn between a positive act and a 'mere omission' to act. However, in a dissenting judgment he said that on the facts of this case the officers' conduct in going on strike could not sensibly be described as a mere omission. While the right to strike was important, the right not to be falsely imprisoned was of fundamental importance. Do you agree with his view that a deliberate refusal to obey a direct order from a prison governor to release a particular prisoner from his cell is not simply an omission, but is fairly described as an act?

11.2.3.3 **Knowledge of the restraint not necessary**

In order to succeed in an action for false imprisonment it is not necessary to have knowledge of the restraint at the time. In *Meering v Grahame-White Aviation Co Ltd* (1919), the plaintiff was suspected of theft from his employers. He was taken by two of the works' police to the company's office for questioning. Unknown to the plaintiff, the police waited outside the office and, if the plaintiff had tried to leave, they would have prevented him from doing so. The Court of Appeal held that there was no need for the plaintiff to have been aware of the imprisonment, but knowledge of the detention might be relevant to the assessment of damages. In *Meering*, the court failed to consider an earlier decision, *Herring v Boyle* (1834), where, because of un-paid school fees, the headmaster refused to allow a mother to take her son home for the Christmas holidays. It was held that, since the boy was unaware of the detention, there was no false imprisonment. The conflict of authority in these cases was resolved in *Murray v Ministry of Defence* (1988), where the House of Lords disapproved of *Herring* and approved *Meering* and ruled that knowledge of the restraint of freedom of movement was not necessary to es-tablish false imprisonment. However, their Lordships noted that a person who is unaware that he has been falsely detained and has suffered no harm can only expect to obtain **nominal damages**. There must, however, be an actual detention. In *R v Bournewood Community and Mental Health NHS Trust* (see 11.2.3.1 A complete restraint on freedom of movement), the House of Lords held that although in cases of false imprisonment it is not necessary for the plaintiff to be aware of the detention, there must be an actual rather than a potential restraint on the plaintiff's liberty.

> **nominal damages**
> refers to a token sum of damages awarded by the court when a legal right has been infringed but where the claimant has suffered no substantial loss.

11.2.3.4 **Detention by an order of the court**

There is no action for false imprisonment where the detention is carried out under an order of the court and until such an order is set aside the detention is legally justified. In *Quinland v Governor of Swaleside Prison* (2003), the claimant had been convicted of certain offences for which a total sentence of two years and three months' imprisonment should have been im-posed. The judge, however, made an arithmetical error in calculating the claimant's sentence and, due to further administrative errors, the claimant's appeal against his sentence was not heard until after his release. In the claimant's action in false imprisonment for the period of detention in excess of his sentence, the prison governor was not held liable in false imprison-ment. Until the court order was set aside the claimant's detention was legally justified as the prison governor had no other option than to obey the warrant and he could not legitimately have acted otherwise.

11.2.3.5 **Relevant intention is intention to detain**

The relevant intention is the intention to detain the prisoner and because false imprisonment is a tort of strict liability, where a prison governor has authority to release the prisoner without an order of the court to terminate the period of custody, there may be liability. In *R v Governor of Brockhill Prison, ex parte Evans (No 2)* (2001), the prison governor appealed from an award of £5,000 compensation for false imprisonment made by the Court of Appeal in favour of a pris-oner who had been detained at Brockhill Prison for fifty-nine days beyond her release date. The prison governor had not been to blame for the miscalculation of the date of the prisoner's release which had been made according to the bad law that existed at the time of the calculation. However, in dismissing the appeal, the House of Lords held that the prison governor's belief that the prisoner was lawfully detained was insufficient justification for the unauthorized detention. Even though the governor's incorrect calculation was based on pre-existing court rulings, the detention amounted to false imprisonment.

Liability for false imprisonment in the case of foreign nationals detained pending deportation under the Immigration Act 1971 was considered in *Lumba v Secretary of State for the Home Department* (2011). Following widespread publicity in April 2006 that more than 1,000 foreign prisoners had been released without being considered for deportation, the Home Office introduced a secret ban on release pending deportation. The Home Office's official stated policy was that a foreign prisoner who had been released from prison would not normally be detained pending their deportation but in spite of this policy, during the period in question, the Home Office implemented an unpublished policy which effectively reversed the presumption in the stated policy. The Supreme Court held that breach of a public law duty authorizing detention is capable of making that detention unlawful and the claimants had therefore been falsely imprisoned. The fact that the appellants would have lawfully been detained in any event did not affect the Secretary of State's liability in false imprisonment. However, since false imprisonment is actionable per se regardless of whether the victim suffers any harm, the question of damages was at issue. Because the prisoners suffered no loss it was held by a majority that they should recover no more than nominal damages. Nevertheless, according to Lord Hope (dissenting):

> There must be some recognition of the gravity of the breach of the fundamental right which resulted in false imprisonment, and account should be taken of the deterrent effect of an award lest there be the possibility of further breaches. But account should also be taken of the underlying facts and circumstances which indicate that it should not be more than a modest one. It should do no more than afford some recognition of the wrong done, without being nominal or derisory.

The decision in *Lumba* was affirmed and applied 'with full force' in *R (on the application of DN (Rwanda)) v Secretary of State for the Home Department* (2020).

In *Kambadzi v Secretary of State for the Home Department* (2011), the appellant, a Zimbabwean national, entered the United Kingdom lawfully, but remained here after his leave to remain expired. He was subsequently convicted of assault and sexual assault and sentenced to one year's imprisonment. Prior to his being released from prison, the Secretary of State decided to make a deportation order against him and he was detained for this purpose under the Immigration Act 1971. However, during the period of his immigration detention proper reviews of that detention were not conducted in line with the written detention policy. The issue here was whether the Secretary of State's failure to comply with a procedural requirement in state policy relating to the detention of foreign national prisoners results in their detention being unlawful, so as to allow the detainee to make a claim in tort for false imprisonment. In finding the failure to conduct the relevant reviews made the detention unlawful, the question of entitlement to damages in tort for false imprisonment was considered. The approach in *Lumba* was adopted on the ground that even if the procedural requirements had been met and the detention justified, the prisoner suffered no loss and no more than nominal damages could be recovered.

> **Q | CASE CLOSE-UP**
>
> ### *Muuse v Secretary of State for the Home Department* (2010)
>
> In this case, the Home Secretary did not dispute that Mr Muuse had been unlawfully detained pending deportation to Somalia, even though there was no right to deport him. However, his treatment by officials during the period of his detention was described by the trial judge as: 'high handed, insulting, malicious and oppressive'. Although verification of his claims that he was Dutch could have been carried out quite simply, nothing was done. During this ordeal Mr Muuse said he was terrified that he would be deported. Since the judge considered his treatment as being particularly deserving of condemnation, in addition to an award of compensatory damages he made a 'significant punitive' award of exemplary damages. In cases of breach of power by government officials exemplary damages are only awarded in cases of oppressive, arbitrary, or unconstitutional conduct. In *Rookes v Barnard* (1964), Lord Devlin said an award of exemplary damages is made where its effect will serve 'a valuable purpose in restraining the arbitrary and outrageous use of executive power'. On appeal, neither the award of compensatory nor aggravated damages for unlawful imprisonment was disputed. but the Home Secretary challenged the award of exemplary damages. In dismissing the appeal the Court of Appeal held that such an award was needed to stigmatize the conduct of the officials at the Home Office as an outrageous and arbitrary exercise of executive power. Sir Scott Baker further said:
>
>> it is to be hoped that the worrying issues raised by this case have been or will be addressed. Nothing less is acceptable in a true democracy.

Because they suffered no loss the prisoners in *Lumba* were awarded no more than nominal damages. Nevertheless, Lord Hope (dissenting) said that despite the deplorable official conduct he did not see this as a case for exemplary damages in the tort of false imprisonment but in view of the importance of the right to be vindicated he thought it was not a case for nominal damages either. We have seen in *Muuse* that the award of exemplary damages for unlawful imprisonment was unanimously upheld because the Court of Appeal found the conduct of the officials calculated to degrade and humiliate, typical of abuses which occur when power is exercised by those who are not competent to exercise that power.

11.2.3.6 **Deprivation of liberty ('kettling')**

Austin and others v United Kingdom (2012) arose from the G20 summit in London in May 2001 which was surrounded by considerable confrontation and widespread violence. Police intelligence identified that the protest would create one of the most serious threats to public order ever seen in the city, with a real risk of serious injury and even death, as well as damage to property. The crowd-control strategy adopted by the police—kettling—was imposed to create an absolute cordon to restrict movement around specific areas.

The appellants, not themselves protestors, were contained within the cordon for up to seven hours during the afternoon and into the evening. They argued that the containment within the cordon amounted to deprivation of liberty within the meaning of Article 5(1) of the ECHR.

This was the first time that the Court in Strasbourg considered the application of the Convention in respect of the 'kettling' carried out by the police on public order grounds. The Court ruled that based on the specific and exceptional facts of this case, the kettling did not amount to a deprivation of liberty so Article 5 was inapplicable. However, the Court went on to say:

> It must be underlined that measures of crowd control should not be used by the national authorities directly or indirectly to stifle or discourage protest, given the fundamental importance of freedom of expression and assembly in all democratic societies. Had it not remained necessary for the police to impose and maintain the cordon in order to prevent serious injury or damage, the 'type' of the measure would have been different, and its coercive and restrictive nature might have been sufficient to bring it within Article 5.

The application of Article 5 in the management of crowd control was considered by the Supreme Court in *R (Hicks and others) v Commissioner of Police for the Metropolis* (2017) in respect of the policing policy for managing crowds at the wedding of the Duke and Duchess of Cambridge on 29 April 2011. Members of the Royal Family, foreign royalty, and other heads of state moving around London that day together with thousands of citizens expected to converge on central London for the event, presented the police with a great challenge.

During a period before the wedding a number of violent disruptions had taken place and the police had intelligence that activities aimed at disrupting the celebrations were being planned through social websites. The threat level from international terrorism at the time was also high.

The four appellants were arrested in separate incidents at various places in central London. The arresting officers had reasonable belief that this was necessary to prevent an imminent breach of the peace. The appellants were taken to four different police stations and later released without charge, once the wedding was over and the police considered there was no longer a risk of breach of the peace. The appellants claimed the detention violated their rights under Article 5 because the planning and execution of the policing operation did not make proper allowance for the democratic rights of anti-monarchist protestors to express their views in a peaceable way.

The Supreme Court unanimously dismissed their appeal. The fundamental principle underlying Article 5 is the need to protect the individual from arbitrary detention, but Article 5 must not be interpreted in such a way as would make it impracticable for the police to perform their duty to maintain public order and protect lives and property. These two requirements are not contradictory, but the principle of proportionality must be applied in determining the lawfulness of deprivation of liberty (as held in *Austin v Commissioner of Police of the Metropolis*). Protecting the public from arbitrary detention needs to be balanced with the reality of the situation and the practical implications of preventing an imminent breach of the peace. The ability of the police to perform their duty would be severely hampered if they could not lawfully arrest and detain a person for a relatively short time.

11.3 Defences to trespass to the person

In addition to the defences outlined in the following text, a number of statutes authorize conduct that would, under different conditions, amount to trespass to the person: the Police and Criminal Evidence Act 1984 provides police with a defence to what might otherwise constitute false imprisonment or battery; the Mental Health Act 1983 makes provision for the compulsory admission to hospital and treatment in relation to mental health; under the Children and Young Persons Act 1933 parents can justify an assault and battery by way of chastisement of their children. Disciplinary powers also remain for the captain of a ship: in *Hook v Cunard Steamship Co* (1953), it was held that reasonable force may be exercised to preserve discipline for the safety of the ship, its crew, passengers, and cargo.

11.3.1 **Consent**

Many cases of physical contact which might otherwise be a battery will be lawful because the claimant expressly consented to the contact. For example, a patient requiring an invasive medical procedure normally gives express consent by signing a consent form authorizing the doctor to carry out the treatment. We will consider the issues surrounding the consent or refusal of medical treatment at the end of this section but at this point we will examine the situations where there is an *implied* consent to a battery.

11.3.1.1 **Implied consent: participants in sporting activities**

> ⏩ **CROSS REFERENCE**
> See 11.2.2 Battery.

Implied consent to battery most frequently arises in the case of participants in sporting activities who are implied to consent to the physical contact that occurs within the ordinary conduct of a game or sport. In *R v Billinghurst* (1978), the plaintiff, in the course of a rugby game, was deliberately punched in the face by an opponent. The plaintiff did not have possession of the ball at the time of the incident and although players are deemed to consent to force of a kind which could reasonably be expected to happen during a game, this conduct went beyond what a reasonable participant would expect in the game and it therefore amounted to a battery. In *Condon v Basi* (1985), it was held that consent to contact which could reasonably be expected is consent only to non-negligent behaviour. In this case the defendant was found liable in negligence when the plaintiff suffered a broken leg as the result of a foul tackle in the course of a game of football. In *Watson v British Boxing Board of Control* (2001), it was held that although a boxer consents to injury caused by his opponent in the boxing ring, he does not consent to injury resulting from inadequate safety arrangements by the sport's governing body after being hit. As we have seen in *Nash v Sheen* there will be a trespass if there is a deviation from the procedure consented to—in that case the application of a tone rinse to a plaintiff who requested a permanent wave was held to be trespass.

11.3.1.2 **Voluntary participants in fights**

Participants who voluntarily involve themselves in fights are taken to have consented to the battery. In *Lane v Holloway* (1968), the plaintiff, a retired gardener aged 64, came back from the pub one night and provoked an argument by calling the defendant's wife 'a monkey faced tart' and striking the 23-year-old defendant on the shoulder. The defendant retaliated by striking the plaintiff a violent blow in the eye, inflicting a wound that needed nineteen stitches. The court held that although there is no action in battery available to those who take part in fights (especially an ordinary fight with fists) because the participants would be taken to have consented to the battery, consent did not apply in the circumstances of this case. The defence will only apply if the force used by the defendant is proportionate and in this case the plaintiff's conduct was trivial and the defendant retaliated with a savage blow out of all proportion to the incident.

In *Barnes v Nayer* (1986), the defendant claimed provocation as a defence after he killed the plaintiff's wife with a machete. The defendant and his family had been subjected to a prolonged course of abuse by the deceased woman and her family. The Court of Appeal held that contributory negligence, **volenti**, and **ex turpi causa** could be a defence to trespass to the person, but the defences did not apply in this case because of the disparity between the deceased's conduct and the defendant's deadly attack.

> ***ex turpi causa (ex turpi causa non oritur actio)***
> where the law will not allow an action to proceed if it is based on an illegal cause

> ***volenti (volenti non fit injuria)*** the translation of this Latin phrase means 'something to which a person consents cannot be considered an injury'. Where a claimant gives his consent with prior knowledge of the risk involved, there is a general defence in tort.

11.3.1.3 **Consent to medical treatment**

Medical treatment involving the direct application of force administered without the patient's consent, or giving treatment different from that for which consent has been given, constitutes a battery. In *Chatterton v Gerson* (1981), the plaintiff was suffering from severe pain caused by a trapped nerve for which the defendant, a specialist in the treatment of chronic intractable pain, gave her spinal injections. This helped the pain for a while but when her right leg became numb she claimed in trespass on the ground that her consent to the injection was invalid as she had not been warned of the risks associated with the injection or informed of the potential consequences. The defendant was not liable in trespass on the ground that if a patient is informed in broad terms of the nature of the procedure this amounts to 'real consent' and any failure to disclose the risks associated with the procedure does not invalidate the consent. However, even where consent is a valid defence to a claim in trespass, it is important to note that an action in respect of a doctor's failure to disclose sufficiently the risks inherent in medical treatment may be taken in negligence. You will see in *Chester v Afshar* that a neurosurgeon who failed to warn a patient of a small inherent risk of injury was held liable in negligence because, the court held, unless that was done, the duty to warn would be a hollow one.

> ❯ CROSS REFERENCE
> *Chester v Afshar* is discussed in Chapter 4.

11.3.1.4 **Lack of mental capacity to consent**

Every mentally competent adult patient has the absolute right to refuse consent to treatment, even if the consequence is that he will suffer serious injury or die. However, where an adult permanently lacks the mental capacity to give a valid consent, the defence of necessity, provided it is in the best interests of the patient, will protect a doctor who gives medical treatment. In *F v West Berkshire Health Authority* (1990), F, a 36-year-old woman, was said to have the mental capacity of a child about the age of 5. She was cared for as a voluntary patient in a mental hospital and was thought by staff to have started a full sexual relationship with a male patient from the same hospital. Although the woman in question did not have the capacity to consent to the operation it was proposed that she be sterilized, and her mother applied to the court for a declaration that the operation would not be unlawful. Holding that the operation would not be unlawful, the House of Lords ruled that surgical procedures in these circumstances are permitted where the doctor was acting in the best interests of the patient. Lord Goff considered the principle upon which medical treatment may be justified without the consent of the patient:

> We are searching for a principle upon which, in limited circumstances, recognition may be given to a need, in the interests of the patient, that treatment should be given to him in circumstances where he is (temporarily or permanently) disabled from consenting to it. It is this criterion of a need which points to the principle of necessity as providing justification . . . . To give a simple example, a man who seizes another and forcibly drags him from the path of an oncoming vehicle, thereby saving him from injury or even death, commits no wrong . . . . We are concerned here with action taken to preserve the life, health or well-being of another who is unable to consent to . . . when a person is rendered incapable of communication either permanently or over a considerable period of time (through illness or accident or mental disorder . . . the basic requirements, applicable in these cases of necessity, that, to fall within the principle, not only (1) must there be a necessity to act when it is not practicable to communicate with the assisted person, but also (2) the action taken must be such as a reasonable person would in all the circumstances take, acting in the best interests of the assisted person.

▶ CROSS REFERENCE

Bolam v Friern Hospital Management Committee is discussed in Chapter 3.

Lord Goff held that in the above circumstances the treatment would be justified if the doctor acted in accordance with a responsible and competent body of relevant professional opinion, on the principles set down in *Bolam v Friern Hospital Management Committee*. These principles also apply where a patient is in a persistent vegetative state and unable to make a decision about whether his life should be prolonged or whether life-sustaining treatment of food and water should be withdrawn.

11.3.1.5 **The Mental Capacity Act 2005**

Guidelines for sanctioning treatment in the best interests of persons over 16 are now set out in the Mental Capacity Act 2005. The 'best interests' principle is an essential feature of the Act, but the notion of best interests is not defined. Nevertheless, the Act builds on the common law and aims to offer further guidance. The Act provides that:

- A person must be assumed to have capacity to consent to treatment unless it is established that he lacks capacity.

- A person lacks capacity if he is unable to make a decision for himself because of an impairment in the functioning of the mind or brain.

- A decision about what is in a person's best interests must not be made merely on the basis of age or appearance, a condition, or an aspect of behaviour which might lead others to make unjustified assumptions. The Act (s 4) makes clear that best interests determinations require a consideration of all relevant circumstances.

Section 5 of the Act provides a defence to a person who does an act in connection with the care or treatment of another if, before doing the act, he takes reasonable steps to establish whether the person lacks capacity. The defendant must also reasonably believe that it will be in the person's best interests for the act to be done.

What is a reasonable belief as to best interests of another?

 CASE CLOSE-UP

Commissioner of Police for the Metropolis v ZH (2013)

In *Commissioner of Police for the Metropolis v ZH* (2013), a severely autistic, epileptic boy of 16 was taken by his school carers to a local swimming pool. He made his way, fully clothed, to the side of the pool where he stood, fixated by the water. He would not move from the water's edge so after half an hour the pool manager called the police. The police officers arrived to find ZH still standing beside the pool. One officer spoke briefly to ZH's carer and learned that he was autistic. A series of incidents in and out of the water then ensued, culminating with lifeguards and the police lifting ZH out of the water.

> **THINKING POINT**
> What is reasonable where there is time to reflect and take measured action may be quite different in an emergency. The context here would have been different if ZH had been standing on a riverbank.

Although his carers urged the officers not to restrain him as he was autistic and epileptic, the officers placed ZH on his back to restrain him. He was then taken to a police van and placed alone in the cage in the rear of the van, still in wet clothes, with handcuffs and leg restraints. He subsequently suffered post-traumatic stress syndrome and his epilepsy worsened. ZH claimed in assault, battery, and false imprisonment. He also claimed violations of his human rights under the ECHR (Article 3 in respect of inhuman or degrading treatment, Article 5 for deprivation of his liberty, and Article 8 for interference with his private life).

The Police Commissioner appealed the judge's finding of liability in assault and battery for:

- touching of ZH before he jumped into the water;
- the force applied to him in lifting him out of the pool and restraining him;
- the force applied to him when he was out of the water by the poolside;
- the false imprisonment of ZH from the time when he was restrained by the poolside until he was released from the police van.

Denying all the claims, the Commissioner accepted that ZH had been imprisoned but relied on the defence in s 5 of the Mental Capacity Act to deny liability. The Court of Appeal found that since there had been no imminent risk of ZH jumping into the pool there had in fact been no emergency when the officers arrived. Section 4 required the officers to consult with ZH's carers about what was in his best interests and having failed to do this, judged objectively, the officers had not reasonably believed that their actions were in his best interests. The defence in s 5, that the officers' actions were in ZH's best interests, was therefore not available.

The court also found that the officers' response had not been proportionate to the likelihood of ZH suffering harm and the seriousness of that harm in dismissing the appeal. Additionally, the Commissioner's finding had breached ZH's rights under the ECHR:

Article 3: Although the police officers were acting in what they thought to be the best interests of ZH, they made serious errors which led them to treat a vulnerable young man in a way which caused him great distress and anguish. The treatment of ZH was so serious that it crossed the threshold of inhuman or degrading treatment under Article 3.

Article 5: The purpose and intention of the police was, in part, to protect ZH's safety. Although this was relevant in determining if there had been a breach of Article 5, there was, on the particular facts of this case, a deprivation of ZH's liberty.

Article 8: The interference with ZH's right to respect for his private life was not justified and amounted to a breach under Article 8.

11.3.2 Self-defence

Self-defence will be a justification to an action in battery if the force used is reasonable and is proportionate to the threat. In *Cockroft v Smith* (1705), the plaintiff, Cockroft, who was clerk of the court, ran his forefinger towards Smith's eyes during a scuffle in court. Smith bit off Cockroft's finger during the incident and the question was whether in these circumstances self-defence was a proper defence. It was held that a person may use reasonable force in self-defence and Smith could not justify biting off Cockroft's finger. Holt LJ said:

> hitting a man a little blow with a little stick on the shoulder, is not a reason for him to draw a sword and cut and hew the other.

Force may be used defensively under the Criminal Law Act 1967; s 3 provides that:

> a person may use such force as is reasonable in the circumstances in the prevention of crime.

Although the defence is available to one who goes to assist another under attack, in *Bici v Ministry of Defence* (2004) self-defence failed in the case of soldiers taking part in United Nations peacekeeping operations in Kosovo who were not being threatened with being shot when they fired their guns and there were no reasonable grounds for them to believe that they were.

The defendant has the burden of proving self-defence and the requirements for what the defendant needs to show to establish this defence in civil law are different from what is required in criminal law. *Ashley v Chief Constable of Sussex Police* (2008) involved the fatal shooting of Mr Ashley by the police during an armed drugs raid at his home in the early hours of the morning. The police admitted negligence and accepted responsibility for all damage flowing from the raid, but disputed liability for battery on the basis that the officer in question had acted in self-defence. One of the questions considered by the House of Lords was whether a defendant who had mistakenly but honestly thought it was necessary to defend himself against an imminent risk could rely on self-defence if his mistaken belief, although honestly held, had not been a reasonable one.

The position in criminal law should be noted at this point. Here, even if the mistake was an unreasonable one, if the defendant genuinely believed himself to be under threat of imminent attack, he is entitled to rely on self-defence. The question before the court was whether the criteria for self-defence in civil law should be the same. In *Ashley* their Lordships confirmed that in a civil law action for battery the burden is on the defendant to prove not only an honest belief that he had been under threat of imminent attack, but also the reasonableness of that belief. If a defendant acts reasonably in assessing whether he is about to be attacked and uses reasonable force in defending himself, then he will be able to rely on the defence. However, an excuse of self-defence based on non-existent facts will not suffice; if the defendant's mistaken belief is unreasonably held, then the defence will not be available in civil law.

11.3.3 Necessity

The defence of necessity to trespass to the person may be invoked where the defendant acts for the purpose of protecting the plaintiff's own health or safety. For example, in *Leigh v Gladstone* (1909), the plaintiff, a suffragette prisoner on hunger strike, was forcibly fed by prison staff. When she claimed damages for trespass the defence was that the acts were necessary to save her life and that the force used was the minimum necessary. Her action failed on the ground it was lawful for prison officials to intervene because they had a duty to preserve the life and health of those in their custody.

11.4 Trespass to land

Trespass to the person, as we have seen, protects against interferences with the person whereas trespass to land is concerned with protection of interests in land. However, as with trespass to the person, the unlawful interference with land must be direct and intentional and it is also actionable per se (although only nominal damages will be awarded without proof of loss).

11.4.1 What 'intention' is required?

An intention to trespass is not required; it is the intention to *enter* the land that is essential for liability. This means that a guest who walks up the drive to the front door of a house in the mistaken belief that it is the home of a family with whom he is staying could be a trespasser. Although he had no intention to trespass, his intention was to *enter* the land of another, albeit in a mistaken belief as to who owned the land. In one old case, *Basely v Clarkson* (1682), when the defendant was mowing his own land he mistakenly went over the boundary and mowed his neighbour's land, believing it to be his own. The defendant's plea of mistake to a claim in trespass to land failed because his act of cutting the grass was intentional even though he made a mistake about where the boundary was. This case shows that it is irrelevant that a defendant has made a reasonable mistake and the fact that the defendant was not negligent is also irrelevant.

In *League against Cruel Sports Ltd v Scott* (1986), the interference was committed by the animals of Scott, who was a master of hounds in a hunting party. The hounds entered the land of the League against Cruel Sports and, in considering the intention required for trespass, the court said that where the defendant intended the entry of the animals on the land or failed to prevent it, there could be liability in trespass to land. In this case, it would have been virtually impossible for the master to prevent the hounds entering the land and on this basis the intention to enter was inferred. An alternative interpretation of this decision is that, in some cases, trespass to land can occur negligently.

11.4.2 What is a 'direct' interference?

> **THINKING POINT**
>
> Which of the following are direct interferences: smoke from a neighbour's bonfire, a farmer's sheep grazing on the land of another, or loud music from a nightclub?

It is important to note that trespass to land protects against *direct* interferences with land which can be committed by: entering someone's house; walking on the land; leaning against a fence; or sitting on a wall. *Indirect* interferences with use or enjoyment of land such as smells, smoke, or noise are protected by the tort of nuisance. Another distinction between trespass and nuisance is that a single unlawful entry can give rise to a claim in trespass whereas public nuisance requires an ongoing state of affairs. Trespass and nuisance are compared in Table 11.1.

11.4.3 What is 'land'?

'Land' includes the surface and anything permanently attached to the land, like houses, walls, or standing crops. It also includes the subsoil and airspace, which means anything above or below the land to a reasonable height or depth in relation to the normal use of the land. Although invasions of airspace are actionable, a landowner's rights in the airspace above his land does not extend to an unlimited height. In *Bernstein v Skyviews* (1978), the issue of intrusion in airspace above the land was in question when Bernstein sued the defendants in trespass for taking aerial photographs from hundreds of metres above the grounds of his house. The court

Table 11.1 Trespass to land and nuisance

Trespass to land	Nuisance
Actionable per se	'Unreasonableness' of the interference is required to establish liability
A single entry can give rise to liability	Continuity of the interference is required
Locality not relevant	If no physical damage is caused by the nuisance, locality may be relevant in a claim for private nuisance
Does not generally give rise to criminal liability but there are exceptions under some statutes	Private nuisance is only a tort but public nuisance can give rise to criminal liability

held that Bernstein had no reasonable use for the airspace at that height and on this ground the defendant was not liable in trespass. However, in *Kelsen v Imperial Tobacco Co* (1957), an advertising sign which protruded a few inches into the airspace over the plaintiff's land amounted to a trespass and in *Woolerton v Costain* (1970) a builder was liable in trespass for a crane which overhung the plaintiff's land.

11.5 Defences to trespass to land

11.5.1 Consent

A defendant who enters with the permission of the person in possession of the land is not committing a trespass, but this permission may be withdrawn. A defendant who does not leave within a reasonable time after permission has been withdrawn will become a trespasser. In *Wood v Leadbitter* (1845), a ticket holder for Doncaster races was ejected forcibly by an employee after refusing a request to leave. Although the ticket holder had wrongfully been asked to leave in breach of contract this wrong was held to be irrelevant in an action in tort, and the court held that the ticket holder had become a trespasser when he refused to leave after being requested to do so. However, in *Hurst v Picture Theatres Ltd* (1915), in similar circumstances, the plaintiff who had paid an entrance fee to a cinema was asked to leave. He initially refused to leave but when the manager called a policeman, Hurst left the cinema and claimed in assault. In reaching its decision the Court of Appeal focused on the equitable aspects of the case and Hurst received substantial damages for assault.

> ▶ **THINKING POINT**
> Why do you think Hurst claimed only in assault? What apprehension or fear might he have experienced in the circumstances? Forcible ejection from the cinema?

11.5.2 Necessity

It is possible to defend an action in trespass on grounds of necessity but for the defence to succeed there must be no reasonable alternative course of action open to the defendant. *Southwark London Borough Council v Williams* (1971) was an action for trespass in unoccupied premises against squatters who were homeless. The squatters were not allowed to rely on the necessity for shelter as a defence.

11.6 Remedies

A claim in damages to recover any financial loss suffered as a result of the trespass may be made or, alternatively, if no damage is suffered, a nominal sum may be awarded. For example, in some cases of trespass to land the claimant may not want financial compensation at all but will instead be seeking an **injunction**, an order of the court to prevent a continuing or future trespass, or perhaps a declaration that the trespass is unlawful.

> **injunction** an order of the court directing a person to refrain from doing an act or continuing to do an act. In some cases an injunction can be used to order something to be done by restraining a defendant from continuing an omission.

Boyd v Ineos Upstream Ltd & others (2019)

In anticipation of future anti-fracking demonstrations, a company applied to the court for an interim injunction against 'person unknown' for, among other things, anticipated trespass to land and obstruction of the highway. This was granted by the High Court but on appeal the Court of Appeal placed a significant emphasis on the potential chilling effect of such legal strategies on freedom of expression and assembly. While the Court did not disagree in principle with 'persons unknown' injunctions, they should be used only sparingly. In accordance with the Human Rights Act 1998, s 12(3), conditions were set out for the granting of such injunctions, including: a real and imminent risk of a tort being committed, the impossibility of naming the persons concerned, and clear limitations on time and locality. The decision in *Boyd* indicates a measure of protection for environmental and other protesters.

 ## Summary

- Trespass covers intentional and direct interference with the person or with land.
- Claims for *indirect* interference with the person must be brought in negligence and claims for *indirect* interference with use or enjoyment of land must be brought in nuisance.
- An assault is the reasonable apprehension of an *immediate* battery; a battery can take place without an assault and even the slightest force may amount to a battery, for example, an unwanted kiss.
- The need to extend the principle of *Wilkinson v Downton* for the deliberate infliction of emotional harm is no longer so important because the Protection from Harassment Act 1997 protects against repeated harassment.

○ Visit the online resources to listen to a podcast summarizing the topics covered in this chapter.

 ## The bigger picture

The practice of granting injunctions against 'persons unknown' has recently come under scrutiny in two cases: *Birmingham City Council v Afsar* (2019) concerning protests about school teaching policy and *Boyd v Ineos Upstream Ltd & others* (2019), concerning anti-fracking demonstrations and discussed above. One aspect is that, because these apply to the world at large, one so affected may not know about it until the time of arrest for breach. Only permitted since 2003, such injunctions must require clear and rigorous conditions before granting. The following article from the Legal Action Group sets out the human rights issues pertaining to such remedies: www.lag.org.uk/article/205728/fracking-and-the-right-to-protest

? Questions

Knowledge-testing questions

1. Identify the individual torts that comprise trespass to person.

2. Is an intention to injure the claimant essential for an action in trespass to the person?

3. Can a defendant ever be liable in trespass for the intentional infliction of harm without making direct contact with the claimant?

4. Is it necessary for the claimant to have knowledge of the unlawful restraint at the time of the false imprisonment to succeed in action?

5. For which breaches of ZH's rights under the ECHR was the Commissioner liable in *Commissioner of Police for the Metropolis v ZH* (2013)?

Problem and essay questions

1. Mayuri was shopping in Arnott music centre when she noticed a number of items on display at greatly reduced prices. She decided to buy a CD player which contained a price label showing £25. As she was leaving the store the security guard at the exit accused Mayuri of switching the labels and claimed that she had replaced the original £50 price label on the CD with the label showing £25 taken from another item on the display. Arnott's manager phoned the police and Mayuri was detained in his office until the police arrived 30 minutes later. The manager's office was unlocked and Mayuri was unaware that the security guard remained outside as they waited for the police to arrive. Mayuri was prosecuted for theft in the magistrates' court but found not guilty of the offence and she now wishes to sue Arnott music centre for false imprisonment.

   Advise Mayuri.

2. Explain the possible defences to a claim that direct application of force has been administered without the person's consent.

   Visit the online resources for guidance on answering these questions.

☰ Further reading

Chamallas, M, 'Will Tort Law Have Its #MeToo Moment?' (2018) 11(1) Journal of Tort Law 39

Keywood, K, 'Vulnerable Adults, Mental Capacity and Social Care Refusal' (2010) 18(1) Med Law 103

Lunney, M, 'Practical Joking and Its Penalty: *Wilkinson v Downton* in Context' (2002) 10 Tort LR 168

Wilson Stark, S, 'Deprivations of Liberty: Beyond the Paradigm' (2019) PL 380

12 Nuisance

┌──┐
│ ☐ │ **LEARNING OBJECTIVES**
└──┘

By the end of this chapter you will be able to:

● define the elements of liability in private and public nuisance;

● identify the differences between private and public nuisance;

● distinguish the relationship between nuisance and fault-based liability; and

● explain the human rights dimension to the law of nuisance.

Introduction

Nuisance is one of the oldest torts and it protects against 'indirect' interference with the claimant's use and enjoyment of land, such as excessive noise and the emission of smells or noxious fumes. For example, smoke emanating from rubbish burning on a defendant's land which interferes with an adjacent neighbour's enjoyment of his garden is an indirect interference which, depending on other factors, may give rise to an action in nuisance. Other examples of indirect interference include encroachment of trees and physical injury to property (such as flooding). In some of the cases we will look at in this chapter you will see that the types of activity outlined below have been held to constitute actionable nuisance:

- the overflow of water onto the land of another constitutes physical damage and is actionable in nuisance: *Sedleigh-Denfield v O'Callaghan* (1940);
- a landslip was held to constitute a nuisance: *Leakey v National Trust* (1980);
- disturbance by noise from a go-cart track was held to constitute a nuisance: *Tetley v Chitty* (1986);
- nauseating smells emanating from a village pig farm were held to constitute nuisance: *Bone v Seale* (1975);

- a sex shop in a residential street was held to constitute an unreasonable interference with enjoyment of property: *Laws v Florinplace* (1981); and
- a fish-and-chip shop was an unreasonable interference (its benefit to local poor inhabitants could not justify its presence in a fashionable street): *Adams v Ursell* (1913).

Direct interferences, such as unlawfully walking across a neighbour's land or dumping rubbish in his garden, are dealt with by the law of trespass to land. Private nuisance is commonly defined as an unreasonable interference with the use or enjoyment of land. The definition of 'land' for the purposes of nuisance was considered in *Crown River Cruises Ltd v Kimbolton Fireworks Ltd* (1996), where, following a fireworks display held by the defendants on the River Thames, the claimants claimed in negligence, nuisance, and under the principle in *Rylands v Fletcher*. They sued for damage to their floating barge and a passenger vessel moored alongside it, but the defendants, Kimbolton Fireworks, argued that the essence of an action in nuisance was based on the use or enjoyment of land, not a floating barge. It was held that a permanently moored barge, occupied under a mooring licence, could give rise to the possibility of an action in private nuisance.

> **CROSS REFERENCE**
>
> *Rylands v Fletcher* is the subject of Chapter 13.

12.1 Public nuisance and private nuisance

You will also see that there are two categories of nuisance: public nuisance and private nuisance. One of the main differences between the two types of nuisance is that in order to sue in private nuisance the claimant must have an interest in the land affected. It is for this reason that, although the types of interference we have seen (such as smoke, fumes, and noise) in nuisance are also an interference with the environment more generally, to be able to bring an action in private nuisance in respect of one these interferences, the claimant must have an interest in the land affected. Another difference between public and private nuisance is that public nuisance can be a crime as well as a tort (for example, obstructing the highway or making it unsafe to use), whereas private nuisance is only a tort. There are statutory forms of nuisance, some of which have been created by Acts of Parliament to cover those nuisances that are most damaging to the environment. These include the Environmental Protection Act 1990 (which creates a whole set of statutory nuisances) and the Public Health Acts. The statutory forms of nuisance are normally enforced by the relevant statutory body and an individual may complain to that body for any environmental breach. These statutory environmental protection measures will not be covered by this chapter, which is mostly concerned with private nuisance. We will start by examining this aspect of nuisance and then move on to discuss public nuisance.

Table 12.1 Characteristics of public and private nuisance

Public nuisance	Private nuisance
Is a crime as well as a tort	Only a tort
The claimant does not need an interest in land to sue	Only those with an interest in land can sue
Damages for personal injury are recoverable	Damages for personal injury are not recoverable
An isolated incident may give rise to a claim	An isolated incident will not give rise to a claim; there must be an ongoing state of affairs
The claimant must be one of a class of Her Majesty's subjects who suffered damage over and above the rest of the class affected	An individual may sue, not as part of a class

12.1.1 Distinctions between public nuisance and private nuisance

The differences between the two categories of nuisance are shown in Table 12.1.

12.2 Private nuisance

Private nuisance, which as we have seen is not the same tort as public nuisance, is commonly defined as an unreasonable interference with the use or enjoyment of land or an interference with rights over land. Although the same state of affairs may constitute both torts, the rules relating to them are not identical: an action in private nuisance requires an 'ongoing' state of affairs, whereas an isolated incident can give rise to an action in public nuisance. Private nuisance seeks to strike a balance between the rights of occupiers to use their property as they choose and the rights of their neighbours not to have their use of land interfered with. Lord Atkin defined it as: 'a wrongful interference with another's enjoyment of his land or premises by the use of land or premises either occupied or in some cases owned by oneself'. Generally, a defendant's activity must be unreasonable and the traditional approach to the protection of the relevant interests is one of compromise, a 'rule of give and take, live and let live'. In *Bamford v Turnley* (1862), a private nuisance was defined as:

> any continuous activity or state of affairs causing a substantial and unreasonable interference with a plaintiff's land or his use or enjoyment of that land.

12.2.1 Damage: proof of damage necessary

To succeed in an action for private nuisance, the claimant must show: (1) that damage has been suffered; and (2) that the interference was unlawful. The need for the claimant to prove damage distinguishes the tort of nuisance from trespass because the tort of trespass is actionable per se.

Damage in nuisance may be proved by either showing indirect *physical* damage to the property as in *St Helen's Smelting Co v Tipping* (1865), where the plaintiff's crops and trees were damaged by the acid rain from the defendant's smelting works, or by showing *loss of amenity* (personal discomfort) in the claimant's use of the premises. In the context of physical damage, in *Hunter v Canary Wharf Ltd* and *Hunter v London Docklands Development Corp* (1997), it was held that a deposit of dust is capable of giving rise to an action in nuisance. You should note here that the tort of nuisance exists for the protection of *interests in land* and therefore an action *for pure personal injury* cannot be taken in private nuisance. We will look at this more closely when we consider who can sue in nuisance, but the important point to note here is that where the claimant suffers loss of amenity, he is not claiming for any personal injury but is seeking a remedy for the inability to use his property to its fullest.

THINKING POINT

In many cases of alleged nuisance, the court is faced with conflicting rights arising from the legitimate use or enjoyment of land and a balance must be struck between neighbours in these circumstances. What factors do you think might be relevant in striking this balance?

12.2.2 **What is an unlawful interference?**

In establishing an unlawful interference, the central issue in the whole law of nuisance is the question of 'reasonableness' and what constitutes an unreasonable interference. Unlike the tort of negligence, in nuisance the law does not concentrate so much on the reasonableness of the defendant's *conduct* but rather on the unreasonableness of the *interference* with the claimant's use or enjoyment of land. In nuisance the claimant's right to a reasonable use of land is balanced with the level of interference that a defendant is reasonably expected to tolerate. This means that not every interference with enjoyment of land will amount to a nuisance; it is only when the defendant's activity, measured by reference to the standards of an ordinary person who might occupy the claimant's property, becomes unreasonable that it becomes unlawful. In *Sedleigh-Denfield v O'Callaghan* (1940), Lord Wright said a useful test is what is reasonable according to the ordinary usage of mankind living in a particular society. Therefore, to be actionable the inconvenience ought to be more than fanciful. It must be:

> an inconvenience materially interfering with the ordinary comfort physically of human existence, not merely according to elegant or dainty modes and habits of living, but according to plain and sober and simple notions among the English people [per Knight-Bruce VC in *Walter v Selfe* (1851)].

In trying to strike a balance between the competing rights of claimants to enjoy their property and defendants' rights to use their land as they wish, the court looks not only at the nature of the interference itself, but at all the circumstances of the particular time and place where it took place.

A modern application of the above cases by the Court of Appeal can be found in *Barr v Biffa* (2012). The claimants, a group of householders on an estate, claimed that the unpleasant smells emanating from a waste tip operated by Biffa affected their enjoyment of their houses and gardens. Planning permission had been obtained by Biffa for operation of the site to be used for landfill and a waste management permit for tipping was granted by the Environment Agency. The judge at first instance dismissed their claims for nuisance. He accepted Biffa's argument that the correct understanding of more recent case law, taken in the context of the modern statutory framework, justified and required the reshaping of conventional principles to fit the modern world. However, in allowing the claim against Biffa the Court of Appeal ruled that this case was governed by conventional principles of the law of nuisance. Carnwath LJ said:

> The common law of nuisance has co-existed with statutory controls, albeit less sophisticated, since the 19th century. There is no principle that the common law should 'march with' a statutory scheme covering similar subject matter. Short of express or implied statutory authority to commit a nuisance . . . there is no basis, in principle or authority, for using such a statutory scheme to cut down private law rights.

This decision is an important reminder that notwithstanding the elaborate modern statutory framework governing smells and other environmental interferences, the nineteenth-century principles in the law of nuisance are still applicable.

Unusually in tort law, the court will consider whether the defendant's conduct in respect of the nuisance was motivated by malice. We will now look at the factors that the court takes into account in analysing the balance between parties' competing positions.

12.2.3 What is unreasonable?

Although there is no set formula for determining what is unreasonable, and much depends on the facts in each case, the following factors are taken into account:

- abnormal sensitivity of the claimant;
- the nature of the locality;
- the time and duration of the interference; and
- the defendant's conduct, taking account of all the circumstances in the case.

12.2.4 What is abnormal sensitivity?

Because, as we have seen earlier, the defendant's activity is measured by reference to the standards of an 'ordinary person' who might occupy the claimant's property, an important factor in determining the reasonableness of the defendant's conduct is the extent to which the claimant's health or property may be abnormally sensitive or particularly prone to damage. This principle is illustrated in respect of sensitive property by the case of *Robinson v Kilvert* (1889), where the defendants manufactured paper boxes in the cellar of a building which required hot and dry air. They heated the cellar accordingly but this raised the temperature on the floor above, which caused the plaintiff's stock of delicate brown paper to dry and diminish in value. The heat did not cause discomfort to the plaintiff's workforce and it would not have harmed ordinary paper, and on this basis the defendant was not liable; the plaintiff had undertaken an exceptionally delicate trade and could not complain because it was injured by his neighbour doing something lawful on his property.

In *Robinson v Kilvert* the action in nuisance failed because ordinary brown paper would not have been damaged by the heat from the defendant's cellar. However, if the heat would have damaged ordinary, non-sensitive paper, the defendant would have been liable. This was the case in *McKinnon Industries v Walker* (1951), where the plaintiff's business of growing delicate orchids was unusually sensitive. The plaintiff was able to recover the full extent of the loss, including the damage to the sensitive orchids caused by the noxious fumes from the defendant's factory, because non-sensitive plants would have been damaged by the fumes.

However, the law's response to what is an abnormally sensitive activity may change over time. In *Bridlington Relay Co v Yorkshire Electricity Board* (1965), sensitivity to television reception was held to be an ultra-sensitive activity and interference with the recreational amenity of television viewing was found not to be a substantial enough interference to give rise to an action in nuisance. However, since television viewing is now an activity enjoyed by a majority of the population, it is unlikely that it would be regarded as abnormally sensitive. In *Nor-Video Services v Ontario Hydro* (1978), on similar facts the Canadian courts refused to follow *Bridlington Relay Co* and held television reception to be a protectable interest.

In *Network Rail Infrastructure Limited v Morris* (2004) the Court of Appeal thought the concept of abnormal sensitivity in *Robinson v Kilvert* was outmoded. The case concerned an appeal by Network Rail against a finding of liability in private nuisance caused by magnetic waves emitting from its rail signalling system. The interference from the magnetic waves had affected the sound of electric guitars in Morris's recording studio some 80 metres away. Network Rail had argued that the recording studio was not protected by the law of nuisance because its 'extraordinary commercial activity' was abnormally sensitive to the magnetic waves.

In allowing Network Rail's appeal, it was held that in modern tort law a broad approach is taken to the existence of a nuisance. In establishing a nuisance, it is now necessary to consider whether it was foreseeable that the interference would cause the specific damage to a specific claimant. The court also noted that the law of nuisance has moved on and when resolving claims involving users of electrical or electronic equipment, the balance may be struck by asking what is reasonable. Network Rail could only be liable in nuisance if they should reasonably have foreseen that the signalling system would cause damage to someone in the position of Mr Morris. The claim failed because on the facts of the case this essential element of the tort of nuisance was not established.

⟩ CROSS REFERENCE

See 12.2.1 Damage: proof of damage necessary.

In *Hunter v Canary Wharf Ltd* and *Hunter v Docklands Development Corporation* the issue was not about an *activity* on the land, it concerned an interference caused by the *existence* of the building itself. The defendant had lawfully built on its land the Canary Wharf Tower, which is 250 metres high and over 50 metres square with stainless-steel cladding and metalized windows. The plaintiff and hundreds of others claimed in nuisance from Canary Wharf Ltd for interference, over a period of years, with reception of television broadcasts at their homes in East London. Although the House of Lords held that in certain circumstances, an action for interference with television reception might be protected, their Lordships said that more is

⟩ THINKING POINT

What might have been the policy reasons behind the House of Lords' decision that static structures could not constitute an actionable nuisance on the facts of *Hunter*?

required than the mere presence of a neighbouring building to give rise to an actionable private nuisance. It is a well-established principle that there is no legal right to a view and, in the same way, the principle applies in the case of the presence of a building in the line of sight between a television transmitter and other properties that it is not an actionable interference with the use and enjoyment of land.

12.2.5 **The nature of the locality**

In assessing whether an interference amounts to an actionable nuisance the nature of the locality is taken into account and what is a reasonable activity in one area may be an unreasonable one in another. In the words of Thesiger LJ in *Sturges v Bridgman* (1879): 'What would be a nuisance in Belgrave Square would not necessarily be so in Bermondsey.' At the time, Belgrave Square comprised genteel residential properties while Bermondsey was the main London centre for leather tanning—a very smelly activity! The nature of a locality may, however, change naturally over time. You may notice that new residential housing is increasingly being developed on 'brownfield' sites, former industrial areas which fell into disuse with the decline in heavy industry. The regeneration of these areas means that their nature will have changed from industrial areas to residential.

The nature of the locality rule does *not* apply in cases where the interference causes physical damage to property. The distinction between nuisances which cause physical damage and those which merely affect the use or enjoyment to land ('amenity' nuisance) can be illustrated in *St Helen's Smelting Co v Tipping* (1865).

🔍 CASE CLOSE-UP

St Helen's Smelting Co v Tipping (1865)

In June 1860, the plaintiff purchased a valuable estate in an area where industrial smelting was a well-established activity. The defendant had acquired neighbouring land for the purpose of engaging in copper works and this activity commenced in September 1860, soon after the plaintiff purchased his property. The plaintiff said that the large quantities of offensive, noxious, and unwholesome smokes emitted from the defendant's smelting works damaged the trees, shrubs, and crops on his land. He claimed this interference prevented him from having a beneficial and healthy use and occupation of his property and he brought an action in nuisance in respect of the harm this caused.

The defendant contended that the whole neighbourhood was devoted to similar manufacturing purposes and that smoke from one manufacturing process was as injurious as the smoke from the other. He claimed that the smoke sometimes united so it was impossible to say to which of the smelting processes caused a particular injury. The defendant also argued that in industrialized areas claims in nuisance claims should take account of the interest of the public generally and the law must not allow persons to bring actions in respect of every matter of annoyance. It was claimed that if such actions were allowed the industrialization of the whole country would be seriously interfered with. The fact that the defendants' smelting works existed before the plaintiff bought the property was also relied on.

The House of Lords upheld an injunction to restrain the defendants from creating the nuisance caused by the smelting works. A distinction was drawn between nuisances causing damage to property and those causing personal discomfort and convenience (loss of amenity). Where there is physical damage to the property the nature of the locality is irrelevant—property damage must not be inflicted wherever the defendant is carrying on the activity. This has become known as the 'character of the neighbourhood' principle expressed by Lord Westbury:

> My Lords, in matters of this description it appears to me that it is a very desirable thing to mark the difference between an action brought for a nuisance upon the ground that the alleged nuisance produces material injury to the property, and an action brought for a nuisance on the ground that the thing alleged to be a nuisance is productive of sensible personal discomfort. With regard to the latter, namely, the personal inconvenience and interference with one's enjoyment, one's quiet, one's personal freedom, anything that discomposes or injuriously affects the senses or the nerves, whether that may or may not be denominated a nuisance, must undoubtedly depend greatly on the circumstances of the place where the thing complained of actually occurs. If a man lives in a town, it is necessary that he should subject himself to the consequences of those operations of trade which may be carried on in his immediate locality, which are actually necessary for trade and commerce, and also for the enjoyment of property, and for the benefit of the inhabitants of the town and of the public at large. If a man lives in a street where there are numerous shops, and a shop is opened next door to him, which is carried on in a fair and reasonable way, he has no ground for complaint, because to himself individually there may arise much discomfort from the trade carried on in that shop. But when an occupation is carried on by one person in the neighbourhood of another, and the result of that trade, or occupation, or business, is a material injury to property, then there unquestionably arises a very different consideration. I think, my Lords, that in a case of that description, the submission which is required from persons living in society to that amount of discomfort which may be necessary for the legitimate and free exercise of the trade of their neighbours, would not apply to circumstances the immediate result of which is sensible injury to the value of the property.

 THINKING POINT

Does the decision in *St Helen's Smelting Co v Tipping* suggest that the courts are willing to give a higher priority to protecting property rights than to protecting a person's rights to enjoyment of land?

12.2.5.1 Nature of the locality: planning permission

Changes to the character of an area may also be part of a deliberate development of the locality brought about by planning permission. This means that planning permission can, in some circumstances, act as a defence (see also the defence of statutory authority). Where planning permission is granted for a large-scale strategic development that may change the character of the locality, the question of whether an interference arising from the activity on the land amounts to a nuisance will be decided with reference to its *present* use (with the development) and not the *previous* nature of the locality. In *Gillingham Borough Council v Medway (Chatham) Dock Co Ltd* (1993) planning permission to develop a commercial dock was held to have changed the character of the neighbourhood, and the local residents were therefore unable to claim in nuisance for the disturbance it created. In *Gillingham* the nuisance was foreseen by the local residents, who objected and petitioned at the time planning permission was under consideration. However, the planning permission was 'not merely permissive' it was granted specifically to enable the operation of a commercial port.

It is important to note, however, that the granting of planning permission to facilitate an activity does not carry with it an immunity in nuisance. Planning permission for a large-scale dockland development which is likely to change the nature of the locality can be distinguished from a small-scale development such as, for example, permission to extend a house or to build an outside greenhouse. In the case of such small-scale developments the granting of planning permission could not be said to alter the nature of the locality. In *Wheeler v JJ Saunders Ltd* (1996), the defendants had obtained planning permission for two pig-weaning houses to facilitate the intensification of pig farming on a site they already used for that purpose. The pig-weaning houses adjoined the plaintiff's holiday accommodation and he claimed in nuisance because of the smell of the pigs. The defendants contended that, since they had obtained planning permission, any smell emanating from the pigs kept in the weaning houses could not amount to a nuisance. It was held that the planning permission did not change the nature of the locality and the defendants were liable. Staughton LJ said:

> It would in my opinion be a misuse of language to describe what has happened in the present case as a change in the character of the neighbourhood. It is a change of use of a very small piece of land, a little over 350 square metres according to the dimensions on the plan, for the benefit of the applicant and to the detriment of the objectors in the quiet enjoyment of their house. It is not a strategic planning decision affected by considerations of public interest. Unless one is prepared to accept that any planning decision authorises any nuisance which must inevitably come from it, the argument that the nuisance was authorised by planning permission in this case must fail.

In *Watson v Croft Promo-Sport Ltd* (2009), the principle in *Wheeler v JJ Saunders Ltd* was applied by the Court of Appeal. Although the appellants (Watson), owners of a home located close to a motor-racing circuit, were awarded damages for the diminution in value of their property and loss of amenity, they failed to obtain an injunction to restrain the nuisance created by the excessive noise and discomfort. In respect of whether the nature and character of the locality had been changed by the planning permission, the judge held that the nature of the locality had not been changed; it remained essentially rural so that the operation of the circuit did constitute an actionable nuisance. In *Barr v Biffa* (discussed in 12.2.2 What is an unlawful interference?) the Court of Appeal rejected the defendant's attempt to rely on the granting of planning permission and permits for the operation of its landfill site as a defence to a claim in nuisance.

CASE CLOSE-UP

***Coventry v Lawrence* (2014)**

In this case the Supreme Court has, for the first time, reviewed the relationship between planning control and the tort of nuisance. The appellants bought a house in a predominantly rural area and sought an injunction to restrain the alleged noise nuisance arising from a nearby speedway racing stadium and a motocross track. Planning permissions covering the activities complained of had been granted and the question for the court was the extent to which planning permission might change the character of the neighbourhood. In overturning the Court of Appeal decision that the grant of planning permission had by itself changed the nature of the locality, the Supreme Court clarified that the grant of planning permission could not authorize a nuisance. It would seem wrong in principle that, through the grant of a planning permission, 'a planning authority should be able to deprive a property owner of a right to object to what would otherwise be a nuisance, without providing her with compensation, when there is no provision in the planning legislation which suggests such a possibility'.

According to Lord Neuberger:

A planning authority has to consider the effect of a proposed development on occupiers of neighbouring land, but that is merely one of the factors which has to be taken into account. The planning authority can be expected to balance various competing interests, which will often be multifarious in nature, as best it can in the overall public interest, bearing in mind relevant planning guidelines. Some of those factors, such as many political and economic considerations which properly may play a part in the thinking of the members of a planning authority, would play no part in the assessment of whether a particular activity constitutes a nuisance—unless the law of nuisance is to be changed fairly radically. Quite apart from this, when granting planning permission for a change of use, a planning authority would be entitled to assume that a neighbour whose private rights might be infringed by that use could enforce those rights in a nuisance action; it could not be expected to take on itself the role of deciding a neighbour's common law rights.

 THINKING POINT

Can you think of an example of a locality where its nature and character have changed over time? For example, since the decline of the shipping industry the dockland areas in many cities have been redeveloped with apartments and houses: consequently, the character of these areas has changed from industrial to residential localities.

12.2.6 **Time and duration**

In determining the reasonableness of the interference, the time and duration of the alleged nuisance will be taken into account. What may be reasonable at one time of day may be

❱ **CROSS REFERENCE**

See 12.2.13 Remedies for private nuisance.

unreasonable if done at another time of day. This point is illustrated by the case of *Halsey v Esso Petroleum* (1961), where the filling of oil tankers at 10am was reasonable but when they undertook this activity at 10pm the court held it was an unreasonable time to do so and it constituted a nuisance. The existence of a nuisance is usually associated with a continuing 'state of affairs' but this does not mean that a temporary state of affairs cannot be a nuisance. In *De Keyser's Royal Hotel v Spicer* (1914), although it was only of temporary duration, piledriving at night was held to be a nuisance. However, rather than impose a complete ban on the activity, where the interference is of a temporary or occasional nature, the court can limit the time of the activity. The remedy granted in this case was an injunction restricting the drilling activity between 10pm and 6.30am. This approach was taken in *Kennaway v Thompson* (1981), where the Court of Appeal allowed an injunction against motor-boat racing by the defendant club, but rather than impose a complete ban on the activity, the court qualified the injunction by limiting the times at which the sporting activities could take place.

12.2.6.1 Ongoing state of affairs

CROSS REFERENCE

For more on *Rylands v Fletcher*, see Chapter 13.

Although a private nuisance normally requires proof of an ongoing state of affairs, if the interference arises from an unreasonable state of affairs on the defendant's land it can constitute a nuisance. For example, in *British Celanese v AH Hunt Ltd* (1969), the defendants, manufacturers of electrical components, stored on their premises thin strips of foil used for making the components. Some of the strips were blown by the wind onto an electricity power station and this caused the power supply to be cut off. The plaintiffs were manufacturers of synthetic yarn which solidified in their machines when the machinery came to a halt as a result of the power cut. A similar incident had arisen three years previously and the defendants had been warned to store the metal strips more carefully. The incident in question was held to create an actionable nuisance because the method of storing the strips interfered with the plaintiffs' beneficial enjoyment of their property: it arose from a 'continuing state of affairs'. Although a single negligent act which damages an electric cable does not necessarily constitute a nuisance, in *SCM v Whittall* (1970), Thesiger J said:

> while there is no doubt that a single isolated escape may cause the damage that entitles a plaintiff to sue for nuisance, yet it must be proved that the nuisance arose from the condition of the defendant's land or premises or property or activities thereon that constituted a nuisance.

Isolated escapes, of course, can give rise to an action under the *Rylands v Fletcher* rule and we have seen earlier in *Crown River Cruises Ltd v Kimbolton Fireworks Ltd* that in addition to negligence and nuisance, an action under this principle was taken in respect of a fireworks display on a river barge. The court held that a fireworks display of about fifteen to twenty minutes' duration creates an actionable nuisance because of the inevitability that some hot and burning debris will fall upon neighbouring property.

12.2.7 The defendant's conduct in all the circumstances of the case

In assessing whether the defendant's use of his own land creates an unreasonable interference with his neighbour's property, the emphasis is generally on the *nature of the interference* and on whether it was unreasonable. However, in certain circumstances the *conduct* of the defendant can be a relevant consideration and the factors taken into account in determining the existence of a nuisance in these situations are: (1) the motives of the defendant; and (2) the reasonableness of his conduct taking into account all the circumstances of the case. The traditional rule is that malice is irrelevant in the law of tort and a lawful act carried out on the defendant's land does not become a nuisance just because it is done with malice. For example, in *Bradford Corporation v Pickles* (1895) the House of Lords held that even though the defendant was deliberately diverting water from his land in order to induce the claimants to buy it at an inflated price, his motive was irrelevant. No legal wrong had been committed because Bradford Corporation had no right to the supply of water which percolated from the defendant's land so he was therefore not liable in nuisance.

There are, however, a small number of exceptions to the rule that malice is irrelevant in the law of tort: the defences of qualified privilege and honest opinion in the tort of defamation can be defeated by malice and, from the cases below, you will see that malice also has relevance in the tort of nuisance. The extent to which malicious behaviour on the part of the defendant makes what would otherwise be a lawful use of his land a nuisance is one of the factors taken into account in determining what constitutes an unreasonable use of land. In considering what is fair and just in the case of an alleged nuisance, the defendant's conduct will, in certain circumstances, give rise to liability in the same way as it is relevant in the tort of negligence and a defendant's failure to act reasonably will be taken into account by the court.

12.2.7.1 Malice: relevance of the defendant's intention

Conduct which is motivated by malice on the part of the defendant may convert what would otherwise have been a reasonable and lawful act into an actionable nuisance. In *Christie v Davey* (1893), the plaintiff, a music teacher, lived in one half of a semi-detached house. The defendant, who lived next door, was annoyed by the music lessons and in retaliation he banged on the party wall, beat trays, whistled, and shrieked in an attempt to make life intolerable for the plaintiff. An injunction was granted on the ground that the series of noises made in the defendant's house was done with the purpose of vexing and annoying his neighbours and this was not a legitimate use of his house. However, North J indicated that he would have taken an entirely different view of the situation if the defendant's acts had been innocent; it may then have been a case of undue sensitivity on the part of the plaintiff. This approach was followed in *Hollywood Silver Fox Farm v Emmett* (1936), where the presence of malice and intention to cause harm in the defendant's conduct in the use of his own land was a relevant consideration. The defendant's premises adjoined the plaintiff's silver fox farm and, when a dispute broke out between the neighbours, the defendant instructed his son to remain on his own premises but to fire his guns as close as possible to the boundary with the plaintiff's adjoining silver fox farm. The defendant's intention was to prevent the foxes from breeding by firing the guns to scare the foxes in the breeding pens. The vixens of these animals are very nervous during breeding time and the noises caused the silver foxes not to breed. Macnaghten J considered the intention of the defendant to be relevant in nuisance and held the firing of the gun to be an unreasonable use of his own land. The plaintiff was granted an injunction and an award of damages.

Christie v Davey and *Hollywood Silver Fox Farm v Emmett* are distinguishable from *Bradford Corporation v Pickles* on the ground that Bradford Corporation had no right to receive the water in question so there was no legal interest to be protected by the tort of nuisance. However, the right to make noise on a person's own land is qualified by the right of their neighbours to the quiet enjoyment of their land. A person who acts with the intention of causing harm to his neighbour is unlikely to establish a reasonable use of land.

A case which vividly illustrates the way the courts approach the finely balanced rights and liabilities of neighbours in the modern world is *Fearn v The Board of Trustees of the Tate Gallery* (2019). In 2016 the Tate Modern art museum in London ('the UK's most popular tourist destination') opened a Viewing Gallery, offering a stunning 360-degree aspect of the London skyline. Those enjoying the views, perhaps with a coffee or glass of wine, can also gaze straight into the flats belonging to residents of the adjacent luxury apartment building: NEO Bankside. Owners of four of the flats launched an action against the Tate for breach of privacy and private nuisance, seeking an injunction to compel preventative measures. In finding in favour of the defendants Mann J cited the need for give and take in modern society and observed, 'In an inner city urban environment with a considerable amount of tourist activity, an occupant can expect less privacy than perhaps a rural occupant might'. Noting concessionary measures already taken by the Tate, he went on to suggest that the claimants had, in choosing architecturally adventurous homes, voluntarily 'submitted themselves to circumstances of increased sensitivity', with parallels being drawn to *Robinson v Kilvert*. Though only a first instance decision, *Fearn* provides a valuable insight into the operation of the law in this area.

12.2.7.2 Nuisance and fault: reasonableness of the defendant's conduct

The issue of fault in nuisance is not so important where the claimant is seeking an injunction to prevent a nuisance from continuing but fault is relevant where the claimant is seeking damages in compensation for a past wrong. The older cases indicated that the liability on the creator of the nuisance is strict and that it is not necessary for the claimant to show fault or carelessness on the part of the defendant. Where a nuisance or a state of affairs is created by a trespasser an occupier is not liable unless he knows about and adopts or continues the nuisance. This is what happened in *Sedleigh-Denfield v O'Callaghan* (1940), where, without the defendants' permission (and therefore technically trespassing), the Middlesex County Council laid a pipe in a ditch on their land. The workmen involved did not place a grid near the mouth of the pipe to prevent leaves and debris blocking it. The defendants were aware of the trespass and the ditch was cleaned out twice a year on their behalf but some years later, after a heavy rainstorm the pipe became blocked and caused flooding on the plaintiff's adjoining land. The House of Lords held the defendants liable because they were aware of the presence of the nuisance. They ought to have appreciated the risk of flooding and taken reasonable steps to abate it.

In *Goldman v Hargrave* (1967) (an Australian case), the nuisance was not caused by a trespasser but arose from the operation of nature on something on the defendant's land. A redgum tree, 100 feet high, on the defendant's land was struck by lightning and caught fire. The defendant cleared the land around the burning tree and the tree was then cut down. However, he did not extinguish the fire after doing this in the belief that the fire would eventually burn itself out. It kept smouldering and subsequently the wind increased and reignited the fire, which spread to the plaintiff's land. Although it had previously been considered that a defendant was not under a duty to abate a natural nuisance on his land, the principle in *Sedleigh-Denfield* was applied and the occupier was liable for failing to take adequate precautions to extinguish the fire in the face of foreseeable risk. The court said there is a positive duty on adjoining landowners to prevent fire or harmful matter from crossing the boundary. Lord Wilberforce said:

> It is only in comparatively recent times that the law has recognised an occupier's duty as one of a more positive character than merely to abstain from creating, or adding to, a source of danger or annoyance.

In *Leakey v National Trust* (1980), the Court of Appeal extended the principle in *Goldman* to include nuisances caused by the natural condition of the land itself. The nuisance was caused by the natural movement of the Trust's land which, because of its geological structure, was prone to subsidence and caused landslips onto the plaintiff's adjoining land below. Although they had been warned of the possibility of a substantial earth slip, the defendants refused to do anything about it and merely gave the plaintiff permission to abate the nuisance at his own expense. The Court of Appeal held that ownership of land carries with it a duty to take whatever steps are reasonable in all the circumstances to prevent hazards, however they might arise, from causing damage to a neighbour. The court recognized that where a hazard is thrust upon an occupier through no fault of his own, the resources available to the defendant may be very modest compared with those of the claimant and the duty to abate it does not require the occupier to do more than what is reasonable in the circumstances. This means that the extension of the duty to take positive action in these cases takes account of the abilities and resources of the particular defendant. An important factor in *Leakey* itself was that, in terms of resources available to it, the National Trust was in a better position than the plaintiff to prevent or control the damage.

In summary, the position now is, whether the state of affairs is created by a trespasser or through the forces of nature, once the occupier becomes aware of the nuisance and fails to remedy it within a reasonable time, he may become liable. Although Lord Wilberforce said that, in cases where the defendant was not himself responsible for creating the nuisance or danger, the duty is to take reasonable care and it is immaterial whether the cause of action is brought in nuisance or negligence because the standard of care required is the same, *Leakey* was decided in nuisance. In *Cambridge Water Co v Eastern Counties Leather plc* (1994) the House of Lords relied on the principle of foreseeability of damage established in *The Wagon Mound (No 1)* and held that the action in nuisance failed because at the time the contamination was taking place it was not foreseen that the quantities of the chemical would accumulate or that, if it did, there would be any significant damage. Their Lordships ruled that foreseeability of damage of the relevant type should now be regarded as a prerequisite of liability in nuisance.

> ❱ **CROSS REFERENCE**
> Discussed in Chapter 13
> *Rylands v Fletcher.*

 THINKING POINT

You should note that the main difference between negligence and nuisance is that in negligence the 'reasonable man' objective standard of care is applied but in nuisance, the subjective standard, which takes account of the individual circumstances of the defendant, is applied.

12.2.8 **The measured duty of care**

 CASE CLOSE-UP

Holbeck Hall Hotel v Scarborough Borough Council (2000)

The considerations of an occupier's measured duty outlined in the cases in this chapter were further discussed in *Holbeck Hall Hotel v Scarborough Borough Council*, where the defendant local authority occupied the cliff adjoining the claimant's hotel. Due to natural coastal erosion, the cliff had become unstable and as the result of a catastrophic landslip, the claimant's hotel was damaged by lack of support and had to be demolished. In arguing that the defendants were liable in nuisance for failing to take steps to prevent the landslip, the claimant sought to apply *Leakey*. The Council, however, argued that *Leakey* was not applicable to the rights of support and claimed that the principle was confined to en-croachment or escapes from the defendant's land. The Court of Appeal said that the measured duty of care to a neighbouring landowner arose out of a danger due to lack of support caused by a landslip in just the same way as it arose out of an escape or encroach-ment of a noxious thing. The scope of the defendant's duty, however, was to avoid damage to the claimant's land, which they ought to have foreseen. Although the Council was aware of marine erosion of the land, it was not liable for an unforeseen catastrophic col-lapse, which could only have been discovered through further investigation by a geological expert. However, even if the extent of the landslip had been identified, the extensive and expensive nature of the work required to support the cliff was such that the Council's duty would not have extended beyond warning its neighbours of the danger and sharing infor-mation. Although it will usually be the owner of the land who is best placed to undertake the remedial work to prevent the damage in these cases, the court held that it would not be fair, just, or reasonable to impose such an onerous requirement in respect of the meas-ured duty of care owed in cases where the defendant has not created the nuisance.

The duties owed by landowners to prevent natural occurrences on their land from causing damage to neighbouring properties were reviewed in *Vernon Knight Associates v Cornwall County Council* (2013). In this case, the owner of a holiday village in Cornwall claimed in nuis-ance in respect of flood water which had surged into his village, causing extensive damage. The local authority, which had responsibility for maintaining adequate drainage on one side of the village, argued that it had taken all reasonable steps to prevent flooding. The Court of Appeal considered what was fair, just, and reasonable between the neighbouring parties and, in bal-ancing the relevant factors, took account of the fact that the defendant was a public authority with substantial resources. The previous authorities were reviewed to set out the current pos-ition in relation to the liability of landowners in respect of natural nuisance. In finding the local authority liable, Lord Justice Jackson outlined liability for natural occurrences as follows:

(1) A landowner owes a measured duty in both negligence and nuisance to take reasonable steps to prevent natural occurrences on his land from causing damage to neighbouring properties.

(2) In determining the content of the measured duty, the court must consider what is fair, just, and reasonable as between the two neighbouring landowners. It must have regard to all the circumstances, including the extent of the foreseeable risk, the available preventive measures, the costs of such measures, and the resources of both parties.

(3) Where the defendant is a public authority with substantial resources, the court must take into account the competing demands on those resources and the public purposes for which they are held. It may not be fair, just, or reasonable to require a public authority to expend those resources on infrastructure works in order to protect a few individuals against a modest risk of property damage.

12.2.9 **Nuisance and the Human Rights Act**

The degree to which the extension of the measured duty to take positive action applies where the activities are carried out under a statutory scheme was considered in *Marcic v Thames Water Utilities Ltd* (2004). This case concerned flooding which discharged both surface water and foul water onto the claimant's garden, where many thousands of other householders were at similar risk from internal or external flooding. Under the Water Industry Act 1991, Thames Water was responsible for the provision of sewers and for the removal of sewage from the affected area. The flooding was caused by overloading of the sewage system which had, over the years, failed to keep pace with the increased demand, and Thames Water sought to rely on lack of resources to justify their decision to take no steps to abate the nuisance. Thames Water argued that in fulfilling its obligations under the Act it was required to determine priorities between competing interests and a fair balance had to be struck between the interests of individual consumers and the interests of the community as a whole. Applying these priorities, Thames Water claimed that in the interests of fairness in devolving its limited resources there was no prospect of carrying out the work for the foreseeable future. At first instance the judge held that: (1) he was bound by authority to dismiss the claims founded in *Rylands v Fletcher*, nuisance, and negligence; and (2) he concluded that the failure by Thames Water to carry out suitable work to repair the sewer gave no action for a breach of statutory duty. Nevertheless, he held that the failure of Thames Water to repair the sewer constituted an interference with the claimant's human rights. A common law nuisance may constitute an interference with a claimant's rights under Article 8 of the European Convention on Human Rights (ECHR) (respect for private and family life) and/or Protocol 1, Article 1 (protection of property). Since the Human Rights Act (HRA) 1998 came into force, such rights may be relied on in domestic courts.

However, the Court of Appeal held that this was not, in fact, a human rights case at all but that the claimant was entitled to succeed under the common law of nuisance. Thames Water was operating the sewerage system for profit in circumstances where it knew or should have known of the hazard. In considering the reasonableness of the conduct of Thames Water, the rules established in the cases of *Sedleigh-Denfield*, *Goldman v Hargrave*, and *Leakey v National Trust* were applied and Thames Water was found to have failed to demonstrate that it was not reasonably practicable for it to prevent the nuisance.

When the case reached the House of Lords, their Lordships allowed the defendant's appeal and rejected liability in common law nuisance, holding that the claim under the HRA 1998 was ill-founded. Their Lordships focused on the statutory regulatory scheme and ruled that where Parliament had established a regulatory scheme in which an independent regulator sought to balance the competing interests and consider overall priorities, liability would not be imposed. Although the flooding did amount to a prima facie breach of Mr Marcic's Convention rights, these rights are subject to limitations of finding a fair balance between the interests of individual consumers and community interests. The limitation on the rights under the Convention was emphasized in the earlier decision of the Grand Chamber of the European Court of Human Rights in *Hatton v UK* (2003), which made it clear that the Convention does not accord absolute protection to property or even to residential premises. It requires a fair balance to be struck between the competing interests of the parties involved.

⟩ **CROSS REFERENCE**

See also Chapter 17 on remedies and limitation.

For aggrieved parties such as Mr Marcic, the statutory scheme provided a complaints procedure which empowered the regulator to issue enforcement notices against sewage providers in appropriate circumstances. (However, Mr Marcic had never approached the regulator or attempted to avail himself of this remedy.) The remedies available under the regulatory scheme in question were held to be compatible with Article 8 and Protocol 1, Article 1 and there had, therefore, been no infringement of his rights under the ECHR. Their Lordships further stated that to expose the defendants to liability in nuisance in these circumstances would cut across the statutory scheme which Parliament had established.

You should note that before the House of Lords made their decision in *Marcic*, the Court of Appeal ruling on the human rights infringement aspect of the case was applied in *Dennis v Ministry of Defence* (2003). In *Dennis*, the flying of RAF Harrier jets caused severe and frightening noise disturbance, which resulted in a reduction in the capital value of the claimant's property. This was held to have been an interference with the claimant's rights under Article 8 for which damages of £950,000 were awarded. *Dennis* was a significant policy decision since it would be contrary to public interest to prevent the RAF planes from flying from their base. It is for this reason that substantial damages were awarded rather than the granting of an injunction. In the context of policy, the financial implications of the possible claims in *Marcic* were vast—£1,000 million damages to 18,000 residents. The potential liability of Thames Water was clear when the case reached the House of Lords.

12.2.10 **Who can sue?**

The traditional view has been that only those who have a legal interest in the land affected can sue in private nuisance: persons with no proprietary interest in the land but with whom householders shared their homes had no cause of action. In *Malone v Laskey* (1907), vibrations on the defendant's property caused the collapse of a cistern in a lavatory in the adjoining premises and caused personal injury to the plaintiff, the wife of the occupier of the premises. She was found to have no claim in private nuisance because she had no proprietary or possessory interest in the land. The Court of Appeal departed from this decision in *Khorasandjian v Bush* (1993) and held that the plaintiff, who lived with her mother and had no proprietary interest in the property, was entitled to an injunction to restrain a private nuisance in the form of telephone harassment. Dillon LJ said:

> To my mind, it is ridiculous if in this present age the law is that the making of deliberately harassing and pestering telephone calls to a person is only actionable in the civil courts if the recipient of the calls happens to have the freehold or a leasehold proprietary interest in the premises in which he or she has received the calls.

Q CASE CLOSE-UP

Hunter v Canary Wharf (1997)

In this case the issue of whether persons who had no interest in the land affected should have a right to sue in private nuisance was considered by the House of Lords. The Court of Appeal, in *Khorasandjian v Bush*, had stated that occupation of a property as a home (by those such as children or relatives) provided a sufficiently substantial link to the property to enable them to sue in private nuisance. However, the category of those having a 'substantial link' was considered by their Lordships who asked: who was this category meant to include? Did it include a lodger, or an au pair girl, or a resident nurse? They concluded that the extension of the tort of nuisance in the way proposed by the Court of Appeal would transform it from a tort to land into a tort to the person. The court pointed out that the criteria for liability in nuisance are not the same as those required in negligence and, if this category of persons were permitted to sue, a plaintiff could recover damages without showing a duty of care or fault on the part of the defendant. The tort of nuisance is not based on a duty of care owed by the defendant; it is concerned with striking a balance between the interests of neighbours in the use of their land. The Court of Appeal decision was overruled because their Lordships ruled that this was not an acceptable way to develop the law and they reinstated the *Malone v Laskey* principle that a proprietary interest in land is required to found an action in private nuisance.

In *Dobson v Thames Water Utilities Ltd* (2009), the Court of Appeal reiterated the principle that damages in nuisance were for injury to the property. Damages for interference with the comfort and enjoyment of the land are not available to those without a legal interest in the land affected. A number of those affected by the odours and mosquitoes that emanated from the defendants' sewage treatment works were unsuccessful because they had no legal interest in the land.

However, although the principle in *Hunter* still remains, the requirement for a claimant to have proprietary interest in land is open to challenge as incompatible with the HRA 1998. In *McKenna v British Aluminium Limited* (2002) the court refused to strike out claims in nuisance brought on behalf of children, who were permanent residents but did not have any proprietary interest in the land affected. Neuberger J (as he then was) said there was a powerful case for saying that effect had not been given properly to Article 8.1 of the ECHR if a person with no interest in the home, but who had lived at the home for some time, was at the mercy of the owner as the only person able to bring proceedings.

▶ THINKING POINT

Does the decision in *Hunter v Canary Wharf* mean that someone like the wife in *Malone v Laskey* would have no legal remedy for her injuries?

12.2.11 Who can be liable?

12.2.11.1 The creator of the nuisance

The creator of the nuisance can always be sued, even if that person is no longer in occupation of the land in question. However, liability extends beyond those in occupation of land themselves and covers those who create a nuisance while on somebody else's land. In *Southport Corporation v Esso Petroleum* (1956), the defendant's oil tanker ran aground and there was a danger that it might break up with the probable loss of the ship and the loss of the lives of its crew. In order to prevent this, the master decided to lighten the ship and 400 tons of oil were discharged into the sea. The river estuary was polluted and the plaintiff corporation alleged that the deposit of oil on the foreshore gave rise to three causes of action: trespass, nuisance, and negligence. The House of Lords held that a nuisance, which need not emanate from private land, had been committed but in this case the defence of necessity succeeded. The defendants were absolved of liability because where life and limb are at risk, any necessary damage to property will be justified.

12.2.11.2 Occupiers

We have seen in *Goldman v Hargrave* that the occupier was liable because he failed to take adequate precautions to extinguish the fire and in *Leakey v National Trust* that an occupier who fails to take reasonable care to abate a nuisance created by nature may also be liable. In *Sedleigh-Denfield v O'Callaghan*, the occupier was liable for a nuisance created by a trespasser because the defendant had known of the nuisance; he had made use of the pipe laid by the trespasser to drain water from his land and he was therefore found liable for having both adopted and continued the nuisance.

12.2.11.3 Landlords

The general rule is that a landlord who has leased premises is not liable for nuisances arising from them when the occupier takes control of the land. However, where the landlord grants the lease for the purpose which constitutes the nuisance there will be liability. In *Tetley v Chitty* (1986), residents in Rochester complained of noise from a go-cart track which could be heard in their houses. The Medway Borough Council had granted planning permission for the go-cart track on its land and had granted a lease to a go-cart club but the local authority argued that having leased the land it was no longer in occupation of it. However, the local authority was held liable because the excessive noise was a very predictable consequence of the use for which the land had been let. In another case involving a local authority as a landlord, *Hussain v Lancaster City Council* (1999), the local authority was held not liable in respect of a long-term campaign of racial harassment of a shopkeeper by other tenants on the council estate. The Court of Appeal found that it was the conduct of the council's tenants as individuals that caused the interference. The acts complained of did not involve the use of the defendants' land; it was 'merely a springboard' for the tenants' actions and the local authority was therefore not liable. This case was distinguished in *Lippiatt v South Gloucestershire Council* (1999), where the local authority was responsible for its own conduct. Here, the local authority had failed to evict travellers who had parked their caravans on a piece of its land bordering the claimant's farm. It was, therefore, liable for the travellers' repeated acts of interference, such as trespass, damage to property, theft, and dumping of rubbish on the claimant's land.

A landlord who has an obligation to repair or who reserves the right to enter and repair a premises may be liable for a nuisance if it is caused by their failure to repair the premises. In *Wringe v Cohen* (1940), the landlord's house, which was let to a weekly tenant, was located next to the plaintiff's shop. The landlord was liable to keep the premises in repair and because of want of repair when a wall of the house had become defective it collapsed and damaged the plaintiff's shop. The landlord argued that he did not know that the wall was in a dangerous condition and that it had become a nuisance because of the lack of repair. The landlord's appeal was dismissed and the Court of Appeal stated:

> if, owing to want of repair, premises on a highway become dangerous and, therefore, a nuisance a passer-by or an adjoining owner suffers damage by their collapse, the occupier, or owner if he has undertaken the duty of repair, is answerable whether he knew or ought to have known of the danger or not.

Where the nuisance is created, not by want of repair but through the act of a trespasser or by an unobservable operation of nature, such as subsidence under the foundations of a house, the occupier or landlord will not be liable unless he knew or should have known of the nuisance and allowed it to continue.

12.2.12 **Defences**

A number of defences are available to an action in nuisance and in *Nichols v Marsland*, when an ornamental lake burst its banks during an unprecedented rainfall and caused damage on the plaintiff's land, 'Act of God' was accepted as a defence. You will see in 12.2.12.1 that some other concepts which have been raised by defendants such as coming to the nuisance and social utility are ineffectual as defences.

12.2.12.1 **Twenty years' prescription**

The continuation of a nuisance for twenty years will, by prescription, legalize a private nuisance (but not a public one); therefore, where the defendant can show he has been committing the nuisance for twenty years continuously and that the claimant has been aware of this and done nothing about it, the defendant has acquired the right. It is not sufficient for the defendant to show only that the activity has been carried on for twenty years; the interference must have amounted to an actionable nuisance for a period of twenty years.

In *Sturges v Bridgman*, the defendant's confectionery business adjoined the premises of the plaintiff, a medical practitioner. For over twenty years the noise and vibrations from the defendant's business had not interfered with the plaintiff's use of land. However, the plaintiff then built a consulting room in the garden of his house and complained of the noise. When prescription was pleaded as a defence it failed because the interference had not been an actionable nuisance for the whole twenty years: time ran from when the new building was erected and the nuisance had only commenced from that date.

Prescription was again considered in *Miller v Jackson*, where the plaintiff bought a house on a recently built estate next to a ground where cricket had been played for seventy years. When cricket matches were taking place at weekends, cricket balls sometimes landed in his garden and the issue of whether the defendant could claim a prescriptive right was considered by the Court of Appeal. The court referred to *Sturges v Bridgman* and decided that the cricket balls constituted a nuisance but defendants had no prescriptive right because the period only started to run from the date when the houses were built as it was from then that the cricket became a nuisance.

12.2.12.2 **Statutory authority**

If a statute authorizes the defendant's *activity* the defendant will not be liable for interferences that are an inevitable result. Many damaging *activities* are carried out in pursuance of some statutory purpose but where the one in question is carried out ***intra vires*** the defendant will not be liable in nuisance. In *Allen v Gulf Oil Refining Ltd* (1981), a private Act of Parliament authorized Gulf Oil to acquire land by compulsory purchase for the building of an oil refinery in order to facilitate the importation and refinement of crude oil and petroleum products.

> ***intra vires***
> within the powers of a party to exercise such a power.

However, the Act contained no express authority for the use and operation of the refinery once it had been built. After the refinery had been in operation, the plaintiff living in the vicinity alleged that it caused a nuisance by smell, noise, and vibration. The House of Lords held that Gulf Oil were entitled to statutory immunity in respect of any nuisance which they were able to prove was an inevitable result of constructing the refinery which conformed to the intention of Parliament. Lord Diplock commented:

> Parliament can hardly be supposed to have intended the refinery to be nothing more than a visual adornment to the landscape in an area of natural beauty.

We have seen in *Wheeler v JJ Saunders*, that the argument that since the defendant had obtained planning permission for two pig-weaning houses, any smell emanating from them could not amount to a nuisance, was rejected. It was held that the granting of planning permission by a local authority did not grant immunity from liability in nuisance and this has now been confirmed by the Supreme in Court *Coventry v Lawrence* (see 12.2.5.1 Nature of the locality: planning permission).

 THINKING POINT

We have seen in *Coventry* that the granting of planning permission by a local authority (under its own statutory powers) does not give immunity to an action in nuisance in respect of that permission. However, these situations should be distinguished from an interference resulting from the implementation of an Act of Parliament, which does carry immunity in nuisance.

12.2.12.3 **Coming to the nuisance**

It is no defence to claim that the claimant came knowingly to an existing nuisance by occupying the land adjoining it. In *Bliss v Hall* (1838), the plaintiff occupied a property adjoining the premises of the defendant candle-maker. The plaintiff alleged nuisance in the emission of smells, fumes, and noxious vapours which resulted from the candle-making process. The defendant argued that the business had been carried on in the same premises for three years before the plaintiff came to the adjoining property. It was held that the plaintiff had a right to wholesome air and it was no defence that the business had been in existence before his arrival. The justification for the rule is that it would be unreasonable to expect someone not to purchase land because a neighbour was abusing their rights.

This rule was confirmed by the Court of Appeal in *Miller v Jackson* (discussed earlier), where Lane LJ stated:

> It is no answer to a claim in nuisance for the defendant to show that the plaintiff brought the trouble on his own head by building or coming to live in a house so close to the defendant's premises that he would inevitably be affected by the defendant's activities where no one had been affected previously.

This principle has now been reaffirmed by the Supreme Court in *Coventry v Lawrence*. The defendant's argument that the speed-racing activities had been ongoing for many years before the claimants acquired their property was rejected. Nevertheless, the court noted that nuisance claims should be considered by reference to the 'give and take as between neighbouring occupiers of land'. Lord Neuberger indicated that it would be open to a defendant to argue that a nuisance claim should fail:

> where a claimant builds on, or changes the use of, her land, I would suggest that it may well be wrong to hold that a defendant's pre-existing activity gives rise to a nuisance provided that (i) it can only be said to be a nuisance because it affects the senses of those on the claimant's land, (ii) it was not a nuisance before the building or change of use of the claimant's land, (iii) it is and has been, a reasonable and otherwise lawful use of the defendant's land, (iv) it is carried out in a reasonable way, and (v) it causes no greater nuisance than when the claimant first carried out the building or changed the use.

THINKING POINT

Is there an inconsistency between the defences of twenty years' prescription and the maxim that coming to the nuisance is no defence?

12.2.12.4 Social utility

Despite the view expressed by Lord Denning in *Miller v Jackson* that balancing the public interest of protecting playing fields to enable people to play cricket with the Millers' private interest in the security of their property should favour the public interest, it seems well established that it is no defence that the activity in question was for the benefit of the public. In *Adams v Ursell* (1913), it was no defence to an action in nuisance that a fish-and-chip shop in a fashionable street was a benefit to the public, especially the poor inhabitants of the neighbourhood. The Court of Appeal more recently rejected the possibility of such a defence in *Kennaway v Thompson* (discussed later).

12.2.13 **Remedies for private nuisance**

There are three remedies available to a claimant in private nuisance:

(1) injunction;

(2) damages; and

(3) abatement (which means self-help).

12.2.13.1 **Injunction**

An injunction is the primary remedy in an action for nuisance. Its objective is to force the defendant to cease or limit the nuisance. However, in many cases the defendant would prefer to pay damages rather than cease or restrict the activities in question, but the traditional view of the courts is that regardless of how beneficial a defendant's activity is, the courts will not allow a wrongdoer to continue the nuisance simply because he is able and willing to pay for harm suffered. In *Shelfer v City of London Electric Lighting Co* (1895), an injunction was granted to a publican to restrain a nuisance caused by excessive vibrations from the defendant's engines. The court rejected the defendant's argument that the plaintiff's remedy should be limited to damages because the result of the injunction would be to deprive many Londoners of electricity.

You should note that an injunction is an equitable remedy and it is not therefore available to the claimant as of right. An injunction is used at the discretion of the court to balance the competing interests of the parties in their use and enjoyment of land. This balancing exercise was undertaken by the Court of Appeal in *Kennaway v Thompson*, where the plaintiff had built a house by a lake and was disturbed by waterskiing and speed-boat racing which the defendant club was beginning to organize. The defendants were held liable for the nuisance created by the noise but they argued that an injunction should not be granted on the ground that there was a public interest in permitting the water sports to continue. The trial judge had taken into account the public's interest in having sports facilities available to it and, exercising his discretion, awarded damages instead of an injunction. However, the Court of Appeal was not prepared to allow the public interest in water sports to prevail and an injunction was granted. The court criticized the decision in *Miller v Jackson*, where damages rather than an injunction was granted, and reasserted the traditional view that if there is an actionable nuisance the plaintiff should win an injunction. Nevertheless, the injunction granted to the plaintiff was obviously influenced by public interest; it was formulated in terms that amounted to a compromise and permitted motor-boat racing to continue on the lake but restricted the number and extent of racing activities in each year and restricted the noise level of boats using the lake at other times.

In respect of remedies for private nuisance, it is important to note that the claimant has no *right* to an injunction; it is a discretionary remedy. When considering whether the grant of a mandatory injunction or an injunction to restrain a continuing nuisance is appropriate, the court may decide to give damages 'in lieu' of an injunction. We have seen above that planning permission does not authorize a nuisance, but *Coventry v Lawrence* has indicated that it may be relevant in determining the remedy. Lord Neuberger identified 'public interest' as a relevant consideration: this means that, in exercising its discretion, the court may take account of public interests and make an award of damages in lieu of an injunction.

Damages in lieu of an injunction are awarded only in very limited circumstances. The Supreme Court in *Coventry v Lawrence* took the opportunity to review the court's power to award damages in lieu of an injunction and to remind judges of their broad discretion beyond the boundaries of the *Shelfer* rules (see 17.6.3 Final injunction). Lord Sumption said:

CROSS REFERENCE

See also Chapter 17 for damages in lieu of an injunction.

> In my view, the decision in *Shelfer* is out of date, and it is unfortunate that it has been followed so recently and so slavishly. It was devised for a time in which England was much less crowded, when comparatively few people owned property, when conservation was only beginning to be a public issue, and when there was no general system of statutory development control. The whole jurisprudence in this area will need one day to be reviewed in this court. There is much to be said for the view that damages are ordinarily an adequate remedy for nuisance and that an injunction should not usually be granted in a case where it is likely that conflicting interests are engaged other than the parties' interests. In particular, it may well be that an injunction should as a matter of principle not be granted in a case where a use of land to which objection is taken requires and has received planning permission. However, at this stage, in the absence of argument on these points, I can do no more than identify them as calling for consideration in a case in which they arise.

12.2.13.2 Damages

Private nuisance is concerned with protecting the claimant's interests in land and therefore recovery for personal injury should not be permitted. We have seen in *Hunter v Canary Wharf* the House of Lords ruled that because nuisance is a tort against the land and not against the person, only those with an interest in land could sue. The court also expressly stated that damages in nuisance are intended to compensate for loss of amenity in the land, which may include the personal discomfort suffered through noise or noxious fumes; damages should not be awarded for personal injury, which is protected by the tort of negligence (although recovery for personal injury is available for public nuisance). Damages will be recoverable for any depreciation in the value of the land, as seen in *Dennis v Ministry of Defence*, where the claimants were awarded £950,000 damages to compensate for the reduction in the value of their property caused by the noise of the Harrier jets. The defendant is only liable for damages which can be reasonably foreseen and the remoteness-of-damage test set out in The *Wagon Mound (No 1)* is applied.

In *Raymond v Young* (2015), assessment of loss and the measure of damages for private nuisance were considered by the Court of Appeal. Here, Raymond owned a cottage and Young owned an adjacent farm. Motivated by resentment that the farmhouse was used as a weekend home, Raymond had engaged in continuous acts of harassment, trespass, and nuisance against Young over many years. These acts included obstructing the driveway, burning noxious materials, dumping rubbish, and physical intimidation.

Young was granted a permanent injunction against Raymond to prevent further nuisance and awarded £20,000 for distress and loss of amenity. Raymond's actions were also found to have caused a diminution in the value of the farm of 20 per cent, amounting to £155,000, and a further award of this amount was made to Young. Raymond appealed, claiming it was wrong to have made an award for diminution in value, because the injunction was sufficient to prevent any future acts of nuisance. The Court found that because of Raymond's character and behaviour his conduct was unlikely to be restrained by the grant of a permanent injunction.

This meant that potential purchasers would not see the injunction as a guarantee that they would not be subjected to the same treatment by Raymond. The award of £155,000 for diminution in value because of the threat of a nuisance to a future purchaser was upheld.

Network Rail Infrastructure v Williams and Waistell (2018)

The claimants owned property bordering the defendants' railway embankment, which was infested with Japanese knotweed, an extremely invasive and damaging wild plant. The homeowners brought an action in private nuisance, applying for a mandatory injunction requiring Network Rail to treat and eliminate the knotweed as well as claiming damages for diminution in value of their homes, due to the encroachment of the plant. At first instance, the judge declined to issue an injunction but damages were awarded for private nuisance.

The defendant appealed, alleging that encroachment could not give rise to compensation unless actual physical damage had been caused to the claimant's land. The appeal was rejected by the Court of Appeal, however it preferred to describe the grounds for damages as loss of amenity and quiet enjoyment rather than diminution in value. The presence of the hazardous plant on the neighbouring defendant's land placed an immediate burden on the claimants and diminished their use and enjoyment of the land. It inhibited their ability to develop or sell their land as well as raising the risk of future physical damage. This was the head under which compensation could be awarded, rather than diminution of value which did not constitute actionable damage in private nuisance; compensation must be tied to the use and enjoyment of land rather than seemingly pure economic loss or protection of land value as a financial asset.

12.2.13.3 **Abatement**

Although generally discouraged by the courts, the remedy of **abatement** is a form of self-help where a claimant takes steps to abate (stop) the nuisance—for example, by cutting overhanging branches from a neighbour's garden. A claimant who wishes to enter the neighbour's property to undertake such an activity must give notice of this intention, otherwise they may be liable in trespass. In *Delaware Mansions Ltd v Westminster City Council* (2001), encroachment of the roots of a tree which was growing on the pavement caused damage under a block of flats. Westminster Council, as highways authority and owner of the tree that created the continuing nuisance, refused to have the tree removed and the claimant was entitled to recover the cost of remedying the damage himself.

> **abatement** a form of self-help. For example, an abatement of nuisance refers to steps taken by the claimant to remove or stop the nuisance. Abatement notices may be served by a local authority in respect of statutory nuisance.

12.3 Public nuisance

While private nuisance protects an individual's interest in land, public nuisance, primarily a crime, is concerned with protecting the interests of the wider public. It is possible for the same conduct to give rise to an action in both public and private nuisance. The activity or interference giving rise to liability must be unreasonable and in this sense the two torts are similar. In *Attorney General v PYA Quarries Ltd* (1957), the defendants used a system of blasting that created dust, noise, and vibrations and also caused stones and splinters to project from their quarry into the neighbourhood. There were two highways and about thirty houses close to the quarry and the defendants contended that there was, at most, a private, and not a public, nuisance. According to Romer LJ, a public nuisance is an act or omission:

> which materially affects the reasonable comfort and convenience of life of a class of Her Majesty's subjects.

Any interference which materially affects a class of Her Majesty's subjects can amount to a public nuisance but the question of whether the number of persons is sufficient to constitute a 'class' is a question of fact in each case. In *Wandsworth London Borough Council v Railtrack plc* (2001), the Court of Appeal held that droppings from feral pigeons roosting under a railway bridge created a hazard over a footpath used by pedestrians and therefore constituted a public nuisance. Other examples include carrying on an offensive trade: in *Laws v Florinplace* (1981), residents were granted an injunction to restrain the operation of a 'sex shop' in their street; or holding a badly organized pop concert and, the most common example, obstructing the highway.

A public nuisance which endangers the life, health, property, or morals of a class of Her Majesty's subjects amounts to a crime as well as a tort. An essential element of the crime of public nuisance is that the act or omission must affect a substantial section of the public; repeated acts of offensive conduct directed at an individual (which may amount to a private nuisance) do not translate into the crime of public nuisance. In *R v Rimmington* and *R v Goldstein* (2006) a large number of separate packages containing racist material were posted by Rimmington to individual members of the public. Goldstein posted an envelope containing salt to a friend as a practical joke. A postal worker raised the alarm when the salt was discovered, fearing it to be anthrax. The question for the House of Lords was whether this series of acts amounted to the crime of public nuisance. According to Baroness Hale (as she then was):

> It is not permissible to multiply separate instances of harm suffered by individual members of the public, however similar the harm or the conduct which produced it, and call them a common injury. Conduct which was not criminal when the first letter was sent would become criminal at some unknown future time when it was thought that enough such letters had been sent to constitute such a common injury.

Related to the crimes of public nuisance involving environmental danger or offensive public behaviour, a form of public nuisance 'outraging public decency' exists to protect against indecent actions or displays that may cause offence to members of the public. The Law Commission Report (2015) *Simplification of the Criminal Law: Public Nuisance and Outraging Public Decency* considered the relationship of public nuisance and the public order offences. It was proposed that both offences should be replaced by statute and that:

- in public nuisance, it should be a requirement that the defendant intended to cause, or was reckless about causing, a nuisance to the public; and

- in outraging public decency, it should be a requirement that the defendant knew that he or she was or might be in a public place and that the act or display was such as to cause outrage to ordinary people.

12.3.1 Who can sue in public nuisance?

As we have seen in private nuisance, a claimant must have an interest in the land affected but an interest in land is not necessary to sue in public nuisance. Because public nuisance is primarily a crime, the **Attorney General**, representing the public interest, may bring a '**relator action**' on behalf of the class of people affected. Not all those in the class affected are permitted to sue; an individual member of the class will only succeed in an action for public nuisance where he suffers 'particular damage' over and above the damage sustained by the public generally. In *Tate & Lyle Food and Distribution Ltd v GLC* (1983), ferry terminals constructed by the defendants in the River Thames caused excessive silting. This disrupted the plaintiff's business by obstructing access to their jetty and they had to spend large sums of money on dredging operations so that they could continue to use the river. Their claim in private nuisance was dismissed because: (1) the jetty itself was unaffected; and (2) they had no private rights of property in the riverbed. The House of Lords held that it was their public right to use the river which had been damaged, and their claim lay in public nuisance alone. The expenditure incurred by the plaintiffs on dredging the riverbed constituted particular damage over and above the ordinary inconvenience suffered by the public at large, and was therefore recoverable.

> **Attorney General and relator actions** where the Attorney General has refused his consent to relator proceedings in the civil courts, a private citizen who asserts that the public interest is involved by threat of a breach of the criminal law has no right to go to the civil courts for a remedy either by way of injunction or a declaration.

> **relator** a private person at whose suggestion a legal action is commenced by the Attorney General (as in the case of a matter of public interest, such as public nuisance).

12.3.2 Who can be sued in public nuisance?

Those who can be liable in public nuisance are the same as the potential defendants in private nuisance. Liability in both situations depends on the reasonableness of the interference and, as we have seen, in public nuisance the reasonableness of the interference is determined by focusing on the interference itself and not on the conduct of the defendant. However, in balancing considerations of reasonableness in public nuisance the conduct of the defendant may be relevant because the defendant may argue that his alleged nuisance is, in fact, an exercise of some other right. For example, a person making a public protest may claim freedom of expression.

12.3.3 Remedies in public nuisance: (1) damage to property

> ❱ THINKING POINT
>
> Why was the noise from the tankers entering and leaving the depot throughout the day held not to constitute a nuisance?

In *Halsey v Esso Petroleum Co Ltd* the defendants operated an oil-distributing depot near to the plaintiff's house in a partly residential area in Fulham. Among other things the defendant was liable (1) in *private* nuisance for acid smuts from a boiler in the depot which damaged the washing on the plaintiff's clothes line; and (2) liability for the same smuts which caused damage to the plaintiff's car standing on the road outside but, because his car was parked on the public highway, the damage caused by the smuts was actionable in *public* nuisance as he was able to show that he suffered damage over and above that suffered by other road users. There was also liability in public and private nuisance caused by noise from tankers on the road outside as they entered and left the depot throughout the night.

12.3.4 Remedies in public nuisance: (2) personal injury

A key difference between public and private nuisance is that damages for personal injury *are* recoverable in public nuisance. We have seen that private nuisance is specifically aimed at protecting the claimant's interests in rights over land. The court in *Hunter v Canary Wharf* distinguished between personal injury, which concerns harm to the person, and interference with use or enjoyment of land, which concerns rights over land. Their Lordships said that the tort of negligence protects against personal injuries and for this reason damages for personal injury should not be awarded in private nuisance. Public nuisance is mainly concerned with unreasonable obstructions to the highway and once a claimant can show that he suffered particular damage over and above the rest of the class affected, he will be able to claim for personal injury and property damage. In *Castle v St Augustine's Links* (1922), a taxi driver was driving on the highway when he was struck by a golf ball hit from the defendant's golf course. Golf balls hit from this particular part of the golf course constantly went onto the highway and this was held to be a public nuisance because it affected a class of persons: the users of the highway. The plaintiff succeeded because he suffered special damage (a serious eye injury) over and above that suffered by the rest of the class.

 CASE CLOSE-UP

Corby Group Litigation Claimants v Corby BC (2008)

The claimants, who had all been born with upper-limb deformities, issued proceedings in negligence and breach of statutory duty against the defendant. They also made a claim in public nuisance alleging that, at a time when the local authority had been following a programme for the development of contaminated land within its area, their mothers, who lived close to the land sites, had been exposed during the embryonic stage of their pregnancies to toxic materials being emitted from the land.

They claimed that this exposure had caused their deformities. The local authority applied to strike out the claim in nuisance on the ground that damages for personal injury could not be recovered in public nuisance.

> **CROSS REFERENCE**
> *Hunter v Canary Wharf* is discussed in Chapter 13.

You will note from the earlier discussion of *Hunter v Canary Wharf*, that non-recovery for damages for personal injury is concerned with damages for personal injury in *private* nuisance rather than *public* nuisance. One of the important questions in *Corby* was whether damages for personal injury were recoverable in public nuisance. The Court of Appeal pointed out that the principle that damages for personal injury were recoverable in public nuisance was not criticized by their Lordships in either *Hunter* or *Transco*. The local authority's striking-out application was therefore rejected because neither *Hunter* nor *Transco* had impliedly reversed the long-established principle that damages for personal injury could be recovered in public nuisance. In stating that public nuisance is a developing area of the law the Court of Appeal emphasized that the precedents in allowing recovery for personal injury in public nuisance to those adversely affected by an unlawful act or omission had not been overruled. The local authority was held to be liable (upon proof of damage in individual cases) for causing, allowing, or permitting the dispersal of dangerous or noxious contaminants.

12.3.5 Defences to public nuisance

The defences in public nuisance are the same as those available in private nuisance but with one exception: because public nuisance is a crime as well as a tort, the defence of twenty years' prescription is not available in public nuisance.

12.4 Summary of the similarities between public and private nuisance

They both protect against indirect interference with use or enjoyment of land.

The rules on who can be sued are the same in each case.

The same conduct may give rise to an action in both public and private nuisance.

They both require that the interference is unreasonable.

Summary

- Nuisance covers *indirect* interferences with use or enjoyment of land and it differs from the tort of trespass, which protects against *direct* interferences.
- Although public nuisance is a crime as well as a tort, private nuisance is only a tort.
- A claimant in private nuisance must have an interest in land to sue; public nuisance is not linked to the claimant's interest in land and it protects against personal injury, which is not recoverable in private nuisance.
- In certain respects nuisance and negligence are similar because they both use the concept of reasonableness. A claimant in nuisance must show a lack of reasonable care.

🔵 Visit the online resources to listen to a podcast summarizing the topics covered in this chapter.

The bigger picture

Private nuisance

You may be interested to read the practitioner's perspective on the Japanese knotweed threat and its insurance implications:

www.dacbeachcroft.com/en/gb/articles/2018/october/an-invasion-of-japanese-knotweed-claims

Public nuisance

As we have seen, public nuisance is a tort as well as a crime, and the definitions of the tort and the crime are identical except that a private individual can sue for the tort only if he or she suffers damage over and above the effect on the general public. Unlike most crimes of comparable seriousness, public nuisance contains no requirement that the defendant intended or was reckless about whether his conduct caused the relevant kind of harm. The fault requirement is the same in the crime as in the tort: namely, that the defendant ought reasonably to have foreseen the consequences of the act or omission. The report below is part of the government's wider project on simplification of old common law offences to consider how public nuisance could be restated in statute in a simpler and more comprehensible form.

Public Law Commission Report on public nuisance, https://s3-eu-west-2.amazonaws.com/lawcom-prod-storage-11jsxou24uy7q/uploads/2015/06/lc358_public_nuisance.pdf

See also N Padfield, 'Public Nuisance and Outraging Public Decency' (2015) 8 Crim LR Aug 561

? Questions

Knowledge-testing questions

1. List the factors taken into account by the courts to determine whether an indirect interference amounts to a nuisance.

2. Who can sue and be sued in private nuisance?

3. Are damages for personal injury available in private nuisance?

4. Under what circumstances is a claimant allowed to recover damages in public nuisance?

Problem and essay questions

1. Outline the requirements for a claim in private nuisance and explain the factors taken into account by the courts when considering such a claim.

2. Discuss the potential liability of Jordan and Edith in respect of the following situation.

   Jordan makes model airplanes in his spare time. He is in the habit of burning the rubbish created by his hobby in his back garden. Jordan's bonfires cause smoke and fumes to drift from his garden onto Edith's land and damage the delicate plants that she cultivates on her patio. The smoke and fumes also create so much unpleasantness for Edith's friend, Jill that she can no longer spend weekends at Edith's house. On one particular occasion, an aerosol can containing a highly inflammable substance was among the rubbish thrown onto the bonfire by Jordan. This created a massive explosion, which shattered the windows in nearby houses. Pieces of flying metal from the container damaged cars parked on the highway and injured Atif, a passing cyclist. When Jordan ignored Edith's requests to stop the bonfires she decided to retaliate by playing music at a very high volume through a loudspeaker close to Jordan's house between 3am and 6am each day.

 Visit the online resources for guidance on answering these questions.

≡ Further reading

Buckley, R, 'The March of Negligence: Has Nuisance a Future?' (2007) 58 Northern Ireland LQ 395

Lee, R, 'Old Iron: Birth Defects Litigation and the Corby Steelworks Reclamation' (2009) 25(4) Journal of Professional Negligence 174

Lee, M, 'The Public Interest in Private Nuisance; Collectives and Communities in Tort' (2015) 74(2) CLJ 329

Nolan, D, 'A Tort Against Land: Private Nuisance as a Property Right' in D Nolan and A Robertson (eds), *Rights and Private Law* (Hart 2012)

Public Law Commission Report, *Codifying Public Nuisance and Outraging Public Decency* (2015), www.gov.uk/government/publications/simplification-of-the-criminal-law-public-nuisance-and-outraging-public-decency

Steel, S, 'The Locality Principle in Private Nuisance' (2017) 76 (1) CLJ 145

Wightman, JA, 'Nuisance: The Environmental Tort?' (1998) 61 MLR 870

13 *Rylands v Fletcher*

Introduction

Since its development in the 1868 case of the same name, the rule in *Rylands v Fletcher* has appeared to impose **strict liability** for damage caused by the escape of dangerous things from land. Much of the legal precedent relating to this tort stems from the nineteenth century and some believe that *Rylands v Fletcher* is of relatively little practical significance today. This is because of the expansion of the torts of nuisance and negligence—as well as developments in statutory liability for environmental wrongs. In many cases liability for hazardous activity is specifically governed by statute—see, for instance, the Nuclear Installations Act 1965 and the Environmental Protection Act 1990.

> **strict liability**
> where liability is imposed without fault having to be proved.

> **THINKING POINT**
>
> Why might statute be a more appropriate form of protection for environmental wrongs than the common law?

The defences which are available to actions in *Rylands v Fletcher* are generous and, when combined with certain requirements, such as the need for foreseeability, raise questions about the extent to which liability is truly strict. Its character as a land-based tort was emphasized in the more recent key cases of *Cambridge Water Co v Eastern Counties Leather plc* (1994) and *Transco plc v Stockport Metropolitan Borough Council* (2004).

⟩ **CROSS REFERENCE**

For more on nuisance and the *Hunter v Canary Wharf* case, see Chapter 12.

The tort in *Rylands v Fletcher* differs from its close cousin, nuisance, in that it does not depend on the defendant being involved in a continuous activity or an ongoing state of affairs. Unlike trespass to land, there will not be direct and intentional interference. The absence of the need for the existence of a duty of care and its breach, along with the questionable place of personal injury as an actionable type of damage, distinguishes *Rylands v Fletcher* from actions in negligence (see Table 13.1).

Table 13.1 *Rylands v Fletcher* compared to other tort actions

	Rylands v Fletcher	Private nuisance	Negligence	Trespass to land
Direct or indirect?	Indirect	Indirect	Indirect	Direct
One-off or continuous?	One-off or continuous	Continuous	One-off or continuous	One-off or continuous
Damage or actionable per se	Damage	Damage	Damage	Actionable per se
Physical injury recoverable?	No	No	Yes	No
Who can sue?	Interest in land required	Interest in land required	Anyone to whom a duty is owed	Interest in land required

 CASE CLOSE-UP

Rylands v Fletcher (1865)

In 1860 the defendant engaged contractors to build a reservoir in Bradfield for his mill. This was built on top of abandoned mine shafts, which collapsed under the weight of water, allowing water to escape through the mine shafts into the colliery leased by the plaintiff.

The defendant was not found to have been negligent and had chosen the independent contractors with care. However, liability was founded upon the following statement by Blackburn J:

> We think that the true rule of law is, that the person who for his own purposes brings on his lands and collects and keeps there anything likely to do mischief if it escapes, must keep it in at his peril, and, if he does not do so, is *prima facie* answerable for all the damage which is the natural consequence of its escape.

When the case was appealed to the House of Lords in 1868, Lord Cairns LC restated the principle as also requiring 'non-natural user' on the part of the defendant as a precondition of liability. 'Non-natural user' has been subject to different interpretations and what is now often referred to as non-natural use has been a significant element in limiting the application of *Rylands v Fletcher*.

13.1 Key ingredients

13.1.1 'for his own purposes brings onto land and collects and keeps there'

In *Rylands*, the accumulation was of water in the reservoir. In *British Celanese v AH Hunt* (1969), metal foil strips had been collected on the defendants' land. In *Mason v Levy Autoparts of England Ltd* (1967), a large quantity of combustible autoparts had been accumulated.

While Lord Blackburn in *Rylands v Fletcher* referred to someone who acts 'for his own purposes', case law indicates that the defendant need not benefit from the accumulation. In *Smeaton v Ilford Corp* (1954), *Rylands v Fletcher* was held to apply to a local authority exercising its statutory power to accumulate sewage on its land, although the local authority could not be said to benefit from this activity.

Can *Rylands v Fletcher* apply to an accumulation of something naturally on the land? In *Giles v Walker* (1890), a farmer's failure to control the spread of thistles growing naturally on his land was held not to be within the rule when their down blew onto neighbouring properties.

> **THINKING POINT**
> Why might this tort exclude liability for natural accumulations?

13.1.2 'something likely to do mischief'

Blackburn J described: 'something likely to do mischief if it escapes'. This 'something' need not be dangerous as such, but the risk lies in its behaviour when it escapes, as seen with the water in *Rylands v Fletcher* itself. Other examples of substances to which this tort has applied are fire (*Jones v Festiniog Railway* (1866)); gas (*Batchellor v Tunbridge Wells Gas Co* (1901)); fumes (*West v Bristol Tramways Co* (1908)); and electricity (*Hillier v Air Ministry* (1962)). In *Crowhurst v Amersham Burial Board* (1878), the branches of a yew tree which the defendant had planted on its land gave rise to *Rylands v Fletcher* liability when their branches grew over the claimant's land and, when eaten, poisoned his cattle. *Attorney General v Cory Bros and Co Ltd* (1921) concerned 'an enormous amount of rubbish' which slipped down a hillside. In one case, *Attorney General v Corke* (1933), travellers living in caravans on the defendant's land were treated as 'something likely to do mischief'; however, this situation would now be addressed by the law of nuisance (see *Lippiatt and Anor v South Gloucestershire CC* (1999)).

The extent of an accumulation might determine its 'mischief-making' potential. In *Mason v Levy Autoparts* it was the large number of greased car components in wooden crates collected in a small yard, along with petrol and paint which made them likely to cause a fire. The likelihood of the danger or mischief can be linked to the issue of foreseeability, which we will consider in more detail in the case of *Cambridge Water Co v Eastern Counties Leather plc*. Lord Bingham in *Transco plc v Stockport Metropolitan Borough Council* considered this aspect of the tort and recognized that the 'danger or mischief test' was also closely related to the issue of non-natural use. He also felt that, given the history of the tort and its strict liability characteristic, the test should not be too easily satisfied.

 CROSS REFERENCE

For discussion of *Cambridge Water*, see 13.3 Foreseeability of harm.

13.1.3 Escape

It is essential that there be an escape of a dangerous thing from the defendant's land or control.

Q CASE CLOSE-UP

Read v J Lyons & Co Ltd (1947)

In this case (see also 13.1.4 Non-natural use), an explosion in a munitions factory during the Second World War killed an inspector working on the premises. As there was held to be no 'escape from a place where the defendant has occupation of or control over land to a place which is outside his occupation or control', *Rylands v Fletcher* did not apply. It was thought that the 'thing' which is accumulated need not always be the thing which escapes. In *Miles v Forest Rock Granite Co (Leicestershire) Ltd* (1918) there was *Rylands* liability when explosives were stored on the defendant's land and led to the escape of rocks in a blast. But more recently, the Court of Appeal in *Stannard (t/a Wyvern Tyres) v Gore* (2012) held that *Rylands* did not apply when flammable tyres were stored in large quantities on the defendant's land and then ignited, causing a fire which spread to neighbouring premises. The things collected were tyres, but what escaped was fire. See 13.5.2 Default of the claimant or contributory negligence for a more detailed consideration of *Stannard*.

 THINKING POINT

What alternative cause of action could have been considered in *Read*?

13.1.4 **Non-natural use**

The requirement of *non-natural use* of his land by the defendant emerged when the rule, first set out by Blackburn J in a lower court, was restated by Lord Cairns LC in the House of Lords. The non-natural use in *Rylands* itself was the construction of a reservoir, at a time when Professor Simpson tells us that such developments were seen as dangerous following the bursting of a reservoir in 1864 that caused great loss of life.

Its meaning was further considered in *Rickards v Lothian* (1913), where Lord Moulton observed:

> It is not every use to which land is put that brings into play that principle. It must be some special use bringing with it increased danger to others and must not merely be the ordinary use of land or such a use as is proper for the general benefit of the community.

According to Lord Porter in *Read v Lyons* (1947):

> all the circumstances of time and practice of mankind must be taken into consideration so that what may be regarded as dangerous or non-natural may vary according to the circumstances.

A review of the cases indicates most vividly that what has been treated as non-natural use at one point in time may be seen as extremely ordinary at another. A surprising example is *Musgrove v Pandelis* (1919), where the fact that the motorcar was a relative newcomer to the transport scene must explain why its presence in a garage with petrol in its tank was considered non-natural use for the purposes of *Rylands v Fletcher* liability. The operation of a wartime munitions factory was held to constitute non-natural use in *Rainham Chemical Works v Belvedere Fish Guano Co Ltd* (1921), but the same point was doubted in the later case of *Read v Lyons*. In *Transco v Stockport*, Lord Bingham put it another way:

> I think it clear that ordinary user is a preferable test to natural user, making it clear that the rule in *Rylands v Fletcher* is engaged only where the defendant's use is shown to be extraordinary and unusual. This is not a test to be inflexibly applied: a use may be extraordinary and unusual at one time or in one place but not so at another time or in another time (although I would question whether, even in wartime, the manufacture of explosives could ever be regarded as an ordinary use of land . . .).

 THINKING POINT

Does the term 'ordinary' rather than 'natural' make it easier to determine what activity would create *Rylands v Fletcher* liability?

The amount of the substance collected and its conditions of storage will be relevant to the assessment of non-natural use in that it may determine the risk which the defendant's activity poses to others. In *Mason v Levy Autoparts of England Ltd* (1967) the fact that the combustible items were being stored in such large quantities contributed to the conclusion that this was non-natural use. *Stannard* (see 13.5.2 Default of the claimant or contributory negligence) calls *Mason* into question. A similar storage of auto parts might not be considered non-natural user today.

The question of wider benefit does not seem to be significant, despite *Rickards v Lothian* (1913). There, where 'ordinary plumbing' did not constitute non-natural use, Lord Moulton said:

> It is not every use to which land is put that brings into play [*Rylands v Fletcher*]. It must be some special use bringing with it increased danger to others, and must not merely be the ordinary use of land or such use as is proper for the general benefit of the community.

In *Cambridge Water* Lord Goff expressed dissatisfaction with the element of community benefit, which he felt might be unnecessarily expansionist. He considered the issue of powerful chemicals stored in drums for use in the tanning process:

> I cannot think that it would be right . . . to exempt [the defendants] from liability under the rule in *Rylands v Fletcher* on the ground that the use was natural or ordinary. The mere fact that the use is common in the tanning industry cannot, in my opinion, be enough to bring the use within the exception, nor the fact that Sawston contains a small industrial community which is worthy of encouragement or support. Indeed I feel bound to say that the storage of substantial quantities of chemicals on industrial premises should be regarded as an almost classic case of non-natural use; and I find it very difficult to think that it should be thought objectionable to impose strict liability for damage caused in the event of their escape.

Lord Goff did, however, acknowledge the 'lack of precision' in the concept of non-natural user. He concluded however, that it would not be his responsibility to refine the concept in the instant case, due to the conclusion that liability under *Rylands* would be denied on the grounds of foreseeability of damage cause. Instead, the challenge was adopted by the House of Lords in *Transco v Stockport Metropolitan Borough Council.*

🔍 CASE CLOSE-UP

Transco plc v Stockport Metropolitan Borough Council (2004)

Water for domestic use was carried by pipes throughout the defendants' block of flats. A pipe failed, without negligence on the defendants' part, and a substantial leak occurred, which remained undetected for a long period of time. The water escaped from the building and seeped into a bank of earth which was supporting the claimants' gas pipe. The bank collapsed, the gas pipe lost support and was at risk of cracking, which could have led to the potential escape of gas. This involved the claimants in an urgent and expensive repair operation.

Lord Bingham addressed the question as follows:

> I think it clear that . . . the rule in *Rylands v Fletcher* is engaged only where the defendant's use is shown to be extraordinary and unusual. This is not a test to be inflexibly applied: a use may be extraordinary and unusual at one time or in one place but not so at another time or in another place . . . . I also doubt whether a test of reasonable user is helpful, since a user may well be quite out of the ordinary but not unreasonable . . . .

Lord Bingham agreed with Lord Goff in *Cambridge Water* that the question of general benefit to the community adds little and may cause confusion. He concluded that the rule in *Rylands v Fletcher* was not applicable in this case for the following reasons:

- the *'danger or mischief test'* was not satisfied—piping a domestic water supply from the mains to storage tanks would not appear to anyone as particularly hazardous;

- it was questionable whether the defendants had been *accumulating* rather than simply supplying the water; and

- the use of its land by the Council was 'entirely normal and routine'. The requirement of *non-natural use* was not fulfilled.

13.2 Parties

Lord Macmillan in *Read v Lyons* described *Rylands v Fletcher* as: 'a principle applicable between occupiers in respect of their land'.

13.2.1 Who may be sued under the rule?

An owner, or occupier of land, including whoever stores or collects the substance in question, can be sued. In *Rainham Chemical Works Ltd v Belvedere Fish Guano Co Ltd* (1921), the House of Lords held that both the licensee who collects the harmful substance (here explosives) and the landlord could be liable.

13.2.2 Who may sue under the rule?

In *Rylands v Fletcher*, and in many subsequent cases, the plaintiff's claim was derived from his interest in land and based upon damage to that interest or physical harm to possessions on that land. In *Hale v Jennings* (1938), a chair from a fairground ride flew off and injured another stallholder. Her *Rylands v Fletcher* claim was based upon the tenancy of her stall. As in *Hale*, several other cases have indicated that plaintiffs could recover in *Rylands v Fletcher* for personal injuries. In *Perry v Kendricks* (1956), the claim was unconnected to any interest in land. The court assumed that passers-by on a highway who were injured by an explosion were entitled to bring an action under *Rylands v Fletcher*, although their claim failed on other grounds.

However, the close relationship with nuisance has led to the more recent conclusion that, in parallel with the House of Lords decision in *Hunter v Canary Wharf*, actions in *Rylands v Fletcher* cannot be based on personal injury. That should be the province of the law of negligence. Rather, *Rylands v Fletcher* actions will address damage to land, loss of value, and damage to things on the land. In *Transco, Rylands v Fletcher* was described as 'a remedy for damage to land or interests in land. It must . . . follow that damages for personal injuries are not recoverable under the rule.'

13.3 Foreseeability of harm

🔍 CASE CLOSE-UP

Cambridge Water Co v Eastern Counties Leather plc (1994)

In this case the House of Lords thoroughly reviewed the status of *Rylands* when dealing with a case of historic pollution. The defendants had for many years operated a tannery in an 'industrial village'. They used a chemical (PCE) to degrease animal skins and had stored it on the premises in 40-gallon drums. The plaintiffs were the owners of a borehole through which water was pumped from its underground sources in order to be supplied to water customers in the Cambridge area. The borehole was located just over a mile away from the tannery.

In 1982, an EC directive required new standards for testing water for human consumption and the claimants' water was found to be unfit. The source of the pollution was the borehole, which had been contaminated by PCE from the defendant's tannery. Spillage had occurred in transferring the chemical into containers or in piping it through the plant and PCE had seeped down into the underground water supply. It was suggested that this contamination had been occurring for up to thirty years. The plaintiffs incurred great expense in finding alternative sources of water and sued in negligence, nuisance, and *Rylands v Fletcher*.

The trial judge dismissed the actions in negligence and nuisance on the grounds that the defendant could not have reasonably foreseen the pollution as a result of the spillages of the chemical and said that *Rylands v Fletcher* could not apply because the use of land was not non-natural. In the Court of Appeal the ruling on non-natural use was upheld. When the case reached the House of Lords, however, Lord Goff stated that 'storage of substantial quantities of chemicals on industrial premises should be regarded as an almost classic case of non-natural use'. He was unimpressed with the argument that the creation of local employment might establish the tannery as a natural use of land. His opinion on this point must, however, be regarded as *obiter* because the Lords went on to reject *Rylands v Fletcher* liability for other reasons.

Lord Goff believed that the origins of the rule and its interpretation in precedent and academic writing indicated that *Rylands v Fletcher* liability is an extension of the law of nuisance, as applied to isolated escapes. As 'foreseeability of damage of the relevant type' was confirmed as essential to an action in nuisance in *The Wagon Mound (No 1)* (1967), then it should be likewise a requirement for liability in *Rylands v Fletcher*. At the time of the collection of PCE on the defendant's land, the damage which it caused to the water supply was not reasonably foreseeable and therefore the plaintiffs were unsuccessful. In such cases the escape itself, however, need not be reasonably foreseeable to establish liability and it is this aspect of the rule which maintains its 'strict liability' nature.

Lord Bingham, in *Transco*, considered the foreseeability aspect of the tort:

> It must be shown that the defendant has done something which he recognized, or judged by the standards appropriate at the relevant place or time, or ought reasonably to have recognized, as giving rise to an exceptionally high risk of danger or mischief if there should be an escape, however unlikely an escape may have been thought to be.

He acknowledged that the 'danger or mischief' requirement was closely related to the issue of non-natural use.

13.4 *Rylands v Fletcher* and liability for fire

The Fire Prevention (Metropolis) Act 1774 governs most incidents of damage caused by fire. According to s 86: 'No one will be liable for a fire which begins on his premises unless he has been negligent in respect of it.' But if the fire arises by accident, then the occupier could be liable if they are negligent in allowing it to spread. Case law indicates that 'accident' is narrowly interpreted and covers only occurrences by chance or of which no cause can be traced. *Musgrove v Pandelis* [1919] 2 KB 43 illustrates the way the 1774 Act operates. The claimant lived in rooms above the defendant's garage. A fire started accidentally (within the Act) in the engine of his car. However, its spread, which caused the claimant's property damage, was due to the negligence of the defendant's employee in failing to take simple steps to extinguish it. This lost the defendant the protection of the Act and he was liable in negligence. It must be noted that the burden of proof remains on the claimant.

It has generally been accepted that the 1774 Act does not govern cases where *Rylands v Fletcher* is applicable. However, the issue was reviewed by the Court of Appeal in *Gore v Stannard* [2012] EWCA Civ 1248.

 CASE CLOSE-UP

Gore v Stannard (2012)

The defendant operated a tyre-fitting business. On his property on an industrial estate he stored approximately 3,000 tyres. One night a fire started accidentally, probably due to faulty wiring. The tyres were ignited and the fire spread rapidly to the claimant's property, which was destroyed. Actions against the defendant were brought in negligence and *Rylands v Fletcher*. The former failed at first instance due to lack of evidence supporting breach of duty by the defendant; however, the latter succeeded.

The Court of Appeal unanimously overturned the finding of liability under *Rylands*. The tyres, brought onto the land were not especially dangerous, carrying a high risk of causing mischief if they escaped, the defendant's business did not constitute non-natural use of land, and perhaps most significantly, it was not the tyres which escaped but rather fire. Fundamentally, following *Stannard*, in order for there to be liability for fire under *Rylands*, it must be the fire which is brought onto the defendant's land and which then escapes.

The Court was divided on the issue of whether or not the 1774 Act could, in theory, provide assistance to the defendant in a case where *Rylands* applied. A strong argument in favour, was made by Lewison LJ in a lengthy judgment which reviewed the history of the relevant law, beginning with the Great Fire of London in 1666. The majority, however, comprising Etherton LJ and Ward LJ upheld the status quo and followed *Musgorve* in replying in the negative. The wider considerations around liability for damage caused by fire are of course closely linked to questions of insurance, although these provide no easy answers.

The decision in *Stannard* is thought to be indicative of a somewhat restrictive trend, following *Transco*, in which the clear founding principles of *Rylands* must be adhered to in order to prevent any creeping expansion of the tort.

13.5 Defences

These are wide-ranging and cover many of the situations in which we would expect *Rylands v Fletcher* to apply otherwise. Some of these defences bring aspects of negligence into what should be a strict liability tort.

13.5.1 **Act of an unknown third party**

In *Perry v Kendricks Transport Ltd* (1956), this defence was successful when a boy threw a match into a petrol tank which exploded, the cap having been removed by an unknown person. The plaintiff failed in *Rickards v Lothian* (1913), when a vandal's 'malicious act' caused a flood in the premises below when he turned on a tap, having first blocked the basin outlet. If the actions of the party responsible for the escape are known to the claimant, then the defendant is likely to be able to deny liability: *Northwestern Utilities Ltd v London Guarantee and Accident Co Ltd* (1936).

13.5.2 **Default of the claimant or contributory negligence**

» CROSS REFERENCE

For more on contributory negligence, see Chapter 6.

The claimant who is wholly or partly to blame will not have the benefit of strict liability. In *Rylands v Fletcher* itself Lord Blackburn stated, 'He [the defendant] can excuse himself by showing that the escape was owing to the plaintiff's default.' In *Dunn v Birmingham Canal Navigation Co* (1892), the owners of a mine under a canal were not successful in their *Rylands v Fletcher* action in respect of the flooding of their property because they were said to have seen 'the danger and may be said to have courted it'. At that time contributory negligence was a complete defence; however, now the Law Reform (Contributory Negligence) Act 1945 will apply and the court may apportion liability.

As in cases of nuisance, the court may also consider that the claimant was using his land in such a way as to make him unusually vulnerable to harm. *Eastern SA Telegraph Co Ltd v Cape Town Tramways Companies Ltd* (1902) concerned an allegation that an escape of electricity stored in the workings of the defendants' trams had affected the sending of telegraphic messages in the plaintiff's cables. The plaintiff failed because no tangible damage was done and the judge stated: 'A man cannot increase the liabilities of his neighbour by applying his own property to special uses, whether for business or pleasure.'

13.5.3 **Act of God**

This defence was first mentioned in *Rylands v Fletcher* itself and has been taken to relate to unforeseeable circumstances, not man-made, which it would be impossible to take precautions against. It has been applied to exceptionally heavy rainfall (*Nichols v Marsland* (1876)) but subsequent cases have doubted that anything other than the most extreme weather conditions would suffice. In practice, the use of the 'Act of God' defence is extremely close to invoking negligence principles relating to fault or its absence. This does not seem appropriate for a strict liability tort and is of little significance.

13.5.4 **Consent of the claimant**

If the claimant can be said to have consented, expressly or impliedly, to the accumulation of the substance in question, he cannot impose liability if it escapes. This defence can be combined with another, that of *common benefit*. In the case of *Carstairs v Taylor* (1871), where the collection of water was for the benefit of a number of occupants of a building, these two issues were treated as one for the purpose of denying liability.

13.5.5 **Statutory authority**

When the defendant's activity is governed by statute, that act may provide him with a defence to an action in *Rylands v Fletcher*. It may specify where responsibility should lie, as with the Water Industry Act 1991. If it does not, it is necessary to pay careful regard to the wording of the legislation in question. The cases show that the determining factor is whether the defendant was acting under a duty, in which case the defence is likely to apply, as in *Green v Chelsea Waterworks Co* (1874) or only under a power, in which case it will not, as in *Charing Cross Electricity Co v Hydraulic Power Co* (1914).

 THINKING POINT

Can the tort in *Rylands v Fletcher* be accurately described as one of strict liability, given the defences described in this chapter?

13.6 Reform of *Rylands v Fletcher?*

In *Cambridge Water*, Lord Goff did not believe that it was appropriate for the Lords to develop the rule in *Rylands*, preferring it to remain in its historical context as an aspect of nuisance law. Furthermore, statutory provision was said to be the most appropriate and adaptable means of addressing environmental losses:

> Like the judge in the present case, I incline to the opinion that, as a general rule, it is more appropriate for strict liability in respect of operations of high risk to be imposed by Parliament, than by the courts. If such liability is imposed by statute, the relevant activities can be identified, and those concerned can know where they stand. Furthermore, statute can where appropriate lay down precise criteria, establishing the incidence and scope of such liability . . . . It is of particular relevance that the present case is concerned with environmental pollution. The protection and preservation of the environment is now perceived as being of crucial import-ance to the future of mankind; and public bodies, both national and international, are taking significant steps towards the establishment of legislation which will promote the protection of the environment, and make the polluter pay for damage to the environment for which he is responsible . . . . But it does not follow from these developments that a common law principle, such as the rule in *Rylands v Fletcher*, should be developed or rendered more strict to provide for liability in respect of such pollution. On the contrary, given that so much well-informed and carefully structured legislation is now being put in place for this purpose, there is less need for the courts to develop a common law principle to achieve the same end, and indeed it may well be undesirable that they should do so.

In the same year, however, in *Burnie Port Authority v General Jones Pty Ltd* (1994), the High Court of Australia held that the differences between *Rylands v Fletcher* and negligence are now so slight that the former should be absorbed as a variation of the latter, while characterized by a non-delegable duty and a high standard of care.

In *Transco*, the House of Lords noted the decision in *Burnie* but rejected the opportunity to permit *Rylands v Fletcher* to be absorbed into the law of negligence or alternatively to extend the reach of strict liability in this area.

Instead, Lord Bingham proposed that the court should retain the rule, as a 'sub-species of nuisance . . . while insisting upon its essential nature and purpose; and . . . restate it so as to achieve as much certainty and clarity as is attainable'. *Rylands* 'has been a part of English law for nearly 150 years and despite a searching examination [by Lord Goff in *Cambridge Water*] there was no suggestion in his speech that it could or should be abolished. I think that would be too radical a step to take.'

 THINKING POINT

Should the tort in *Rylands v Fletcher* be simplified and converted into a form of strict liability for ultra-hazardous activities, as in the United States?

Lord Bingham's summary (from *Transco*) of the current status of *Rylands v Fletcher* is thought-provoking:

> I pause at this point to summarise the very limited circumstances to which the rule has been confined. First, it is a remedy for damage to land or interests in land. As there can be few properties in the country, commercial or domestic, which are not insured against damage by flood and the like, this means that disputes over the application of the rule will tend to be between property insurers and liability insurers. Secondly, it does not apply to works or enterprise authorised by statute. That means that it will usually have no application to really high risk activities. As Professor Simpson points out (1984) 13 J Leg Stud 225 the Bradfield Reservoir was built under statutory powers. In the absence of negligence, the occupiers whose lands had been inundated would have had no remedy. Thirdly, it is not particularly strict because it excludes liability when the escape is for the most common reasons, namely vandalism or unusual natural events. Fourthly, the cases in which there is an escape which is not attributable to an unusual natural event or the act of a third party will, by the same token, usually give rise to an inference of negligence. Fifthly, there is a broad and ill-defined exception for 'natural' uses of land. It is perhaps not surprising that counsel could not find a reported case since the second world war in which anyone had succeeded in a claim under the rule. It is hard to escape the conclusion that the intellectual effort devoted to the rule by judge and writers over many years has brought forth a mouse.

THINKING POINT

(1) How is protection currently provided against high-risk activities?

(2) Why is the prevalence of insurance in this area seen as significant?

(3) Can non-natural use be described as a restricting or widening factor?

(4) Why might *Rylands v Fletcher* have given rise to so much thought and writing?

Summary

- The action in *Rylands v Fletcher* is a land-based tort.
- It remains a strict liability tort, although this aspect has been modified by *Cambridge Water*.
- *Transco* held that the action in *Rylands v Fletcher* is of limited practical importance.
- Underlying legal developments in this area is the policy issue: where should loss due to hazardous activities lie?

 Visit the online resources to listen to a podcast summarizing the topics covered in this chapter.

The bigger picture

The tort in *Rylands v Fletcher* must be understood in the wider context of the law of nuisance and both are part of the bigger legal world of environmental protection. Although much of this is now controlled by statute law, the common law still holds an important role. In her article 'The Public Interest in Private Nuisance: Collectives and Communities in Tort' (2015) CLJ 329, Maria Lee analyses the way regulatory decisions are made and the way the public interest is incorporated into private law decision-making on environmental matters.

? Questions

Knowledge-testing questions

1. To what extent might negligence be a factor in determining liability under the tort in *Rylands v Fletcher?*

2. What is the significance of the decision in *Transco v Stockport?*

3. What are the main defences to the tort in *Rylands v Fletcher* and how do they relate to the ingredients of the tort itself?

Problem and essay questions

1. Robert and Linda Snow moved in the winter of 2012 into a scenic riverside bungalow which featured a jetty where they moored their rowing boat. At the bottom of the long garden was a small group of allotments, provided for the last thirty years by Avonmere District Council, where local residents can grow fruit, vegetables, and flowers on small plots.

   When spring arrived, they realized that Arthur, the allotment holder nearest to their garden, burned his refuse in a bonfire on the other side of their wall. Smoke and ash frequently blew into their garden. When they put out their garden furniture and sun canopies, they often became stained and smelly. The situation became even worse when Robert realized that someone on the allotment must be growing marijuana, the seeds of which had blown into his garden and self-seeded.

   In 2014 their jetty became unusable when it was blocked by silt from a small industrial quarry upstream, Rocks R Us having obtained planning permission to do so from Avonmere DC.

   In 2015 Robert and Linda were horrified to realize that sewage was seeping into the basement of their bungalow. Neighbours told them that Avon Water has been failing for years to maintain the local sewage works for which they are responsible.

   Advise Linda and Robert.

2. What is the future of the tort in *Rylands v Fletcher*, following recent key cases?

 Visit the online resources for guidance on answering these questions.

☰ Further reading

Bagshaw, R, '*Rylands* Confined' (2004) 120 LQR 388

Law Commission, *Civil Liability for Dangerous Things and Activities* (Report No 32, 1970)

Murphy, J, 'The Merits of *Rylands v Fletcher*' (2004) 24(4) OJLS 643

Newark, F, 'The Boundaries of Nuisance' (1949) 65 LQR 480

Nolan, D, 'The Distinctiveness of *Rylands v Fletcher*' (2005) 121 LQR 421

Simpson, AWB, 'Bursting Reservoirs and Victorian Tort Law: *Rylands and Horrocks v Fletcher*' in Simpson, *Leading Cases in the Common Law* (OUP 1996) 195

Tofaris, S, 'Case Comment: Rylands v Fletcher Restricted Further' [2013] 72 CLJ 11

14 Elements of defamation

Introduction

The other aspects of tort law contained in this textbook are mainly concerned with the protection of personal safety or protection against some other form of physical interference but defamation is different because it is concerned with protecting against harm caused by words. The aim of the law of defamation is to provide compensation for those whose reputations are harmed by untrue statements and to enable those threatened with loss of reputation to obtain an **interim injunction** to prevent the publication of a potentially defamatory statement. Defamation is different from other torts in terms of the complicated legal procedures involved in taking or defending an action and, because it is one of the oldest torts, a large body of case law has evolved in protecting against wrongful loss of reputation. You will further see in Table 17.1 that the limitation period for defamation claims is one year from the date on which the cause of action accrued, which is much shorter than the limitation period for other torts. However, in studying this topic you will also find that many of the cases involve celebrity litigants such as Elton John and Victoria Beckham; these cases will provide you with helpful and interesting 'live' illustrations of the different aspects of an action in defamation. A difference that previously existed between defamation and other torts

interim injunction
an order which is temporary, until the issue can be determined at a full hearing—this was previously known as an interlocutory injunction.

was that defamation was the only tort in which trial by jury was used. The judge and the jury had separate and distinct functions: the role of the judge was to direct the jury on the legal meaning of a defamatory statement, but it was the role of the jury to decide whether the words in question were, in fact, defamatory. Removal of the presumption in favour of trial by jury was one of the key provisions in the Defamation Act 2013; s 11 provides that trials for both libel and slander are now to be without a jury unless the court orders otherwise. This places full responsibility on the judge to determine issues such as defamatory meaning, as in *Stocker v Stocker* (2018) (see 14.3.1.4).

You will see in *Lewis v Daily Telegraph* (1964) that a company, as well as a human person, can sue for a defamatory statement affecting its business or trading reputation. The scope for companies to sue for reputational damage is significantly limited by the Defamation Act 2013; s 1(1) provides that a statement is not defamatory unless its publication has caused or is likely to cause serious harm to the reputation of the claimant but, in the case of corporate claimants, s 1(2) provides that harm to the reputation of a body that trades for profit is not 'serious harm' unless it has caused or is likely to cause that body serious financial loss.

It is only untrue words which cause harm to the claimant's reputation that are covered; for example, regardless of how much emotional distress or injury to feelings is suffered as the result of a true statement, this will not be relevant to the question of whether the statement is defamatory.

Tony Weir (*Casebook on Tort*, 10th edn, 2004, p 520) points out:

> The law has an extraordinary regard for truth, and just as it makes a person liable for a white lie, it makes a person immune in respect of a black truth.

When we are looking at the defences to defamation in Chapter 15 you will see that the law presumes that a defamatory statement is untrue so that in order for a statement to be actionable it is not necessary for the claimant to show that the statement was false. Once the claimant can show that the statement was defamatory, the burden is on the defendant to show that the statement was true by way of a defence. This is yet another example of the ways in which defamation is different from other torts; the general rule in tort is that the burden of proving the case against the defendant is on the claimant. In effect this means that, in defamation, the claimant may succeed, not because the statement made by the defendant was false, but because the defendant failed to produce sufficient evidence to prove the truth of the allegation. The reality is, however, that because of the lack of legal aid for actions in defamation and the very high costs incurred in these cases, it is usually only the wealthy who can use the law of defamation as a remedy for damage to their reputation. This also explains why litigants in defamation actions tend to be celebrities or well-known public figures, leading to widespread media attention in these cases. In addition to the common law developments in this tort, you will see that many of the changes in the law of defamation have been brought about by legislation. Defamation is also an area of law where the influence of the Human Rights Act 1998 has been increasingly evident in the context of freedom of speech and protection of reputation. Partly because of the large body of case law built up following the growth of mass-circulation newspapers in the late nineteenth and twentieth centuries, together with complicated substantive and procedural rules, defamation is one of the most complex torts. The main reasons for the complexities surrounding the tort of defamation are summarized below:

- the complicated rules of evidence and procedure;
- the historical evolution of liability for defamatory words which has produced a large volume of case law on defamation;
- the rules on awards of damages;
- the need to balance protection of reputation with freedom of speech; and
- the enactment of the Human Rights Act 1998.

For the above reasons, the law on libel had been criticized as being antiquated, costly, and unfair, the effects of which resulted in a chilling effect on freedom of expression and the stifling of legitimate debate. An ongoing high-profile campaign for law reform seeking better protection for freedom of speech and demands for legal recourse for damage to reputation led to the enactment of the Defamation Act 2013. We shall see throughout this chapter and Chapter 15 on defences to defamation that the Act aimed to offer clearer, better protection for individuals, members of the press, scientists, and academics who wish to publish information and views without the threat of libel action. The Act reformed and codified the libel laws in England and Wales to meet the needs of the digital age and provide the protections and freedoms required in the twenty-first century.

14.1 Defamation Act 2013: presumption in favour of jury trials removed

Defamation proceedings in jury trials took longer than cases heard by a judge alone and significantly increased the costs of defamation claims. We will see in the following chapter that juries were also unpredictable in assessing damages. The delay and cost in defamation actions were factors criticized for restricting free speech and stifling legitimate debate. The removal of the presumption in favour of jury trials under s 11 of the 2013 Act aims to rebalance the law and make access to justice in defamation cases quicker and cheaper. However, you will see later (14.3.1 What is a defamatory meaning?) that a defamatory statement is one which 'lowers a person in the eyes of right-thinking people'. Since juries represent ordinary members of society, the question as to whether they are in a better position than a judge alone to decide whether or not a statement is defamatory could be asked. Should the meaning attached to a statement made by an individual or a journalist be determined by a judge alone?

This is one of the questions that arose in *Yeo v Times Newspapers Ltd* (2015), the first decision on removal of the presumption of trial by jury. Mr Yeo, a member of Parliament, claimed that articles published by *The Times* and the *Sunday Times* contained the defamatory meaning that in return for cash he was prepared to act in breach of the rules of the House of Commons. The newspaper sought a jury trial on the ground that 'members of the public are best placed to decide whether publication was legitimate given [Mr Yeo's] role in public life and the role of the press in holding those in public life to account'. The court concluded that the factors supporting the statutory presumption in favour of trial by judge alone to be powerful and not outweighed by those supporting a jury trial, which were unpersuasive. In refusing to exercise his discretion to order a trial by jury the judge pointed out that 'Parliament no longer regards jury trial as a right of "the highest importance" in defamation cases. It is no longer a right at all.' This decision indicates that the possibility of a jury trial in any future defamation claim is highly unlikely. In *Stocker v Stocker* (2019), at 14.3.1.4, the Supreme Court implied satisfaction with the judicial ability to put itself in the place of the average Facebook or Twitter reader.

14.2 Libel and slander

Historically, the tort of defamation has evolved as the two separate torts of libel (which is a crime as well as a tort) and slander (which is only a tort). The distinction between the two torts is that libel is a defamatory statement made in a 'permanent' form; this can be a written statement or visual representation such as pictures, statues, and waxwork effigies, such as those seen in waxworks museums like Madame Tussauds in London. In *Youssoupoff v Metro-Goldwyn-Mayer Pictures* (1934), the court found that a film which contained photographic scenes accompanied by recorded speech, which implied that a woman had been seduced, constituted a libel.

Increasingly, through electronic means of communication, words, gestures, and visual images are transmitted and in these situations statute has intervened to provide guidance. The Defamation Act 1952 specifically provided that offending items in radio and television broadcasts constitute libel and now the Broadcasting Act 1990, s 166 provides that defamatory words, pictures, and visual images on radio or television or any other programme service are to be treated as libel. The Theatres Act 1968, s 4(1) provides that defamatory statements made in the course of a public performance of a play shall be treated as publication in a permanent form, but under s 7 of the Act this provision does not apply to statements made in the course of a performance in a domestic occasion in a private dwelling. As far as defamatory statements on records, recorded tapes, and discs is concerned, there is doubt as to whether they are potentially libel or slander and, although not the sole criterion in determining the issue, the judicial comments in *Monson v Tussauds* (1894) suggest that 'permanency' is an important consideration in these situations. The case concerned a waxworks exhibition situated close to the Chamber of Horrors in Madame Tussauds, where it was held that displaying a model of the plaintiff and his gun in a murder scene was capable of being a libel.

Lopes LJ stated that:

> Libels are generally in writing or printing, but this is not necessary; the defamatory matter may be conveyed in some other permanent form. For instance, a statue, a caricature, an effigy, chalk marks on a wall, signs or pictures may constitute a libel.

Libel, because it takes a permanent form, is deemed to be the more serious wrong and was always actionable per se. This meant that until recently damage did not need to be proved; all a claimant needed to show was that a defamatory statement about him was published and once this was established there was no need to show that damage was suffered as a result.

However, a serious harm threshold for defamation claims is now required to be met under the Defamation Act 2013. Unless publication of a statement has caused or is likely to cause serious harm to the reputation of the claimant it is not defamatory. The 'serious harm' requirement under s 1(1) of the 2013 Act means that defamation is no longer actionable per se (as it was under the previous common law). This provision in s 1(1) of the Act aims to restrict misuse of the law and stop trivial or non-viable claims from commencing.

Slander is a statement made in a transitory or temporary form such as words spoken and gestures or mimicry made without being recorded.

Slander generally requires proof of **special damage**, which means that the claimant must show some loss or harm of monetary value, or damage assessable in monetary terms. So, for example, a claimant bringing an action in respect of a statement made in the form of a slander alleging dishonesty would need to show some loss, such as the denial of employment or the refusal of another to enter into a contract with him as a result of the words or gesture. However, because with certain types of allegation, damage is so likely to result as a consequence, a number of exceptions to the rule that damage needs to be proved in cases of slander have been established. Three of the former rules of exception originated in the common law (only one of which survives the Defamation Act 2013) but the fourth, 'imputation of incompetence', which is the exception most frequently relied upon by claimants, is provided by s 2 of the Defamation Act 1952.

> **special damages**
> these will not be presumed, such as the loss of earnings or medical expenses. They must be stated and proved.

The two exceptions to the general rule that slander requires proof of special damage are:

(1) *Imputation of a crime*: words imputing that a claimant has committed a criminal offence punishable by imprisonment give rise to a slander actionable per se. In *Webb v Beavan* (1883), the statement 'I know enough to put you in gaol' was actionable per se. The statement must be a direct imputation of a criminal offence punishable in the first instance with imprisonment. However, words conveying a mere *suspicion* that a claimant has committed the offence are not actionable per se and an action in these circumstances will not succeed unless damage is proved.

(2) *Imputation of incompetence*: an imputation that a person is incompetent, dishonest, or unfit for any office, profession, trade, or calling is the second remaining exception to the rule that, for slander, damage must be proved. At common law this exception applied only where the words spoken related directly to the person's trade or calling and because of this, in *Jones v Jones* (1916), an accusation that a headmaster had committed sexual misconduct with one of the school cleaners was not actionable per se: there was no allegation that this conduct would lower his *professional* reputation. However, if the imputation of impropriety with a pupil at the school had been alleged the position might have been different. This common law requirement that the statement had to be specifically in the context of the plaintiff's calling or professional activities has been removed by s 2 of the Defamation Act 1952. If, therefore, the natural tendency of the statement is to harm the professional reputation of the claimant it will be actionable per se, whether or not the words are spoken in the way of his office, profession, calling, trade, or business. A claimant in similar circumstances as the teacher in *Jones* would today have a claim (subject to the Defamatory statement: serious harm requirement 14.3.1.1).

The Defamation Act 2013 s 14(1) repeals the Slander of Women Act 1891, which provided the exception that words imputing unchastity or adultery in any woman or girl (but not in a man) were actionable per se and s 14(2) of the Act provides that imputation of a contagious or infectious disease no longer gives rise to a cause of action for slander unless special damage is shown.

> **THINKING POINT**
>
> Read the following extracts from *McManus v Beckham* (2002) (which was settled with Victoria Beckham paying the claimant £55,000 compensation) and identify which of the statements were (1) slander; and (2) libel.

The defendant, Victoria Beckham, is alleged to have said to others in the defendant's memorabilia shop: 'Excuse me but do not buy any autographs from this shop, they are all fakes. That is not my husband's signature out there. . . . I just don't want to see you people being ripped off.'

> **sting**
>
> the specific hurt or harm caused by the words.

The defendant's publication of the words complained of foreseeably led to extensive media coverage, repetition, and republication of the words and/or their **sting**, including articles published in the *Daily Mirror* and on their website entitled, 'Posh goes stropping—Beck's "forgery fury"'(www. peoplenews.com an article entitled, 'Posh Spice in Feud with Shopkeeper—Owner Fears Her Rant Could Ruin Business'). Similar statements circulated between dealers, collectors, and other individuals in the specialist celebrity autograph memorabilia market. In their natural and ordinary meaning the (said) words, or some of them, meant, and were understood to mean that in the course of conducting their business the claimants were and would continue to be in the habit of dishonestly and fraudulently 'ripping off' their customers by knowingly selling fake autographs.

14.3 Elements of defamation

Defamation consists of the 'publication' of a statement bearing a 'defamatory' meaning which 'refers' to the claimant. The approach taken in this chapter to examining the elements of liability in defamation is to explore the following three questions: (1) What is a defamatory meaning? (2) What is publication? (3) What is 'reference' to the claimant?

14.3.1 What is a defamatory meaning?

There is no exhaustive definition of what makes a statement defamatory but words critical of a person's conduct, competence, or character are likely to cause others to think worse of him. In determining whether the words in question are capable of bearing a defamatory meaning, the court distinguishes between words that amount to vulgar insults and are not capable of being defamatory, and words deliberately intended to hold the claimant up to mockery and ridicule, which are capable of bearing a defamatory meaning. An old definition of a defamatory statement in *Parmiter v Coupland* (1840) was said to be one which is calculated to injure the reputation of another by exposing him to 'hatred, contempt or ridicule'. However, this test was thought not to be satisfactory because words can adversely affect a person's reputation without exposing him to hatred, contempt, or ridicule. For example, an allegation that a person had used a very skilful method to commit internet fraud might harm his reputation without creating feelings of hatred, contempt, or ridicule.

A broader test was proposed by the House of Lords in *Sim v Stretch* (1936): 'Would the words tend to lower the plaintiff in the estimation of right-thinking members of society generally?'

The standard, applied by judge (or jury), would be an objective assessment of the meaning which the ordinary reasonable reader would give the words, that is, whether they would have the *tendency* to so lower the claimant's reputation. Thereafter damage would be an irrebuttable presumption.

Prior to the Defamation Act 2013, the courts had begun to establish a threshold of required damage to the claimant's reputation before a defamation action could be brought (see *Jameel (Yousef) v Dow Jones & Co Inc* (2005)). The threshold at that time was low, requiring only that damage be more than minimal. According to *Thornton v Telegraph Media Group* [2011] 1 WLR 1985, 'defamatory' incorporates a qualification or threshold of seriousness:

> the publication of which [a claimant] complains may be defamatory of him because it [substantially] affects in an adverse manner the attitude of other people towards him, or has a tendency to do so.

14.3.1.1 Defamatory statement: serious harm requirement

The issue was then addressed by s 1(1) of the Defamation Act 2013:

STATUTE

s 1 Serious harm

(1) A statement is not defamatory unless its publication has caused or is likely to cause serious harm to the reputation of the claimant.

(2) For the purposes of this section, harm to the reputation of a body that trades for profit is not 'serious harm' unless it has caused or is likely to cause the body serious financial loss.

> **THINKING POINT**
>
> What sort of evidence might a claimant produce to show that 'serious harm' has been caused, or is likely to be caused, to his reputation?

The aim of the statutory provision is to tip the balance in favour of freedom of expression by removing the threat of proceedings being used indiscriminately to silence those who wish to speak out.

The case of *Cooke v MGN Ltd* (2014), was the first to come before the courts on interpretation of the Act's new '*serious harm*' threshold. Here, the claim concerned the broadcast of a television series *Benefits Street*, which featured the lives of its residents dependent on social security benefits. The *Sunday Mirror* published an article about the series which focused on the exploitation of the residents by unscrupulous landlords, containing a front-page headline 'Millionaire Tory Cashes in on TV *Benefits Street*'. The statements about the claimants published in the article would have been defamatory under the old common law. On the Sunday following the publication, the *Sunday Mirror* published an apology. Bean, J found the apology sufficient to eradicate, or at least minimize, any unfavourable impression created by the original article. The claimants accepted that there was no specific evidence that the article had caused serious harm to their reputations so they failed to meet the threshold requirement under s 1(1). The judge considered that such serious harm could not be inferred:

> I do not accept that in every case evidence will be required to satisfy the serious harm test. Some statements are so obviously likely to cause serious harm to a person's reputation that this likelihood can be inferred. If a national newspaper with a large circulation wrongly accuses someone of being a terrorist or a paedophile, then in either case (putting to one side for the moment the question of a prompt and prominent apology) the likelihood of serious harm to reputation is plain, even if the individual's family and friends knew the allegation to be untrue. In such a case the matter would be taken no further by requiring the claimant to incur the expense of commissioning an opinion poll survey, or to produce a selection of comments from the blogosphere which might in any event be unrepresentative of the population of 'right thinking people' generally. But I do not consider that the Article in the present case, with the meaning relating to the claimants which I have held it to have, comes anywhere near that type of case.

The decision in *Cooke* indicated that the threshold of the previous common law test for serious harm had been raised significantly by the 2013 Act.

The application of s 1(1) to the context of tweets was considered in *Monroe v Hopkins* (2017). The claimant, who comes from a family with military connections, alleged that the defendant's tweets accused her of vandalizing a war memorial and desecrating the memory of those who fought for her freedom. She claimed that the tweets also suggested that she approved of or condoned that vandalization. The defendant argued that tweets are an accepted part of social media activity; they are intended to be provocative and should be treated with less credibility than 'serious' media publications. It was claimed that the tweets in question did not bear the meanings complained of and, because tweets are transient in nature, the claimant had not shown the statements to have caused serious harm to her reputation.

This argument was rejected. The abuse Monroe had received in respect of the tweets from other Twitter users caused distress and injury to feelings, additionally, the tweets:

> not only caused Ms Monroe real and substantial distress, but also harm to her reputation which was serious. . . .

Neither the limited extent nor the transience of the publication led to a finding against serious harm. Equally unacceptable was the argument that because Twitter is the 'Wild West' of social media, statements published there lacked sufficient authority to cause serious harm.

CASE CLOSE-UP

Lachaux v Independent Print Ltd (2019)

A number of newspaper articles were published by the defendants alleging that Lachaux had been physically abusive during his marriage, having caused his former wife to flee with their son, and then having falsely accused her of kidnapping the child. The question for the courts was to what extent the new law had altered, if at all, the common law presumption of damage in libel.

At first instance the appellants' case was that s 1(1) had effectively abolished the common law presumption of damage by introducing a new hurdle to be satisfied before the statement could be regarded as defamatory, and that the words complained of must not only be inherently injurious but 'must also be shown to produce serious harm in fact', which may require extraneous evidence to be submitted. Warby J held that under s 1(1) serious harm to the claimant's reputation must be proved and cannot be assumed on the basis of the 'tendency' of the words. It must be proved on the balance of probabilities that the publication has in fact caused serious harm to the claimant's reputation, or would probably do so in the future. He concluded, based on a combination of: the meaning of the words, the situation of Mr Lachaux, the circumstances of publication, and the inherent probabilities ('is more probable than not'), that (with one exception) the defamatory meanings in the articles had caused serious harm to the claimant's reputation. The defendants appealed.

The Court of Appeal upheld the judge's ruling but on different grounds. Davis LJ basically agreed with the claimant's contention that the Act left unaffected the common law presumption of general damage and the associated rule that the cause of action is made out if the statement complained of is inherently injurious or, as in *Jameel* and *Thornton*, the relevant words carry a 'tendency' to injure the claimant's reputation. The change brought about by the Act was that the tendency must be, not just towards some damage to reputation, but rather serious harm. The Court of Appeal concluded that serious harm had been proved.

On appeal to the Supreme Court, Lord Sumption gave the lead speech of the unanimous decision. The Court of Appeal's analysis had not given sufficient effect to the language of s 1. More was needed than the common law presumption of damage based on the tendency of the words:

> [It] not only raises the threshold of seriousness above that envisaged in *Jameel (Yousef)* and *Thornton*, but requires its application to be determined by reference to the actual facts about its impact and not just to the meaning of the words . . . This is a proposition of fact which can be established only by reference to the impact which the statement is shown actually to have had. It depends on a combination of the inherent tendency of the words and their actual impact on those to whom they were communicated.

It was important to read s 1(1) with s 1(2) concerning defamation of a body trading for profit—the Court's interpretation of that provision made it clear that more proof of damage is required than simply the tendency of the words used. Parliament's intention in the Act's preamble was to 'amend the law of defamation', implying again a departure from *Jameel* and *Thornton*.

THINKING POINT

Is publication of a swift apology, offsetting the likelihood of serious harm to the claimant's reputation, likely to act as a deterrent to claimants in future defamation claims?

In this instance, the absence of direct evidence from readers did not harm the claimant's case. The judge had been entitled to draw inferences which confirmed serious harm from: (i) the scale of the publications; (ii) the fact that the statements complained of had come to the attention of at least one identifiable person in the United Kingdom who knew Mr Lachaux; (iii) that they were likely to have come to the attention of others who either knew him or would come to know him in future; and (iv) the gravity of the statements themselves.

14.3.1.2 Who are right-thinking members of society generally?

The test of what 'right-thinking members of society' think appears to be determined by what they should think rather than what in fact they do think. In *Byrne v Deane* (1937), the police removed a number of illegal gambling machines from a golf club after somebody had informed them that the machines were in the club house. Soon after this happened, a verse appeared on the noticeboard of the club which ended with the lines: 'But he who gave the game away, may he byrne in hell and rue the day.' Mr Byrne brought an action for libel, alleging that by these words the defendants meant, and were understood to mean, that he was guilty of underhand disloyalty to his fellow club members. In addressing the question of whether the words were defamatory, the Court of Appeal held that an allegation that the plaintiff had reported a crime to the police could not be regarded as lowering his reputation because right-thinking members of society would regard this as commendable. The fact that disloyalty would damage the plaintiff's reputation among his fellow club members was irrelevant and his claim failed. In *Hartt v Newspaper Publishing plc* (1989), the Court of Appeal described the ordinary reader as someone who is not unduly suspicious, but who can read between the lines. Although he might engage in a certain amount of loose thinking, he is not to be treated as someone avid for scandal, and he will not select one bad meaning where other non-defamatory meanings are available.

14.3.1.3 Ridicule

The question of whether it was defamatory to say that a man was 'hideously ugly' was considered by the Court of Appeal in *Berkoff v Burchill* (1996). Stephen Berkoff, an actor and film director, argued that two statements made in a review by a well-known journalist, Julie Burchill, to the effect that he was hideously ugly, would tend to expose him to ridicule or would tend to cause other people to shun or avoid him and were, as such, defamatory.

> **THINKING POINT**
>
> Neill LJ thought that to describe a person in the public eye, who earns his living as an actor, as 'hideously ugly' is capable of lowering his standing in the estimation of the public and of making him an object of ridicule. Do you think this statement would meet the 'serious harm' threshold to Mr Berkoff's reputation as now required by s 1(1) of the Defamation Act 2013?

A majority of the Court of Appeal dismissed the defendant's case that the words were not capable of being defamatory. There was no entirely satisfactory definition of the word 'defamatory' and the exact borderline may be difficult to draw. Although a statement that a person was hideously ugly did not fall into that category of statements that were defamatory because they tended to make people shun or avoid the claimant, where the statement damaged the claimant's reputation by exposing him to ridicule it is relevant to consider the circumstances in which the words were used. In the circumstances of this case it was open to a jury to conclude that the remarks about Mr Berkoff gave the impression that he was not merely physically unattractive in appearance, but actually repulsive. Neill LJ said that the word 'reputation' is to be interpreted in a broad sense taking account of all aspects of a person's standing in the community. It was clearly relevant that Berkoff was an actor, and the words might impact on his employability.

In a dissenting judgment, Millett LJ said that 'chaff and banter' are not defamatory, and even serious imputations are not actionable if no one would take them to be meant seriously. He pointed out that the words were an attack on Mr Berkoff's appearance and not his reputation and said that people must be allowed to poke fun at one another without fear of litigation. Although Ms Burchill made a cheap joke at Mr Berkoff's expense, his Lordship thought the legal proceedings to be as frivolous as her article and that the time of the court should not be taken up with either of them.

 THINKING POINT

Read the following extract from the judgment of Phillips LJ in *Berkoff v Burchill* and consider the extent to which you agree with his judgment or the dissenting opinion of Millett LJ that: 'People must be allowed to poke fun at each other without fear of litigation.'

Phillips LJ:

> Where the issue is whether words have damaged a plaintiff's reputation by exposing him to ridicule, that question cannot be answered simply by considering whether the natural and ordinary meaning of the words used is defamatory per se. The question has to be considered in the light of the actual words used and the circumstance in which they are used. There are many ways of indicating that a person is hideously ugly, ranging from a simple statement of opinion to that effect, which I feel could never be defamatory, to words plainly intended to convey that message by way of ridicule. The words used in this case fall into the latter category. Whether they have exposed the plaintiff to ridicule to the extent that his reputation has been damaged must be answered by the jury.

14.3.1.4 **The meaning of words**

There are a number of factors to consider when establishing whether or not the words in the statement bear a defamatory meaning. In deciding the issue the judge must first consider the meaning of the words in their natural and ordinary sense. Where an explicit allegation of criminal conduct, dishonesty, or immorality is made, the words are clearly defamatory and the natural meaning of the words can be relied on.

Stocker v Stocker (2019) was based on the effects of the breakdown of an unhappy marriage combined with social media. In a Facebook exchange with her ex-husband's new partner, the defendant recounted a number of incidents from the marriage, including alleged 'gun issues' and the possibility that the claimant ex-husband had breached a non-molestation order. She went on to describe an argument during which he had 'tried to strangle' her. The claimant's defamation action alleged that the words implied that he had intended to kill her. The defendant argued that instead they implied 'merely' that he had gripped her hard by the throat, causing fear.

The judge at first instance, relying on the dictionary definition of the word 'strangle', found in favour of the claimant. According to Sharp LJ in the Court of Appeal, 'The use of dictionaries does not form part of the process of determining the natural and ordinary meaning of words, because what matters is the impression conveyed by the words to the ordinary reader when they are read, and it is this that the judge must identify.'

A unanimous Supreme Court agreed. In Lord Kerr's opinion, '[The] meaning is to be determined according to how it would be understood by the ordinary reasonable reader. It is not fixed by technical, linguistically precise dictionary definitions, divorced from the context in which the statement was made.' The context of the publication is important. In his view:

> the ordinary Facebook reader does not splice the post into separate clauses, much less isolate individual words and contemplate their possible significance. Knowing that the author was alive, he or she would unquestionably have interpreted the post as meaning that Mr Stocker had grasped his wife by the throat and applied force to her neck rather than that he had tried deliberately to kill her.

On this basis, the defendant was able to avail herself of the complete defence of justification, now 'truth' under s 2(1) Defamation Act 2013.

14.3.1.5 Innuendo

However, in some cases, words innocuous in themselves may bear another meaning which causes them to become defamatory. An 'innuendo' is the term used to describe words that are not defamatory in their natural and ordinary meaning but which may have a hidden meaning when put into context.

We shall now look at a case where the House of Lords found that words which were totally innocent in their ordinary meaning transformed into a defamatory statement because of the extrinsic facts known to those to whom it was made. The plaintiff in *Tolley v Fry* (1931) was a well-known amateur golfer. Without his knowledge, the defendants advertised their chocolate on a poster which depicted Tolley playing golf with a bar of their chocolate protruding from his pocket. This picture was accompanied by a verse which named him and compared the excellence of their chocolate to the excellence of his golf. Although the words seemed innocuous in themselves, the plaintiff claimed that people would think that he had agreed to advertise the defendants' chocolate for some financial gain or reward. This was held to be defamatory as it implied that he had prostituted his reputation and been guilty of conduct unworthy of his status as an amateur golfer. This is an example of a true innuendo (or legal) innuendo, which is one of the two types of innuendo, true and false, that are outlined below.

True (or legal) innuendo

A true innuendo is where the words in their ordinary meaning are innocent and only become defamatory when combined with extrinsic facts and circumstances which are known by some of the people to whom the statement is published. In these cases, the claimant must specifically show the meaning attributed to the words and prove the existence of the extrinsic facts to support this meaning. A further illustration of a true innuendo can be seen in the case of *Cassidy v Daily Mirror Newspapers Ltd* (1929) (discussed in the next paragraph).

False (or popular) innuendo

A false innuendo is where a defamatory inference can be drawn from the words themselves in their natural and ordinary meaning. The court does not have to be informed of any extrinsic facts to draw this inference. An illustration of a false innuendo can be seen in the case of *Lewis v Daily Telegraph* (1964).

14.3.1.6 Defamatory statement: true innuendo

A defendant may be liable for a statement which he does not know to be defamatory and it is no excuse that the defendant has no actual knowledge of the external facts that transform an innocent statement into a defamatory one. In *Cassidy v Daily Mirror Newspapers Ltd*, the defendant published a picture of Mr Cassidy with a young woman, together with a statement announcing their engagement. However, Mr Cassidy was already married and, although he lived apart from his wife, he was in the habit of visiting her at the shop where she was employed and he sometimes stayed at her flat. His wife brought an action for libel against the defendants alleging that she had suffered damage to her reputation through the publication. It was understood by several people to mean that Mr Cassidy was not the plaintiff's husband but that he was living with her in immoral cohabitation. The majority of the Court of Appeal held that the publication was capable of a defamatory meaning as it conveyed to reasonably minded people an aspersion on her moral character.

As we have already seen, defamation is a tort of strict liability and therefore the fact that it was Mr Cassidy who provided the reporter with the information about his engagement was irrelevant. The photographer sent the information to the defendants for publication and then took no further steps to verify its accuracy. You should note that when we are looking at unintentional defamation in Chapter 15 you will see that if similar circumstances were to arise in a publication now, in the absence of negligence, a defence under ss 2–4 of the Defamation Act 1996 might be available to the defendant.

14.3.1.7 Defamatory statement: false innuendo

 CASE CLOSE-UP

Lewis v Daily Telegraph (1964)

This case concerned an action brought by a company and its managing director and chairman, Lewis, which alleged that newspaper articles reporting that the Fraud Squad was carrying out an investigation into the affairs of the company contained a false innuendo. Although it was true that the company was being investigated by the Fraud Squad, Lewis claimed that the publication of the article implied that there were grounds for suspicion about the way in which the company conducted its business that could be understood by the ordinary reader to mean that the company's affairs were being conducted fraudulently or dishonestly. The Court of Appeal and the House of Lords held that the words complained of were incapable of meaning that either the company or the plaintiff, Lewis, had behaved fraudulently. Three possible meanings in respect of the statements were considered by the House of Lords: (1) that there was an investigation in progress; (2) that the plaintiffs were suspected of fraud; and (3) that the plaintiffs were guilty of fraud. The statement about an investigation into the company was true, so the only possible actionable meanings in this case were the second two and Lord Reid pointed out that there is a great difference between saying that a man has behaved in a suspicious manner and saying that he is guilty of an offence. In considering the task of deciding how a reasonable person would view a statement containing a range of possible meanings, he said:

> What the ordinary man, not avid for scandal, would read into the words complained of must be a matter of impression. I can only say that I do not think that he would infer guilt of fraud merely because an inquiry is on foot.

In these circumstances the statement is looked at in context and the court will consider the publication as a whole. In *Charleston v News Group Newspapers* (1995), a newspaper published a photograph of two television actors who appeared in *Neighbours*, an Australian soap opera. Pictures of the actors' faces were superimposed on bodies depicted in a pornographic pose. The picture was accompanied by explanatory text which made it clear that the faces of the actors were used without their knowledge or consent. The House of Lords dismissed the actors' allegation that in its ordinary meaning the newspaper article conveyed the meaning that they had posed for pornographic images because: (1) the photographs could not be considered in isolation from the article itself which, in this case, negated the libel; and (2) the meaning which the article, taken as a whole, conveyed to ordinary, sensible, and fair-minded readers could not rely on the fact that the defamatory statement might be conveyed to those who would only read the headline and not read or take account of the rest of the article.

14.3.2 What is publication?

The first thing to note is that the word 'publication' in the law of defamation has a technical meaning that is not related to newspapers or to the printed press. Publication of a statement in defamation simply means communication of the statement to at least one person other than the claimant. (As Tony Weir points out, you can be as rude as you like if no one is listening.) In this sense, defamation is a three-party tort. Defamation is concerned with the protection of a person's reputation in the eyes of others and therefore a statement communicated to the person about whom it is made will not constitute publication. The statement does not have to be in writing. Publication can take place in a variety of ways such as by letter, through conversation, or through the media.

Those who actively create and issue the material—the author and responsible editor—are primary publishers. They are strictly responsible for what they issue. 'A printer and publisher intend to publish, and so intending cannot plead as a justification that he did not know the contents': *McLeod v St Aubyn* (1899). Those who merely distribute material created by others are secondary publishers, and may be able to rely on the defence of innocent and non-negligent publication under s 1 of the Defamation Act 1996. This will cover printers, libraries, wholesale and retail newsagents, and others who handle print media. It would cover the situation in *Byrne v Deane* where publication took place through omission. It was not the presence of the poem (created and posted by an anonymous person), but the golf club's failure to remove it from its noticeboard within a reasonable time which amounted to publication, because of negligence. Under s 10 of the Defamation Act 2013, a secondary publisher may only be sued if it is not practicable to sue the primary publisher.

Secondary publication is a major issue with digital media. Much content is created by individual posters, but it appears on websites which are created and managed by service providers of various kinds. These providers are clearly not creating and issuing the material. It is not always possible to identify the primary publisher, as much content is published anonymously or using pseudonyms. In *Godfrey v Demon Internet* (1999) it was held that service providers who actually hosted the material could be liable if they had notice that the material was defamatory, as they could not then rely on the defence under s 1 of the 1996 Act. In *Bunt v Tilley* (2007) it was held that an internet service provider which did not host any material, but merely allowed it to appear on the internet and be accessed, was not a publisher—it was equated to a telephone company, which provides facilities for messages to be transmitted, but has no responsibility for them. Similarly in *Metropolitan International Schools Ltd v Designtechnica Corpn* (2011) search engines were also held not to be publishers of the information which they retrieved.

In *Tamiz v Google Inc* (2013) the defendant provided a blog platform. This did not make it a primary publisher:

> Google plainly facilitates publication of the blogs (including the comments posted on them) but its involvement is not such, however, as to make it a primary publisher. Google does not create the blogs or have any prior knowledge of, or effective control over, their content. It is not in a position comparable to that of the author or editor of a defamatory article.

However, by providing tools to help a blogger design the layout of his part of the notice board, the Court of Appeal said that Google went further than providing a notice board, and was a facilitator of the publication. It could therefore be liable, as in *Godfrey*, if it had notice and failed to take action. Nevertheless, the trial judge's finding was upheld and the appeal failed because the claimant could not show 'a real and substantial tort' since the period between notification to Google and removal of the blog was so short that damage to the appellant's reputation arising out of continued publication must have been trivial. Section 5 of the 2013 Act explicitly provides that there is to be no liability for material not posted by the operator unless he has been notified that the material is defamatory, and has failed to respond to a notice of complaint appropriately.

In *Stocker v Stocker* (2019), above, one limb of the defence case was that the defendant was not liable as a publisher, given that the allegations had been in a comment attached to a third-party's Facebook status. This was firmly rejected by the Court of Appeal. The defendant was the originator of the libel and she had deliberately posted it on a Facebook platform which she knew to be semi-public. Nor was this a republication; when she posted her comment it was instantly accessible to all of the recipient's 'friends'. *Stocker* confirms that the Facebook wall clearly exists in the realm of 'real world' noticeboards.

The words must be intelligible to the recipient, so there is no publication if the statement is in a foreign language he does not understand, or if he is too deaf to hear it or too blind to see it. Neither is there publication if a person gets to know of the statement through his own wrongful act, such as theft or deception.

THINKING POINT

As Roxi and Soo were driving alone in Roxi's car, Soo accused Roxi of fraud and theft. Is Soo's statement capable of bearing a defamatory meaning? Has the statement been published?

14.3.2.1 No publication between spouses

There is a rule that communication to the defendant's spouse does not amount to publication. This is an arbitrary rule which can partly be explained by the reluctance of the courts to have spouses give evidence about one another. However, there are situations where communication to the claimant's spouse can give rise to liability. In *Theaker v Richardson* (1962), the defendant wrote a letter to the plaintiff, a married woman and a fellow member of the local district council, which stated that she was: 'a lying, low down brothel keeping whore and thief'. The letter was placed in a sealed brown envelope similar to those used for election addresses and sent to the plaintiff. Her husband, thinking it was an election address, opened the letter. The Court of Appeal held that this amounted to publication on the ground that a natural and probable consequence of the defendant's writing and delivery of the letter was that it would be opened and read by her husband. The rule is, therefore, that where the defendant knew or ought to have foreseen that the statement would come to the attention of a third party, there is publication, even if that third party is a spouse.

A defendant will not be liable if it is not foreseeable that the third party will hear or see the defamatory statement. In *Huth v Huth* (1915), a man sent a letter in an unsealed envelope to his wife which contained defamatory statements about her and about her children. In an admitted breach of duty her butler, acting out of curiosity, opened and read the letter. At that time, the legal existence of a wife was incorporated into that of her husband and this meant that the woman was unable to sue her husband in tort, so the action in defamation against her husband was brought by the children. The plaintiff argued that since there was a presumption that postmen read open postcards, even though they have no business doing so, the same presumption ought to apply to unsealed envelopes. The Court of Appeal held that, even though the envelope was unsealed, there was no publication. It was not part of the butler's duty to open the letter and it was not foreseeable that he would open his employer's mail.

THINKING POINT

Ali and Bella are members of the Olympic Leisure Club. Ali writes a letter to Bella in which he accuses her of dishonesty and puts it into a sealed envelope. He plans to post the letter to Bella's home address. What could he write on the envelope in order to avoid publication of the potentially defamatory statement to someone other than Bella?

14.3.2.2 Repetition of a defamatory statement

In the context of the internet, a significant change is contained in s 8 of the Defamation Act 2013, which abolishes the long-standing common law principle that each publication of defamatory material gives rise to a new cause of action. This meant the twelve-month limitation rule for bringing an action in defamation started afresh each time the defamatory statement was published.

 CASE CLOSE-UP

***Loutchansky v Times Newspapers Ltd (Nos 2–5)* (2002)**

The particular difficulties this posed for internet publication and for those operating online archives can be illustrated in *Loutchansky v Times Newspapers Ltd (Nos 2–5)* (2002). In this case a Russian businessman brought a libel action in respect of statements in a printed newspaper and also contained on *The Times* newspaper's website article which alleged that he was the boss of a major Russian criminal organization and was involved in money laundering and other criminal activity. A settlement between the parties was reached in respect of the printed newspaper article but the claimant brought a second claim in respect of the same story which had been placed in the newspaper's online archive.

The Times contended that the harshness of the common law should be mitigated because enabling a claimant to sue every time an online article is accessed exposes website providers to repeated claims in defamation. Exposing newspapers which maintained a website of back numbers to indefinite vulnerability to claims in defamation was bound to affect their preparedness to provide readers with an internet archive of back numbers.

The effect of s 8 will limit such claims against a single defendant to publications that are not 'substantially the same' as the original defamatory publication. In effect this will prevent an action being brought in relation to publication of the same material by the same publisher after a one-year limitation period. This provision is particularly important to those operating websites and online archives because the multiple-publication rule required costly and time-consuming monitoring of archive content.

The single-publication rule which prevents an action being brought in relation to publication of the same statement by the *same publisher* does not apply where the manner of the subsequent publication is 'materially different' from the manner of the first publication. Furthermore, where a defamatory statement is published, it is no defence for the defendant to claim that he is merely repeating what he heard from another person. Where an unauthorized repetition of defamatory material takes place, the publication will normally be treated as a *novus actus interveniens* breaking the chain of causation. However, in certain circumstances, even an unauthorized repetition may make the original publisher liable. In *Slipper v British Broadcasting Corporation* (1990), the plaintiff, a senior police officer, claimed that he was defamed in a film about his unsuccessful attempts to secure the extradition from Brazil of one of the Great Train robbers who had fled there following his escape from jail. Slipper claimed that a press review of the film broadcast by the BBC, which portrayed him as incompetent, had caused widespread repetition of the sting of the libel through reviews in the television columns of newspapers. The Court of Appeal held that in appropriate cases, repetition of the sting of a libel by an unauthorized third party may be treated as the 'natural' or the 'natural and probable' consequences of the original publication, thus making the original publisher liable in damages in respect of the repetition.

> **novus actus interveniens** a new intervening act which breaks the chain of causation between the defendant's negligence and the harm suffered by the claimant. A *novus actus interveniens* can constitute a general defence in an action in tort. Where the act or omission of a third person intervenes between the original statement and the publication, and the act of the third person could have been expected in the particular circumstances, it is considered to be the direct cause of the damage.

In *McManus v Beckham* the Court of Appeal held that it might not be necessary to show that the defendant was actually aware of the risk of repetition, provided it was foreseeable to a reasonable person that further publication of the defamatory statement would take place. A reasonable person would have recognized that the words spoken by Victoria Beckham would receive widespread media coverage. The case was settled with Victoria Beckham paying the claimants £55,000 compensation and giving them a set of items signed by David Beckham.

14.3.2.3 Innocent dissemination

It is not just the author of a defamatory article published in a book, journal, or newspaper that may be liable for publication of the defamatory material, but the printer, publisher, bookseller, and newsagent can also be liable. However, to overcome the potential harshness of this rule, a distinction is drawn between:

- 'republication'—those who produce the libel (author, publisher, etc); and
- 'mechanical distributors'—those who merely disseminate the material (booksellers, newsagents, etc): Defamation Act 1996.

Mechanical distributors are those concerned with mere distribution of such material in the course of their business. Newsagents, libraries, and booksellers, for example, had a common law defence of 'innocent publication' if they did not know, or ought not to have known, that the material was defamatory. The distinction was explained in *Vizetelly v Mudie's Select Library* (1900). The defendants, proprietors of a circulating library, allowed people to use a book which, unknown to them, contained a libel on the plaintiff. Romer LJ held that mechanical distributors of such matter would have a defence if they could show that:

(1) they were innocent of any knowledge of the libel in the work in question;

(2) there was no reason for them to be aware that the work contained a libel; and

(3) it was not through negligence on their part that they failed to know it contained a libel.

The defendants in this case failed because they were negligent in that they did not have procedures for checking whether the books they lent contained libels and they had overlooked the publisher's circular requesting the return of the books in question.

14.3.2.4 Defamation Act 1996

Statute has also intervened to mitigate the harshness of the strict liability rule for those who inadvertently become involved in the dissemination of defamatory material and to reflect modern technology through the updated provisions contained in the Defamation Act 1996 and the Defamation Act 2013. The 1996 Act extends the principle of 'innocent defamation' to 'mechanical distributors'—namely, those who disseminate the material, such as printers, distributors, sellers, broadcasters of live programmes, and the operators of a communications system by which a defamatory statement is published, such as an internet service provider.

Section 1 deals with responsibility for publication and provides a defence in defamation proceedings where a person can show that:

(1) he was not the author, editor, or publisher of the statement complained of;

(2) he took reasonable care in relation to its publication; and

(3) he did not know, and had no reason to believe, that what he did caused or contributed to the publication of a defamatory statement.

A defendant who has innocently published defamatory words and can establish the above factors will be able to make an offer of amends and so escape liability for damages in a general action for defamation.

14.3.2.5 Defamation Act 2013

The principle of 'innocent defamation' is extended to include website operators in s 5(1) of the Defamation Act 2013. Where the website operator can show that it did not itself post the statement a new defence is created in respect of a statement posted by a third party. However, the defence will fail where the claimant can show:

(1) it was not possible for it to identify who posted the statement;

(2) it gave the operator a notice of the defamatory content; and

(3) the operator failed to respond in accordance with the regulations.

The defence will also fail if the claimant can show malice on the part of the website operator in relation to posting of the statement. For further discussion on internet publication, see *Godfrey v Demon Internet* (1999) and *Tamiz v Google* (2013).

> **CROSS REFERENCE**
> For more on offer of amends, see Chapter 15.

14.3.3 What is 'reference' to the claimant?

The test for whether a statement referred to the claimant is not about what the defendant intended; the question is whether reasonable people would believe the words complained of to refer to the claimant. Where a person is named in a publication there is usually no difficulty in showing that the words referred to him or her, but the reference to a claimant in defamation cases is not always express and direct. Special facts or circumstances known only to certain readers may identify the claimant and, as we have seen above, the test of whether a statement has referred to the claimant is whether an ordinary reasonable person, in the light of the special facts, would understand the words as referring to the claimant. The claim in *Morgan v Odhams Press* (1971) concerned a follow-up story to a report about dog doping which was published at a time when the young girl in question was staying at Mr Morgan's flat close to Finchley. *The Sun* newspaper reported: 'dog-doping girl was kidnapped last week by members of the gang and kept in a house in Finchley'. Mr Morgan produced six witnesses who said that they had seen him and the girl together and understood from the newspaper article that he was connected with the dog-doping gang.

Although a close reading of the article would have shown discrepancies that would have indicated that it could not refer to Morgan, the court held that in determining the impression in the mind of the reader, the character of the article and the class of reader likely to read it should be considered. An ordinary reader would not give a sensational article in a popular newspaper the same scrutiny that would be given to it by a lawyer. The court pointed out that the ordinary sensible man 'reading an article in a popular newspaper is not expected to analyse it like a Fellow of All Souls'. In overruling the Court of Appeal decision that the plaintiff must find in the words used some key or pointer to him, the House of Lords said the story was capable of a defamatory meaning. In determining whether the words referred to the plaintiff, the question is whether by reading casually and not expecting a high degree of accuracy would:

- a sensible reader,
- having knowledge of the special circumstances,
- understand the article as referring to the claimant.

14.3.3.1 **Words not intended to refer to the claimant**

The defendant may be liable even if he intended to write about a fictitious character. In *Hulton v Jones* (1910), the defendants published a humorous story about a motor festival in Dieppe which implied that a fictitious character, 'Artemus Jones' a churchwarden at Peckham, was behaving in a discreditable way with a woman who was not his wife. The plaintiff, a barrister also called Artemus Jones, was not a churchwarden nor did he live in Peckham. Although he had not visited the motor festival in Dieppe, friends of his swore they believed that the article referred to him. The defendant argued that they had invented a fictitious character and claimed they had never intended to refer to the real Artemus Jones. The House of Lords held that what mattered was how the words were understood by others, not what they meant in the minds of the writer and the publisher. Similarly, in *Newstead v London Express Newspapers Ltd* (1940), the defendants were liable for a newspaper article stating that: 'Harold Newstead, thirty-year old Camberwell man' had been convicted of bigamy. This statement was true of a barman of that name but not of the plaintiff, Harold Newstead, an unmarried hairdresser from Camberwell, also aged about 30.

You will see in Chapter 15 that the Defamation Act 1996 has substantially changed the rules regulating unintentional defamation but, if the Act is not applicable or the defendant chooses not to use it, the common law applies. However, the above cases must now be considered in the context of the Human Rights Act 1998 as they are likely to be challenged under Article 10, as can be seen in *O'Shea v MGN Ltd* (2001) (discussed below in 14.5.2 The Human Rights Act 1998). This case dealt with an allegation that the photograph accompanying an advertisement of adult material on the internet, although actually of 'Miss E', was the 'spit and image' of the claimant, such that her friends and relatives thought it was her. It was held that in this context, at least, the 'strict liability rule' was inconsistent with Article 10. It would be impossible to check whether other people resembled those being illustrated in news stories, etc and the burden imposed on the media would be disproportionate.

THINKING POINT

How does the decision concerning the statement in *Cassidy v Daily Mirror Newspapers Ltd* (see 14.3.1.6 Defamatory statement: true innuendo) compare with the case of *O'Shea v MGN Ltd* in respect of the argument about 'lookalike' photographs not being defamatory?

14.3.3.2 **Group defamation**

As a general rule, where a statement is directed to a group, body, or class of persons, no individual belonging to that class is entitled to sue. An old example is the statement that 'all lawyers are thieves', which has been said to give no cause of action on the part of any individual lawyer. In respect of a defamatory statement where the class is too large to permit each individual member to sue, if something in the words or the circumstances in which they were published identifies a particular individual in the class, the test for liability is whether a sensible ordinary reader who knew the claimant would believe the words to refer to him. The House of Lords in *Knuppfer v London Express Newspapers Ltd* (1944) was considering an allegation of defamation in respect of a newspaper article published at the time of the Second World War which criticized the Young Russian political party and linked them with fascism. The party was an international organization consisting of thousands of members, but the British branch consisted of only twenty-four members. The plaintiff, a Russian resident in London, alleged that, as the person responsible for the politics of the party, the libel personally affected him. On the basis of the evidence, his claim was rejected; the article made no specific mention of Knuppfer from beginning to end and it was therefore not capable of referring to him, or being understood by others to refer to him personally. In determining liability to an individual for words directed to a group, body, or class of persons, Lord Porter said:

> In deciding this question the size of the class, the generality of the charge and the extravagance of the accusation may all be elements to be taken into consideration, but none of them is conclusive.

In *Aspro Travel Ltd v Owners Abroad Group* (1996), the principles in *Knuppfer* were applied in respect of an allegation that a family business was going 'bust'. The Court of Appeal held that the statement in question was capable of bearing a defamatory meaning and, since it was a family business, the company and each individual member was permitted to sue because the words might be understood to refer to the company and to them as individual directors of the company.

In summary, where a statement refers to a class of persons, no individual belonging to that class is entitled to sue unless:

- the words were published of the claimant in the sense that he can be said to be personally pointed at; and

- the class is so small that the statement must refer to each person in it.

▶ CROSS REFERENCE
See 14.5.2 The Human Rights Act 1998.

THINKING POINT

During a television interview about higher education Samira said that the lecturers in Hibernian Law School were unprofessional and incompetent. Would Dr Doubt, one of the lecturers who has just won the Law Teacher of the Year Award, have a claim in defamation?

14.4 Who can sue?

Defamation is the only tort in which the action does not survive the death of either party. As a personal wrong, the tort concerns the publication of a false statement that is capable of injuring the reputation of the person to whom it refers, and only living persons can sue. Even where a claim has been commenced, the cause of action will be extinguished by the death of either party. As well as a human person, a company can sue for a defamatory statement affecting its business or trading reputation but, in order to bring a successful defamation claim, corporate claimants will now have to overcome a heavy burden of proof.

The scope for companies to sue for reputational damage is significantly limited by the Defamation Act 2013; s 1(1) provides that a statement is not defamatory unless its publication has caused or is likely to cause serious harm to the reputation of the claimant. However, in the case of corporate claimants, s 1(2) provides that harm to the reputation of a body that trades for profit is not 'serious harm' unless it has caused or is likely to cause that body serious financial loss. The need to show 'serious financial loss' will restrict companies from using the threat of defamation proceedings to silence critics who wish to speak out. You will see shortly that a government department performing public functions may not sue in defamation. This is because the public interest in discussing and criticizing public authorities is seen as paramount. Removing the right of companies to sue was seriously considered during the legislative process of the Defamation Act, but finally rejected.

We have seen earlier in *Lewis v Daily Telegraph* that the defamation action was brought by the company and its managing director and chairman in respect of newspaper headlines in the *Daily Mail* which read: 'Fraud Squad Probe Firm'.

However, because the threat of a civil action restricts freedom of speech, a government department may not sue in defamation; nevertheless, a statement directed at an individual member of such a department may be actionable if it can be shown that the words would be understood to refer to him.

Q CASE CLOSE-UP

Derbyshire County Council v Times Newspapers (1993)

In this case, the House of Lords laid down a specific rule that a local authority, or the government itself, could not sue for libel. Here, the local authority had taken an action in defamation in respect of articles published by the defendant in *The Times* newspaper questioning the propriety of dealings in the Council's pension fund.

The House of Lords ruled that it is contrary to the public interest to permit organs of government, whether central or local, to sue for libel. There are rights available to private citizens which institutions of central government or local authorities are not in a position to exercise unless they can show that it is in the public interest to do so. *Derbyshire* is another illustration of the need to balance free speech and press freedom with protection of reputation. Their Lordships said that to admit such actions in defamation would place an undesirable restriction on freedom of speech and held that the 'chilling effect' of libel might prevent the publication of matters about which the public ought to be informed. Lord Keith said:

> It is of the highest public importance that a democratically elected governmental body, or indeed any governmental body, should be open to uninhibited public criticism. The threat of a civil action for defamation must inevitably have an inhibiting effect on freedom of speech.

Nevertheless, the continued existence of the right for companies to sue means that if public services are outsourced, the service providers will be able to sue, even though the governmental bodies previously responsible could not. The chilling effect of such claims is significant.

14.4.1 'Libel tourism'

The multiple-publication rule and the presumption of falsehood, together with the global dimension to internet publication, created very favourable conditions for claimants to bring defamation actions in English courts for statements mainly published outside the United Kingdom. This encouraged rich and powerful claimants, not domiciled in the United Kingdom or another EU member state to pursue their case in the English courts. This so-called 'libel tourism' led to the criticism that English libel law has a negative impact on freedom of expression, both in the United Kingdom and around the world. The Libel Reform Report (2009) states:

> A book that would once have been available only in the United States can now be bought here. An online publication or article can be downloaded anywhere. The number of cases that can be, and are, brought to the English courts has multiplied as a result. This exposes the English legal system to abuse by claimants with no reputation to defend in this country.

Libel tourism is addressed in s 9 of the Defamation Act 2013, which prevents claims by those with a tenuous link to England and Wales being heard in domestic courts by giving the court power to refuse jurisdiction. Section 9(2) states that 'a court does not have jurisdiction to hear and determine an action . . . unless the court is satisfied that, of all the places in which the statement complained of has been published, England and Wales is clearly the most appropriate place in which to bring an action in respect of the statement'.

Although the case of *Karpov v Browder* (2013) commenced before the enactment of the 2013 Act, it is one of two similar rulings concerning abuse of process. Karpov, a retired senior Moscow policeman, brought an action in defamation against Browder, a British-based investment fund manager, over allegations in relation to the death of a fellow Russian, Sergei Magnitsky, an anti-corruption activist. In dismissing the claim, Mr Justice Simon said that Karpov could not establish a reputation within this jurisdiction sufficient to establish a real and substantial tort. He also thought it would have been more appropriate for Karpov to have brought the claim in Russia; he found 'a degree of artificiality' about Karpov's attempt to protect his reputation in this country. This ruling is in line with the provisions of the 2013 Act and it demonstrates the attempts of the UK courts to end London's reputation as the libel capital of the world. A further example of the Court of Appeal's attempt to curb abuse of process can be seen in *Tamiz v Google Inc* (2013) (discussed earlier, and also in Chapter 15).

14.5 Current issues in defamation

14.5.1 **Balancing protection of reputation and freedom of expression**

▶ CROSS REFERENCE

For more on privacy, see Chapter 16.

The starting point when considering the protection of reputation is to remember that the competing right of freedom of expression is highly valued by society and this right is also protected by law. Where a conflict between these two competing rights arises, the courts must strike a balance between the protection of reputation and the freedom of speech. Traditionally, the common law protected freedom of expression through the defences available to a claim in defamation. (It is for this reason that in studying the topic, an understanding of the defences to defamation is equally important as understanding the elements of liability of the tort.) As well as the protection afforded to free speech through the defences to defamation, the right is given further protection under the European Convention on Human Rights (ECHR). Article 10(1) provides that everyone has the right to freedom of expression and gives individuals the right to hold opinions and receive and impart information and ideas without interference by public authorities. However, freedom of expression is just one of the individual rights which must be upheld and the Convention acknowledges the potential conflict between freedom of expression and an individual's right to the protection of their reputation. In order to strike a balance between freedom of expression and protection of reputation, Article 10(2) places certain restrictions on the exercise of freedom of expression. It provides that the exercise of freedom of expression may be subject to:

> formalities, conditions, restrictions or penalties as prescribed by law and are necessary in a democratic society, in the interests of national security of public safety, for the prevention of disorder or crime, for the protection of health or morals or for the protection of the rights and freedoms of others.

14.5.2 **The Human Rights Act 1998**

▶ CROSS REFERENCE

See Chapter 15 for more detail on 'the *McLibel* case'.

The need to balance the right to freedom of expression and the protection of reputation most frequently arises in claims involving statements made by the press and, in these cases, the sanctity of free speech is vehemently invoked by the press. It was thought that in preserving the balance between freedom of speech and protecting an individual's reputation, the law of defamation gave too much protection to reputations at the expense of free speech, but you will see from the cases discussed later in this chapter that the approach taken by the courts to the interpretation of Article 10 has been to tip the scales in favour of more free speech and less protection of reputation. The enactment of the Human Rights Act 1998 incorporated Article 10 of the Convention and, as a consequence, Article 10 can be invoked in a defamation action under domestic law, which must now be interpreted by English courts to give effect to the Convention rights. In *Steel and Morris v UK* (2005), 'the *McLibel* case', the denial of legal aid to two campaigners to defend a defamation action was found to be a breach of Article 10 (freedom of expression) and a violation of Article 6 (right to a fair hearing) of the ECHR. Another example of the approach taken by the English courts to Article 10 can be seen in the case of *O'Shea v MGN Ltd* (2001), where the question of liability for unintentional defamation in the case of a 'lookalike' picture was being considered by the court.

The case involved an advertisement in a Sunday newspaper for pornographic internet services which contained a picture of a woman who, it was alleged, was the 'lookalike' or 'spit and image' of the claimant. The woman in the picture was holding a telephone to her ear and saying, 'See me now at www . . . internet.com if you have access to the net, join online now'. The claimant alleged that the photograph was defamatory because a number of people who knew her had identified her with the photograph, and thought that the advertisement meant that she was appearing or performing on a pornographic website. At this point you should note that when we were examining liability for defamation earlier in this chapter we saw that in *Hulton v Jones*, the House of Lords established the principle of **strict liability** for unintentional defamation, and under the common law this case would have fallen within the strict liability principle.

However, the question arose as to whether the imposition of strict liability for unintentional defamation by the publication of a 'lookalike' photograph was an infringement of the right to freedom of expression under the Human Rights Act 1998. The court held that notwithstanding the position in common law, to hold the defendant strictly liable in this case would amount to an unjustifiable interference with the right to freedom of expression. Strict liability in circumstances such as these would impose an impossible burden on a publisher if he were required to check if the true picture of someone resembled someone else; it would be an unjustifiable interference with the right to freedom of expression disproportionate to the aim of protecting the reputations of 'lookalikes'. Also, because no claim had been made in respect of a 'lookalike' picture in over a century, strict liability could not be justified under Article 10(2) as *necessary* in a democratic society.

> **strict liability**
> liability for a wrong that is imposed without the claimant having to prove that the defendant was at fault.

 THINKING POINT

As you read the following extracts from the judgment of Morland J consider these questions:

(1) What is the effect of the strict liability principle in the tort of defamation?

(2) Why could the strict liability principle not be justified in this case?

Morland J:

> In ascertaining the meaning of the words, the criterion is not: 'What did the defendant intend the words to mean?' It is: 'What would the words reasonably be understood to mean in the light of the surrounding circumstances as known to the persons to whom they were published?' That is the common law rule. A considerable body of criticism has been

directed against it. This is only to be expected in view of the fact that in the past, heavy damages have been awarded in libel actions against defendants who had no idea that the words published would be defamatory of any existing person and, in some cases could not, by the exercise of any reasonable care, have ascertained that they would be. The result offends one's sense of justice.

[J]urisprudence of the European Court of Human Rights has established that 'necessary' requires the existence of a pressing social need . . . . Photography and filming play a major role in modern journalism in newspapers, magazines and television in getting the message across. Pictures are necessary, effective, and telling adjuncts to a story. It would impose an impossible burden on a publisher if he were required to check if the true picture of someone resembled someone else who because of the context of the picture was defamed. Examples are legion: unlawful violence in street protest demonstrations, looting, hooliganism at football matches, people apparently leaving or entering court with criminal defendants and investigative journalism into drug dealing, corruption, child abuse and prostitution.

14.5.3 Cyber-defamation

We have looked at defamatory material in the traditional contexts of publication but 'cyber-opportunities' for the publication of defamatory material on websites, mobile platforms, and applications are enormous. It is possible for a person with access to a website to publish the most damaging libel and disseminate it via the internet within seconds. A person defamed on the internet can find it very difficult to identify the maker of the statement and, even where the party who published the statement can be identified, he or she is often not worth suing. The party defamed may seek to have the defamatory statement removed from the public domain as quickly as possible and will immediately approach those responsible for providing the 'conduit' for publication and dissemination such as the internet service provider. However, as well as providing the defence of innocent dissemination to those who innocently disseminate printed material, s 1 of the 1996 Act extended the principle of innocent defamation to operators of communications systems (such as the internet), where a defamatory statement is published electronically. Section 5(1) of the Defamation Act 2013 extends the principle of innocent defamation to website operators and persons who are not the author, editor, or publisher of a statement. An internet service provider is not considered to be the 'publisher' of the defamatory statement in these circumstances but is treated as a secondary publisher (distributor) and may be able to rely on the defence of innocent dissemination.

The case of *Godfrey v Demon Internet* (1999), illustrated how the s 1 defence under the 1996 Act applied in the case of a defamatory statement posted on the internet. Statements defamatory of the claimant were posted by an unknown person on an internet newsgroup hosted on the defendant's server. The defendant was notified by the claimant but did not remove the material from the internet for about two weeks. In an action for damages in libel the defendants argued that they were not the publishers of the defamatory statement and that, even if they were, the defence of innocent dissemination under s 1 was available to them. Morland J noted the traditional position under common law in respect of publication in these cases as set out in the golf club noticeboard case, *Byrne v Deane* (1937):

> It may very well be that, in some circumstances, a person, by refraining from removing or obliterating the defamatory matter, is not committing any publication at all. In other circumstances, he may be doing so. The test, it appears to me is this: having regard to all the facts of the case, is the proper inference that, by not removing the defamatory matter, the defendant really made himself responsible for its continued presence in the place where it had been put.

Morland J said that although the defendants in *Godfrey v Demon Internet* successfully showed that they were not the author, editor, or publisher of the defamatory statement within the meaning of the Defamation Act 1996, they could not show that they had taken reasonable care in relation to its publication. The defence in s 1(b) of the Act requires that the defendant did not know, and had no reason to believe, that what they did caused or contributed to the publication of a defamatory statement. The internet service provider in this case had been informed of the libel on the internet and had failed to remove it and the s 1(b) defence was defeated.

14.5.3.1 Search engine liability

Online defamation in respect of search engine liability for publication of statements claimed to be defamatory was considered in *Metropolitan International Schools Ltd v Designtechnica Corporation, Google UK and Google Inc* (2009).

The first judicial analysis of search engine liability for defamation under UK law was made when a company, which operates learning courses in the development of games, claimed that Google was responsible for defamatory comments on a website which appeared on its search results page. The question was whether Google should be regarded as a 'publisher' of the words complained of (whether before or after Google had been notified of their defamatory comments) or whether it was a mere facilitator. Mr Justice Eady found that Google was not liable for publication of the statements because it had no control over the search terms entered by users of the search engine or over the material which is placed on the web by its users. He confirmed that mere facilitators, like telephone carriers, are generally not liable for defamatory content. He further noted that in the *Godfrey* case (discussed earlier in the context of internet service providers), in which Demon Internet was found liable for defamatory postings that it had failed to remove from a site it hosted in spite of warnings, 'the acquisition of knowledge was regarded as critical'. In distinguishing the facts of *Godfrey* he said in that case: 'the defendant stored information posted by other people, transmitted it to subscribers, and had knowledge that the words complained of were defamatory. It also had the ability to take them down from the Web.' Mr Justice Eady also pointed out that a search engine is different from a website host; merely pressing a button will not ensure that the offending words will never reappear on a Google search snippet and there is no control over the search terms typed in by future users. In considering the role of search engines he said:

> It would be impossible for Google to search every page available on the web in real time and then deliver a result in a time frame acceptable to users. What happens is that Google compiles an index of pages from the web and it is this index which is examined during the search process. Although it is well known, it is necessary to emphasise that the index is compiled and updated purely automatically (i.e. with no human input). The process is generally referred to as 'crawling' or the 'web crawl'.

He further said that if someone feels they have been defamed by material on a website, then they should address their complaint to the person who actually wrote and published the material. The operator of a search engine simply compiles an index of pages from the web and it is this index which is examined during the search process.

14.5.3.2 Liability of website operators

The evolving liability of website operators has given rise to concerns about the chilling effect on freedom of speech in respect of internet publication. To strike a balance between protection of reputation and free speech where publication takes place online, the law is developing to provide greater protection for website operators and online intermediaries from liability for online content for which they are not responsible. We shall see in Chapter 15 that the Defamation Act 2013 has introduced a new defence for the protection of website operators and the case of *Tamiz v Google Inc* (2013) (below) will show the judicial approach to online publication. This is the first time the Court of Appeal has examined the law on the liability of providers of internet platforms such as Google as potential publishers of defamatory comments.

 CASE CLOSE-UP

Tamiz v Google Inc (2013)

This case concerned statements posted on a 'London Muslim' blog operated by Google Inc. After the claimant had complained to Google about the defamatory content of the blog, Google failed to remove it promptly from the website. The claim against Google was in relation to the period after Google was notified of the comments, but prior to their removal. Although some of the comments were arguably defamatory, the trial judge held that Google was not the publisher. He went on to say that, in any event, even if Google was found to be the publisher, it could successfully rely on the defence under s 1 of the Defamation Act 1996 in respect of the statements remaining on the blog. Nevertheless, he ruled that the continuance of the proceedings could not be justified because the period of time between Google being notified of the words complained of and the removal of the blog was so short, any potential liability was so trivial that the continuance of the proceedings could not be justified. Tamiz appealed against this finding.

The questions for the Court of Appeal were:

(1)   *whether there was an arguable case that Google Inc was a publisher of the comments*

The Court of Appeal agreed that Google could not be said to be either a primary or a secondary publisher. However, after being notified of the words complained of, there was an arguable case that Google was a publisher. The facts were found to come within the scope of *Byrne v Deane* (discussed earlier); the Court made an analogy with a giant notice board provided by Google on its own terms and conditions. Arguably, the time taken to respond to notification of the defamatory blog was sufficiently long to leave room for inference adverse to Google. By failing to remove the blog it might be inferred that Google had made itself responsible for the continued presence of the defamatory material and had become the publisher.

(2) *in the event of Google Inc being found to be the publisher of the comments, whether it would have a defence under s 1 Defamation Act 1996*

On the basis that once Google had been notified that failure to remove the blog caused or contributed to the continued publication of the comments, the Court was not satisfied that s 1(c) would provide Google with a watertight defence.

(3) *whether any potential liability was so trivial as not to justify the maintenance of proceedings and to amount to abuse of process*

The Court agreed that any reputational damage during the relevant period must have been so trivial that 'the game would not be worth the candle' and concluded that the trial judge's decision to dismiss the claim had been correct.

This case makes it clear that, once notified, an internet service provider can be a publisher of a defamatory statement posted by a third party and, if they do not act promptly in response to notification to remove the material, they may not have a defence under s 1 of the Defamation Act 1996.

As we have seen, in the context of protection against harm caused by words or images which are true, there is no remedy in defamation. However, you will see that in the context of human rights, claimants in these cases may be able to rely on the protection of privacy.

> **CROSS REFERENCE**
Privacy is the subject of Chapter 16.

 Summary

- Interests in reputation are protected by the tort of defamation.
- In balancing protection of reputation and free speech, Article 8 and Article 10 of the ECHR are of crucial importance.
- The law of defamation draws a distinction between libel and slander.
- A successful defamation action requires that a claimant proves: (1) a defamatory statement; (2) publication to a third party; and (3) that it referred to him.

  Visit the online resources to listen to a podcast summarizing the topics covered in this chapter.

 The bigger picture

See A Mullis and A Scott, 'Tilting at Windmills: The Defamation Act 2013' (2014) 77(1) MLR, 77(1), 87–109, which considers the main changes introduced by the new law of defamation. Of relevance to this chapter is the discussion of the costly and burdensome process in libel claims, and the criticism that the core problem of overcomplication of disputes, and the cost of embroilment in legal proceeding has been barely touched by the 2013 Act.

You may wish to visit Inforrm's Blog, https://inforrm.org, to keep abreast of developments in defamation. Guy Vassall-Adams and Hugh Tomlinson's *Online Publication Claims: An Practical Guide* (Matrix Chambers, 2017) considers the global communications revolution brought about by the internet.

The article below on Inforrm's blog examines the 'serious harm' requirement in the Defamation Act 2013, which was supposed to make it more difficult for those who felt that they had been defamed to bring a successful claim. It examines the statistics and concludes that it is too early to tell whether they tell the whole story because, with the one-year limitation period within which defamation claims should be brought, defamation claims heard in 2014 may simply relate back to publications where the old law applies: A Stephenson, 'Libels, Damned Libels and Statistics' (2015), https://inforrm.wordpress.com/2015/09/18/libels-damned-libels-and-statistics-andrew-stephenson

See also Inforrm on the impact that the SC decision in *Lachaux* might have on costs:

https://inforrm.org/2019/06/13/case-law-lachaux-v-independent-print-supreme-court-abolished-common-law-presumption-of-damage-in-libel-cases-mathilde-groppo

? Questions

Knowledge-testing questions

1. List the main elements required to establish a claim in defamation.

2. Does the Defamation Act 2013 make significant changes to the elements required?

3. Has the Defamation Act 2013 maintained the distinction between libel and slander?

4. Which tests are applied to determine if the statement complained of has a 'defamatory meaning'?

Problem and essay questions

1. When may a defendant be liable for a statement which is not directly defamatory of the claimant but from which the claimant alleges a defamatory inference may be drawn?

2. The *Morning Star* featured a story about Rory, the manager of an animal rescue centre, claiming that the centre is facing ruin because of his financial mismanagement. Even though the *Morning Star* published a prominent apology four days later, Rory has discovered that one of the centre's donors has withdrawn its annual donation but refused to disclose the reason for this.

What is the likely effect of the apology on any potential claim in defamation which Rory may consider?

⊙ Visit the online resources for guidance on answering these questions.

Further reading

Bennett, T, 'Why So serious? *Lachaux* and the Threshold of "Serious Harm" in Defamation Act 2013' (2018) 10 JML 1

James, S and L McCormack, 'Closing the Floodgates: Google Is Granted Immunity from Defamation Claims in Landmark Decision for Search Engines' (2010) 21(1) ELR 1

Kaye, JM, 'Libel or Slander: Two Torts or One' (1972) 91 LQR 524

Soto-Miranda, D, 'Fame and Fortune: All Reputations Are Equal, But Some Reputations Are More Equal Than Others' (2017) 2 Communications Law 51

15 Defences to defamation

LEARNING OBJECTIVES

By the end of this chapter you should be able to:

- analyse the functions of the defences to defamation;
- distinguish between the different levels of protection afforded by the 'absolute' and 'qualified' defences;
- outline the defences available for unintentional or innocent publication;
- explain the reforms introduced by the Defamation Act 2013.

Introduction

It is through the defences to defamation that freedom of speech is protected in English law and specific defences protect a defendant where it is in the public interest that the statement should be published. Reforms in the Defamation Act 2013 aimed to strike a fair balance between the right to freedom of expression and protection of reputation. We have seen in Chapter 14 that claimants are now required to show that they have suffered serious harm before suing for defamation, a single-publication rule has been introduced, and the presumption in favour of a jury trial has been removed. The provisions in the Act relevant to this chapter were amendments to the existing common law defences to defamation and added new defences to protect operators of websites that host user-generated content.

Some of these defences are 'absolute' defences, which means that regardless of how careless the defendant has been in publishing the statement or whether he has been motivated by malice, the defence provides complete protection. Other defences are 'qualified' defences which apply to a wider range of situations, but these defences fail where the claimant can show that the statement was made 'maliciously'. Malice in this context can be defined as ill will, spite, and improper motive or a lack of honest belief in the truth of the statement. However, before we go on to look at the three main defences to defamation—truth, honest opinion, and privilege—we will look at the statutory 'offer of amends' defence which is available in cases of unintentional or innocent defamation.

15.1 Unintentional defamation defence 'offer of amends'

As we have already seen in *Hulton v Jones*, as far as reference to the claimant is concerned, liability in defamation does not depend on the intention of the person responsible for the publication of the statement. We have also seen in *Cassidy v Daily Mirror Newspapers* that a defendant's lack of knowledge in relation to facts which make a statement, which is innocent on its face, defamatory of the claimant is no defence. The application of the 'strict liability' rule in these cases of 'unintentional defamation' can result in hardship for the defendant, especially if the defendant happens to be a writer or publisher of fiction, and this has led to complaints by the press and publishers. The harshness of these principles has been mitigated by statute and where a defendant has 'innocently' published a defamatory statement he may offer to make amends.

The Defamation Act 1996 (ss 2–4) created a formal procedure to enable a defamation dispute to be resolved at an early stage with the agreement of the parties. In order to encourage parties to settle before the trial commences, the Act provides that a person who has published a statement alleged to be defamatory of another may offer to make amends.

In making an offer of amends the defendant must:

- offer a suitable correction of the statement complained of;
- make a sufficient apology to the aggrieved party; and
- include an agreement to pay appropriate compensation and costs.

If the defendant publishes a suitable correction and sufficient apology in a reasonable manner but the parties cannot agree about the amount to be paid in compensation, the amount will be determined by the court. Where a defendant's offer to make amends in respect of the publication is accepted, the claimant may not bring or continue with the defamation proceedings. If the offer is not accepted the proceedings may continue but the rejection of the defendant's offer may be used as a defence in subsequent proceedings and as a factor in determining the amount of any award of damages. The offer to make amends is *not* a defence where the person making the offer 'knew or had reason to believe' that the statement complained of referred to the claimant or was likely to be understood as referring to him and was both false and defamatory. The burden of proving that the defendant 'knew or had reason to believe' is on the claimant.

15.2 Truth (replaces the common law defence of 'justification')

Truth is a complete defence to an action in defamation. Where the statement complained of is substantially true, s 2(1) of the Defamation Act 2013 provides a statutory defence of truth to replace the common law justification defence.

We have seen that the law presumes a defamatory statement to be untrue and the onus is not on the claimant to prove the statement was false; the burden of showing the truth of the statement is on the defendant. Where a statement is shown to be true, even if the statement was made with malice, there is no liability in defamation (but see also the Rehabilitation of Offenders Act 1974). The reason for this can be summarized by comments in one case, *McPherson v Daniels* (1829), where the judge said:

> the law will not permit a man to recover damages in respect of an injury to a character which he does not or ought not to possess.

The burden of proving the truth of a statement can be a heavy one for defendants as they may not have access to the evidence or to credible witnesses to support their version of events. There is also a risk in raising this defence. If the defendant is unable to prove that the statement was substantially true, the injury to the claimant will be aggravated by the claimant's persistence with the allegation and the award of damages will therefore be increased. However, the burden of proving truth is somewhat reduced because the defendant does not have to prove the literal truth of every word in the facts of the defamatory statement if he can justify the sting in the libel. In *Alexander v North Eastern Railway Co* (1865), the plaintiff was charged before magistrates for travelling on a train from Leeds for which his ticket was not valid and for his refusal to pay the proper fare. He was convicted and sentenced to fourteen days' imprisonment in default of payment of the fine and costs. The statement published by the defendant said that the plaintiff was sentenced to three weeks' imprisonment for the offence. Nevertheless, the defence of justification succeeded because the statement was not sufficiently inaccurate to defeat the defence. The defendant had shown the statement to be substantially true and to prove the sting of the libel.

Section 2(1) of the 2013 Act confirms this approach: if the defendant can establish the 'essential' or 'substantial' truth of the sting of the libel there is no need to prove that every word of the statement was true.

> **THINKING POINT**
>
> The *Morning Express* published the headline: 'Homer Is a Thief, Liar and Can't Play the Piano'. Homer has convictions for fraud and theft but he is a talented amateur musician. Would the defence of truth be available to the *Morning Express* if Homer sues in defamation in respect of the statement that he 'can't play the piano'?

The success of the defence of truth will turn on the facts of each case and what constitutes a minor inaccuracy is ultimately a matter of interpretation of the facts. In *Wakley v Cooke and Healy* (1849), the defendant called the plaintiff a 'libellous journalist' and in support of the defence of justification he showed evidence that the plaintiff had once been successfully sued for libel. The defence failed because, in the context of the words, the meaning conveyed was that the plaintiff had a habit of libelling others and an instance of such conduct on one occasion only did not justify this meaning.

> If the defendant has alleged that the claimant has committed an offence, s 13 of the Civil Evidence Act 1968 (as amended by s 12 of the Defamation Act 1996) provides that evidence of the conviction is proof that it is true.
>
> The fact that the claimant's conviction is 'spent' under the Rehabilitation of Offenders Act 1974 does not prevent the defendant from relying upon the defence of truth. However, in these circumstances malice is relevant; if a defamatory statement concerns a 'spent' conviction and the claimant can show malice on the part of the defendant, the defence will fail.

15.3 Honest opinion

A new defence of honest opinion, which replaced the common law defence of fair comment, was introduced by s 3 of the Defamation Act 2013. Honest opinion, like justification, is a complete defence to an action in defamation. However, unlike justification, the defendant is not required to show the truth of the statement. A purely factual statement is either true or false but the same cannot be said for expressions of opinion. Although the statutory defence of honest opinion is largely a restatement of the current law, the cases discussed here, interpreting what amounts to a statement of fact and what is a statement of opinion, continue to be relevant.

Honest opinion is also unlike the defence of qualified privilege (discussed later) as honest opinion is not limited to those who have a duty to publish the information; any person is entitled to comment on a matter of public interest. The requirement for the opinion to be on a matter of public interest is not contained in the 2013 Act, which gives protection to all opinion. Prior to the Act, honest comment failed if the claimant could show malice on the part of the defendant. However, all the defendant now needs to show is an honest belief in the truth of the opinion.

Honest opinion, which protects honest expressions of opinion based on true fact is viewed as one of the fundamental rights of free speech. It is important to note that honest opinion does not mean that the opinions protected must be fair-minded or reasonable. Honest opinion protects opinions honestly held, however obstinate, prejudiced, or exaggerated if the following requirements are met:

- the statement was a statement of opinion (not a statement of fact);
- the statement indicated the basis of the opinion; and
- an honest person could have held the opinion on the basis of any fact which existed at the time the statement was published or asserted to be a fact in a privileged statement published beforehand.

The statement complained of must be recognizable as comment (as distinct from an imputation of fact). The assessment is made on the basis of how the ordinary person would understand the statement and reflects the test approved by the Supreme Court in *Spiller v Joseph* (discussed below) that 'the comment must explicitly or implicitly indicate, at least in general terms, the facts on which it is based'.

15.3.1 **Opinion based on true facts**

The defence of honest opinion must be based on true facts. In *London Artists Ltd v Littler* (1969) the four top performers in a play simultaneously terminated their contracts through their agents, the plaintiffs. The defendant, Littler, the producer, was convinced that there was a plot to force the end of a successful play and he wrote to each of the actors deploring their conduct and published the contents of the letter at a press conference. The defence of fair comment failed because the defendant could not prove the correctness of the underlying fact that there had been a plot between the theatre owners and the actors to put an end to his play. Although the statement must be a comment based on true facts, it is not necessary that all the facts upon which the comment is based should be specified in the alleged libel. In *Kemsley v Foot* (1952), the defendant attacked a newspaper by publishing an article headed: 'Lower than Kemsley'. Lord Kemsley, a newspaper proprietor not connected with the newspaper and attacked in the article, sued the defendants, alleging that the article's heading imputed that his name was a byword for false and foul journalism. The House of Lords took a very broad view of the headline and held that the words implied the conduct of the Kemsley Press were the relevant facts upon which the comment was made and, because this was sufficiently clear in the article, the defence of fair comment was available.

🔍 CASE CLOSE-UP

Spiller v Joseph (2010)

In this case the Supreme Court considered the defence of fair comment in proceedings involving the claimant (a band called the Gillettes) and the defendant (Spiller's entertainment booking agency). The agency arranged a booking for the Gillettes at a restaurant in Leeds but when the band made a repeat booking directly with the restaurant without reference to the agency, Spiller claimed the Gillettes had breached a 're-engagement' clause of the contract between them. The defendant then posted a notice on its website which included statements that they were 'no longer able to accept bookings for this artist as The Gillettes c/o Craig Joseph are not professional enough to feature in our portfolio and have not been able to abide by the terms of their contract . . . . For this reason, it may follow that the artists' obligations for your booking may also not be met.'

The Gillettes sued for libel in respect of the website posting and the defendant claimed that the statements were protected by the defence of fair comment. At first instance the judge found that fair comment was not available on the grounds that the allegations were fact, not comment, and there was no public interest. The Court of Appeal held that the words were, indeed, comment and arguably in the public interest, but it rejected the defence of fair comment on the basis that the posting on the defendant's website had not gone into enough detail to specify the facts upon which the statement was made.

The question therefore for the Supreme Court was whether the defence of fair comment could be based on facts not referred to in the publication. In allowing the defendant's appeal to have fair comment reinstated, the court reviewed the law of 'fair comment' and renamed it 'honest comment'. It also ruled that the burden of proof on the defendant to prove the facts upon which the comment is based should be reduced. Although the comment must explicitly or implicitly indicate, at least in general terms, the facts on which it is based, it does not have to identify the facts to the extent necessary to enable readers to verify for themselves that the comment was well founded. According to Lord Philipps, the underlying justification for the defence is the desirability that a person should be entitled to express his view freely; if the subject matter of the comment is not apparent from the statement, this justification will be lacking.

> It is a requirement of the defence that it should be based on facts that are true. This requirement is better enforced if the comment has to identify, at least in general terms, the matters on which it is based. The same is true of the requirement that the defendant's comment should be honestly founded on facts that are true . . . More fundamentally, even if it is not practicable to require that those reading criticism should be able to evaluate the criticism, it may be thought desirable that the commentator should be required to identify at least the general nature of the facts that have led him to make the criticism. If he states that a barrister is 'a disgrace to his profession' he should make it clear whether this is because he does not deal honestly with the court, or does not read his papers thoroughly, or refuses to accept legally aided work, or is constantly late for court, or wears dirty collars and bands.

As we have seen earlier, the Defamation Act 2013 has adopted this approach in the statutory defence.

15.3.2 **Distinguishing fact and opinion**

The line between what is fact and what is opinion is not always clear but, as a rule of thumb, fact is capable of objective proof, whereas opinion is not. One of the questions which arose in *London Artists Ltd v Littler* was whether the allegation of a plot was a statement of fact or comment; the court concluded that, on balance, it was a fact. In *Dakhyl v Labouchere* (1908), the plaintiff described himself as a 'specialist for the treatment of deafness, ear, nose and throat diseases' and when the defendant described him as 'a quack of the rankest species' the question arose as to whether the defendant's statement was comment or fact. The House of Lords held that the defendant was entitled to raise the defence of fair comment (now known as honest opinion) as the statement could be comment rather than fact.

In considering whether the statement is one of fact or comment the court must confine itself to the subject matter of the publication and cannot have regard to the wider context of the material.

In *Telnikoff v Matusevitch* (1992), when considering whether the statements were fact or comment, the House of Lords examined the context in which the words had to be assessed. In this case the defendant had written an angry and critical letter to the *Daily Telegraph* complaining about an article written by the plaintiff which concerned recruitment to the BBC Russian service. In his letter the defendant had quoted from the article he criticized. In determining which parts of the letter constituted allegations of fact and which were merely comments, the question arose as to whether the letter could be read alongside the offending article. In the context of honest comment, the House of Lords held that the court should not look at the article and ruled that it was confined to considering the letter itself; readers of the letter would not necessarily have read the original article and the publication in question must be judged on its own merits.

The 2013 Act gives protection in situations such as this, where the defendant is not the author of the statement but is publishing statements made by others. In these circumstances the defence of honest opinion will succeed unless the claimant can show that the defendant ought to have known that the opinion stated was not held by the author.

The question of whether the statement was fact or a statement of opinion that would entitle an individual to rely on the former defence of fair comment was examined in *British Chiropractic Association v Singh* (2010). Dr Singh, a scientist and science writer, wrote an article in *The Guardian* which included the following statement: 'The British Chiropractic Association claims that their members can help treat children with colic, sleeping and feeding problems . . . even though there is not a jot of evidence. This organisation is the respectable face of the chiropractic profession and yet it happily promotes bogus treatments.'

In its claim for defamation in respect of this statement the British Chiropractic Association (BCA) did not bring the case against *The Guardian*, but sued the science writer instead on the ground that to a reasonable reader, the words would mean that the association knowingly claimed the treatments were effective, although it knew that there was absolutely no evidence to support this claim. The trial judge held that the words amounted to assertions of verifiable fact, not expressions of opinion protected by the defence of fair comment. Dr Singh appealed against the finding that the words were a statement of fact. In allowing his appeal the Court of Appeal held that evidence of the efficacy of the treatments which depended heavily on context, and whether such evidence amounted to proof, are what scientific opinion is there to debate. A view that there was no worthwhile or reliable evidence for the efficacy of the treatments expressed in the course of this debate was as much a value judgement as a contrary viewpoint and it therefore fell within the scope of fair comment. Lord Judge remarked:

> By proceeding against Dr Singh, and not the Guardian, and by rejecting the offer made by the Guardian to publish an appropriate article refuting Dr Singh's contentions, or putting them in a proper prospective, the unhappy impression has been created that this is an endeavour by the BCA to silence one of its critics.

This case highlighted attempts by large corporations to stifle scientific and academic debate with the threat of libel proceedings. Public concerns about defamation laws being used to frustrate robust scientific and academic debate, or to impede responsible investigative journalism were addressed in the Defamation Act 2013. The Act creates a new defence of qualified privilege (discussed later) relating to material in scientific or academic journals, whether published in electronic form or otherwise, which has undergone a responsible peer-review process.

15.3.3 Could an honest person have held the opinion?

The test whether an 'honest person' could have held the opinion is an objective test. The question is not whether the opinion is reasonable; it is whether an honest person would have been able to hold the opinion on the basis of any fact which existed at the time the statement was published. The new defence broadly reflects existing case law which established that opinions which are not reasonable may nevertheless be honestly held. In *Cheng v Tse Wai Chun* (2000) Lord Nicholls said that the comment must be one which could have been made by an honest person, however prejudiced he might be, and however exaggerated or obstinate his views. Honest opinion will fail if the claimant shows that the defendant did not hold the opinion.

15.4 Publication on a matter of public interest

Section 4 of the Defamation Act 2013 created a new public interest defence. This new defence was intended to reflect the principles established in *Reynolds v Times Newspapers* (discussed below) and in subsequent case law. Section 4 replaces the '*Reynolds* privilege' defence developed by the courts in order to provide a wider and more effective statutory public interest defence. It may be relied on irrespective of whether the statement complained of is one of fact or opinion. The Act does not say that the defence is defeated by malice, but since it is based on 'reasonable belief' that publication was in the public interest, the presence of malice should be a relevant factor in determining the defendant's belief when he published the statement.

The s 4 defence applies where the defendant can show:

- the statement was, or formed part of, a statement on a matter of public interest; and
- the defendant reasonably believed that publishing the statement was in the public interest.

Although the Act abolished the *Reynolds* defence and the courts are required to apply the words used in the statute, it does not, for example, define what is meant by 'the public interest'. The common law principles established in *Reynolds* are set out below because the current case law would constitute a helpful (albeit not binding) guide to interpreting how the new statutory defence should be applied.

 CASE CLOSE-UP

Reynolds v Times Newspapers Ltd (2001)

Although in *Reynolds v Times Newspapers Ltd*, the House of Lords considered whether a 'political information' category of qualified privilege should be created to protect political information or debate, the new 'publication on a matter of public interest' defence created under the Act does not refer to privilege in this context. Albert Reynolds, a former prime minister of the Republic of Ireland, brought an action against the *Sunday Times* newspaper concerning an article which he claimed contained defamatory statements about his handling of a political crisis and political events leading up to his resignation from office. The article did not give an account of Reynolds's version of the events. He succeeded at first instance, but the jury awarded no damages and Reynolds sought a retrial because of errors in the judge's summing-up. *The Times* cross-appealed against the judge's ruling that the publication was not protected by qualified privilege and argued that media reporting of political issues should be protected by a new category of qualified privilege for 'political speech' to protect the right of freedom of expression under the European Convention on Human Rights (ECHR) and the Human Rights Act.

On *The Times*'s cross-appeal, the Court of Appeal held that there is no special version of qualified privilege in respect of 'political information' because the existing tests for the defence were still to be applied. However, the court developed an additional test, the 'circumstantial test' which asks whether the nature, status, and source of the material published, and the circumstances of the publication, were such that, in the public interest, the publication should be protected by privilege in the absence of proof of malice. The House of Lords rejected the special 'political information' defence; their Lordships were unanimous in the view that the common law should not develop 'political information' as a new category of the qualified privilege defence. It would be unsound in principle to distinguish political discussion from discussion of other matters of public concern. The established common law approach to qualified privilege (the test of whether there was a duty to disseminate the information and an interest in receiving it—discussed at 15.7.2 Qualified privilege) continues to apply, and there is no separate and additional 'circumstantial test'. Lord Nicholls identified ten factors which are not exhaustive, but should be taken into account when making a detailed factual inquiry into the circumstances of each case. The *Sunday Times* could not rely on qualified privilege because the article contained serious allegations in a hard-hitting article about Mr Reynolds but had failed to mention his own explanation of his conduct to the Irish Parliament.

In recognizing that it is the duty of the media to inform the public on matters of public interest, their Lordships said that a newspaper's unwillingness to disclose the identity of its sources should not be held against it and it should always be remembered that journalists act without the benefit of clear hindsight. Lord Nicholls stated that the press performs vital functions as a 'bloodhound as well as a watchdog' and that interference with freedom of speech should be confined to what was necessary in the circumstances of the case. He said:

> The court should be slow to conclude that a publication was not in the public interest and, therefore, the public had no right to know, especially when the information is in the field of political discussion. Any lingering doubts should be resolved in favour of publication.

15.4.1 Interpreting the new 'public interest' defence

The new s 4 defence from the Defamation Act 2013 broadly reflected the common law principles established in *Reynolds* and their application in subsequent cases. It is expected that the courts take into account the judicial analysis of these principles and the guidance provided by the Supreme Court in *Flood v Times Newspapers Ltd* (see the case close-up below) where appropriate. Although it only applied in respect of the media, the *Reynolds* test for 'responsible journalism' was not restricted to political matters, but applied to any matter of public interest. As we have seen earlier, the emphasis in the s 4 defence is not on responsible journalism but on whether a journalist or other publisher acted with 'reasonable belief' in publishing the statement. There is no express requirement in the Act for the publisher to establish a standard of responsible journalism or meet any or all of the *Reynolds* principles.

When deciding whether the media has a duty to publish the words to the world at large, the relevant interest is that of freedom of expression and the public interest in a free and vigorous press. The Court of Appeal considered the *Reynolds* test in *Loutchansky v Times Newspapers Ltd (No 2)* (2002) and stated that setting the standard of journalistic responsibility too low would encourage a readiness to publish defamatory matter but setting the standard too high would be no less damaging, because this would deter newspapers from discharging their duty to keep the public informed. The *Reynolds* test was applied in *Loutchansky*, where it was held that although the matters published by the newspaper were of legitimate public interest, the defendant had not engaged in responsible journalism because the accuracy of the statements had not been sufficiently investigated and, as with *Reynolds*, the newspaper had failed to give the claimant's side of the story.

However, in *Jameel v Wall Street Journal Europe* (2006), the House of Lords focused on the 'public interest' aspect of *Reynolds* and said that the defence was being applied too cautiously by the lower courts. In this case the newspaper published an article (naming Jameel) stating that the bank account of the company was being monitored to prevent it being used for the channelling of funds to terrorist organizations. The jury held that the defendants were not entitled to qualified privilege because they failed to delay publication of the claimants' names long enough for them to comment on the contents of the article. This finding was upheld by the Court of Appeal but the House of Lords allowed the defendants' appeal and held that denying the defence in the circumstances in question subverted the liberalizing intention of the decision in *Reynolds*. The first question in *Reynolds* is whether the contents of the article were a matter of public interest: in this case they were. The next question is whether the steps taken to gather and publish the information were responsible and fair. In deciding this issue those engaged in responsible journalism should be given a wide margin of discretion and the standard of conduct required must be applied in a practical and flexible manner. The House of Lords held that in this case the defendants had satisfied the requirements of responsible journalism.

🔍 CASE CLOSE-UP

Flood v Times Newspapers Ltd (2012)

The *Reynolds* principles were considered by the Supreme Court in *Flood v Times Newspapers Ltd* (2012) in respect of an article headed: 'Detective Accused of Taking Bribes from Russian Exiles', which named Flood as a senior officer whom police were investigating as having accepted bribes in exchange for confidential police information. The article, published by *The Times* in its print edition and on its website, set out the details of what had been alleged. The trial judge held that the defendant was entitled to rely on *Reynolds* qualified privilege, but the Court of Appeal was of the view that because the steps taken to verify were inadequate the defendant was not protected by *Reynolds* privilege. In the context of human rights Lord Neuberger MR said:

> The fair balancing of Article 8 and Article 10 would normally require that such allegations should only be freely publishable if to do so is in the public interest and the journalist has taken reasonable steps to check their accuracy. If they are true, a claim for defamation will fail; if they are untrue, but their publication was in the public interest, and a reasonable check was carried out, there is good reason why a claim for defamation should fail, even though it is hard on the claimant; if they are untrue and their publication cannot be said to be in the public interest or no reasonable check was carried out, it seems quite unjust that the claimant should have no remedy in law.

However, the Supreme Court unanimously disagreed and ruled that the requirements of responsible journalism had been satisfied in *Flood*. In the context of human rights, it was held that where Article 8 rights have to be balanced against rights under Article 10, the public interest in receiving the information has to be weighed against the public interest in preventing the dissemination of defamatory allegations. It was emphasized that 'the degree of defamation involved' and 'the question of knowing at what point the media might reasonably consider sources as credible for the allegations' had to be considered from the viewpoint of the journalists at the time, and not with the benefit of hindsight. Here, it was in the public interest that both the accusation about Flood and most of the facts that supported it were published. In considering whether or not a publication was in the public interest, the court gives weight to the ordinary standards of responsible journalism in a broad and practical way, and in contexts going beyond the steps taken to check material. Lord Mance explained:

> The courts therefore give weight to the judgment of journalists and editors not merely as to the nature and degree of the steps to be taken before publishing material, but also as to

the content of the material to be published in the public interest. The courts must have the last word in setting the boundaries of what can properly be regarded as acceptable journalism, but within those boundaries the judgment of responsible journalists and editors merits respect. This is, in my view, of importance in the present case.

The importance of flexibility within *Reynolds* privilege was highlighted and even though the statutory defence s 4 replaces *Reynolds*, the analysis in *Flood* of the steps that a reasonable journalist should take to verify information is likely to be influential. There is no express requirement in the s 4 defence for the publisher to prove that it acted both fairly and responsibly in gathering and publishing information. However, in considering whether the defendant's belief that publishing the information was in the public interest was reasonable the court must make such allowance for editorial judgement as it considers appropriate. This expressly recognizes the discretion given to editors in judgments such as *Flood*, but this discretion is not limited to editors in the media context.

The first major case testing the boundaries of the s 4 public interest defence was *Economou v de Frietas* (2018). A bereaved father made a statement to the press giving his view as to the circumstances of his daughter's suicide. This contained implied allegations against the claimant, although their primary focus had been about the Crown Prosecution Service. In the defamation action, the trial judge concluded that the statements had been on a matter of public interest and that the defendant had reasonably believed them to be so. The *Reynolds* criteria were considered, including the defendant's careful investigations, measured tone, unique perspective, and the urgency to make the statement. As a non-journalist, the defendant would be held to a lower standard than a professional, rather closer to that of a source or contributor. When the issue of 'reasonable belief' was appealed by Mr Economou, the Court of Appeal upheld Warby J's reasoning and conclusion.

15.5 The 'reportage' defence

The s 4(3) defence encapsulates the 'reportage' defence developed by the common law. This has been described as a 'convenient word to describe the neutral reporting of attributed allegations rather than their adoption by the newspaper'.

Where the statement complained of was an accurate and impartial account of a dispute to which the claimant was a party, the defendant does not need to have verified the information before publication. This means that a defendant newspaper, for example, would not be prejudiced for a failure to verify.

An illustration of the approach to reportage can be seen in *Roberts v Gable CA* (2008), where the Court of Appeal explored the nature and extent of the emerging 'reportage' defence and its place in the libel law landscape. Reportage emerged as an element of the former privilege defence in cases where the media neutrally reported the allegations made by one party against another without adopting, embellishing, or endorsing the allegations. Here, the claimants, members of a political party, alleged that the defendants had libelled them in an article in a monthly magazine which reported that other members of the same party had publicly accused them of stealing money and brought an action for libel against the author of the article, the editor of the magazine, and its publisher, who pleaded the defences of justification and qualified privilege. Although still subject to the *Reynolds* test, provided that the report met the standards of responsible journalism and reported both sides in a disinterested way, this special species of qualified privilege protects the reporting of news by the press and the broadcasting media. Where an article viewed objectively constitutes reportage, responsible journalism does not require the defendants to establish the truth of what was reported and, in certain circumstances, it may be unrealistic to expect the defendants to have sought comment from the claimants before publication.

15.6 New defence for website operators

In the context of social media and other online platforms, individuals and companies need to be provided with effective measures to protect their reputations in respect of online defamation. We have seen in Chapter 14 that claims in defamation are now being taken against website operators and other intermediaries in respect of statements posted by third parties. This is a particular problem where statements are posted by anonymous authors. Section 5 of the Defamation Act 2013 aimed to protect the website operator by shifting more responsibility for defamatory content to the author of web posts.

This defence, together with the single-publication rule, gives website operators greater protection from defamation claims arising from user-generated comments. Section 5 does not replace the existing law; it is a new defence aimed at forums and blog sites who print, distribute, and host user-generated content. The defence is available where an action for defamation is brought against a website operator in respect of a statement which it did not post. The defence is defeated where the operator acted with malice in respect of posting the statement. However, the defence is not defeated just because the website operator moderates the statements posted by others.

In terms of procedure, the Act specifies that a complainant is required to send a notice of complaint to the website operator which contains the following information:

- where the material is located (usually the URL);
- why it is claimed to be defamatory;
- what defamatory meaning the complainant ascribes to the material; and
- what specific aspects of the statement are untrue or comment based on untrue facts.

The website operator is then required to communicate the complaint to the poster of the statement (if it has the means to do so). The poster then has a chance to respond and provide their contact details. In respect of the s 5 procedure the Defamation (Operators of Websites)

Regulations 2013 are designed to be as straightforward as possible for people to use, and there is no requirement on anyone involved to seek legal advice. They specify when and how a website operator must respond to a notice of complaint in respect of timescales for taking the post down and revealing the identity or contact details of the poster. Where the website operator complies with the regulations by taking down the post and/or providing the complainant with the identity or contact details of the poster the defence will be established.

The s 5 defence is defeated if the claimant shows that it was not possible for the claimant to identify the person who posted the statement. In this context 'identify' means that the claimant has sufficient information to bring proceedings against the poster of the statement. The defence will also fail if the claimant gave the operator a notice of complaint and the website operator failed to respond to the notice of complaint in accordance with the regulations.

In addition to s 5, an intermediary who can show that it was not the author, editor, or publisher of a defamatory statement is provided with a defence under s 1 of the Defamation Act 1996; and Regulation 19 of the Electronic Commerce (EC Directive Regulations) 2002 provides a defence where an intermediary does not have actual knowledge in respect of unlawful statements.

15.7 Privilege

The law recognizes that on certain occasions the public interest requires that freedom of speech must outweigh the protection of individual reputations, and this is achieved through the defence of privilege. There are two kinds of privilege: *absolute* privilege, which is very narrow in scope and only applies on limited occasions; and *qualified* privilege, which has a wider scope but provides a weaker form of protection. The defence of absolute privilege protects statements made on occasions where freedom of speech is essential, such as statements made in Parliament or in a court of law. As we will see, on the occasions where absolute privilege applies, no matter how untrue the statement or how malicious the defendant's motivation, he is immune from liability in defamation. The main difference between absolute and qualified privilege is that the defence of qualified privilege is defeated by malice.

15.7.1 **Absolute privilege**

The defence of absolute privilege only applies on the following occasions:

---

(1) Statements in Parliament

The Bill of Rights 1668 states that:

the freedom of speech and debates or proceedings in Parliament ought not to be impeached or questioned in any court or place out of Parliament.

- This privilege is to prevent members of both Houses of Parliament from being sued for statements or opinions expressed during parliamentary debate or proceedings. The protection applies to proceedings in committees, and reports, papers, and proceedings ordered to be published by Parliament are also protected. In *Makudi v Triesman* (2014), following the failure of the English 2018 Football World Cup bid, an inquiry into football governance was set up by the Culture, Media and Sports Committee (CMSC) of the House of Commons. At the inquiry, the former chairman of the Football Association (FA) reported his concerns about improper conduct, which included lucrative TV rights, which he believed to be linked to a promise to vote for the English bid. He also gave an undertaking to the CMSC to take his concerns to the FA, which subsequently set up its own inquiry. During the FA inquiry the chairman repeated his evidence and the question was whether those statements attracted immunity under the Bill of Rights 1689. The Court of Appeal held that the protection provided to statements made in the Houses of Parliament could extend to speech outside Parliament where there was a public interest in the repetition of the statement and where it was reasonably foreseeable that the maker of the statement would be obliged to repeat it on subsequent occasions.

- Statements made *outside* the House will not be protected. In *Church of Scientology of California v Johnson-Smith* (1972), in an action for a defamatory statement made by an MP outside Parliament the defence of fair comment was available to the defendant. This defence is defeated by evidence of malice on the part of the defendant in making the statement. The plaintiff wanted to rely on a speech made in Parliament to show evidence that the defendant was motivated by malice when he made the statement outside Parliament. However, it was held that parliamentary privilege prevented the plaintiff from using the statement made in Parliament as evidence.

- The defence of absolute privilege is to prevent members of Parliament from being sued, but under s 13 of the Defamation Act 1996 this privilege may be waived. In *Hamilton v Al Fayed* (2001), the House of Lords held that the waiving of parliamentary privilege means that proceedings in Parliament can be used as evidence in court.

(2) Judicial privilege

- Statements made by a judge, jury, counsel, or witnesses in proceedings in an ordinary court of law or in any tribunal recognized by law are protected by privilege.

- All relevant communications between solicitor and client relating to judicial proceedings are also protected.

Fair and accurate newspaper or broadcast reports of proceedings in public before a court are protected provided that they are published *contemporaneously* with the proceedings. *Contemporaneously* means as soon as practicable after the hearing; to be *fair* the report must present a summary of both sides of the case; to be *accurate* it must contain no inaccuracies, as even a slight inaccuracy will destroy absolute privilege.

(3) Executive privilege

- Statements made by one officer of state to another in the course of their duty are protected by absolute privilege as it is believed that they should be able to perform their duties without fear of litigation.

15.7.2 **Qualified privilege**

Although it affords less protection than absolute privilege, the defence of qualified privilege is much wider in scope than absolute privilege. The defence of qualified privilege is frequently relied on by the media and the situations covered by qualified privilege are many and varied. A complete list of the possible situations in which it arises is not possible, but it is important to remember that the defence of qualified privilege is destroyed by malice. In the context of qualified privilege 'malice' does not require hostility or ill will. Where the claimant can show that the defendant did not honestly believe the truth of what he said or if there was some improper motive on the part of the defendant, other than fulfilling a duty to communicate the information or in protecting an interest, the defence will fail. Qualified privilege applies to honestly held opinions. The crucial issue is the honesty of the defendant's belief in the truth of the statement and if the defendant honestly believed the statement to be true, qualified privilege will not be lost, even if the belief is arrived at from unreasonable prejudice or was irrational. *Horrocks v Lowe* (1975) provides an illustration of the House of Lords approach to honesty and the effects of 'malice'. Here, the plaintiff, a Conservative Party councillor, complained that at a meeting of the Bolton town council Lowe, a leading Labour Party opposition member made defamatory remarks in respect of his interests as a property developer. The sting of Lowe's statement was contained in the words:

> I don't know how to describe his attitude whether it was brinkmanship, megalomania or childish petulance . . . I suggest that he has misled the town, the Leader of the party and his political and club colleagues some of whom are his business associates. I therefore request that he be removed from the committee.

The trial judge held that the occasion was privileged but that Lowe, being in the grip of 'gross and unreasonable prejudice', was guilty of malice and therefore the privilege was lost. The Court of Appeal and the House of Lords disagreed. Their Lordships ruled that however prejudiced or irrational, the plaintiff's belief in the truth of what he said on that privileged occasion entitled him to succeed in his defence of privilege. Where the defendant positively believes in the truth of the statement, the courts are reluctant to find malice. Lord Diplock said regardless of the mental process by which 'the belief is arrived at it may still be "honest", that is, a positive belief that the conclusions they have reached are true. The law demands no more.'

15.7.2.1 **Qualified privilege at common law: legal, moral, or social duty**

In *Reynolds v Times Newspapers Ltd* (2001), Lord Nicholls emphasized that the categories of qualified privilege are not exhaustive and said:

> The list is not closed. The established categories are no more than applications, in particular circumstances, of the underlying principle of public policy. The underlying principle is conventionally stated in words to the effect that there must exist between the maker of the statement and the recipient some duty or interest in the making of the communication. Lord Atkinson's dictum in *Adam v Ward* [1917] is much quoted:
>
> > 'a privileged occasion is . . . an occasion where the person who makes a communication has an interest or a duty, legal, social, or moral, to make it to the person to whom it is made, and the person to whom it is made has a corresponding interest or duty to receive it. This reciprocity is essential.'

From the above extract it can be seen that where one person has a legal, moral, or social duty to communicate a statement and the person to whom it is made has a corresponding interest in receiving it, the defence of qualified privilege will apply. Although the law recognizes that there are occasions where it is necessary for people to feel free to communicate information without fear of litigation, an occasion is privileged only if the person to whom the statement is made also has an interest or duty to receive the information. The next case illustrates that reciprocity is essential. In *Watt v Longsdon* (1930), the defendant, a company director, received a letter from the foreign manager of the organization. The letter alleged that Watt, who was the overseas managing director, was immoral and dishonest. The defendant informed the company chairman of his suspicion that Watt was misbehaving with women. Without waiting for any verification of the information, the defendant also communicated the statements, which were false, to Watt's wife. When Watt sued in libel in respect of these statements the defendant sought to rely on the defence of qualified privilege.

The Court of Appeal held that the communication to the company chairman was covered by qualified privilege because both publisher and receiver had a common interest in the affairs of the company which entitled them to discuss the conduct of the plaintiff. However, the publication to Watt's wife was not protected by qualified privilege because, even though she might have an interest in hearing them, the defendant had no social or moral duty to inform her about unsubstantiated allegations. If the allegations had been verified, it is arguable that the wife would then have had an interest in hearing about her husband's misconduct and there may then have been a moral or social duty on the part of the defendant (who was on old friend of the wife) to inform her.

15.7.2.2 **Qualified privilege and references**

CROSS REFERENCE
See also Chapter 5 on duty of care problem areas.

An employment reference is a common example of a statement that is protected by qualified privilege because, although not a legal duty, there is a reciprocal social duty between a current or past employer and a prospective employer. This means that a person about whom a defamatory statement is made in a reference may have difficulty in obtaining a remedy (unless malice can be shown by the maker of the statement) because the defendant will be protected by qualified privilege. However, in *Spring v Guardian Assurance*, although the reference was protected against an action in defamation by qualified privilege, Spring was successful in his action in negligence under the *Hedley Byrne* principle.

 THINKING POINT

In *Spring v Guardian Assurance*, Lord Keith said that imposing liability in negligence for defamatory statements would inhibit those asked to give references from speaking frankly. You will see in Chapter 5 that the duty of care in negligence is breached where a defendant fails to take reasonable care. Do you agree with Lord Goff that those providing references should be expected to take reasonable care?

15.7.2.3 **Qualified privilege under statute**

The Defamation Act 1996 sets out the statements protected by qualified privilege in respect of newspaper or media broadcasting of news or other matters of public interest and in the following circumstances:

Court reporting

- We have seen that absolute privilege only applies to reports published *contemporaneously* with the proceedings. Qualified privilege covers fair and accurate *non-contemporaneous* reports of judicial proceedings anywhere in the world.

Parliamentary proceedings

- Again, we have seen that absolute privilege only applies to proceedings in committees and reports, papers, and proceedings ordered to be published by Parliament. Qualified privilege covers fair and accurate reporting of parliamentary proceedings.

- It is important to note that a statement will not be protected by qualified privilege if it is proved that the defendant has been requested by the claimant to publish an explanation or contradiction and has refused to do so.

Other official bodies and registers

- Statutory qualified privilege extends to reports of public proceedings of a foreign legislature, international organizations, and courts.

- Fair and accurate copies or extracts from official registers and notices published by courts are also protected.

Section 6 of the Defamation Act 2013: qualified privilege extended to scientific or academic journals

The case of *British Chiropractic Association v Singh* (see 15.3.2 Distinguishing fact and opinion) illustrates the public concerns about defamation laws being used to obstruct scientific and academic debate that this section aims to address. *Singh* also shows the vulnerability of individual scientists or academics to a claim in defamation in respect of debate and comment. Section 6 provides that statements in scientific or academic journals are privileged if: (1) the statement relates to a scientific or academic matter; and (2) before publication in the journal an independent review of the statement's scientific or academic merit was carried out by an editor and persons with relevant expertise. The second requirement of this defence would have prevented Dr Singh relying on it because his statement was published in a newspaper article, which is unlikely to have undergone the necessary peer review.

As with other forms of qualified privilege, the defence can be defeated by malice.

🔍 CASE CLOSE UP

Singh v Weayou (2017): specific defences illustrated

This claim in defamation arose from email messages sent to the HR Manager and another senior manager of the hospital where the claimant was employed as the Night Services Coordinator and the defendant was employed as a Health Care Assistant. In the email exchange Weayou (the defendant) alleged that Singh had committed sexual advances against him and said that when he rejected the sexual advances, Singh victimized him by seeking to have him unlawfully dismissed from his job.

The elements of Singh's claim in libel were: the allegations against him were fabricated and untruthful; the statement was 'published' in the email; the natural and ordinary meaning of the words complained were defamatory—they were understood to mean that being in a position of trust and authority he was guilty of sexual harassment; publication of the email caused or was likely to cause serious harm to his reputation (s 1 of the 2013 Act).

The defendant sought to defend the claim by raising the following three defences:

Truth

As to the defence of truth in respect of libel the court noted:

> The burden of proof is upon the defendant. The claimant accepts that section 2 of the 2013 Act means that the defendant need only prove that his allegations are substantially true however he will not avoid liability by avoiding the truth entirely.

The judge was satisfied that the claimant was a witness of truth. His evidence was consistent and supported by written and oral evidence of witnesses and email documentation. However, the defendant was not thought to be a credible witness. There were inconsistencies in his original allegations, his witness statement, and his oral evidence. He was found to have embellished his evidence in court and altered it to suit the times and dates of documentation. Not only did the court find the defendant's allegations to be false, they were also found to have been made maliciously.

Honest opinion

We have seen (in 15.3 Honest opinion) that the first condition that must be met is that the statement complained must be a statement of opinion. In this case the defence was defeated because the court found that the statements contained in the original publication were not statements of opinion, they were statements of fact.

Qualified privilege

Qualified privilege at common law (15.7.2.1) arises where the person making the statement has a legal, moral, or social duty to disclose the information and the person receiving the information has a corresponding interest or duty to receive it. Qualified privilege can

> be defeated where the defendant acts with malice and it failed in this case because, according to the judge:
>
>> A complaint to a manager at the hospital would have constituted an occasion of qualified privilege had the statements complained of been believed to be true, they were not. I have found that the statements were made maliciously.

15.8 Damages: general principles

The primary remedy for defamation is an award of damages. The court seeks to compensate the claimant for loss of reputation, injury to feelings, and the anxiety suffered during the litigation. The assessment of damages depends on the facts in each individual case. The award should reflect the seriousness of the allegation, the extent of the publication, and the nature of the defendant's conduct, both in publishing the defamatory statement and in his conduct afterwards. For example, as we shall later in this section, an apology and retraction will generally be taken into account in mitigation of damages but, conversely, where a defendant persists with an unfounded defence of justification the distress to the claimant will be increased and this will be reflected in the award of damages. If the case of defamation is proved but the claimant has suffered little damage a nominal amount of compensation may be awarded.

For example, in *Singh v Weayou* (above) the claimant was a respected professional who enjoyed his work at the hospital for seventeen years before the defamatory allegations were made. In addition to the harm he suffered in the workplace the court held:

> The allegations have also impacted upon his personal life and health. In my view he is entitled to be compensated for these matters and for the distress of having been defamed. My figure for general damages is £15,000. I award a further £5,000 for aggravated damages to reflect the defendant's persistence in taking this matter to trial on defences he would have known were not true. Special damages (pecuniary loss) are granted in the sum of £30 plus relevant interest and £5,501.10 plus relevant interest.

In this case the court did not have confidence that the defendant would not repeat the defamatory statements. Therefore, an injunction for a period of five years was also granted to restrain the defendant from repeating the defamatory statements, the court said:

> The defendant has fought this case to the end, there has been nothing in his behaviour which gives this Court confidence that the fact of these proceedings of themselves will be sufficient to restrain the defendant from further publication.

The approach to assessing damages for a libellous statement posted on a website was considered in *Woodward v Grice* (2017) EWHC 1292 (QB). The defendant (a football fan) admitted that he had posted statements on the website 'Fansonline.co.uk' which contained the words, 'The well-known struck off solicitor Graham Woodward'.

The claimant, an in-house solicitor employed by Blackpool Football Club, maintained that the untrue allegation as to his being a struck-off solicitor would result in highly charged gossip and rumour:

> A fans website such as these reaches and circulates information to people with a keen interest in Blackpool Football Club. This means any false statement upon such a notice board or website can quickly spread through the Blackpool community.

The initial publication, published on a second website, was found to be a foreseeable repetition of the initial libel so the damages were based on the harm to the claimant's reputation as the result of both posts. In assessing the appropriate level of award, the court took account of: the hostile motivation of the defendant; his refusal to retract the statement until he was shown positive evidence that he was wrong; and the damaging slurs he made against the claimant in the course of the defamation proceedings. Damages of £18,000 were awarded to the claimant.

However, if the publication had stood alone without the aggravating factors, the judge said the amount of damages in vindication of the claimant's reputation and compensation for distress and hurt feelings would have been £10,000. The court also granted a permanent injunction to prevent a repetition of the libel (the risk of the defendant repeating the words complained of was considered to be a real and continuing one).

15.9 Functions of awards in defamation

⟩ CROSS REFERENCE

The emerging law on privacy is the subject of Chapter 16.

The function of an award in damages for personal injury and an award in damages for defamation serve different purposes. The main objective of a personal injury award is to compensate the claimant for financial loss or harm suffered and although there is an element of compensation for injury to feelings in defamation, we have seen earlier that an award in damages for defamation is intended to serve other important functions. It is intended to vindicate the claimant's good reputation and also to act as a deterrent. The levels of awards in damages for defamation can be said to be effective as a deterrent as relatively few defamation actions actually reach the court. However, the emphasis on deterrence from pursuing an action in defamation needs to be balanced with the rights of those who have been defamed. In the context of human rights in a modern society this approach is unlikely to achieve the right balance between protection of reputation and freedom of speech.

You should note that inadequacy of the law of defamation to protect against invasion of privacy has led the courts to develop the law on privacy.

15.9.1 **Level of damages**

A significant issue in the law of defamation in the past was that the level of damages was set by the jury. The Court of Appeal had previously been reluctant to interfere with jury awards, except in very rare cases where the court came to the conclusion that the jury was manifestly wrong. As we will (see 15.9.1.3 Damage awards in relation to ordinary values of life), a number of controversial awards in the late 1980s gave rise to serious criticism summarized by Tony Weir, *A Casebook on Tort* (Sweet & Maxwell, 2004): 'juries in England have long awarded ridiculous sums of money in defamation cases'. These criticisms prompted a change in the approach of the courts to the control of damages.

15.9.1.1 Nominal damages

Before going on to look at cases where **nominal damages** have been awarded it is important to note that damages for personal injury are to compensate the claimant and the aim is to put him in the position he would have been in (in as far as money can do so) if the accident had not happened. Awards in defamation are primarily intended to: (1) compensate the claimant for the damage to his reputation; (2) vindicate the claimant's good reputation; and (3) act as a deterrent. We have seen in Chapter 14 that removal of the presumption in favour of trial by jury is one of the key provisions in the Defamation Act 2013 so juries are no longer likely to be awarding damages in defamation claims.

> **nominal damages** token sum of damages awarded when the court finds that a legal right has been infringed but where the claimant has suffered no substantial loss.

THINKING POINT

One of the functions of damages is to act as a deterrent to publication of a defamatory statement, so how might restricting the levels of compensation by placing a 'cap' on awards reduce the effectiveness of this function?

In *Grobbelaar v News Group Newspapers Ltd* (2002), *The Sun* newspaper published articles alleging that the claimant, a well-known footballer, had taken bribes and was involved in match fixing. The articles were based on information given to one of *The Sun*'s reporters and on covert audio and video recordings in which Grobbelaar confessed to accepting bribes and fixing matches. Although the evidence at trial showed that he had taken bribes, the sting of match fixing was not made out. The defence of justification failed and the jury awarded Grobbelaar £85,000 in damages. On the defendant's appeal against this decision, the jury's finding in respect of liability was upheld but the House of Lords found that an award of £85,000 to a footballer who acted in a way that no decent or honest sportsman would act was an affront to justice. In view of the proven corruption against Grobbelaar, the amount of damages was reduced to £1.

> **CROSS REFERENCE**
> See also Chapter 17 on remedies and limitation.

15.9.1.2 Defamation awards and human rights

In *Tolstoy Miloslavsky v UK* (1995), Count Tolstoy was ordered to pay £1.5 million for a libel in respect of comments he made about Lord Aldington's conduct at the end of the Second World War. The European Court of Human Rights unanimously held that this disproportionately high award had been in breach of Count Tolstoy's freedom of expression under Article 10 of the Convention. In *Rantzen v MGN Ltd* (1993), the jury awarded the claimant (founder of ChildLine) £250,000 for the defendants' false allegation that she had knowingly protected a person who had committed sexual abuse. The newspaper appealed against this award on the ground that it was wholly disproportionate to the damage done to Esther Rantzen's reputation and the Court of Appeal, influenced by the freedom of expression arguments, substituted an award of £110,000. You should note that until 1990 the Court of Appeal had no power to reduce any award made by the jury but, exercising powers conferred under s 8 of the Courts and Legal Services Act 1990, the Court of Appeal was enabled to reduce the award of damages in this case. This power was also exercised by the House of Lords in *Grobbelaar*.

15.9.1.3 Damage awards in relation to ordinary values of life

The case of *John v Mirror Group Newspapers Ltd* (1997) involved an allegation in the *Sunday Mirror* that Elton John was suffering from an eating disorder and that he had been seen at a party in California chewing food and disposing of it in his napkin. The story was completely false and because the defendants had not even checked whether Elton John was actually at the party in question, the jury awarded compensatory damages of £75,000 and £275,000 in exemplary damages. The Court of Appeal reduced the award of compensatory damages to £25,000 and the award of exemplary damages to £50,000 and said that despite the *Rantzen* ruling there was continuing evidence of libel awards which appear so large as to bear no relation to the ordinary values of life. Making reference to damages in cases of personal injury, Sir Thomas Bingham MR said:

> there can be no precise correlation between loss of a limb, or of sight, or quadriplegia, and damage to reputation. But if these personal injuries respectively command conventional awards of, at most, about £52,000, £90,000 and £125,000 for pain and suffering . . . juries may properly be asked to consider whether the injury to his reputation of which the plaintiff complains should fairly justify any greater compensation.

However, in *Kiam v MGN* (2002), the Court of Appeal declined to reduce an award of £105,000 made by the jury, even though the trial judge had recommended an amount of between £40,000 and £80,000.

 THINKING POINT

Before the Court of Appeal reduced the amount, compensatory damages of £75,000 and exemplary damages of £275,000 were awarded to Elton John in respect of a defamatory statement. Lord Bingham noted that a personal injury award for the loss of a limb is about £52,000 and subsequently *Cairns v Modi* held that reference to pain and suffering in personal injury cases could be made when considering defamation awards. Bearing in mind the reference to personal injury awards as a yardstick for damages in defamation, how does personal injury equate in value with reputation?

The above cases illustrate that extent of control which the Court of Appeal began to exercise over the levels of award in damages. This has resulted in very substantial reductions in the amounts awarded. In *Cairns v Modi* (2012) the Court of Appeal reflected on the wide parameters for damages in libel cases and the highest level of awards currently considered appropriate and noted:

> reference could be made to the current conventional scale of compensatory damages being awarded in respect of pain and suffering in personal injury cases, not because there could be any precise correlation, but merely as one check on the reasonableness of any figure being considered as an award in libel proceedings. It has now become conventional also to recognise in effect a 'ceiling' figure, allowing periodically for inflation, corresponding to the current maximum level of damages for pain and suffering and loss of amenity in personal injury cases.

However, Mullis and Scott express concern about this approach. Their research shows that in reality most libel actions involve instances of damaging inaccuracy perpetrated by multinational media corporations and challenged by relatively impecunious claimants. They make the point that libel damages have been substantially reduced over the past 20 years and observe:

> We are concerned, however, that the critique of the libel regime is too broad and the reforms proposed too sweeping and indiscriminate. The public commentary on libel law has been remarkably one-sided, and in some respects dangerously oversimplified. We are nervous that the important societal functions performed by libel law have been underplayed. Libel reform should be coherent, not piecemeal and un(der)-principled.

Notwithstanding the significant reforms introduced by the Defamation Act 2013 the costs associated with trials in defamation together with the complicated rules and procedures involved in bringing a claim mean that criticisms about the high legal fees continue. Although public funding has never been available either to bring or defend a defamation action, lawyers are increasingly willing to act under a 'conditional fee agreement' (CFA) which is popularly known as a 'no win, no fee' basis. However, before a lawyer will act under a 'no win, no fee' arrangement the merits of the case and prospects of success must be sufficiently good. You should note that although the party to a CFA action in defamation will not be liable for the lawyer's costs whether they win or lose the case, if they do lose the case they will almost certainly be ordered to pay the successful party's legal costs. Although it is possible to obtain insurance to protect against the risk of paying the opponent's legal costs, the way in which the insurance premiums are calculated and payable on such policies is complicated. *Campbell v Mirror Group Newspapers* is an example of a privacy case which was taken under a CFA.

CROSS REFERENCE
See Chapter 16.

CROSS REFERENCE
See Chapter 1 for conditional fee agreements.

A further development in reducing the costs of litigation is a pre-action protocol for defamation, which implements procedures to enable the early resolution of claims, and there is also the possibility of summary judgment in certain cases. The serious harm requirement under the 2013 Act aims to reduce trivial claims, but it is still generally the case that only the very rich can afford to sue in defamation.

15.10 Lack of public funding for defamation actions

Steel and Morris v UK the 'McLibel' case (2005)

▶ CROSS REFERENCE

discussed in Chapter 14.

Because there is no public funding either to bring or defend an action in defamation it is often seen as a tort for the wealthy. In 'the *McLibel* case' the denial of legal aid to two campaigners to defend a defamation action was found to be a breach of Article 10 and a violation of Article 6 of the ECHR. As part of an anti-McDonald's campaign in the mid-1980s, the applicants had distributed a six-page leaflet entitled: 'What's wrong with McDonalds?' McDonalds sued them for libel allegedly contained in statements published in the leaflet relating to destruction of the rainforest, responsibility for Third World starvation, cruelty to animals, and exploitation of children. Throughout the trial, which lasted for 313 court days and was the longest trial in English legal history, the applicants represented themselves, with only some help from volunteer lawyers, whereas McDonalds was represented by experts in the law of libel. Although Mr Morris was unemployed and Ms Steel was either unemployed or on a low wage during the period, they had been refused legal aid to defend the action. The European Court of Human Rights ruled that in an action of such complexity, neither the help given by the volunteer lawyers nor the extensive judicial assistance provided during the hearing was any substitute for representation by expert lawyers. The absence of legal aid by itself would not necessarily amount to a breach of Article 6 but the burden of proving that the statements were true was on the defendants and, in such a complex case, this resulted in an unacceptable inequality of arms with McDonalds. In these circumstances, assistance should have been provided.

↻ Summary

- English law protects free speech through the defences to defamation.
- Even if defamatory and malicious, certain statements are of such social and political importance that the law provides absolute protection.
- The application of the 'strict liability' rule in cases of 'unintentional' publication is mitigated for an 'innocently' published statement.
- The Defamation Act 2013 introduced major reform of the law of defamation and provided new protection for website operators.

  ◐ Visit the online resources to listen to a podcast summarizing the topics covered in this chapter.

The bigger picture

A Mullis and A Scott, 'Tilting at Windmills: The Defamation Act 2013' (2014) 77(1) MLR 87–109.

This article provides detailed discussion of reforms to the main common law defences and the impact of the new legislation on scientific discourse and online speech. The authors are critical that more attention has not been paid to remedies for defamation and that new technology has not been fully used to embrace the remedies of apology, correction, and right of reply.

It may help your understanding of the new statutory defences to read, Dan Tench, 'Defamation Act 2013, A Critical Evaluation, Part 3, "Truth" and "Honest Opinion"' (2014) on Inforrm's website, https://inforrm.wordpress.com/2014/07/28/defamation-act-2013-a-critical-evaluation-part-3-truth-and-honest-comment-dan-tench

? Questions

Knowledge-testing questions

1. List the new defences introduced by the Defamation Act 2013.

2. Explain the difference between the defences of absolute privilege and qualified privilege.

3. The courts will now be required to apply the words used in the statute when considering the defences to defamation, so is the judicial analysis of the principles and guidance provided by the Supreme Court in cases such as *Flood v Times Newspapers Ltd* still relevant?

4. Explain how the Defamation Act 2013 aims to provide website operators with greater protection from claims in defamation.

Problem and essay questions

1. Do the reforms to defences in the Defamation Act 2013 strike a fair balance between freedom of expression and the protection of reputation?

2. Before taking up a new appointment as editor-in-chief of a national newspaper, Graeme was the editor of the *Fern Hill Gazette*. Hilary, a freelance sports journalist, writes a weekly column for the *Fern Hill Gazette* and also for a rival newspaper, the *Globe Observer*. Hilary has never forgiven Graeme for his refusal to make her a member of the permanent staff on the *Fern Hill Gazette*. Two months ago Rhodri provided Hilary with information to suggest that Graeme had been implicated in a 'cash for lobbying scandal' involving Sir Arthur, a Member of Parliament. In her latest column in the *Globe Observer* Hilary refers to Graeme's new appointment and states that: 'his career has advanced considerably since his cash for lobbying deal with Sir Arthur'. The allegation is untrue and Graeme has started legal proceedings against the *Globe Observer*.

   Explain any defences that may be available to the Hilary and the *Globe Observer* in respect of Graeme's claim in defamation.

 Visit the online resources for guidance on answering these questions.

Further reading

Balin, R et al, 'Libel Tourism and the Duke's Manservant: An American Perspective' (2009) 3 European Human Rights LR 303

Complaints about defamatory material posted on websites: Guidance on Section 5 of the Defamation Act 2013 and Regulations: www.gov.uk/government/uploads/system/uploads/attachment_data/file/269138/defamation-guidance.pdf

Hooper, D, K Waite, and O Murphy, 'Defamation Act 2013: What Difference Will It Really Make?' (2013) 24 Ent LR 199–206

Howarth, D, 'The Cost of Libel Actions: A Sceptical Note' (2011) 70(2) CLJ 397

Lock, O, 'Is It Interesting? New Judgment Considers the Scope of the "Public Interest" Defence under the Defamation Act 2013 s. 4' (2017) 28 Ent LR 16

16 Privacy and misuse of private information

LEARNING OBJECTIVES

By the end of this chapter you should be able to:

- understand the history of the protection of privacy in English law;
- describe the range of current legal approaches to privacy;
- understand that the courts now recognize the separate tort of misuse of private information;
- appreciate the impact of the Human Rights Act 1998 on this developing area of law; and
- see the English law on privacy in an international context.

Introduction

Privacy is a difficult concept to clearly define and this is one reason why in the past English law has appeared reluctant to regulate invasion of privacy. We may think of sunbathing in our garden as a private activity; similarly going out to eat with a friend, sending a personal email, or consulting a doctor about a medical condition. Yet what unites these diverse examples?

THINKING POINT

In the United States Judge Cooley, in 1888, defined privacy as 'the right to be left alone'. In what way might this definition of privacy be found wanting?

According to the US Restatement of the Law of Torts, 2d, 1977:

> The right of privacy is invaded by:
>
> (a) unreasonable intrusion upon the seclusion of another . . . or
>
> (b) appropriation of another's name or likeness . . . or
>
> (c) unreasonable publicity given to another's private life . . . or
>
> (d) publicity that unreasonably places another in a false light before the public.

 THINKING POINT

List some of the many different activities which could be described as involving a breach of privacy.

What effect might the current practice of 'sharing' on social media have on legal controls in this area?

A number of government bodies have reviewed this subject and made recommendations concerning legislation on privacy, see: the Younger Committee, Report on Privacy (1971); the Calcutt Committee, Report on Privacy and Related Matters (1990); and, on the subject of regulation of the press, the Leveson Inquiry: Culture, Practice and Ethics of the Press (2011–12).

The Calcutt Report adopted the following working definition of privacy:

> The right of the individual to be protected against intrusion into his personal life or affairs, or those of his family, by direct physical means or by publication of information.

We will see later that there are a number of different torts which indirectly address wrongful intrusion into another's privacy. However, English law has characteristically not directly protected privacy in its own right. It was the coming into force of the Human Rights Act 1998 that provoked significant litigation which tested the extent to which Article 8 of the European Convention might require courts to develop a law of privacy and, if so, how this might be accomplished. The aspect of privacy that is the main concern of the cases discussed in this chapter pertains to the *publication of private information*.

The traditional approach of English law to the question of privacy was well summarized in the case considered next.

 CASE CLOSE-UP

Kaye v Robertson (1991)

Gorden Kaye was a popular television star of the series *Allo!, Allo!* who suffered serious head injuries when a tree fell through the windscreen of his car during a wind storm. While he was recovering in a semi-conscious state in his private hospital room, a journalist and photographer from the *Sunday Sport* newspaper entered the room (despite signs excluding them), photographed him, and attempted to interview him, before being ejected by staff. An interim injunction was granted prohibiting publication of the picture and the interview, which the *Sport* claimed had been exclusively granted by Mr Kaye. The newspaper appealed to the Court of Appeal.

Glidewell, LJ began by stating:

> in English law there is no right to privacy, and accordingly there is no right of action for breach of a person's privacy. The facts of the present case are a graphic illustration of the desirability of Parliament considering whether . . . statutory provision can be made to protect the privacy of individuals.

He went on to consider the 'well-established rights of action which might indirectly be used to justify an interim injunction to protect privacy'.

(1) *Libel*: The claimant argued an analogy with *Tolley v JS Fry & Sons Ltd* (1931), where an implication that an amateur golfer had accepted payment for endorsing a product constituted a defamatory innuendo. In this case, the court doubted whether a jury would find that the implication that Mr Kaye had granted an interview to the *Sunday Sport* while lying injured in hospital was defamatory.

(2) *Trespass to the person*: In the view of the court it was possible that deliberately flashing a bright light, such as a flash bulb, in someone's eyes could constitute a battery, although it was not necessary to decide this point in *Kaye*.

(3) *Passing off*: This 'economic tort' is committed when a defendant trader uses a misrepresentation calculated to deceive the recipients in order to cause foreseeable injury to the business interests of the claimant trader. The court did not believe that Mr Kaye could be described as a 'trader' in relation to his interest in the story of his accident.

(4) *Malicious falsehood*: 'The essentials of this tort are that the defendant has published about the plaintiff words that are false, that they were published maliciously and that special damage has followed as the direct and natural result of their publication.' Malice was inferred on the basis that the defendants knew that it was false to state that Mr Kaye had knowingly granted the interview. The special damage was the claimant's loss of the valuable right to sell his story. Damages would not be an adequate remedy and so the case for an interim injunction was made on the basis of malicious falsehood.

Unfortunately for Gorden Kaye, the interim injunction could only prohibit publication of the falsehood, which was that permission to publish had been given. The *Sunday Sport* published the article in a different form, along with a photograph of the claimant asleep in bed.

For Bingham LJ, *Kaye* highlighted:

> the failure of both the common law of England and statute to protect in an effective way the personal privacy of the individual citizen.

Legatt LJ observed:

> it is to be hoped that the making good of this signal shortcoming in our law will not be long delayed.

▶ THINKING POINT

Can you think of other
causes of action which might
indirectly protect someone's
interest in privacy?

In 1995 some took the view that the common law should develop a right to privacy. In *Hellewell v Chief Constable of Derbyshire* (1995), Lord Irvine suggested 'the courts will be able to adapt and develop the common law by relying on existing domestic principles in the laws of trespass, nuisance, copyright, confidence . . . to fashion a common law right to privacy'.

16.1 Human rights

The passing of the Human Rights Act 1998 brought about a new perspective on the question of protection of privacy. One matter for debate has been the extent to which the Act can be said to have **horizontal effect**.

horizontal effect

the application of human rights law to actions between individuals, in contrast to actions brought against public authorities. It has been argued that the ECHR creates a positive duty upon the state to protect individual Article 8 rights.

According to Lord Nicholls in the important case of *Campbell v MGN*:

> The values embodied in Articles 8 and 10 are as much applicable in disputes between individuals or between an individual and a non-governmental body such as a newspaper as they are in disputes between individuals and a public authority.

16.1.1 European Convention on Human Rights, Articles 8 and 10, incorporated into English law by s 1 Human Rights Act 1998

 STATUTE

Article 8: Right to respect for private and family life

(1) Everyone has the right to respect for his private and family life, his home and his correspondence.

(2) There shall be no interference by a public authority with the exercise of this right except such as in accordance with the law and is necessary in a democratic society in the interests of national security or the economic well-being of the country, for the prevention of disorder or crime, for the protection of health or morals, or for the protection of the rights and freedoms of others.

 STATUTE

Article 10: Freedom of expression

▶ CROSS REFERENCE

See 16.2.2 The *Campbell* case.

(1) Everyone has the right to freedom of expression: This right shall include freedom to hold opinions and to receive and impart information and ideas without interference by public authority. . . .

(2) The exercise of these freedoms, since it carries with it duties and responsibilities, may be subject to such formalities, conditions, restrictions and penalties as are prescribed by law and are necessary in a democratic society . . . for the protection of the reputation or rights of others. . . .

16.1.2 **Human Rights Act 1998**

 STATUTE

Human Rights Act 1998, s 12(1)–(4): Relief

(1) This section applies if a court is considering whether to grant any relief which, if granted, might affect the exercise of the Convention right to freedom of expression.

(2) If the person against whom the application for relief is made . . . is neither present nor represented, no such relief is to be granted unless the court is satisfied—

   (a) that the applicant has taken all practicable steps to notify the respondent, or

   (b) that there are compelling reasons why the respondent should not be notified.

(3) No such relief is to be granted so as to restrain publication before trial unless the court is satisfied that the applicant is likely to establish that publication should not be allowed.

(4) The court must have particular regard to the importance of the Convention right to freedom of expression and, where the proceedings relate to material which the respondent claims, or which appear to the court, to be journalistic, literary or artistic material (or conduct connected with such material), to—

   (a) the extent to which—

      (i) the material has, or is about to, become available to the public; or

      (ii) it is, or would be, in the public interest for the material to be published,

   (b) any relevant privacy code.

See 'The bigger picture' at the end of this chapter for discussion of press regulation in the United Kingdom.

The primary foundation for legal developments in this area, since 2000, is the action based upon breach of confidence. This is a well-established cause of action which has recently undergone a process of reinterpretation and adaptation. You should remember that, in contrast to actions in defamation, those concerning issues of privacy are not based on allegations that the subject matter concerned is *untrue*.

16.2 Breach of confidence

16.2.1 **Background**

This is a wrong, arising from the breach of a duty to keep confidence arising from either a confidential situation, transaction, or relationship. Its status is unclear. Originally breach of confidence was actionable in equity and the remedy sought was an injunction, but now it is equally likely to result in a claim for damages. According to *Douglas v Hello!* (2005), breach of confidence is not a tort but a **restitutionary** claim for **unjust enrichment**.

> **restitutionary** a payment made in order to restore an unjust enrichment; distinguished from compensation.

> **unjust enrichment** where one party wrongly makes a material gain at the expense of the other; for example, when an overpayment has been made by mistake. This can give rise to an obligation upon one party to make restitution; that is, to restore that gain to the rightful party.

Traditionally, the action has been founded upon the unauthorized use of information of a confidential nature when the defendant is said to be under a duty of confidentiality. In *Prince Albert v Strange* (1849), the royal family obtained an injunction prohibiting unauthorized publication of family caricatures made for family and friends by Prince Albert and Queen Victoria. Here, the information was disclosed to a printer by a servant. Intimate aspects of a marriage were the subject of the successful breach-of-confidence action in *Duchess of Argyll v Duke of Argyll* (1967). The duty of confidentiality was seen to be intrinsic to the relationship of husband and wife.

In other cases, the nature of the confidential information may have commercial aspects. That was the situation when the film stars Michael Douglas and Catherine Zeta-Jones sold the exclusive rights to publish a selection of photos of their wedding to *OK!* magazine. An unauthorized photographer secretly managed to take photos of the occasion, which were later published by *OK!*'s rival *Hello!* magazine. This gave rise to a series of legal actions. The first concerned the attempt to obtain an interim injunction to prevent the photos' publication in *Hello!*

Q CASE CLOSE-UP

Douglas v Hello! (2001)

In *Douglas v Hello!* (2001), the Court of Appeal decided that the interim injunction obtained at first instance was unnecessary because the claimants' interests would be adequately protected by damages, while the magazine would suffer disproportionate losses should the injunction be upheld. Given that the couple had already given permission for their wedding to have a certain amount of publicity, any residual interest in privacy did not warrant an injunction. The law of breach of confidence was said to cover this situation. Significantly, Sedley LJ believed:

> [W]e have reached a point where it can be said with confidence that the law recognises and will appropriately protect a right of personal privacy . . . . [T]he law has to protect not only those whose trust has been abused but also those who find themselves subject to an unwanted intrusion into their personal lives. The law no longer needs to construct an artificial relationship of confidentiality between intruder and victim: it can recognise privacy itself as a legal principle drawn from the fundamental value of personal autonomy.

▶ CROSS REFERENCE

See also Chapter 17 on remedies and limitation.

For him this was an example of the common law being developed in accordance with the principles of s 6 of the Human Rights Act, but we will see that subsequently the House of Lords rejected his sweeping assertion regarding protection of privacy.

The main focus of *A v B* (2002) was the balancing of Article 8 rights as against those of Article 10 in an application to prevent an embarrassing publication. Here, an interim injunction was granted (and subsequently confirmed) to prevent publication in the defendant newspaper of an article containing the accounts by two women of their brief extramarital affairs with the prominent footballer Gary Flitcroft. The newspaper's appeal was successful. The Court of Appeal stressed that the remedy of injunction requires the justification of being in the public interest. Transitory relationships such as the affairs in question did not carry with them an equivalent degree of confidentiality to those within marriage. This situation was at the 'outer limits' of relationships requiring protection and the granting of an injunction would be an unjustified interference with the freedom of the press and the women's freedom of expression. It was significant that the claimant was a public figure. One who has 'courted publicity' must expect a degree of intrusion into his affairs in which the public will have a 'legitimate interest'.

Lord Woolf CJ took a conservative approach to the possible extension of the law into a new right to privacy:

> In the great majority of situations, if not all, where the protection of privacy is justified . . . an action for breach of confidence now will provide the necessary protection. This means that at first instance it is not necessary to tackle the vexed question of whether there is a separate cause of action based upon a new tort involving the infringement of privacy.

He did, however, give a generous interpretation to the scope of the action for breach of confidence:

> A duty of confidence will arise whenever the party subject to the duty either knows or ought to know that the other person can reasonably expect his privacy to be protected. If there is an intrusion in a situation where a person can reasonably expect his privacy to be protected, that intrusion will be capable of giving rise to liability in an action for breach of confidence unless the intrusion can be justified.

However, another adulterous liaison did receive protection in *CC v AB* (2006). The defendant was partly motivated to write of the claimant's affair out of spite and greed. The court was of the opinion that each case must be examined on its own merits and was persuaded to grant an interim injunction for the erring husband by evidence that the publication would pose a threat to the emotional well-being of the applicant's wife and to his efforts to repair his marriage and family life. It has now been recognized by the courts that many such 'kiss-and-tell' stories concerning sports or entertainment celebrities resemble little more than an attempt to blackmail the subject, and as such are not deserving of Article 10 protection (see *CTB v NGN* (2011)).

16.2.2 **The *Campbell* case**

The House of Lords decision in *Campbell v Mirror Group Newspapers* (2004) clarified the circumstances in which there will be legal protection regarding publication of private information. Since *Campbell*, case law has developed which focuses on *misuse of private information.* That this is now a tort in its own right has been recognized, at least for procedural purposes, in the case of *Google v Vidal-Hall* (2015), but its precise status in relation to equitable wrongs is still developing.

 CASE CLOSE-UP

Campbell v Mirror Group Newspapers (2004)

The model Naomi Campbell had publicly claimed that she did not use drugs. The *Mirror* subsequently published an article detailing Miss Campbell's 'courageous bid to beat her addiction to drink and drugs' accompanied by a photo of her leaving a Narcotics Anonymous meeting. She claimed damages for breach of confidence, succeeding at first instance, and was awarded a modest sum, including aggravated damages. The defendant appealed and the Court of Appeal held that regardless of whether the claim fitted more properly within breach of confidence or privacy, the publication was justified as being in the public interest. The *Mirror*'s correction of her earlier misleading statements, when viewed according to the Human Rights Act, s 12(4) criteria regarding balancing the right to privacy and freedom of expression, should not give rise to compensation.

Miss Campbell's appeal resulted in a very important and detailed consideration of the matter by the Law Lords. In their speeches, all five judges approached the case on the basis that in English law, while 'there is no over-arching, all-embracing cause of action of "invasion of privacy"', there can now be said to be a right against wrongful disclosure of private information. Lord Hoffmann described the cause of action as a new variant of breach of confidence, but one which has 'firmly shaken off the limiting constraint of the need for an initial confidential relationship'.

What information should be protected by this new cause of action? According to Lord Nicholls, 'Essentially the touchstone of private life is whether in respect of the disclosed facts the person in question had a reasonable expectation of privacy.' Thus, the test is basically a subjective one (based on the claimant's expectation) limited by the requirement that this expectation be reasonable and that the defendant knew or ought to have known about that expectation.

The aspects of the publication which were complained of were as follows:

- the fact of Miss Campbell's drug addiction;
- the fact that she was receiving treatment;
- the fact that she was receiving treatment at Narcotics Anonymous;
- the details of the treatment; and
- the photograph of her leaving a meeting.

Accepting that each of the five aspects were of an essentially private nature, it was then necessary for the court to embark upon balancing the Article 8 right of Miss Campbell to private life with the Article 10 right of the newspaper to inform the public. The tests applied were:

(1) Did the publication pursue a legitimate aim?

(2) Were the benefits which would be achieved by publication proportionate to the harm that might be done by interference with privacy?

The balancing exercise was a difficult one. However, by a majority of three to two the appeal was allowed. The Law Lords accepted that a line could be drawn between the first two and the last three aspects of the claim. The fact of drug addiction and treatment was 'open to public comment in view of her denials' and not unduly intrusive. However, the disclosure of details of her treatment accompanied by the secretly taken photograph were more than just 'peripheral' to the main story and went beyond merely setting the record straight. This could have disrupted her necessarily confidential course of therapy at a 'fragile' stage and as such could not be justified. Miss Campbell's damages were reinstated.

THINKING POINT

Hale LJ, as she then was, described the *Campbell* case as involving 'a prima donna celebrity against a celebrity-exploiting tabloid newspaper. Each in their time has profited from the other. Both are assumed to be grown-ups who know the score.' In what way should the privacy rights of the celebrity be different from those of the ordinary citizen?

16.2.3 **Applying the principles of *Campbell***

As in *Albert v Strange* in the nineteenth century, royalty again had recourse to the law relating to privacy in the twenty-first century. In *HRH Prince of Wales v Associated Newspapers* (2006), Prince Charles brought an action claiming damages for breach of confidence when the *Mail on Sunday* published extracts from his personal diary. The extracts in question covered his state visit to the Far East in 1997 and in particular focused on the Prince's views on the handover of Hong Kong to China and opinions on various Chinese officials he met at formal events. In an action

❯ THINKING POINT

The Law Lords considered it to be significant that the story about Naomi Campbell was accompanied by a photograph. Why might that be important? Do you agree?

for **summary judgment** Blackburne J applied the law as laid down by the House of Lords in *Campbell v MGN*.

> **summary judgment** where the court decides a particular issue without a full trial.

▶ CROSS REFERENCE
Discussed at 16.4 Photos.

First, did the claimant have a *reasonable expectation of privacy* in relation to the information in question? If so, then Article 8 would be engaged. Despite the fact that it was not of a 'highly personal or private nature' and that it had been circulated to between twenty and seventy-five recipients, the contents of the journal were held to raise a reasonable expectation of privacy. The envelopes in which this was circulated had been sealed and marked 'Private and Confidential', and even public figures were entitled in some circumstances to expect privacy in expressing thoughts, even about issues of an essentially political nature.

Second, having accepted this 'threshold expectation', the court had to conduct a *balancing exercise* between the Article 8 right to private and family life and the Article 10 right to freedom of expression. Neither of these rights takes precedence over the other and any restriction or interference must be in accordance with law, pursue a legitimate aim (as set out in Articles 8(2) and 10(2)), and be 'necessary in a democratic society', meet a 'pressing social need', and 'be no greater than is proportionate to the legitimate aim pursued'. Blackburne J pointed out that 'what may be in the public interest to know . . . is not to be confused with what is interesting to the public'. The fact that the claimant in this case was a well-known public figure did not mean that he was not entitled to have a private life. Both the *Campbell* case and that of *Von Hannover* indicate a shift towards legal recognition of the 'protection of human autonomy and dignity' and the need for those in the public eye to control information about their private life. It was the latter fact that led the judge to conclude that given the nature of the journal, publication of its contents could not be said to be 'necessary in a democratic society' when weighed against the prince's interest in a 'private space' in which to think and write.

The decision in favour of the Prince of Wales was upheld by the Court of Appeal, which was of the opinion that it was significant that the material had been disclosed by an employee in breach of his own duty of confidence:

> The test to be applied when considering whether it was necessary to restrict freedom of expression in order to prevent disclosure of information received in confidence was not simply whether the information was a matter of public interest but whether in all the circumstances it was in the public interest that the duty of confidence should be breached.

In *McKennitt v Ash* (2006), the defendant had written a biography of a folk singer, revealing details of the singer's personal life which had been obtained during her close friendship with the author. These included details of her sex life and her feelings about the death of her husband. An injunction was obtained against further publication and was upheld by the Court of Appeal. The information was of a confidential nature and was obtained in a relationship of confidence based upon friendship; therefore it carried with it 'a reasonable expectation of privacy'. On the facts, any Article 10 rights of the author must yield to the Article 8 rights of the subject of the book. In contrast, in *Napier v Pressdram Ltd* (2009), an action brought against *Private Eye*, the professional adjudication proceedings of the Solicitors' Regulation Authority were held not to hold any reasonable expectation of privacy.

The 'reasonable expectation of privacy' can, of course, be undermined by the subject's own conduct. In *Trimingham v Associated Newspapers* (2012), the bisexual lover of a politician was held to have compromised her own expectation of privacy by taking risks in her personal life.

16.3 Physical intrusion

 CASE CLOSE-UP

Wainwright v Home Office (2003)

In *Wainwright v Home Office*, a woman and her son were subjected to a strip search conducted by a prison officer while they were visiting a prison inmate. The woman was distressed and humiliated by the incident and her son, who suffered from a learning disorder and whose penis was touched by the officer, suffered post-traumatic stress disorder. They brought actions based upon battery (see Chapter 11, *Wilkinson v Downton*), and a proposed tort of invasion of privacy.

The claimants were successful at first instance, where the judge awarded damages for battery (compensatory and aggravated) to both claimants. The events took place before the coming into force of the Human Rights Act 1998; however, the common law was to be developed by analogy with the European Convention on Human Rights (ECHR) and the judge framed his conclusions in terms of protection of privacy. The Court of Appeal held that, because Mrs Wainwright had not been touched but only forced to undress, the tort of battery could not be extended to satisfy her claim. On the subject of privacy, Buxton LJ was of the opinion that the future shape of the law should be determined by Parliament, not the courts. Before the House of Lords, the cause of action was based upon *Wilkinson v Downton* and invasion of privacy. According to Lord Hoffmann, 'mere distress' was insufficient to found an action for intentional causation of harm under *Wilkinson v Downton*. On the second point, he reviewed recent developments and concluded that privacy can be regarded as a fundamental *value* of law which may indicate its future development, rather than founding a tort in its own right. Despite Sedley LJ's view in *Douglas*, there was no 'principle of privacy so abstract as to include the circumstances of the present case'. In *Wainwright v UK* (2007) the European Court of Human Rights (ECtHR) held that the Home Office had been in breach of both Articles 8 and 13 of the ECHR. This indicates the future approach for cases of this sort.

> **CROSS REFERENCE**
>
> For more on trespass to the person, see Chapter 11.

16.4 Photos

The powerful impact of visual images has been noted and was frequently cited in *Campbell* in the following terms: 'In general photographs of people contain more information than textual description' and 'publishing the photos contributed both to the revelation and to the harm that it [the story] might do'. For Lord Hope, the inclusion of the covertly taken photos in the *Campbell* story tipped the balance against the publication. According to Lord Carswell, the mere fact of covert photography was not enough in itself to make the information conveyed confidential; however, the photographs were a 'powerful prop to a written story', thus much valued by paparazzi, and thus not to be dismissed too readily as adding to the total effect of the publication.

Jamie Theakston, a TV presenter, applied for an interim injunction to prevent a Sunday newspaper from publishing an article containing the fact of his visit to a brothel, details of his activities there, and a photograph of the latter. In *Theakston v MGN* (2002), the judge at first instance believed that it was only the prevention of publication of the photograph which would be upheld at full trial. It involved 'no particular extension of the law of confidentiality and . . . publication of such photographs would be particularly intrusive into the claimant's own individual personality . . . in a peculiarly humiliating and damaging way'. In refusing an injunction regarding the article itself, note was taken that Theakston 'had already placed various aspects of his private life in the public domain in order to enhance his reputation as a man physically and sexually attractive to many women'.

Privacy can also be threatened when someone is photographed in a public or semi-public space. In *Peck v UK* (2003), a man was photographed by CCTV on a London street late at night, holding a large knife, having recently attempted suicide. This footage was later broadcast widely as part of a crime-prevention and detection initiative. Having failed in his legal actions at the domestic level, Peck successfully applied to the ECtHR, which found that his Article 8 rights had been breached.

Despite the fact that he had been photographed in a public place, the publication had been 'viewed to an extent which far exceeded any exposure to a passer-by or to security observation'. Public interest in demonstrating the effectiveness of CCTV in crime prevention did not warrant the intrusion. Mr Peck was awarded damages for the distress caused by the interference in his private life.

Q   CASE CLOSE-UP

Von Hannover v Germany (No 1) (2005)

A long-standing problem with persistent paparazzi lay behind *Von Hannover v Germany (No 1)* (2005). Various German tabloid publications had published photos and accompanying articles showing Princess Caroline of Monaco engaged in different activities, such as practising sports, leaving a restaurant, or on holiday. Many of the photos in question had been taken in France, whose legal system is generally protective of public figures, but published in Germany, where the press is treated more leniently.

In a markedly pro-privacy decision, the ECtHR found that the German court which had ruled against her application had failed to take the positive steps necessary to protect her Article 8 rights. The Court noted the context: 'photos taken in a climate of continual harassment that induces in the persons concerned a very strong sense of intrusion into their private life or even of persecution'. According to the court, the decisive factor in the balancing exercise lay in assessing whether the photographs could make any meaningful contribution to a debate of general interest.

> The Court considers that a fundamental distinction needs to be made between reporting facts . . . capable of contributing to a debate in a democratic society relating to politicians in the exercise of their functions . . . and reporting details of the private life of an individual who . . . does not exercise official functions.

Here it was concluded that because Princess Caroline held no public office and the photos related to her private life, there was no such justification for the intrusion.

 THINKING POINT

Princess Caroline, a prominent socialite, would have been visible to members of the public when some of these photos were taken. Should that make a difference to her claims for protection? Could claims like hers ever be motivated by commercial considerations?

In a subsequent action, *Von Hannover v Germany (No 2)* (2012), the ECtHR held that photographs of the Princess and her family in a ski resort, at the time when her father, the Head of State of Monaco was seriously ill, were justifiably published in the public interest, given an impetus to discuss the appropriateness of her holiday.

 CASE CLOSE-UP

Mosley v News Group Newspapers (2008)

In *Max Mosley*, the Chairman of Formula One and son of the late Oswald Mosley, a fascist sympathizer at the time of the Second World War, sued the defendants for breach of confidence and unauthorized publication of personal information contrary to Article 8 of the European Convention. The now defunct *News of the World* had published photos (clandestinely taken) of him partaking in a sadomasochistic 'orgy' and these were accompanied by an interview with one of the female participants. The action was founded upon the pre-existing relationship of confidentiality between the participants, and it cited as authority *McKennitt v Ash*.

Mr Justice Eady in the High Court carried out the now familiar balancing exercise between Articles 8 and 10 and was not convinced by the defendant's allegation that there had been a Nazi or 'death camp' theme evident in the session, thereby creating a public interest in its revelation. He concluded that the claimant had had a reasonable expectation of privacy in relation to sexual activities ('albeit unconventional') carried out between consenting adults on private property. He commented particularly on the potency of visual images. In relation to the defence of public interest, the judge observed:

> The facts of this case are far removed from those in *Von Hannover*. There can be little doubt that intimate photographs or recording of private sexual activity, however unconventional, would be extremely difficult to justify at all by Strasbourg standards: see e.g. Dudgeon v UK (cited above) at [49]–[53]. It is those to which we are now required by the Human Rights Act to have regard. Obviously, titillation for its own sake could never be justified. Yet it is reasonable to suppose that it was this which led so many thousands of people to accept the *News of the World*'s invitation on 30 March to 'See the shocking video at notw.co.uk'. It would be quite unrealistic to think that these visits were prompted by a desire to participate in a 'debate of general interest' of the kind contemplated in *Von Hannover*.

Mosley was awarded £60,000 damages for the distress suffered and as recognition that his right to privacy had been breached. In doing so the judge was guided by the comparable tariff in defamation cases but declined to extend damages to include any exemplary or deterrent aspect.

Q CASE CLOSE-UP

Sir Cliff Richard v BBC and the Chief Constable of the South Yorkshire Police (2018)

Interests in privacy and in public broadcasting came into sharp conflict in this case. Sir Cliff Richard is a well-known singer and entertainer, self-identified as a Christian, who began his recording career in the 1950s and still actively pursued this into his eighth decade. Unknown to him, he was under investigation by the South Yorkshire Police (SYP) for a historic sex offence. When it was decided to search the claimant's home (at a time when he was abroad), someone from within the investigation secretly notified the BBC in advance. There was extensive coverage of the search including live filming from overhead, which was broadcast worldwide. The coverage had a serious emotional and physical impact on Sir Cliff, as well as damage to his reputation and professional status. He remained under investigation for two years until he was notified that no charges would be brought.

Sir Cliff brought actions for damages against the BBC and SYP for violation of his rights in privacy and under the Data Protection Act 1998. SYP accepted liability, apologized and reached a settlement for £400,000 plus legal costs. The BBC contested the claim and there followed a thirteen-day trial, which also dealt with contribution proceedings between the BBC and SYP.

The *McKennitt v Ash* (2008) balancing exercise was applied, asking:

1. Is this a situation in which the information is protected by Article 8?

2. If so, in all the circumstances, must the interest of the owner of the private information yield to the right of freedom of expression conferred on the publisher by Article
   10? That is, was there a countervailing public interest in publishing the information?

Mr Justice Mann reviewed the facts in detail in his judgment which went on to cite the
balancing exercise of *McKennitt v Ash* (2008). He held that, as a general principle and
based on authorities, a suspect has a reasonable expectation of privacy in relation to a
police investigation and this need not be compromised in the course of a search. This is a
fact-sensitive issue but Richard's was not a situation in which the police sought publicity in
order to alert other potential victims to come forward. There was nothing about the claimant's position as an entertainer or a Christian which compromised his expectation of
privacy.

The balancing exercise between Article 8 and 10 rights and in the light of s 12 then proceeded according to a format set out by the Grand Chamber of the European Court of
Human Rights in *Axel Springer AG v Germany* [2012] EMLR 15. The criteria were:

(a) Contribution to a debate of public interest

   The general fact of active investigations involving public figures was of general public
   interest but this was not enhanced by identifying the individual concerned.

(b) How well known is the person concerned and what is the subject of the report?

(c) Prior conduct of the person concerned

   (b) and (c) were taken together. The judge recognized that one who puts himself in
   the public eye can expect to lose privacy to some extent, but this depends on the
   nature of the public persona adopted. The claimant's Christian position might make
   certain proven conduct appropriate for disclosure but unsubstantiated allegations
   were not enough.

   Although in certain special circumstances the public's right to be informed can even
   extend aspects of the private life of public figures . . . This will not be the case—even
   where the persons concerned are quite well known to the public—where published
   photographs and accompanying commentaries relate exclusively to details of the
   person's private life and have the sole aim of satisfying the curiosity of a particular
   readership in that respect.

(d) The method of obtaining the information and its veracity

   The accuracy of the report was not in question. But there were aspects of the relationship between SYP and the BBC with the disclosure by the former of a secret tip-off
   plus the compromised opportunity for reply by the claimant or his representative.

(e) Content, form, and consequences of the publication

The content was sensationalist and with a certain urgency, lending false drama with shots of officers entering the building and the helicopter footage, which added to the sensationalism. The judge stated, 'The BBC went in for an invasion of Sir Cliff's privacy rights in a big way.' The consequences were immensely serious and likely to have been magnified by the style of broadcast.

The conclusion of the balancing exercise was resolved in Sir Cliff's favour. The judge observed that if the BBC felt that the decision was unduly restrictive of freedom of the press, that was as a result of the Human Rights Act 1998, and so a matter for Parliament to consider.

On the issue of damages, the judge rejected the defendant's assertion that damages for loss of reputation were the sole province of defamation.

It is therefore quite plain that the protection of reputation is part of the function of the law of privacy as well the function of the law of defamation. That is entirely rational. As is obvious to anyone acquainted with the ways of the world, reputational harm can arise from matters of fact which are true but within the scope of a privacy right.

The claimant was awarded £210,000 in damages. The judge regarded this case as more serious than *Mosley*, while commenting that damages should not be so high as to have an undesired chilling effect on freedom of expression. On the contribution issue, damages were allocated 65 per cent against the BBC and 35 per cent against SYP. In 2019, the BBC's liability to Sir Cliff for costs was agreed at £2 million, although the full extent of his costs may have been nearer £4.5 million.

16.5 Children and privacy

The principles of *Campbell* were applied to *Re S (A Child)* (2004), where the question of what is private information and the delicate nature of the balancing process was considered. The claimant's mother was a defendant in a murder trial, charged with the murder of the claimant's brother. He had applied for a High Court injunction prohibiting publication of information which could lead to his identification (including the identity of his mother and deceased brother). On appeal to the House of Lords, Lord Steyn applied four principles, arising out of *Campbell*, on the interplay between Articles 8 and 10. First, neither article took automatic precedence over the other. Second, where the values under the two articles are in conflict, an intense focus on the comparative importance of the specific rights being claimed in the individual case is necessary. Third, the justifications for interfering with or restricting each right must be taken into account. Finally, the proportionality test must be applied to each. Here, there was a traditional recognition of the importance of freedom of the press in unrestrained reporting of the progress of criminal trials and the importance of this, in promoting public confidence in the administration of justice, outweighed the child's claim for anonymity under Article 8.

There are particular sensitivities around the media approach to children whose parents are in the public eye. The case of *AAA v Associated Newspapers Ltd* (2012) concerned an attempt by a mother, to prevent publication of the paternity of her daughter, who was conceived in an extramarital affair. It was held that the father's identity—he was Boris Johnson, then Mayor of London—meant that it was a 'public matter which the electorate was entitled to know when considering [his] fitness for public office'. Further, the mother had spoken of the paternity in the press, thereby indicating an 'ambivalent and inconsistent attitude' towards the privacy of this issue.

The child is unable to consent to such public exposure and in the cases below there was no suggestion of parental approval. In *Murray v Express Newspapers* (2008), the author J K Rowling and her husband brought an action for breach of the Article 8 right to privacy, on behalf of their son, regarding the publication of a photo (taken with a telephoto lens) that had been published of her child in a pushchair on a public street. In the light of *Von Hannover*, the Court of Appeal held that the law should protect children from intrusive media attention, to the extent of holding that a child had a reasonable expectation that he would not be targeted in a public place in order to obtain photographs for publication.

 CASE CLOSE-UP

Weller v Associated Newspapers (2015)

Weller v Associated Newspapers (2015) concerned a photo of the musician Paul Weller and his three children, taken on a day out in California, and published online. Not only had no consent been given, but the paparazzi had been requested to stop, despite assurances that the children's faces would be pixelated. This was not done, and the children were identified by surname.

An injunction against further publication was granted. The fact that this would not have been actionable in California was given little weight by the Court of Appeal, which followed *Von Hannover* and *Murray*.

According to Tomlinson LJ, 'A person's age is an important attribute. It cannot reasonably be said that young children even when they are in public, lay themselves open to the possibility of their privacy being invaded.'

In balancing the children's Article 8 rights to privacy against those of the publisher under Article 10, the following factors were determinative: that the publication did not contribute to a current debate of general interest; the children had little or no public profile and were only of interest to the publisher because of their father; the photographs related exclusively to their private lives and had the sole purpose of satisfying public curiosity; the mere fact that their father had mentioned them in interviews could not justify publication; images of the younger two of the children had not previously been published, and the father had genuine security concerns for his family. The Court acknowledged not only these security concerns but also the vulnerability of celebrities' children to embarrassment and bullying.

16.6 Remedies

When the subject of a story wants to prevent its publication, time may be of the essence and he may want to seek a remedy which will take effect immediately. An award of damages after the story has been made public may well be inadequate. An **interim injunction** can be applied for and granted without a full trial, which could take a number of months to arrange. The interim injunction, however, has great implications for freedom of expression and will virtually never be granted in a defamation case in which the defendant proposes to raise the defence of justification.

CROSS REFERENCE

See also Chapter 17 on remedies and limitation.

Privacy cases may be different, however. You will recall that s 12(3) of the Human Rights Act 1998 requires that 'No . . . relief is to be granted so as to restrain publication before trial unless the court is satisfied that the applicant is likely to establish that publication should not be allowed.' In *Cream Holdings v Banerjee* (2004), the court recognized that exceptionally 'there will be cases where it is necessary for a court to depart from this general approach and a lesser degree of likelihood will suffice as a prerequisite. Circumstances where this may be so include those where the potential adverse consequences of disclosure are particularly grave'.

🔍 CASE CLOSE-UP

Venables v News Group Newspapers (2001)

One such case was *Venables v News Group Newspapers* (2001). Here, an injunction was granted against the world at large (*contra mundum*) prohibiting publication of information which would reveal the identity and 'past, present and future' whereabouts of Venables and Thompson, the killers of James Bulger. It was feared that their guilt in the notorious case could make them vulnerable to retaliatory acts when they were released from prison. According to Butler-Sloss LJ, the common law of confidentiality was the basis for the remedy:

> The duty of confidence may arise in equity independently of a transaction or relationship between parties. In this case, it would be a duty placed upon the media. A duty of confidence does already arise when confidential information comes to the knowledge of the media, in circumstances in which the media have notice of its confidentiality. An example is the medical reports of a private individual which are recognised as being confidential . . . The issue is whether the information leading to disclosure of the claimants' identity and location comes within the confidentiality brackets . . . . Under the umbrella of confidentiality there will be information which may require a special quality of protection. In the present case the reason for advancing that special quality is that, if the information was published, the publication would be likely to lead to grave and possibly fatal consequences. In my judgment, the court does have the jurisdiction, in exceptional cases, to extend the protection of confidentiality of information, even to impose restrictions on the Press, where not to do so would be likely to lead to serious personal injury, or to the death, of the person seeking that confidentiality and there is no other way to protect the applicants other than by seeking relief from the court.

Following his success in the High Court in 2008, Max Mosley took his case to the ECtHR, arguing that the *News of the World* had breached a positive duty under Article 8 to notify him of the story in advance of publication, so that pre-emptive action, such as contradiction or even application for interim injunction, could be taken. The ECtHR agreed that this constitutes good practice in many cases but concluded that to impose it as a legal requirement upon publishers would be too restrictive of their Article 10 freedom.

For a time, there was a perceived explosion of so-called super injunctions, which aimed not only to prevent publication of the story but even the revelation of the names of the parties involved in any legal action, in order to protect reputations, often of celebrities (see, for instance *LNS v Persons Unknown* (2010)). Because of the threat to freedom of information posed, these non-disclosure orders have been the subject of Court of Appeal guidelines to restrict their use. The increasingly widespread use of social media has also reduced the practical likelihood of anonymity being maintained.

The indirect impact on children and families can be focused on as justification for interim relief.

The Court of Appeal, in *O v A* (2014) granted an interim injunction to stop publication of an autobiography giving accounts of abuse which it was argued could harm the author's son. This was held to have been wrongly granted, when the Supreme Court held that any future claim based on the tort in *Wilkinson v Downton*, had 'no prospect of success'.

CROSS REFERENCE

See Chapter 11: *Rhodes v OPO* (2015).

CASE CLOSE-UP

PJS v NGN (2016)

A celebrity who was married with young children was allegedly involved in extramarital sexual relations with another couple. He obtained an interim injunction against a magazine which proposed to publish the story on the grounds of breach of confidence and misuse of private information. This was effective for eleven weeks until the story was published in the United States and Canada, in both hard copy and online. The Court of Appeal set aside the injunction on the grounds that the information was already in the public domain.

However, the Supreme Court held that the appeal court's balancing exercise between Articles 8 and 10 had been wrongly premised on giving undue weight to right of freedom of expression, the story already having been published. Rather, 'an intense focus on the comparative importance of the rights being claimed in the individual case was needed'. There was a huge difference between the appellant's children learning about the matter in due course, and 'the media storm' which was likely to meet the discharge of the injunction. It was concluded that the interim injunction would be maintained on the grounds of misuse of private information.

> An interim injunction concerning the identity of a party involved in the criminal justice system was the issue in *Khuja v Times Newspapers* (2017). The appellant was one of nine men arrested for very serious child sex grooming offences in Oxford. He obtained an interim injunction until such time as he was charged or released. When notified that he was to be released without charge he applied for a non-disclosure order concerning his identity, to protect himself and his family from 'misuse of private information'. The denial was approved by the Supreme Court. The public interest in allowing the free and open press reporting of court proceedings extended to the issue of appellant's identity. These matters would have been discussed in open court and raised no reasonable expectation of privacy.

16.7 International comparisons

The case of *Von Hannover (No 1)* (2005) was an example of the way in which some privacy cases can have multinational implications. We saw that a princess from Monaco complained about photos which were taken in France but published in Germany and the case was ultimately determined by the ECtHR in Strasbourg.

There is no constitutional right to privacy in Australian law; however, some statutes may protect disclosure of private information. In the case of *ABC v Lenah Game Meats* (2001), the High Court of Australia was not prepared to rule out the possibility that a common law right to protection of privacy might be accepted in the future, despite earlier case law to the contrary. Such a tort would be available for the protection only of individual people, not companies or other such bodies.

⟩ CROSS REFERENCE

See Introduction to this chapter.

The position in the United States was favourably commented on in *ABC*. The judge referred to the US Restatement of Torts 2d (1977), particularly to Dean Prosser's 'four distinct kinds of invasion'. In the United States, although there is a variation in the law between the different states and a highly respected constitutional First Amendment right protecting freedom of speech, there is generally a more extensive legal protection for private information in the kinds of situations discussed in this chapter.

Although, unlike freedom of expression, privacy is not specifically protected by the New Zealand Bill of Rights Act 1990, it is recognized as a necessary restriction upon freedom of expression. In *Hosking v Runting and Pacific Magazines Ltd* (2005), the New Zealand Court of Appeal held that there does exist a tort of invasion of privacy founded upon the existence of facts in respect of which there is a reasonable expectation of privacy, followed by publicity given to those facts that would be considered highly offensive to an objective, reasonable person. In *Hosking*, the court responded to the unauthorized publication of photos of a celebrity's children by an award of damages; injunctions were held to be wholly exceptional in such cases.

Summary

- Privacy has traditionally not been directly protected in English law.
- The Human Rights Act 1998 opened the way for creation of the tort of misuse of private information.
- The Article 8 right to respect for privacy must be balanced with the equally powerful Article 10 right to freedom of expression.
- *Campbell v MGN* (2004) provides a detailed consideration of this area of law by the House of Lords.

⊙ Visit the online resources to listen to a podcast summarizing the topics covered in this chapter.

The bigger picture

Facial recognition technology and privacy

Facial recognition technology (FRT) has been increasingly employed by law enforcement as a tool of crime detection and prevention. An improvement over the well-established CCTV, it enables the identification of individuals in real time, with links to databases of individuals who may be sought for a variety of reasons. In London in August 2019 it was discovered that this technology was in place 'for public safety' in the 67-acre King's Cross Central development which encompasses shops, restaurants, offices, and colleges as well as a major transport hub. This raised human rights concerns, like those occurring worldwide in places as diverse as San Francisco (which has become the first US city to ban the police use of FRT), Sweden, Scotland, and Singapore. Questions have been raised about the extent to which citizens in public have a 'reasonable expectation of privacy'. Additional concerns are the accuracy of the identifications, racial and political profiling, chilling effects on lawful public protest, and the retention of biometric data. In the United Kingdom it remains to be determined what position the Information Commissioner's Office, the government, and the courts should take on the use of FRT for security and law enforcement.

To what extent should personal privacy be sacrificed to the aims of public protection? The main legal issues are discussed in Purshouse, J and L Campbell, 'Privacy, Crime Control and Police Use of Facial Recognition Technology' (2019) 3 Crim LR 188.

Questions

Knowledge-testing questions

1. What is the difference between breach of confidence and misuse of private information?

2. The *Campbell* case involved the balancing of which interests? What tests did the court apply and what factors were significant in reaching the final decision?

3. What two key cases are indicative of the ECtHR general position on privacy?

Problem and essay questions

1. Arthur, 19, is the son of Vicky and Bert, who are household names due to the fact that they host one of the most popular daytime talk shows on national television and have recently jointly published a book on 'Parenting Your Teen'. Arthur has been suffering from an eating disorder for several years and has been receiving intensive therapy at The Abbey, a prestigious clinic. In the course of his therapy, Arthur has revealed to his therapist Linda that Bert had abused him over several years when he was a child. *The Spectre*, a tabloid newspaper, has now published a photo of Arthur (in which he is recognizable, despite wearing a hoodie) entering The Abbey. Accompanying the photo is an article saying, 'sources close to The Abbey have revealed that all was not what it seemed in Vicky and Bert's household'.

Disregarding the law of defamation, what tort actions might be brought by Arthur, Vicky, and Bert?

2. It has been claimed that the public's right to be informed, which is an essential right in a democratic society, can even in some circumstances extend to the private life of public figures.

Comment on the development of the right to privacy in British law.

 Visit the online resources for guidance on answering these questions.

 Further reading

Brennan, C, 'O v A' (2015) 31 Journal of Professional Negligence 33

Eady, D, 'Injunctions and the Protection of Privacy' [2010] 29 CJQ 411

Hughes, K, 'The Public Figure Doctrine and the Right to Privacy' (2019) 78(1) CLJ 70

Moreham, N, 'Privacy in the Common Law: A Doctrinal and Theoretical Analysis' (2005) 121 LQR 628

Moreham, N, 'Beyond Information: Physical Privacy and English Law' (2014) 73(2) CLJ 350

Moreham, N, 'Unpacking the Reasonable Expectation of Privacy Test' (2018) LQR 134 651

Phillipson, G, 'Privacy' in D Hoffman (ed), *The Impact of the UK Human Rights Act on Private Law* (CUP 2011)

Warren, SD and LD Brandeis, 'The Right to Privacy' (1890) 4 Harv LR 193

17 Remedies and limitation

LEARNING OBJECTIVES

By the end of this chapter you should be able to:

- have an overview of the types of remedies which are utilized in tort actions;
- understand the basic principles of calculation and payment of tort damages;
- appreciate the effect of death upon tort compensation claims; and
- understand the basic rules regarding limitation periods in tort.

17.1 Remedies

The most commonly sought type of remedy for torts, such as negligence, is the award of *damages* as compensation for what the claimant has lost. The other remedy which frequently arises in tort is that of the *injunction*, which might be relevant in a nuisance or defamation action, when the claimant hopes to obtain an order that the defendant cease a particular activity. This chapter will focus on damages but will also consider injunctions and briefly look at other remedies.

17.2 Damages

The main category of damages is compensatory. There are, however, three other types of damages which are non-compensatory. These are as set out below.

17.2.1 **Contemptuous**

Contemptuous damages are awarded in some cases, commonly defamation, where there is a desire to indicate that although the claimant has been successful technically, the court feels that

CROSS REFERENCE

For more on the *Reynolds* case, see Chapter 15.

the action should never have been brought. The claimant will usually receive the smallest coin in circulation at the time and is unlikely to have a costs award made in his favour. In *Reynolds v Times Newspapers* (2001), the former prime minister of Ireland was awarded 1p (and was ordered to pay the newspaper's costs) when he won his libel action.

17.2.2 **Nominal**

In some cases, the claimant will be held to have had his rights violated but will not have actually suffered any loss. Vindicated and not blameworthy for bringing the action, he will be awarded nominal damages, typically £2, and will not necessarily be awarded costs. In *Watkins v Secretary of State for the Home Department* (2006), the House of Lords held that the award of nominal damages would only be permissible in relation to torts which are actionable per se, such as trespass.

17.2.3 **Exemplary/punitive**

Exemplary damages are sometimes described as punitive and are imposed over and above any compensatory damages in order to teach the defendant that 'tort doesn't pay'. This reminds us that one of the functions of the tort system is deterrence.

🔍 CASE CLOSE-UP

Rookes v Barnard (1964)

In this case Lord Devlin in the House of Lords itemized the restricted situations in which exemplary or punitive damages are appropriate:

(1) where there are oppressive, arbitrary, or constitutional actions by servants of the government. This includes not only local or central government bodies but, significantly, the police and prison officers. The torts in such cases would typically be trespass to the person or malicious prosecution. In *Thompson v Commissioner of Police for the Metropolis* (1997), some judicial limits were set on exemplary damages against the police. The usual minimum in cases where such damages were appropriate was £5,000, and £25,000 would be the usual maximum, with up to £50,000 appropriate only when high-ranking officers were implicated; and

(2) where the conduct has been calculated to make a profit. This typically applies in some defamation cases. In the case of *John v Mirror Group Newspapers* (1997), exemplary damages were awarded when the court felt that consideration of the effect on newspaper sales of the revelations of Elton John's habits had been a motivating factor upon the publishers.

CROSS REFERENCE

For more on trespass to the person, see Chapter 11.

CROSS REFERENCE

For more on defamation, see Chapter 15.

Exemplary damages have been somewhat controversial as it has been argued that they represent a confusion between civil and criminal law. The burden of proving a case in tort law is that of the balance of probabilities, and there are questions about the extent to which juries should 'punish' a defendant financially without his being found guilty of conduct according to the higher criminal standard of beyond reasonable doubt. In *AB v South West Water Services* (1993), the Court of Appeal took a restrictive view of any possible extension of the *Rookes* categories, saying that exemplary damages could only be awarded in torts which had been contemplated at the time Lord Devlin set out his categories. This restriction was rejected by the House of Lords in *Kuddus v Chief Constable of Leicestershire Constabulary* (2001). For them, inclusion in the list depended not upon the name of the tort, or of the cause of action, but the nature of the conduct involved. The tort in question, **misfeasance in public office**, although virtually forgotten at the time of *Rookes*, involved similar conduct to that described in Lord Devlin's first category and so could give rise to exemplary damages in appropriate cases. The Law Commission in 1997 recommended that the law regarding aggravated and exemplary damages be simplified and rationalized but that punitive damages should be awarded in an expanded range of cases, when a judge feels that this adequately reflects conduct of the defendant. This would bring English law more in line with other common law jurisdictions in which they have a more extensive role; however, the government has shown no inclination to introduce legislation to this end.

> **misfeasance in public office**
>
> the tort allows an action in damages by one who is injured by the unlawful act, in bad faith, of the holder of public office.

17.2.4 Compensatory damages

Aggravated damages are compensatory in nature but indicate that the claimant's position has been made worse because of the defendant's malice or bad motivation and reflect injury suffered to the claimant's feelings as a result of the tort. They are not a separate category of damages but will be part of the overall compensation which the successful claimant is awarded. They have been awarded in cases of battery, trespass to the person and to land, defamation, and deceit, among others, but, according to *Kralj v McGrath* (1986), are not available in personal injuries actions arising out of the tort of negligence.

The case of *Appleton v Garrett* (1996) concerned a dentist who was liable in trespass to the person to a number of patients for whom he had carried out extensive but unnecessary dental work, in order to extend his financial gain. Here the judge said that 15 per cent of the awards made for pain, suffering, and loss of amenity should constitute aggravated damages for the claimant's anger, indignation, and mental distress resulting from discovering that the treatment was unnecessary.

The recent privacy case of *Sir Cliff Richard v BBC* (2018), above, saw aggravated damages of £20,000 awarded against the BBC due to the fact that it nominated its story of the search of Sir Richard's home for the award of 'Scoop of the Year'. This implied pride and lack of repentance from the defendant.

In actions against the police for false imprisonment or malicious prosecution *Thompson v Commissioner of Police for the Metropolis* (1997) tells us that in cases when there has been aggravation due to injury to feelings, the starting point for damages should be £1,000.

In *KD v Chief Constable of Hampshire* (2005), a police officer behaved inappropriately in relation to a victim of crime. He visited her frequently, questioned her about her sexual history, and cuddled her. He was found liable for harassment under the Protection from Harassment Act 1997 and for battery. The claimant was awarded £10,000 in compensatory damages and an additional

> **THINKING POINT**
>
> Why might it have been necessary for the court in the *Thompson* case to introduce limits on exemplary damages?

£10,000 in aggravated damages; the latter on the basis that the defendant's repeated denials had resulted in the claimant having to undergo prolonged and distressing cross-examination.

The objective of *compensatory damages* is, as far as possible, to restore to the claimant what has been lost. This was traditionally represented by the Latin phrase: **restitutio in integrum**. The extent to which this is possible depends very much on what the claimant has suffered. When the loss is a damaged car, financial means of restoration will seem more appropriate than when the loss is that of a limb or a sense, such as eyesight. Additionally, the practice of making a once-and-for-all assessment of the claimant's needs for compensation at the time of the trial can involve the need to guess what is likely to happen in the future—for instance, regarding the course of his physical condition or of his employment prospects. Lord Scarman, in *Lim Poh Choo v Camden & Islington Health Authority* (1980) described the process in this way:

> The award, which covers past, present and future injury and loss, must, under our law, be of a lump sum assessed at the conclusion of the legal process. The award is final; it is not susceptible to review as the future unfolds, substituting fact for estimate. Knowledge of the future being denied to mankind, so much of the award as is to be attributed to future loss and suffering (in many cases the major part of the award) will almost surely be wrong. There is really only one certainty: the future will prove the award to be either too high or too low.

In personal injury cases, damages awarded by the judge to the successful claimant can be divided into categories or *heads of damage:* pecuniary loss (pre- and post-trial) and non-pecuniary loss (already experienced or anticipated).

17.3 Pecuniary damages

The claimant may have suffered loss of earnings, and incurred medical and care expenses (sometimes over a period of years) up to the date of trial. For instance, due to a disability, his home may need adapting. These should be capable of being specifically itemized in his claim, unlike future such monetary loss, and are required to be specifically pleaded.

The claimant can only recover for expenses *reasonably* incurred. The courts will not regard it as unreasonable to choose private medical care in preference to that available from the National Health Service (Law Reform (Personal Injuries) Act 1948, s 2(4)). In that situation, however, statute requires that any saving which the claimant makes while relying on public services, for instance, on his food while in an NHS hospital, should be deducted from his damages (Administration of Justice Act 1982, s 5). There may be a considerable period of time between the accident and the claimant's receiving his compensation. For that reason in most cases the court will now include interest for that period in the damages awarded.

The more problematic aspect of pecuniary loss is that which must be anticipated for the future but awarded at the time of the trial, due to the 'once-and-for-all' nature of damages payments. These may include loss of future earnings or earning capacity and the cost of future care.

---

restitutio in integrum

'restored to the original condition'; that is, the payment of damages is intended to put the claimant back to his pre-tort position, as far as is possible.

THINKING POINT

What changes to the system of payment of damages could help to avoid the uncertainty which Lord Scarman describes?

17.3.1 **Loss of earnings**

Loss of earnings, up to the date of the trial, are calculated according to an average of the net (after tax) amount which it is estimated that the claimant would have earned during the years between the accident and the trial. Loss of future earnings is a more complicated matter. That is because what would have happened in the future is unknown and unknowable. A 35-year-old salesman who is rendered unable to work again may have been promoted to sales director and worked until retirement at 65, or he may have been made redundant in two years' time. He may have contracted a disease and died at 50. As a recipient of a lump sum he also gains certain investment advantages.

The courts have devised a system in order to avoid as far as possible Lord Scarman's scenario in *Lim* where the payment is too high or too low. A sum is calculated which represents the likely future net average annual income of the claimant, taking into account such factors as promotion possibilities. This is known as the *multiplicand*. This is multiplied by a sum known as the *multiplier*, which is the notional number of years which the claimant has been prevented from working. In the case of the 35-year-old salesman above, you might imagine that his multiplier would be 30—that is, that he would be expected to work until retirement at 65. But as we have seen, life brings with it a number of contingencies which may intervene, leading the courts to significantly discount the multiplier to the extent that 18 years is the highest, and even that is rarely used.

▶ **THINKING POINT**

What sorts of 'contingencies' lead to the lowering of the multiplier?

One factor taken into account by courts in choosing the multiplier was the rate of return the claimant could expect when he invested his lump sum to provide an annual income. In the case of *Wells v Wells* (1998), the House of Lords ruled that claimants could only be expected to make relatively low-risk, low-return investments, and consequently the multipliers which courts were adopting had been resulting in under-compensation. The Damages Act 1996, s 1 gave the Lord Chancellor the power to give directions on prevailing rates of return. This rate was set at 2.5 per cent in 2001, leading to higher multipliers and consequently higher loss of earnings awards.

17.3.2 **'Lost years'**

One issue which may arise in calculation of loss of future earnings is the situation in which the injury has reduced the life expectancy of the claimant. How can damages reflect money not earned in the years in which he would have worked, had he lived? *Pickett v British Rail Engineering* (1980) established that pecuniary losses may include loss of earnings for the years by which the claimant's life expectancy is shortened. This must include a deduction for his living expenses which are saved during these 'lost years'. The ruling in *Pickett* replaced the former situation in which non-pecuniary damages could include a standard sum representing damages for the claimant's knowledge that he would die early: loss of expectation of life. This was abolished by the Administration of Justice Act 1982, s 1(1)(a). According to s 1(1)(b) the mental suffering caused by the claimant's own awareness of his reduction in life expectancy will be included under damages for 'pain and suffering'.

▶ **CROSS REFERENCE**

See 17.4 Non-pecuniary damages.

17.3.3 **Pecuniary losses suffered by others**

It is not uncommon for those who are injured to be looked after either by a publicly funded body such as the National Health Service, a local authority, or by a relative. In such cases, although the benefit goes to the victim of the tort, financial loss will be suffered by someone other than the injured party.

In *Donnelly v Joyce* (1974), a child was seriously injured due to the defendant's negligence. His mother had to give up work in order to assist in treating his injuries. Her lost earnings were held to be recoverable by the child, as part of his tort claim. It remained, however, a matter of debate as to whether the financial loss was truly that of the injured party or of the person who gave up work to care for him.

 CASE CLOSE-UP

Hunt v Severs (1994)

This question was considered by the House of Lords in *Hunt v Severs* (1994). Here, the injured party's boyfriend was liable in negligence for causing her serious injury in a motorcycle accident. He gave up work in order to care for her, and eventually they were married. The question which arose in her tort action was whether there could be recovery against the defendant for care which he in fact was providing. It must be remembered that it would be the defendant's insurers who would be meeting the cost. The House of Lords held that, contrary to the reasoning in *Donnelly*, the claimant in such cases was in reality obtaining compensation on behalf of the carer. According to Lord Bridge:

> By concentrating on the plaintiff's need and the plaintiff's loss as the basis of an award in respect of voluntary care received by the plaintiff, the reasoning in Donnelly v Joyce diverts attention from the award's central objective of compensating the voluntary carer. Once this is recognised it becomes evident that there can be no ground in public policy or otherwise for requiring the tortfeasor to pay to the plaintiff, in respect of the services which he himself has rendered, a sum of money which the plaintiff must then repay to him.

 THINKING POINT

In *Hunt*, what would have happened if, in the future, the plaintiff's husband was unwilling or unable to care for her? How would she then recover the costs of her care?

17.3.4 **Rights of recovery by public and private bodies**

The Road Traffic (NHS Charges) Act 1999 provides that a central body, the Compensation Recovery Unit (CRU), will have responsibility for recovering from tortfeasors the costs of NHS care given to their victims. In *Islington BC v University College London Hospital Trust* (2005), it was attempted to extend this principle to other bodies under the common law. The defendant hospital had negligently caused injury to its patient, who consequently required ongoing care from the claimant local authority. As the patient had no means, the local authority could not recoup its costs from her. Instead it decided to sue the hospital in negligence for the loss it had indirectly caused. In applying the *Caparo* 'three-stage' test for duty of care, the Court of Appeal held that although Islington could be said to be a foreseeable victim of the hospital's negligence, there was insufficient proximity between the claimant and defendant. Further, it would not be fair, just, and reasonable to find a duty of care in respect of the claimant's pure economic loss. The patient had suffered no loss as she was cared for at public expense, and it was not possible for the local authority to claim its expenses from the wrongdoer.

17.4 Non-pecuniary damages

These cannot be easily itemized by reference to tangible financial realities as pecuniary losses. How much is your ability to play tennis worth? If you could never play again, your enjoyment of life may be significantly diminished; however, unless you are a professional, you will not have suffered any financial loss. Similarly, courts must put sums on the physical and psychological effects of the injury itself. In practice the non-pecuniary award will represent a combination of the injury itself, accompanied by *pain and suffering and lack of amenity* (commonly referred to by lawyers as PSLA). Compensation for the injury itself is based upon a published tariff. You may wish to consult Norris (ed), *Kemp & Kemp: The Quantum of Damages* (2019) or the Judicial Studies Board: *Guidelines for the Assessment of General Damages in Personal Injury Cases* (2019) for details on how this very injury-specific tariff system operates in practice.

Pain and suffering is, as it sounds, a subjective concept and it reflects what the claimant has experienced. In *Wise v Kaye* (1962), a victim who had been unconscious continuously since the accident was presumed to have experienced nothing of her injuries and received nothing under this head. Loss of amenity or faculty, however, refers to loss of the experience of life, including personal relationships, hobbies, sports, and specific physical capacities. It is objectively measured and thus a sum to reflect this was awarded in *Wise*, despite the limited awareness of the plaintiff.

This award was controversial and was referred for consideration to the House of Lords in *H West & Son v Shephard* (1964).

 CASE CLOSE-UP

H West & Son v Shephard (1964)

A 41-year-old woman was severely injured in a car accident which was caused by the defendant's negligence. Her condition was not as extreme as that in *Wise*; however, she was rendered quadriplegic and was left with little or no ability to communicate and doubtful awareness of her surroundings. Her life expectancy at the time of the trial was five years.

The House of Lords considered two questions:

(1) To what extent could this plaintiff recover damages for loss of amenity as part of her overall award for non-pecuniary damages, which also included pain and suffering and loss of expectation of life?

(2) To what extent was the use to which the plaintiff would be able to put the damages after they were awarded a factor which must be considered in the award?

On question (1), Lord Pearce joined with the majority, who confirmed the correctness of the decision in *Wise v Kaye*:

> If a plaintiff has lost a leg, the court approaches the matter on the basis that he has suffered a serious physical deprivation no matter what his condition or temperament or state of mind may be. That deprivation may also create future economic loss which is added to the assessment. Past and prospective pain and discomfort increase the assessment. If there is loss of amenity apart from the obvious normal loss inherent in the deprivation of the limb—if, for instance, the plaintiff's main interest in life was some sport or hobby from which he will in future be debarred, that too increases the assessment.

Question (2) was based on an argument which was made in *West* that non-pecuniary damages in this case should be lowered to reflect the fact that the claimant would not be in a position to directly enjoy or spend the money. Lord Morris said:

> If damages are awarded to a plaintiff on a correct basis, it seems to me that it can be of no concern to the court to consider any question as to the use that will thereafter be made of the money awarded. It follows that if damages are assessed on a correct basis, there should not then be a paring down of the award because of some thought that a particular plaintiff will not be able to use the money. In assessing damages there may be items which will only be awarded if certain needs of the claimant are established. A particular plaintiff may have provision made for some future form of transport: a particular plaintiff may have to have provision made for some special future attention or some special treatment or medication. If, however, some reasonable sum is awarded to a plaintiff as compensation for pain endured or for the loss of past or future earnings or for ruined years of life or lost years of life, the use to which a plaintiff puts such a sum is a matter for the plaintiff alone. A rich man, merely because he is rich and is not in need, is not to be denied proper compensation: nor is a thrifty man merely because he may keep and not spend.

THINKING POINT

Is it right that defendants might be required to pay lower damages for more serious injuries which render their victims unconscious as opposed to less serious injuries of which victims are aware?

❱ THINKING POINT

What might be the outcome if damages were to reflect the financial status of the claimant or his ability to enjoy his money?

The Pearson Report recommended a change in the law in cases of permanent unconsciousness such as that in *Wise*; however, when the House of Lords reviewed the position in *Lim Poh Choo v Camden and Islington Area Health Authority*, it refused to reverse the ruling in *West* on questions (1) and (2).

In *Damages for Personal Injury: Non-pecuniary Loss* (1998) the Law Commission noted a gradual proportionate fall in the value of non-pecuniary damages awards due to inflation and it was recommended that awards generally be increased. *Heil v Rankin* (2000) gave a five-judge Court of Appeal the opportunity to review the situation and it responded in slightly different terms from those proposed by the Law Commission. *Heil* decided to require rises of up to 33 per cent for the most serious injuries, tapering down to awards of £10,000, below which there would be no change. It should be noted that it is this lower category which makes up the vast majority of tort claims. The top limit of awards for 'catastrophic injuries' was raised from £150,000 to £200,000. In order that damages keep pace with the changes in funding of litigation brought about by the Jackson Reforms (as implemented in the Legal Aid, Sentencing and Punishment of Offenders Act 2012) the Court of Appeal, in *Simmons v Castle (Note)* (2013), stipulated a uniform 10 per cent increase in damages for all cases involving pain, suffering, and loss of amenity in respect of personal injury, nuisance, defamation, or 'any other tort that causes suffering, inconvenience or distress to individuals'. In *Shaw v Kovac* (2017) it was confirmed, in a medical negligence case, that 'loss of autonomy' resulting from not having given informed consent could not be introduced as a new, separate head of damage. Any distress suffered by a patient in such circumstances could be accounted for under the head of pain and suffering.

The relationship between non-pecuniary and pecuniary damages in nuisance was discussed by the Court of Appeal in *Raymond v Young* (2015), where it was held that damages for diminution of value of land included within it loss of amenity, so the two could not be awarded to the same claimant.

CROSS REFERENCE

For more on the case of *Raymond v Young*, see Chapter 12.

17.5 The nature of the damages award

You will recall that historically tort damages have been paid as a once-and-for-all lump sum. Although this has the advantage of bringing finality to the proceeding for both claimant and defendant (usually an insurer), this system of payment has had a number of disadvantages. Because the claimant's physical and financial future cannot be known, the lump sum amount awarded at the time of trial is likely to be either inadequate or excessive. The impact of future inflation on the amount awarded will also be unpredictable. Finally, some claimants may find it difficult to handle a large sum of money in terms of saving or investment for future needs.

Since the Supreme Court Act in 1981, courts can, in some cases, address the problem of uncertainty about the claimant's future health. Section 32A gives a statutory power to award *provisional damages* in cases where there is a known chance that, as a result of the tort, the claimant's health may suffer a 'serious deterioration' in the future. A provisional award will be made based on his current medical position at the time of the trial but allowing him to return to the court (once only) for additional compensation should the deterioration occur.

In *Willson v Ministry of Defence* (1991), it was held that the future 'serious deterioration' must take the form of a 'clear and servable medical occurrence' rather than an 'ordinary deterioration'. The possibility that the plaintiff's ankle injury might lead to progressive arthritis or to a general weakness which might cause a fall, did not qualify for the application of s 32A.

Structured settlements began to be utilized in the early 1990s as a way of allowing the amount of compensation to be paid on a periodical basis, which can be variable over time according to estimates of the future changing needs of the claimant. Taxation rules made this arrangement advantageous to both parties and they were given statutory footing in the Damages Act 1996, s 5.

> **annuity**
>
> an investment of money which will produce payments in the form of a series of equal sums over a certain period.

Structured settlements gave the recipient the benefit of an **annuity** which is purchased for him by the defendant's insurers, enabling him to receive compensation in monthly or annual instalments for life, or longer if there were dependants. They could not be imposed by the court, but depended on agreement between the two parties and were limited in practice to large awards, often when the claimant was a child.

 STATUTE

Damages Act 1996, s 5(1)

a 'structured settlement' means an agreement settling a claim . . . for personal injury on terms whereby—

a. the damages are to consist wholly or partly of periodical payments; and

b. the person to whom the payments are to be made is to receive them as the annuitant under [annuities] purchased for him by the person against whom the claim is brought . . . or his insurer.

Structured settlements were rendered largely obsolete by the innovation of *periodical payments* which were established in the Damages Act 1996, s 2 (as amended by the Courts Act 2003, ss 100 and 101). From 1 April 2005, in all cases involving future pecuniary loss, courts must consider whether periodical payments are appropriate. In what was a significant change, they can be ordered by the court without the consent of the parties (although their preferences will be taken into account) on the basis of a calculation of the claimant's expected yearly financial requirements, which must then be met by the defendant as long as the claimant lives. In considering if periodical payments are appropriate the court must take into account the defendant's likely future financial resources, unless insured or a government or health service body. The court may make a variable order in circumstances similar to those described above concerning provisional damages or apply periodical payments to only a proportion of the award.

 THINKING POINT

It is likely that this shift away from the once-and-for-all approach to payment of damages will be more popular with claimants than defendants. Why might this be?

17.5.1 **Deductions**

Due to the personal injury in question, a claimant may receive financial benefit from sources other than tort compensation. The sources of these *collateral benefits* could include his own, charity, insurance, employers' schemes, or, most importantly, state benefit. To what extent will they be taken into account in the calculation and payment of damages? To answer this question, it must be recalled that the objective of tort damages is *restitutio in integrum* and that under this principle it would not be intended to either over- or under-compensate the claimant. This must be balanced, however, by a policy concern that the claimant who plans ahead to provide for himself in adversity is not penalized for his prudence and foresight.

According to Lord Reid in *Parry v Cleaver* (1970):

> It would be revolting to the ordinary man's sense of justice and therefore contrary to public policy, that the sufferer should have his damages reduced so that he would gain nothing from the benevolence of his friends or relations or the public at large, and that the only gainer would be the wrongdoer.

Benefits derived from a tort can be divided into two categories: the first which will not be deducted from compensation and the second which will. Included in the first category are gifts and charity, the claimant's own insurance, or occupational schemes contributed to by his employer, payable after the end of employment.

Social security benefits can be contrasted with the examples above in that they are earned as of right rather than as the result of any effort or luck on the claimant's part. Since they were first established in 1948, there has been a gradual trend towards deducting them from the damages paid to a claimant. Until recently, however, the defendant or his insurers benefited from this policy in that they were liable to pay a claimant lower damages than if he had not received state benefits. This was changed by the Social Security (Recovery of Benefits) Act 1997, which provided that almost all social security benefits (such as income support and attendance allowance) received by a claimant for five years following the event be deducted before compensation is made and paid directly to the government's Compensation Recovery Unit. In this way the claimant does not receive double payment, but the state rather than the tortfeasor benefits. Social security benefits cannot be deducted from damages for pain, suffering, and loss of amenity. Long-term occupational sickness benefits are treated as akin to earnings rather than insurance and are also deducted.

17.5.2 **Property loss or damage**

While most of the law in this chapter pertains to personal injury, the basic principles of compensation regarding property should briefly be considered. When property is lost or destroyed, the starting point is that the defendant will be liable for all the costs incurred in that loss. This will include replacement of the property at current market prices and costs incurred by the claimant, which are consequential upon, and not too remote from, the destruction; for example, the short-term hire of a replacement. If the property is not lost but damaged, then the claimant will be entitled to the amount by which the piece of property has been diminished in value. This is usually but not always equivalent to the repair costs of the property. Again, consequential damage will be recoverable.

17.6 Injunctions

An injunction is an order of the court requiring the defendant either to do something (mandatory injunction) or to cease doing something (prohibitory injunction). An injunction may be appropriate in cases in which the tort is of an ongoing nature; for instance, nuisance caused by noise. Another example of a typical injunction case would be that concerning defamation or, more recently, privacy, when the claimant is concerned to prevent publication in order to keep certain information out of the public domain.

Because it is an **equitable remedy** the injunction is not available by right but rather at the court's discretion. The factors which will influence how this discretion is exercised are determined by the type of injunction being sought.

> **equitable remedy**
> as distinguished from one based in the common law. Remedies that originated in the Court of Exchequer Chamber, which was abolished in the late nineteenth century, were more discretionary and less precedent-bound than those of the common law.

17.6.1 *Quia timet* injunction

This is sought when it is anticipated that a tort might be committed in the future. Courts are understandably reluctant to interfere in such cases, when no wrong has yet been committed, and so will generally only grant this remedy if the claimant can prove that the tort is highly likely and imminent.

17.6.2 Interim (or interlocutory) injunction

Here, the tort will have been committed and will be ongoing. The claimant will urgently want to prevent further damage until such time as the merits of the dispute can come to trial. The court will be concerned to balance the rights of both parties, on the basis that the claimant could ultimately lose the case.

In *American Cyanamid v Ethicon* (1975), the House of Lords set out the principles which are relevant to the granting of an interim injunction. There must be a 'serious question' to be tried and the balance of convenience must favour the granting of an injunction. Also, the claimant may be required to give an undertaking to pay damages and costs to the defendant should he ultimately lose the case.

> **CROSS REFERENCE**
> See *Douglas* (Chapter 16) and *Rhodes* (Chapter 11).

Interim injunctions are rare, particularly regarding publication, as the courts will be aware of the public interest and the value of freedom of expression. This has been explicitly reinforced by the Human Rights Act 1998, which stipulates that no interim relief is to be granted without, under s 12(3), the court being 'satisfied that the applicant is likely to establish that publications should not be allowed'; and under s 12(4), the court 'having particular regard to the importance of the Convention right to freedom of expression'. It is interesting to note that in *Douglas v Hello!*

(2001) Michael Douglas and Catherine Zeta-Jones were successful in obtaining an interim injunction against *Hello!* magazine to prevent publication of their wedding photos; however, despite this, they went on to lose the privacy case when the issue came to trial. The surprising decision of the Court of Appeal to grant an interim injunction in *Rhodes v OPO* (2014), which constituted a significant restriction on freedom of artistic expression, was unanimously over-ruled by the Supreme Court in 2015.

17.6.3 **Final injunction**

This may be granted when a judge has heard all the relevant facts and both parties have had their say in court. When an application has been made for an injunction, the defendant may try to convince the court that damages would be a preferable remedy.

Q CASE CLOSE-UP

Shelfer v City of London Electric Lighting Co (1895)

In this case an injunction was granted to an occupier to prevent continued noise and vibra-tion caused by the defendant, despite its significant impact upon the local electricity supply. It was held that 'damages in lieu' of an injunction would only be justified if the injury to the claimant's legal right:

- is small;
- is capable of being estimated in money;
- can be adequately compensated by a small money payment; and
- where it would be oppressive to the defendant to grant an injunction.

The Court of Appeal, in Dennis Reagan v Paul Properties Ltd (2006), had to review a judge's decision to award damages in lieu of an injunction, when the defendant's property develop-ment blocked the light coming into the claimant's living room, thereby creating a nuisance. It was confirmed that the effect of *Shelfer* was to create a prima facie right to an injunction and the burden was not upon the claimant to show why the remedy should not be damages. Al-though the injunction would have a serious effect upon the defendant, this was more than outweighed by the extent of the light blockage upon the claimant, which would not be ad-equately compensated by the payment of a small sum of money.

In *Coventry v Lawrence* (2014) the Supreme Court indicated that the above '*Shelfer* criteria' should not continue to be applied 'mechanically', as in *Dennis*; instead, a more flexible ap-proach should prevail in favour of the alternative award of damages in cases of nuisance and other interference with property rights.

⟩ CROSS REFERENCE
Refer to *Coventry v Lawrence*, Chapter 12.

Future judicial consideration of the tension between the rights of the private landowner or entrepreneur and public interest in quiet enjoyment was predicted by Lord Sumption:

> The whole jurisprudence in this area will need one day to be reviewed in this court. There is much to be said for the view that damages are ordinarily an adequate remedy for nuisance and that an injunction should not usually be granted in a case where it is likely that conflicting interests are engaged other than the parties' interests. In particular, it may well be that an injunction should as a matter of principle not be granted in a case where a use of land to which objection is taken requires and has received planning permission.

> **CROSS REFERENCE**
>
> For more on nuisance, see Chapter 12.

It is unclear the extent to which courts are justified in considering the impact on public interest in exercising their discretion to grant final injunctions. In *Kennaway v Thompson* (1981) an injunction was granted to prevent noisy powerboat racing events on Lake Windermere. Previously, however, in *Miller v Jackson* (1977), Lord Denning had waxed lyrical about the beauties of village cricket when he refused to countenance an injunction in respect of the nuisance it caused. Damages were awarded in lieu 'to cover any past or future damage'.

> **THINKING POINT**
>
> Could it be argued that damages in a case such as *Dennis* permit the wrongdoer to 'buy' his right to continue his tort?

The case of *Dennis v Ministry of Defence* (2003) was one brought by a landowner against the government because of the noise caused by low-flying aircraft from the nearby RAF training base. It was alleged that, in addition to causing common law nuisance, the defendants had also infringed the claimant's rights to privacy (Article 8 of the European Convention on Human Rights) and to quiet enjoyment of his property (Article 1, First Protocol). An injunction was sought, but when the court considered the wider implications of restrictions on RAF training, it was decided to award damages instead for loss of property value and to compensate for future disturbance. It appears that the requirements of the Human Rights Act are likely to lead to an extension in the requirements laid down in *Shelfer*.

17.7 Self-help

> **abate**
>
> to put to an end or suppress

This remedy basically involves the injured party taking steps on his own to address or **abate** the wrong. For instance, in a nuisance case (*Lemmon v Webb* (1895)) a landowner was justified in chopping off (but not keeping) branches of the defendant's tree overhanging his property. If you are falsely imprisoned you may attempt escape and in some circumstances can use reasonable force to protect yourself from trespass to the person or to eject someone who is trespassing on your property. Self-help as a remedy is treated with caution by the law!

17.8 Compensation and death

The legal position following on from the death of either a claimant or defendant must now be considered.

17.8.1 **Survival of existing cause of action**

Until 1934, the common law rule was that any existing tort actions would cease with the death of either the claimant or the defendant. The Law Reform (Miscellaneous Provisions) Act 1934, s 1(1) provides that such causes of action, with the exception of defamation, will survive the death of either party. This means that an injured party who has a viable cause of action against someone who then dies can sue his estate. Conversely, if a cause of action is in existence at the time someone dies, his estate can continue that action for damages sustained before his death.

17.8.2 Death creating a new cause of action for loss of dependency

When a tort causes a fatality, there may be serious financial consequences for those close to the victim. The Fatal Accidents Act 1976 allows those who were financially dependent on the deceased to have the benefit of a claim against the wrongdoer, providing that the deceased himself would have had a claim if he had not died. You may recall the case discussed earlier in terms of causation: *Corr v IBC Vehicles Ltd* (2008). Here, the House of Lords held that the defendant will only be liable under the 1976 Act if the deceased's death was a foreseeable consequence of his tort. We have seen, earlier, that s 1(1)(b) of the Administration of Justice Act 1982 allows damages to be recovered for the mental suffering caused by the claimant's own awareness of his reduction in life expectancy. However, when death is virtually instantaneous, as with the plaintiff's daughters in the crush at Hillsborough Football Stadium in 1989 in *Hicks v CC South Yorkshire* (1992), it was held that such a time interval is not sufficiently long to justify damages. Here the damage and the death were one and the same.

> **CROSS REFERENCE**
> See Chapter 4.

Who count as dependants? The categories of dependants for the purposes of the Act are set out in s 1(3). They include a spouse or cohabitee, children, parents, siblings, and specific other types of relation.

There are two categories of damages. The most important is for *loss of support* and this is based upon the claimant's reasonable expectation of support from the deceased—either currently or in the future. The action will usually be brought on behalf of all dependants by the executor or administrator of the deceased's will and the sum awarded is divided proportionately between the recipients, according to their relative expectations. Any benefits, such as insurance, gained as a result of the death are deducted. The second category is known as *bereavement*. Spouses (including a partner or civil partner) and parents of a minor who has never married are entitled to one lump sum fixed by statutory instrument. Currently this is £12,980. According to s 5 of the 1976 Act any contributory negligence by the deceased in relation to his death will be taken into account in the calculation of damages.

> **THINKING POINT**
> What do bereavement damages represent? Is £12,980 an adequate sum? If not, what sum would you recommend?

17.9 Limitation

It would not be convenient or workable for claimants to have an unlimited time in which to bring their tort claims. Evidence would be lost, memories would fade, and insurers would never be able to update or close their books. Limitation periods have been laid down by statute in order to restrict the amount of time within which the claimant must begin his action. It is a complex area for practitioners and one in which as a student you will need only to understand the basic principles.

Table 17.1 Limitation

Damage	Personal injury	No personal injury	Defamation
Time	3 years Limitation Act 1980 s 11	6 years Limitation Act 1980 s 2	1 year Defamation Act 1996 s 5
Extendable?	Yes	No	No

They are as follows:

- For tort claims which involve personal injury caused by 'negligence, nuisance or breach of duty' (including trespass to the person), actions must be started within three years of the cause of action accruing (Limitation Act 1980, s 11). In some circumstances the court will have the discretion to extend this period, which will be considered later.

- For tort claims not involving personal injury, claims must be begun within six years of the cause of action accruing (Limitation Act 1980, s 2). This period is not extendable.

- Some torts have special provisions. Defamation, for example, requires that actions must be begun within one year of accrual (Defamation Act 1996, s 5).

The limitation periods for different types of claim are summarized in Table 17.1.

'Accrual' is the earliest time at which an action can be commenced. For instance, in the average road traffic accident, accrual takes place at the time of the accident, when the property and/or personal injury takes place and damage is suffered. Imagine, however, that one of the passengers sustains a type of injury which is not immediately apparent at the time of the accident or he learns six months later that he is suffering from depression as a result of his experience. This would be known as *latent damage* and in such cases the law may allow the limitation period to be extended. Where the damage in question is personal injury, s 11(4) of the 1980 Act gives the claimant three years from the 'date of knowledge' in which to claim, if it is later than the date of accrual.

According to s 14(1), knowledge is achieved when the claimant knows:

(a) that the injury in question was significant; and

(b) that the injury was attributable in whole or in part to the act or omission which is alleged to constitute negligence, nuisance, or breach of duty; and

(c) the identity of the defendant; and

(d) if it is alleged that the act or omission was that of a person other than the defendant, the identity of that person and the additional facts supporting the bringing of an action against the defendant;

(e) and knowledge that any acts or omissions did or did not, as a matter of law, involve negligence, nuisance, or breach of duty is irrelevant.

The court also has a discretion to waive the limitation period for claims covered by s 11 when it is felt that it would be equitable to the claimant to do so and where the claimant has been prejudiced by the limitation provisions (Limitation Act 1980, s 33(1)). Further, time will not begin to run against a claimant until he reaches what is known as his 'majority': his eighteenth birthday.

Latent damage can also arise in non-personal injury cases. For instance, that a building has been negligently designed may only become apparent, for example, by it beginning to crack, years after its construction. This is dealt with by the Latent Damage Act 1986, which applies to latent damage in all negligence claims other than those concerning personal injury and death. The 1986 Act inserts ss 14A and 14B into the Limitation Act 1980. Section 14A uses 'knowledge' (similar to personal injury) as the starting date for latent damage to property, after which the claimant has three years in which to begin his action. According to s 14B, there is a 'long-stop' of fifteen years from the act or omission constituting the negligence, after which the claimant cannot begin any action.

It has not always been clear which category of limitation applies in a particular case. In some cases, claimants have been forced to attempt to adapt their claim because they are trying to take advantage of a longer time span.

In *Letang v Cooper* (1964) a woman suffered personal injury when a car ran over her legs while she was sunbathing in a car park in 1957. In 1961, she framed her tort action against the driver in trespass to the person, because negligence was statute-barred as being outside the three-year period. According to Lord Denning, 'when injury is not inflicted intentionally but negligently . . . the only cause of action is negligence, not trespass'. Claiming under the tort of unintentional trespass was not permitted to be used to circumvent the limitation rules, and after *Letang* actions under this tort ceased.

Q | CASE CLOSE-UP

Stubbings v Webb (1993)

Stubbings v Webb (1993) presented a different problem. The adult plaintiff wished to bring a trespass action against her father and stepbrother for sexual assaults over a period of 18–28 years earlier. She described her action as one for 'breach of duty' because, if it could be brought under s 11(4) of the 1980 Act, then she could have the advantage of the latent damage provisions as well as the court's discretion to extend time under s 33. The House of Lords held that the wrongs committed against her could only be regarded as intentional trespass to the person: the tort of battery. This could not be described as 'breach of duty' for the purposes of applying s 11(4) and thus her claim must fail. Lord Denning said:

> I should not myself have constructed breach of duty as including deliberate assault. The phrase lying in juxtaposition with negligence and nuisance carries with it the implication of a breach of duty of care not to cause personal injury, rather than an obligation not to infringe any legal right of another person. If I invite a lady to my house one would naturally think of a duty to take care that the house is safe but would one really be thinking of a duty not to rape her?

THINKING POINT

Do you agree with Lord Denning's interpretation of s 11? How might this section have been drafted if it was intended to include assault?

One of the issues for the plaintiff in *Stubbings* was the impact of certain psychological conditions, caused by the tort, which led to a delay in the claimants bringing proceedings. One known characteristic effect of certain kinds of abuse is to create an attitude of denial, either intentional or subconscious, in the victim. The Law Commission, in its report *Limitation of Actions* (2001), recommended statutory change which, among other purposes, would address this inequity, but as yet this has not been a matter of legislative priority.

In the absence of any parliamentary response, the House of Lords took the opportunity in *A v Hoare and others* (2008) to amend the law.

CASE CLOSE-UP

A v Hoare and others (2008)

In this case, six different victims of childhood sexual abuse challenged the ruling in *Stubbings*, according to which their actions for damages were time barred by s 2 of the Limitation Act 1980—given that the cause of action accrued more than six years before the bringing of proceedings. In *A v Hoare*, the defendant had been convicted in 1989 of the attempted rape of the claimant. He was sentenced to life imprisonment and in 2004, while serving his sentence, he won £7 million in the national lottery. The claimant then decided to sue him for compensation for the damage she suffered as a result of this serious sexual assault. But her action was initially struck out because, according to *Stubbings*, the action was commenced outside the six-year time limit.

The House of Lords exceptionally chose to depart from its earlier approach, holding that both because uniformity in limitation periods regarding all forms of personal injury was desirable and, because of the obvious anomalies illustrated in the case of *Lister v Hesley Hall, Stubbings* had been wrongly decided.

The position of *Letang v Cooper* was reinstated, according to which trespass to the person could be included within 'breach of duty'. Therefore, s 11 of the 1980 Limitation Act applied and the court had a discretion under s 33 to extend the limitation period for claimants whose 'knowledge' of their injury satisfied the s 14 test. According to Lord Hoffmann, the s 33 discretion to exclude time limits is 'unfettered'.

> The judge is expressly enjoined by subsection (3)(a) to have regard to the reasons for delay and, in my opinion this requires him to give due weight to evidence, such as there was in this case, that the claimant was for practical purposes disabled from commencing proceedings by the psychological injuries which he had suffered.

This discretion was applied in the claimant's favour in *Raggett v Preston Catholic College Governors* (2010), indicating the courts' growing awareness of the effects of repression of child sexual abuse, a trend which proceeded apace in the vicarious liability case of *A v Trustees of the Watchtower Bible and Tract Society* (2015), where expert evidence as to post-traumatic stress disorder suffered by the claimant following sexual assault when a child was one of the key reasons that the High Court disapplied the limitation period.

A similarly generous approach to limitation was demonstrated towards claimants suffering from a different type of personal injury, linked to nuclear testing in the 1950s, in *B v Ministry of Defence* (2009).

> **CROSS REFERENCE**
> Refer to *Lister v Hesley Hall* in Chapter 9.

 ## Summary

- Compensatory damages are the main remedy in tort. They are intended to restore to the claimant what he has lost.

- Compensatory damages are divided into pecuniary and non-pecuniary damages. They are usually awarded as a lump sum.

- Statute provides that tort actions can survive the death of either the claimant or the defendant. Dependants have a right to sue in the case of a death when they have lost support from the victim.

- The limitation period for all personal injury cases is three years and for non-personal injury cases is six years.

  ◐ Visit the online resources to listen to a podcast summarizing the topics covered in this chapter.

The bigger picture

The *Jackson Review of Civil Litigation Costs* (2010) gave valuable insight into the calculation and payment of damages in different aspects of tort law: www.judiciary.gov.uk/wp-content/uploads/JCO/Documents/Reports/jackson-final-report-140110.pdf

A research study by Oswald and Powdthavee at the University of Warwick in 2007 presented extensive statistical data on the effects upon mental well-being of different types of bereavement.

https://warwick.ac.uk/fac/soc/economics/research/workingpapers/2008/twerp_827.pdf

Could so-called happiness regression equations be used to provide more scientifically based tort compensation?

? Questions

Knowledge-testing questions

1. What benefits are, and are not, deducted from a claimant's compensation award?

2. What factors will determine whether or not a final injunction will be granted?

3. In what circumstances will punitive damages be awarded?

4. Does the law of limitation invariably benefit the defendant?

Problem and essay questions

1. Susie, aged 32, lived with her children, Topsy and Tim, along with her elderly father Olu. She was working as a taxi driver when, due to Pam's negligence, she was badly injured in a motoring accident. Susie was hospitalized at Edenvale NHS Trust, in a coma, until she died six weeks later.

   What damages will Pam be liable for? Give details, including any deductions.

2. What are the policy issues which have recently been influential in the development of the law relating to limitations in tort?

🌐 Visit the online resources for guidance on answering these questions.

☰ Further reading

Brennan, C, 'An Instrument of Injustice?' (2006) 17 CFLQ 1

Judicial College, *Guidelines for the Assessment of General Damages in Personal Injury Cases*, 15th edn, 2019 [available on Lexis Nexis]

Law Commission, *Aggravated, Exemplary and Restitutionary Damages* (Report No 247, 1997)

Law Commission, *Claims for Wrongful Death* (Report No 263, 1999)

Law Commission, *Damages for Personal Injury: Non-pecuniary Loss* (Report No 257, 1999)

Law Commission, *Limitation of Actions* (Report No 270, 2001)

Lewis, R, 'Increasing the Price of Pain: Damages, The Law Commission and *Heil v Rankin*' (2001) 64 MLR 100

Murphy, J, 'Rethinking Injunctions in Tort Law' (2007) 27(3) OJLS 509

Norris, W (ed), *Kemp & Kemp: Personal Injury Law, Practice and Procedure* (Sweet & Maxwell 2019)

Steele, J, 'Damages in Tort and under the Human Rights Act: Remedial or Functional Separation?' (2008) 67 CLJ 606

Index

Q

R

U

V

W